HAWKS. *Top, left to right: Red-tailed hawk, immature; Cooper's hawk, immature; pigeon hawk, adult. Bottom, left to right: Sparrow hawk, adult; goshawk, immature and adult.*

THE UNIVERSAL
STANDARD
ENCYCLOPEDIA

THE UNIVERSAL STANDARD ENCYCLOPEDIA

VOLUME 11

GILBERT—HANSON

An abridgment of The New Funk & Wagnalls Encyclopedia
prepared under the editorial direction of
JOSEPH LAFFAN MORSE, Sc.B., LL.B., LL.D.
Editor in Chief

STANDARD REFERENCE WORKS
PUBLISHING COMPANY, INC., NEW YORK

THE UNIVERSAL
STANDARD
ENCYCLOPEDIA

LIST OF ABBREVIATIONS USED

abbr., abbreviated
A.D., Anno Domini
alt., altitude
A.M., ante meridiem
anc., ancient
approx., approximately
Ar., Arabic
AS., Anglo-Saxon
A.S.S.R., Autonomous Soviet Socialist Republic
at.no., atomic number
at.wt., atomic weight
b., born
B.C., before Christ
b.p., boiling point
B.T.U., British Thermal Unit
Bulg., Bulgarian
C., centigrade, syn. Celsius
cent., century
Chin., Chinese
cm., centimeter
Co., County
colloq., colloquial
cu., cubic
Czech., Czechoslovakian
d., died
Dan., Danish
Du., Dutch
E., east, easterly, eastern
ed., edition
e.g., for example
Egypt., Egyptian
Eng., English
est., estimated
et seq., and following
F., Fahrenheit
fl., flourished
fr., from
Fr., French
ft., foot

Gael., Gaelic
Gen., General
Ger., German
Gr., Greek
Heb., Hebrew
Hind., Hindustani
Hon., Honorable
h.p., horsepower
hr., hour
Hung., Hungarian
I., Island
i.e., that is
in., inch
Ind., Indian
Ir., Irish
It., Italian
Jr., junior
kg., kilogram
km., kilometer
lat., latitude
Lat., Latin
lb., pound
lit., literally
long., longitude
m., mile
M., Middle
min., minute
M.L., Medieval Latin
mm., millimeter
mod., modern
m.p., melting point
M.P., Member of Parliament
m.p.h., miles per hour
Mt., Mount, Mountain
N., north, northerly, northern
N.T., New Testament
OE., Old English
OF., Old French
OHG., Old High German
ON., Old Norse

ONF., Old Norman French
O.T., Old Testament
oz., ounce
Phil., Philippine
P.M., post meridiem
Pol., Polish
pop., population
Port., Portuguese
prelim., preliminary
pron., pronounced
q.v., which see
R., River
rev., revised, revision
Rev., Reverend
Rom., Romanian
Russ., Russian
S., south, southerly, southern
sec., second
Skr., Sanskrit
Sp., Spanish
sp.gr., specific gravity
sq., square
S.S.R., Soviet Socialist Republic
Sum., Sumerian
Sw., Swedish
syn., synonym
temp., temperature
trans., translation, translated
Turk., Turkish
U.K., United Kingdom
U.N., United Nations
U.S., United States
U.S.A., United States of America
U.S.S.R., Union of Soviet Socialist Republics
var., variety
W., west, westerly, western
yd., yard

Note.—The official abbreviations for the States of the Union are used throughout. For academic degrees, see article DEGREE, ACADEMIC. Other abbreviations or contractions are self-explanatory.

GILBERT, Sir Humphrey (1539?–83), English soldier and navigator, a half brother, on his mother's side, of Sir Walter Raleigh, born in Compton, Devonshire, and educated at Eton and Oxford University. Though his family wished him to become a lawyer, he joined the English army. He saw active service in the war with France (1562–64) and, in 1566, was commissioned a captain in the English army in Ireland. He was appointed governor of Munster (Ireland) in 1569, and in the following year was knighted. During 1571 he sat in Parliament as the member for Plymouth and, in 1572, was sent to the Netherlands with an English force in an unsuccessful attempt to aid the Dutch in the campaign against Spain.

Gilbert spent the period from 1572 to 1578 in retirement, mainly engaged in writing. As early as 1566, and again a year later, he had petitioned Queen Elizabeth I to be allowed to seek the Northeast and Northwest Passages to the Orient. In consequence, during his period of literary activity his most important production was *A Discourse of a Discovery for a New Passage to Cataia* (1576). In 1578 his efforts were finally rewarded by a royal charter granting the privileges of exploration and colonization in North America. Gilbert and Sir Walter fitted out an expedition the same year, but their ships were dispersed by the Spaniards off Cape Verde and they were forced to return. A second expedition sailed from Plymouth in 1583 and, after a voyage of fifty days, reached the north coast of Newfoundland, where Gilbert founded the first English colony in America. The colonists were, however, mutinous and unwilling to co-operate, and the expedition decided to return to England. On the return voyage, Gilbert decided to sail in the small ten-ton frigate, the *Squirrel,* rather than in his forty-ton flagship, the *Golden Hind.* In a storm off the Azores, the *Squirrel* went down with its entire crew.

GILBERT, William (1540–1603), English physicist and physician, born at Colchester, and educated at Cambridge University. He was admitted to the College of Physicians about 1576, and in 1601 was appointed physician to Queen Elizabeth.

Gilbert is known primarily not as a physician, but as the first experimentalist to make a scientific study of the nature of electricity and magnetism. He found that a great number of substances other than amber had the power to attract light objects when rubbed (see ELECTRICITY: *History*), and applied the term "electric" to the force these substances exert after being rubbed. He was the first to use the terms "electric force", "electric attraction", and "magnetic pole", and he distinguished between magnetic and electric action. Perhaps Gilbert's most important contribution was the experimental demonstration of the magnetic nature of the earth. The unit of magnetomotive force, the gilbert, was named after him. Gilbert was also the first exponent of the Copernican system (q.v.) in England. His most important works are *De Magnete, Magneticisque Corporibus, et de Magno Magnete, Tellure, Physiologia Nova* (1600), probably the first great scientific work written in England, and *De Mundo Nostro Sublunari Philosophia Nova* (published posthumously, 1651).

GILBERT, Sir William Schwenck (1836–1911), English playwright, born at London, and educated principally at London University. In 1861, while a clerk in the education department of the privy council office, he began to contribute humorous poetry to the periodical *Fun;* these and other poems were later published as *Bab Ballads* (1869) and *More Bab Ballads* (1873), with both books achieving immediate and lasting popularity. In 1864 Gilbert was admitted to the bar, but practiced little as an attorney, his attention being given more and more to literary work. His first play, *Dulcamara* (1866), was a burlesque of Donizetti's opera *L'Elisire d'Amore.* Subsequently he wrote a number of plays, most of them comedies, including *The Palace of Truth* (1870), *Pygmalion and Galatea* (1871), *The Happy Land* (in collaboration with Gilbert à Beckett, 1873), *Sweethearts* (1874), *Engaged* (1877), and *Gretchen* (1879). He also wrote the librettos for the comic operas *The Mountebanks* (1892, music by Alfred Cellier) and *Fallen Fairies* (1909, music by Sir Edward German).

Gilbert is best known for his long and rewarding collaboration, from 1871 to 1896, with the composer Sir Arthur Seymour Sullivan (q.v.). The collaboration resulted in the creation of fourteen comic operas, which were produced by the noted theatrical manager Richard D'Oyly Carte (q.v.), and which rank among the best and most popular comic operas ever written. In his librettos (Sullivan wrote the music) Gilbert showed himself a master at creating fantastically absurd characters and satiric and paradoxical stage situations. Since his time, the term "Gilbertian" has come into use to describe any similarly humorous writing. Gilbert was knighted in 1907.

Gilbert and Sullivan Operas is the name given to the entire group of operas created by the two collaborators. Because they were produced after 1881 at the Savoy Theatre, London, which was especially built to house them, the works are also sometimes known as the *Savoy Operas*. These include *Thespis* (1871); *Trial by Jury* (1875, a satire on the English law courts); *The Sorcerer* (1877); *H.M.S. Pinafore* (1878, a satire on the British navy and also on grand opera); *The Pirates of Penzance* (1879); *Patience* (1881, a satire on the esthetic movement led by the poet Oscar Wilde); *Iolanthe* (1882, in which the British House of Lords is held up to ridicule); *Princess Ida* (1884, which pokes fun at the contemporary movement for greater women's rights in political and social life); *The Mikado* (1885); *Ruddigore* (1887); *The Yeomen of the Guard* (1888); *The Gondoliers* (1880); *Utopia, Limited* (1893); and *The Grand Duke* (1896). The most popular of the group are *H.M.S. Pinafore, The Pirates of Penzance, Patience, Iolanthe, The Mikado, Ruddigore, The Yeomen of the Guard,* and *The Gondoliers.*

GILBERT AND ELLICE ISLANDS COLONY, a colony of the Western Pacific Islands administration of Great Britain (see BRITISH WESTERN PACIFIC). The colony is composed of the Gilbert Islands, the Ellice Islands, Ocean Island, the Phoenix Islands, and the Line Islands. Ocean Island, formerly the capital, is the one island of the colony which is not a coral atoll. The present seat of administration is Tarawa, in the Gilberts. The colony was proclaimed a protectorate in 1892 and was given colonial status in 1915. The principal products of the colony are high-grade phosphate, pandanus fruit, and coconuts. During World War II most of the islands of the colony were captured by the Japanese. Total area of colony, about 460 sq.m.; pop. (1952 est.) 37,832.

GILBERT ISLANDS, an archipelago composed of sixteen coral atolls, located on the equator between 174° and 178° E. long., and comprising part of the Gilbert and Ellice Islands Colony (q.v.) of Great Britain. The inhabitants of the Gilberts are a mixture of the races of Melanesia and Polynesia. Pandanus fruit and coconuts are the chief crops of the islands. During World War II many of the Gilberts were captured by the Japanese. In Nov., 1943, Tarawa (q.v.), one of the islands, was the site of one of the fiercest battles in the history of the U.S. Marine Corps. Area, about 114 sq.m.; pop. (1952) 28,958.

GILDERSLEEVE, BASIL LANNEAU (1831–1924), American classical scholar, born in Charleston, S.C., and educated at the College of New Jersey (now Princeton University) and abroad. He was professor of Greek at the University of Virginia from 1856 to 1876, and at Johns Hopkins University from 1876 to 1915. In 1880 he founded and from 1880 to 1920 he edited the *American Journal of Philology*. His works include *A Latin Grammar* (1867), *Odes of Pindar* (1885), *Syntax of Classical Greek* (Pt. I, 1900; Pt. II, 1911), and *Creed of the Old South* (1915).

GILDERSLEEVE, VIRGINIA CROCHERON (1877–), American educator, born in New York City, and educated at Barnard College. She was an instructor in English at Barnard from 1900 to 1910, assistant professor in 1910–11, and professor and dean until 1947. In 1945 she was the only woman delegate to the United Nations Conference on International Organization. She was a member of many learned societies, including the Modern Language Association of America and the Classical Association of the Atlantic States, and was chairman of the American Council on Education. In 1946 she went to Japan as a member of the American Education Mission. She wrote *Many a Good Crusade* (1954), an autobiographical work.

GILEAD, a word appearing several times in the Old Testament. **1.** A mountainous but fertile region situated between the Jordan R. on the W., the Arabian plateau on the E., the plateau of Moab on the S., and the Bashan region on the N. **2.** A mountain W. of the Jordan R., in central Palestine. **3.** The grandson of Manasseh, Joseph's eldest son. **4.** The father of the judge Jephthah.

GILES, SAINT (fl. 7th century), Grecian-born saint, probably of noble Athenian descent. Following his parents' death, he distributed his possessions to the poor and became a hermit in a desert region near Arles, France. He was discovered in his retreat by the Gothic king Flavius, who constructed a monastery and made Giles the first abbot.

British Information Services

Native houses in the Gilbert Islands

Giles's hermitage subsequently developed into the town of Saint-Gilles, Gard. Giles is the patron saint of beggars, cripples, and lepers; St. Giles's Church, Cripplegate, London, is named in his honor. His feast is celebrated on Sept. 1.

GILGAL, the name of several geographical locations mentioned in the Old Testament. **1.** The first camping site of the Israelites after their crossing of the Jordan R., undoubtedly near the city of Jericho. **2.** A city visited by the Hebrew prophets Elisha and Elijah. It is identified with the modern village of Jiljilia, near Bethel. **3.** A city mentioned in the list of the chiefs overthrown by Joshua, successor of Moses.

GILGIT. See KASHMIR.

GILIAKS or **GILYAKS,** a Paleo-Asiatic tribe of about 4500 persons, inhabiting a region of Siberia in the vicinity of the mouth of the Amur R., which empties into Tatarskie Strait, and the N. part of Sakhalin Island across the strait. The Giliaks are of two racial types, one resembling the Ainus, and the other the Tungus (qq.v.). They are brachycephalic and of average height, with well-proportioned bodies, and are primarily a hunting and fishing people. Their religion is Shamanism (q.v.).

GILL, or BRANCHIA, one of the paired respiratory organs found in all animal forms which breathe air dissolved in water. In general, gills are outgrowths of the body wall and are, characteristically, thin-walled structures plentifully supplied with blood vessels. The gill structure is arranged so that it is constantly bathed in water, and the oxygen in the dissolved air passes through the thin membranes of the gill and into the animal's blood stream. At the same time the waste carbon dioxide in the animal's blood passes out through the gill membranes and into the water. Annelid worms, brachiopods, mollusks, echinoderms, certain arthropods, fishes, and the larvæ of amphibia are equipped with gills. Although the gills of all these animals function in a similar manner, the gill structures differ widely. The gills of the various groups mentioned above are described in separate articles.

GILL, ERIC ROWLAND (1882–1940), English sculptor, type designer, engraver, and author, born at Brighton, and educated at the art school in Chichester. He was apprenticed to an architect but turned to carving inscriptions on tombstones. The first exhibition of his stone carvings was held in London in 1911. Two years later he joined the Roman Catholic Church and was commissioned to carve the Stations of the Cross in Westminster Cathedral. These carvings are in low relief, and their apparent archaism, largely dictated by the nature of the hard stone Gill used, was the subject of much controversy when they were first unveiled. His relief, "Christ Driving the Moneylenders out of the Temple", executed as a war memorial at Leeds University in 1922–23, caused a further outcry as the figures were depicted wearing top hats and frock coats. The sculptures on Broadcasting House, London, were among his major works. His interest in lettering led him to design new type faces for book printing, outstanding being the faces known as "Gill-Sans" and "Perpetua". Gill wrote many books on his philosophical approach to art and life, including *Sculpture, An Essay on Stone Cutting—with a Preface about God* (1917); *Christianity and Art* (1927); *Beauty Looks after Herself* (1933); *Money and Morals* (1934); *Work and Leisure* (1935); and *Work and Property* (1937). His *Autobiography* was published in 1940, and his *Letters* appeared in 1944.

GILLENIA, genus of perennial herbs of the Rose family. Gillenias have attractive white or pale-rose flowers and graceful three-parted leaves, and are often planted in borders and rock gardens. Two species, both called Indian physic, are native to the U.S. The bowman's root, *G. trifoliata,* is a small herb with awl-shaped stipules at the base of each leaf. The dropwort or American ipecac, *G. stipulata,* has large, leaflike stipules. A fluidextract, used as an expectorant and mild emetic, is manufactured from the roots of both species.

GILLETTE, WILLIAM (1855–1937), American actor and playwright, born in Hartford, Conn., and educated at the Massachusetts Institute of Technology, and at Boston and New York universities. He spent some years touring the United States with various stock companies, and in 1881 produced and starred in his play, *The Professor,* performed at the Madison Square Theater in New York City. Subsequently he appeared in fourteen plays which he had either written or adapted from earlier works. He is best known for and was most favorably received in his dramatization of *Sherlock Holmes* (1899), which he adapted from the celebrated stories of A. Conan Doyle. Gillette made recurrent appearances in the title role of this play, the last in New York City in 1932. He also appeared in Barrie's *The Admirable Crichton* in 1903, in Henri Bernstein's *Samson* in 1908, and in Victorien Sardou's *Diplomacy* in 1921.

GILL-OVER-GROUND. See GROUND IVY.

GILLYFLOWER (Middle English *gilofre,* "clove"), common name given to several aromatic plants. The name was first applied to the clove, *Eugenia aromatica.* This application was extended to the clove pink, *Dianthus caryophyllus,* from which the cultivated carnation is derived. The common wallflower, *Cheiranthus cheiri,* and members of the stock genus, *Matthiola,* are commonly called gillyflowers. See STOCK.

GILMAN, DANIEL COIT (1831–1908), American educator, born in Norwich, Conn., and educated at Yale University, where from 1856 to 1872 he was professor of physical and political geography. In 1861 he founded the Sheffield Scientific School at Yale. He was president of the University of California from 1872 until 1875 when he became the first president of Johns Hopkins University, Baltimore. He served in the latter capacity until 1901. In that year he became the first president of the Carnegie Institution in Washington, D.C. In 1896–97 he was a member of the international commission which settled a boundary dispute between Venezuela and Great Britain. He was the author of *Life of James Monroe* (1883) and *University Problems* (1898).

GILMER, ELIZABETH MERIWETHER, popularly known by her pseudonym, DOROTHY DIX (1870–1951), American journalist and author, born in Montgomery Co., Tenn. She was editor of the women's department of the New Orleans *Picayune* from 1896 to 1901. During that period she began to write her celebrated column, published under the title "Dorothy Dix Talks", counseling readers who asked her advice about their unhappy love affairs. Subsequently her column appeared as a daily feature in hundreds of newspapers in the United States. She became a feature writer for the New York *Journal* in 1901, and a member of the staff of the Wheeler Syndicate in 1917, of the Ledger

Syndicate in 1923, and of the Bell Syndicate in 1933. Her writings include *Mirandy* (1902) ; *Dorothy Dix, Her Book* (1926) ; and *How to Win and Hold a Husband* (1939).

GILMORE, PATRICK SARSFIELD (1829–92), American bandmaster and composer, born near Dublin, Ireland. At the age of twenty-one he emigrated to the United States, and in 1859 he organized Gilmore's Band in Boston. He became internationally famous in 1869 when, for the National Peace Jubilee held in Boston, he organized and directed an orchestra of 1000 players and a chorus of 10,000 singers. Three years later, at the World's Peace Jubilee held in the same city, he organized and directed an orchestra of 2000 players and a chorus of 20,000. In 1874 he settled in New York City and began a series of successful tours with his band, appearing in many cities in Canada, the United States, and Europe. Under the pseudonym Louis Lambert, he composed the famous Civil War marching song *When Johnny Comes Marching Home.*

GILSONITE. See ASPHALT.

GILYAKS. See GILIAKS.

GIN, an alcoholic liquor, distilled from grain, and deriving its flavor principally from an infusion of juniper berries. The name is an abbreviation of the word "geneva", a corruption of either the French *genièvre* or the Dutch *junever,* both meaning "juniper". The two principal kinds of gin are the American or English variety, usually described as "dry gin", and the Dutch type, called "Geneva", "Schnapps", or "Hollands". Dry gin is prepared from grain alcohol which has been purified by fractional distillation. The purified alcohol is then mixed with juniper berries and other flavoring agents, distilled once more, and diluted to approximately 80 or 90 proof. Dutch gin is prepared in much the same way as dry gin, except that the grain alcohol is less highly purified, and thus retains more of the flavor of the grain. Sugar syrup is sometimes added to the final product. Gin drinking became a social evil in England in the 18th century, necessitating the levying of increasingly heavy taxes, beginning with the Gin Act of 1736. See DISTILLED LIQUORS; LIQUORS, FERMENTED AND DISTILLED.

GIN, COTTON. See COTTON: *Processing*; COTTON GIN.

GINGER, name applied to plants of the genus *Zingiber,* belonging to the family Zingiberaceae, and to a flavoring obtained from one species, *Z. officinale.* The genus is native to the East Indies and includes about twenty species. Its flowers, borne in compact spikes subtended by bracts, are white with purple streaks. The rhizomes or underground stems of ginger are perennial, but the aboveground portions of the stem die back each autumn. The rhizome is a knotty, fibrous structure which is fleshy when fresh. Cultivated ginger, being sterile, is propagated wholly from these rhizomes. The stems are reedlike, generally 3 to 4 feet tall, and covered with the sheaths of lance-shaped, smooth leaves.

All members of the genus have aromatic rhizomes, but the spicy flavor is especially strong in *Z. officinale,* the common or narrow-leaved ginger, which has been cultivated in the East Indies for thousands of years. It is now cultivated in the West Indies (particularly Jamaica), w. Africa (particularly Sierra Leone), South America, Australia, and China, in addition to its original habitat.

When the stems have withered, the rhizomes are harvested and prepared for market either by scalding and subsequent drying, which produces black ginger, or by scraping and washing, which produces white ginger. White and black ginger are commonly used as condiments and as flavors for ginger ale and ginger beer. When used to make candied ginger, the rhizomes are gathered when still young and are preserved in sugar.

The principal constituents of ginger rhizomes are starch, an oleoresin, and a pale-yellow essential oil called "oil of ginger". Ginger is used in medicine as fluidextract, oleoresin, tincture, and powder, or as a constituent of various compounds. Ginger is taken internally to relieve dyspepsia and flatulence, and is used externally to reduce local skin irritation.

Certain species of ginger, other than *Z. officinale,* are used as condiments and drugs in the regions to which they are native. Several plants unrelated to *Zingiber,* especially wild ginger, *Asarum canadense,* are called ginger because of similarity of flavor; see ASARUM.

GINGILI OIL. See SESAME.

GINKGO, genus of gymnospermous trees of the family Ginkgoaceae. *G. biloba,* the maidenhair tree, is the only living representative of this family and of the order Ginkgoales, although other plants of this order were abundant in the Mesozoic era. The ginkgo has been preserved as a sacred tree in Chinese temple gardens since ancient times. Botanists long believed that the species would have become extinct without this care, but

Leaves and cones of the ginkgo tree

wild ginkgos have been found in recent years in inaccessible valleys of western China.

Ginkgo trees grow 40 to 120 feet tall. The ginkgo leaf is a fan-shaped structure with veins arising from the base and branching dichotomously throughout. The common name, maidenhair tree, is derived from the resemblance in venation between the ginkgo and the maidenhair fern. Larger branches of the ginkgo are covered with dwarf branches, called spurs, which grow slowly and bear leaves yearly. Ginkgos are dioecious; male and female cones are borne on separate trees. Male cones produce pollen which is distributed by wind; female cones bear seeds which contain a malodorous pulp. The seed, called the ginkgo nut, is roasted and eaten by the Chinese, who regard it as a delicacy. Ginkgos are frequently planted in parks and ornamental gardens and on streets in large cities. Female trees are rarely so planted because of the unpleasant odor of the seeds.

GINSENG, name given to dicotyledonous plants of the family Araliaceae, particularly those of the genus *Panax*. The family comprises over fifty genera and five hundred species of trees, shrubs, and herbs, most of which have aromatic foliage. The appearance and specific botanical characteristics of the family are almost identical with those of the Umbelliferae (q.v.), excepting that the fruit is a one-seeded drupe. The principal genera are *Aralia*, the spikenard and sarsaparillas; *Hedera*, the ivy (q.v.) ; *Panax*, the ginseng; and *Fatsia* (*Echinopanax*), the devil's club.

The genus *Panax* includes the Chinese ginseng, *P. schinseng*, an herb having small green flowers, scarlet berries, and leaves composed of five leaflets. The root of ginseng, which has a flavor similar to that of licorice, is regarded by the Chinese as possessing extraordinary virtues as an "elixir of life". It is used as a remedy in China for almost all diseases and for relief of fatigue of both body and mind. The demand, in China, for ginseng root is so great that large quantities of American ginseng, *P. quinquefolia*, are normally imported from the U.S. Pharmacologists have been unable to discover any useful medical properties in either species, and ginseng does not appear in the U.S. Pharmacopoeia.

GINZBERG, ASCHER (1856–1927), Russian writer, born in Kiev, and better-known under his pen name *Achad Ha-am* (Heb., "one of the people"). In 1889 he founded the Zionist League at Odessa. He emigrated to England in 1906, living there until 1921, when he settled in Palestine. His writings, which center upon the problem of the Jewish peoples dispersed throughout the world, expressed his belief in the desirability of a Jewish homeland in Palestine based upon the common cultural and ethical heritage of the Jews. Ginzberg's philosophy, adopted by numerous writers since his time and now called "cultural Zionism", was designated to bring about not a national state, similar to other national states, but a religious center in which the principles enunciated by the Prophets could be reaffirmed. Ginzberg wrote a collection of essays, *Al Parashat Derachim* (1895), and a collection of letters *Igeroth* (1923).

GIOLITTI, GIOVANNI (1842–1928), Italian statesman, born at Mondovi, Cuneo Province, Piedmont, and educated in the law at Turin University. He was appointed councilor of state and elected to the chamber of deputies in 1882. In 1889 he was made treasury minister and in the following year finance minister. He became prime minister in 1892 but was forced to resign in the following year for withholding records relevant to a bank scandal. After several years in private life he again entered and became influential in politics, receiving the post of home secretary in 1901. Two years later he was named to the premiership, which office he held four successive times between 1903 and 1921. While he was premier, Italy gained control of Tripolitania and Cyrenaica by means of a war with Turkey. On the advent of World War I Giolitti counselled neutrality for Italy, feeling that his country was unprepared for war. Nevertheless, in 1917, after the Italian defeat at Caporetto, he urged a firm Italian stand against

the Central Powers. In 1920 he aided in ne-
gotiating the treaty of Rapallo, which resolved
the Italo-Yugoslav conflict over Fiume (q.v.)
and other Adriatic territories. During Giolitti's last term as prime minister he allowed
Fascists to fill various administrative posts,
and in 1924 he approved the Fascist rise to
power. However, after a period in the chamber of deputies under Benito Mussolini's government, he became an opponent of the Fascist regime. He was the author of *Memorie
della Mia Vita* (2 vols., 1922).

GIONO, Jean (1895–   ), French novelist, born at Manosque, in Provence. At the
age of nineteen he was inducted into the
French army and fought in World War I.
Later he wrote about the horrors of war in
Le Grand Troupeau (1931). His pacifist creed
was fully expounded in *Refus d'Obeissance*
(1937). The majority of his books are concerned with man's relationship to the soil,
as in his novel *Les Vraies Richesses* (1936).
Among his other works are *Colline* (1920),
Regain (1930), *Le Chant du Monde* (1934),
Batailles dans la Montagne (1937), *Le Hussard
sur le Toit* (1951), and *Le Moulin de Pologne*
(1953). His book of short stories, *La Femme
du Boulanger* (1935), was widely read, and
his play, *Lanceurs de Graine*, was successfully
produced in 1937.

GIORDANO, Luca (1632–1705), Neapolitan painter. He was known as *Fa Presto*
("Hurry Up") because of the speed with
which he worked. He studied with José Ribera
and Pietro da Cortona, and his style was derived from those of Cortona and of Paolo
Veronese. Giordano lived and worked mainly
in Naples; he also executed commissions in
Florence and from 1692 to 1700 resided and
worked in Madrid under the patronage of
King Charles II of Spain. Giordano painted
innumerable pictures, which are in most of
the important galleries of Europe, including
galleries in Madrid, Naples, Dresden, Vienna,
and Munich. His work is characterized by
harmonious color, charm, and facile invention. Among his frescoes are those in the
cupola of the Corsini Chapel, Florence;
"Christ Expelling the Traders from the Temple" (church of San Philippo da Girolami,
Naples); and "The Battle of Saint-Quentin"
and "The Taking of Montmorency" (Escorial,
Madrid). His easel paintings include "St.
Francis Xavier Baptizing the Indians" (Naples Museum), reputedly painted in a day and
a half; "Venus and Mars" (Louvre, Paris);
and "Birth of John the Baptist" (Metropolitan Museum of Art, New York City).

GIORGIONE, IL, also Giorgione da Castelfranco, originally Giorgio Barbarelli
(1478?–1511), Venetian painter, born at
Castelfranco. He was brought up in Venice,
and apprenticed to the painter Giovanni Bel-
lini. He achieved an early success, being commissioned in 1500 to paint the portrait of the
Doge Agostino Barberigo. Giorgione was the
leader of the Venetian school of his period,
and he influenced several contemporaries, including Titian. In 1504 he executed the altarpiece in the cathedral at Castelfranco, which
still exists, though much restored. This trip-
tych shows the Virgin enthroned in the center, supported on either side by St. Francis
and St. Liberale. Other works of about this
period which also can be definitely assigned
to him are the twin paintings, "Trial of
Moses" and "Judgment of Solomon" (Uffizi
Gallery, Florence), and the "Portrait of a
Young Man" (Kaiser Friedrich Museum,
Berlin). Giorgione's mature style can be seen
in the "Knight of Malta" (Uffizi), the "Sleep-
ing Venus" (Dresden Gallery), and the "Pastoral Symphony" (Louvre, Paris). The last
of these was once attributed to Titian, because
the painting of the two Venetian artists was
sometimes so similar that their works are easily confused. Giorgione died of the plague in
Venice.

GIOTTO, in full Giotto di Bondone
(1276?–1337?), Florentine painter, sculptor,
and architect, born at Vespignano, near Florence. He studied with Cimabue. He was the
greatest Italian painter immediately preceding
the Renaissance, and was celebrated for his
arrangement of groups and the vividness of
the gestures of his figures. Four early works,

U.S.D.A., Bur. Plant Ind., Soils, & Agric. Eng.

Leaves and root of American ginseng

"Flight into Egypt," fresco by Giotto in the Arena chapel, Padua

a series of frescoes depicting the life of St. Francis, are in the lower church at Assisi, and can be decisively credited to him; these include the "Marriage of St. Francis to Poverty", the "Triumph of Obedience", the "Triumph of Chastity", and the "Glorification of St. Francis". The "Navicella", a mosaic by him depicting Christ saving St. Peter from the waves, was executed in 1298, and is in the sacristy of St. Peter's, Rome; it has been much restored and altered. In the same church is an altarpiece showing Christ acclaimed by angels, and depicting the martyrdoms of St. Peter and St. Paul on the side panels. In the Cathedral of St. John Lateran, Rome, is the much repainted fresco fragment entitled "Boniface VIII Proclaiming the Jubilee". In 1306 Giotto started his most ambitious work, the series of frescoes in the Annunziata dell' Arena chapel, Padua; the series includes "The Ascension of the Savior", "The Last Judgment", and other frescoes depicting the life of Christ. In 1330 Giotto became the guest of

Robert of Anjou, King of Naples, but no trace remains of the works he painted under the royal patronage. In 1334 he became chief architect of the building of the Florentine cathedral of St. Reparata (now Santa Maria del Fiore), for which he designed the west façade and the detached campanile; the latter bears sculptured ornament from his designs.

GIRAFFE, common name for any of the long-necked and long-limbed members of the African genus *Giraffa*, the tallest of the terrestrial mammals, which together with the okapi (q.v.) and several fossil genera constitute the ruminant family Giraffidae. Male giraffes sometimes reach a height of nineteen feet, and females reach a height of seventeen feet, measured from the top of the head to the ground. This height is due to the long legs and to the long, stiff neck which contains only seven vertebrae, the same number as in the necks of humans and other mammals. Because the body slopes sharply down to the tail, the forelegs appear to be longer than the hind legs, but all four legs are actually equal in length. On the forehead of both sexes are skin-covered horns. The upper lip of the giraffe is long and muscular, and the tongue reaches 18 inches in length. The animal is adapted to procure its food from the leaves of trees, especially the acacia. In order to lower its head to the ground, the giraffe stands with forelegs wide apart on the rare occasions when it drinks or grazes. It can go without water for at least a month. The giraffe moves both legs on one side simultaneously when it walks or runs, and reaches a running speed of over thirty miles an hour. Valued for its hide and flesh, the giraffe was slaughtered indiscriminately in former times; it is now protected by law. It is timid, but when cornered shows fierce resistance, being capable of delivering powerful kicks with its hind legs. The typical cry of the giraffe, which has only rudimentary vocal cords, resembles the lowing of a cow. Only one fawn is produced at birth.

Two species of giraffes are known. The Nubian giraffe, *G. reticulata,* is found in N.E. Africa from Somaliland to Kenya and eastward to the Nile River. It is red-chestnut in color with a fine network of white lines over its entire body. It has a third horn, midway between the other two, lower down on the forehead. The southern giraffe, *G. camelopardalis,* ranges from the Union of South Africa northward to Kenya and the Sudan. It is pale brown or cream-colored, with large, lemon-yellow, red, or brown blotches. These blotches grow darker with age. The southern giraffe has only two horns. The coloring of both species camouflages them in their natural surroundings. Though presently confined to the regions of Africa s. of the Sahara Desert, fossil remains indicate that the giraffes were once common in s. Europe and Asia.

GIRARD, STEPHEN (1750–1831), American businessman and philanthropist, born at Bordeaux, France. The son of a sea captain, at twenty-three Girard had become captain and part-owner of a ship engaged in the West Indian and American coast trade. In 1776 he settled in Philadelphia, and became a merchant. At the outbreak of the Revolutionary War he supported the colonial cause. He became a citizen of Pennsylvania in 1778 and resumed his trading activities with the West Indies, accumulating a sizable fortune. In 1810 he invested about $1,000,000 in shares of the Bank of the United States. In 1812, when the bank's charter lapsed, he purchased a con-

trolling interest in its stock and continued the business as the Bank of Stephen Girard. During the War of 1812 he was an important financial supporter of the United States government; in 1814 he subscribed for about 95% of the war loan of $5,000,000. When the Second Bank of the United States was chartered in 1816, Girard became one of its principal stockholders and had a dominant influence on its policy for many years.

At his death Girard's fortune was probably the largest in the United States, amounting to about $7,500,000, the bulk of which he left for philanthropic purposes. His will, which made legal history, provided money for the improvement of the Philadelphia police system, for municipal improvements, and for the erection of a school or college for "poor, white, male orphans". In the regulations for the management of the college the will provided that no minister or ecclesiastic of any sect could hold office in the college or enter upon its premises, and that there was to be no inculcation of religious doctrine in a denominational sense. The heirs-at-law contested the will in 1836, and in 1844 Daniel Webster argued for the heirs before the U.S. Supreme Court, making a famous plea for the Christian religion. The Supreme Court nevertheless held that the will was valid, and the school was organized. See GIRARD COLLEGE.

The southern giraffe

GIRARD COLLEGE, an industrial school for orphan boys, founded in 1848 at Philadelphia, Pa., in accordance with the will of Stephen Girard (q.v.). Girard left the residue of his estate, amounting to $5,260,000, for the establishment of the school, which was formally opened in 1848 with one hundred pupils and seventeen instructors. Since 1869 the school has been controlled by twelve directors chosen for life by a board consisting of judges of the courts of common pleas of Philadelphia, the mayor of the city, and the president of the city council. The same board also manages the Girard estate. The school has a normal capacity of about 1500 students, and its endowment has grown to over $30,-000,000. It has more than twenty buildings covering an area of about forty acres. It comprises a primary school, a grammar school, and a high school in which mechanical and commercial trades are taught.

GIRASOL. See OPAL.

GIRAUD, HENRI HONORÉ (1879–1949), French general, educated at St. Cyr. During his service in World War I, he was captured by the Germans, but escaped after a short imprisonment. He fought against the Riffs in Morocco in the campaign of 1925–26. In 1940 Giraud was in command of allied defenses in Northern France, and after the fall of Sedan he was again a prisoner of the Germans. He escaped from Germany to unoccupied France in April, 1942, and made his way to Algeria in November. After the assassination of Admiral Jean-François Darlan (q.v.) in December of that year, General Giraud was appointed high commissioner of French North and West Africa. In June, 1943, Giraud became copresident of the French Committee of National Liberation with General Charles de Gaulle (q.v.). In July Giraud was named commander in chief of all French forces and in November resigned his political office. After the liberation of France Giraud was a deputy in the second Provisional Assembly in 1946.

GIRAUDOUX, JEAN (1882–1944), French writer and diplomat, born at Bellac, Haute-Vienne, and educated at the École Normale Supérieure in Paris. He became head of the press service in the French foreign office and in 1912 secured an appointment in the diplomatic service. His experiences in the first World War furnished him with material for several novels, including *L'Adorable Clio* (1920). He won the Goncourt prize in 1926 for *Siegfried et le Limousin* (1922). In 1939 he became chief of propaganda for France. His works display originality and wit and

are literary parallels to the impressionist trends in music and painting. Giraudoux was particularly successful in the field of drama, and contributed to the freeing of French theater from the bonds of realism. Many of his plays, such as *Amphitryon 38* (1929), were based on ancient Greek myths. Among other important works of his are the novels *Simon le Pathétique* (1918), *Suzanne et le Pacifique* (1921), and *Églantine* (1927); the plays *Intermezzo* (1933), *Électre* (1937), and *La Folle de Chaillot* (1945). An English version of his play *Ondine* was produced in the United States in 1954.

GIRDLE OF VENUS or **VENUS'S-GIRDLE,** common name for any of the semitransparent, ribbon-shaped marine animals of the family Cestidae of the phylum Ctenophora (q.v.). The ends of the ribbon are actually the left and right sides of the animal's body. Members of the typical genus, *Cestus,* are about two inches long, five feet wide, and a fraction of an inch thick from front to back. The mouth is situated in the center of the animal on one border of the "ribbon". The girdle of Venus swims with an undulating action. The best-known species, *C. veneris,* is found in the Mediterranean and in the Atlantic.

GIRGA, city and capital of the administrative division of the same name, Upper Egypt. The city is situated on the w. bank of the Nile, 313 m. by rail S.S.E. of Cairo. Girga is the former capital of Upper Egypt. It contains one of the oldest Roman Catholic monasteries in Egypt, and is the seat of a Coptic bishopric. Girga is noted for the excellent quality of its ceramics. Pop. of city, about 20,000. Area of administrative division, about 595 sq.m.; pop. (1947) 1,283,468.

GIRL SCOUTS OF THE UNITED STATES OF AMERICA, a nonsectarian, nonpolitical, interracial organization founded in 1912 by Mrs. Juliette Low for the general purpose of building good character and citizenship among girls from the ages of seven to eighteen. The aims of the Girl Scouts are expressed in the Girl Scout promise, to which candidates for membership are expected to subscribe: "On my honor, I will try to do my duty to God and my country, to help other people at all times, and to obey the Girl Scout laws." In accordance with their promise, members are required to practice honesty, courtesy, humanity, obedience, cheerfulness, thrift, and other worthy qualities. To aid in inculcating these traits, the organization carries on activities under the following general categories: homemaking, arts and crafts, music and danc-

National Girl Scout News Bureau

ACTIVITIES OF THE
AMERICAN GIRL SCOUTS

Above: Wing Scouts, a branch of Senior Girl Scouts, taking flying lesson. Right: Scout leader giving a cooking lesson. Below: Attending a class in first aid.

ing, literature and dramatics, health and safety, sports and games, nature study, outdoor projects, community life, and international friendship. For Senior Girl Scouts, a classification including members between the ages of fifteen and eighteen, vocational guidance is added to the list of activities. Members between the ages of seven and ten are known as Brownie Scouts or Brownies; those between ten and fifteen are known as Girl Scouts.

The Girl Scouts are organized into troops, with membership ranging from sixteen to thirty-two girls. The activities of each troop are performed under the guidance of a leader, who must be at least twenty-one years old, and who may have one or more assistants. The leaders are selected and trained under the supervision of local councils of men and women; these councils also exercise over-all guidance on the activities of most of the troops, and elect the members of the national council, the highest governing body of the organization.

In June, 1954, membership in the Girl Scouts was 1,748,561, and the number of troop leaders, associate Girl Scouts, and other adults serving in the organization was 532,411. The Girl Scouts organization, with headquarters in New York City, publishes two monthly magazines, *The Girl Scout Leader* and *The American Girl.*

GIRONDE, a maritime department of s.w. France, formed of part of the ancient province of Guienne. It is watered by the rivers Garonne and Dordogne. The department is level and extremely fertile, with the exception of small wooded hills in the E. Gironde is one of the principal wine-producing departments of France, with over one seventh of its total area devoted to vineyards. Other agricultural products are corn, rye, oats, wheat, tobacco, vegetables, and fruits. In addition, pitch, resin, and turpentine are obtained from large pine forests; milch cows, cattle, and horses are bred; and limestone is quarried. Fishing and oystering are commercially important on the coast. The principal cities of Gironde are Bordeaux (q.v.), the capital, and Caudéran (pop. in 1946, 24,637), Bègles (22,289), Talence (20,412), Mérignac (19,-550), Le Bouscat (17,809), Libourne (14,563), and Pauillac (2320). Area of the department, 4141 sq.m.; pop. (1953 est.) 898,000.

GIRONDE ESTUARY, the largest estuary of France and one of the largest in w. Europe, located in the department of Gironde, France. It is formed by the confluence of the Garonne and Dordogne rivers, 45 miles s.w. of the Bay of Biscay. Its mean depth is 21 feet and its widest point, near the mouth, is 6 miles. The estuary is divided by small islands and mud banks into an E. and a W. channel. At the mouth of the estuary stands the famous lighthouse, the Phare de Corodouan, built in 1585 and enlarged in the 18th century.

GIRONDISTS, members of the moderate republican party, the *Gironde,* formed in the French legislative assembly in 1791. The leaders were deputies to the assembly from the Department of Gironde. See FRENCH REVOLUTION.

GIRTIN, THOMAS (1775–1802), English water-color painter and etcher, born at Southwark, and apprenticed to a mezzotint engraver. With his friend Joseph Mallord William Turner he developed the art of water-color painting from the mere application of tints over monochrome washes to the use of the full range of pure color which it now employs. In his etchings he made a skillful use of aquatint to obtain the effects formerly shown in monochrome water color. His early death, from consumption, caused Turner to remark, "Had Tom Girtin lived, I should have starved." There are representative collections of his works in the British Museum and the Victoria and Albert Museum, London, and the Whitworth Institute, Manchester.

GIRTY, SIMON (1741–1818), American frontiersman and scout, born in what is now Dauphin Co., Pa. He was known as "The Great Renegade" because he turned traitor during the American Revolution. From 1759 until the outbreak of the Revolution he served as interpreter and scout at Fort Pitt. At the beginning of the Revolution he acted as interpreter for the Continental Army. However, in 1778 he deserted to the British and was consequently attainted by the Pennsylvania legislature. During the rest of the war he led raiding parties of British and Indians along the northern and western frontiers. After the war he settled near Detroit, which remained in British hands, and continued to lead Indian raids on American outposts. In 1791 he participated in the attack on Fort Jefferson and the defeat of Major General Arthur St. Clair, first American governor of the Northwest Territory. In 1796, when Detroit was ceded to the United States under the terms of the Jay Treaty, Girty escaped to Canada, where he lived for the rest of his life. Although the stories circulated concerning Girty's savagery were exaggerated, he was greatly feared in the western settlements and is known to have permitted the torture and burning of whites by Indians.

GISH, DOROTHY (1898–), American actress, born at Massillon, Ohio, sister of Lillian Gish. She made her stage debut at the age of four, in *In Convict Stripes,* and in the following year played Little Willie in *East Lynne,* in New York City. She continued to play juvenile roles until 1912, when she began her long career in motion pictures. Between that year and 1928 she appeared in many films, including *Hearts of the World, The Orphans of the Storm, Nell Gwyn,* and *Madame Pompadour.* Returning to the stage in 1928, she played in numerous productions, mostly in New York City; among them are *Young Love* (1928), *Comedienne* (1934), *Missouri Legend* (1938), *Life With Father* (1940), *The Magnificent Yankee* (1946), and *The Man* (1950). She also appeared in the motion pictures *Our Hearts Were Young and Gay* (1944) and *Centennial Summer* (1946).

GISH, LILLIAN (1896–), American actress, born in Springfield, Ohio, sister of Dorothy Gish. At the age of six she made her first appearance on the stage in *In Convict's Stripes,* a play in which her four-year-old sister Dorothy also appeared. She danced in a Sarah Bernhardt production in New York City in 1903, and in 1913 appeared in *A Good Little Devil,* with Mary Pickford. From 1912 to 1930 she played leading roles in numerous motion pictures, including *The Birth of a Nation, Intolerance, The Hearts of the World, Broken Blossoms,* and *Way Down East.* She then returned to the stage, subsequently appearing in such plays as *Uncle Vanya* (1930), *Camille* (1932), *Hamlet* (1936), and *Life With Father* (1940). Later motion pictures in which she appeared include *Commandos Strike at Dawn* (1942), *Duel in the Sun* (1948), *Portrait of Jenny* (1949), and *The Night of the Hunter* (1955).

GISSING, GEORGE ROBERT (1857–1903), English novelist, born at Wakefield, and educated at Owens College, Manchester. He became a teacher, but made only a meager living at teaching, first in London and then in the United States, suffering the deprivations of poverty which later supplied material for many of his works. His novels deal chiefly with the lives of London's lower middle classes, and his favorite theme is the degrading and brutalizing effect of poverty on human beings. His first novel was *Workers in the Dawn* (1880), but he received no popular

recognition until the publication of his fourth novel, *Demos* (1886), an imaginary account of the effect of Socialism upon poverty-stricken people. Among his other writings are the novels of contemporary life *Thyrza* (1887), *New Grub Street* (1891), *In the Year of Jubilee* (1894), and *The Whirlpool* (1897); the semiautobiography *The Private Papers of Henry Ryecroft* (1903); and *Veranilda* (posthumously published, 1904), a historical novel of 6th-century Italy which reflects Gissing's scholarly knowledge of the work of the late Latin historians.

GITANOS. See GYPSIES.

GIULIO ROMANO. See ROMANO, GIULIO.

GIZA or **GIZEH,** city and capital of the administrative division of the same name, Upper Egypt. The city is located on the w. bank of the Nile, 3 miles s.w. of Cairo. The great pyramids (q.v.) are situated 5 miles w. of the city. Pop. of city (1947) 66,156. Area of administrative division, 397 sq.m.; pop. (1947) 818,168.

GJELLERUP, KARL (1857–1919), Danish author, born in Roholte, on the island of Zealand. He studied theology in his youth, but later became an atheist, under the influence of the Danish literary critic Georg Morris Brandes (q.v.). After 1892 he lived in Germany; many of his writings are in the German language and demonstrate his admiration for that country and its culture, expressing the broad humanistic spirit of Schiller and Goethe. In 1917 the Nobel Prize for literature was awarded jointly to Gjellerup and another Danish writer, Henrik Pontoppidan (q.v.). Gjellerup's works include *En Idealist* (1878), *Minna* (1889), and *Den Gyldne Gren* (1917).

GLACE BAY, a town in Cape Breton County, Nova Scotia, Canada, situated on the coast, about 15 miles N.E. of Sydney, with which it is connected by rail. Glace Bay is a transatlantic wireless station and an important coal-mining center. Pop., about 25,000.

GLACIAL EPOCH. See QUATERNARY PERIOD.

GLACIER, a large, usually moving mass of ice formed in high mountains or in high latitudes where the rate of snowfall is greater than the rate of melting of the snow. Glaciers can be divided into four well-defined types, Alpine, Piedmont, Spitzbergen, and Greenland, according to the topography and climate of the region in which the glacier was formed.

Alpine Glaciers. The snow that falls on the walls and floors of valleys in high mountain regions tends to accumulate to a great depth, because the rate of melting, particularly in wintertime, is far less than the rate at which the snow falls. As a result the earlier snows, compressed by later falls, are changed into a compact body of ice having a granular structure. This body of ice is often composed of well-defined layers resulting from successive snowstorms and from the deposition of layers of atmospheric dust on the surface of new falls of snow. When the depth of the glacier reaches approximately 100 ft., the whole mass begins to creep slowly down the valley in which it is formed. This flow continues as long as a superabundance of snow reaches the top of the glacier. As the glacier flows down the valley to a lower altitude where it is not replenished by snowfall, it melts or wastes away, and the meltwater forms the source for streams and rivers.

In cross section, the structures of all glaciers are similar. At the bottom of the glacier is a layer of clear ice which is subject to great pressure and which flows like a viscous fluid. Above the ice is a thick layer of *névé* or *firn,* composed of snowflakes which have become compacted into granular balls of ice by a combination of melting and pressure. Over the névé is a mantle of new snow. The flowing of the glacier is confined to the compact ice at its base, and, because of the unconformity between this ice and the upper layers of the glacier, cracks known as *crevasses* commonly are formed in the glacier's upper surface. These crevasses, which may be many feet across and many yards deep, are frequently covered and masked by new-fallen snow and form a hazard to anyone walking across the surface of the glacier. A large crevasse known as the *bergschrund* is usually formed in the shape of a semicircle at the head of the glacier, between the glacier itself and the headwall of the valley in which it lies.

Glaciers are usually bordered at their sides by zones of rock debris which have fallen from the side walls of the valley as a result of frost wedging action; see EROSION. These zones of rock fragments on the glacier's surface are called *moraines.* At the lower end of the glacier the moraines increase in size. When two glaciers from neighboring valleys meet, the moraines at their adjoining sides coalesce to form a *medial moraine* in the middle of the resulting glacier. As the ice melts at the lower end of a glacier, rock and debris that it has plowed up in its progress over the valley floor, in addition to rock material that may have fallen into crevasses, are deposited in a series of semicircular hillocks which

are called the *terminal moraine* of the glacier.

As a glacier moves down its valley it eventually reaches a point at which the melting and evaporation from its surface exceed the amount of snow falling upon it. At this point, often called the *firn-line,* the surface of the glacier is névé or firn rather than snow. Rocks or boulders falling on the surface of the glacier below this point often insulate the ice beneath them from the heat of the sun and, as the glacier wastes away, are left supported on columns of ice. Such structures are known as *ice-tables.*

The speed of flow of glaciers varies between wide limits. Most glaciers move downward at the rate of a few feet per day, but observation of the Black Rapids Glacier in Alaska during the years 1936–37 showed that it was moving at the rate of 115 ft. per day. This is the swiftest advance ever recorded for any glacier in the world and was probably due to extremely heavy snowfalls which occurred in the area some years earlier.

With variations in climate, glaciers shrink and expand to a marked extent. An excess of precipitation causes a situation analogous to a river flood and the glacier increases in size. Similarly, when precipitation decreases, the glacier shrinks.

Glaciers of the alpine type are found in high mountain ranges throughout the world, even in the tropics. In the U.S., alpine or valley glaciers exist on the slopes of Mt. Rainier, Mt. Baker, and Mt. Adams in Washington, Mt. Hood in Oregon, and Mt. Shasta in California. The Hubbard glacier in Alaska, 80 m. long, is the longest glacier of the alpine type in the world. Glaciers of the N.W. United States were observed in 1955 to be advancing for the first time since the middle of the 19th century.

Piedmont Glaciers. When a number of valley glaciers flow together in the valley at the foot of a range of mountains they frequently form extensive glacier sheets known as piedmont glaciers (after the department of Piedmont in Italy). Glaciers of this type are especially common in Alaska. The largest of the piedmont glaciers is the Malaspina Glacier which has an area of about 1500 sq.m. The lower portion of this glacier is almost flat and is covered with so much soil and rock debris that it supports a thick forest.

Spitzbergen Glacier. The glacier system which covers a large portion of the island of Spitzbergen in the Arctic sea north of Europe is unique in form, being a type intermediate between the alpine glacier and the

Can. Pac. Ry.; Can. Nat. Rys.

GLACIERS OF NORTH AMERICA

Above: Crevasses in Athabaska Glacier, Alberta. Right: Long tongue of Yoho Glacier, Alpine type, moves down valley in British Columbia. Below: Edge of Taku Glacier in Alaska, having reached sea, forms icebergs.

Greenland glacier described below. The entire center of the island is covered with an ice sheet which overlies a high plateau. At the edges of the plateau the sheet breaks up into a series of valley glaciers which move down steep valleys, sometimes reaching the sea.

Greenland Glaciers. Covering almost the entire extent of Greenland is a huge glacial blanket over 700,000 sq.m. in area and about 6200 ft. in maximum thickness. This gigantic glacier flows slowly outward from two centers, one on the southern part of the island and one in the north. Because of its thickness the Greenland ice sheet rises far above both the valleys and hills of the land beneath it, and the underlying rock is exposed only near the seacoast where the glacier breaks up into tongues of ice somewhat resembling valley glaciers. From the ends of the these tongues where they reach the sea large and small fragments of ice break off during the summer, forming icebergs. A glacier of a similar type covers the whole of the Antarctic continent and has an area of about 5,000,000 sq.m. Continental glaciers covered much of North America during the Quaternary period (q.v.).

Glacial Erosion. As a glacier moves down a valley (or across country in the case of a large ice sheet) it sculptures the land in a characteristic manner. Rocks in its path are plowed out of the way and rocks beneath it are broken up by frost action and picked up and carried away. Furthermore the rocks imbedded in the bottom of the glacier act as abrasive particles, scratching and scouring the rocks over which the glacier is moving.

At the head of a valley in which a glacier is formed, the headwalls are eroded into a characteristic semicircular form called a cirque (q.v.). Valleys down which glaciers have traveled are eroded to a U shape rather than the V shape caused by stream erosion. Frequently the valley is excavated so deeply that the mouths of tributary valleys are left high above the new valley floor as *hanging valleys*. *Fiords* are glaciated valleys which have been partly flooded by the sea. See DEPOSIT; GEOLOGY.

GLACIER BAY NATIONAL MONUMENT, a national monument in S.E. Alaska, w. of Juneau, established in 1925. Its area of nearly 2,300,000 acres, noted for its tidewater glaciers, extends inland to include several peaks of the St. Elias range, in particular mounts Fairweather, La Perouse, and Lituya. Among the great glaciers discharged by the mountains into Glacier Bay are Brady and Muir. The latter is about 50 m. long, 3 miles broad at the sea, and 1500 ft. deep; it has an area of over 350 sq.m. The monument area is of value for scientific research on the performance of glaciers and the conditions existing after glacial retreat. In 1939 the area of Glacier Bay National Monument was increased from about 1,135,000 acres to its present size.

GLACIER NATIONAL PARK, a national park established in 1910, in N.W. Montana, extending southward from the Canadian boundary and occupying portions of Glacier and Flathead counties. Together with Waterton Lakes National Park in Alberta, Canada, it forms the Waterton-Glacier International Peace Park, established jointly by the U.S. and Canadian governments in 1932; the two areas are connected by an international highway opened in 1938. Glacier National Park covers an area of 1583 sq.m. in the Lewis and Livingston ranges of the Rocky Mountains, and contains more than 60 glaciers and over 200 glacier-fed lakes. The Continental Divide traverses the park from northwest to southeast.

Extraordinary scenic beauty distinguishes the region included in the park; particularly notable are precipices thousands of feet in depth, carved by erosion, and broad U-shaped valleys which were formed by glaciers. The small remaining glaciers are among the few in the U.S. which are readily accessible. The E. and W. sides of the park are connected by the Going-to-the-Sun Highway, which crosses the Continental Divide through Logan Pass at an elevation of 6654 ft. above sea level. The highest peak among the mountains within the park area is Mount Cleveland (10,438 ft. above sea level). Lake McDonald, 10 miles long and a mile wide, is the largest lake in the park. The western slopes of the mountains are thickly forested, and the park contains about thirty species of trees. More than a thousand varieties of flowers bloom in the valley floors and alpine meadows. Among the animals within the park are moose, bighorns, elk, mountain goats, mountain caribou, bears, deer, bobcats, beavers, marmots, otters, and martens. The many varieties of birds found there include the osprey, ptarmigan, and the golden and bald eagles. The lakes and streams of the area abound in fish, especially mackinaw and several species of trout. Adjoining the park on the E. is the Blackfeet Indian Reservation.

GLACKENS, WILLIAM JAMES (1870–1938), American painter, born at Philadelphia, and educated at the Pennsylvania Academy of Fine Arts. He was the leading exponent of the French Impressionist style of painting in the United States. Most of his works are landscapes; they include "The Bathers", "Central Park—Winter", "Bal Martinique", and "Chez Mouquin". Glackens is represented by paintings in a number of leading American museums, including the Metropolitan Museum of Art, New York City; the Corcoran Gallery of Art, Washington, D.C.; and the Museum of History, Science, and Art, Los Angeles.

GLADIATOR (Lat. *gladius*, "sword"), in ancient Rome, a professional fighter, who took part in public contests of skill at armed combat, in arenas built for the purpose. The spectacle of men fighting to the death originated in Etruria, and enjoyed vast popularity in Rome and its provinces. The first exhibition of gladiators at Rome was held in 264 B.C. at the Forum Boarium, and was organized by the brothers Marcus and Decimus Brutus during the funeral celebration for their father. At that time only three pairs of gladiators fought, but by 174 B.C., at a three-day spectacle arranged by Titus Flaminius, there were 37 pairs. Julius Cæsar presented exhibitions of such proportions that the Roman senate was impelled to limit the number of contestants; this ruling did not prevent his exhibiting 300 pairs on one occasion. The largest contest of gladiators recorded was that given by the Emperor Trajan to celebrate his victory over Decebalus of Dacia in 106 A.D., with no fewer than 5000 pairs of contestants. Freak shows were occasionally given, such as the combats organized by the Emperor Domitian in 90 A.D. at the Saturnalia, between women and dwarfs.

The first gladiators were slaves, condemned criminals, and prisoners of war, the last-named including Britons, Moors, African Negroes, and Thracians, but later freemen and Roman citizens also entered the arena. One emperor, Commodus, actually fought in the arena himself. The gladiators were trained in *ludi*, or schools. Hardened criminals were forced to become swordsmen, and special measures were taken to discipline them and to prevent them from committing suicide. In the *ludus gladiatorius* discovered in the ruins of Pompeii, 63 skeletons were found, many of them in chains. On the other hand, a successful gladiator received great acclaim; he was praised in verses by poets, his portrait appeared on gems and vases, and patrician ladies pampered him.

According to the arms they used, or their methods of fighting, gladiators were divided into different classes. The *Retiarius,* clad in a short tunic, was armed with a net and a trident; he attempted to entangle his opponent, the *Secutor,* with the net, *iaculum,* and then to kill him with the trident. The *Samnites* used their national weapons, a short sword and an oblong shield, and wore a plumed helmet. The *Thraces,* with a small sword or dagger, generally curved like a scythe, were as a rule matched with the *Mirmilliones,* carrying a sword and shield and wearing a helmet crested with a fish. When a gladiator had his opponent at his mercy he would turn to the crowd of spectators who, if they considered the defeated man had fought well, would wave their handkerchiefs as a signal that he should be spared; however, when the crowd considered that he had shown cowardice, they turned down their thumbs to indicate that the victor should kill him.

Although the emperor Constantine attempted to abolish gladiatorial contests in 325 A.D. by issuing an edict against them, they continued to be held until about the year 500.

GLADIATOR'S WAR. See SPARTACUS.

GLADIOLUS, genus of herbs belonging to the Iris family, having spikes of flowers and sword-shaped leaves. The flowers are funnel-shaped and have corolla lobes which are narrowest at the base and become progressively wider toward the tip. Most of the approximately two hundred species of gladioli have flowers of great beauty. Gladioli display an extensive range of colors, but each type is restricted to a single color. A few species are native to Eurasia, but the bulk of them originated in South Africa. The great development in gladiolus cultivation in the U.S. has resulted in production of a profusion of horticultural varieties, most of them hybrids, which are important commercial flowers all year round. Botanists do not attempt to classify this confusing array into the usual species and varieties, and so the various kinds of gladiolus are classified by "type" and are given common names. Some of the most beautiful gladioli have been derived from the wild species *G. primulinus, G. cardinalis, G. blandus,* and *G. oppositiflorus.*

Gladioli may be grown from bulbous rhizomes which are commonly called bulbs but are actually corms. Gladiolus corms are not hardy and must be protected from freezing temperatures, but may be planted any time after the soil becomes warm in early spring. They are planted six inches apart and three inches deep in soil that has been deeply spaded. Several plantings may be made dur-

A variety of Gladiolus blandus

ing the spring and early summer to provide a succession of flowers throughout the growing season.

Gladiolus corms used for planting are usually propagated from small structures known as cormels. Cormels, which are produced at the bases of corms, are small, hard-shelled structures about the size of corn grains. The shells are usually broken by cracking, or softened by soaking in water, before the cormels are planted. Cormels do not require as much space as corms, but are planted at the same depth. They develop into full-sized corms in one to three years.

Gladioli are occasionally grown from seeds. Seeds are sown in March or April, and grown in plots under glass until summer. In temperate climates, the plants must be taken indoors for the winter and replanted in the spring. Gladioli grown from seeds attain maturity in three or four years.

The common fungus diseases of gladiolus are hard rot, dry rot, scab, and yellow. Hard rot, caused by the fungus *Septoria gladioli,* attacks gladiolus leaves and corms, appearing first as brown spotting and later drying the corms into hard, wrinkled masses. Dry rot, caused by the fungus *Sclerotium,* produces brown spotting of corms similar to hard rot. Scab, caused by certain bacteria, appears as brownish or purple spots near the bases of the leaves. Yellows, produced by members of the fungus genus *Fusarium,* causes yellowing of leaf-sheaths and death of leaves in midsummer, especially during hot, dry periods. Fungicides (q.v.) are effective in controlling most fungus and bacterial diseases of gladiolus, but no preventive treatment has been found for yellows.

Small gladiolus thrips (slender black insects which develop from yellow or orange larvae) suck plant juices from gladiolus leaf sheaths and flower buds, causing small grayish spots which eventually turn brown. Flower buds attacked by thrips when young become distorted; when attacked at a later stage they develop white spots. Thrips are controlled by destruction of all plant debris at the end of a growing season, by dusting corms intended for use the following season with D.D.T., and by spraying or dusting plants with D.D.T. during growth; see INSECTICIDE.

GLADSTONE, WILLIAM EWART (1809–98), British statesman, born in Liverpool and educated at Eton and Christ Church College, Oxford University. While still a student, Gladstone manifested an oratorical brilliance and a sympathy with the Tory Party that brought him to the attention of the Duke of Newcastle; in 1831, the Duke procured him a seat in Parliament. Gladstone took his seat as the member for Newark a year later and attached himself to the Tories, led by Sir Robert Peel (q.v.). The new M.P. made his maiden speech in defense of his father, a wealthy merchant, against whom charges had been brought concerning the mistreatment of slaves on a plantation in Demerara, British Guiana. A succession of notable speeches opposing reform measures brought Gladstone into political prominence; during the first Peel ministry of 1834–35, he was appointed to two minor administrative posts, in the colonial and treasury offices. After the fall of the Peel cabinet, which had lasted only five months, Gladstone again became a member of the opposition. During the next six years, he devoted a great part of his time to writing two books: *The State in Its Relations with the Church* (1838) and *Church Principles* (1840). The first of these books, which aroused unfavorable comment even in the Tory Party, advocated the establishment of a single church under the control of the state, of which the church should be the moral guide.

When Peel became prime minister for the second time in 1841, Gladstone was appointed vice-president of the Board of Trade, and two years later he became its president and a member of the cabinet. In this capacity, he played a leading role in the revision of the tariff in accordance with the policies of Peel who, reversing his earlier position, had become an advocate of free trade. In early 1845, refusing to compromise the religious principles outlined in his first book, Gladstone resigned from the cabinet over a question of subsidies to an Irish Catholic seminary, which he refused to support. He had, however, already proved his value and, in December, 1845, when Peel revised his cabinet to prepare for repeal of the Corn Laws (q.v.), the prime minister prevailed on Gladstone to accept the secretaryship of state for the colonies. As a result the Duke of Newcastle, who was opposed to free trade, refused to support him in the borough of Newark; for more than a year, the only hiatus in his long legislative career, Gladstone was not a member of Parliament. The Tory cabinet fell in 1846; in the general elections of the following year, Gladstone was elected an M.P. for Oxford University, a coveted honor.

In the next few years, a revolution took place in Gladstone's political thinking. His early conservatism relaxed, and he became progressively more liberal in his speeches. In 1852 he first clashed with the conservatism of Benjamin Disraeli (q.v.), who became his greatest political rival. Disraeli, then chancellor of the exchequer, outlined a budget for that year which Gladstone so decried, in a notable speech, that the government fell. In the new cabinet formed by George Hamilton Gordon, Earl of Aberdeen, Gladstone himself became chancellor of the exchequer. He filled his office with such brilliance that, when the Aberdeen cabinet resigned in 1855, he was asked to continue as chancellor in the cabinet formed by Viscount Henry George Temple Palmerston (q.v.).

Differences with cabinet policy led him to resign after three weeks, but his political stature remained undiminished and four years later, at the request of Queen Victoria, he returned to Palmerston's cabinet as chancellor. His budgets for the years 1860 and 1861 were regarded as marvels of financial statesmanship; moreover, the 1860 budget, which included a marked increase in the number of duty-free imports, indicated that Gladstone had definitely adopted the policies of the Liberal (formerly Whig) Party. When Lord John Russell (q.v.), the leader of the Liberal Party, formed a cabinet in 1865, Gladstone became a member. Two years later Russell retired and Gladstone became the undisputed Liberal

leader. In this capacity he assailed the Conservative (formerly Tory) ministry of Disraeli in 1868 concerning an Irish question; the elections which followed gave the Liberals an overwhelming majority and Gladstone became prime minister for the first time in December, 1868.

The new administration began at once to propose reforms in Irish affairs, one of Gladstone's greatest interests. Despite bitter opposition in Parliament, the disestablishment of the Irish Church was effected in 1869. A year later the Irish Land Act was passed, giving Irish tenants more rights and a measure of protection from unscrupulous landlords. The next few years witnessed the passing of outstanding reforms in civil service, the army, and, notably, education (see EDUCATION, NATIONAL SYSTEMS OF: *United Kingdom*). About 1873 the Liberal government began to experience difficulties in Parliament; its handling of the *Alabama* Claims (q.v.) was exceedingly unpopular, and the new reforms tended to alienate large groups of the English population. The defeat of a proposal to establish an Irish national university forced the prime minister to dissolve Parliament in 1874. The resulting general election brought the Conservatives, under Disraeli, into office. Gladstone resigned his leadership of the Lib-

William Ewart Gladstone (photograph, 1896)

eral Party in 1875 and retired from public life.

He was not long silent, however. In 1876 Bulgaria revolted against the Turkish Empire, and Turkey permitted its irregular troops to quell the rebellion; the resulting massacres became internationally notorious as the Bulgarian Atrocities. Disraeli, as prime minister, insisted that England maintain an official pro-Turkish attitude, but Gladstone aroused public feeling against the Turks to a pitch of excitement by a series of speeches and pamphlets. In 1879, once more a prominent public figure, he toured England in a great political campaign. The Liberals, opposing Disraeli's foreign policy, were voted into office and, in 1880, Gladstone became prime minister for the second time.

The foreign policy of the Gladstone government, committed to reversing the aggressive imperialism of Disraeli, soon became as unpopular as its predecessor. In 1881 the prime minister withdrew the British troops occupying Afghanistan, but Russia moved troops into the country and war was narrowly averted. In the same year the government ended a revolt of the Boers (q.v.) in South Africa by giving the Transvaal its independence, a step contrary to public opinion. Moreover, despite its disavowal of imperialism, the government found itself deeply and unwillingly involved in Egyptian affairs (see EGYPT: *History*). In 1885 the cabinet suffered a severe loss in prestige from the British failure to relieve Khartoum in the Anglo-Egyptian Sudan, to which Gen. Charles Gordon had been sent to evacuate Egyptian troops following a Sudanese revolt.

Gladstone's domestic policy was equally unpopular, particularly in regard to Ireland. One of the prime minister's first acts, following his appointment, was the introduction of a new Irish land bill, passed in 1881. Irish political affairs were at a crucial stage at the time because of the increasing Irish agitation for Home Rule, led by Charles Stewart Parnell (q.v.). Gladstone himself was converted to a belief in Home Rule, but a series of incidents involving Irish terrorism led his government to enact harsh and restrictive measures against the Irish population. The Irish members of Parliament joined with the Conservatives against the prime minister, and he was forced to resign in 1885. Despite this check, Gladstone was convinced that satisfactory relations between Britain and the Irish patriots were possible, and he announced his full adherence to the Irish nationalist

cause. In 1886 he became prime minister for the third time and, in April, had a Home Rule bill introduced; it was, however, opposed by all factions and was defeated both then and later, when it was reintroduced. Parliament was thereupon dissolved and the Liberals were voted out of office.

Home Rule became the focus of Gladstone's entire political activity. Though the Liberals carried the elections of 1892, their majority was small; the fourth Gladstone ministry, which was devoted to the Irish nationalist movement, carried its plan through largely because of the prime minister's personal effort and speeches. In 1893 a new, amended Home Rule bill was introduced in the House of Commons and Gladstone, making the last great official fight of his life, carried the act to a triumphant passage. The House of Lords, however, refused to pass it, and the prime minister's extraordinary campaign ended in failure. His last speech in Parliament was devoted to a prediction of the coming struggle between the House of Commons and the House of Lords, which consistently opposed measures put forward by the Liberal government. Weary of the tumults of Parliamentary life, Gladstone resigned his office in 1894. His last participation in public affairs was an attempt to rouse the British public, as he had twenty years before, against the Turkish massacres, this time involving the Armenians, in 1896. He died two years later, and was buried in Westminster Abbey.

Gladstone is considered the outstanding political leader and prime minister of Victorian England. His intellect, powers of concentration and study, and oratorical ability resulted in his attainment of political stature equaled by few men in British history. His ability as a financier and an economist gave new life to British commerce, and his broad knowledge of colonial problems was invaluable at a time when Britain was building its vast colonial Empire. His work contributed greatly to the eventual settlement of the Irish problem. He will be remembered also as a defender of the liberties of all classes of British subjects.

Gladstone's literary labors were as prodigious as his political labors. In addition to writing books, he contributed articles to periodicals throughout his life. Gladstone was an intensive scholar; when he was over eighty, he lectured on Homer, and during his great Irish battle of 1894, he completed a translation of the *Odes* of Horace. Even those who opposed him bitterly respected and admired him and, when Gladstone resigned in 1894, his chief political opponents stated that his retirement resulted in the loss of the greatest intellect in the history of parliamentary government.

GLAMIS CASTLE, an ancient castle, the seat of the Earl of Strathmore and Kinghorne, situated near Strathmore, Angus County, Scotland. The original structure dated from the 11th century; the present structure dates from the 17th century. The castle is a good example of the Scottish baronial style of architecture, with a certain admixture of the French château style. Glamis is the castle of Shakespeare's *Macbeth*, and the scene of Duncan's murder. It is the ancestral estate of the house of Bowes-Lyon, the family of Queen Elizabeth, wife of King George VI of Great Britain.

GLAMORGANSHIRE, the southernmost county of Wales. It borders the Bristol Channel on the s. and s.w., and is watered on the N.W. by the Neath R. and on the E. by the Taff. Glamorganshire is the most economically important county of Wales, because of its great coal fields and large iron industry. In the fertile s. portion of the county wheat, barley, oats, potatoes, and turnips are grown; horses, cattle, and sheep are raised in the hilly area of the N. The most important trade and commercial centers of the county are Barry; Cardiff, the county seat and a county borough; Port Talbot; and the county borough of Swansea, all on the Bristol Channel. Area of county, including county boroughs, 818 sq.m.; pop. (1951 prelim.) 1,201,989.

GLANDERS or **EQUINIA,** highly contagious febrile disease of horses and donkeys, caused by the bacillus *Pfeifferella mallei*. It is transmissible to carnivores, goats, sheep, and man, but cattle are immune. Glanders attacks the mucous membranes and the lymphatics and, in animals, is characterized by ulceration of the nose, involving the cartilages and bone, with the emission of a sticky discharge. Advanced cases involve the bronchi, lungs, liver, and spleen. In one form of glanders, called *farcy,* primary symptoms appear in the form of swollen lymph nodules called *farcy buds* in the skin, especially of the legs. These farcy buds later ulcerate, emitting viscid pus. Animals found to be affected with glanders are usually immediately destroyed. Glanders, allowed to run its course, is usually fatal; pleurisy, pneumonia, and prostration precede death.

Man may contract glanders by inhalation, by ingestion of contaminated food or water, or by the infection of an open wound with pustular material from a sick animal. Veterinarians, bacteriologists, and horse handlers most frequently catch the disease. The incubation period varies widely but averages from four to seven days. The symptoms appear in the membranes of the eye and on the skin, where nodules form. The patient feels generally ill; there is pain in the arms, legs, and back; abscesses break out over the body; and fever is high. The disease is often mistaken for smallpox. Mallein, a substance discovered in 1888 produced from cultures of *P. mallei,* is used in a skin test to prove the presence of glanders. Injection of guinea pigs is a recent, more accurate diagnostic method. In acute cases, surgery or cautery of localized areas and vaccine therapy have proven helpful. The mortality rate is high, death occurring in from two days to two weeks. No treatment has been found for chronic cases, which may recover spontaneously, or persist for many years. Glanders is world-wide in distribution. See DISEASES OF ANIMALS.

GLANDULAR FEVER. See MONONUCLEOSIS.

GLANVILLE or **GLANVIL,** RANULF DE (d. 1190), English statesman and jurist, born at Stratford, Suffolk. He was sheriff of Yorkshire from 1163 to 1170, and of Lancashire after 1173. In 1176 he was appointed justice of the king's court and in 1180 he became justiciar (chief political and judicial officer) to Henry II (q.v.). During Henry's frequent sojourns in France, Glanville ruled England. He reformed the English judicial system, and was the author of the first work embodying a systematic codification of English law, *Tractatus de Legibus et Consuetudinibus Regni Angliæ.* This work was compiled about 1181, and was first printed in 1554.

GLARUS (Fr. *Glaris*), city and capital of the Swiss canton of the same name. The city is situated on the w. bank of the Linth R., about 42 m. by rail S.E. of Zurich. It lies 1578 ft. above sea level, at the foot of the mountains Vorder Glärnisch (7648 ft. above sea level) and Schild (7501 ft.). Glarus is chiefly industrial, producing, with its suburb Ennenda (pop., about 2800), cotton yarn, printed calico, woolen textiles, and Schabziger, a green cheese. Cattle raising and the quarrying of slate are other occupations of the city's inhabitants. The canton is composed of the deep upper valley of the Linth. A number of small villages occupy the flat valley floor.

British Information Services

Sauchiehall Street in Glasgow, Scotland

Cattle raising is the chief industry of the canton, because of the excellent mountain pasturages. Glarus canton entered the Swiss Confederation in 1352. Pop. of city (1950) 5695. Area of canton, 265 sq.m.; pop. (1950) 37,663.

GLASGOW, city, royal and parliamentary burgh, and port of Scotland, situated in Lanark County, on both banks of the Clyde R., 47 m. by rail w.s.w. of Edinburgh. Glasgow is the largest city in Scotland and the third-largest city in the British Isles. The city, originally centered on the N. bank of the Clyde, spread to the s. bank and now covers the hills surounding the valley floor. The N. and the s. banks of the Clyde at Glasgow are connected by eleven bridges, two of which are for railroads and two for pedestrians; by an underground subway; and by steam ferryboats. George Square, on the N. bank of the river, is considered the center of the city. The square contains an eighty-foot fluted column surmounted by a statue of Sir Walter Scott. Also in the square are equestrian statues of Queen Victoria and Prince Albert, and statues of Sir John Moore, James Watt, Sir Robert Peel, William Pitt, Thomas Campbell, Robert Burns, David Livingstone, Lord Clyde, and William Gladstone. Around George Square are grouped some of the most important buildings of the city, including the municipal buildings, the general post office, and the bank of Scotland. The outstanding building of Glasgow is St. Mungo's Cathedral, dedicated in 1197 and completed in the middle of the 15th century. It was designed in the form of a Latin cross; its transepts, however, were never completed. The cathedral, built in the Early English style of architecture, is particularly noted for its beautifully proportioned and elaborately decorated crypt. Other public buildings are the Corinthian-styled Royal Exchange, in front of which stands an equestrian statue of the Duke of Wellington; the Early English buildings of the University of Glasgow (q.v.); the Institute of Fine Arts; and the art gallery and museum in Kelingrove Park, considered among the finest galleries in the United Kingdom.

Glasgow owes its industrial and commercial importance to its advantageous situation in the center of an important coal and iron district and to its position on the Clyde. The city possesses an excellent harbor, covering an area of 368 acres. Over $40,000,000 has been spent in the improvement of the harbor, which has a minimum depth of 26 ft. The harbor has 12 m. of wharves, two patent slips, five graving docks, and a dry dock. The chief articles of export are woolen, cotton, and linen goods, machinery, millwork, foundings, coal, paper, alcoholic beverages, and chemicals. The imports are largely raw products, such as wheat, corn, flour, sugar, wool, metal ores, lumber, tobacco, and petroleum. Shipbuilding is the most important industry of Glasgow; ocean liners, battleships, freighters, yachts, barges, and many other types of craft are built in the shipyards of the city. Other industries include the manufacture of steel and brass, the smelting of lead and zinc, the forging of builder's ironwork, and the manufacture of batteries, electric appliances, motor trailers, sewing machines, welding equipment, clothing, boots and shoes, cotton cloth, pottery, rubber goods, glass, paper, and alcoholic beverages.

Glasgow traces its beginnings to a small church built by St. Kentigern, apostle to the Scots, in 560 A.D. Nothing is known of the town until 1116, when David, prince of Cumbria (later King of Scotland as David I), rebuilt its church for the episcopal see of Glasgow. In 1450 the town was made a regality; in 1611 it gained by charter the right of electing its magistrates, and in 1636 became a free royal burgh. The great commercial growth of Glasgow dates from Scotland's union with England in 1707. The town was given equal freedom of trade with English ports and soon obtained a large share of the American trade, for which its position on the w. coast was particularly suited. It soon became the chief center of the tobacco trade; this trade, however, ended as a result of the American Revolution. The subsequent introduction of cotton manufacture and sugar trade with the West Indies eventually made Glasgow one of the most important ports of the British Isles. Shipbuilding and the tremendous development of the iron industry, during the 19th century, insured the commercial superiority of the city. During World War II Glasgow, because of its great industrial concentration, was an important target for bombing by enemy aircraft. Pop. (1953 est.) 1,084,300.

GLASGOW, ELLEN (ANDERSON GHOLSON) (1874–1945), American author, born in Richmond, Va. Her family belonged to the Southern aristocracy, but in her novels she rebelled against the idealization of the genteel traditions of the antebellum South. She attempted a realistic interpretation of the South and its problems, showing the contrast between the old society and the new which rose in the period following the Civil War. Among her most important works are *The Battle-Ground* (1902), *Virginia* (1913), *Life and Gabriella* (1916), *Barren Ground* (1925), *The Sheltered Life* (1932), and *Vein of Iron* (1935). She won the Pulitzer Prize for her last novel, *In This Our Life* (1941). Her autobiography *The Woman Within* was published posthumously in 1954.

GLASGOW UNIVERSITY, a coeducational institution of higher learning, founded at Glasgow, Scotland, in 1450, under a papal bull of Pope Nicholas V. In 1460 the school was moved from its original site on Rottenrow to High Street, where it remained for four centuries. For the first two hundred years of its existence the university's standing fluctuated, but it acquired a distinguished academic reputation in the 18th century. The university was moved to its present site on Gilmore Hill in 1870, after a reorganization of the entire corporation. The ruling body now includes a chancellor, elected to a life tenure of his post by a general council; a principal, similarly appointed; and a lord rector, elected for a three-year term by the students. The faculty numbers over 550 members, 50 of whom are professors, and the student body numbers some 6800. There are two colleges, Queen Margaret and Muirhead, for women, who were first admitted to the university in 1893. The university grants degrees in arts, science, medicine and surgery, divinity, and law. In the 20th century several new chairs and lectureships in branches of medicine, chemistry, physics, history, and literature were founded. The endowments of the university have been supplemented by grants from the Carnegie Trust and the British government. The library has benefited from several bequests, including the collection of the anatomist William Hunter (1718–83), consisting of coins, medals, anatomical exhibits, and black-letter books.

GLASPELL, SUSAN (1882–1948), American author, born at Davenport, Iowa, and educated at Drake University and the University of Chicago. She worked for a time as legislative reporter for newspapers in Des Moines, and used her experiences as the basis for her first short stories. In 1913 she married George Cram Cook, with whom she founded the Provincetown Players (q.v.) in 1915. While with the Players she was instrumental in presenting the plays of Eugene O'Neill for the first time. For this group also she wrote a number of one-act plays, including *Trifles* (1916) and *Tickless Time* (1918). In 1931 she was awarded the Pulitzer Prize for her play *Alison's House* (1930). After 1933 she confined her writing to novels and short stories. Among her other works are the plays *Bernice* (1920), *Suppressed Desires* (with her husband, 1920), and *The Verge* (1922); and the novels *The Glory of the Conquered* (1909), *Brooks Evans* (1928), *Ambrose Holt and Family* (1931), and *Judd Rankin's Daughter* (1945).

GLASS, a noncrystalline "rigid liquid" (see CRYSTAL) formed by the supercooling of a number of substances, especially compounds of silicon dioxide with metallic oxides. Characteristically glass is a brittle solid which breaks with a conchoidal fracture, i.e., with a shell-like pattern on the broken face. In appearance glasses vary from black opaque substances such as the mineral obsidian to colorless, transparent manufactured glasses such as optical glass. The physical properties of glasses also vary within a wide range according to their composition. Melting points are between 500° and 1510° C. (932° and

2750° F.) ; tensile strength from 4000 lb. per sq. in. up to the strength of steel; and specific gravity between 2.125 and 8.12 (a range from less than the specific gravity of aluminum to greater than that of most steels). Similar wide variations occur in thermal expansion, optical, and electrical properties. Because the properties of glass can be controlled in manufacture, it is possible to use the material for many purposes, from walls of buildings to optical instruments.

Composition. Although the composition of individual specimens of glass may differ widely, all manufactured glasses can be grouped into five general classifications. *Fused quartz* or vitreous silica is a form of glass composed entirely of silicon dioxide. It has a very low coefficient of expansion, which would make it highly valuable for cooking utensils and other objects subjected to heat, but its high melting point (1650° C. or 3180° F.) makes it extremely difficult to produce and fabricate, particularly in quantity production. The use of this type of glass is, therefore, confined almost entirely to scientific instruments where the importance of its properties outweighs considerations of cost. *Alkali silicates,* potassium silicate, sodium silicate, and mixtures of the two, have the important property of being soluble in water. These silicates are sold commercially as *water glass* and are used extensively for food preservation, fireproofing, and adhesives. *Lime glasses* or lime-soda glasses are alkali glasses which have been made insoluble by the addition of a small amount of lime. Most of the glass used for windows, light fixtures, and containers fall into this category. Lime glasses often contain both sodium and potassium silicates, but sometimes contain only the former. *Lead glass,* which is usually a complex potassium-lead silicate, is one of the heaviest of glasses, weighing as much as cast iron. Because of its high refractive index, lead glass, sometimes called flint glass, is useful in making lenses and prisms. Lead glass is also used for the finest tableware and decorative glass, as well as for the "paste" used for imitation diamonds, because of the high brilliance of the material, particularly when cut. *Borosilicate glass,* as the name indicates, is largely a mixture of silica and boric oxide, usually with some admixture of sodium silicate. Glasses of this type are extremely resistant to chemical action and also have low expansion coefficients. Sold as Pyrex and under other trademark names, borosilicate glasses are extensively used for cooking utensils, laboratory glassware, and resistant linings for pipes and tanks containing corrosive liquids.

Besides these general types of glass, a number of special glasses have been developed. One of the most recent of the special glasses is a form of specially treated borosilicate glass known by the trade name of Vycor. The glass is fabricated and then treated with an acid solution which dissolves and removes most of the nonsiliceous components; it is then shrunk by heat treatment, producing a glass that is approximately 96% silica and that has many of the desirable qualities of vitreous silica. Molten lead can be poured into a Vycor dish resting on a block of ice without cracking the dish.

The chief raw material in the manufacture of glass is sand. Glass sands must be as nearly as possible pure silica and should contain a minimum of impurities. Sodium is usually added in the form of soda ash (sodium carbonate), although salt cake (sodium sulfate), sodium bicarbonate, or sodium nitrate are also sometimes used. Potassium is intermixed in carbonate, nitrate, or oxide form, and lime as calcium carbonate.

In addition to the basic components of the various glasses, small quantities of other compounds are often added to the melt to color or decolorize the glass and to improve its texture. Various oxides are used as coloring agents, including copper oxide for red and blue, cobalt salts for blue, nickel oxide for purple and brown, selenium or uranium oxides for yellow, and chromium oxides for yellow and green. Iron oxides, which are often present as impurities, give an undesirable greenish or brownish tinge to glass. To mask this tint, manganese, nickel, and selenium oxides are sometimes used as decolorizers. Ruby-red glass is usually produced by the addition of selenium, but colloidal gold and copper are also sometimes used to give this color. "Opal glass" is made by the admixture of phosphates and fluorides. The addition of antimony and arsenic and other substances to melted glass lessens the tendency of the glass to form bubbles. Substances used for this purpose in glassmaking are known as *fining agents.*

Glass Manufacture. The first stage in any form of glass manufacture is the melting together of the sand and other raw materials. In the early days of glassmaking, clay pots were employed for this purpose, heated in ovens stoked with wood or coal. Similar pots, made of fire clay and holding between ½ and 1½ tons of glass, are still occasionally employed. For the mass production of such items as window glass, the modern practice is to use tank furnaces holding more than 1000 tons of glass at a time. Both pot and tank furnaces are heated by oil or gas. In tank furnaces the raw materials are fed continuously into an opening (called the doghouse) in one end of the tank, while the molten glass is drawn off at the other end. A typical charge for a modern glass furnace making a lime-soda glass consists of one-half broken glass fragments, called *cullet,* and one-half of a mixture of raw materials. The raw materials include about 63 percent sand, 19 percent soda ash, 10 percent lime, 7.5 percent sodium sulfate, and traces of arsenic as a fining agent and of powdered cannel coal as a reducing agent.

In forming or working glass in its plastic state five basic methods are employed: pressing, casting, blowing, drawing, and rolling. By using these techniques alone or in combinations it is possible to produce an almost limitless variety of shapes from broad sheets of plate glass to complex laboratory glassware and delicate cups and vases. Subsidiary processes, used chiefly for decoration, include polishing, engraving, cutting, and enameling.

Historically, pressing and casting are the oldest forms of glassworking. In pressing, the semifluid glass is taken from the melting pot and worked into shape by means of paddles or other hand tools. Crude shapes of glass have been made in this way for many millennia. In more recent times hand-operated or machine-operated presses have been employed to force the glass into molds. In this form of pressing, the outside surface of the object is formed by the mold itself and the inside by a plunger to which pressure is applied. Modern presses are equipped with automatic devices for delivering a gob of glass to the mouth of the mold and for removing the finished article after forming. Molds are also employed for casting glass, but in this method of working no pressure is employed.

The invention of the blowpipe, which is credited to the Phenicians, made possible a great expansion in the variety and utility of the objects which could be fabricated from glass. The ordinary blowpipe is an iron pipe about four feet long with a mouthpiece at one end. In using it the glass blower dips up a small amount of molten glass on the end of the pipe. He then rolls or presses the gob of glass against a paddle or metal plate to shape its exterior and cool it slightly. This cooling is necessary because, unless the surface is slightly cooler and hence slightly stronger than the inside of the mass of glass, blowing into the pipe will simply blow a hole in the gob. The worker then blows into the mouthpiece, producing a bubble of glass. By twisting the blowpipe while blowing, and by rolling and shaping with a paddle, a great variety of shapes can be made. Intricate forms are manufactured by adding more glass to the original mass and shaping the whole. When the object is completed but still soft, it is cut away from the pipe by means of shears.

In the ordinary technique of glass blowing only round vessels can be formed, but by employing molds into which the glass can be blown, hollow pieces with angular or irregular outlines may be made. A subsidiary form of glass blowing, known as *lampworking,* is employed for making elaborate glass structures such as vacuum pumps and decorative figures. The lampworker uses rods and cylinders of preformed glass and shapes and joins them after heating them as required in the flame of a gas lamp or Bunsen burner. "Offhand" glass blowing and lampworking are highly skilled crafts. The vast majority of hollow glassware is now blown by machines as described below.

Drawing is a process used for the production of tubing, sheets, fibers, and rods of glass. The techniques of drawing glass sheets and fibers is discussed below. Tubing is drawn by pulling out a cylindrical mass of semifluid glass and at the same time blowing an air blast into the center of the cylinder. This operation is almost always performed by a machine in which molten glass is fed continuously over a nozzle through which a blast of air is forced. The size of the tubing depends on the strength of the air blast and the viscosity of the glass. Rods are produced on the same machine without the use of an air blast.

After forming, all glass objects are subjected to an annealing treatment to relieve strains which are set up within the glass as it cools. The treatment in general consists of reheating to a temperature high enough so that the strains are eased by flow within the object, and then cooling slowly, so that very little new strain is set up. In the preparation of strong glass for special purposes, such as electrical insulators, a form of reverse annealing or tempering is sometimes employed. In this process, the glass is heated almost to the softening point and then cooled rapidly in an oil bath or by some other means that applies pressure on the exterior of the glass

Owens-Illinois Glass Co.; American-Swedish News Exchange

Left: Making a glass bottle in an American glass factory. First a hollow bubble is blown on the end of a blowpipe. It is then put into a mold and blown again to fill out the form. Right: A glass blower in a Swedish factory performing a similar operation.

during cooling. The exterior pressure counterbalances the interior strains set up in cooling and produces a glass of great toughness. This glass specially processed for strength is sometimes called chilled, case-hardened, or tempered glass.

Window Glass. Flat sheets of window glass were formerly made by glass blowers who formed long cylinders approximately 15 in. in diameter, cut lengthwise and flattened to form sheets which could then be cut into individual windowpanes. The hand method of manufacture was later superseded by the machine-cylinder method in which the cylinder was drawn by machine and then cut. All modern processes for the formation of sheet glass, however, produce flat sheets by drawing. In one typical process a long narrow trough with a longitudinal slit in its bottom is forced down into the surface of the molten glass in a tank furnace. The sheet of glass squeezed upward through the slit is caught by asbestos-covered rollers and carried upward through further sets of rollers to a height of about 25 ft. The temperature in the area of the rollers is carefully controlled so that the sheet is annealed as it is drawn upward. In a continuous process a metal rod called a *bait* is lowered into the glass, and the glass adhering to it is drawn upward and then horizontally around a metal roller as a sheet. The continuous sheet is then passed over a flattening table and through a *lehr* or annealing oven 200 ft. long. Leaving the lehr, it reaches a cutting table where it is automatically cut into large sheets, which are later cut into commercial sizes of windowpanes.

Plate Glass. Ordinary drawn window glass cannot be entirely uniform in thickness because of the nature of the process by which it is made. The variations in thickness cause distortion of objects viewed through panes of this type of glass. Such distortions are not important when the glass is used in the windows of houses, but they are undesirable in mirrors, the display windows of shops, or the windshields of automobiles. For all purposes where optical distortion must be avoided another kind of sheet glass called plate glass is used. Plate glass is produced by rolling rather than drawing, and is often ground and polished after cooling. An old method of producing plate glass consisted of pouring single sheets on a metal table and flattening them by passing a single roller over the sheet. In a typical modern process, molten glass is poured on a level table and then is passed between two water-cooled rollers which press the glass out into a continuous sheet of even thickness. After annealing and cutting, the sheets of glass are set firmly on a level bed in plaster of Paris and are ground with successively finer grades of sand and emery and finally brought to a high polish by buffing with rouge. The grinding and polishing process may have as many as eleven stages.

Several specialized types of glass are also produced by the rolling process, including wire glass and figured glass; the latter is composed of glass sheets with a pressed surface design which are sometimes used for interior office partitions and doors. Wire glass has the valuable property of not shattering under the action of heat although it does crack. It is made by feeding wire mesh into the molten glass just before it passes beneath the roller. Rollers with a pebbled or corrugated surface are employed to give a pressed design to figured glass.

Safety glass, which is universally employed in the windshields and windows of automobiles, is made by laminating a sheet of transparent plastic between two sheets of plate glass. When safety glass is broken it does not shatter like ordinary glass, even under the impact of a hard blow. Instead, the broken pieces of glass are held in place by the adhesive plastic layer between them. Cellulose nitrate, the plastic originally employed in the manufacture of safety glass, had the property of becoming brittle at low temperatures and soft at high temperatures. As a result glass laminated with this plastic was unsafe at extreme temperatures. It also tended to turn yellow under the action of the sun. Modern safety glass uses plastics which do not have these drawbacks, chiefly vinyl resins.

Optical Glass. Most kinds of ordinary glass have various internal imperfections which render them unsuitable for use in eyeglasses, lenses, and optical instruments. Small air bubbles and inclusions of tiny unfused bits of sand or other raw material cause distortion in a lens. Even more serious is the distortion which results from *striae,* streaks caused by lack of complete chemical homogeneity in the glass. In addition, strains in glass caused by imperfect annealing impair its optical qualities. For these reasons the manufacture of optical glass is a far more delicate operation than any other type of glass making. The various ingredients used in the making of optical glass are carefully chosen for purity, and the pots in which the glass is melted are made from special clay. The most damaging impurity in optical glass is iron oxide, which tends to give the glass an undesirable color. Pots of optical glass are kept in the melting furnace for a prolonged period, sometimes several days, during which the glass is constantly stirred by a refractory rod. This stirring mixes the glass thoroughly and avoids striae in the finished glass. After it has been removed from the melting furnace the pot of glass is cooled by degrees in an annealing furnace, a process which often takes many days. Finally the pot and the glass within it are broken to pieces. The most perfect of the fragments are sawed up into smaller pieces, remelted, and cast into forms from which lenses and prisms can be ground.

To produce optical elements that are free from aberrations it is necessary to use glasses of varying refractive index and dispersions. The simplest form of corrected lens employs two elements, one with comparatively low refractive index and low dispersion, and one with a comparatively high refractive index and high dispersion. Optical glasses of the former type are known as crown glasses, and those of the latter type as flint glasses. Because of recent improvements in glass-making technology the index of refraction and other optical characteristics of individual batches of glass may be varied through fairly wide limits. Prior to World War I the technique of making good optical glass was a trade secret closely held by a comparatively small number of European factories; but research in the U.S. during and after the war resulted in the development of a high-quality optical-glass industry in this country.

Glass Fibers. By drawing out molten glass to diameters of a few ten-thousandths of an inch, it is possible to produce fibers that can be woven or felted like any textile fiber. In general, glass fibers are produced in two different ways. In one method, long single-filament fibers are manufactured by drawing out a thread of molten glass over a revolving drum. Short-staple fibers from ten to twelve in. in length are made by blowing an air or steam blast past a narrow tongue of glass as it is extruded through a nozzle. The action of the air blast draws out the glass to a thin thread. This latter method of producing the fibers has virtually supplanted the earlier drum-drawing technique.

Glass fibers have been employed for a number of purposes. Woven into textile fabrics, they make excellent drapery and upholstery materials because of their chemical stability and resistance to fire and water. Glass fabrics are not as yet, however, suitable for clothing. Woven-glass fabrics also find numerous applications in the field of electrical insulation. Mats produced by felting glass fibers are used extensively in storage batteries as insulating spacers. Because these mats are not attacked by the battery acids, batteries that last twice as long as those using other forms of insulation can be built. Other uses of matted fibers include heat insulation and acoustical materials for building construction.

By impregnating layers of glass fabric with plastics, it is possible to produce solid molded objects which combine the inertness of glass with great mechanical strength. In World War II armor plate (q.v.) which was more

effective weight-for-weight than steel was made by this process, and since the war glass-and-plastic boat hulls have been molded in the same way. These hulls are completely unaffected by the action of salt water or the attacks of marine borers.

Yarns made of glass fibers usually consist of several twisted strands, each containing about a hundred single filaments of glass. The yarns are not shiny like ordinary glass but have a dull finish caused by the appearance of the broken ends of the individual filaments. Glass yarns are as flexible and as easily woven as wool or cotton. The thin filaments, each about two ten-thousandths of an inch in diameter, are in themselves flexible and will not break until they are bent to a radius of a thousandth of an inch or less. In practice none of the filaments are bent so sharply, even when the fabric is folded on itself and creased.

Bottles and Containers. The general method of producing bottles, light bulbs, cosmetic jars, and other glass containers is by blowing glass into a suitable mold which shapes the outside of the hollow object. Formerly all such products were hand-blown, but today the great majority of them are automatically mold-blown by machine. A skilled glass blower is able to produce as many as 300 bottles a day, but some of the modern bottle-making machines have a capacity of 6000 bottles in the same time and one form of bulb-blowing machine operated by one man produces 700 electric-light bulbs per minute.

In a typical automatic bottle-blowing machine, a gob of molten glass is dropped into a narrow inverted mold and forced down into the lower portion of the mold, which represents the neck of the finished bottle, by an air blast. A baffle then drops over the top of the mold, and a blast from the bottom of the mold partially forms the bottle. The bottle, held by its neck, is then inverted and lowered into a second finish mold where a further air blast blows it out to its finished dimensions. The process of annealing is carried out in a conventional lehr through which the bottles pass in a period of about two hours.

In the manufacture of some large bottles a combination of pressing and mold-blowing is employed, and wide-mouthed containers are sometimes pressed rather than blown.

Miscellaneous Glass. Glass bricks are square, hollow, construction blocks with ribbed or patterned sides which can be laid in mortar like any form of masonry. These

Pittsburgh Plate Glass Co.

Top: Reaching into furnace with electrically-operated tongs to withdraw a pot of molten glass. After removal, glass is allowed to stand until it attains proper consistency for casting. Bottom: Liquid glass is slowly passed between rollers to form plate glass.

bricks are used extensively to construct translucent outside walls and partitions. Two pressed halves are fused together while hot to produce such bricks.

Foam glass is an extremely light, solid glass product of cellular structure, which floats on water. It is made by adding to an ordinary glass melt materials which vaporize when the glass reaches the melting point, leaving a large number of bubbles within the glass. Foam glass has excellent heat-insulating qualities and comes in the form of rigid panels that can be sawed or drilled.

Thermopane is a trade-mark name for a pane of glass consisting of two plate-glass panels sealed together at their edges, with the space between them evacuated. It is chiefly for large "picture windows" which cause serious heat losses if made from ordinary glass. Thermopane has the added property of not clouding over with condensed moisture during cold weather.

Frosted glass is made by etching ordinary plate glass with hydrofluoric acid to give a white, mat finish. Patterns are sometimes etched into frosted glass by covering portions of the glass with paraffin which resists the action of the acid. Although etched glass is often called *ground glass,* true ground glass is made translucent by grinding with abrasives. Lead glass containing a high proportion of lead silicate is sometimes called *X-ray glass,* because the lead offers protection from radiation, and such glass is used in shields to protect persons who work with X rays. A new type of glass shielding was developed in 1956 for use in atomic-energy plants. It has three layers, one made of beryllium, lithium, and boron oxides, which absorb neutrons, a central sheet of glass with a high melting point, and a third of lead-boro-silicate glass, which absorbs beta and gamma radiations. All layers are transparent, so that the shield not only provides protection from radiation, but also permits the observation of nuclear reactors in operation.

Ordinary glass does not transmit the invisible ultraviolet rays of sunlight. In order to obtain the benefits of this radiation inside buildings, windows are sometimes made of special glasses, often called *health glasses,* which admit the passage of these rays. Health glasses include certain borosilicate, phosphate, and quartz glasses.

See also GLASS, PAINTED AND STAINED; WINDOWS.

GLASS, CARTER (1858–1946), American legislator, born in Lynchburg, Va., and educated in the public and private schools of that city. After working in a printing office for several years, he became the owner of two Lynchburg newspapers, the *Daily News* and the *Daily Advance.* He served in the Virginia State senate from 1899 to 1903, and from 1902 to 1918 was a Democratic member of the U.S. House of Representatives. While serving in the latter capacity, he was the chief author of the Federal Reserve Bank Act and played a decisive role in its passage in 1913. He resigned from the House in 1918 and became secretary of the treasury in the cabinet of President Woodrow Wilson. Two years later he resigned the secretaryship when he was appointed to fill a vacancy in the U.S. Senate. He was elected senator in 1924 and subsequently re-elected three times. In 1933 he was cosponsor of the Glass-Steagall Banking Reform Act. He was voted president *pro tempore* of the Senate in 1941, and was chairman of the Appropriations Committee and a member of the Foreign Relations Committee. Glass was one of the foremost Congressional experts on banking, and the author of *Adventures in Constructive Finance* (1927).

GLASS, PAINTED AND STAINED, colored glass made by applying pigments to molten glass and the surfaces of glass panes. Stained glass is made by adding metallic oxides to molten glass; painted glass is made by applying pigments to glass sheets, and fusing the pigments with the surfaces of the sheets by heating. Pieces of colored and colorless glass are cut into appropriate shapes and joined by lead strips to form mosaic representations of scenes or patterns, used as windows. Although pictorial windows are usually composed of both stained and painted glass, they are commonly called "stained-glass windows".

The process of making colored glass, which probably originated in the Near East about the 9th century, was adopted by Italian artists about the 10th century. The earliest record of use of stained and painted glass in making pictorial windows occurs in an account of the rebuilding of Rheims Cathedral in the late 10th century. The stained-glass windows of Augsburg Cathedral, executed about the end of the 11th century, are probably the oldest in existence. Extensive use of stained glass began in the 12th century.

Technique. Many improvements in technique have been made since the 12th century, but the fundamental operations involved in making stained-glass windows have not changed. The 12th-century artist made a cartoon of the design on a white board

Brit. & Irish Rys.; Can. Info. Ser.; Brit. Info. Ser.

PAINTED AND STAINED-GLASS WINDOWS

Above: Making a stained-glass window. Left, laying out glass pieces on an outline, much the same as a jigsaw puzzle; right, joining the pieces together with lead strips.
Right: Modern painted window in a chapel in Westminster Abbey, London, a memorial to the men of Great Britain's flying forces.

which was identical in size and shape with the proposed window. He then cut pieces of white and colored glass to fit the shapes required by the cartoon. Each piece was shaped approximately by cutting with a hot iron, and then finished by breaking off the edges to exact size with an instrument called a *grozing iron*. The grozing iron had a slot at one end which resembled the notch in a wrench. Small details which could not be brought out by shaping the pieces of glass were added by painting. A brown paint, called *grisaille*, was made of a metallic oxide (probably iron oxide) and powdered glass in a gum medium. High lights were added by cutting through the paint layer with a sharp stick, and shading effects were stippled with a brush. The painted glass was fired in a kiln to fuse paint and glass.

After all the individual glass pieces of the mosaic had been completed, they were arranged on top of the cartoon, and joined together with H-shaped strips of lead. When the glass was completely leaded, the lead strips were soldered at the places where they intersected, and the spaces between glass and lead were filled with putty. At the completion of this step the window was ready for installation.

Many improvements and refinements in technique were introduced after the 12th century. Artists of the 14th century discovered that silver salts would produce a clear yellow color when applied to glass, and 16th century artists discovered that metallic oxides could be used to produce blue and green colors. The use of grozing irons was discontinued, in the 16th century, in favor of diamond-pointed cutting tools. Glassmakers of the 16th century developed methods of making thin, translucent glass. Makers of stained-glass windows used two layers of thin glass, each of a different color, to produce an intermediate color. Swiss artists of the 17th century developed methods of enameling glass. Enameled-glass windows became popular in Switzerland and England, but their popularity declined for the reason that the enamel chipped off easily.

Stained Glass as Art. Extensive use of stained glass began in the early 12th century and included such beautiful examples as the windows at Chartres Cathedral and at St. Denis Abbey. The series of stained-glass windows in Canterbury Cathedral, made about 1180 and depicting the genealogy of Christ, exemplify typical color patterns of the period; the tints are quiet blues, greens, and browns, with flesh tints represented by pink glass. The *grisaille* method of painting on clear glass is typified by the windows of the Chapter House at York, made during the late 13th century. In the 13th-century Sainte Chapelle in Paris, the artists used a latticework of blue and red glass as a background. Latticework backgrounds became popular in France, but were not used to any great extent in England. A common feature of windows of the 14th century was the use of carefully detailed representations of plants, such as ivy and strawberries. During the middle of the 14th century the Black Death (q.v.) disrupted Europe, and many of the secrets of making brilliantly colored glass were lost; as a result, use of silver stain and *grisaille* increased. At about the same time the use of borders composed of small angels, heraldic badges, crowns, and mythological animals, all surrounded by foliage, became popular.

Glass windows of the late 15th century, such as those created for Ulm Cathedral by a German artist, Hans Wild, are characterized by a remarkable sense of color and boldness of design. The finest stained-glass windows of the 16th century were made in the Netherlands. Dutch artists often treated a series of adjacent windows as if it were a single large space, ignoring the intervening stone supports. Barnard Flower, a Dutch artist who was appointed glazier to Henry VII in 1505, made four windows for King's College Chapel at Cambridge University and the windows of Henry VII's Chapel at Westminster Abbey. On the Continent fine windows were being made by artists of Rouen in France and by glaziers employed in the building of Cologne Cathedral.

During the 17th and 18th centuries most "stained-glass" windows were made of unleaded, painted panes. The use of leaded mosaics was revived in the middle 19th century by the work of Sir Edward Burne-Jones in collaboration with William Morris. The windows of Holy Trinity Church in London, made in 1887, are probably the finest products of this collaboration. German artists of the 20th century, working before 1933, were influenced by the same modernism that was apparent in the painting and sculpture of their contemporaries. Modern work with stained glass in the U.S. is exemplified by four windows, symbolizing *The Divine Comedy, Pilgrim's Progress, Paradise Lost,* and *Le Morte d'Arthur,* made by the American artist Charles Jay Connick (1875–1945), for the Chapel of Princeton University. See WINDOW.

GLASS SNAKE, common name for any lizard of the genus *Ophisaurus,* family Anguidae, characterized by smooth, hard, highly polished, shinglelike scales which ring its body, and by the absence of limbs. The glass snakes move in the manner of snakes, but are less graceful, being restricted by their hard scales. Members of this genus, like other lizards of the same family (see BLINDWORM), possess fragile tails; their tails are twice as long as their bodies, and break off without the shedding of blood when handled, writhing and twisting for some time after separation from the body. The posterior portion of the tongue is thick and fleshy; the anterior portion is thin and forked, and retracts into the posterior portion. There is a deep fold running along each side of the snake's body.

The American glass snake, *O. ventralis,* is found from North Carolina and s. Illinois to s. Mexico. The color varies among members of the species; some are black with a green spot on each scale, others are olive-colored with clusters of yellowish dots on each scale. In some specimens the dots coalesce and form a longitudinal stripe. The American grass snake reaches a length of 2 to 3 ft., and subsists almost entirely on insects.

The largest species of glass snake is the Old World scheltopusik, *O. apodus,* which reaches a length of 4 ft. and a diameter in its thickest portions of 1½ in.

GLASSWORT, common name of plants of the genus *Salicornia,* belonging to the family Chenopodiaceae. Glassworts occur in salty marshes and shores on the coasts of Eurasia and North America. The burned ash of glassworts, called barilla, was formerly used in the manufacture of glass. Barilla is an impure soda ash and has been supplanted, in glassmaking, by commercial sodium carbonate.

Species of *Salicornia* are leafless and have succulent, jointed stems with opposite branches. The flowers, which lack calyx and corolla, are borne in spikes on small branchlets. The most common glasswort, *S. europaea,* also called the marsh samphire, is an erect, branching plant with green stems which turn red in the fall.

The name prickly glasswort is sometimes applied to *Salsola kali,* a closely related species similar in habitat and characteristics, which is more often called the saltwort.

GLASTONBURY, a market town and municipal borough of Somersetshire, England, situated on the Brue R., 6 miles s. of Wells and 25 miles s.w. of Bath. Its leading industries are tanning and the manufacture of boots, leather articles, and tiles. Glastonbury is thought to be the site of the first English Christian church, established in the 1st century A.D. by Joseph of Arimathea. In the 2nd century, two missionaries there established a fraternity of anchorites, which was organized under monastic rule three centuries later by St. Patrick. St. Dunstan became abbot of a monastery in Glastonbury in 946. Between 1120 and 1172 the old buildings of the monastery were replaced; when these were destroyed by fire, a few years later, King Henry II ordered the building of a larger abbey and church.

In 1892, in the vicinity of the town, the so-called Glastonbury lake village was discovered, yielding knowledge of the life of the British people at the time of the Roman invasion. The village, consisting of sixty mounds, was built over a swamp on timber piles which were covered with mounds of clay. The houses had from one to ten circular dwelling floors ranging from fourteen to forty feet in diameter. Palisades of wattle work enclosed the entire village. The fibulæ, bronzes, combs, ladders, and other items found in the mounds date from Celtic to Romano-British times. Pop. of town (1951 prelim.) 5081.

GLAUCOMA, a disease of the eye characterized by increased pressure within the eyeball, gradual hardening of the eyeball, and failing vision. When glaucoma has no apparent cause, it is called *primary* glaucoma; when accompanied or preceded by injury to the eye, it is called *secondary* glaucoma.

Primary glaucoma may be chronic (noninflammatory) or acute (inflammatory). When the eye is completely hard, and blindness has set in, the condition is known as *absolute glaucoma.*

Ordinarily the contents of the eyeball press outward with a pressure of about ½ lb. per sq. in. This pressure preserves the shape of the eyeball, and is consequently an important factor in regulating the optics of the eye. The pressure is produced by the aqueous and vitreous humors and by the nutritive fluids constantly circulating between them and the capillaries supplying the eye. In glaucoma the outflow of these nutritive fluids is obstructed. Glaucoma usually develops in middle age or later, though congenital glaucoma has often been observed.

In chronic glaucoma the patient has attacks of blurred vision, and often sees colored halos around distant lights. In acute glaucoma there is reddening of the eye, dilation of the pupil, and headache. The cornea and humors are cloudy, often leading to confusion of this disease with cataract. The field of vision is reduced, a phenomenon which is demonstrated for diagnostic purposes with an ophthalmic instrument called a *perimeter.* Another instrument, the *tonometer,* is used to demonstrate the increase in pressure.

Medical treatment of glaucoma can sometimes stop the progress of the disease. Present-day treatment includes the use of Diamox, a drug chemically related to sulfanilamide. According to medical reports (1954), Diamox taken regularly may relieve the pressure indefinitely. In advanced cases of the disease, surgery may be indicated.

GLAZIER, WILLARD (1841–1905), American soldier, explorer, and author, born in Fowler, N.Y., and educated at State Normal College, Albany. He served during the Civil War in the Second and Twenty-sixth New York cavalry regiments. In 1863 he was captured by Confederate forces. He escaped, was recaptured and tried as a spy, and escaped again, succeeding on this occasion in reaching the Federal lines; he spent a total of fourteen months in Confederate prisons. These experiences were described by him in *Capture, Prison-Pen and Escape* (1865). In 1876 he made the trip from Boston to San Francisco on horseback, a journey which furnished the basis for his *Ocean to Ocean on Horseback* (1896). In 1881 he discovered the lake (later named after him) which is the source of the Mississippi River, and verified his discovery ten years later. During the Spanish-American

Aleksandr Glazunov

War he formed and served as colonel of a provisional regiment of Illinois volunteers. He explored the coast and interior of Labrador in 1902.

GLAZUNOV, ALEKSANDR KONSTANTINO-VICH (1865–1936), Russian composer, born at St. Petersburg. He studied principally with the eminent Russian composer Nikolai Rimski-Korsakov. Glazunov was a precocious student, completing an entire course in composition in eighteen months and composing his *Symphony No. 1* at the age of sixteen. Success came to him early; his first symphony was performed in 1882, and in 1884 the noted Russian music publisher Mitrofan Petrovich Belyaev (1836–1904) contracted to publish all of his works. Glazunov was the last important composer of the Russian national school founded by Mikhail Glinka; his work also shows the influence of Liszt and Wagner. Together with Rimski-Korsakov, Glazunov completed (1889) *Prince Igor,* the opera left unfinished by Alexandr Borodin at his death (1887), which became one of the best-known Russian operas. Glazunov was professor of music at the St. Petersburg Conservatory from 1900 to 1906 and its director from 1906 to 1917. He left Russia in 1928; except for a visit to the United States, where he conducted the Detroit Symphony Orchestra (1929) and other leading orchestras, he lived in Paris

until his death. Among his numerous compositions are much program music, including the symphonic poems *Stenka Razin* and *The Kremlin* (1892); a number of overtures, including *Overture on Greek Themes* (No. 1, 1881–84; No. 2, 1882–85); ballets, including *Raymonda* (1898) and *The Seasons* (1901); concertos, including *Violin Concerto* (1904); eight symphonies (1881–1907); chamber music; and music for piano and for voice.

GLEDITSIA. See HONEY LOCUST.

GLEE (from Anglo-Saxon *gligge,* "music"), a piece of unaccompanied vocal music, for at least three voices, usually male. A glee may be either sprightly or melancholy. The glee differs from the madrigal in that the glee contains a number of musical themes, which are developed harmonically, whereas the madrigal generally has few themes, which are treated contrapuntally. The glee is an English musical form and was popular chiefly between 1700 and 1825. The important composers of glees include Benjamin Cooke (1734–93), Johan Danby (1757–98), John Hindle (1761–96), Stephen Faxton (1735–87), Reginald Spofforth (1770–1827), and the most noted of all, Samuel Webbe (1740–1816). The famous London Glee Club (1787–1857) had as its purpose glee singing and the encouragement of glee writing.

GLENDALE, a city of Los Angeles Co., Calif., situated 6 miles N. of the center of the city of Los Angeles, at the entrance to the fertile San Fernando Valley. It is served by three railroads, and has a municipal airport. The city is a residential suburb of Los Angeles, and is also an important manufacturing center, producing airplanes and airplane engines, furniture, hospital supplies, medicinal goods, tools and dies, and pottery and tile. Forest Lawn Memorial Park Cemetery in Glendale contains reproductions of several noted churches in England, including the Little Church of the Flowers modeled after the Stoke Poges church in Buckinghamshire, where Thomas Gray wrote his celebrated poem, *Elegy Written in a Country Churchyard.* The site of the present city of Glendale was a part of the former Rancho San Rafael, first land grant in California made by the king of Spain. Glendale was incorporated in 1906; the population of the city has grown from 2746 in 1910 to 82,582 in 1940. Pop. (1950) 95,702.

GLENDOWER, OWEN, in Welsh, OWAIN AB GRUFFYDD (1359?–1416?), lord of Glyndwr, in Wales, and the last Welsh chief to claim the title of independent Prince of Wales. He is a Welsh national hero and historically famous as a rebel against the English during the reign of Henry IV. Glendower was originally a partisan of the English and was in the service of Henry of Bolingbroke before Henry became king, following the deposition of Richard II (see ENGLAND: *History*). The Welsh remained strongly attached to Richard. A year after the deposition, Glendower's feudal lord failed to summon him to join an expedition against Scotland and later declared him a traitor for his absence. This unfair charge, combined with Welsh sympathy for Richard, incited Glendower to lead a major revolt against the English.

On his return from Scotland, King Henry led an army against the Welsh, but his campaigns in 1400 and 1401 were ineffectual. Glendower, gaining control of most of Wales, negotiated for aid with the Irish, the Scots, and the French, all enemies of England, and intrigued with prominent English lords, notably Henry Hotspur (see PERCY, SIR HENRY). In 1402, Glendower's army captured Sir Edward de Mortimer, one of the greatest lords in England, who had been suspected by the English of plotting with the Welsh; soon afterward Mortimer married one of Glendower's daughters. The Welsh chief began to style himself Prince of Wales; he called a parliament, established his own government for Wales, and entered a formal alliance with France in 1404. A year later, an English army under Prince Henry (later Henry V) defeated Glendower's forces in three successive battles. The fortunes of the Welsh chief began to wane, and his battles assumed the aspect of petty mountain warfare. He was pardoned by Henry V in 1415; nothing is known of him after that date.

Glendower was the last great champion of Welsh independence, and the one who came closest to realizing it. The Welsh have invested him with a mythology that has tended to obscure historical fact. Shakespeare's *Henry IV* (Part I) presents Glendower as this idealized hero.

GLENNON, JOHN JOSEPH (1862–1946), American Roman Catholic prelate, born in Kinnegad, Westmeath, Ireland, and educated at All Hallows College, Dublin. He later emigrated to the United States where he was ordained in 1884. From 1884 to 1892 he officiated at Saint Patrick's Cathedral in Kansas City, Mo., and from 1892 to 1894 was vicargeneral of the diocese of Kansas City. He was subsequently made coadjutor bishop of Kansas City, with right of succession. In 1903 he was consecrated coadjutor archbishop of St. Louis, and later the same year, archbishop. He was responsible for the erection of a new cathedral in St. Louis, dedicated in 1914. Fourteen days before he died he was elevated to the Sacred College of Cardinals.

GLENS FALLS, a city of Warren Co., N.Y., situated on the Hudson R., and on the eastern outskirts of the Adirondack Mts., 52 miles N. of Albany. It is served by a railroad, and has a municipal airport. In the vicinity are limestone and black-marble quarries. The city is an important manufacturing center, producing paper and pulp, newsprint, wallpaper, cement, brick, shirts, collars, dresses, blouses, silk gloves, lace, chemicals, paper-mill machinery, and toys. Considerable power is supplied the manufacturing plants by the falls from which the city derives its name. A staircase from a concrete bridge across the Hudson R. at Glens Falls leads down to the river bank and the entrance to Cooper's Cave, made famous by the American author James Fenimore Cooper in *The Last of the Mohicans.* The region surrounding the city abounds in points of interest connected with the French and Indian War and the American Revolution. Lake George (q.v.), site of numerous battles, lies a few miles N. of Glens Falls. The site of the present city was settled in 1763 by Abraham Wing, who built a tavern there. The settlement was known as Wing's Falls until 1788, when it received its present name. Glens Falls was incorporated as a village in 1837. It was partially destroyed by fire in 1780 and again in 1884, but was rebuilt, and became a city in 1908. Pop. (1950) 19,610.

GLIDER, a heavier-than-air aircraft which has no engine, deriving its motive power from the aerodynamic forces acting upon it. In form gliders resemble ordinary airplanes, but are characterized by extreme lightness, by low wing loading (the ratio of weight to wing area), and by high aspect ratio. A good modern glider of the sailplane type (see below), when flying level in still air, will sink at a rate less than three feet per second, and therefore will be capable of climbing in an air current which is rising at the rate of about two miles per hour.

Experiments with gliders laid the foundations for the design of the first powered aircraft. Beginning in the 1870's a number of pioneer aeronauts built gliders that made successful flights and provided much information as to the efficient design of wings and control systems. Among these pioneers were

Institute of the Aeronautical Sciences

Top: A troop-transport glider of the type used in World War II. Middle: Model of glider designed by Octave Chanute in 1894. Bottom: Primary gliders used for training.

the German Otto Lilienthal and the Americans Octave Chanute, James J. Montgomery, and Wilbur and Orville Wright (qq.v.). The first powered airplane to fly successfully was designed by the Wrights as a direct result of their earlier work with gliders.

The chief impetus to the modern development of gliders, and the art of flying them, came from the Germans. In the years following World War I, Germany, which was forbidden by the Versailles Treaty to manufacture powered airplanes suitable for military use or for the training of pilots, turned to the building of gliders and to research in glider flight. German aeronautical engineers discovered the great efficiency of light craft with long, birdlike wings, and the meteorological conditions under which soaring flight could be successful.

Upcurrents in the atmosphere, on which the

glider pilot depends for motive power, are principally of two kinds: ridge currents and thermal currents. Ridge currents are formed when a steady wind blows against the side of a ridge or a range of hills. Such currents can be quite strong but are limited to an area a few hundred feet high over the windward edge of the ridge. Thermal currents are formed by heat rising from the ground, as for example over a bare field on a hot day. These currents are always present under cumulus clouds and to a marked extent under and in the towering, anvil-shaped clouds of thunderstorms. Within such a thunderhead the upward currents may reach a speed of 100 miles per hour.

In gliding flight, the craft must be launched from the ground by some exterior force. In practice this launching is usually accomplished by catapulting the glider by means of long elastic cords or by towing it aloft by means of a winch, an automobile, or a powered airplane. When a glider is launched by a tow, the pilot cuts loose his towline when he has reached the desired altitude above the ground. Once in the air the pilot directs his glider in search of upcurrents. If he simply wishes to remain in the air, he may fly back and forth along a ridge where there is a suitable current. If, however, he is making a cross-country flight, he flies by "cloud chasing" or "thermal sniffing", searching for thermal currents which will give him lift. When he has found such a current, he will spiral his craft to remain within the current while gaining altitude. After reaching the maximum altitude to which the current will lift him, he glides away to find another current. High-performance gliders can glide twenty miles horizontally for every mile of altitude they have attained. Such flights are generally restricted to daylight hours, because of meteorological conditions as well as lack of visibility.

Experienced pilots frequently fly under or into thunderheads in their efforts to gain altitude. This procedure is hazardous because of the violence of the currents encountered and the extreme turbulence of the air within the clouds. In one instance a pilot forced by the violence of the storm to abandon his glider in the middle of a thunder cloud found himself being borne upward within the cloud, when his parachute opened, because of the speed of the upcurrent.

Glider Types. In general, gliders are of three types. Primary gliders, used entirely for instruction purposes, consist of little more than a girder framework to which the wings and control and stabilizing surfaces are attached. In them the pilot sits on an open seat at the front of the framework. Secondary gliders or sailplanes are built like ordinary airplanes with a fuselage and an enclosed cockpit seating one or two persons. They are designed for the maximum of aerodynamic efficiency. The third type of gliders, cargo gliders, are used for military or peacetime purposes and are large craft designed to carry heavy loads. They are built not to soar but to be towed in groups behind a powered plane to increase the pay load of the plane. The chief advantages of the cargo glider are its carrying capacity, and its low landing speed, which makes possible the landing of a heavy pay load in a space too restricted for the operation of conventional planes.

Prior to World War II, gliding was regarded largely as a sport. Annual glider meets at Elmira, N.Y., and elsewhere attracted hundreds of participants and thousands of spectators. During the war, however, gliders were put to extensive logistic use for carrying supplies and airborne troops. Notable glider operations were the German invasion of Crete and the Allied attack on Myitkyina in Burma. In the same period was developed the technique of glider "pickups", in which a plane in flight hooks on to the towrope of a glider on the ground and lifts it into the air. Glider pickups have been successfully employed for the rescue of airmen forced down on terrain where conventional aircraft could not be landed.

Glider Records. International records for gliders include: duration of flight, 56 hrs. 15 min.; distance of flight, 535.169 m.; and altitude, 30,100 ft.

GLIÈRE, REINHOLD MORITZOVICH (1875–1956), Russian composer, born at Kiev. He studied composition at the Moscow Conservatory under the noted Russian composers Anton Arenski, Sergei Taneev, and Mikhail Ippolitov-Ivanov. Glière was one of the most facile and popular of modern Russian composers. In his early years he followed the traditions of the national Russian school; later he became a follower of the European romantic school. He subsequently incorporated elements of Impressionism into his work, and finally became a successful composer of music on themes of a revolutionary or folk nature in accordance with the policies laid down for composers by the Soviet government. His best-known works are *Symphony No. 3; Ilya Murometz* (1909–11), which narrates in music the tale of a legendary Russian hero; and the ballet *Red Poppy* (1926–27), including the *Sailors' Dance.* Among his other compositions are the symphonic poems *The Sirens* (1908) and *Cossacks of Zaporozh* (1921); the opera *Shakh-Senem* (1923–25), based on the folk music of Azerbaijan; *March of the Red Army* (for wind orchestra, 1924); the overture *For the Happiness of the Fatherland* (1942); *Concerto for Horn and Orchestra* (1952); chamber music; compositions for violin and piano; and numerous songs and piano pieces.

GLINKA, MIKHAIL IVANOVICH (1803–57), Russian composer, born at Novospasskoi. His musical education, which comprised the study of the piano, violin, and singing, and lessons in theory, counterpoint, and composition, was protracted over many years (about 1817–33) and was obtained from various teachers in a number of European countries, including Rus-

Mikhail Glinka

sia, Italy, and Germany. Until 1835 his compositions consisted mainly of songs. In that year he began the composition of his opera *A Life for the Tsar,* the story and music of which are based on Russian folk tales and songs. The opera, produced in St. Petersburg in 1836, was the first Russian opera of a national character. The music of Glinka's second opera *Russlan and Ludmilla* (1842), based on a poem by the Russian poet Aleksander Pushkin, was also drawn largely from Russian folk music. Glinka established himself as the founder of the Russian national school of music, which was subsequently carried on by such composers as César Cui, Aleksandr Borodin, Modest Musorgski, and Nikolai Rimski-Korsakov. Glinka was also interested in the popular music and dancing of Spain, where he lived from 1845 to 1847; in addition to his operas, his works include the overtures *Jota Aragonesa* and *Night in Madrid* (1851). His other works include the orchestral fantasia *Kamarinskaya* (1848); a valse-fantaisie (1839); chamber music, including a string quartet (1830) and a sextet for piano and strings (1833–34); about forty pieces for piano; and about eighty-five songs.

GLOBEFLOWER, common name of the perennial genus *Trollius,* belonging to the family Ranunculaceae. Flowers of this genus, borne in globe-shaped clusters, have large, yellow, petal-like sepals and small, linear petals. Globeflowers are native to the colder parts of the Northern Hemisphere. The common

globeflower, *T. europaeus,* called lucken gowan in Great Britain, is cultivated in flower gardens in the U.S. and Europe. The spreading globeflower, *T. laxus,* grows in swampy areas of northeastern U.S. and the Rocky Mountain region. An unrelated plant, a double-flowered variety of *Kerria japonica,* is called the Japanese globeflower.

GLOBE, THE, name of a 17th-century English theater in London, notable for the initial and contemporary productions of Shakespeare's plays and of the dramatic works of Ben Jonson, Francis Beaumont, John Fletcher (qq.v.), and others. The Globe was constructed in 1599 by the famous actors Richard and Cuthbert Burbage in partnership with Shakespeare and others. The octagonally-shaped outer wall of the theater enclosed a roofless circular inner pit into which the stage projected, and three galleries one above the other, the topmost of which was roofed with thatch. In 1613 a cannon, discharged during a performance of Shakespeare's play *Henry the Eighth,* set fire to the thatched roof, resulting in the destruction of the building. The theater was rebuilt in 1614 but, thirty years later, was razed by the Puritans to make room for dwellings. A brewery now stands on the site formerly occupied by The Globe.

GLOBIGERINA. See FORAMINIFERA.

GLOBUS HYSTERICUS. See HYSTERIA.

GLOCKENSPIEL, a percussion instrument consisting of a series of steel bars tuned to the chromatic scale and played by means of a pair of hammers. The instrument has a range of two to three octaves and gives out a brilliant, high-pitched, bell-like tone. The two principal types are the orchestral, which is placed in a horizontal position in front of the performer; and the military, used in marching bands. The bars of the latter type are mounted in a lyre-shaped frame, and the instrument is carried and placed in a perpendicular position. A notable orchestral use of the glockenspiel is in the magic fire music in the third act of the opera *Die Walkure* by Richard Wagner. The term "glockenspiel" is also used for an organ stop which consists of bells, rods, or tubes that are struck by a hammer action and emit a sound like that of the orchestral or military glockenspiel.

GLOMMA, the largest river of Norway, issuing from Lake Aursundsjö, near the town of Röros, E. central Norway. The river flows in a southerly direction, emptying into the Skagerrak at the city of Fredrikstad after a course of about 375 m. The Glomma's most important tributary is the Vormen. Navigation on the Glomma is possible for 10 miles N. from the river's mouth to the first waterfall and then for 20 m. between the first and second fall.

GLONOIN. See NITROGLYCERIN.

GLORIOUS REVOLUTION, the name applied to the English Revolution of 1688. James II (q.v.), the English king, had publicly avowed Roman Catholicism in 1672, thirteen years before his accession to the throne. From the commencement of his reign, he undertook to remove the religious and political disabilities to which Roman Catholics in Great Britain were subject. To achieve this end he decreed special dispensations designed to nullify the Test Act; James also issued two proclamations suspending penalties against dissenters which he commanded to be read aloud from the pulpit of every Anglican Church on two successive Sundays. Seven prominent bishops who refused to comply with the royal order, and who circulated protest petitions against it, were brought to trial on charges of libel and sedition. The bishops were tried in an atmosphere of mounting excitement, and their acquittal was greeted with widespread rejoicing.

Opposition to James' arbitrary policies had become general, and fear of their continuance in the person of the monarch's newborn son (see STUART, JAMES FRANCIS EDWARD) impelled the opposition leaders to solicit help from the Netherlands ruler William (see WILLIAM III), husband of James' daughter Mary, and the foremost defender of Protestantism in Europe. William accepted the invitation to be English king, sailed for England with a Dutch army, and marched on London. James, alarmed by the disaffections in his army, and recognizing the untenability of his position, fled to the court of Louis XIV in France. A year later, however, aided by a small contingent of French troops, he proceeded to Ireland and made an attempt to regain the British throne, but was decisively defeated at the Battle of the Boyne (see BOYNE, BATTLE OF THE). James thereupon returned to France, where he passed the remainder of his life. Meanwhile William had accepted the Declaration of Rights (1689), which later became the Bill of Rights (q.v.), and the Act of Toleration (1689), and with his wife, Mary, acceded to the British throne.

GLOSS (Gr. *glōssa*, "a word needing explanation"), as used in literary, scientific, and other works, a marginal or interlinear interpretation or explanation of obscure expressions. Such expressions comprise foreign words, archaic or obsolete words, provincialisms, dialect words, technical terms, and other words unfamiliar to the average reader. The earliest use of glosses occurred in ancient Hebrew, Greek, and Latin manuscripts; these were at first interlinear, but were subsequently marginal, probably for the sake of convenience. Because of their number, in some instances these glosses amounted to running commentaries on entire works. Such marginal commentaries became distinguishing features of a number of versions of the Bible and, in many cases, were incorporated into the Biblical texts. In Bologna from the 12th to the 14th century, running commentaries on the texts of the Civil Law, which later became important, were called *glossæ* or *glossemata*. Many modern works contain systematic lists of glosses, usually at the end of the published text; such a list is called a *glossary* and is, in effect, a specialized and limited dictionary; see DICTIONARY.

GLOTTIS. See LARYNX.

GLOUCESTER, a city and port of entry of Essex Co., Mass., situated on Cape Peninsula, 28 miles N.E. of Boston. It is served by a railroad and by steamers. Gloucester has a fine harbor formed by Eastern Point, a peninsular section of the city extending into the

N.Y. State Museum
The spreading globeflower

Stand. Oil (N.J.); Mass. Devel. & Indus. Comm.

Above: Fishermen mending nets on a dock in Gloucester, Massachusetts. Left: Fishing trawlers tied up in Gloucester harbor.

ocean for about 3 miles. The city is a noted summer resort and fishing center. Cape Ann's rocky coast and the city's picturesque old houses and fishing wharves attract many artists as well as vacationists. Gloucester's fish industry, more than three centuries old, is still the most important commercial enterprise of the city. Cod, mackerel, haddock, halibut, rosefish, pollock, cusk, and hake comprise the principal catch of the Gloucester fishing fleets, which range the Atlantic Ocean from the Capes of Virginia to Greenland and Iceland. Other industries in the city include the manufacture of glue, oilskins, cod-liver oil, paint, nets and seines, and wooden boxes. At one time, dark granite of a fine quality was quarried at Gloucester, and was used in the construction of such noted edifices as the Brooklyn Bridge and the Woolworth Building in New York City.

The city contains a Fishermen's Memorial, erected in 1923, which commemorates the men of Gloucester lost at sea, numbering approximately 8000 since 1830. Other interesting structures in Gloucester are a cooper's shop, built in 1658, and a house dating from 1768 and containing exhibits of old china and glassware. Off the coast of Gloucester is a large sunken rock, the "reef of Norman's Woe" in

Henry Wadsworth Longfellow's poem *The Wreck of the Hesperus.* Many other authors have described the life of Gloucester's fishermen, including Rudyard Kipling in his novel *Captains Courageous.* The French explorer Samuel de Champlain sailed around the Cape in 1605 and named it *Cap aux Isles,* and in 1606 he mapped the harbor, calling it *Le Beau Port.* One of the oldest towns in Massachusetts, Gloucester was settled in 1623 by English fishermen and was incorporated as a town in 1642. During the American Revolution the town was unsuccessfully attacked by the English in 1775. It served as a port for American privateers during the Revolution and during the War of 1812. Gloucester was chartered as a city in 1874. Pop. (1950) 25,167.

GLOUCESTER, name of an English earldom and dukedom. The earldom was created about 1121 for Robert, illegitimate son of King Henry I. About the end of the 12th century the title passed to Gilbert de Clare (see CLARE), 7th Earl of Clare and 6th Earl of Gloucester, who inherited it through his mother. It was held by his descendants until Gilbert de Clare, 10th Earl of Clare and 9th Earl of Gloucester, was killed at the battle of Bannockburn in 1314. The dukedom of Gloucester was created in 1385 for Thomas of Woodstock (q.v.), youngest son of King Edward III. It was bestowed in 1414 on Humphrey (q.v.), youngest son of King Henry IV, and in 1461 on Richard (later King Richard III), younger brother of King Edward IV. Since the beginning of the 18th century, the title has been bestowed on the sons of the British sovereigns.

GLOUCESTER (anc. *Glevum*), county town, county and parliamentary borough, and port of Gloucestershire, England, located on the Severn R., 114 m. by rail w. of London. The city was founded about 97 A.D. by the Romans. In 681 Ethelred, king of Mercia, established the abbey of St. Peter in the city. By 1066, the date of the Norman Conquest, Gloucester had borough status and contained a royal residence and a mint. In 1483 Gloucester was incorporated, and in 1541 it became the seat of an episcopal see. Many fine examples of Gothic architecture are found in the city. Among them are the cathedral built during the late 11th century, and the West Gate, built during the 12th century. Other buildings of interest are the 15th-century New Inn, the 16th-century Bishop Hooper's Lodging, and the 19th-century shire hall. The industries of Gloucester include the manufacturing of chemicals, agricultural implements, and cordage. Foundries, sawmills, flour mills, marble and slate works, fisheries, and shipbuilding yards are also found in the city. The port is connected to the Gloucester-Berkeley ship canal, opened in 1827. The chief exports are coal, iron, salt, and the articles manufactured in the city. Imports include grain and lumber. Pop. (1953 est.) 66,400.

GLOUCESTERSHIRE, a w. midland county of England. In the eastern part of Gloucestershire are the Cotswold Hills, on the eastern slopes of which rise the Severn, the

Wye, the Stratford Avon, the Bristol Avon, and the Thames rivers. The Severn estuary, which connects the Severn R. with the Bristol channel, is an important trade route. Coal, iron, limestone, and clay are the chief mineral resources of Gloucestershire. The county's principal industry is dairying. Leading crops are grains, turnips, apples, and pears. Shipbuilding, aircraft manufacturing, iron founding, and the production of locomotive and railway cars, textiles, and lumber are among the manufacturing industries of Gloucestershire. Bristol (q.v.) is the most important industrial city and port of the county. Other important towns are Gloucester, the county town, and Cheltenham and Tewkesbury. Area of county, 1258 sq.m.; pop., including the county boroughs of Bristol and Gloucester (1951 est.) 938,618.

GLOVE, a covering for the hand, with an individual sheath for each finger. The wearing of gloves is generally believed to date from prehistoric times, but the first record of their use appears in the writings of such ancient Greek authors as Homer and Xenophon. Both the Greeks and the Romans, living in comparatively mild climates, had little need of gloves as protection against the cold; the Greeks wore them chiefly when doing heavy work, and the Romans as a sign of rank. The

Right: The village of Chalford in the Cotswold Hills of the county of Gloucestershire, England. Below: The 11th-century cathedral in the city of Gloucester, England.

British Information Services

Romans introduced the use of gloves into Britain soon after their conquest of that island in the 1st century B.C. By the 8th and 9th centuries A.D., gloves were in general use among the Anglo-Saxons, the Germans, and the Scandinavians.

In the early Middle Ages, the use of richly jeweled and embroidered gloves became common among monarchs, noblemen, and high ecclesiastical officials; gloves of this type were made a part of the papal vestments. Heavy leather gloves, armored with iron plates, were used for hunting and fighting during this period. Ornamental, elbow-length linen gloves became fashionable among ladies in England in the 13th century.

The Middle Ages also gave rise to a number of symbolical uses of gloves. A glove was customarily cast to the ground as a challenge to battle; picking up the glove indicated acceptance of the challenge. When worn in the hat, the glove symbolized the fealty of the wearer to the owner of the glove. A folded glove was commonly presented to an individual with whom a contract had been arranged, as a token of intention to carry out the terms of the contract in good faith. In Oriental countries, the glove possessed a legal significance in connection with the transfer of property, the handing over of the seller's glove to the purchaser being the recognized token of investiture.

In England, during the 16th and 17th centuries, gloves made from the skins of birds were used to some extent; chicken-skin gloves were common during the 18th century. Modern gloves are made from a wide variety of materials, including woven and knitted fabrics; and leather, made chiefly from the hides of sheep, kids, goats, lambs, and deer.

Various specialized types of gloves are used in modern scientific and industrial establishments. Among these are the sterile rubber gloves, of exceptionally fine texture, used by surgeons and nurses to preserve antiseptic conditions during surgical operations; the heavy rubber gloves worn by electrical workers, and the leaded rubber gloves worn by X-ray technicians, both for purposes of insulation; and the asbestos-covered gloves worn by workers in steel mills and similar establishments, as a protection against the extreme heat of the furnaces near which they work.

Glove Manufacturing in the United States. The manufacture of gloves was introduced into the American colonies by Sir William Johnson (q.v.), who in 1760 brought a number of glovemakers from Perthshire, Scotland, to his estates in what is now Fulton County, N.Y. The settlement later became the town of Gloversville (q.v.), which has persisted to the present day as a leading center of the glove-making industry.

GLOVERSVILLE, a city of Fulton Co., N.Y., situated in the foothills of the Adirondack Mts., 45 miles N.W. of Albany. Gloversville is the leading center of the glove industry in the U.S., and together with the neighboring city of Johnstown and other industrial areas of Fulton County manufactures most of the gloves produced in the U.S. In addition to eighty or more factories producing leather and fabric gloves and mittens, the city contains large silk mills, tanneries, knitting mills, lumber mills, a hair mill, machine shops, foundries, and factories manufacturing wooden articles, paper boxes, men's and women's overcoats, sporting goods, leather pocketbooks, and leather and fabric novelties. Potatoes are the principal crop grown in the surrounding agricultural area. The Sacandaga Reservoir, the largest in the State, is situated 6 miles from Gloversville. The Adirondack Forest Preserve, which commences within a few miles of the city, contain numerous lakes and mountains and provides excellent facilities for fishing, hunting, and winter sports. Gloversville was first settled about 1752. The making of gloves was first introduced in the region by a group of colonists from Perthshire, Scotland, who were settled there by Sir William Johnson about 1760. Gloversville, formerly called Stump City, received its present name in 1828. In 1851 it was incorporated as a village, and in 1890 as a city. Pop. (1950) 23,634.

GLOWWORM. See FIREFLY.

GLOXINIA, common name of *Sinnangia speciosa* (formerly *Gloxinia speciosa*, named after Benjamin Peter Gloxin, an 18th-century German botanist), belonging to the family Gesneraceae. Gloxinias are herbs native to tropical Brazil. They have large, downy leaves with conspicuous veins. The showy bell-shaped flowers have solid, marbled, or spotted corollas of purple, violet, pale red, or white. The leaves grow in a rosette just above the ground and the flowering stems rise from the center of the rosette to a height of about six inches. Gloxinias are cultivated as home and hothouse plants in the U.S.

GLUCASE. See MALTASE.

GLUCINUM. See BERYLLIUM.

GLUCK, CHRISTOPH WILLIBALD (1714–87), German operatic composer, born at Erasbach,

Bavaria. He studied music at the Jesuit seminary at Komotau and also in Prague and Milan; in the last-mentioned city he studied with the Italian composer Giovanni Battista Sammartini. Gluck's first opera, *Artaserse,* was produced at La Scala, Milan, in 1741. During the following nine years he wrote and produced approximately twelve operas in various European cities, including Venice, London, Dresden, Vienna, Prague, and Copenhagen. Among them were *Sofonisba* (1744), *Artamene* (1746), *Semiramide Riconosciuta* (1748), and *Ezio* (1750). In 1750 he took up residence in Vienna and thenceforth, except for periods spent in Naples, Rome, and Paris, the capital of Austria-Hungary was the center of his musical activities. In 1754 the Empress Maria Theresa appointed him *kapellmeister* of opera at the theater of her court. Among the operas Gluck wrote during the period between 1750 and 1760 were *La Clemenza di Tito* (1752), *Antigono* (1756), and *Tetide* (1760).

Up to 1762 Gluck had composed in the contemporary operatic style, cultivated chiefly in Italy, which was marked by music written primarily to give virtuoso singers opportunity to display their skill. As his career progressed, however, Gluck grew dissatisfied with the conventionalities of Italian opera, characterized by surface brilliance and overornamentation. He began to develop a style intended to restore opera to its original purpose of expressing in music the meaning or emotion conveyed by the words (see OPERA). About 1760 he became acquainted with the Italian poet Raniero da Calzabigi (1714–95), who wrote for Gluck a libretto that admirably suited the composer's ideas concerning proper balance between words and music. The opera Gluck wrote on this text was *Orfeo ed Euridice,* which surpassed in grandeur, dignity, dramatic quality, and naturalness anything he had written before; it was produced in Vienna in 1762 with great success. Among subsequent operas Gluck wrote in his "grand" manner were *Alceste* (1767) and *Paride ed Elena* (1770), both on texts by Calzabigi; *Iphigénie en Aulide* (1774); and *Armide* (1777).

The reforms he inaugurated in opera met with violent opposition from composers, singers, critics, and others devoted to the Italian operatic style. This opposition was particularly manifest in Paris, where a veritable war was waged (1774–81) between those who believed in Gluck's reforms and those who championed Italian opera. Even

Christoph Gluck at the harpsichord

after the success of *Iphigénie en Aulide* in Paris in 1774, the partisans of Italian opera in the city criticized Gluck's music severely and claimed that a certain composer of Italian opera resident in Paris, Nicolò Piccini, was Gluck's superior. The director of the Opéra commissioned the two rivals each to compose an opera on the same text, *Iphigénie en Tauride.* Gluck's version turned out to be his masterpiece. Produced in Paris in 1779, it met with tremendous success, and Piccini's version, produced in 1781, was adjudged much inferior.

Gluck's operatic reforms made a lasting mark on opera. The principles for which he stood influenced the work of many later composers, including Mozart, Cherubini, Spontini, Beethoven, and Wagner.

GLUCOSE, DEXTROSE, or GRAPE SUGAR, a monosaccharide sugar, formula $C_6H_{12}O_6$; see CARBOHYDRATE; SUGAR. It is found in honey and the juices of many fruits; the name "grape sugar" is derived from its presence in grapes. It is the sugar most often produced upon hydrolysis of natural glycosides (q.v.). Glucose is a normal constituent of the blood of animals: see SUGAR, METABOLISM OF.

Glucose is a white crystalline solid, less sweet than sucrose. Solutions of glucose rotate the plane of polarization of polarized light to the right; hence the name "dextrose" (Lat. *dexter,* "right"). Glucose crystallizes in three different forms. The degree of rotation of polarized light is different for each form.

α-glucose, the most common form, has a melting point of 146° C. (295° F.).

Glucose is formed by the hydrolysis of many carbohydrates, including sucrose, maltose, cellulose, glycogen, and starch. Fermentation of glucose by yeast produces ethyl alcohol and carbon dioxide.

Glucose is made industrially by the hydrolysis of starch in the presence of dilute acid. About 500,000 tons of glucose are produced annually in the United States by this method. The commercial form of glucose, obtained as an intermediate in the production of pure glucose, is a sirup containing maltose and dextrin in addition to glucose. Glucose is used as a sweetening agent in candies, jellies, and other foods, in chewing gum, and in pharmaceutical preparations. It is also used in dyes and in weighting silk. Commercial glucose, by itself or with cane sugar, is used as a table sirup.

GLUCOSIDE. See GLYCOSIDES.

GLUE, an impure form of gelatin (q.v.), used as an adhesive for a variety of materials including wood, paper, and leather. It is a yellow-brown, hard, brittle, semitransparent substance, which dissolves in warm water to form a viscous, mucilaginous fluid. Most commercial glue is made from the waste products of slaughterhouses, especially animal bones and scraps of hide. The glue is extracted with boiling water or steam after the glue stock has been processed for removal of mineral matter and fat in the case of bone, and of blood, hair, and fat in the case of hide. The extract is then clarified with alum, bleached, and dried.

Fish glue is made in a similar manner from the skins, swimming bladders, and offal of fish. It is a strong adhesive, but has an offensive odor and is usually deodorized.

Glue in flake or powder form must be dissolved in hot water and applied while still hot to the surfaces to be joined. Certain reagents, such as lead sulfate together with acetic acid or nitric acid, check the tendency of glue to gelatinize in cold water without diminishing its adhesive qualities. The glue can thus be used in a cold, liquid form, known as liquid glue. Waterproof glue is made by adding tannins and formaldehyde to ordinary glue. Marine glue, a waterproof cement used in shipbuilding, is not technically glue. It is made of rubber and shellac dissolved in naptha or benzene. For other types of adhesive materials, see CEMENT.

The adhesive strength of glue is determined by measuring the force necessary to pull apart two wooden blocks which have been glued together. Best-quality animal glue is the strongest adhesive. Glue is used extensively in furniture-making, bookbinding, veneering, rug-sizing, and in making match tips and abrasive papers. It is used with shreds of waste leather to make a type of imitation leather.

The glue industry in the United States dates from 1837, when Peter Cooper (q.v.) established a glue factory on Long Island. Since that time the industry has developed steadily, and in a recent year 158 million pounds of glue were manufactured in this country.

GLUME. See SPIKELET.

GLUT HERRING, the summer herring or blueback. See HERRING.

GLUTTON, an animal of the Weasel family. See WOLVERINE.

GLYCEMIA. See SUGAR, METABOLISM OF.

GLYCERIN or **GLYCEROL,** $C_3H_5(OH)_3$, an alcohol (q.v.) containing three hydroxyl groups. It is a colorless, odorless, sweet-tasting, sirupy liquid, with density 1.26 and boiling point 290° C. (554° F.). Although its melting point is 20° C. (68° F.), glycerin is rarely seen in the solid state, as it ordinarily remains liquid even under low temperatures, which sometimes solidify it into crystals. Once frozen, it does not melt unless heated above its melting point. It is extremely hygroscopic, and is soluble in water and alcohol in all proportions.

Fats and oils are esters of glycerin and fatty acids (q.v.). In the manufacture of soap (q.v.), fats and oils are treated with alkali, producing soap and glycerin. The crude glycerin thus obtained is purified by distillation. In recent years the annual production of glycerin obtained as a by-product in soap manufacture has been over 200,000,000 pounds. Glycerin is obtained from carbohydrates, such as glucose, fructose, treated starch, and molasses, by fermentation with yeast in an alkaline medium under special conditions. It is being synthesized on a large scale from petroleum products such as allyl alcohol and propylene. Plants with an annual production capacity of 37,000,000 pounds of glycerin have been built within the petroleum industry.

Large quantities of glycerin are used in making the explosive nitroglycerin (q.v.), and in the manufacture of synthetic resins (see PLASTICS). Glycerin is used as a skin-softener in cosmetics, as a preservative for tobacco and meat, and as a sweetening agent in beverages and medicines. It is also used in perfumery, in ink for stamp pads, in automobile hydraulic brakes, and as a solvent and a lubricant.

GLYCON. See FARNESE ART.

GLYCOSIDES, a class of complex chemical compounds which occur in plants. They are broken down by the action of plant enzymes into sugars, among which glucose is generally included, and other substances. The term "glucoside" is often used synonymously with glycoside, but in its more specific meaning it refers to glycosides which yield glucose.

Each glycoside in a plant is hydrolyzed by an enzyme, usually a specific enzyme found in the same plant. The enzyme emulsin, however, causes hydrolysis of several glycosides. The enzymes and glycosides are stored in separate plant cells until the reaction products of the glycosides are needed by the plant and the glycosides are hydrolyzed.

Glycosides are believed to serve several purposes in the plant. Inasmuch as the glycosides, which are bitter-tasting, have been converted to sweet sugars by the time the fruits ripen and the seeds mature, it is believed the glycosides help keep birds and insects from eating seeds and fruit before they achieve full growth. When a plant tissue is bruised the plant enzymes hydrolyze the glycosides. The products of the hydrolysis other than sugars, such as phenol compounds and acids, have an antiseptic action and prevent decay of the damaged tissues.

Glycosides are soluble in water and are obtained from plants by water-extraction. They are mostly colorless crystalline solids with a bitter taste. Simple glycosides have been synthesized in the laboratory, and several hundred glycosides, many of which are used in medicine and as a source of natural dyes, have been extracted from plants and isolated. Among the important glycosides are indican, the traditional commercial source of indigo (q.v.), the cardiac glycosides, such as strophanthin (see STROPHANTHUS) and digitalin (see DIGITALIS), and the saponins (q.v.).

GLYCYRRHIZA. See LICORICE.

GNAT, common name loosely applied to any biting, dipterous fly. In America, the term is most often used for members of the following families: Simuliidae, containing the black fly (q.v.), buffalo gnat, and turkey gnat; Mycetophilidae, containing the fungus gnat; and Psychodidae, containing the moth fly or sand fly (q.v.). In England, mosquitoes are commonly called gnats.

The blue-gray gnatcatcher

GNATCATCHER, common name for any small, insectivorous, New World, oscine bird in the genus *Pelioptila,* of the same family as the Old World warblers. Gnatcatchers are found in the dense foliage of short trees, where they build unique mossy nests, covered with lichen. The names flysnapper and flycatcher are sometimes erroneously applied to these birds.

A common gnatcatcher of southeastern U.S. is the blue-gray gnatcatcher, *P. caerulea,* also called the sylvan flycatcher. This slender, graceful bird averages five inches in length. The back of the adult male is a dull blue-gray; the head is somewhat brighter, with a black line crossing the forehead and running along the sides of the crown. The wings are gray-black bordered with gray, the tail black bordered with white, and the underside ash-white. The adult female is similar in coloring except for a brownish-gray back and the absence of the black line on the head. The song of the blue-gray gnatcatcher is a complex strain, weak in volume. Western gnatcatchers belong to the species *P. melanura.* A variety, the black-tailed gnatcatcher, found in southwestern U.S., is famous for its call, which resembles the mew of a kitten.

GNAWING ANIMALS. See RODENTIA.

GNEISENAU, COUNT AUGUST NEITHARDT VON (1760–1831), Prussian soldier, born at Schildau. He studied at the University of Erfurt for two years, and at the age of nineteen enlisted in the Austrian army. In 1782–83, during the American Revolutionary War, he served in a regiment of mercenaries, under British command. Later, during the Napoleonic Wars, he entered the Prussian service, took part in the battle of Jena (1806), and conducted a masterly and successful defense of the city of Colberg. Between 1807 and 1809 he collaborated with General Gerard von Scharnhorst in reorganizing the Prussian army, as a result of which it became one of the most formidable fighting forces in Europe. By 1813, when Germany began the War of Liberation against Napoleon's rule, Gneisenau had become a major general. He served under General Gebhard von Blücher and played an important role in the victories won by the Prussian armies and their allies over the French. He later became Blücher's chief of staff and, in that capacity, helped devise the strategy which culminated in the final defeat of Napoleon at Waterloo in 1815. Gneisenau was named governor of Berlin in 1818, and became a field marshal in 1825.

GNEISS, metamorphic rock in which the mineral constituents have been segregated into parallel layers, giving a banded or laminated structure to the rock. The metamorphosis of many igneous and sedimentary rocks has resulted in a banded structure in which the quartz and feldspar are segregated into layers which alternate with layers of dark minerals. The different varieties of gneiss are named after the type of rock from which they have been formed (as granite gneiss and diorite gneiss) or after a mineral in which the rock is unusually rich (as biotite gneiss and hornblende gneiss). See METAMORPHIC ROCKS.

GNOMON. See MAP; SUNDIAL.

GNOSTICISM (Gr. *gnostikos,* "man of knowledge"), a term applied to several religious philosophies, both Christian and pagan, which stressed the revelation of mystical knowledge as the key to salvation. Gnosticism was syncretistic in character, drawing its inspiration from diverse and often opposed sources. The chief elements of gnostic religion and philosophy were Greek philosophy, Jewish cabalistic mysticism, Babylonian mythology, Mithraism, and Persian dualism. Various gnostic sects differed widely in their beliefs and practices. Gnostic groups were important in the Christian Church, particularly during the 2nd century A.D., but gradually came to be regarded as heretical.

A fundamental doctrine of the gnostics was a clear-cut dualism between good and evil, between the divine and the material worlds. In some gnostic teachings evil is supposed to have been generated by God or the supreme being by a series of emanations. According to this belief a less perfect world emanated from the divine world, and from this less perfect world a succession of inferior worlds, until, as the divine good dwindled and became diluted by distance, the creation of evil was possible. Generally the material world in which men live was regarded as the creation of seven powers, half-angel, half-devil, called Eons, who represented the last link in the chain of emanations. The seven Eons were clearly identified with the sun, moon, and five planets of the Babylonian mythology. In some gnostic systems the place of the Eons is taken by a single creative being having similar attributes, the Demiurge.

An important link between gnosticism and Christianity was the stress which both creeds laid on personal salvation. The gnostics believed that such salvation was attainable by ignoring the material world and concentrating on the divine world of light. As aids in their journey through the intermediate worlds to the perfect world, the gnostics made use of many symbols and sacraments, including sacred formulas, the names of the demons of the lower world and of the Eons, and anointment with holy oil.

In certain gnostic systems Sophia (Gr., "wisdom") or the Great Mother played a prominent part. She was regarded as the goddess of heaven and the mother of the stars. This goddess was obviously the equivalent of the mother goddess of a number of Asiatic faiths who was worshipped under such names as Aphrodite, Astarte, Cybele, and Isis. A parallel figure was the Primal Man, who existed before the creation of the world, appeared on the earth in many forms, and finally became a man in the form of Christ. The resurrection of the Primal Man and his ascent into heaven served as the basis for the hope of personal salvation among the gnostics.

GNOSUS. See KNOSSOS.

GNU or **WILDEBEEST,** common name for the large, buffalo-faced, horse-tailed, African antelope comprising the genus *Connochaetes.* The wide head of the gnu is black, with small, keen eyes, hairy nostrils, and tufts of hair on the face and chin. The broad smooth horns, present in both sexes, curve downward, outward, and upward, and grow to a length of thirty inches, measured along the curve. In old adults the horns cover and protect the forehead. The body of the gnu is dark brown, the females being lighter in color than the males. The back slopes downward from the shoulders to the hindquarters. The neck is arched and bears an erect, bristling mane. The hairy tail reaches three feet in length. The legs are graceful, like those of other antelopes, and gnus can run swiftly for long distances.

The white-tailed gnu or black wildebeest, *C. gnu,* was once common in South Africa, but has now become almost extinct. This beast stood forty-two inches at the shoulder and had long hairs on its throat. Its tail was white. The larger brindled gnu or blue wildebeest, *C. taurinus,* standing fifty-four inches high at the shoulders, is still common in the interior of South Africa. Its shoulders and neck are marked with dark, vertical stripes. The tail is black and there is no long hair on the throat. The brindled gnus are found in herds of ten to twenty, but gather together in large droves of more than two hundred toward the end of the dry season. Another species, the white-bearded gnu, *C. albojubata,* is found in British East Africa. The hair on the face of this species is white. See ANTELOPE.

GNU GOAT. See TAKIN.

GOA (Port. *Gôa*), district of Portuguese India (q.v.), situated on the Malabar coast, and bounded on the N. by the Terakhul R., on the E. by the Western Ghats, on the S. by the Kanara district of India, and on the W. by the Arabian Sea. It has 62 m. of coastline, and possesses a generally hilly terrain, especially in the interior, where some of the peaks of the Western Ghats attain an altitude of nearly 4000 ft. above sea level. The principal rivers by which the district is traversed are the Mandavi and the Juari, which completely encircle the small island of Goa on the coast, forming the harbors of Agoada, or Aguada, at the Mandavi on the N., and Mormagao at the Juari on the S. A breakwater and a quay have been added to the harbor facilities recently, and an extensive export trade is carried on in manganese, cotton, coconuts, fruits, spices, fish, and salt. The district comprises four subdistricts known as Velhas Conquistas (Old Conquests), where the population is predominantly Christian, and seven others called Novas Conquistas, which contain a largely Hindu population. Konkani is the chief language spoken by the inhabitants native to the region. Goa was conquered by the Portuguese soldier Affonso de Albuquerque in 1510 from the kingdom of Bijapur, and became the first Portuguese territorial acquisition in Asia.

Several cities in the district have been called Goa on various occasions in the past.

The brindled gnu

The first was the ancient Hindu city (Skr. *Gove, Govapuri,* or *Gomant;* Ar. *Sindabur* or *Sandabur*) on the southernmost part of the island, of which scarcely any relics or ruins remain. Velha Goa (Old Goa), founded about 1440, also lies largely in ruins. Of its remaining buildings, the most important are the cathedral founded by Albuquerque in 1511, the convent of St. Francis (1517), and a converted mosque with a portal of carved black stone, dating from the early 16th century. The mosque is the only specimen of early Portuguese architecture in India. Old Goa became the capital of the entire Portuguese empire in the east, and was granted the same civic rights as Lisbon. However, between 1695 and 1775, the fortunes of the city declined, and the population decreased from 20,000 to less than 2000 because of numerous attacks and sieges by the Dutch and the Mahrattas. In 1759 the capital was moved to its present site and is now called Panjim or Nova Goa. Area, 1348 sq.m.; pop. (1940) 540,925.

GOAJIROS or **GOAJIRAS,** one of the Arawakan South American Indian tribes, numbering about 30,000 and inhabiting the Goajira peninsula northwest of Lake Maracaibo, in Colombia. The Goajiros build their houses on piles in Lake Maracaibo and in the various lagoons of the region. They engage in fishing and in rudimentary agriculture, and are expert in featherwork and in weaving fabrics from cotton and processed palm.

GOAT, common name for any of a number of species of ruminant, cloven-hoofed, horned animals constituting the genus *Capra* of the family Bovidae. The females, which have smaller horns than the males, are properly called *does,* but in ordinary usage they are often termed goats or nanny goats. The young are called *kids.* Male goats are called *bucks,* or, colloquially, billy goats. Goats are closely related to sheep (q.v.), but differ from them

Left: The bezoar goat or pasang, a wild goat. Right: The Toggenburg, a domestic Swiss goat.

in that the hollow horns are long and directed upward, backward, and outward, while those of the sheep are spirally twisted. Goats also have shorter tails than sheep. Male goats have beards, unlike sheep, and differ further by the characteristic strong odor they give off in the rutting season.

In the wild state, goats are nomadic, and are generally found in mountainous habitats. They are agile at making long, flying leaps from rock to rock, landing with both front feet close together. Their sure-footedness is due partly to the construction of their hoofs. The subunguis (inner layer of material of the hoof) is softer than the unguis (outer layer), and wears away more quickly. Acting as a shock absorber, the subunguis takes the punishment from the pounding which rocky terrain gives the hoofs, wears away, and keeps the hoofs continuously supplied with a hard edge. Goats are gregarious, except for the old bucks, which tend to live by themselves, and which serve sometimes as sentinels or scouts on the outer edges of herds. Wild goats feed on greens in pastures, and, in the mountains, on the branches and leaves of shrubbery. They breed in the fall, generally between October and December. The gestation period is five months, or, in some species, a few weeks longer. Two kids are usually produced at birth. They are able to move with the herd in a short period of time, and mature sexually at six months. Among the most important of the wild goats is the bezoar goat, or pasang, *Capra aegagrus*, a brownish-gray goat about 36 inches high at the shoulder, found from Asia Minor to N.E. India. For other wild goats, see the articles IBEX; MARKHOR.

A number of breeds of goats are raised domestically throughout the world. They belong to the species *C. hircus*, probably descended from the bezoar goat. Several million are raised in the U.S. They are used for meat, as milk producers, as pets, and as beasts of burden. Many parts of the animal are economically valuable for a variety of purposes, such as the skins for leather and the pelts for rugs and robes. One variety of domestic goat, important for its commercial value, is the Angora. The best Angoras are covered with long, fine, silky hair called mohair over the entire body except for the face and the legs below the knees. The brilliant, transparent texture of mohair has made it a useful material from which imitation fur and ladies' dresses are made. The Cashmere goat, a small animal native to Kashmir, India, is the source of the fine wool, cashmere, from which the famed Cashmere shawls are made.

The U.S. Rocky Mountain goat (q.v.) is properly a goat antelope (q.v.), and is more closely related to the European chamois than to goats and sheep.

Goat's milk compares very favorably in nutritive value with cow's milk. As it is more easily digested than cow's milk, it is frequently recommended by physicians for infants and invalids. Goat's milk is also used extensively in the making of cheeses.

GOAT ANTELOPE, common name for animals of the subfamily Rupicaprinae, family Bovidae (q.v.), which are intermediate in characteristics between goats and antelopes. Most of the goat antelopes have short tails, and relatively small cylindrical horns; some, such as the Rocky Mountain "goat", have beards. For representative goat antelopes, see

CHAMOIS; ROCKY MOUNTAIN GOAT; SEROW; TAKIN.

GOATFISH. See MULLET.

GOAT ISLAND, an island of New York State, situated in the Niagara R., at the brink of Niagara (q.v.) Falls, dividing the falls into the American Falls and the Horseshoe (Canadian) Falls. It is about three quarters of a mile long, and is a part of the Niagara State Reservation of 425 acres. A bridge connects Goat Island with the American shore.

GOAT MOTH. See CARPENTER WORM.

GOATSBEARD. See SALSIFY.

GOATSUCKER, common name for any wide-mouthed bird in the family Caprimulgidae. Goatsuckers are found in all parts of the world except Australia. American goatsuckers include the chuckwill's widow, the nighthawk, and the whippoorwill (qq.v.). The common European goatsucker is called a nightjar. Goatsuckers get their name from an erroneous assumption that their food consists of goats' milk. Actually goatsuckers are insect eaters; their wide-spreading mouths, framed by a network of long, stiff bristles on the lower margin, specially adapt them for the capture of insects while in flight. The bill is very short and weak, the wings long and narrow, and the legs short. Female goatsuckers build no nests, laying their eggs in any convenient cavity in the ground. The eggs are white, sometimes blotched with black, brown, or purple. A clutch usually consists of two eggs.

GOBAT, CHARLES ALBERT (1843–1914), Swiss statesman, born in Tramelan. In 1882 he was elected a member of the Great Council of Bern. Two years later he became a member of the *Ständerat* or Council of States, one of the two chambers comprising the national legislature of Switzerland. From 1890 to 1914 he was a member of the *Nationalrat* or National Council, the other chamber of the legislature. During his entire political life Gobat worked in behalf of international peace; in 1902, in recognition of his efforts, the Nobel Peace Prize was awarded jointly to him and to a compatriot, the editor Élie Ducommun.

GOBI, an extensive desert area in central Asia, principally in Mongolia, sometimes called by the Chinese name *Shamo,* "sand desert". The Gobi, which is approximately 1000 m. in extent from east to west and 600 m. from north to south, is bounded by the Great Khingan Mountains on the east, the Altyn Tagh and Nan-shan Mountains on the south, the Pamir Mountains on the west,

and the Altai, Kangai, and Yablonoi Mountains on the north. The general form of the Gobi is that of a plateau depressed between higher mountains. The height of the plateau ranges from 3000 ft. above sea level in the eastern portion to 5000 ft. in the west. The surface of the Gobi plateau consists in the main of rolling gravel plains, interspersed occasionally with low, flat-topped ranges and isolated hills which are the result of faulting action. Only the southeastern portion of the Gobi is completely waterless. The remainder of the region, or approximately three quarters of its area, has a thin growth of grass, scrub, and thorn sufficient to feed the flocks of the nomadic herdsmen who live there; water is available in wells and occasional shallow lakes. The borders of the Gobi to the north and northwest are fertile, and grassy steppes or prairies lie at the southeastern edge of the desert area. Several caravan trails of great antiquity cross the Gobi region. Among the more important are the routes from Su-chan to Hami and Kalgan to Urga.

The first Europeans to traverse the Gobi were Marco Polo (q.v.) and his father and uncle, who crossed the region about 1275. The next recorded crossing is that of the Jesuit priest Gerbillin in the years 1688 to 1698. In modern times a number of expeditions have explored the Gobi, including those of the Swedish explorer Sven Hedin (q.v.). In the years 1921 through 1930 the

Nature Magazine

The tawny frogmouth, a goatsucker

American Museum of Natural History sponsored a series of expeditions under the leadership of Roy Chapman Andrews (q.v.). The American Museum expeditions discovered fossilized dinosaur eggs in the Gobi; see DINOSAURIA. Archeological finds in the Gobi area include remains of Eolithic, Upper Paleolithic, Azilian, Neolithic, and Bronze Age civilizations.

GOBY, common name for the small, tropical, semiterrestrial fish in the families Gobiidae and Periophthalmidae of the suborder Acanthopterygii. Gobies are widely distributed in the tropics and include the smallest fish known. One Philippine species, *Pandaka pygmea,* is only $\frac{1}{3}$ to $\frac{1}{2}$ in. long when fully grown, and another, *Mistichthys luzonensis,* is only about $\frac{1}{2}$ in. long. The latter species is used as food; one pound consists of 16,000 individuals. Species of the typical genus *Periophthalmus* reach four inches in length. The gobies usually have broad, flattened heads with large mouths. Their pelvic fins are often united to form a sucking disk by means of which they climb mangrove roots when out of water. Their scales may be ctenoid, cycloid, or entirely absent. Coloring varies from species to species. Gobies normally live near beaches and in the mouths of rivers, but during the breeding season they usually go out to sea. The young, born at sea, return to the shores, rarely leaving them until mature and ready to breed.

The most unusual of these fish are the skipping gobies, or mudskippers, found in Asia and the Pacific, which can skip more swiftly over sand and mud than they can swim in water. The mudskippers have strong tails and fins with elbowlike bases, which adapt them to traveling over land. Their respiratory organs are modified for air breathing so that they can remain out of water for an entire day in search of small crustaceans and insects. Their eyes are also specially adapted; their range of vision out of water is thirty feet. They are almost completely deaf to sounds in air. The mudskippers live in individual burrows in the mud into which they dive when frightened. During the dry season, members of one genus, *Pseudapocryptes,* estivate (see HIBERNATION) in these burrows, often remaining for weeks with their heads out of water. Members of another genus, *Periophthalmodon,* often engage in a harmless form of fighting-play which terminates when one mudskipper is completely exhausted.

GOD, the Supreme Being, creator and ruler of the universe, in all monotheistic religions, especially Judaism, Christianity, and Mohammedanism; see MONOTHEISM. God is omnipotent, omniscient, infinite in time and space, immanent in the material world but transcendant over it; He is good, loving mankind, and righteous, demanding righteousness from His people. By most believers God is regarded as a personality, but not necessarily in the human sense; see ANTHROPOMORPHISM. The great majority of Christians believe that God existed in human form in the person of Jesus Christ (q.v.; see also TRINITY, DOCTRINE OF THE).

The early Hebrew concept of God was that of a tribal deity; see HENOTHEISM. Under the prophets the concept became strongly moral, and the national God, named variously in the Scriptures *Adonai, Elohim,* or *Jehovah,* in time became a God of righteousness and morality; see JUDAISM. Influenced by their increasing contact with other peoples, the Jews came to regard Jehovah as Lord of Nations, ruling the entire world, but having special care for the Jewish nation. This concept of God was adopted by Christianity, which, however, emphasized the idea of God as a loving Father, and substituted the Christian Church for the Hebrew nation as the object of His special care. Mohammedanism (q.v.), in turn, substituted the followers of the Prophet Mohammed.

The traditional arguments for the existence of God are: (1) the *ontological* argument, formulated by St. Anselm and later restated by René Descartes, that the gradations of perfection evident in the material world imply an absolute perfection, which is God; (2) the *cosmological* argument of Aristotle and St. Thomas Aquinas that, inasmuch as every effect in the material world has a cause and an infinite regression of finite causes is inconceivable, the chain of cause and effect must ultimately extend back to a First Cause, which is God; (3) the *teleological* argument proceeding from the order and arrangement in the universe, which postulate the existence of an intelligence and power as the fountainhead of order; and (4) the *moral* argument of Immanuel Kant, which holds that the moral law inherent in human nature implies an external lawgiver, who is God. See THEISM. Modern philosophers have introduced such arguments as that from *entropy,* which holds that, because the availability of energy in the material universe is constantly decreasing, it must at one time have been at a finite maximum. Such a condition implies creation in that state or the application of an extracosmic

God creating the world, a fresco by Michelangelo on the Sistine Chapel ceiling, Rome

force. Several independent branches of science also give evidence that the universe had a cataclysmic beginning about three billion years ago; see RELATIVITY.

Modern objection to the traditional proofs was begun by Kant, who claimed to have refuted not only the traditional arguments but also their antitheses; he thus became the founder of modern agnosticism (q.v.; see also DEISM; ATHEISM).

In polytheistic religions a god is regarded as a being possessed of supernatural qualities and powers, a higher intelligence controlling forces of good or evil, or a personification of any of the forces of nature; see GREEK RELIGIOUS MYTHOLOGY; RELIGION, COMPARATIVE; ROMAN RELIGIOUS MYTHOLOGY; SCANDINAVIAN MYTHOLOGY. See also THEOLOGY.

GODAVARI, a river of India, rising in the Nasik district in the Western Ghats Mountains, and flowing 900 m. generally S.E. to its delta, about 60 m. from the Bay of Bengal, into which seven mouths of the river empty. Just above the entrance of the river into the delta, the Godavari courses through a gorge 200 yards wide. Every twelve years the great bathing festival, called *Pushkaram*, is held on the banks of the Godavari by the Hindus, to whom the river is sacred. The waters of the river, chiefly in the delta, are used for irrigation. A dam at Dowlaishweram, a village at the head of the delta, provided three canals with sufficient water in 1920 to irrigate nearly 1,000,000 acres. Sections of the lower Godavari are open for water communication; rapids hinder navigation on the upper part of the river. The Godavari R. ranks in agricultural and commercial utility, as well as in scenic beauty, with the Ganges and Indus rivers.

GODDARD, HENRY HERBERT (1866–1957), American psychologist, born at Vassalboro, Me., and educated at Haverford College, at Clark University, and in Germany. He was director of research of the Training School for Feeble-Minded Children at Vineland, N.J., from 1906 to 1918, and director of the Ohio State Bureau of Juvenile Research from 1918 to 1922. He was professor of abnormal and clinical psychology at Ohio State University from 1922 to 1938, when he retired. An authority on feeble-mindedness, the education and problems of juveniles, and eugenics, Goddard was the first to use the word "moron". His many writings include *The Kallikak Family* (1912), *Feeble-Mindedness* (1914), *Psychology of the Normal and Subnormal* (1919),

Juvenile Delinquency (1921), *School Training of Gifted Children* (1927), and *How to Raise Children in the Atomic Age* (1948).

GODFREY, ARTHUR (1903–), American radio and television entertainer, born in New York City, and educated in the public schools of Hasbrouck Heights, N.J. At the age of 17 he enlisted in the U.S. Navy. He attended the Naval Radio School, Great Lakes, Ill. After completing (1924) his naval service he worked in various fields until 1927, when he joined the U.S. Coast Guard. He secured his discharge from the Coast Guard in 1930, and having been favorably received as an amateur and part-time radio singer and broadcaster in Baltimore, Md., obtained employment as a staff announcer for the Washington, D.C., station of a national network. Early in his radio career Godfrey originated the technique of mildly ridiculing his sponsors' commercial announcements. Acquiring a reputation for informality and humorous ad libs, he soon became one of the most popular performers in radio. He was a free-lance broadcaster after 1934, appearing at first as a "disc jockey" and later as master of ceremonies of *Talent Scouts,* a weekly program featuring beginners in the entertainment field. Subsequently televised on a nationwide network, *Talent Scouts* was adjudged (1952) one of the most popular shows on the air. In January, 1953, Godfrey was named "man of the year" in radio for 1952.

GODFREY OF BOUILLON (1061?–1100), French nobleman, soldier, and leader in the First Crusade, born in Baisy. In 1088 he was created Duke of Lower Lorraine by the Holy Roman emperor Henry IV, with his capital at Bouillon. He and his brothers Eustace and Baldwin led a body of about 40,000 Germans in the First Crusade, beginning in 1096. Arriving at Constantinople in November of that year, he succeeded in establishing friendly relations with Emperor Alexius I Comnenus. In 1099 Godfrey participated in the siege and capture of Jerusalem; upon being offered the title "King of Jerusalem", he refused it for religious reasons, and was instead named "Baron and Defender of the Holy Sepulcher". In August, 1099, when Egyptian forces moved to attack Jerusalem, Godfrey defeated them at Ascalon. As the first Christian ruler of Jerusalem, Godfrey later became the hero of many songs, legends, and literary works, including several *chansons de geste* and the epic poem *Jerusalem Delivered* (1575), by Torquato Tasso. See CRUSADES.

GODIN, JEAN BAPTISTE ANDRÉ (1817–88), French social reformer and industrialist, born at Esquehéries, Aisne. He worked in his father's blacksmith shop until 1834, and later became a manufacturer of an industrial oven of his own design. He then discovered a new method of enameling cast iron, and acquired great wealth from this process.

About 1842 he became interested in the ideas of the French utopian socialist François Marie Charles Fourier (q.v.). When a Fourierist colony was founded in Texas in 1848, Godin presented 100,000 francs to its organizers. In 1859 he established a Fourierist settlement at his iron foundry at Guise; the workers were provided by Godin with a community store, nursery, hospital, recreation rooms, and a large theater, in addition to a pension plan and health insurance. Later he initiated a profit-sharing plan, and in 1880 the foundry, the largest manufactory of enamelware in France, became the property of the workers employed in it. In 1871, after the formation of the Third Republic, Godin was elected a deputy to the National Assembly, in which he worked to establish laws for the protection of women and children in industry, and became a leading advocate of trade unionism. His economic and social ideas are expressed in his books *Solutions Sociales* (1871), *Les Socialistes et les Droits du Travail* (1874), *Mutualité Sociale* (1880), and *La République du Travail et la Réforme Parlementaire* (1889).

GODIVA or **GODGIFU** (1040–80), English noblewoman, wife of Leofric, Earl of Mercia. She is known to have persuaded her husband to found monasteries at Coventry and Stow. According to popular legend she obtained for people of Coventry a lowering of the excessive taxes levied by her husband, who agreed to reduce the taxes on condition that she ride naked through the town. Lady Godiva, mounted on a white horse and covered only by her long hair, carried out his demand. Only one person disobeyed her orders to remain indoors behind closed shutters; this man, a tailor known afterward as Peeping Tom, peered through a window and immediately became blind. The oldest form of the legend is quoted from earlier writers by Roger of Wendover (d. 1236), in *Flores Historiarum.* A festival in honor of Lady Godiva was later instituted as a part of Coventry Fair in 1678, and was celebrated at intervals until 1826. The festival was again revived in 1848 and 1929.

GOD SAVE THE KING. See NATIONAL ANTHEMS: *Great Britain and Colonies.*

GOD'S TRUCE. See TRUCE OF GOD.

GODUNOV, Boris Fëdorovich (1551?–1605), Czar of Russia from 1598. A boyar and the descendant of an ancient Tatar family, Boris became a favorite of Czar Ivan IV, called Ivan the Terrible. His influence on the imperial court was strengthened by the marriage of his sister to Ivan's feeble-minded son, Fëdor Ivanovich. On his deathbed, in 1584, Ivan appointed Boris a guardian of Fëdor, and regent during his son's reign. Boris became the most powerful man in Russia, recognized as head of the state. He recolonized Siberia and gave the Muscovite Church a status equal to that of other Eastern churches by making Moscow a patriarchate. Extremely autocratic, he was the first Russian ruler to use Siberia as a place of banishment for political exiles; moreover, he legalized serfdom in its grimmest form by an edict of 1587, which forbade the transfer of serfs from one landowner to another and thus bound them to the land. When Demetrius (Dmitri), another son of Ivan, menaced his rule, Boris reportedly had him murdered.

On the death of Fëdor in 1598, the *Zemsky Sobor* (National Assembly) elected Boris czar. The new czar banished the Romanovs, his chief rivals, and proceeded to further policies he had already begun; strengthening Russian commerce, introducing various aspects of Western civilization, and struggling against the privileged nobility. Despite his power, Boris was exceedingly suspicious and felt himself insecure; informers kept him constantly advised of all political activities and increasing numbers of Russians became the victims of his persecutions. In 1604 a pretender to the throne, who claimed to be the murdered Demetrius, appeared in Poland, and thousands of supporters joined a revolt against Boris. The czar, however, died suddenly in the midst of the civil war. The story of Boris Godunov became the basis of the play *Boris Godunov* by Aleksandr Pushkin, later made into the opera of the same name by Modest Musorgski.

GODWIN, Mary Wollstonecraft (1759–97), English author and feminist, born probably at Hoxton, London. Soon after 1780 she left home to earn her living, running a school for two years with her sisters Eliza and Everina, and subsequently serving for a year as a governess in Ireland. In 1788 her first novel, *Mary, a Fiction,* was published with moderate success, and she then decided to devote herself to a literary career. She settled in London, where she was employed by a publisher as a reader and translator. At this time she became a member of an intellectual group which included William Blake, Thomas Paine, Joseph Priestley, and Henry Fuseli. In 1788 appeared her best-known work, *A Vindication of the Rights of Woman,* asserting that intellectual companionship was the ideal of marriage and pleading for equality of education and opportunity between the sexes. Shortly thereafter she went to France to observe the French Revolution. In Paris she established a liaison with an American, Captain Gilbert Imlay, to whom she bore a daughter in 1794. Imlay subsequently deserted her and she returned to England, where in 1797 she married William Godwin (q.v.). She died at the birth of their daughter Mary, later Mary Wollstonecraft Shelley (q.v.). Her works include *Original Stories from Real Life* (1791) and *A Vindication of the Rights of Man* (1793). Her letters were published in *Memoirs of the Author of the Rights of Woman* (1798) by William Godwin.

GODWIN, William (1756–1836), English novelist and political economist, born at Wisbech, Cambridgeshire, and educated at Hoxton Academy, London. His parents were strict Calvinists, and Godwin became a follower of John Glas, founder of the Sandemanian sect, and a Sandemanian minister. By 1785, however, he had become an atheist, and in his best-known work, *The Inquiry Concerning Political Justice, and Its Influence on General Virtue and Happiness* (1793), expounded the theories of philosophical anarchism (q.v.). He expanded these theories in his novel *Caleb Williams, or Things as They Are* (1794). Godwin was later converted to theism by Samuel Taylor Coleridge.

In 1797 Godwin married Mary Wollstonecraft (see Godwin, Mary Wollstonecraft), who died in giving birth to a daughter (see Shelley, Mary Wollstonecraft) who later became the wife of Percy Bysshe Shelley. In 1801 Godwin married Mary Jane Clairmont, and with her help established himself as a bookseller and publisher under the pseudonym Edward Baldwin. He wrote several books for children, and published others, notably the *Tales from Shakespeare* of Charles and Mary Lamb. His business failed in 1822, and he devoted himself to writing one of his best works, *The History of the Commonwealth* (1828).

Godwin exerted a profound influence, both as a person and as a writer, upon the authors of the time, especially Shelley and the novelist Edward Lytton Bulwer (later Bulwer-Lytton). His other works include *The En-*

quirer, a Series of Essays (1797); *St. Leon, a Tale of the Sixteenth Century* (1799); and *Thoughts on Man, a Series of Essays* (1831).

GODWIN-AUSTEN, HENRY HAVERSHAM (1834–1923), British soldier and topographer, born at Teignmouth, Devonshire, and educated at the Royal Military College, Sandhurst. After his graduation he was sent with his regiment to India, where he participated in the Punjab and Burmese wars. In 1856 he joined the Great Trigonometrical Survey of India. Between that date and his retirement from the army in 1877, he conducted topographical surveys in Kashmir in 1857, in Ladakh in 1862, in the Pang Kong Lake district in 1863, and in Bhutan from 1863 until 1865. Mt. Godwin-Austen, the second-highest peak in the world (28,251 ft. above sea level) in the Karakoram range of the Himalayas, India, was named for him. He wrote numerous articles and treatises on scientific subjects.

GOEBBELS, JOSEPH PAUL (1897–1945), German fascist propagandist and politician, born at Rheydt, Rhineland, and educated at the University of Heidelberg and other institutions. He joined the National Socialist or Nazi party (see NATIONAL SOCIALISM) in 1922 and undertook the direction of students who joined the party. Until 1925 Goebbels looked upon the Nazi movement as socialist and proletarian, but a year later he met Adolf Hitler and adopted all the beliefs of German fascism. In 1926 he was made *gauleiter,* or party leader, for the region of Berlin, and in 1927 he founded and became editor of the official Nazi periodical *Der Angriff.* He was elected to the Reichstag in 1928 and a year later became propaganda leader of the Nazi party, in which capacity he became the apostle of unreasoning hatred of the Jews and other groups. His work as a propagandist was a contributing factor to Hitler's success in acquiring power. In 1933 he was appointed Reich minister for propaganda and national enlightenment. From that time until his death, Goebbels used all media of education and communications to further Nazi propagandistic aims, instilling in the Germans the concept of their leader as a veritable god, and of their destiny as the rulers of the world. In 1938 he became a member of Hitler's cabinet council. During World War II, in 1944, he became Reich trustee for total mobilization. Goebbels killed himself in 1945, shortly before the fall of Berlin to the Russian troops.

GOERING, HERMANN. See GÖRING, HERMANN.

GOETHALS, GEORGE WASHINGTON (1858–1928), American army officer and engineer, born in Brooklyn, N.Y., and educated at the College of the City of New York and the U.S. Military Academy at West Point. Upon graduating in 1880 he was appointed second lieutenant in the Corps of Engineers in the U.S. Army. During the Spanish-American War he was chief of engineers of U.S. volunteers.

Goethals' early engineering projects (1882 to 1905) included the Tennessee River improvement, the Muscle Shoals canal, and the fortification of Narragansett Bay. In 1907 President Theodore Roosevelt appointed him chairman and chief engineer of the Panama Canal Commission. With the help of William C. Gorgas (q.v.), the sanitation problem in the canal region was successfully combatted, and Goethals' capable handling of personnel problems in addition to his engineering skill contributed greatly to the rapid and successful completion of the project. Goethals was governor of the Canal Zone from 1914 to 1916, and was promoted to the rank of major general in 1915. He was on active duty during World War I as quartermaster general and director of purchase, storage, and traffic. After the war he retired from active duty to become a civil-engineering consultant in New York City. The Goethals Bridge between Staten Island, N.Y., and Elizabeth, N.J., is named after him.

GOETHE, JOHANN WOLFGANG VON (1749–1832), German poet, dramatist, novelist, and scientist, born at Frankfort on the Main. From 1765 to 1768 he studied law at Leipzig; there he also experienced the first of the numerous love affairs which served as material for many of his literary works. This first romantic attachment was with Anna Katharina Schönkopf, the daughter of the owner of the tavern at which he dined; her influence was reflected in one of his earliest works, the one-act comedy in verse *Die Laune des Verliebten.* During the Leipzig period he also wrote a tragedy in verse, *Die Mitschuldigen* (1768). Goethe's health broke down in Leipzig and he returned to Frankfort, where, during his convalescence, he studied occult philosophy, astrology, and alchemy. Through the influence of a friend of his mother's, Susanne Katharina von Klettenberg, who was a member of the religious cult known as Pietism (q.v.), Goethe gained some insight into religious mysticism. From 1770 to 1771 he continued his study of law in Strasbourg; in addition, he took up the study of music, art, anatomy, and chemistry.

Two friendships he formed in Strasbourg were of great influence on his literary life. One was with Friderike Brion, the daughter of a pastor of the town of Sesenheim; she later was the model for feminine characters in several of Goethe's most important works, including that of Gretchen in his poetic drama *Faust*. The other friendship was with the German philosopher and critic Johann Gottfried von Herder. Through Herder, an ardent advocate of a German national school of literature, Goethe rid himself of the influence of the principles of French classicism which largely prevailed in Germany at the time, including the principles of the three dramatic unities which the French classical school had adopted from ancient Greek drama (see DRAMA). Goethe also learned from Herder to appreciate the plays of Shakespeare, in which the classic unities are largely discarded for the sake of complete emotional expression; and to realize the value of German folk poetry and German Gothic architecture as sources of inspiration for German literature.

As a result of Herder's influence, Goethe, after he had received his law degree and returned (1772) to practice law in Frankfort, wrote the tragedy *Götz von Berlichingen* (1773). The play, modeled on those of Shakespeare, is an adaptation of the story of a German robber knight of the 16th century; to his exploits Goethe gave the significance of a national German revolt against the authority exerted by the Roman Catholic Church over Germany in the early part of the 16th century. *Götz von Berlichingen* was of great significance in German literary history. Together with the pamphlet *Von Deutscher Art und Kunst* (1773), to which Goethe, Herder, and others contributed, the play inaugurated the important German literary movement known as *Sturm und Drang,* the forerunner of the German romantic movement (see GERMAN LITERATURE: *The Classical and Romantic Period*); the play also served to establish in the tradition of German drama the Shakespearean type of play. The following year (1774), as the result of an unhappy love affair with Charlotte Buff, the fiancée of one of his friends, Goethe wrote the romantic and tragic tale *Die Leiden des Jungen Werthers.* This work was the earliest important novel of the *Sturm und Drang* movement and became the model for numerous novels, characterized by an excessive sentimentality, subsequently written in Germany, France, and elsewhere. Among Goethe's other works writ-

Sculptured head of Johann Wolfgang von Goethe

ten during the years 1772 to 1775 were the plays *Clavigo* (1774) and *Stella* (1776), both of which belong to the German *Sturm und Drang* period.

In 1775 occurred an event which proved to be a turning point not only in the life of Goethe, but in the literary history of Germany. In that year Charles Augustus, heir apparent to the duchy of Saxe-Weimar, invited Goethe to live and work in the capital of the duchy, Weimar, at that time the intellectual and literary center of Germany. From 1775 to the year of his death Goethe's life centered at Weimar, from which city his influence as a writer spread throughout Germany. However, the first ten years of his connection with the court of Weimar formed for him a period of intellectual development rather than of literary production. Through association at Weimar with Herder and the poet Christoph Martin Wieland, and through correspondence and association with Charlotte von Stein, the wife of a Weimar official and a woman of great intellectual gifts, Goethe's intellectual life was broadened. Experience in public office, which included service in important posts in the Weimar war department and department of bridges as well as a term of office as privy councilor, gave Goethe an extensive knowledge of practical affairs. In addition he continued his interest in science during this period, studying nat-

ural science, mineralogy, geology, and oste-
ology. It was during this period, also, that
he was ennobled. He wrote little during the
first ten years of his stay at Weimar, except
for some notable poems, including the lyric
Wanderers Nachtlied and the ballad *Der Erl-
könig;* however, he began the composition of
some of his most notable works, including the
poetic dramas *Iphigenie auf Tauris* (in a prose
version), *Egmont,* and *Faust,* for all of which
he derived a new point of view during the
next important event of his life, his visit to
Italy from 1786 to 1788.

Several reasons impelled Goethe to make
this Italian journey. He was wearied of the
life of the Weimar court, his relationship with
Charlotte von Stein was beginning to pall, and,
above all, he had outgrown the *Sturm und
Drang* point of view and felt the need of a
new set of principles upon which to base
future writings. He found them in Italy. After visiting several cities in northern Italy, he
settled in Rome, where, except for a short trip
to Naples and Sicily, he remained until 1788.
He studied the art and literature of ancient
Greece and Rome and those Renaissance
works of art and literature which had been
most strongly influenced by the ancients, and
he achieved an understanding of the classic
spirit, which stressed balance and perfection
of form rather than emotional content;
thenceforth his work had a balance, calm-
ness, and dignity previously lacking. The writings dating from his Italian stay and the period shortly following it included an iambic
version of the drama *Iphigenie auf Tauris*
(1787); the poetic dramas *Egmont* (1788)
and *Torquato Tasso* (1790); and some work
which he did on *Faust,* part of which appeared as *Fragment* (1790). These works inaugurated for German literature the period
of stability in ideas and form that succeeded
the *Sturm und Drang* period and was known
as the classical period.

Goethe returned to Weimar in 1788. The
following three years were disturbed ones for
him. He found opposition to his new literary
principles at Weimar, and enmity from Frau
von Stein because of his loss of interest in her.
He further antagonized court circles by taking
to live with him a young girl, Christiane Vulpius (1765–1816), who in 1789 bore him a
son. He might have abandoned Weimar but
for two interests: the directorship of the ducal
theater, in which he served from 1791 to
1813; and renewed absorption in scientific
studies, for which he had the facilities at
Weimar. Previously, in 1784, he had made the

discovery, by methods which foreshadowed
the science of comparative morphology, that
the human jawbone contained traces of a
structure similar to the intermaxillary bone
in apes. In 1790 he wrote *Versuch, die Meta-
morphose der Pflanzen zu Erklären,* which
further developed his ideas on comparative
morphology and to some extent foreshadowed
Darwin's ideas on organic evolution. Goethe
was also the author of a treatise on optics,
Beiträge zur Optik (2 parts, 1791 and 1792).
His absorption in scientific work caused him
for the time being to lose interest in literature. This interest was revived through his
friendship with Friedrich von Schiller, one
of the greatest of German dramatists and, after
Goethe, the foremost figure of the German
classical period. The friendship, which lasted
from 1794 to Schiller's death in 1805, was in-
tellectually greatly profitable for Goethe;
Schiller's criticism and suggestions stimulated
him to a new creative period. Its chief products were Goethe's contributions to Schiller's
periodical *Die Horen,* which included *Rö-
mische Elegien* (1795); the novel *Wilhelm
Meisters Lehrjahre* (1796), which became a
model for German fiction for the following
thirty years; and the epic idyll in verse *Hermann und Dorothea* (1798). Schiller also encouraged Goethe to take up again the writing
of *Faust,* a work which Goethe had put aside
for some time. The first part of *Faust* was
published in 1808.

The period from 1805 to his death was one
of comparative tranquility for Goethe. In
1806 he married Christiane Vulpius and remained happy with her until her death ten
years later, although his marriage did not
prevent his having love affairs with several
women, including Bettina von Arnim, the
daughter of one of his former mistresses, and
Minna Herzlieb, foster daughter of a publisher of Jena. Even the upheavals of the
French Revolution and the succeeding Napoleonic period did not interrupt either his literary or scientific work. In politics Goethe
was conservative. While not opposing the War
of Liberation (1813–15) waged by the German people against Napoleon, he stood aloof
from the effort to unite the various parts of
Germany into one nation, advocating instead
the maintaining of small states ruled by benevolent despots. Among his writings of the
period between 1805 and 1832, the most important are the novels *Die Wahlverwandt-
schaften* (1809) and *Wilhelm Meisters Wan-
derjahre* (1821–29); the autobiography *Aus
Meinem Leben, Dichtung und Wahrheit* (4

vols., 1811–33); the book of lyrics *West-östlicher Diwan* (1819); and the second part of his great drama *Faust* (published posthumously, 1832).

The completion of *Faust* was the crowning act of Goethe's long life. The work is one of the masterpieces of German and of world literature. It is not only a new rendition of the well-known legend of the medieval magician Johann Faust (q.v.), but an allegory of human life in all its ramifications. In style and in point of view toward life it reflects the complete range of Goethe's development from the overemotional days of the *Sturm und Drang* period to the calm classicism and deep understanding of his mature years. Its emphasis on the right and power of the individual to inquire freely into affairs both human and divine, and to work out his own destiny in life, accounts for its universal reputation as the first great work of literature in the spirit of modern times.

Among the literary geniuses of modern times, Goethe was the most catholic in his intellectual interests. By the success with which his poetry expresses the deepest spiritual feeling of the German people, by the profound understanding and creation of character in his plays and novels, because of the literary movements he inaugurated and of which he was the chief figure, and because of the vast influence of his dramas and novels upon contemporary and later world literature, Goethe must be considered not only the greatest of German writers, but one of the most eminent in all world literature.

GOETHITE, a common ore of iron, and one of the most commonly occurring minerals in nature. It generally contains about 63 percent iron, 27 percent oxygen, and 10 percent water. Manganese is often present in amounts up to 5 percent. Goethite is formed as a weathering product of other iron minerals. It is also precipitated from water and deposited at the bottom of bogs and springs in a form known as bog-iron ore. Such deposits are usually associated with foreign materials and are too impure to be worked commercially for the iron. Goethite is widely distributed; some of the most notable workable deposits are found, usually associated with other iron minerals, in Alsace-Lorraine, Westphalia, Bohemia, and in the Lake Superior and Appalachian Mountain regions in the United States. The ore is yellow brown to dark brown in color, has a hardness of 5 to 5½, and a specific gravity of 4.3. It crystallizes in the rhombic system in acicular crystals

Museum of Modern Art
Self-portrait, Vincent van Gogh

and in stalactitic aggregates. Goethite was named in honor of the German poet Johann Wolfgang von Goethe.

GOGGLES. See EYEGLASSES.

GOGH, VINCENT VAN (1853–90), Dutch painter, born at Groot-Zundert, in North Brabant, son of a Dutch Protestant pastor. Early in life, he displayed a moody, restless temperament which was to thwart his every pursuit. By the age of twenty-seven he had been in turn a salesman in an art gallery, a French tutor, a theological student, and an evangelist among the miners at Wasmes, in Belgium; his experiences as a missionary are reflected in his first paintings of peasants and potato diggers. Dark and somber, sometimes crude, these early works evidence Van Gogh's intense desire to express the misery and poverty of humanity as he saw it.

In 1886 he went to Paris to live with his brother Théo, an art dealer, and became familiar with the new art movements developing at the time. Influenced by the work of the Impressionists (see IMPRESSIONISM), Van Gogh began to experiment with current techniques and subsequently adopted the brilliant hues found in the paintings of the French Impressionist Camille Pissaro (1831–1903) and those of Georges Seurat (q.v.).

In 1888 Van Gogh left Paris for southern France, where, under the burning sun of

Nikolai Vasilievich Gogol

Provence, he painted scenes of the fields, cypress trees, peasants, and rustic life characteristic of the region. During this period, living at Arles, he began to use the swirling brush strokes and intense yellows, greens, and blues associated with such typical works as "L'Arlesienne", "Room at Arles", and "Landscape With Cypress Trees". For Van Gogh all visible phenomena seemed to be endowed with a physical and spiritual vitality. In his enthusiasm he induced the painter Gauguin, whom he had met earlier in Paris, to join him. After awhile they began to have violent disagreements, culminating in a quarrel in which Van Gogh wildly threatened Gauguin with a razor; the same night, in deep remorse, he cut off his own ear. This episode marked the beginning of a periodic insanity which continued until his death. For a time he was in a hospital at Arles; then he spent a year in the nearby asylum of St. Remy, working between repeated spells of madness. Under the care of a sympathetic doctor, whose portrait he painted ("Dr. Gachet"), Van Gogh spent three months at Auvers, and then shot himself.

Van Gogh's letters to his brother Théo (published in 1911) constitute a remarkably illuminating record of an artist's life. The French painter Haim Soutine and the German painters Oskar Kokoschka, Emil Nolden,

and Ernst Ludwig Kirchner (qq.v.) owe more to Van Gogh than to any other single source. Van Gogh, in fact, represents the archetype of Expressionism (q.v.), the idea of emotional spontaneity in painting. His paintings hang in most of the prominent museums of the world; the largest single collection is in the Museum of Modern Art at The Hague.

GOGOL, NIKOLAI VASILIEVICH (1809–52), Russian writer, born in Poltava Province, of Ukrainian Cossack parents. In 1820 he went to St. Petersburg, where he eventually secured employment in the civil service and became known in literary circles. Enthusiastic praise greeted his volume of short stories of Ukrainian life, *Evenings in a Farm near Dikanka* (1831). Then followed another collection, *Mirgorod,* (1835), containing *Taras Bulba,* which was expanded in 1842 into a full-length novel; this latter work, dealing with 16th-century Cossack life, revealed Gogol's great ability for accurate and sympathetic character portraiture and his sparkling humor.

In 1836 appeared Gogol's play *The Inspector General,* regarded by many critics as the greatest play in Russian literature and one of the finest in European literature. It is a rollicking satire on the cupidity and stupidity of contemporary bureaucratic officials, as seen through the eyes of a traveler who arrives unknown in a small town; he is mistaken by the local officials for an expected government inspector, and is offered propitiatory bribes to induce him to overlook their misconduct in office.

From 1836 to 1848 Gogol lived in Rome, where he worked on a novel which is considered his greatest creative effort and one of the finest novels in world literature, *Dead Souls* (1842), also published under the alternative title *Chichikov's Journey.* In structure, *Dead Souls* is akin to *Don Quixote* by Cervantes. Its extraordinary humor, however, derives from a unique and sardonic conception: Collegiate Councilor Pável Ivanovich Chichikov, an ambitious, shrewd, and unscrupulous adventurer, goes from place to place, buying, stealing, and wheedling from their owners the titles to serfs whose names appeared on the preceding census lists but who had since died and were, accordingly, called "dead souls". With this "property" as security he plans to raise loans with which to buy an estate with "live souls".

Chichikov's travels constituted the occasions for profound and objectively stated insights into the degrading and stultifying influence of serfdom on both owner and serf. The work also contains a large number of brilliantly depicted Russian provincial types. *Dead Souls* exerted an enormous influence on succeeding generations of Russian writers. Many of the witty sayings expressed in its pages have become Russian maxims.

As published, *Dead Souls* was intended by its author to constitute the first part of a larger work; Gogol began its sequel but in a fit of hypochondriacal melancholy destroyed the manuscript. His *Selected Passages from a Correspondence with Friends* appeared in 1847. In the following year he made a pilgrimage to the Holy Land, and on his return a priest, Matthew Konstantinovsky, persuaded him that his fictional work was sinful. Gogol thereupon destroyed a number of his unpublished manuscripts. Gogol is ranked with the novelists Lev Tolstoi, Ivan Turgenev, and Fëdor Dostoevski, and the poet Aleksander Pushkin (qq.v.), as one of the five greatest writers of Russian literature.

GOGRA, a river of N. India, and one of the largest affluents of the Ganges R. It rises in the S. slopes of the Himalayas in Tibet, at an altitude of 13,000 ft. above sea level. The river flows S.W. through Nepal as the Kauriala. In Uttar Pradesh State the Gogra flows in a S.E. direction to the town of Chapra, where, after its total course of 570 m., it joins the Ganges R. The river is one of the most important commercial waterways of Uttar Pradesh.

GOITER, a disease of the thyroid gland (q.v.), characterized by an enlargement of the gland, visible externally as a swelling on the front of the neck. In many cases the basal metabolic rate (see METABOLISM) is elevated, and nervousness is a common associated symptom.

Simple goiter. This disease is characterized by an enlargement of the entire gland, or of one of its two lobes, caused by a deficiency of iodine (q.v.) in the diet. The disease is especially apt to appear in adolescence. Simple goiter occurs in inland areas of all continents and in Derbyshire, England, where it is called Derbyshire Neck. It is common in the U.S. "goiter belt", which includes the Great Lakes region and the N. Pacific coast. The administration of iodine, or of the iodine-containing hormone thyroxin, acts both to prevent and to cure the disease. Prevention requires the taking of small doses of iodine for long periods. Ingestion of iodine during pregnancy prevents development of the disease in the infant as well as in the mother.

Public health measures, including the addition of iodine to water supplies and to table salt, have proved of benefit in reducing the incidence of simple goiter in certain areas. Iodine is most effective when administered to children who have the disease. Thyroidectomy, or surgical removal of the gland, may be necessary in cases where the gland has become greatly enlarged.

Toxic goiter. This disease, also called exophthalmic goiter, and Graves' disease, for the Irish physician Robert James Graves (1796–1853), is caused by an excess of thyroid secretion. The cause of the excessive secretion is obscure. In some cases it may result from excessive stimulation by the pituitary body (q.v.). The symptoms of toxic goiter are similar to those of simple goiter, except that the eyes generally protrude and have a fixed and staring appearance, and there is a rapid heartbeat and a fine tremor. Thiouracil and iodine are sometimes used in the treatment of toxic goiter. Irradiation of the gland by radioactive iodine is among the more recent methods of treatment. See also CRETINISM; HORMONES; MYXEDEMA; THYROID GLAND; THYROXINE.

GOLD, metallic element, symbol Au, atomic number 79, atomic weight 197.2, m.p. 1063° C. (1945° F.), b.p. 2600° C. (4712° F.), and valence 1 or 3. The metal has been known and highly valued from earliest times. The unit used in weighing gold is the troy ounce (see WEIGHTS AND MEASURES). In terms of dollars, a troy ounce of gold was for many years worth $20.67. Since January, 1934, gold has been purchased by the U.S. Treasury at $35.00 an ounce. See DOLLAR; GOLD STANDARD.

Occurrence. Gold is found in nature in quartz veins and secondary alluvial deposits (see GEOLOGY, ECONOMIC) as a free metal or in a combined state. It is very widely distributed, although it is rare, being 58th in order of abundance of the elements in the earth's crust. It is almost always associated with varying amounts of silver; the naturally occurring gold-silver alloy is called *electrum.* Gold occurs, in chemical combination with tellurium, in the minerals calaverite and sylvanite along with silver, and in the mineral nagyagite along with lead, antimony, and sulfur. It occurs with mercury as gold amalgam. It is generally present to a small extent in iron pyrites; galena, the lead sulfide ore which usually contains silver, sometimes also contains appreciable amounts of gold. Gold also occurs in sea water to the extent of 5 to 250 parts by weight to 100 million parts of water.

Library of Congress

Gold miners in California in 1860 using cradle to wash earth from gold ore (from old woodcut)

Although the quantity of gold present in sea water is over 10 billion tons, the cost of recovering the gold would be far greater than the value of the gold obtained.

Properties. Pure gold is the most malleable and ductile of all the metals. It can easily be beaten or hammered to a thickness of a two hundred-thousandths of an inch, and a single ounce can be drawn into a wire sixty miles long. It is one of the softest metals (hardness, 2.5 to 3), and is extremely dense (specific gravity, 19.3). It is a good conductor of heat and electricity. Gold is bright yellow and has a high luster. Finely divided gold, like other metallic powders, is black; colloidally suspended gold ranges in color from ruby-red to purple.

Gold is inactive chemically. It is unaffected by air, heat, moisture, and all ordinary solvents. It dissolves in aqua regia, a mixture of three parts hydrochloric and one part nitric acid, forming chlorauric acid. The most important compounds are the chlorides and the cyanides.

Uses. The major portion of the gold produced is used in coinage and jewelry. For these purposes it is alloyed with other metals to give it the necessary hardness. Coinage gold is composed of 90 parts gold to 10 parts silver. Green gold used in jewelry contains copper and silver; white gold contains zinc and nickel, or platinum metals.

The gold content in alloys is expressed in carats. Gold is also used in the form of gold leaf in the arts of gilding and lettering. Purple of Cassius, a precipitate of finely divided gold and stannic hydroxide formed by the interaction of auric chloride and stannous chloride, is used in coloring ruby glass. Chlorauric acid is used in photography for toning

silver images. Potassium gold cyanide is used in electrogilding. Gold is also used in dentistry (q.v.). Radioisotopes of gold are used in biological research and in the treatment of cancer; see TRACERS.

Gold Mining. The process used for mining gold in early civilizations and by individual prospectors in the various "gold rushes" was extremely simple. It consisted of "panning", the use of a circular dish often with a small pocket at the bottom. The prospector filled the dish with gold-bearing sand or gravel, held it under a gentle stream of water, and rotated it. The lighter parts of the gravel were gradually washed off and the gold particles were left in the pocket.

As gold mining developed, more elaborate methods were introduced and hydraulic mining was invented. The hydraulic method consists of directing a powerful stream of water against the gold-bearing gravel or sand. This operation breaks down the material and washes it away through specially constructed sluices where the gold settles while the lighter gravel is floated off. For mining on rivers, elevator dredges are generally used. The elevator dredge is a flat-bottomed boat employing an endless chain of small buckets which scoop up the material from the river bottom and empty it on the dredge into a container built of screening called a *trommel*. The material is rotated in the trommel as water is played on it. The gold-bearing sand sinks through perforations in the trommel, and drops onto shaking tables, where it is further concentrated. Dredging may also be used in dry beds of ancient rivers if there is ample water within a reasonable distance. A pit is dug, and the dredge moved in and floated by water pumped from the adjacent source.

Extensive underground deposits of gold-bearing rocks are often discovered by a small outcrop on the surface. Shafts are sunk, as in coal mining, and the ore brought to the surface. It is then crushed in special machines.

Gold is extracted from gravel or from crushed rock by dissolving it either in mercury (the amalgam process) or in cyanide solutions (the cyanide process). Some ores, especially those in which the gold is chemically combined with tellurium, must be roasted before extraction. The gold is recovered from the solution and melted into ingots. Gold-bearing rock with as little as one part of gold to 300,-000 parts of worthless material may be worked at a profit.

The rarest form of gold is a nugget. The largest known nugget, the "Welcome Stran-

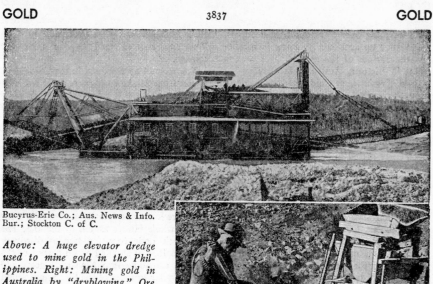

Bucyrus-Erie Co.; Aus. News & Info. Bur.; Stockton C. of C.

Above: A huge elevator dredge used to mine gold in the Philippines. Right: Mining gold in Australia by "dryblowing." Ore is first shaken, then dust and dirt is blown away. Below: A stream of water is used in hydraulic mining in California.

ger", weighing over 150 pounds avoirdupois, was turned up accidentally, a few inches below the surface of the ground, by a wagon wheel in Victoria, Australia, in 1869.

Gold Production. Gold production dates from the earliest civilizations, the Etruscan, Minoan, Assyrian, and Egyptian, when placer gold was derived from alluvial sands and gravels by simple processes of washing or panning. Gold was produced in this manner at an early period in India, Central Asia, the s. Urals, and in the regions bordering the E. Mediterranean. With progress in mining technique, primary auriferous veins were exploited; this type of gold mining attained some importance before the opening of the Christian Era. During the Middle Ages gold production and mining made little progress.

At the time of the discovery of America, the value of the total gold stock of Europe was probably less than $225,000,000. During the succeeding 350 years, from the end of the 15th century to about 1850, total world gold output amounted to about 150,000,000 oz. South America and Mexico became large producers of gold during this period. The acquisition of South America by Spain resulted, in the 16th century, in a large increase in gold produced in the New World. Some of this production resulted from simple seizure of gold from the Indians of Peru, who had long mined the metal. In the same century, Mexico contributed about 9% of the total world production. Gold was discovered in Australia in February, 1851, and in the following months rich fields were found there.

By the middle of the 19th century, the U.S. produced a considerable percentage of the world's gold. In the U.S., gold is produced in two regions: the E. region along the Appalachian Mountains and the w. region along the Rocky Mountains, Sierra Nevada, Coast, and Cascade ranges. Gold has been found at numerous localities on the E. slope of the Appalachians from Newfoundland to Alabama, although workable deposits occur only in Nova Scotia, Canada, and the s. States. In the U.S., the auriferous belt, varying from a few miles to 75 miles in width, extends from Virginia through N. Carolina, S. Carolina, and Georgia into Alabama. Both veins and surface deposits are worked. Some pockets of ore are exceptionally rich. The first gold shipped to the mint for coinage from the s. States was from N. Carolina in 1804. For the next twenty years N. Carolina's annual output amounted to less than $2500. In 1829 Virginia and S. Carolina, in 1830 Georgia, in 1831 Alabama and Tennessee, and in 1868 Maryland shipped gold to the mint for coinage.

The w. gold fields extend in the Cordilleran region from Alaska to Mexico. Gold was discovered first in this region at Sutter's Mill, Calif., January 24, 1848. During the next five years gold valued at more than $285,000,000, an amount twenty-one times greater than the value of the total previous production of the entire country, was produced in California (see CALIFORNIA). The "gold rush" took place at this time, when men from all parts of the world rushed to the new gold district; see FORTY-NINERS. The discovery furnished the incentive for the exploration and development of the whole far w. section of the U.S. The Comstock Lode (q.v.), a famous discovery made in 1859, is situated on an E. spur of the Sierras, extending into Nevada. Placers and veins similar to those of the Sierras are found also in Oregon and Washington. The Rocky Mountain and the outlying ranges, which were first prospected by Californian miners in the early sixties, include an immense area of gold-bearing territory. Rich gravels have been worked near Leadville, Fairplay, and in San Miguel Co., Colo.; near Helena and Butte, Mont.; along the Snake and Salmon rivers, Idaho; near Deadwood, S. Dak.; at Santa Fe, N. Mex.; and in Alaska.

Placer deposits of gold were discovered on the Yukon River in Canada and Alaska in 1869. The discovery in 1896 of a rich gold deposit in the Bonanza Creek, a headwater of the Klondike, which in turn is a tributary of the Yukon, led to another gold rush. In 1910 gold discoveries were made on Bitter Creek, near Stewart, British Columbia. In 1911 rich gold was also discovered in Alaska, some 20 miles from the Canadian boundary at the source of the Sixty Mile River, which rises in Alaska and flows into the Yukon River. Since 1911 the production of gold in Ontario, Canada, in the Porcupine and Kirkland Lake districts, has gone ahead rapidly. Important discoveries of gold mixed with copper were made in the N.W. part of Quebec.

The gold production of Australia has been famous since 1851; the chief centers of production are in w. Australia and Victoria. The Union of South Africa is the world's largest producer of gold, with a total production in 1952 of $410,758,255. The U.S. production usually amounts to less than $100,000,000; in 1952 it totaled approximately $67,400,000. Peak production in the United States occurred in 1940, amounting to about $210,-

Natives on a tropical beach near Accra, the capital of the Gold Coast territory, Africa

000,000, including Philippine production. In that year world gold production also reached a peak, amounting to $1,311,450,000. The Philippine Islands produced about $40,000,000 in some prewar years, but the mines were destroyed by the Japanese in 1944 and 1945, and recovery has been slow. The U.S.S.R. is probably the second largest producer of gold; output in 1952 was estimated at 9,500,000 fine ounces. Canada usually ranks third among world gold producers; output in 1952 was valued at $156,500,000. Other important producers (estimated value of production in 1952) are Australia, $34,300,000; West Africa, $23,800,000; Rhodesia, $17,400,000; Mexico, $16,100,000; Colombia, $14,800,000; India, $8,900,000; and Nicaragua, $8,900,-000.

GOLDBERGER, Joseph (1874–1929), Austrian-American physician, born in Austria, and educated at the College of the City of New York and New York University College of Medicine. In 1904 he was assigned, as a surgeon in the U.S. Public Health Service, to the Hygienic Laboratory in Washington, D.C., to do special research in diseases. He studied many diseases, including dengue fever, Mexican typhus, and cholera, but his most important contributions were in connection with pellagra. He showed that the substance known as vitamin B was a complex, consisting of more than one factor, one of which showed specific action in the treatment of pellagra. This factor, which he called the "pellagra preventive" factor, was later shown to be nicotinic acid or its derivatives. See VITAMIN: *Niacin.*

GOLD COAST, a British West African territory extending about 335 m. along the Gulf of Guinea eastward from the French Ivory Coast. The Gold Coast comprises the Gold Coast Colony (23,937 sq.m.), the colony of Ashanti (24,379 sq.m.), the Northern Territories protectorate (30,486 sq. m.), and, for administrative purposes, the United Nations trust territory of Togoland (British mandate, 13,041 sq.m.) ; see ASHANTI; TOGOLAND. The important towns are the capital Accra, Takoradi (qq.v.), Sekondi, Cape Coast, and Kumasi in Ashanti. Total area of the Gold Coast, 91,843 sq.m.; pop. (1956 est.) 4,255,000.

The terrain of the Gold Coast is covered for the most part by dense tropical jungle, in which are valuable cabinet woods, notably African mahogany. The so-called bush growth includes the bamboo, mimosa, and rubber vine. Chief among the flowering plants are the lily and the orchid. Northeast of the dense forest belt is a region of orchardlike country containing cacao, shea, wild plum, kola nut, and baobab trees, and the fan and dwarf date palms. Other fruit trees and plants are the banana, pineapple, orange, papaw, avocado, and mango. Ginger, tobacco, and cotton plants are also found. The fauna includes the antelope, panther, leopard, hyena, jackal, potto lemur, wild hog, and many varieties of monkey. The principal snakes are the puff adder, poisonous water snake, python, horned adder, and cobra. Birds, diversified but not numerous, include the kingfisher, parrot, pigeon, hornbill, osprey, woodpecker, curlew, crossbill, pelican, vulture, heron, dove, stork, and swallow. Among the myriads of insects are the mosquitoes, transmitting yellow fever and malaria.

With the exception of some 7000 non-Africans, the native population of the Gold Coast is entirely Negro. The Accra, noted as sailors and artisans, and believed to be descended from the aboriginal inhabitants, dwell in the eastern part of the territory; the Fanti (q.v.) tribesmen inhabit the west; the gold-mining Akim occupy the N.E.; and the Akwapim, engaged in trade and agriculture, dwell to the s. of the Akim. Other native peoples are the Ahanta, Adangme, Apollonia, and Krobos. The principal language of the Gold Coast is Tshi, which contains many dialects.

The chief agricultural products are cacao (in the cultivation of which the Gold Coast leads the world), palm oil and palm kernels, and kola nuts. Other products are copra, rubber, citrus fruits, rice, and groundnuts. The timber exports in 1952 totaled more than 10,500,000 cu.ft., consisting chiefly of African mahoganies, cedars, and walnut. Minor forest products include oils, fibers, rattans, gums, resin, rubber adulterants and coagulants, various medicinal substances, and raw leopard, reptile, and monkey skins. A considerable fishing industry, for domestic consumption, exists along the coastal areas. The leading commercially exploited mineral deposits of the Gold Coast are gold, diamonds, manganese ore, and bauxite. Manufacturing industries are negligible.

The balance of trade is generally favorable. Imports in 1952, valued at about $186,000,-000, were chiefly cotton piece goods, clothing, shoes, foodstuffs, cigarettes and unmanufactured tobacco, machinery, and petroleum products. Imports were largely from the United Kingdom, also from the Netherlands, the United States, and Japan. Exports, valued at about $242,000,000, and consisting principally of cacao, gold, manganese ore, bauxite, logs, diamonds, palm oil, and palm kernels, were to the United Kingdom, the United States, Germany, and the Netherlands.

The total mileage of railways is (1953) 535. Roads suitable for automobile traffic cover almost 7400 m., approximately 3000 m. of which are all-weather roads maintained by the Public Works Department.

Educational facilities in the Gold Coast Colony, Ashanti, and the Northern Territories comprised in 1953 some 3190 primary schools (1953 enrollment, 344,022), 832 middle schools and secondary schools (87,247), 27 colleges and normal schools (3294), and several technical and trade schools giving training in agriculture, metalwork, carpentry, and allied crafts. The dominant religion of the Gold Coast natives is fetishism (q.v.), but the Protestant, Roman Catholic, and Mohammedan faiths are also represented.

The Gold Coast is governed according to the provisions of the constitution of 1951. By the terms of this document, which extends a large measure of self-government to the native populations, administrative authority is vested in a governor. This official, an appointee of the British government, is assisted by an executive council, consisting of 11 members, and a legislative assembly, consisting of 84 members; 38 assembly members are elected by direct adult suffrage, 37 are elected by native councils, and 9 are appointed by the colonial government. Eight members of the executive council are appointed with the approval of the assembly.

Portuguese navigators first explored the Gold Coast toward the end of the 15th century, establishing the settlement of Ora del Mina, or "Mouth of the (gold) Mine". A century and a half later, the Dutch effected the withdrawal of the Portuguese, but were themselves challenged by the English, who established forts at Kormantyne and Cape Coast. The ensuing rivalry between the two powers culminated in war, from which the Dutch emerged victorious. The English, however, continued to pursue their interest on the Gold Coast, developing by 1750 a flourishing slave trade. In 1821, fourteen years after the abolition of the slave traffic, the British settlements on the West African coast were taken over by the crown. By the terms of a convention negotiated in 1871, the Dutch coastal settlements were transferred to the British. The subsequent history of the Gold Coast is characterized by the extension and consolidation of British power, the demarcation of spheres of influence with the French and the Germans, and the development of native resources. In World War I the Gold Coast Regiment of the West African Frontier seized German Togoland (August, 1914).

The Regiment served in the German Cameroons until 1916, and subsequently in German East Africa. In World War II, battalions of the Regiment operated against the Italians in Italian East Africa.

GOLDEN AGE, in Greek and Roman mythology, the earliest age of the world's history, the ideal period when the earth produced its fruits without cultivation, when warfare was nonexistent, and sinless man lived in perfect health and happiness. The Greek poet Hesiod, in his *Theogony,* makes the Golden Age under Cronus the first of five successive ages, the others being respectively the silver, the bronze, the heroic, and the iron. In the Roman tradition, as described by the poet Ovid (*Metamorphoses*), the Golden Age under the reign of Saturn is followed by the silver, the bronze, and the iron, the heroic being omitted.

GOLDEN BIBLE. See SMITH, JOSEPH (1805–44).

GOLDEN BULL (Lat. *bulla aurea*), the imperial edict or constitution promulgated by the Holy Roman emperor Charles IV in 1356, for the purpose of establishing the form of the Imperial election and coronation, the persons to whom the right of election belonged, and the obligations and privileges of such electors. This constitution prevailed until the downfall of the Holy Roman Empire in 1806. See BULL.

GOLDEN CALF, according to the Biblical account in Exodus, a molten idol cast at the foot of Mt. Sinai from the earrings of the Israelites by Aaron, brother of Moses, while Moses was on the Mount. Later, when Moses accused him of sinning, Aaron explained (Exodus 32:23) that he had made the calf to satisfy the people's desire for visible objects which they could worship.

GOLDEN CARP. See GOLDFISH.

GOLDEN CREST. See HAEMODORACEAE.

GOLDEN-CRESTED WREN. See KINGLET.

GOLDENEYE, a duck of the genus *Glaucionetta,* found in Europe, Asia, and North America, characterized by a slight crest on its crown. The goldeneyes are expert divers and rapid fliers. The beating of their wings in flight produces a sharp whistling sound, and they are often called whistlers. The American goldeneye or whistlewing, *Glaucionetta clangula,* is twenty inches long. The tail and back of the adult male are black. The head is blackish, showing green reflections in sunlight; a large white spot lies just below each of the golden-yellow eyes, and the bill is black. A wide ring of white encircles the neck. The wings are black with some white feathers, the underparts are white, and the legs and feet are orange. The back of the adult female is brownish gray; the head is brownish red and has no spot. The American goldeneye is found in summer from the Arctic to northernmost U.S. In winter it migrates southward, reaching Mexico and Cuba. It eats small fish, crayfish, mussels, and vegetation. A less common, more widely distributed American species is Barrow's goldeneye, *G. islandica,* similar to the American goldeneye, but with a purplish-blue head. The common European species is *G. clangula.* See DUCK.

GOLDEN-EYED FLY, common name for any small, adult, lacewing insect characterized by eyes with a gilt luster. About 40 species in the genus *Chrysopa* are found in the U.S. The adults are about ½ in. in length; they have broad, light-green, many-veined wings more than 1 in. long. They emit a disagreeable odor, so that they are often called "stink flies". The larvae, commonly called *aphis lions,* are carnivorous and eat aphids, or plant lice, and other insects. The female adult places each egg on the tip of an individual stalk of stiff silk which she has spun to prevent cannibalism by the first larva hatched. Often the adult female will devour her own eggs. The larva spins a delicate cocoon which is chewed open at the end of pupation by the new adult. See NEUROPTERA.

GOLDEN FLEECE, in Greek legend, the fleece of the ram Chrysomallus. Athamas, king of Orchomenus in Bœotia, and Nephele, goddess of the clouds, had two children, Helle and Phrixos. When Athamas fell in love with Ino, daughter of the hero Cadmus, Nephele disappeared. Ino, who hated Phrixos and Helle, was about to dispose of them, when the spirit of Nephele intervened, sending Chrysomallus to help the children escape. They bestrode the ram's back and were transported high above the Ægean Sea, but Helle fell off and was drowned in the narrow channel which thereafter was known as the Hellespont. Phrixos arrived safely in the ancient country of Colchis E. of the Black Sea, where he sacrificed the ram to Zeus and presented its golden fleece to King Aeëtes, who hung it in the sacred grove of Ares, where a sleepless dragon watched over it. Jason, nephew of Athamas and hero of the Argonauts (q.v.), finally obtained the Golden Fleece with the aid of the sorceress Medea, daughter of Aeëtes. The foregoing story is related by Hesiod, and by Apollonius Rhodius in his *Argonauts.*

GOLDEN GATE, a strait at the entrance to San Francisco Bay, California, separating

North American goldenrod (S. canadensis)

the bay from the Pacific Ocean. It is about five m. long and varies in width from one to two m. The famous Golden Gate Bridge, longest single-span suspension bridge in the world, crosses the strait to connect San Francisco, on the s., with Marin Co., on the N. Although the English explorer Sir Francis Drake visited the region of San Francisco Bay in 1579, and Sergeant José Francisco Ortega, a scout for the Spanish colonial governor, Don Gaspar de Portola, may have explored as far as the Golden Gate in 1769, the first persons of European origin known to have seen the famous channel were a party of soldiers dispatched by Portola under Pedro Fages in 1772. John Charles Frémont, the American explorer, gave the strait the name Golden Gate in an official report to the U.S. Congress in 1846.

GOLDEN GLOW. See RUDBECKIA.

GOLDEN HORDE (Tatar *āltŭn ordŭ,* "golden army"), the name applied to a great body of Tatars who, under Batu Khan, grandson of Genghis Khan, overran eastern Europe; and to the khanate, or empire, which the Tatars established on the banks of the Volga R., and which is also known as Kipchak. The army led by Batu was one of three dispatched to Russia in 1235 by Ogadai Khan, the successor of Genghis. The Tatars crossed the Ural R. in 1237, and penetrated to the very center of the country, pillaging, burning, and killing. Moscow, Kiev, and other cities were taken and razed, and their inhabitants put to the sword. From Russia, the Tatars passed into Poland, Silesia, and Hungary, carrying destruction and bloodshed wherever they went. Lublin and Cracow were laid waste in 1240, and Breslau was burned the following year. At Liegnitz, on the field since known as the Wahlstatt, Batu defeated an army of Silesians, Poles, and Teutonic knights, under Henry II, duke of Silesia, in April, 1241. Unsuccessful in the siege of Neustadt, the Horde turned eastward, and Batu pitched his gorgeously embroidered silk tent (which gave rise to the name "Golden") on the banks of the Volga R., summoning the Russian princes to his presence to do him homage. This settlement was called *Sir Orda* (Golden Camp). The empire which Batu established over the Russians was maintained until the power of the khans was broken by Ivan the Great toward the close of the 15th century.

GOLDEN HORN. See ISTANBUL.

GOLDEN MOLE or **CAPE MOLE,** common name for any burrowing member of the family Chrysochloridae of the order Insectivora. This molelike animal is found only in South Africa and takes its name from the brilliant, bronze luster of its fur. The type genus is *Chrysochloris.* Each foreleg of the golden mole has two long, powerful claws for digging purposes, but the hand is not broad, as in the true moles. See MOLE.

GOLDEN NUMBER. See METONIC CYCLE.

GOLDENPERT. See GRATIOLA.

GOLDEN RETRIEVER. See RETRIEVER.

GOLDENROD, common name of plants of the genus *Solidago,* belonging to the Thistle family. They are typical autumn flowers of the U.S. which grow in a great variety of habitats, such as woods, meadow, hills, and rocky ground. Goldenrod was, for many years, considered a major cause of hayfever, but experiments with goldenrod pollen have indicated that plants of this genus are virtually harmless. Goldenrods are occasionally transplanted to gardens, but are too coarse and weedy for ordinary cultivation.

Goldenrods are perennial herbs with wandlike stems and stalkless leaves. Their yellow flowers are borne in graceful clusters or racemes. The genus contains more than 50 species, most of which are North American. *S. canadensis,* one of the commonest species, grows three to four feet tall and has large panicles of small yellow flowers. The sweet goldenrod, *S. odora,* grows one to four feet tall and has anise-scented leaves used to make an herb tea. The wreath goldenrod, *S. caesia,* grows about two feet high in shady places.

The November goldenrod, *S. serotina*, grows two to seven feet high and bears large hairy panicles of flowers. Several goldenrod species are State flowers in the U.S.; *S. canadensis* is the State flower of Alabama, *S. patula* is the State flower of Kentucky, and *S. serotina* is the State flower of Nebraska. Only one goldenrod species, *S. virgaurea*, is native to Europe. Several species of goldenrod which have white ray flowers, such as *S. bicolor*, are commonly called silverrod.

GOLDEN ROSE, a golden, gem-encrusted ornament, blessed by the pope and awarded by him to a city, church, or person, in recognition of unusual loyalty to or distinguished service on behalf of the Holy See. The ornament comprises a thorny branch to which is attached a rose. It is awarded annually on the fourth Sunday of Lent, which, in consequence, is sometimes called *Dominica Rosæ*.

The presentation of a papal gift to an especially meritorious recipient dates from the earliest history of the Church. Such gifts assumed the form of a rose in the 11th century; the use of a full branch and flowers began at a later date, probably early in the 14th century. It has been customary, since the 16th century, to send a letter with the rose, recounting those qualities or deeds of the recipient which have merited the award.

GOLDEN WARBLER, a greenish-yellow wood warbler, *Dendroica aestiva*, about five inches long, abundant throughout the U.S. in summertime and often called the summer warbler. The golden warbler migrates to Central and South America for the winter. The head and underparts of the adult male are a solid yellow; its sides are lightly blotched with rust. In the dense, wet foliage which the golden warbler usually inhabits, the greenish tinge of its plumage enables the bird to blend into its surroundings, but in broad daylight it appears entirely golden. The golden warbler feeds on minute insects. The female builds the nest out of plant fibers, placing it in low shrubs less than 5 ft. above the ground; the nest is steel gray in color and is sturdily built. The golden warbler is known under four other common names in different regions of America: Alaskan warbler, California warbler, Sonora warbler (s.w. United States), and eastern yellow warbler.

GOLDEYE. See MOONEYE.

GOLDFINCH, any of several small, singing birds in the Finch family which are prominently marked with yellow. The British goldfinch, *Carduelis carduelis*, is kept as a pet because of its beautiful coloring and canary-like song; it has been imported into the U.S. This bird is about six inches long. Its face and throat are a brilliant red; its crown, neck, tail, and wings are black; and a broad band of gold marks each wing. Its back is reddish brown; its lower parts and the sides of its head and neck are white. The native American goldfinches belong to the genus *Spinus*. The most common of these, the eastern goldfinch, *S. tristis*, is found throughout the U.S. east of the Rocky Mountains. It is three and one-half to four inches long. Adult males are a brilliant yellow, black-crowned, and with black tail and wings. Each wing is marked by two bands of white. The eastern goldfinch is distinguished by its undulating flight. The female goldfinch builds her nest in late summer and eats seeds which she regurgitates and then feeds to her young. See FINCH.

GOLDFISH or **GOLDEN CARP,** a species of soft-finned, fresh-water fish, *Carassius auratus*, belonging to the Carp family. Goldfish are small fish, usually measuring about five or six inches in length, though some have attained a size of twelve inches. Goldfish, like all carp, are exceptionally long-lived, and have been reported to reach an age of seventy years. Originally goldfish were native to E. Asia, but they have been successfully introduced throughout the world. In their native state goldfish are olive green in color and subsist on weeds and small invertebrates.

Goldfish which are artificially reared undergo changes in color and form which may be perpetuated among domestic varieties by careful breeding. Upon escaping to a less favorable environment, such as a river, natural

Eastern goldfinch, female (left) and male

The telescope fish, a type of goldfish developed by Japanese breeders

selection reverses this breeding process and the species reverts to its natural, olive-green color. The best-known domestic varieties of goldfish are golden red. Blind, albino forms have been produced by the Chinese, and varieties of these, completely white, white with red fins, or silvery, compose the important fancy breeds of *silverfishes*. The *telescope fishes* are another important breed, developed by the Japanese, which are characterized by short, round bodies, broad heads with protruding eyes, and large bilobed or trilobed tails. In common varieties of this breed the eyes are turned outward, but in the *celestial telescopes* they are directed upward. The *veiltails*, or *fringetails,* are a fancy breed characterized by long, veil-like fins; the *calicoes* are spotted goldfishes of any breed; and the *fantails* are goldfishes with two tails and two top fins.

Goldfish have been bred for centuries by the Chinese. Japanese culturists learned the art from the Chinese and carried their interest in the species to the point of holding annual goldfish exhibits in Tokyo. The fish are reported to have been introduced into England in 1691, and into France in the middle of the 18th century when specimens were received as gifts by Mme. de Pompadour, mistress of King Louis XV. During World War I they were found to be of use in chemical warfare in identifying certain types of poison gas. Today they are produced in many countries on a sizable commercial scale. One goldfish hatchery, near Frederick, Md., occupies over 100 acres and has an annual production of 5,000,000 fish.

Goldfish thrive in large tanks or outdoor pools supplied with clean, well-aerated water kept at a temperature of slightly over 80° F. Their optimum diet consists of weeds, crumbs ot bread, worms, small shellfish, and insects.

Under such conditions they breed several times a year.

GOLDIE, SIR GEORGE DASHWOOD TAUBMAN (1846-1925), British colonial administrator, founder of the British colony of Nigeria (q.v.), born on the Isle of Man, and educated at the Royal Military Academy, Woolwich. After serving for two years as a lieutenant in the Royal Engineers, Goldie began to travel, particularly in Africa. He first visited the region of the Niger R. in 1877 and, seeing its commercial possibilities, devoted himself thereafter to adding the territory to the British Empire. By 1879 he had succeeded in forming a merger of all the British commercial interests in the region as the United African Co. To fulfill the necessary conditions for a royal charter, which would enable it to govern the region, the company, renamed the National African Company, increased its capitalization, opened new stations, and, under Goldie's direction, bought out the interests of French traders on the lower Niger. Under the name of the Royal Niger Company, the enterprise received its charter in 1886, with Goldie as vice-governor and, in 1895, governor. In 1887 the administrator was knighted for his services. Despite the disruptive activities of France and Germany, which also sought to acquire the territory, Goldie built up the Nigerian state and maintained the unity of the region as a British dependency. In 1900 the company sold its interests to the British government for £865,000, and the territory became a British colony under the name of Nigeria. After his retirement, Goldie engaged in various activities, being president of the Royal Geographical Society in 1905 and, in 1908, an alderman of the London City Council. From 1905 to 1920, except for the year 1914-15, he was president of the National Defense Association.

GOLDMAN, EDWIN FRANKO (1878-1956), American band conductor and composer, born at Louisville, Ky. He studied music at the National Conservatory of Music, New York City, and the cornet with private masters. Goldman was the founder in 1911 of the Goldman Band, and was its conductor from the year of its organization. The band became one of the foremost in the United States; it was particularly noted for its performances of symphonic music arranged for all-wind band, an innovation in band music first introduced on a large scale by Goldman. Of the two annual series of free concerts given by the Goldman Band, one was started in 1918 in Central Park, New York City, and the other in 1934 in Prospect Park,

Brooklyn. Goldman composed more than ninety marches and other compositions for band; among his marches are *On the Air, On the Mall, Central Park, On the Farm,* and *Indian March.* He was the author of *The Band Guide and Aid to Leaders* (1916), *Band Betterment* (1934), and *The Goldman Band System for Developing Tone, Intonation, and Phrasing* (1935).

GOLDMAN, EMMA (1869–1940), Russian anarchist, born in the province of Kovno (now Kaunas). She spent her youth in Königsberg and St. Petersburg (now Kaliningrad and Leningrad, respectively). In 1886 she emigrated to the United States, where she became a leader of the anarchist movement, working in close association with Alexander Berkman. After attacking the government in numerous speeches, she was arrested in 1893 and was sentenced to a year's imprisonment on Blackwell's Island, in New York City, for incitement to riot. Following her release in 1894, she lectured in England and Scotland. She also made lecture tours throughout the United States, and after 1906 was a publisher of and one of the principal contributors to *Mother Earth,* an anarchist periodical.

She expressed strong pacifistic views during World War I, denouncing the war as an imperialistic venture. In 1917 she was tried and convicted on a charge of conspiracy to violate the conscription laws, and was sentenced to two years' imprisonment and a fine of $10,000. Shortly after her release in 1920 she was deported to Russia. At first a stanch admirer of the Soviet regime, she later voiced vehement criticisms of its policies and was expelled from the country. She spent some time in England, becoming a British subject through marriage to James Colton. In 1926 she went to Canada, and in succeeding years lectured widely in that country and in the United States. During the Spanish Civil War (1936–39), she worked for the Spanish Republican government in London and in Madrid. She died in Toronto, Canada. She stated the reasons for her changed opinion of the Soviet government in two books, *My Disillusionment in Russia* (1923–24) and *My Further Disillusionment in Russia* (1925). Her other writings include *Anarchism and Other Essays* (1910), *The Social Significance of the Modern Drama* (1914), and an autobiography *Living My Life* (1931).

GOLDMARK, KARL (1830–1915), Hungarian composer, born at Keszthely. He studied the violin in Vienna with the Bo-

hemian virtuoso Leopold Jansa and later studied harmony at the Vienna Conservatory. Goldmark's musical activities, which included composing, the writing of music criticism, and teaching, took place mainly in Vienna. His best-known compositions are the overtures *Sakuntala* and *Penthesilea;* the symphony *Die Ländliche Hochzeit* ("Rustic Wedding") ; and the opera *Die Königin von Saba,* which was first produced in Vienna, in 1875, and subsequently was performed throughout Germany and Italy, and also in Madrid, Manchester, and New York City. Among his other works are the overture *Im Frühling;* the operas *Merlin* and *Ein Wintermärchen,* the symphonic poem *Zrinyi,* two violin concertos, chamber music, choral works, and piano music.

GOLDONI, CARLO (1707–93), Italian playwright, born in Venice, notable in the history of the drama as the founder of modern Italian comedy; see DRAMA: *Italian Drama.* At an early age Goldoni ran away from home to join a company of traveling comedians. After assiduous study of the works of the classic Greek and Latin comic poets he began to write plays, but his first dramatic works were tragedies, at that time the only seriously regarded form for dramatic composition. Although his tragedies met with some success, Goldoni was dissatisfied with this medium of theater; he conceived the idea of reforming the Italian stage by eliminating the masques (q.v.) and buffooneries with which it abounded and by writing comedies in the manner of the French dramatist Molière, but based on Italian characters and Italian life.

About 1737, after settling in Venice, he produced his first comedies; the first of these was the celebrated play *La Donna di Garbo* (1741). During the next twenty years he completed a total of about 150 comedies, including *La Botega di Caffè, Pamela Nubile, Le Baruffe Chiozzotte, I Rusteghi, Todero Brontolon, Gli Innamorati, Il Ventaglio, La Casa Nova, Il Bugiardo,* and *La Locandiera.* In his comedies Goldoni depicted the social life of his time. He wrote the comedy *Una delle Ultime Sere di Carnevale* (1761), an allegorical farewell to his native city, upon his departure to assume the managership of the Italian theater in Paris.

In Paris he also tutored the princesses of the royal household, and for the wedding of King Louis XVI and Marie Antoinette he composed a comedy in French, *Le Bourru Bienfaisant,* which was well received. Later, after retiring to Versailles, where he wrote his *Memoirs* (1787), Goldoni received a pension from the French king. During the French Revolution he was reduced to penury and he died a pauper. His comedies still occupy a prominent place in the repertoire of the Italian theater and several are frequently performed in other countries.

GOLDSBORO, county seat of Wayne Co., N.C., situated on the Neuse R., 50 miles S.E. of Raleigh. It is served by three railroads, and has a municipal airport. The city is an important tobacco market, and one of the leading manufacturing, distributing, and shipping centers of E. North Carolina. The surrounding agricultural area yields about 50% of the bright leaf tobacco produced in the State, and about 25% of the cotton; corn, fruits, and melons are also produced. Among the industrial establishments in Goldsboro are textile plants, brickworks, and factories manufacturing fertilizer, furniture, and agricultural implements. The city is the site of a branch of the State Orthopedic Hospital, the State Hospital for the Negro Insane, and the North Carolina Grand Lodge Odd Fellows Orphan Home. Goldsboro was settled in 1838 and incorporated in 1841.

Pop. (1950) 21,454.

GOLDSCHMIDT, JENNY LIND. See LIND, JENNY.

GOLDSMITH, OLIVER (1728–74), British poet, playwright, novelist, and essayist, born in Ireland. He received a general education at Trinity College, Dublin, and studied medicine, without receiving a degree, at Edinburgh University and at the University of Leiden. He subsequently wandered through Europe, supporting himself by playing the flute and by begging. Later in England he worked as a pharmacist, practiced as a physician, taught school, and eventually worked for various publishers, writing miscellaneous literary works on order. As a hack writer he was the author of translations, essays, childrens' books, and articles for newspapers, reviews, and magazines. The works were anonymous and were characterized by readability, humor, picturesque descriptions, and a graceful style. Among them was a series of letters, supposedly written by a Chinese traveler describing London, later reprinted as *The Citizen of the World* (1762). These anonymous writings of Goldsmith achieved considerable popular success; after his authorship became known in London literary circles he made many friends among influential people, including

Dr. Samuel Johnson, the foremost literary figure of the day, Sir Joshua Reynolds, the greatest British painter of the time, and the statesman and orator Edmund Burke. In 1763 Goldsmith became one of the original nine members of the celebrated literary society known as The Club, of which Johnson was the central figure.

The years 1761 to 1773 were the most productive of Goldsmith's life. In 1764 his philosophic poem *The Traveller* was published and definitely established him as an important writer. The publication of his novel *The Vicar of Wakefield* (1766) is believed to have been

Oliver Goldsmith

hastily arranged by Dr. Johnson in order to save Goldsmith from going to jail for debt. This work is outstanding among early examples of the modern English novel (see ENGLISH LITERATURE: *Eighteenth Century*). The year 1770 saw the publication of Goldsmith's best poem, *The Deserted Village,* distinguished for its pastoral atmosphere and felicity of phrasing; the poem was one of the important poetic works that marked the transition in English literature from neo-classicism to Romanticism. Goldsmith also produced dramatic works at this time. His first play, the comedy *The Good Natur'd Man* (1768), was a failure, but *She Stoops to Conquer* (1773) was an immediate success; it is today one of the best-known comedies in the history of the British drama. In addition to original works,

Goldsmith continued writing popular miscellaneous books to order, including biographies, histories of Rome, Greece, and England, and books on natural history. Toward the end of his life Goldsmith made an ample income from his writings, but through extravagance, and munificence to friends in financial distress, he spent far more than he earned. His worries over his heavy debts gradually broke his health and were responsible for his last illness.

Goldsmith was buried in the churchyard of the church of St. Mary (known as The Temple), London; subsequently The Club had a memorial erected to him in Westminster Abbey.

GOLD STANDARD, in economics, a monetary system wherein all forms of legal tender may be converted, on demand, into fixed quantities of fine gold, as defined by law. Until the 19th century, most of the countries of the world maintained a bimetallic monetary system (see BIMETALLISM). The widespread adoption of the gold standard during the second half of the 19th century was largely a result of the Industrial Revolution (q.v.), which brought about a vast increase in the production of goods and widened the basis for world trade. The countries which adopted the gold standard were motivated by three principal aims: to facilitate the settlement of international commercial and financial transactions; to establish stability in international exchange rates; and to maintain domestic monetary stability. They believed these aims could best be accomplished by the establishment of a single standard of universal validity and relative stability; hence the gold standard is sometimes also called the single gold standard.

The first country to go on the gold standard was England, which did so in 1816. The United States made the change in 1873, and most other countries had followed suit by 1900. With some exceptions, the prevalence of the gold standard lasted until the economic crisis of 1929 and the ensuing depression. Between 1931 and 1934, the governments of virtually all countries found it expedient or necessary to abandon the gold standard. An important factor motivating this policy was the theory that the exports of a country could be stimulated by devaluating its currency in terms of foreign exchange; see DEVALUATION. In time, however, the advantage thus gained was offset as other countries also abandoned the gold standard. In the United States, a policy of devaluation of the currency was initiated by President Franklin D. Roosevelt shortly after his inauguration in 1933, and in April of that year the country went off the gold standard. See CURRENCY; DOLLAR; MONEY: *Monetary System of the United States.*

GOLF, an outdoor game, played on a stretch of ground known as a course or links, by two or more players, each player using a small, hard, white ball which he propels by means of specially designed clubs. The object of the game is to drive the ball around the course, using as few strokes as possible and playing successively from the beginning, or "tee", to the end, or "cup", of each of the eighteen sections, known as "holes", into which the course is divided. The individual holes vary in length from 110 to 650 yards and each contains, at the end farthest from the tee, a cup or ironed-lined cylindrical container, 4¼ inches in diameter and about 6 inches deep, which is placed in the ground and into which the ball must be propelled in order to complete the play of each hole. An average eighteen-hole course is about 6000 yards long, and if the available terrain permits no more than nine different holes the players go around the course twice.

The players begin at the first "tee", a level area of turf or sand, generally raised slightly above the surrounding terrain, and each player successively drives his ball onto the "fairway" or main part of the course, a strip of land on which the grass has been cut to provide a good lie for the ball. On either side of the fairway is an area left in its wild or natural state, generally consisting of long grass and sometimes of sandy, rough, or marshy land; this area, known as the "rough", is one of the natural obstacles or "hazards" retained in the planning of a golf course to compel the golfer to use additional skill and judgment in playing his shots. If few or no natural hazards exist, artificial ones are constructed. Among these are "traps", hollows dug in the earth and filled with loose sand; "bunkers", earthen embankments; and "water hazards", generally water-filled ditches across the fairway. At the far end of the fairway is the "green", an area of closely cropped grass surrounding the cup; its smooth surface is designed to facilitate the progress of the ball into the cup after the ball has been given a tap or gentle stroke known as a "putt".

In addition to this specialized stroke used on the green, two main types of shots are played on each hole: the "drive", a long shot from the tee onto the fairway, necessitating

A. G. Spalding & Bros.

GOLF: THE DRIVE. *Left: Correct stance for the drive. Middle: 1, hands in overlapping grip on the shaft; 2, side view of correct stance for drive; 3, the top of the swing, side view. Right: At finish of the swing the body has turned to face line of flight.*

power; and the "approach", a short shot from the fairway to the green, necessitating great accuracy. Shots of various lengths are played, according to the distance desired, with different clubs. A standard set includes fourteen clubs, divided into two main types, those with heads made of wood (the "woods"), and those with heads made of forged steel, usually chromium plated (the "irons"); the shafts of both types are either of wood or metal. Each club formerly was known by a name, but to-day is designated by a number. The following is a list of the set of fourteen clubs, giving both their old names and current numbers:

The "Woods"

No. 1 Driver
No. 2 Brassie
No. 3 Spoon
No. 4 Cleek

The "Irons"

No. 1 Driving Iron
No. 2 Midiron
No. 3 Mid Mashie
No. 4 Mashie Iron
No. 5 Mashie
No. 6 Spade Mashie
No. 7 Mashie Niblick
No. 8 Lofter
No. 9 Niblick
No. 10 Putter (head may also be made of wood, aluminum, brass, or plastic)

The clubs are variously useful in regard to achieving distance, height, or accurate placement of the ball. In general, the distance a ball may be driven depends on the angle between the face (the front surface of the head) of the club and the shaft, and upon the length of the shaft; the sharper the angle and the greater the length of the shaft, the greater distance the stroke will drive the ball. For making drives and distance shots on the fairway, three wooden clubs, the No. 1, No. 2, and No. 3, and one iron club, the No. 1, are used; on the drive, the ball is "teed up", that is, placed on a "tee", a small wooden, rubber, or plastic peg which the player carries with him, so that the ball is lifted about half an inch off the ground, allowing the clubhead to strike it with greater force when the player swings. For long, low shots on the fairway, the No. 2 wood is used, and for long, high shots the No. 3 wood is employed. An approach shot, played with a No. 5 or a No. 7 iron, is customarily used when the ball has been driven to within 100 or 150 yards of the green; for shorter approaches, known as "chip shots", the same clubs are played with a shorter swing. The putter, the No. 10 iron, is used on the green only.

Two methods of play exist in golf. In *match play,* the player (or if more than one player, the side) taking the fewer number of strokes to sink the ball into any particular hole is the winner of the hole; and the contest is won by the side winning the greater number of holes. If each side takes the same number of strokes to a hole, the hole is said to be "halved" and does not count in the scoring. In *medal play,* the winner of the contest is the side requiring the fewer number of strokes for the total number of holes agreed upon; although a game usually consists of nine or eighteen holes, for championship contests, thirty-six or seventy-two holes are played.

"Par" is the term applied to the number of strokes in which an excellent player should be able to make any particular hole or the number in which he should be able to play the entire course; par for each hole or for the entire course is usually calculated by the architect who lays out the course. Par for a hole varies from three strokes for a hole up to 250 yards long to six strokes for a hole of over 600 yards. Par-six holes, however, are rare. Occasionally, on a par-three hole, a player makes a "hole in one", i.e., drives it from the tee into the cup; it has been calculated that the odds against any player doing this are 10,331 to 1. A score of one less than par on a hole is referred to as a "birdie" and two less than par (a three on a par-five hole)as an "eagle". Par for an entire course depends on the number of long and short holes.

History. Some historians claim that golf originated in the Netherlands, but it has been fairly well established that the game actually was devised by the Scotch, in the 14th or 15th century. The game became so popular in Scotland that in order to keep people from playing golf and football (q.v.) during the time which should have been employed in practicing archery, a military necessity, the Scottish Parliament in 1457 passed a law prohibiting the two games. However, the Scottish people largely ignored this and similar laws, and in the early part of the 16th century their king, James IV, himself took up the game of golf. His granddaughter Mary, later (1542) Queen of Scotland, took the game to France where she was educated. The young men who attended her on the golf links were known as *cadets* (pronounced cad-day), "pupils"; the term and its pronunciation were adopted later in Scotland and England, the spelling becoming "caddy" or "caddie". In England the game was made popular by the attention given it by the Stuart kings James I (James VI of Scotland) and Charles I. The 18th century saw the establishment, in Scotland, of the first golf associations, including the Honourable Company of Edinburgh Golfers (1744); the St. Andrews Golf Club (1754), which in 1834 took its present name, the Royal and Ancient Golf Club of St. Andrews; and the Royal Blackheath (1787). The first clubs established outside of Scotland were the Calcutta Golf Club of East India (1829) and the Royal Bombay Club (1842). The first golf club established in England was the Golf Club of Westward Ho, in Devonshire (1864). It is believed that golf was played in the United States during the colonial period, but no club came into existence until 1888, when the St. Andrews Golf Club of Yonkers was established.

Three types of ball have been used in golf. The game was originally played with a ball made of tightly packed feathers enclosed in a leather cover. About 1850 a ball made of gutta-percha came into use; and about 1902 the ball with a rubber core enclosed in gutta-percha, in use today, was developed. The present accepted ball is 1.68 inches in diameter and weighs 1.62 ounces.

The governing body of golf for the world, with the exception of the United States, is the Royal and Ancient Golf Club of St. Andrews. In the United States the game is controlled and regulated by the United States Golf Association, founded in 1894. Previous to 1913 the game was played chiefly by people of wealth and leisure. The victory that year over two outstanding British professionals in the United States championship tournament open to both amateurs and professionals (the U.S. Open) by the American amateur Francis Ouimet, who learned the game as a caddy, brought the game to the attention of the general public; since that time the popularity of the game has steadily increased in the United States. In a recent year there were about 5000 golf courses in the U.S.; and well over two million players played at least ten rounds of

Seymour Dunn

GOLF: APPROACHING THE GREEN. *Above, left: Back swing for a chip shot onto the green. Above: The correct stance for a chip shot. Left: Follow-through on a chip shot. Bottom, left: The back swing for one-quarter stroke iron shot. Bottom, right: Follow-through on a one-quarter stroke iron shot.*

Seymour Dunn

GOLF: APPROACHING THE GREEN. *Above: Back swing for one-half stroke iron shot. Above, right: Follow-through on a one-half stroke iron shot. Right: Back swing for a three-quarter stroke iron shot. Below: Explosion shot from sand trap adjacent to the green.*

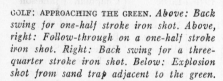

golf each and many thousands more played fewer rounds.

Each year a number of golf championship tournaments take place in the United States and Great Britain. The most important of these are the United States Open, the United States Amateur, the United States Professional Golfers' Association tournament, the British Open, and the British Amateur. The above-mentioned are for men players; for women, one of the most important tournaments is the United States Women's Amateur. From time to time matches take place be-tween teams from the United States and Great Britain. The Walker Cup matches (amateur) and the Ryder Cup matches (professional) are for men; the Curtis Cup matches are for women (amateur). The most famous feat in the history of golf was achieved in 1930 by the American amateur player Robert Tyre Jones, Jr., who in that year won both the British Open and Amateur and the United States Open and Amateur.

Below are listed the records of some of the more important tournaments that have been held.

NATIONAL GOLF CHAMPIONS OF THE UNITED STATES

Year	Open	Amateur	Women's Amateur	Year	Open	Amateur	Women's Amateur
1917	Hutchinson	No match	No match	1936	Manero	Fischer	Barton
1918	No match	No match	No match	1937	Guldahl	Goodman	Page
1919	Hagen	Herron	Stirling	1938	Guldahl	Turnesa	Berg
1920	Ray	Evans, Jr.	Stirling	1939	Nelson	Ward	Jameson
1921	Barnes	Guilford	Hollins	1940	Little	Chapman	Jameson
1922	Sarazen	Sweetser	Collett	1941	Wood	Ward	Newell
1923	Jones, Jr.	Marston	Cummings	1942-5	No matches due to World War II		
1924	Walker	Jones, Jr.	Hurd	1946	Mangrum	Bishop	Zaharias
1925	Macfarlane	Jones, Jr.	Collett	1947	Worsham	Riegel	Suggs
1926	Jones, Jr.	Von Elm	Stetson	1948	Hogan	W. Turnesa	Lenczyk
1927	Armour	Jones, Jr.	Horn	1949	Middlecoff	Coe	Porter
1928	Farrell	Jones, Jr.	Collett	1950	Hogan	Urzetta	Hanson
1929	Jones, Jr.	Jones, Jr.	Collett	1951	Hogan	Maxwell	Kirby
1930	Jones, Jr.	Jones, Jr.	Collett	1952	Boros	Westland	Pung
1931	Burke	Ouimet	Hicks	1953	Hogan	Littler	Faulk
1932	Sarazen	Somerville	Van Wie	1954	Furgol	Palmer	Romack
1933	Goodman	Dunlap, Jr.	Van Wie	1955	Fleck	Ward	Lesser
1934	Dutra	Little, Jr.	Van Wie	1956	Middlecoff	Ward	Stewart
1935	Parks, Jr.	Little, Jr.	Vare	1957	Mayer	Robbins	Gunderson

PROFESSIONAL GOLFERS' ASSOCIATION CHAMPIONSHIPS

Year	Winner	Year	Winner	Year	Winner	Year	Winner
1921	Walter Hagen	1931	Tom Creavy	1941	Vic Ghezzi	1951	Sam Snead
1922	Gene Sarazen	1932	Olin Dutra	1942	Sam Snead	1952	James Turnesa
1923	Gene Sarazen	1933	Gene Sarazen	1943	No match	1953	Walter Burkemo
1924	Walter Hagen	1934	Paul Runyan	1944	Bob Hamilton	1954	Chick Harbert
1925	Walter Hagen	1935	Johnny Revolta	1945	Byron Nelson	1955	Douglas Ford
1926	Walter Hagen	1936	Denny Shute	1946	Ben Hogan	1956	Jack Burke, Jr.
1927	Walter Hagen	1937	Denny Shute	1947	Jim Ferrier	1957	Lionel Herbert
1928	Leo Diegel	1938	Paul Runyan	1948	Ben Hogan		
1929	Leo Diegel	1939	Henry Picard	1949	Sam Snead		
1930	Tom Armour	1940	Byron Nelson	1950	Chandler Harper		

WALKER CUP RECORDS

Year	Score	
1922	United States 8	Great Britain 4
1923	United States 6	Great Britain 5
	(one match halved)	
1924	United States 9	Great Britain 3
1926	United States 6	Great Britain 5
	(one match halved)	
1928	United States 11	Great Britain 1
1930	United States 10	Great Britain 2
1932	United States 8	Great Britain 1
	(three matches halved)	
1934	United States 9	Great Britain 2
	(one match halved)	
1936	United States 9	Great Britain 0
	(three matches halved)	
1938	Great Britain 7	United States 4
	(one match halved)	
1947	United States 8	Great Britain 4
1949	United States 10	Great Britain 2
1951	United States 6	Great Britain 3
1953	United States 9	Great Britain 3
1955	United States 10	Great Britain 2
1957	United States 8	Great Britain 3

RYDER CUP RECORDS

Year	Score	
1927	United States 9½	Great Britain 2½
1929	Great Britain 7	United States 5
1931	United States 9	Great Britain 3
1933	Great Britain 6½	United States 5½
1935	United States 9	Great Britain 3
1937	United States 8	Great Britain 4
1947	United States 11	Great Britain 1
1949	United States 7	Great Britain 5
1951	United States 9½	Great Britain 2½
1953	United States 6½	Great Britain 5½
1955	United States 8	Great Britain 4
1957	Great Britain 7	United States 4

GOLGI, CAMILLO (1844–1926), Italian physician, born at Corteno, and educated at the University of Pavia. He was a professor of histology and pathology at the universities of Siena and Pavia. Golgi's great contributions were in the study of nerve tissue. He was the first investigator to use silver nitrate for staining nerve tissue for microscopic examination, and was able to demonstrate the structure of nerve-cell processes; see NERVOUS SYSTEM. In the field of pathology, Golgi demonstrated the existence of three different varieties of malarial parasites corresponding to different types of malaria. He received half of the Nobel Prize for medicine and physiology in 1906.

GOLGOTHA, the site at which Jesus Christ was crucified. The word is from the Hebrew for skull, and the site, a hillock or rock, is so called either from its form or from the skulls of executed persons found there. The Latin *calvaria* ("a bare skull") is a translation of the word *kranion,* which the Greek Evangelists used to interpret the Hebrew *Golgotha* (see CALVARY). The actual site may have been near the Church of the Holy Sepulcher within the present walls of Jerusalem, but most religious scholars hold that it is outside the Damascus gate north of the city.

GOLIARD, a member of the bands of students who wandered through England, Germany, and France in the 12th and 13th centuries, composing and singing satirical Latin verses and serving as minstrels and jesters. Most of their verses contained attacks on the Church; others were paeans of praise for the pleasures of the flesh.

GOLIATH, Biblical giant of Gath who, as representative of the Philistines, challenged the Israelites to send a champion against him

David slaying Goliath (by Peter Paul Rubens)

In order to decide the issue of the war being waged at that time between the armies of the two tribes. According to the account in 1 Samuel 17:50, Goliath was killed in the resulting contest by a stone shot from the sling of David (q.v.), the Israelite champion. In some versions of the Bible, 2 Samuel (21:19) records that Goliath was killed by Elhanan, an Israelite warrior in the service of David, after the latter was made king of the Israelites; other versions of the Bible designate a brother of Goliath as the victim of Elhanan.

GOLLANCZ, SIR HERMANN (1852–1930), British rabbi, philanthropist, and Semitic scholar, the brother of Sir Israel Gollancz, born in Bremen, Germany. He was educated at University College, London, and was the first Jew to receive the degree of Doctor of Literature at that institution. In 1892 he became preacher at the Bayswater Synagogue, serving until 1923, when he retired. From 1902 until 1923 he was professor of Hebrew at University College. In the latter year he was knighted, being the first British rabbi to receive this honor. He was famous for his philanthropic activities, notably the establishment of a number of synagogues in working-class areas. He contributed many articles to learned publications and translated several works from Hebrew and Aramaic into English. Among his writings are *Russia and the Alien Question* (1905) and *The Foundation of Religious Fear* (1915).

GOLLANCZ, SIR ISRAEL (1864–1930), English scholar and educator, born in London and educated at University College, London, and at Cambridge University. He was the brother of Sir Hermann Gollancz (q.v.). From 1896 to 1906 he was lecturer in English at Cambridge, and in 1906 became professor of English language and literature at University College. He was editor of the *Temple Classics* of English literature, the *Temple Shakespeare* (1894–96), *Exeter Book of Anglo-Saxon Poetry* (1895), *The Sources of Hamlet* (1926), and *The Caedmon Manuscript of Anglo-Saxon Biblical Poetry* (1927). He was knighted in 1919.

GOLTZ, BARON KOLMAR VON DER (1843–1916), Prussian soldier and military writer, born at Bielkenfield, and educated at the Berlin Military Academy. In 1870, on the outbreak of the Franco-Prussian War, he joined the staff of the Prussian commander Prince Frederick Charles, and later participated in a number of major battles of that war. He became professor at the Potsdam military school, and was attached to the historical section of the

Prussian general staff, in 1871. Within the next few years he wrote several notable military histories, including *Die Sieben Tage von Le Mans* (1873) and *Léon Gambetta und Seine Armeen* (1877). From 1878 to 1883 he lectured on military history at the Berlin Academy, and subsequently was adviser to the Turkish government concerning a reorganization of the Turkish army. Returning to Germany in 1896, he received several promotions thereafter, becoming field-marshal in 1911. He was appointed aide-de-camp general to the Sultan of Turkey in 1914, and commander of the First Turkish Army in the following year; he died while serving in the latter post. His writings include *Rossbach und Jena* (1883), *Das Volk in Waffen* (1883), *Kriegführung* (1895), and *Kriegsgeschichte Deutschlands im 19ten Jahrhundert* (2 vols., 1910–14).

GOMARUS, FRANCISCUS (1563–1641), Dutch Calvinist theologian, born at Bruges and educated at the universities of Strasbourg, Neustadt, Oxford, and Cambridge. He became pastor of the Dutch Reformed Church at Frankfort in 1587, and in 1594 was appointed professor of theology at the University of Leiden, where he remained until 1611. During this period he became the foremost opponent of the Arminians (see ARMINIUS, JACOBUS), and gathered around him a group of followers who became known as Gomarists. In 1608 he debated with Arminius before the Assembly of the Estates of Holland, and in the following year he led four of his disciples in a similar dispute with five Arminians. At the Synod of Dort (see DORT, SYNOD OF), Gomarus succeeded in causing the expulsion of the Arminians from the Reformed Church. He was at various times preacher at the Reformed church in Middleburg, and professor at the Illustre Schule in that city and at the universities of Saumur and Groningen. His collected works were published at Amsterdam in 1645.

GOMEL, a town of Byelorussian Soviet Socialist Republic, located on the Sozh R. about 115 miles N.E. of Kiev. Gomel is an important railroad and river-boat junction. Its industries include paper and sawmilling, brewing, iron founding, the processing of bristles, and the manufacture of agricultural machinery. Pop. (1939) 144,169.

GOMERA. See CANARY ISLANDS.

GÓMEZ, JOSÉ MIGUEL (1858–1921), Cuban revolutionist and politician, born in the province of Santa Clara. He participated in the Ten Years' War (1868–78) and the successful revolution of 1895, both against Spain. From

1899 until 1901 he served as governor of Las Villas. In 1906 he was imprisoned for a short time for taking part in the revolt against President Tomás Estrada Palma. Two years later he was elected president of Cuba, retaining that post until 1913. Gómez led an unsuccessful revolt against the government in 1917 because he claimed that his defeat by Mario García Menocal in the presidential election of 1916 was fraudulent.

GÓMEZ, JUAN VICENTE (1857?–1935), Venezuelan dictator, born in San Antonio de Tachira. In 1899 Gómez took a prominent part in the revolution that brought Cipriano Castro to power. When Castro was elected president in 1902, Gómez was made vicepresident. He soon found himself in disagreement with some of the policies of the Castro regime. After growing opposition forced Castro into exile, Gómez became provisional president in 1908. From that time until his death he was supreme dictator of Venezuela, and from 1915 he was commander in chief of the army. Gómez occupied the presidency from 1910 until 1915, from 1922 until 1929, and from 1931 until 1935. In the intervening periods he was also elected president but declined the honor. However, he is known to have controlled the provisional presidents V. M. Bustillos (1915–22) and Juan Bautista Pérez (1929–31). With aid of foreign capital the exploitation of the petroleum resources of Venezuela became the most important industry in the country during the long Gómez regime. Petroleum became a source of great wealth for the dictator and his friends, who owned the majority of the petroleum concessions. Agriculture and other forms of industry, and social and educational improvements were neglected by Gómez, with the result that the people of Venezuela suffered severely during his rule. See VENEZUELA: *History.*

GOMORRAH. See SODOM AND GOMORRAH.

GOMPERS, SAMUEL (1850–1924), American labor leader, born in London. After only four years of attendance at elementary school, he was apprenticed to a cigar maker in the East End of London, where he learned the trade which he followed for a quarter of a century. In 1863 he accompanied his family to New York City. There he later became active in the social clubs, fraternal orders, and labor unions of the city's East Side, then teeming with immigrants from Europe. Unlike many of the other immigrants who were the bearers of European revolutionary traditions and who stood outside the main stream of American life, Gompers entered that stream. His de-

Samuel Gompers

velopment comprised a steady process of Americanization and an evolution in labor unionism from militancy to conservatism.

He became a member of the Cigar Makers' International Union in 1864 and ten years later helped found Local 144 of the International Union, of which he remained a member for the rest of his life. Elected president of Local 144 in 1874, he was ousted from that position by socialist opponents in the local in 1881. He took a leading part in founding and became the first president of the Federation of Organized Trades and Labor Unions, which was established solely to influence legislation in behalf of labor. During the following years he was a leader in the movement to organize a national federation of labor unions. When the American Federation of Labor (q.v.) was constituted in 1886, Gompers was elected its president; thenceforth until his death, except in 1895, he was re-elected annually to that position.

Gompers was the chief exponent of the policies which gave to the AFL its characteristic feature of a conservative federation of autonomous craft unions; see TRADE UNIONS IN THE UNITED STATES. He resisted the efforts of socialists to infiltrate and control the Federation, and fought the openly antagonistic and more militant Industrial Workers of the

Edmond de Goncourt

World. Gompers laid a progressively greater emphasis on co-operation between capital and labor than on strike action as a means of obtaining labor's demands, and exerted the growing influence of the AFL to secure the passage of Federal and State legislation favorable to labor. He was the formulator of the Federation's policy of urging its members to support candidates for public office, regardless of political affiliations, who were considered friendly to labor, and to vote against those considered hostile. This policy has since become known as "rewarding our friends and punishing our enemies".

During World War I, President Woodrow Wilson appointed Gompers a member of the Advisory Commission to the Council of National Defense. After the war, on a tour of Europe in 1918, when that continent was experiencing revolutionary upheavals, Gompers was hailed as a statesmanlike labor leader by the heads of various governments, but encountered great hostility from masses of workers. At the Versailles Peace Conference in 1919 Gompers served as the chairman of the Commission on International Labor Legislation. Returning to the United States, he later played a leading role in establishing the influence of the Federation in various Latin American countries.

GONAÏVES, town and seaport of Haiti, situated on the w. coast, about 65 miles N.N.W. of Port-au-Prince, with an excellent harbor on the Bay of Gonaïves. The principal exports of the port are coffee, raw cotton and sugar, bananas, and tropical woods. Pop. (1950) 165,635.

GONCHAROV, IVAN ALEKSANDROVICH (1812–91), Russian novelist, born in Simbirsk, and educated at the University of Moscow. After a period of employment in the civil service as secretary to the governor of Simbirsk Province, he worked in the finance ministry of the Czarist government in St. Petersburg (now Leningrad). There he was attracted to literature by his contact with a brilliant circle of literary figures, including the poet Nikolai Nekrasov and the critic Vissarion Belinski. In 1856 he served as secretary to the head of a governmental commercial mission to Japan, and two years later was appointed a government censor.

As a literary creator Goncharov worked slowly and consequently produced little. His place in literature rests on two masterpieces: *Oblomov* (1857), on which he spent ten years, and *The Precipice* (1868), on which he worked for twenty years. *Oblomov* is the story of an indolent Russian provincial landed proprietor, and the term *Oblomovism* entered into the Russian language as a designation of habitual laziness. *The Precipice*, which depicts a Russian household presided over by a kindhearted but tyrannical grandmother, contains an unsympathetic treatment of nihilism (q.v.), then a widely held doctrine in Russia. Among his other works are *A Common Story* (1847) and *The Frigate "Pallada"* (2 vols., 1856–57), an account of his Far Eastern voyage.

GONCOURT, EDMOND LOUIS ANTOINE DE (1822–96) and JULES ALFRED HUOT DE (1830–70), French brothers and literary collaborators. Edmond was born at Nancy, Jules in Paris. Both were educated at the Collège Bourbon, Paris. Their mother, shortly before her death in 1848, extracted from them a promise that they would spend their lives in the closest association. Reputedly, they carried out this promise so faithfully that they were never apart, except for a single 24-hour period, until the death of Jules.

They were financially independent as the result of a small legacy, which enabled them to devote themselves to art for a brief period, and subsequently to literature. The first results of their literary collaboration was a series of historical works, including *Histoire de la Société Française pendant la Révolution* (1854) and *Portraits Intimes du XVIIIe Siècle* (2 vols., 1857–58). Concerning themselves exclusively with the 18th century, they sought to present history not as the relation and analysis of great movements and events, but rather as an analysis of society derived from the study of intimate, unpublished documents, social customs, popular music, costumes, and other details. Their approach to art criticism, as displayed in *L'Art du XVIIIe Siècle* (3 vols., 1859–75), was fundamentally the same, based on an intimate study of the personal lives of the artists. Similarly, the outstanding characteristic of the novels written by the Goncourts is a painstaking and varied presentation of the details of physical reality, with the aim of examining and explaining the emotional lives of the characters in terms of their reactions to reality. Novels by the Goncourts include *Soeur Philomene* (1861), *Renée Mauperin* (1864), *Germinie Lacerteux* (1864), and *Madame Gervaisais* (1869). The novels written by Edmond after the death of Jules, closely resembling in style those written jointly, include *La Fille Élisa* (1877) and *La Faustin* (1882).

Edmond bequeathed his entire estate for the foundation and maintenance of the Académie Goncourt, an association consisting of ten literary figures who award annually a monetary prize (the Prix Goncourt) to the author of the best prose work of the year.

GONDS, an aboriginal tribe of Dravidian (*q.v.*) origin, inhabiting the hill country of India, in the State of Madhya Pradesh. The Gonds, who call themselves Koitur or "highlanders", number about 2,300,000, and are the largest stock of the Dravidian people in India. The Rajgonds, who claim Rajput ancestry, are generally followers of the Hindu religion, but the majority of the Gonds practice an animistic religion.

GONDWANA LAND, hypothetical continent in the Southern Hemisphere, thought by geologists to have existed from the Proterozoic to the end of the Mesozoic era. The name of the continent is derived from the name of its characteristic geological formation, which is exposed in Gondwana. The continent covered the area now occupied by the South Atlantic and Indian oceans, all of Antarctica, Falkland Islands, Australia, Tasmania, and Madagascar, and most of Africa, South America, and the peninsula of India. The entire area is characterized by the presence, in Permian and Triassic beds, of the index fossil *Glossopteris*. The presence of this continent during the Paleozoic and Mesozoic eras supplied a land bridge which explains the distribution of many animals which now live in widely separated areas, such as manatees in w. Africa and the Amazon and Orinoco river basins, and lemurs in Africa, Madagascar, and India.

GONGORA Y ARGOTE, LUIS DE (1561–1627), Spanish poet and dramatist, born at Cordova and educated at the University of Salamanca. He was a son of Francisco de Argote, chief magistrate of Cordova, and of Leonora de Góngora, a member of an ancient noble Spanish family. After writing several noteworthy plays and lyrics, he became the innovator of a literary style of exaggerated elegance, artificiality, and florid use of figures of speech, a style known at first as *Gongorism* and later as *cultism*. Despite these eccentricities, his poems indicate his essential genius; the style did not come to be viewed with disfavor until his imitators, lacking his gifts, abused it. Among his writings are the long poems *Soledades*, *Pyramo y Thisbe*, and *Polifemo*; the play *Las Firmezas de Isabel*; and a number of odes, sonnets, and other works in verse.

GONORRHEA, a venereal disease of man characterized by a purulent discharge, caused by a bacterium, the gonococcus. The bacterium usually attacks the mucous membranes of the urogenital tract, but may infect other parts of the body, especially the eyes. The gonococcus tends to involve the urethra and its appendages in the male and the genital system in the female. Infection of adults usually follows sexual intercourse with an infected individual, and rarely follows exposure to material freshly contaminated by one suffering from this disease.

The incubation period of gonorrhea is two to five days. In males symptoms include a burning sensation during urination and a purulent discharge, but in females little discomfort is felt so that a woman suffering from gonorrhea may be unaware of her disease and of her infectiousness. Modern advances in chemotherapy, especially the development of the antibiotics sulfathiazole and penicillin, which are specific for the disease, have made possible the eventual complete elimination of gonorrhea.

GONSALVO DI CORDOVA. See GONZALO DE CÓRDOBA.

GONTAUT, DE. See BIRON.

GONVILLE AND CAIUS COLLEGE, one of the colleges of Cambridge University, England. It was founded by Edmund Gonville in 1348, probably as an institution for the study of theology, and originally bore the official title Hall of the Annunciation of the Blessed Virgin (usually known as Gunnell or Gonville Hall). In 1557 the physician John Caius, a former student at the school, enlarged its lands, expanded its curriculum to include medical studies, and gave the institution its present name. The college charter subsequently underwent several revisions, the most recent occurring in 1923, when the composition of the college was set at one master, a minimum of fifteen fellows, and a varying number of students. The college offers six scholarships in the field of physics, and two scholarships to graduates of Harrow. Famous historical figures who attended the college include the financier Sir Thomas Gresham, the physician William Harvey, the jurist George Jeffreys, and the prelate Jeremy Taylor.

GONZAGA, SAINT ALOYSIUS (1568–91), Italian Jesuit priest, born at Castiglione and educated at the Florentine court of the Medici, in Rome, and at the court of Philip II of Spain. In 1585 he renounced his right to the marquisate of Castiglione and became a member of the Society of Jesus. He took holy orders two years later. Upon the outbreak of famine and pestilence in Rome in 1591, he devoted himself to caring for the afflicted, and was himself stricken and killed by the plague. He was canonized in 1726; June 21 is his feast day.

GONZALO DE BERCEO (1180?–after 1246), Spanish poet, born at Berceo. Little is known of his life. He was the author of about 13,000 verses, and his importance to Spanish literature stems from the fact that he was the first Castilian writer whose name is known, and also from his use of a new poetic form, the *cuaderna vía,* consisting of four-line stanzas with rhyming lines. His poetry is religious, dealing mainly with the miracles of the Virgin and the lives of the saints.

GONZALO DE CÓRDOBA (It., GONSALVO DI CORDOVA), HERNÁNDEZ (1453–1515), Spanish military commander, born at Montilla. He entered the service of Queen Isabella, and took part in the civil wars which were being fought at the time of her accession in 1474, and in the war with Portugal in 1475–76. From 1486 to 1492 he was engaged in the war against the Moors, which culminated successfully in the latter year when he negotiated the surrender of Granada. Three years later he was dispatched by the queen as commander of a Spanish expeditionary force sent to Italy to assist Ferdinand II of Naples in his struggle against Charles VIII of France. During this campaign he became known by the sobriquet *El Gran Capitán,* "The Great Captain". By 1495 he had achieved victory, and in 1498 returned to Spain. He was again in Italy in 1501, and

later allied himself with Louis XII of France against the Neapolitan monarch Frederick III. After conquering Naples he drove out the French, and until 1507 was governor of Naples under King Ferdinand III (see FERDINAND, "the Catholic" of Spain). Meanwhile, in 1504, his patroness Isabella had died, and he was subsequently recalled to Spain by Ferdinand and forced to spend the remainder of his life in retirement.

GOOBER. See PEANUT.

GOOCH, GEORGE PEABODY (1873–), British historian, educated at King's College, University of London, Trinity College, Cambridge University, and the universities of Berlin and of Paris. He was a member of Parliament from 1906 untl 1910 and in 1913. From 1911 he edited the *Contemporary Review*. From 1922 until 1925 he served as president of the Historical Association and from 1933 until 1936 as president of the National Peace Council. Gooch was an authority in the field of modern German history, and was employed as joint editor of the *Cambridge History of Foreign Policy* and of *British Documents on the Origins of the War,* 1898–1914. Among his writings are *Germany and the French Revolution* (1920), *History of Modern Europe, 1878–1918* (1923), *Germany* (1925), *Recent Revelations of European Diplomacy* (1927), *Maria Theresa and Other Studies* (1951), *Catherine the Great, and Other Studies* (1954), and *Louis XV* (1956).

GOOD FRIDAY, the Friday immediately preceding Easter, celebrated by Christians as the anniversary of the crucifixion of Christ. The name Good Friday is generally believed to be a corruption of the older "God's Friday". This day has, since the early days of the Church, been given over to penance, fasting, and prayer. In the Roman Catholic and Orthodox churches, neither communion nor the Mass is performed, and the priests and altar are clothed in black. The Catholic ceremonies on Good Friday include the reading of the Passion according to St. John, prayers for the Church and for all mankind, the unveiling and adoration of the Cross, and the Mass of the Presanctified, which differs from the ordinary Mass in that it includes no consecration of the Host. Customarily, the hours between noon and three P.M. are devoted to sermons, meditations, and prayers centering about the three-hour agony of Christ on the Cross and the seven last words spoken by Him. The last-mentioned custom has been adopted by the Anglican Church, as have several other Catholic practices, including the reading of the Gospel of St. John. In most of Europe, in South America, in the British Empire, and in several States of the United States, Good Friday is a legal holiday.

GOOD HOPE. See CAPE OF GOOD HOPE.

GOODHUE, BERTRAM GROSVENOR (1869–1924), American architect, born in Pomfret, Conn., and educated at Russell's Collegiate and Commercial Institute, New Haven. In 1889 he joined the architectural firm Cram and Wentworth. He was a partner of the firm from 1891 to 1913, when it was dissolved. Thereafter he practiced his profession independently. Goodhue attained renown initially for the Gothic spirit he infused in his otherwise modern designs for churches and university buildings. Outstanding examples of his early work are the churches of St. Thomas, St. Bartholomew, and St. Vincent Ferrer, all in New York City, and many of the buildings of the United States Military Academy, West Point, N.Y. He is famous chiefly, however, for the buildings of his later years, when he developed a greater freedom from tradition and expressed contemporary needs in modern forms and materials. The Nebraska State Capitol is considered his masterpiece. Other buildings Goodhue designed include the Los Angeles Public Library and the National Academy of Sciences, Washington, D.C.

GOODMAN, BENNY (1909–   ), American jazz musician and orchestra leader, born in Chicago, Ill., and educated at Hull House and at Lewis Institute, in that city. He began to study the clarinet at the age of ten, and within four years was appearing with local dance orchestras. For some years he studied with Franz Schoepp, of the Chicago Symphony Orchestra. He subsequently played with several dance orchestras in Chicago and New York City, and in 1933 organized his own orchestra, which by 1936 had become the most popular jazz group in the United States. In addition to his full orchestra, he organized smaller groups, particularly for recording purposes, such as the Benny Goodman Trio, Quartet, and Sextet. He was known for his technical virtuosity and for the melodic inventiveness displayed in his jazz improvisations, and gained popular recognition also for his ability to perform traditional concert music, particularly that of Mozart; he appeared as clarinet soloist with the New York Philharmonic Orchestra, the Budapest String Quartet, and the Philadelphia Orchestra. At various times Goodman conducted his orchestra in "swing concerts" at leading concert halls. A transcription of the first concert,

which took place in Carnegie Hall, New York City, in 1938, became a best-selling record in 1950. He also performed on radio and television and in motion pictures. Though he disbanded his orchestra in 1949, he retained the Sextet. The latter appeared in Chicago and New York City in 1954. After forming a new orchestra, he toured the U.S. and the Far East in 1956. He wrote an autobiography, *The Kingdom of Swing* (*with I. Kolodin,* 1939).

GOODNOW, FRANK JOHNSON (1859–1939), American legal scholar, born at Brooklyn, N.Y., and educated at Amherst College, Columbia Law School, the École Libre des Sciences Politiques, Paris, and the University of Berlin. He was professor of administrative law at Columbia University from 1891 to 1907, served as legal adviser to the government of China in 1913–14, and was president of Johns Hopkins University from 1914 to 1929, when he resigned. Among his writings are *Municipal Home Rule* (1890), *Principles of the Administrative Law in the United States* (1905), *Principles of Constitutional Government* (1916), and *China: An Analysis* (1926).

GOODSPEED, EDGAR JOHNSON (1871–   ), American Greek and Biblical scholar, born at Quincy, Ill., and educated at Denison and Yale universities, and at the universities of Chicago and of Berlin, Germany. From 1898 to 1937 he taught at the University of Chicago, becoming professor of Biblical and Patristic Greek in 1915 and chairman of the New Testament department in 1923. From 1938 to 1947 he lectured on history at the University of California at Los Angeles. He wrote and edited numerous works, including *The Story of the New Testament* (1916); *Strange New Gospels* (1931); *The Apocrypha, An American Translation* (1938); *How to Read the Bible* (1946); *Apostolic Fathers; an American Translation* (1950); the autobiography *As I Remember* (1953); *Modern Apocrypha* (1956); and *The Twelve* (1957).

GOOD TEMPLARS, INTERNATIONAL ORDER OF, a fraternal society founded at Utica, N.Y., in 1851, for the propagation of the principle of total abstinence from all intoxicating liquors, and for the maintenance of world peace. A Right Worthy Grand Lodge of North America was formed in 1858, and ten years later the Order was introduced into England. It subsequently spread to the Scandinavian countries and thence to most of the countries of the world. In the United States, the Order played an important part in the organization of the Prohibition Party in 1869, and of the Women's Christian Temperance Union in 1874. At present it is organized into local, county, and national lodges, and an international lodge which serves as the highest governing body of the Order and has its headquarters in Sweden. The headquarters of the National Grand Lodge of the United States are in West Hartford, Conn. The Order maintains a home for orphans at Vallejo, Calif., and a home for inebriates at Chicago, Ill. In a recent year the total membership in the Order was about 600,000.

GOOD WILL, in law and accounting, an intangible asset comprising a value over and above the valuation of the tangible assets of the business, and representing all benefits derived from the distinctive location, trade name, credit rating, reputation, and patronage of the business. It attaches to the business and cannot be transferred apart from it.

GOODYEAR, CHARLES (1800–60), American inventor, born at New Haven, Conn. He had no formal education, and in 1821 went into partnership with his father in a hardware business that later failed. Goodyear experimented for many years, with no success, to find some means of improving the quality of natural India rubber so that it would not become brittle when cold, or soft and sticky when hot. He purchased from a rival inventor,

Goodyear News Service

Charles Goodyear

Nathaniel Manley Hayward (1808–65), the patent rights to a process for impregnating rubber with sulfur, although this process had not been particularly successful. In 1839 Goodyear discovered, by accidentally dropping on a hot stove a piece of rubber that had been treated with sulfur, that when India rubber and sulfur are heated together at a high temperature a rubber with the desirable properties results. This process, called *vulcanization,* is still the basis of the rubber-manufacturing industry; see RUBBER. Goodyear sold his patent rights for a small sum. He lived in Europe from 1851 to 1859, and established a rubber business there. He died in poverty.

GOOSE, common name for the female of any of a number of species of water birds constituting the subfamily Anserinae in the same family as ducks and swans. The males are properly called ganders, but in ordinary usage they are often also termed geese. Geese differ from swans in having the space between the bill and the eye feathered, and in having shorter necks. They differ from ducks in having longer necks and legs, and in having their legs covered with scales in the back rather than the front. Geese vary in length from about 26 to 45 ins. The feet are fully webbed. The plumage, which is the same in both sexes, consists of feathers and quills which are moulted once a year. Most species have short, heavy bills. The majority nest on the ground, although some make their homes in trees. Their call is a honking sound, often emitted while flying.

A number of species are migratory, nesting in the summer in Canada and wintering near inland waters and along the coasts of the United States. When migrating, geese, like ducks, fly in a V-shaped formation, probably to make it possible for the flock to see the leader clearly.

About thirty species of true geese exist, of which ten or twelve are found in the U.S. Among species which are found in both Europe and North America are the snow goose (q.v.) and the barnacle goose. The blue goose, *Chen caerulescens,* a bluish-gray bird with a white head, is found in North America. Among well-known species which frequent the U.S. is the common Canada Goose, *Branta canadensis,* also known as the wild goose, a gray-brown bird with a black head, famed for its migrations, which in American folklore are regarded as a sign of spring. See also BRANT.

A number of breeds of geese are raised domestically. They probably originated from

Canadian National Railways

GEESE OF NORTH AMERICA
Above: The common Canada goose.
Right: The wild blue goose.

the graylag, *Anser anser,* a wild, gray, European goose. Among the most important domestic geese are the Toulouse, an all-gray breed originating in France, the White Emden, an all-white goose originating in Germany, and the gray African, a tall goose which fattens more rapidly than any other breed. Both the flesh and the eggs of geese are eaten. Geese are the source of the delicacy *pâté de foie gras,* made from goose livers morbidly enlarged by overfeeding the geese and depriving them of exercise. Domestic geese are also commercially valuable for their feathers, which are used in pillows. See POULTRY.

GOOSEBERRY, common name of the fruit of members of the genus *Grossularia* and of the family *Grossulariaceae* (q.v.), to which the genus belongs. *Grossularia* is a genus of about 60 species of shrubs growing in the north temperate zone. Plants of this genus were formerly included in the genus *Ribes* (q.v.), the currants, but differ from *Ribes* in having spines at the bases of the leafstalks. Gooseberry fruits are acid berries used in North America and Europe for making jams, jellies, and pies. Berries of the European species, *G. reclinata,* are superior in size and quality to those of American species, but cannot withstand hot, dry American summers or attacks of powdery mildew. The American species, a hybrid between *G. reclinata* and *G. hirtella,* is mildew-resistant and can withstand hot weather when adequately protected.

Gooseberry bushes grow best in rich, heavy, well-drained soil. They are easily propagated by cuttings, suckers, and layers. Cuttings give the best results, readily producing well-formed plants.

Gooseberries are subject to attack by several insect pests. The currant worms, *Pteronidea ribesii, Pristiphora grossulariae,* and *Epochra canadensis,* are sawfly larvae which strip currant and gooseberry bushes of their leaves. They may be controlled by spraying with lead arsenate solutions or hellebore powders. The gooseberry fruitworm, *Zophodia grossulariae,* is a moth caterpillar which attacks gooseberry fruits. Gooseberries are an intermediate host of white-pine blister rust, and are sometimes intentionally destroyed to preserve pine forests.

U.S.D.I., Fish & Wildlife Service

A pocket gopher at the mouth of its burrow

Many plants which bear fruit similar to gooseberries are called gooseberry. In the U.S., the southern gooseberry is *Vaccinium melanocarpum,* a close relative of the blueberries and cranberries.

GOOSEFISH. See ANGLER.

GOOSEFOOT. See CHENOPODIUM.

GOOSSENS, SIR EUGENE (1893–   ), British conductor and composer, born in London. He studied at the Bruges Conservatory, the Liverpool College of Music, and the Royal College of Music, London. In the first part of his career he was active mainly in England; from 1923, largely in the United States. He was assistant conductor of the Queen's Hall Orchestra, London, from 1915 to 1920, and in 1921–22 conducted opera and the Russian Ballet at Covent Garden, London. Goossens was conductor of the Rochester (N.Y.) Philharmonic Orchestra from 1924 to 1931 and of the Cincinnati Symphony Orchestra from 1931 to 1947. He also appeared as guest conductor with other leading American orchestras. After 1947 he was conductor of the Sydney, Australia, Symphony Orchestra and director of the New South Wales Conservatorium of Music. He was knighted in 1955. His compositions include the operas *Judith* (one-act, 1925) and *Don Juan de Mañara* (1937), orchestral works, chamber and piano music, and songs. He is the author of *Overture and Beginners* (autobiography, 1951).

G.O.P., the abbreviation for the expression "Grand Old Party", a popular name for the Republican Party in the United States.

GOPHER (Fr. *gauffre,* "honeycomb"),common name for three unrelated American burrowing animals, the pocket gopher, ground squirrel, and gopher tortoise, so called because they "honeycomb" the soil. Technically, the term "gopher" refers to the pocket or pouched

gophers (also known as pouched rats) which form a family, Geomyidae, of rodents containing three genera and over seventy species and subspecies. Pocket gophers are widely distributed throughout western, central, and southern U.S. They are chubby, ratlike animals, 10 to 14 inches in over-all length, and covered with soft, short fur. They are characterized by two large, fur-lined pockets, one on the outside of each cheek, in which they store food. Their heads are wide and depressed; the eyes and ears are small and underdeveloped; the incisor teeth are well developed for gnawing, and are fluted in the eastern varieties of pocket gophers. The limbs are short and have powerful claws, which are especially long on the forelimbs. The thick tail is about 3 inches long; it is a sensitive organ, and the pocket gopher uses it in finding its way about the underground tunnels in which it lives. Pocket gophers are voracious and feed on any type of vegetation found underground. They destroy food trees by gnawing away the roots, and ravage tuber and bulb gardens. The damage they do is such that they have become serious economic pests, and steps are taken toward their destruction wherever they are found. Female gophers give birth once a year, producing two to six offspring.

The largest pocket gopher is the camass rat, which reaches a length of 14 inches. One of the most common pocket gophers is the dark-brown prairie gopher, *Geomys bursarius,* found in the upper Mississippi valley. This gopher is a danger to the flood-controlling structures of the Mississippi, because it often builds its burrows in the levees. See GROUND SQUIRREL; GOPHER TORTOISE.

GOPHER SNAKE or **INDIGO SNAKE,** the largest snake in eastern U.S., found in the S.E., and especially abundant in Florida. The gopher snake takes its name from its habit of frequenting the burrow of the gopher tortoise (q.v.). It is a harmless snake, bluish-black in color, with a crimson throat. It has a thick body covered with glassy scales, and reaches a maximum length of nine feet. The gopher snake is a subspecies of the cribo, *Drymarchon corais,* a common brownish-yellow colubrine snake of Central and South America; its scientific name is *D. corais couperi.* It feeds on frogs, toads, lizards, rodents, and the young of other snakes.

The name gopher snake is also sometimes given to the bull snake (q.v.), which feeds on gophers and on other harmful rodents.

GOPHER TORTOISE, a turtle, *Gopherus polyphemus,* inhabiting the arid, coastal regions of southern U.S. from Florida to w. Texas. The gopher tortoise lives in burrows dug in sand and is often erroneously called gopher. The smooth, brown shell of the adult is about one foot long. The inner borders of the forelimbs, which are flattened from front to back, are covered by overlapping, bony plates. Gopher tortoises are herbivorous.

GORAKHPUR, city of Uttar Pradesh (United Provinces), India, on the Rapti R., 100 miles N.E. of Benares. It is thought to have been founded in the 15th century A.D., and is noted for its 17th-century mosque. Gorakhpur is the headquarters of the Bengal and Northwestern railroad, and is a trade center for grain and timber. Pop. (1941) 84,650.

GORAMY. See GOURAMI.

GORBODUC or **FERREX AND PORREX,** the first tragedy written in English and the first drama in blank verse, produced in 1561. The authors of this work were Thomas Norton, who is believed to have written the first three acts, and Thomas Sackville (qq.v.), to whom the last two acts are generally attributed. Gorboduc was a legendary British king who bequeathed his realm to his sons, Ferrex and Porrex, during his lifetime. A dispute ensued between the sons over their legacy, and Porrex murdered his brother, who was the favorite of Videna, their mother. She took vengeance by killing Porrex; the enraged populace then revolted and slew both king and queen. This story is derived ultimately from the 12th-century English chronicle *Historia Regum Britanniæ* by Geoffrey of Monmouth (q.v.).

GORDIAN KNOT, in classical mythology, a complex knot tied by Gordius, the eponymous founder of the ancient town of Gordium, the capital of Phrygia in Asia Minor. According to the myth, the Phrygians consulted an oracle of Zeus concerning the choice of a king. The oracle instructed them to select as their ruler whoever should first appear riding in a cart. The person so specified proved to be the peasant Gordius, and he was forthwith elevated to the throne. In gratitude, Gordius dedicated his cart to Zeus, whereupon another oracle declared that whoever should untie the intricate knot which bound the pole of the cart to the yoke would be ruler of all Asia. Alexander the Great, failing to unloose the knot, cut it in two with his sword and applied the prophecy to himself. Hence, in figurative usage, a Gordian knot is a great difficulty that can be overcome only by bold and resourceful measures.

GORDIUS. See GORDIAN KNOT.

GORDIUS, in zoology. See HAIRWORM.

GORDON, name of a Scottish family important in the history of Scotland and England since the 14th century. Genealogists have traced more than 150 main lines of the family, including the earls and marquises of Huntly and the dukes of Gordon, the earls of Sutherland, the viscounts Kenmure, the earls and marquises of Aberdeen, and the barons Stanmore. The family traces its ancestry to Adam de Gordon (fl. early 12th cent.), a cadet of a noble Anglo-Norman family, who settled in the village of Gordon in Berwickshire, during the reign (1124–53) of David I. Among the important members of the family are the following. **1.** SIR ADAM DE GORDON (d. 1333), soldier and statesman. He assisted King Edward I of England in his effort in 1305 to take the Scottish throne, and was justiciar of Scotland from 1310 to 1314. After the Battle of Bannockburn, however, he supported Robert Bruce, and was rewarded with the lordship of Strathbogie, Aberdeenshire; he renamed his domain Huntly, and it was thenceforth the chief seat of the family. Sir Adam was the ancestor of nearly all the eminent Gordons of Scotland. From his elder son sprang the earls of Aberdeen and the Seton-Gordon line of Huntly (see below); from his younger son, the viscounts Kenmure and the lords of Lochinvar, celebrated in poetry and song, and the Irish and Virginian lines of the Gordon family.

2. ALEXANDER SETON-GORDON (d. 1470), 1st Earl of Huntly. In 1436 he accompanied the daughter of James I, Margaret of Scotland (1425–45), to France for her marriage to the Dauphin (later Louis XI). He was created earl in 1449, and in 1460 he was commander at the siege that won Roxburgh Castle for the Scottish crown. Among his descendants were the Gordons of Gight, turbulent ancestors of the English poet Lord Byron. **3.** GEORGE GORDON (1514–62), 4th Earl of Huntly. He became lieutenant of the north, and in 1544 defeated the Camerons and the Macdonalds, traditional enemies of his house. He was given the earldom of Moray in 1548, but when it was taken from him because of Queen Mary's alarm at the growth of his power, he joined forces with the lords of the congregation (the Scottish Protestant nobility) and lost his life fighting the queen's forces. **4.** GEORGE GORDON (d. 1576), 5th Earl of Huntly. He regained in 1567 the lands and titles that his father had lost. Allying himself with Queen Mary and James Bothwell, he aided in the murder of

Lord Henry Darnley, and helped secure the divorce of his own sister from Bothwell to clear the way for the marriage of Bothwell and Mary. In 1572, however, Gordon abandoned Mary's cause, thereby causing Mary to surrender herself to Elizabeth of England. **5.** GEORGE GORDON (1562–1636), 1st Marquis and 6th Earl of Huntly, son of the 5th earl. He was the leader of the Scottish Roman Catholics against James VI (later James I of Great Britain), and defeated a royal army at Glenivat. The next year James destroyed his castle of Strathbogie, and Gordon left Scotland, but returned secretly and agreed to join the Kirk (the Established Church of Scotland). For a time he was in favor at court, and was created marquis in 1599. Suspicions of the Kirk authorities as to the sincerity of his conversion, and the enmity of powerful families, caused his imprisonment several times; before his death he again professed faith in Roman Catholicism. **6.** GEORGE GORDON (1643–1716), 1st Duke of Gordon and 4th Marquis of Huntly, great-grandson of the 1st marquis. He was created duke in 1684, and in 1688 attempted unsuccessfully to aid James II in the Glorious Revolution (q.v.).

7. LORD GEORGE GORDON (1751–93), third son of the 3rd Duke of Gordon. When in 1778 Parliament passed the Catholic Relief Act, he organized the Protestant associations in opposition to the Act, and became their leader in the following year. On June 2, 1780, he headed a mob of 50,000 persons who marched from St. George's Field to the House of Commons to present a petition against the Act; rioting broke out and raged for several days, during which the mob ruled London. For his part in the riot, Gordon was arrested on a charge of treason, but the skillful defense by Thomas Erskine of Restormel (q.v.) won him an acquittal. In 1787 Gordon was convicted of libeling the Queen of France, the French Ambassador, and the English courts; he escaped to Holland, but returned the following year and was sentenced to a term of five years in Newgate prison. There he lived in comfort, giving dances and dinner parties. On the expiration of his term he was unable to find anyone willing to give surety for his good behavior, and remained in Newgate; he was converted to Judaism shortly before his death. **8.** GEORGE GORDON (1770–1836), 5th Duke of Gordon and 8th Earl of Huntly. He raised and commanded the famous regiment known as the Gordon Highlanders. He was created Baron Gordon Huntly in 1807. Upon his death, his cousin George Gordon (1761–1835)

succeeded as 9th Earl of Huntly; the barony and dukedom expired with him. The dukedom was revived, however, for Charles Henry Gordon-Lennox, grandson of the sister of the 5th earl.

9. ADAM GORDON OF ABOYNE (d. 1537), second son of the 2nd Earl of Huntly. Through his wife Elizabeth, Countess of Sutherland, he acquired the earldom for himself and his descendants. One of his remote descendants, another Elizabeth, Countess of Sutherland in her own right, married in 1785 George Granville Leveson-Gower, who was created Duke of Sutherland in 1833.

GORDON, CHARLES GEORGE, popularly known as CHINESE GORDON and GORDON PASHA (1833–85), British colonial soldier and administrator, born at Woolwich and educated at Taunton School and the Royal Military Academy, Woolwich. In 1852 he entered the Royal Engineers with the rank of second lieutenant. He served in the Crimean War (1854–56) against Russia, and returned to England in 1858. Two years later he was sent to China, which was then partly occupied by British and French forces, and participated in the seizure of Peking.

During the Taiping Rebellion (q.v.) against the Chinese emperor Kuang Hsü, Gordon fought on behalf of the emperor. He served on the staff of the British commander, General Staveley, and in 1863 assumed command of the Chinese troops formerly under the American soldier-of-fortune Frederick Townsend Ward, who had been killed. With this force, which was known as the Ever-Victorious Army, he captured a large number of rebel-occupied towns, and, with the fall of Nanking in 1864, effected the complete suppression of the rebellion. The emperor rewarded Gordon for his military successes by naming him a mandarin of the first class; the sobriquet "Chinese" was first applied to Gordon at about this time.

He spent the years from 1864 to 1874 in military service in England and in carrying out various diplomatic missions on the Continent. In 1874, with the approval of the British government, he entered the service of the khedive of Egypt, Ismail Pasha, who named him governor of his equatorial provinces. Until 1876 Gordon served in that capacity, establishing numerous trading posts, mapping large areas, and suppressing the slave trade. Following Gordon's return to England, in 1877, the khedive increased his powers by appointing him governor of the Sudan, the equatorial provinces, and the regions bordering on the

Red Sea, and Gordon re-entered the service of the Egyptian government.

During the ensuing three years Gordon busied himself in administrative reforms, in attempting to establish peaceful relations between Abyssinia (now Ethiopia) and Egypt, and in the establishment of communications, the exploitation of natural resources, and further suppression of the slave trade.

Subsequently he served the British government in various administrative capacities in India, China, on the island of Mauritius, and in South Africa. He was in England in November, 1883, when rebellious forces led by Mohammed Ahmed inflicted a disastrous defeat on the Anglo-Egyptian forces in the Sudan. The British government ordered the Egyptians to abandon the Sudan in the following month, and Gordon was immediately dispatched to the Sudan, charged with the task of supervising the evacuation of the beleaguered Egyptian garrisons.

He arrived at Khartoum, in the Sudan, in February, 1884, and succeeded in evacuating about 2500 women, children, and sick and wounded persons before the city was surrounded by Ahmed's troops. In March, when his request that the forces of the Egyptian soldier Zobeir Rahama Pasha be brought to bear against the Mahdi was refused by the British government, and when several additional requests for aid were refused, Gordon found himself isolated. Despite the fact that the fortifications of Khartoum were weak, food supplies insufficient, and his garrison woefully small, he withstood the siege for ten months. The British government did not send an expedition to relieve him until November, and this force arrived only after Khartoum had fallen and Gordon had been killed.

A difference of opinion exists among historians with regard to the value of Gordon's services to his country. While some regard him as one of the greatest military leaders in British history, others criticize him for a tendency to impulsive, quixotic behavior, even asserting that his death might have been avoided had he been more mindful of his government's policies in Egypt. Gordon's collected writings include *Reflections in Palestine* (1884), *The Journals of Major-General Gordon at Khartoum* (1885), and *Letters of General C. G. Gordon to His Sister M. A. Gordon* (1888). He is the subject of a biography by Laurence and Elizabeth Hanson, *Chinese Gordon: The Story of a Hero* (1954).

GORDON, JEHUDA LEB or LEON (1830–92), Russian-Jewish poet and novelist, born in Wilno. He spent some twenty years teaching Hebrew in the government schools of his native city, and in 1872 was appointed secretary of the Jewish community at St. Petersburg (now Leningrad), and of the Society for the Dissemination of Culture Among the Jews of Russia. In 1879 he was accused of complicity in the plot to assassinate Czar Alexander II, and with his family was imprisoned and then exiled, but was soon cleared of the charges and allowed to return to St. Petersburg. He contributed heavily to the revival in Hebrew language and literature, expending great effort on the cultural enlightenment of the oppressed Russian Jews. His works, written in classical Hebrew, include the collection of verse *Kol Shire Yehuda* (1883–84), and the collection of novels *Kol Kithbe Yehuda* (1889).

GORDON, RUTH (1896–   ), American actress and playwright, born at Wollaston, Mass., and trained at the American Academy of Dramatic Arts. She made her debut in *Peter Pan,* at the Empire Theatre, New York City, in 1915. She later appeared in a wide variety of roles, and was known especially for her performances as Bobby, the oversensitive girl in *Saturday's Children* (1927); as Elizabeth Rimplegar in the comedy-romance *Three-Cornered Moon* (1933); and as Nora Helmer in Ibsen's classic tragedy *A Doll's House* (1937). Among the other notable plays in which she appeared are *Seventeen* (1918), *Ethan Frome* (1936), *The Three Sisters* (1942), *Over Twenty-One* (1944), and *The Matchmaker* (1955). She is the author of *Over Twenty-One,* a light comedy, and *Years Ago* (1946), a nostalgic, semiautobiographical play which was later made into a motion picture, *The Actress* (1953). She collaborated in the writing of screenplays with her husband, Garson Kanin, and also appeared in a number of motion pictures.

GORDON BENNETT TROPHY RACES. See BALLOON.

GORDON HIGHLANDERS. See HIGHLANDERS.

GORDON RIOTS. See GORDON, family.

GORDON SETTER, a breed of field dog (q.v.) used chiefly in hunting birds, particularly woodcock; see SETTER. Because of its color, a deep black with markings of tan, mahogany, or chestnut, it is sometimes known as the black-and-tan setter. The dog originated in Scotland in the first quarter of the 19th century and takes its name from its reputed first breeder, one of the dukes of Richmond and Gordon. The Gordon setter has a round skull; a fairly long muzzle and a large nose; bright,

Photograph by Mary Eleanor Browning

Gordon setter

dark-brown eyes; a long, lean neck; a deep chest; straight forelegs and long, muscular hind legs; and a short tail which it carries horizontally. Its coat is silky and glossy. The male is from 22 to 25 inches high at the shoulder; the bitch, 21 to 24 inches. The dog is loyal and dependable, but gives its devotion exclusively to its master and cannot be used for hunting by anyone else.

GOREMYKIN, Ivan Longinovich (1839–1917), Russian statesman, born at Novgorod. After a number of years in various administrative posts he became minister of the interior in 1895 and served in that capacity until 1899. In 1906 he succeeded Count Sergei Yulievich Witte as prime minister. Goremykin again occupied that post between 1914 and 1916, during World War I. Because he was a supporter of the czar, he was arrested after the revolution in 1917 and imprisoned and murdered in the Caucasus by the Bolsheviks.

GORGAS, William Crawford (1854–1920), American sanitarian and army surgeon, born at Mobile, Ala., and educated at the University of the South at Sewanee, Tenn., and Bellevue Medical School. He entered the United States Army in 1880 as an officer in the medical corps. From 1898 until 1902 he was chief sanitary officer of Havana, Cuba. He there did research work on yellow fever; and after Walter Reed (q.v.) discovered that the yellow fever germ is carried by mosquitoes, Gorgas organized and carried through a campaign to destroy swamps and all other breeding places of mosquitoes, thus succeeding in ridding Havana of yellow fever. In 1904 he was sent to Panama as chief sanitary officer of the Panama Canal Commission to combat yellow fever and malaria, which were the greatest obstacles to the building of the Panama Canal. Within two years Gorgas succeeded in eliminating yellow fever from the Canal region, and

bringing malaria under control. In 1914 he was appointed surgeon general in the United States Army with the rank of brigadier general, and in 1916 he became a major general. He was retired from the army in 1918, and became director of the work on yellow fever at the Rockefeller Foundation. He was accorded many honors by various countries and universities.

GORGES, Sir Ferdinando (1566?–1647), English soldier, mariner, and colonizer, born at Ashton, in Somersetshire. He founded two Plymouth companies (1606–20 and 1620–35) for acquiring and colonizing lands in New England. In 1629 he received the land between the Kennebec and Piscataqua rivers; and in 1639 the king granted him a charter constituting him proprietor of the Province of Maine. His son neglected the province, which finally placed itself under the jurisdiction of Massachusetts, to which colony Sir Ferdinando's grandson sold his rights in 1677 for $6250. Sir Ferdinando described his hopes and accomplishments in *Briefe Narration of the Originall Undertakings of the Advancement of Plantations into the Parts of America* (1647).

GORGET, patch of contrasting color on the throat of a bird. The blue-throated hummingbird, for example, has a bright-azure gorget, and the ruby-throated hummingbird has a ruby-red gorget. The term gorget, to describe throat markings, is derived from the similarly

William C. Gorgas

named part of a suit of armor which protected the neck (Fr. *gorge*, "neck").

GORGON (Gr. *gorgos*, "grim"), in Greek mythology, the name of a hideous, demonic creature. The Greek epic poet Homer mentions only one Gorgon, represented as inhabiting the lower world. According to the later Greek poet Hesiod, however, the Gorgon, named Medusa (the queen), had two sisters, Euryale (the far-leaper) and Stheno (the strong). Of the three, Medusa alone was mortal. She was also the most terrible, and one glance from her eyes sufficed to turn any human being to stone. Medusa was beheaded by the hero Perseus (q.v.), and from her blood sprang Chrysaor, of the golden sword, and the winged horse Pegasus. The Gorgon's head, with its petrifying power, was used by Perseus against his enemies, and was later taken by the goddess Athena and fastened in the center of her ægis.

Representations of the Gorgon's head were used by the ancient Greeks as talismans to ward off evil influences. The Gorgon figures in Greek art as a winged creature, having a round face, snaky hair, huge staring eyes, and a wide mouth with projecting tongue and tusklike teeth.

GORILLA, the largest known anthropoid ape (see APE). Gorillas are closely related to chimpanzees (q.v.), but are as distinct in structure from the other member of the anthropoid ape family, the orangutan, as they are widely removed in habitat. Two species of gorillas are generally recognized: the common gorilla, *Gorilla gorilla,* and the mountain gorilla, *Gorilla beringei.* The mountain gorilla has heavier fur than the common gorilla, to protect it at the high altitudes (10,000 feet) it frequents in the Belgian Congo. The common gorilla inhabits the forests of w. Africa.

Gorillas approach and may exceed man in size, frequently assume an erect attitude, and resemble man in structure more closely than they do the apes and monkeys of other families. Young gorillas, like all young apes, resemble humans more than adult apes do. The skeleton is substantially similar to the human skeleton, but the bones are thicker, the arms are much longer, and the legs are shorter. The spine lacks those curvatures in the lower part which enable man to stand erect with ease. The teeth are of the same number and character as man's, but not set in horseshoe shape, the front teeth making a decided angle with the cheek teeth, where the canines are developed into tusks. The brain case is smaller, and

Ancient Greek relief of a Gorgon head

the bulk of brain far less than that of man. The ears are smaller than those of man, the nose flat, and the lower jaw strongly developed and protruding. The ribs consist, as in the chimpanzee, of thirteen pairs, in contrast to man and the orangutan, which have twelve. The hair has a grizzled, brownish-gray appearance: the stem of each hair is black; the tip, white. The skin, on hairless portions such as the face, is black.

Gorillas live in families of one male and one female and their young. They build crude shelters in trees and on the ground. Naturalists have observed that these shelters are used generally for a single night. The animals feed mainly on vegetables, but also consume small mammals, birds, and birds' eggs.

The male gorilla may attain a height of about six feet, and may weigh about 400 lbs. It is many times stronger than man because of its massive build and enormous muscles. When excited, gorillas have a peculiar habit of beating their chests in rapid rhythm in the hollow just below the breastbone with alternate action of their slightly cupped hands, producing a drumming noise. Gorillas also emit a few short, sharp barks, and then a loud roar prior to attacking.

Female gorillas are much smaller than the males, generally averaging about 4½ ft. in height, although in other apes the sexes rarely differ in size. The canine teeth of the females are not developed into tusks. Both males and females walk on all fours, turning the fingers of the hands under, and sometimes also the toes of the hind legs. They walk erect with difficulty unless they can steady themselves by grasping a branch or other support.

The gorilla's mentality has been extensively studied, notably by Robert Mearns Yerkes, who published his account of a young female gorilla under the title *The Mind of the Gorilla* (1927). He observed that this gorilla as "compared with chimpanzees and orangutans of like age is remarkably slow in adaptation,

American Museum of Natural History

Museum model of a large male mountain gorilla in its natural surroundings

limited in initiative, originality, and insight".

The largest gorilla ever in captivity, Gargantua, a male acquired by Ringling Bros., Barnum & Bailey Circus, had the following measurements at the age of nineteen: weight, 550 lbs.; height, 5 ft. 6½ in.; arm spread, 9 ft. 5 in.; chest girth, 76 in.

GÖRING, HERMANN (1893–1946), German soldier and National Socialist (Nazi) leader, born at Rosenheim, Bavaria, and educated at the officer's school of Lichterfelde, near Berlin. During World War I he served in the German air force, and in April, 1918, at the death of Baron Manfred von Richthofen (q.v.), he became leader of the latter's famous squadron. Göring met Adolf Hitler in 1921, and a year later was a leader of the National Socialist

Party (see NATIONAL SOCIALISM). He took part in the unsuccessful beer-hall putsch of November, 1923, and was forced to flee to Italy, where he stayed for four years. In 1928 he was elected a member of the Reichstag, and became president of that body in 1932.

Göring became Reich minister for air forces on the success of the Nazi coup d'état in 1933, and early the next year was appointed premier of Prussia and general of the infantry. In November, 1937, he became economic dictator of the German Reich. Three months later he was appointed field marshal, and in 1940, following the outbreak of World War II, Hitler created the rank of reichsmarshal for him. As commander in chief of the German air force, Göring planned much of the strategy, involving close and highly effective co-ordination between the German ground and air forces, which resulted in the rapid conquests of Poland, Norway, Denmark, France, and the Low Countries in 1939 and 1940. He also devised the policy of "terror bombing", whereby entire cities, such as Rotterdam, Holland, and Coventry, England, were leveled by aerial bombardment as a means for the subjugation of their civilian populations. He surrendered to U.S. forces in 1945, and was tried, with other German war leaders, by the International Military Tribunal at Nuremberg (see NUREMBERG TRIALS). At the trial the prosecution stated that "He was the leading war aggressor, both as political and as military leader; he was the director of the slave labor program and the creator of the oppressive program against the Jews and other races, at home and abroad." He was found guilty on all counts and was sentenced to death by hanging. He escaped this fate by poisoning himself on the morning appointed for his execution.

GORIZIA, capital of the province of the same name, Venezia Giulia, Italy, located on the Isonzo R., 25 m. by rail E. of Udine. Prior to World War 1 Gorizia was the capital of the Austrian crownland of Görz and Gradisca. During World War I the city suffered severe damage in the course of fighting between Austro-German and Italian forces. Silks, cottons, leather goods, and soap are manufactured in Gorizia, and a large trade in wine is carried on. The city was occupied by the British Eighth Army in May, 1945, during World War II. Pop. (1951) 43,974. Area of province, 181 sq.m.; pop. (1936) 115,252.

GORKI, formerly NIZHNII NOVGOROD, capital of the Region of the same name, Soviet Russia. The city is located at the confluence of the Oka and Volga rivers, 237 m. by rail E. of Moscow. It is the principal industrial center of the Region, producing automobiles, Diesel engines, chemicals, linen, meat products, electrical equipment, machine tools, precision instruments, lathes, and ships. Libraries, museums, and a large university make the city culturally important. Pop. of city (1946 est.) 900,000. Area of Region, 29,100 sq.m.; pop. (1946 est.) 3,600,000.

GORKI or **GORKY,** MAKSIM or MAXIM, pseudonym of ALEKSEI MAKSIMOVICH PESHKOV (1868–1936), Russian novelist, playwright, and essayist, born in Nizhnii Novgorod (later renamed Gorki in his honor), and self-educated. Although he was known principally as a writer, he was also prominent in the Russian revolutionary movement; and, through his association with its leaders and with the later Soviet government, occupies an important place in Russian and Soviet history.

Compelled to earn his own living from the age of nine, Gorki was for many years a jack-of-all-trades, and tramped over a great part of European Russia. During this time he contracted tuberculosis, from which he suffered for the rest of his life. In 1899 he became associated with the revolutionary activities of the Marxists and in 1906 went abroad on a revolutionary mission for the Russian Social Democratic Labor Party. In 1907, because of failing health, he settled on the Italian island of Capri. In spite of his precarious health and his professions of pacifism, Gorki fought for a time in the Czarist army during World War I.

He supported the revolution of 1917; became a Soviet official in charge of the government propaganda bureau in 1918; and, in the following year, was elected a member of the Petrograd Soviet. During these and the immediately following years, Gorki exerted himself to alleviate the harsh lot of the prerevolutionary intellectuals. Compelled by illness to leave his native land in 1922, Gorki spent six years in Sorrento, Italy, and on his re-

Maksim Gorki

The American goshawk. At left, an immature bird; at right, the adult.

turn to the Soviet Union was received with official honors.

In his writings Gorki exhibited a deep sense of reality and a profound sympathy with the downtrodden and oppressed. He invested the lowliest person in his works with a redeeming spark of hope for a better life; society, not the individual, was the villain in Gorki's philosophy.

His volumes of short stories *My Fellow Traveler* and *Twenty-Six Men and a Girl* (both published in 1901) are generally regarded as masterpieces. His novels include *Foma Gordeev* (1899), *Mother* (1907), and the tetralogy comprising *Bystander, The Magnet, Other Fires,* and *The Specter* (1927–38), which constitutes a cavalcade of Russian history from 1880 to 1924. The best known of his plays is *Lower Depths* (1903), which depicts men reduced to the ultimate depths of degradation but nevertheless retaining estimable qualities innate in humanity; others include *Yegor Bulychov* (1932) and *Dostigaeff and the Others* (1934). His autobiographical works include the trilogy *Childhood* (1913), *In the World* (1915), and *My Universities or Reminiscences of My Youth* (1924); *Recollections* (including the celebrated *Recollections of Tolstoi,* 1920); and *Fragments of My Diary* (1924). Gorki also wrote biographies of the writers Andrei Andreev and Count Lev Tolstoi, and of the Bolshevik leader Nikolai Lenin.

GORLOVKA, a city of the Ukrainian S.S.R., located in the Donets Basin, about 125 miles s.e. of Kharkov. Gorlovka, one of the industrial cities constructed in the Donets Basin

since 1930, is noted for the production of chemicals, nitrogenous fertilizers, and mining machinery. Pop. (1939) 108,693.

GORSE. See FURZE.

GOSHAWK, any large, yellow-eyed, short-winged hawk in the genus *Astur.* Goshawks fly rapidly and maneuver skillfully in their persistent chase of the birds, rabbits, and squirrels which constitute their chief quarry. The keen-sighted goshawks have long legs and large, grasping feet with which they hold their prey.

The American goshawk, *A. atricapillus,* is about twenty-two inches long. It is found in Alaska and Canada in the summer, but travels as far south in the winter as s. New Jersey, Missouri, Kansas, and California. The back of this bird is metallic gray; its underparts are barred with thin, transverse, irregular lines of gray on a white background. Its head is black with a white line over each eye. The long tail is banded with black. A smaller hawk, *Asturina plagiata,* commonly called the Mexican goshawk, is not a true goshawk though its color and markings are similar. This bird is seventeen inches long and is found in s. Arizona, s. Texas, Mexico, and Guatemala. It lives in open country and eats small rodents, lizards, fish, and large insects. Goshawks found in the Old World are used in falconry (q.v.). They include the European goshawk, *Astur gentilis,* and the Indian shikra, *A. baduis.* The Australian goshawk, *A. novaehollandiae,* is completely white. See HAWK.

GOSHEN, in the Old Testament, that part of ancient Egypt settled by the Israelites between the time of the immigration of Jacob and the Exodus. The exact location of the region has not been established. It was a fertile land, free of the plagues of Egypt.

GOSHENITE. See BERYL.

GOSNOLD, BARTHOLOMEW (d. 1607), English explorer and colonizer. In 1602 he was in command of the ship *Concord,* which sailed along the North American coast from Maine to Narragansett Bay. On that voyage he named Cape Cod, some of the islands in Nantucket Sound, including Martha's Vineyard, and the Elizabeth Islands. When he returned to England Gosnold promoted the establishment of colonies in the areas he had explored and aided the merchants who secured a charter from James I to colonize Virginia. He was appointed to command the *God Speed,* one of three ships which transported English settlers in 1606–07 to Jamestown. In 1607 Gosnold was appointed by the king to the council of the colony. After several months in James-town he died of swamp fever.

GOSPEL, term applied to the spoken doc-trine of Jesus of Nazareth, to any of the first four books of the New Testament which contain the doctrine, and to readings from these New Testament books during divine service.

The first three Gospels, those of St. Mat-thew, St. Mark, and St. Luke, are called the Synoptic Gospels because they contain a great deal of similar narration which can be brought together to form a single synopsis. They re-semble one another in both language and con-tent. They give the same general outline of the life of Jesus, narrate almost the same inci-dents, and are uniformly silent on many points. They often agree in the order of narra-tion of events, even when the events them-selves are loosely connected. In many in-stances, they use identical phrasing.

Three major hypothetical explanations have been proposed to explain the origin of the Synoptic Gospels. The *successive dependence theory* is based on the assumption that one of the three Gospels was the basis for the second, and that either or both of the first two were used as bases for the third. Under this theory, the earliest Gospel would prob-ably be either St. Matthew or St. Mark. The Gospel of St. Luke is part of a larger work by St. Luke, comprising the Gospel according to St. Luke, and the Acts of the Apostles, and so is unlikely to have preceded either of the first two Gospels. The *documentary theory* assumes that all three Gospels were written from one or more pre-existing sources. The two documents most often proposed as sources are a collection of the sayings of Jesus known as the *Logia* of Matthew (usually designated "Q"), and a narrative of the ministry of Jesus which is practically, if not completely, iden-tical with the Gospel of St. Mark. The *oral theory* assumes that all three Gospels made use of a common oral tradition which had become fixed through usage. The conclusions of most modern New Testament critics agree most closely with the documentary theory. These critics believe, however, that the two primary sources were supplemented by sources peculiar to each writer, and that the latest of the three writers may have used the earlier of the Synoptic Gospels as sources.

The Gospel of St. John is different, in many respects, from the first three Gospels. The narrative covers many incidents not included in the Synoptics, and omits many others which are included. In the discourses of Jesus the differences are even more radical. Synoptic Gospel discourses are simple talks on the level of everyday speech; those in St. John are far more abstruse. The Synoptics present most illustrative discussion in the form of parable; St. John presents such discussion in allegorical form. Finally, the subjects discussed in the Synoptics are practical, everyday religious and ethical problems; the subject of discourse in St. John is the divinity of Jesus. Modern theologians of all Christian sects agree that St. John was written later than any of the Synoptic Gospels.

In the liturgical sense, the term Gospel is applied to the short selections from the four Gospels which are read or sung, in the Catholic mass and the Anglican communion service, between the Epistle and the Creed. In the early centuries of the Christian era, Gospel reading was continuous; the reading began at the point in the Gospel at which it had been interrupted in the previous service. The Gos-pel selection now used for the purpose is determined, for each day, by the order of worship set forth in the Missal (q.v.). The "Last Gospel", which concludes the modern Roman Catholic Mass, is usually the first fourteen verses of the Gospel of St. John.

GOSPORT, a seaport and municipal bor-ough of England, in Southampton, Hamp-shire, situated on a peninsula 86 m. by rail s.w. of London, and opposite Portsmouth, with which it is connected by a bridge. It is the site of a naval depot and a royal victual-ing yard. Gosport was a borough as early as 1462, and in the 16th century it was noted as a fishing center. During the Napoleonic Wars and the American Revolution and War of 1812, Gosport was of considerable importance as a supply station. In 1894 it became an urban district and in 1922 it was incorporated. Pop. (1951 est.) 58,246.

GOSSAERT, JAN. See MABUSE, JAN.

GOSSART, JENNI. See MABUSE, JAN.

GOSSE, SIR EDMUND WILLIAM (1849–1928), English man of letters, born in Lon-don, and educated privately. He joined the British Museum as assistant librarian in 1867. In 1875 he became translator to the Board of Trade and, in 1904, librarian to the House of Lords. His most important work was the auto-biographical *Father and Son,* published anonymously in 1907, in which he described his relationship with his father, the naturalist Philip Henry Gosse.

Gosse was the first to introduce many Scandinavian authors to the English-speaking world. He was known for his translations of

American-Swedish News Exchange

A canal in the city of Göteborg, Sweden

the works of the Norwegian dramatist Henrik Ibsen, of whom he also wrote a biography (1907). He was knighted in 1925, and received several honorary degrees from British and European universities. A collected edition of his poems appeared in 1911. He was the author of numerous volumes of literary criticism and biography, including *Seventeenth Century Studies* (1883), *Life of William Congreve* (1888), *A History of Eighteenth Century Literature* (1889), *The Jacobean Poets* (1894), *Life and Letters of Dr. John Donne, Dean of St. Paul's* (1899), *Jeremy Taylor* (1904), *Life of Sir Thomas Browne* (1905), and *Life of Algernon Charles Swinburne* (1917). He recorded his memories of the prominent English literary figures of his time in several autobiographical works.

GOSSON, STEPHEN (1554–1624), English clergyman and writer, born probably at Canterbury, and educated at Corpus Christi College, Oxford University. He is best known for his *Schoole of Abuse, Containing a Pleasaunt Invective against Poets, Pipers, Plaiers, Jesters and such like Caterpillers of a Commonwelth* (1579), a violent attack on the theater and on poetry. This work, which contained an unauthorized dedication to Sir Philip Sidney, was answered by the latter in his *Apologie for Poetrie* (written about 1581; published 1595). Gosson became rector at Great Wigborough, Essex, in 1591, and at St. Botolph's, Bishopgate, in 1600.

GOSSYPIUM. See COTTON.

GÖTA, a river and canal of Sweden. The river (Swed. *Götaälv*) is 50 m. long and drains Lake Väner into the Kattegat at Göteborg. It is navigable throughout its entire length, although it contains a number of falls and rapids. Navigation has been made possible past the famous falls of Trollhättan by a series of locks. The Göta canal, of which the river forms a part, was constructed between 1810 and 1832, and leads from Lake Väner through a succession of lakes, rivers, and canals to Stockholm. It contains 58 locks, 20 of which raise it to its extreme height of 300 ft. between lakes Väner and Vätter, and extends a total distance of about 360 m. from Göteborg to Stockholm.

GOTAMA. See GAUTAMA, family; BUDDHA.

GÖTEBORG or **GOTHENBURG**, city, port, and capital of the county of Göteborg and Bohus, Sweden, located on the Göta R., 285 m. by rail s.w. of Stockholm. The city was founded in 1619 by King Gustavus Adolphus.

It is noted for the Göteborg System, a plan of municipal licensing of liquor sales under which profits are used for public projects. The city is connected with the interior of the country by the Göta Canal, opened in 1832. Göteborg is the principal port of Sweden. Exports include iron, steel, zinc, manganese, lumber, matches, oats, fish, and pork. Imports are chiefly sugar, coffee, grain, cotton and cotton goods, and coal. The industries of Göteborg include sawmilling, flour milling, brewing, distilling, cabinetmaking, and the processing of textiles, leather, and tobacco. The city is the site of a large university and library. The Gustavii Domkyrka, the city's cathedral, was built in 1633. Pop. (1953 est.) 363,000.

GOTHA. See Saxe-Coburg-Gotha.

GOTHA, town of Thuringia, East Germany, on the Leine Canal, 17 m. by rail s.w. of Erfurt. It belonged to the landgraves of Thuringia in the 12th century. In 1440 it passed to the electors of Saxony. In 1485, during the partition of the Saxon dominions, it came into the possession of the Ernestine line of the dukes of Gotha, and in 1640 became the capital of the duchy of Gotha. The industries of the town include the manufacture of machinery, mechanical instruments, musical instruments, rubber goods, shoes, furniture, porcelain, and toys. After World War II, Gotha was assigned to the Soviet Zone of Occupation. Pop. (1946) 57,639.

GOTHAM, a village of Nottinghamshire, England, situated 7 miles s.w. of the city of Nottingham. It is traditionally the home of the "Wise Men of Gotham", in satirical allusion to the reputation for foolishness acquired by the early inhabitants. The legend relates that in the beginning of the 13th century King John intended building a castle at Gotham but the villagers, averse to the expense of maintaining royalty, feigned to be fools and engaged in idiotic pursuits in order to divert him from his purpose. The ruse succeeded and King John changed his plans, whereupon the Gothamites are supposed to have said, "We ween there are more fools pass through Gotham than remain in it." Many tales of the follies of the Gothamites have been collected. One of the earliest collections is *The Merry Tales of the Mad Men of Gotham,* compiled about 1568. The name Gotham is popularly applied to New York City, which received the name for the first time in *Salmagundi,* a series of humorous essays published by the American authors Washington Irving, William Irving, and James Kirke Paulding.

GOTHARD. See Saint Gotthard.

GOTHENBURG. See Göteborg.

GOTHIC ARCHITECTURE, the term used to describe the architecture which, developing from the Romanesque, spread throughout Europe during the 12th and 13th centuries; for derivation of the term "Gothic", and allied information, see Gothic Art. The features which serve to distinguish the Gothic style are the buttress (q.v.) and the flying buttress, the pointed arch, and the ribbed vault (q.v.). Minor features are the use of tracery to divide large windows, to make easier the glazing of the panes; the purely decorative use of forms which were originally structural; and a frequent tendency to employ vertical rather than horizontal lines. Although most of these features had been separately employed earlier, the anonymous architect of St. Denis Abbey, near Paris, begun in 1140, was the first man to make use of them together, and was consequently the inventor of the Gothic style. In this building, for the first time, the masses of masonry were enlivened by the use of shafts, and ribbed vaults were employed to give an effect of decorative lightness. With the great communal cathedral-building movement which took place in France at this time, the building of St. Denis Abbey was soon followed by construction of the cathedral of Notre Dame in Paris and the cathedrals at Chartres, Reims, Amiens, and Beauvais; see Cathedral; French Art and Architecture.

The works of the Romanesque architects had been decorated with frescoes and other wall paintings, but the development of the technique of stained glass led to the use of larger and wider windows, until the whole of the clerestory became one glowing window, divided by the lightest of tracery. The Greek architects, and their Roman and Romanesque successors, striving for an ideal in technical engineering, had attempted to give an impression of a load carried successfully and strongly. The Gothic builders, however, influenced by the religious fervor which pervaded medieval thought, attempted to convey an upward drive, symbolic of a reaching up to God.

From France, Gothic spread across Europe. One of the first countries to adopt the style was England, where the Cistercian monastic houses adopted the pointed arch and the French architect William of Sens exploited the new style in the choir of Canterbury cathedral. Built between 1175 and 1178, Canterbury cathedral was, like St. Denis, an innovation in architecture, though in certain

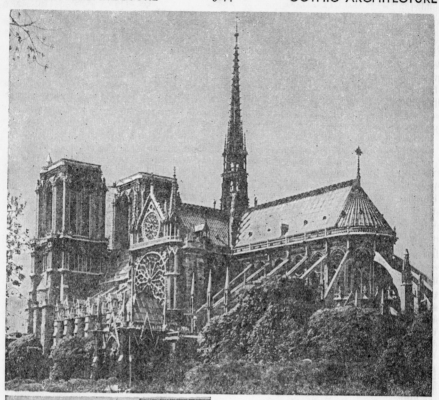

GOTHIC ARCHITECTURE IN FRANCE

Above: Notre Dame cathedral in Paris, built at the beginning of the Gothic movement in French architecture. Left: Cross section and part of side elevation of Reims cathedral, showing typical Gothic features, such as flying and pinnacled buttresses, large windows, intricate tracery, and pointed arches.

respects it derived from the cathedral at Sens, the architect's home town. A curiosity of the English style of early Gothic is the duplication of the transepts, which in France were almost always single. Whereas Canterbury cathedral cannot be called absolutely English in style, the cathedrals that were built shortly afterward, such as those at Lincoln and Wells, are genuine examples of a national expression. A comparison of the cathedral at Lincoln with that at Amiens makes the difference obvious; the bays in the English cathedral are wide, whereas those in the French are narrow; the arches in the triforium are low, almost round, in comparison with the French model; and the vault at Lincoln gives the highly imaginative impression of a series of stars set along the roof, derived from the transverse ribs which separate bay from bay and the rib which runs along the center of the vault, whereas the French cathedral, omitting the central rib, shows only a logical and strictly utilitarian division of bay from bay. The style known as Early English is distinguished by the great length of the nave and the square east end of the cathedral, the latter being rounded in almost every French example in accordance with the plan of Romanesque architecture. Toward the middle of the 13th century, ornament became an important part of English Gothic architecture, the tracery becoming more and more elaborate, as in the great window of the church of St. Mary, at Tilty in Essex, where the long, slender uprights carry a great weight of stone decoration which, at the

Interior of the nave of Lincoln cathedral, an example of the Gothic style in England

same time, conveys an impression of lightness (see DECORATED STYLE).

Although the Gothic style is usually associated only with religious architecture, a Gothic symmetry appears in purely secular buildings, such as Harlech Castle in Wales, the Tower of London, and the Palais de Justice, in Rouen, France.

Toward the end of the 13th century, late French Gothic, known as flamboyant (q.v.), became static, repeating and elaborating the motifs which had been invented by the earliest architects. In England, however, the style progressed, reaching heights of intricate beauty which the Continental syles never achieved. In Germany, Gothic was an imported style which showed none of the transitional features developed in France and England. The national character emerged early, with an exaggeration of vertical lines, such as those in the choir at Erfurt cathedral, and the use of high windows, shown in the cathedral of St. Stephen at Vienna. Another German peculiarity was the use of brick, instead of stone, with consequent variations in style dictated by the material, as in the Marienkirche at Danzig.

In the middle of the 14th century, the English architects, few of whose names have survived, introduced the modification known as perpendicular (q.v.), in which the ornament, a characteristic of the middle Gothic period, was reduced and flattened. The fan vault was employed also, reaching its supreme expression in the chapel at King's College, Cambridge University, and the chapel of King Henry VII at Westminster Abbey, London. The perpendicular style was used not only in cathedrals but also in parish churches, as in the church of St. Peter and St. Paul at Lavenham in Suffolk, which had a square tower characteristic of the use of the rectangle as a decorative form. Another remarkable feature of the period was the use of freestone and flint, which gave a many-colored effect later copied by the 19th-century architects of the "Gothic Revival" in their employment of encaustic brick and glazed tile.

Late Gothic in Germany followed the example of earlier English churches in its use of the starlike vaulting and columns without capitals. German craftsmen were responsible for the use of Gothic in Spain, where the star vault was received as a variation of the Mohammedan dome, which was ribbed to show stars of different kinds. One of the widest single vaults in medieval Europe was built in Spain, in the nave of the Gerona cathedral, designed by Guillermo Boffiy in 1417; the nave is 73 feet wide, with the weight of the vaulting carried by buttresses inside the building.

In Portugal, at the start of the 16th century, Gothic developed an extravagance of ornament, as in the Chapter House at Tomar, with forms derived from marine life and tropical plants clustered around the windows and the columns; Portuguese Gothic was probably the first European architecture to be influenced by the Far East.

In Flanders and the Netherlands, Gothic was a combination of French and German styles and, like the latter, showed no transitional phase. Italian architects made use of certain Gothic features, the pointed arch and the pinnacle, but employed them merely as decoration upon Romanesque buildings. With the spread of the Renaissance from Italy, and the consequent use of classical models, Gothic declined and did not reappear until the 19th century, when, under the influence of Augustus Welby Pugin (q.v.), a revival was started in England and spread across Europe. This revival made use of the industrial materials of the time, such as iron and glazed earthenware, and can be seen at its most extravagant in buildings such as St. Pancras Station in London; in the United States the Gothic revival influenced the construction of churches, college and university buildings, and the decorative details of office buildings such as the Woolworth Building in New York City.

GOTHIC ART, the term applied to the architecture, sculpture, painting and allied arts, and decorative arts of Europe from the 12th to the 15th century. The art of this period was derisively termed "Gothic" by Italian artists and critics of the Renaissance, who used the term as synonymous with "barbaric" and not in association with any tribe or nation of Goths (q.v.) or Germans. The use of the term "Gothic" established the long-held erroneous belief that the European arts of the 12th to 15th century originated in Germany, whereas in truth Gothic art originated in France and spread from France throughout Europe.

Since by far the most important art of the period was architecture, to which both sculpture and painting were adjuncts, the subject of Gothic architecture has been treated in a separate article.

Gothic Sculpture, French. The sculpture of this period existed only as part of an archi-

GOTHIC ART IN FRANCE

*Above: Four of a series of zodiacal signs
in relief on a façade of Amiens cathedral.
Right: A plaster reproduction of sculptured
figures on transept of Chartres cathedral.*

tectural structure, usually a church. The earliest examples of Gothic sculpture, dating from the 12th century and found in the Île de France where Gothic architecture originated, were the statues decorating the lower portions of the portals of various churches. The best period of Gothic sculpture in France was the 13th century, during which the earlier stiff and unlifelike statues gave way to figures more natural in aspect and also more esthetically satisfying. The use of statues to decorate buildings rapidly increased, and often hundreds or even thousands of statues adorned the exterior of a church. They were placed mainly in and about the portals, both front and side, and, in order to accommodate the great number of statues desired, a porch was sometimes added to the doorway; these porches were lined with rows of statues, and the tympanums of the porches were filled with reliefs. The subjects represented in statues and reliefs were of two general types: ecclesiastical and Biblical, including figures of saints and martyrs, or depicting tales from either the Old or New Testament, such as "The Creation"; or allegorical, depicting such concepts as "The Fall of Man", or figures representing the virtues and vices, and the various trades and industries of the time. The statuary decorating the

projecting waterspouts, or gargoyles (q.v.), of Gothic buildings included representations of angels, demons, witches, and animals. Among the French churches noted for 13th-century sculpture are the cathedrals of Notre Dame, in Paris, and of Chartres, Reims, Amiens, and Laon. French Gothic sculpture of this century is characterized by realism, especially in the use of drapery; by expert adaptation of the sculptural form to fit the architectural design; and by dignity and deep religious feeling. Much of the dignity of French Gothic sculpture vanished in the late 13th and in the 14th century, when the aim of the sculptor became the close imitation of life and the production of humorous effects rather than the creation of forms satisfying from both the esthetic and the religious point of view. A notable collection of French Gothic sculpture is contained in "The Cloisters", New

GOTHIC ART IN FRANCE

Above: Decorative figures flanking the door of Strasbourg cathedral. Left: Carvings on the roof of Notre Dame cathedral, Paris. In the background appears the central spire.

York City, a branch of the Metropolitan Museum of Art.

German. The 13th century was the great age of Gothic sculpture in Germany. Contemporary German churches were built in the Romanesque style (see GERMAN ART AND ARCHITECTURE); because the exterior of Romanesque churches, characterized by rounded arches and unbroken walls, was not well adapted to sculptural decoration, the sculpture was confined mainly to the interiors of the churches, between the arches, on the walls of the choir, and also on the altar and pulpit. The principal schools of German Gothic sculpture, all showing the influence of contemporary French sculpture, were the South Saxon school, the Franconian school, and the Rhenish school. Important works of the South Saxon school are the reliefs of the pulpit in the church of Wechselburg, the sculptures of the portal of the cathedral of Freiburg entitled "Revelation of the Kingdom of God to

Man by Christ"; and the tomb of Henry the Lion, Duke of Saxony and Bavaria, and his wife, in the cathedral of Brunswick. The school reached its culmination in the latter part of the 13th century in the simple, realistic, and dignified statues of the benefactors of the church in the cathedral of Naumburg. The best examples of the Franconian school are the statues of the late 13th century in the cathedral of Bamberg, of which the best known is "Ancient Sibyl". Notable examples of the Rhenish school, which was particularly influenced by French sculpture, are in the church of the Virgin, Trier, and in the cathedrals of Freiburg and Strasbourg. In the 15th century, throughout Germany, sculptures in wood largely replaced those in stone, with a change of style toward the mannered and overrefined. The two principal schools of wood sculpture were the Franconian, with Nuremberg as its center, and the Swabian, which centered at Ulm. The principal artists of the Franconian school were Michel Wohlgemuth and Veit Stoss. The chief master of the Swabian school was Jörg Syrlin, whose principal work (1469–74) is the choir stalls in the cathedral of Ulm.

Italian. Sculpture in 13th-century Italy centered at Pisa. The earliest great sculptor

of the Pisan school, Nicola Pisano, was influenced by the sculpture of antiquity; his work marked the culmination of Romanesque sculpture in Italy and immediately preceded the Gothic movement. The work of his son Giovanni, who is regarded as the founder of Gothic sculpture in Italy, was marked by the naturalism and dramatic force characteristic of the Gothic sculpture of France and Germany. The Gothic movement in Italian sculpture reached its culmination in the 14th century, in the work of Andrea Pisano, unrelated to the two above-mentioned sculptors. Andrea Pisano was active chiefly in Florence. He is particularly noted for his sculptures for the façade of the cathedral of Orvieto, and for the reliefs, representing Christian virtues and scenes from the life of St. John the Baptist, on the bronze doors of the baptistery of

the cathedral of Florence. The Florentine school of sculpture inaugurated by Andrea Pisano was carried on after his time by Andrea Orcagna, who is particularly distinguished for the tabernacle in the church of Or San Michele, Florence. Other centers of sculptural activity in Italy, in the 13th and 14th centuries, were Siena and Verona. The latter city was the center of the Lombard school, which was noted chiefly for its sepulchral monuments. A Roman school (12th century) and a South Italian school (early 13th century) were not properly schools of Gothic sculpture, since they based their work on the sculpture of ancient Greece.

Flemish and Burgundian, English, and Spanish. In the 14th century, the center of sculptural activity in Western Europe shifted from France to Flanders and northern Burgundy. The center for sculpture in Burgundy was Dijon, where the art was patronized by the dukes of Burgundy. The principal sculptor of Dijon was the Dutch sculptor Claus Sluter, whose masterpiece (1404–11) was the tomb of Philip the Bold, Duke of Burgundy. English Gothic architecture (see GOTHIC ARCHITECTURE) was not well adapted to sculptural ornament. Few English churches dating from Gothic times are decorated with sculptures; an exception is the Cathedral of Wells, the façade of which contains a number of statues. The characteristic English sculptural works of the period are the sepulchral monuments, engraved or sculptured plaques of brass, the subjects of which are treated with great realism. In northern Spain, the sculpture of the Gothic period was at first greatly influenced by French Gothic sculpture; the numerous statues decorating the façade of the cathedral of Santiago de Compostela are considered as beautiful as those decorating most French cathedrals. In the 15th century in Spain the influence of contemporary German sculpture was added to that of the French.

Painting and Allied Arts. See FRENCH ART AND ARCHITECTURE; FLORENTINE SCHOOL; GERMAN ART AND ARCHITECTURE; SIENESE SCHOOL; GLASS, PAINTED AND STAINED; ILLUMINATED MANUSCRIPTS.

Decorative Arts. The Gothic was a period of importance in the decorative arts, which were employed on articles both for ecclesiastical and for lay use; see such subjects as COSTUME; ENAMEL; FURNITURE; INTERIOR DECORATION; IVORY CARVING; JEWELRY; TAPESTRY. For detailed treatment of ecclesiastical objects in particular, see such subjects as COSTUME, ECCLESIASTICAL; CRUCIFIX.

GOTHIC LANGUAGE, a dead language constituting the eastern branch of the Teutonic subfamily of Indo-European languages. Gothic was spoken by the Ostrogoths of ancient Germany; it was replaced by other Germanic tongues in the period between the 7th and the 9th century A.D. It is older than any other Germanic language excepting, possibly, several of the Norse dialects. As late as the 16th century, Gothic words (Crimean Gothic) were used in the Black Sea region.

The main body of present-day knowledge of the Gothic language stems from a 4th-century Moesian manuscript, known as the Gothic version of the Bible (q.v.), written by the Gothic bishop Ulfilas, and considered the earliest work of German literature. The few other Gothic records which are available include several Italian manuscripts, dating from the time of Gothic rule; a 10th-century Austrian manuscript, found in Salzburg, which contains the Gothic alphabet; and several inscribed spearheads and neck chains.

The Gothic alphabet, which also was devised by Ulfilas, consists of modified Greek capital letters (uncial letters) and of several letters taken from the Norse runic alphabet. Present-day German print uses a modification of the Gothic alphabet. Many words in the Gothic language, derived from Sanskrit, Latin, and Greek, show a peculiar but consistent shifting from the parent languages in the pronunciation of consonants, which has been carried over into the Low Germanic and English languages of today; see GRIMM'S LAW. See also GOTHS; INDO-EUROPEAN LANGUAGES.

GOTHIC ROMANCE, a type of novel which predominated in English fiction in the last third of the 18th century and the first two decades of the 19th, and the setting for which was usually a ruined Gothic castle or abbey. The Gothic romance emphasized mystery and horror and made particular use of the elements of the Gothic castle or abbey which lent themselves to producing these effects, such as ghost-haunted wings, underground passages, and secret stairways. The principal writers of the Gothic romance were Horace Walpole, author of *The Castle of Otranto* (1764); Clara Reeve (*The Champion of Virtue,* 1777); Ann Radcliffe (*The Mysteries of Udolpho,* 1794); Matthew Gregory Lewis (*Ambrosio, or the Monk,* 1796); Charles Robert Maturin (*The Fatal Revenge,* 1807), and Mary Wollstonecraft Shelley (*Frankenstein,* 1818). The Gothic romance was one phase of the Romantic movement in English literature (see ENGLISH LITERATURE:

The Eighteenth Century), and was also the forerunner of the modern mystery novel. The term "Gothic" is used to designate narrative prose or poetry of which the principal elements are violence, horror, and the supernatural. Among well-known literary works containing "Gothic" elements are the novels *The Bride of Lammermoor* (1818) by Sir Walter Scott; *Wuthering Heights* (1848) by Emily Brontë; and *Fanny by Gaslight* (1940) by the English writer Michael Sadleir (1888–), which was made into the American motion picture *Gaslight* (1944).

GOTHIC VERSION OF THE BIBLE, a translation of the Bible done by Ulfilas (q.v.). While serving as a missionary among the Goths of Moesia during the 4th century, Ulfilas translated the Bible into Gothic, using an alphabet composed of Greek uncial letters supplemented by Gothic runic letters; see GOTHIC LANGUAGE. The version was made from a Greek text obtained in Constantinople. A few fragments of this Bible, all from the Old Testament, still exist. The fragments constitute the earliest written Germanic language in existence.

GOTHS, an ancient Teutonic people who, according to the earliest historical accounts, inhabited a region on the Baltic Sea, between the Elbe and Vistula rivers. The origin of the tribe has never been positively ascertained; traditionally, the Goths came from Sweden, according to the Gothic historian Jordanes, who wrote a history of his people in 551. Pytheas, a Greek geographer of the 4th century B.C., described the tribe as dwelling on the Baltic. A 1st-century A.D. account, in *Germania,* by the Roman historian Tacitus, placed the tribe farther south, in the basin of the Vistula. Tacitus called them "Teutons Gothones", and stated that they possessed great independence of spirit.

By the 3rd century A.D. the Goths had migrated as far south as the region of the lower Danube, around the Black Sea. As early as the reign of the Emperor Alexander Severus (222–35 A.D.), the Goths constituted a formidable menace to outlying provinces of the Roman Empire. Gothic armies and fleets ravaged Thrace, Dacia, and cities in Asia Minor and along the coast of the Ægean Sea. They captured and plundered Athens in 262, and Italy itself was threatened. For about a century thereafter, wars between the Roman emperors and Gothic kings devastated the Balkan territory and the northeastern Mediterranean. Other tribes joined the Goths and, in the second half of the 4th century, under the great

king Ermanaric, a kingdom was established which extended from the Baltic Sea to the Black Sea.

About 370, dissensions among themselves led the Goths to divide into two separate groups, each with its own kingdom. The Ostrogoths (Low Lat. *Ostrogothæ,* from *Austrogoti,* "the splendid Goths") were the eastern tribe, inhabiting a kingdom on the shores of the Black Sea. The Visigoths (Low Lat. *Visigothi,* "the good or noble Goths") were the western Goths, with a kingdom extending from the Dniester R. to the Danube.

Visigoths. In 376 the Visigoths, threatened by the Hun invasion, sought the protection of the Roman Emperor Valens, and were given permission to migrate to Moesia (modern Bulgaria and southeastern Yugoslavia). Many Visigoths enlisted in the Roman army but a dispute began over the mistreatment of the Goths by Roman officers. The Goths revolted and the resulting war was climaxed by a decisive battle in 378, near Adrianople, in which the emperor Valens was killed. The victorious Goths then threatened Constantinople, but they were not able to capture it. Theodosius, who succeeded Valens, made peace with the Teuton migrants and incorporated the Gothic army into the Roman forces; from that time on, the Visigoths were an important influence in the Roman Empire. Many who had settled in Moesia became farmers, and were known as Moeso-Goths. For the most part, moreover, the Goths became Christians, adopting the Arian form of belief (see ARIUS).

Upon the death of Theodosius in 395, and the subsequent partition of the Empire between his two sons, Honorius and Arcadius, the Visigoths renounced their allegiance to Rome. They chose Alaric (q.v.) as their king and again became an independent people. In 395–96 Alaric invaded Greece, but was persuaded to retreat by an appointment as prefect of Illyricum. At the beginning of the 5th century, the Visigoth king invaded Italy and, in 410, captured and pillaged the city of Rome. He was preparing to attack Sicily when he died; he was succeeded by Ataulphus, who had married Galla Placidia, half sister of the emperor Honorius. The new king withdrew from Italy and, about 412, led the Visigoths across the Pyrenees into Spain, where he was assassinated.

Under the next king, Wallia, the realm of the Visigoths was extended over a great part of Spain and southern Gaul, with Toulouse as the capital of the new kingdom. Wallia was succeeded by the reputed son of Alaric, Theodoric I, who lost his life fighting, as an ally of Rome, against the Huns (q.v.) at Châlons in 451. The most notable of the Spanish Visigoth kings was Euric; during his reign (466–84) the kingdom of Toulouse came to include almost all of Spain and the greater part of Gaul west of the Rhone R. and south of the Loire. Euric introduced many of the aspects of Roman civilization into the kingdom of Toulouse, and drew up a code of law combining Roman and German elements. The kingdom was, however, continually beset by both internal and external difficulties. The kingship was, nominally, elective, and the powerful Visigothic nobles stood against attempts to found a hereditary royal house. Externally, the Byzantine or Eastern Roman Empire, the Franks, and the increasing forces of Islam menaced the Visigothic lands. In order to instill greater loyalty in his rebellious Roman and Catholic subjects, Alaric II in 506 introduced the collection of laws known as the Breviary of Alaric (q.v.). A year later, Clovis was victorious over the Visigoths at the battle of Vouillé, and most of Provence was separated from the Gothic lands. From about that time, the Visigothic kingdom was confined almost entirely to Spain. Despite the attempts of a long line of Gothic kings to hold the kingdom together, the power of the Visigoths steadily declined. The last king, Roderic (q.v.), was defeated, and probably killed, by the Moslems in the battle of Río Barbute in 711. By 713, Spain was a part of Islam and the Visigothic power was at an end. See SPAIN: *History*.

Ostrogoths. When the Hunnish invaders swept into Europe about 370 A.D., many of the Ostrogoths were conquered and compelled to aid their conquerors; they joined Attila in his expedition against Gaul in 451 and fell by thousands under the swords of their kinsmen, the Visigoths, at the battle of Chalôns. When the Huns were finally forced back, the Ostrogoths again became independent. With the permission of Rome, they settled in Pannonia (modern western Hungary, northern Yugoslavia, and eastern Austria), where they were joined by other Ostrogoths who had taken refuge within the Roman Empire at the coming of the Asiatics. In 476, Theodoric (q.v.), the greatest of the Ostrogoth kings, succeeded to the throne. After his accession, he declared war on Zeno, emperor of the Eastern Roman Empire, and, after successes in battle, was granted some of the richest Roman provinces. Later, he became an ally of Zeno and in 488, with the consent and advice of the emperor,

planned a great expedition against Odoacer, the king of Italy, who had dethroned Romulus Augustus, last of the Western emperors, in 476. Theodoric won a great victory in 493, slew Odoacer himself, and became the ruler of Italy. The Ostrogoth ruler held the power, though not the title, of the Western Roman emperors; a Roman consul was given nominal authority, and the two peoples lived together amicably, with Roman culture greatly influencing the Teutons. Theodoric also ruled the Visigoths from 507 to 526, as regent during the minority of the Visigoth king Amalaric, son of Alaric II.

A ruler of the stature of Theodoric was necessary to preserve the unity of Romans and Goths. Upon the king's death in 526, disruption in Italy became so violent that the Eastern Roman emperor Justinian, in 535, declared war on Italy and sent the general Belisarius (q.v.) to reconquer the country. The wars of the Byzantines against the Ostrogoths, which lasted until 555, broke the Gothic power. The Ostrogoth kingdom ceased to be a separate entity, the throne of Italy being filled by the exarchs (Byzantine governors) of Ravenna.

The Ostrogoths themselves gradually became absorbed into other tribes, such as the Alani, Vandals, Burgundians, and Franks, who had from time to time established themselves in the dominions of the old Roman Empire. See GOTHIC LANGUAGE; ULFILAS.

GOTLAND or **GOTTLAND,** the largest island in the Baltic Sea, located about 44 m. off the E. coast of Sweden, and forming, together with the adjacent islets of Fårö, Karlsöe, and Gotska Sandö, the Swedish county of Gotland. The greatest length of the island, from N. to S., is about 80 m., and its maximum width is about 35 m. The surface is level, the soil fertile. A great part of the surface is forested, the arable land constituting about a fifth of the total area. Sugar beets, rye, barley, wheat, and oats are the principal crops of the island. The important industries are fishing, sugar refining, and the manufacture of lime for cement. Visby (pop. in 1950, 14,770), located on the w. coast, is the most important seaport of the island and capital of the county. The island was in the possession of Sweden as early as the 9th century. In the Middle Ages Visby was an important member of the Hanseatic League. The island was taken several times by Denmark. It came again into the possession of Sweden in 1645.

Area of county, 1225 sq.m.; pop. (1952 est.) 58,508.

GOTTFRIED VON STRASSBURG, German poet of the thirteenth century. Little is known of his life, except that he was a contemporary of the German poets Hartmann von Aue, Wolfram von Eschenbach (qq.v.), and Walther von der Vogelweide (1170?–1230?). The only work that can be attributed to Gottfried with certainty is the Middle High German epic *Tristan und Isolde* (1210); this work places him among the great German poets of the Middle Ages. The legend of Tristan had been used by French trouvères of the early twelfth century. Gottfried's *Tristan und Isolde,* which was based on the version of a French trouvère, Thomas, gave the story the form in which it was used many times by later poets and by Richard Wagner in his opera, *Tristan und Isolde.* Gottfried's poem is particularly notable for fluency and artistry of style and for psychological insight into the characters. The poem was unfinished at Gottfried's death, and two minor poets of his time made attempts to finish it.

GOTTHARD, SAINT. See SAINT GOTTHARD.

GOTTHELF, JEREMIAS. See BITZIUS, ALBERT.

GÖTTINGEN, UNIVERSITY OF, an institution of higher education, established at Göttingen, Germany, by Georg August, Elector of Hanover, later King George II of England. After the opening of the university in 1737, it became a center of academic and literary activity, particularly during the *Sturm und Drang* movement at the close of the 18th century (see GERMAN LITERATURE). It lost popularity for a time after the expulsion, in 1837, of seven professors, including the brothers Jacob and Wilhelm Grimm (qq.v.), Georg Ewald, and Georg Gottfried Gervinus, for protesting King Ernest Augustus' action in revoking the liberal constitution granted four years earlier. Several of the professors returned to the university after the revolution of 1848 and the institution regained its former academic reputation. It was, in the 19th and the early part of the 20th century, especially noted for its courses in philology, history, mathematics, and law. The library, containing more than 600,000 volumes, has one of the finest collections of modern German literature, and well over 6000 ancient and medieval manuscripts.

GOTTSCHALK, LOUIS MOREAU (1829–69), American pianist and composer, born in New Orleans, La. He received a musical education in Paris and made several professional tours as a pianist in Europe. In 1853 he returned to the United States and gave his first concert in New York City in the same year. Subsequently he toured in the United States and Latin America. Among his hundred or more compositions are *Bamboula, Banannier, Bango,* and other works reflecting the color of Negro and Creole folk songs.

GOUACHE, a medium for pictorial painting consisting of a gum or water tempera which, when applied to paper, is opaque. Light is obtained by the addition of white pigment, rather than by reliance upon the transparency of the medium, as in water color. The word is also used to describe a painting in the medium.

GOUCHER COLLEGE, a private college for women in Baltimore, Maryland, founded by the Methodist Episcopal Church. It was opened, under the name of the Woman's College of Baltimore, in 1888, but its name was changed to the present one in 1910 in honor of Rev. Dr. John F. Goucher. Goucher gives courses in the liberal arts and awards a bachelor's degree. In a recent year Goucher had a faculty of about 60 and a student body of about 625.

GOUDA, a town in the province of South Holland, the Netherlands, located at the confluence of the Gouw and Ijssel rivers, 12½ m. by rail N.E. of Rotterdam. Its late-Gothic town hall, 15th-century church of St. John, and 17th-century weighhouse are of architectural interest. The Groote Markt, the market square of the town, is the largest in the country. The chief industries in Gouda are the manufacture of brick, pottery, clay pipes, candles, cigars, and Gouda cheese. Pop. (1953 est.) 39,811.

GOUDSMIT, SAMUEL ABRAHAM (1902–), Dutch-American physicist, born at The Hague, Netherlands, and educated at the universities of Leiden and Amsterdam. He emigrated to the United States in 1927, and taught physics at the University of Michigan, becoming a professor in 1932. He did work at the radiation laboratory at the Massachusetts Institute of Technology from 1942 to 1944. In 1944 and 1945 he was in charge of a scientific intelligence mission in Europe, called ALSOS, under the War Department, which investigated German progress in the field of atomic energy. Goudsmit joined the faculty of Northwestern University in 1946. In 1948 he became senior physicist at Brookhaven National Laboratory, and after 1950 served also as chairman of Brookhaven's physics department. At the age of 23 Goudsmit made an outstanding contribution to theoretical physics; together with his fellow student George Eugene Uhlenbeck (q.v.), he discovered (1925) the phenomenon of electron spin (see SPIN). Goudsmit is the author of *The Structure of Line Spectra* (with L. Pauling, 1930), *Atomic Energy States* (with R. F. Bacher, 1932), and *ALSOS* (1948), an account of the scientific mission in Europe.

GOUIN, FÉLIX (1884–   ), French lawyer and Socialist politician, born at Pepyin, Bouches-du-Rhône, and educated at the Law Faculty, Aix-en-Provence. He was in active military service during World War I. In 1924 he became deputy and mayor of Istres, and in that same year became a member of the national chamber of deputies. At the treason trials held at Riom by the Vichy government of France after French capitulation to the Nazis, Gouin was defense attorney for Léon Blum (q.v.). In London, 1942, he joined the French National Committee led by General Charles de Gaulle (q.v.). In 1943–44 he headed the French Parliament Group in London. He served for a time in 1944 as president of the consultative assembly at Algiers; after the liberation of France in Sept., 1944, Gouin held the same office, in Paris, until 1946. In January, 1946, Gouin was elected by the constituent assembly premier and minister of defense, but resigned in June of that year, when the new constitution, drafted during his premiership, was rejected. On the subsequent

French Embassy, Information Division

Félix Gouin

formation of a new cabinet under Georges Bidault (q.v.), Gouin was made vice-premier **without portfolio.** He became minister of the four-year economic plan in the Léon Blum cabinet in December, 1946. When the government of the Fourth Republic was formally established in 1947, Gouin was appointed minister of state in the cabinet of Paul Ramadier (q.v.).

GOUIN, SIR LOMER (1861–1929), Canadian lawyer and statesman, born at Grondines, Quebec, and educated at Laval and McGill universities. He was admitted to the Quebec bar in 1884, and in 1897 was elected to the provincial parliament of Quebec province, holding his seat until 1908. From 1905 until 1920 he was prime minister and attorney general of his native province, and from 1921 to 1924 minister of justice of Canada. He received his knighthood in 1913. In 1924 Gouin was a Canadian representative at the Imperial and Economic Councils in London. He served as lieutenant governor of the province of Quebec for the two months preceding his death.

GOUJON, JEAN (1510?–68?), French sculptor and architect, probably born in Normandy. He is considered the greatest sculptor of the Renaissance in France and was distinguished for his ability to harmonize his works with the structures they decorated. In 1541, and from 1547 to 1562, Goujon collaborated with the noted architect Pierre Lescot in a number of architectural and sculptural projects, principally the restoration and decoration of the church of St. Germain l'Auxerrois, Paris, and the construction and decoration of a portion of the palace of the Louvre, later the Louvre museum. Two bas-reliefs made by Goujon for the church are today in the Louvre. Notable features of the Louvre for which Goujon was responsible are the Henry II staircase; the figures decorating the sides of the round windows; and the four caryatids (1562) supporting the gallery for musicians. Among the important independent works of Goujon are the two columns supporting the organ of the church of Saint Maclou, Rouen (1541); the statue of Archbishop Georges II d'Amboise (monument to Georges I d'Amboise, cathedral of Rouen); the decorations of the château at Écouen (1545–46); the bas-reliefs "Nymphs" (Fountain of the Innocents, Paris); and decorations of the château of Arrèt, including the group "Diana, the Huntress" (now in the Louvre), a fountain piece for a courtyard of the château.

GOULD, GEORGE JAY (1864–1923), American capitalist, eldest son of Jay Gould (q.v.), born in New York City, and privately educated. He became a member of the New York Stock Exchange in 1886, and was subsequently employed in various positions in his father's network of railroads extending over a great part of the United States. When he was only 24 he became president of the Little Rock and Fort Smith Railroad. In 1892 he inherited his father's railroad properties, and fought a long financial battle for their control against a group of financiers led by Edward H. Harriman. During the panic of 1907 he was unable to support the stock of his various railroad companies. One of them, the Missouri Pacific, was immediately lost to the Harriman interests, and four others were forced into bankruptcy.

GOULD, JAY, originally JASON (1836–92), American financier, born at Roxbury, N.Y., and educated at Hobart College. He worked some years as a surveyor, and later was a leather merchant and a banker. Immediately after the financial panic of 1857 he began buying railroad bonds, and soon controlled the Rensselaer and Saratoga Line. In 1859 he became a broker in New York City, beginning at this time his association with James Fisk (q.v.) and Daniel Drew. They gained control of the Erie Railroad, through stock manipulation, from Cornelius Vanderbilt, and in 1868 Gould became president of the line. In 1869 he entered a scheme to corner the gold market, which resulted in a sudden drop in the price of gold and one of the worst panics in American financial history, on "Black Friday" (q.v.). Gould, Fisk, and Drew gained about $11,000,000 from this venture. Litigation was begun against Gould for his $5,000,000 sale of worthless Erie Railroad stock, and in 1872 he was forced to give up control of the line. During the 1880's, however, he was still in control of an estimated 13,000 miles of railroad, including the Union Pacific; and he owned dominant interests in the New York *World* and the Western Union Telegraph Co.

GOUNOD, CHARLES FRANÇOIS (1818–93), French composer, born in Paris. He studied at the Paris Conservatoire under Jacques Halévy, Ferdinand Paer, and Jean François Le Sueur. Gounod won the Prix de Rome in 1839. During his stay in Rome he studied particularly the works of the early composers of sacred music, notably Palestrina, and composed his own first important religious composition *Messe a Tre* (performed in Rome, 1841). Subsequently he was organist and choirmaster at the Église des Missions

Detail from "Nymphs," relief by Jean Goujon

Estrangères, Paris, and studied for the priesthood; but in 1851 he gave up this study and henceforth devoted himself to musical composition, especially that of opera. His first two operas, *Sapho* (1851) and *La Nonne Sanglante* (1854), were failures, but his light opera *Le Médecin Malgré Lui* (1858) was a success. His fame, however, rests upon his next opera, *Faust* (produced at the Théâtre-Lyrique, Paris, 1859). Although *Faust* was not immediately successful, it became in time one of the most popular operas ever composed. It has been performed innumerable times throughout the world. His two other important operas, neither of which achieved the fame of *Faust*, are *Mireille* (1864) and *Roméo et Juliette* (1867). Gounod also composed the operas *Philémon et Baucis* (1860), *La Colombe* (1860), *La Reine de Saba* (1862), *Cinq-Mars* (1877), *Polyeucte* (1878), and *Le Tribut de Zamora* (1881). Gounod's operatic music is more distinguished for lyric than dramatic quality; it has charm and melodic

Charles François Gounod

invention, and is expertly orchestrated. Gounod was also the composer of distinguished sacred music, including the oratorios *Tobie* (about 1850), *La Rédemption* (1882), and *Mors et Vita* (1885); the cantata *Gallia* (1871); several Masses, motets, and hymns; a *Stabat Mater,* a *Te Deum,* and an *Ave Maria,* based on the first *Prelude* of Johann Sebastian Bach. Gounod was elected to the French Institute in 1866. Among his writings is *Mémoires d'un Artiste* (posthumously published, 1896).

GOUPIL, SAINT RENÉ (1607?–42), French Jesuit lay brother, missionary, and martyr, born at Anjou. He went to Canada in 1640, and in August, 1642, was captured and tortured by the Iroquois, who executed him with a tomahawk a month later at Auriesville, N.Y. He was canonized on June 29, 1940; his feast is celebrated on September 26.

GOURAMI or **GORAMY,** common name for several large, flattened, fresh-water fish in the Fighting-Fish family. They are found in Africa, S.E. Asia, and the Malay Archipelago. *Osphronemus goramy,* a typical gourami, is about three feet long, brightly colored, with a long, trailing, sensory thread hanging from the forward portion of its ventral fin. It eats all types of food and is a tasty food fish. Gouramis, like true fighting fish, are partial air-breathers; a complex respiratory chamber, situated between the mouth and the gill arches, receives swallowed air bubbles and extracts oxygen from them. The gouramis are noted for their nests built of air-filled bubbles of saliva.

Gouramis of the genus *Helostoma* are frequently kept in aquaria as curiosities. They have large, backward-curving lips which are utilized in their natural habitat to grasp seaweed from coral or rocks. In aquaria they often rub their lips against other fish; this habit has earned them the name of kissing gouramis. The three-spot gourami, *Trichogaster trichopterus,* so called because of two black spots over its eyes and one yellow spot on its abdomen, is another aquarium gourami. This fish, which attains a maximum length of five inches, is shining olive gray in color and is characterized by a hairlike ventral fin. The croaking gourami, *Trichopsis vittatus,* makes a distinctly audible sound (see GRUNT), and is often kept in aquaria. It is about three inches long, brownish olive, ringed with broad bands of dark brown.

GOURAUD, HENRI JOSEPH EUGÈNE (1867–1946), French army commander, born in Paris and educated at St. Cyr. Upon the outbreak of World War I, he was appointed general of division. He commanded the 10th Division in the battles in the Argonne Forest in 1914, and in May of the following year was placed in command of the French expeditionary force in the Dardanelles. While taking part in the Dardanelles campaign he suffered a severe wound, which resulted in the amputation of his right arm. In Dec., 1915, he was named commander of the 4th Army which in 1918 halted the last great German offensive in the Champagne sector. From 1919 to 1923 he was high commissioner in Syria and commander in chief of the Army of the Levant, and in 1922 became a member of the Supreme War Council. He represented the French government at the reunion of the Rainbow Division of the American Expeditionary Force, held at Baltimore, Md., in 1929.

GOURD, common name of the family Cucurbitaceae (q.v.), and of several genera which it comprises. Fruits of all members of the Gourd family, such as cucumber, muskmelon, pumpkin, squash, and watermelon (qq.v.), are called gourds, but in the U.S. the term is usually restricted to Cucurbitaceae which have inedible, hard-shelled fruits. The more common gourds in the United States are the bottle gourd, *Lagenaria vulgaris,* and the yellow-flowered gourd, *Curcurbita pepo* var. *orifera.* Less common gourds are the loofah, *Luffa cylindrica;* wax gourd, *Benincasa hispida;* cranberry gourd, *Abobra tenuifolia;*

gooseberry gourd, *Cucumis anguria;* hedge-hog gourd, *Cucumis dipsaceus;* and ivy gourd, *Coccinia cordifolia.* All of these are annual plants which either trail along the ground or climb by means of tendrils. They grow best in full sunlight on rich, well-drained soil. The ripe fruits of many varieties are oddly shaped and marked, and are often used as household ornaments. The loofah, which has a spongelike fibrous "skeleton", is used as a bath sponge in Britain.

GOURMONT, REMY DE (1858–1915), French author and critic, born at Bazoches-en-Houlme, Orme, and educated at the University of Caen. He joined the staff of the Bibliothèque Nationale, in Paris, in 1883. Seven years later he founded the noted periodical *Le Mercure de France,* with which he remained associated for many years. He was compelled to resign his position at the Bibliothèque in 1891 because of an allegedly subversive article, *Le Joujou: Patriotisme,* which he had written. His later writings include several notable series of essays, such as the *Épilogues* (1903–13), dealing in rather cynical terms with contemporary life; and *Promenades Littéraires* (1904–13), comprising perceptive criticisms of contemporary writing. In *L'Esthétique de la Langue Française* (1899), *La Culture des Idées* (1900), and *Le Problème du Style* (1907), Gourmont concerned himself with general problems of esthetics and literary craftsmanship. He was also the author of several novels; the most important of these include *Sixtine* (1890), *Le Songe d'une Femme* (1899), and *Un Cœur Virginal* (1907).

GOURNAY, JEAN CLAUDE MARIE VINCENT DE (1712–59), French economist, born at Saint Malo. At seventeen he went into business, and during the following years his enterprises led him to travel extensively in Western Europe. In 1746, he sold his business and retired to Paris. His commercial background placed him apart from the main body of 18th-century French economists, who were physiocrats (see ECONOMICS). They believed that the land was the sole wealth of the state, but Gournay realized the value of industry as well. His influence was chiefly felt through his conversations with his contemporaries, especially his pupil, Anne Robert Jacques Turgot, later finance minister of France; he also translated several works of English economists. In 1757, Gournay was appointed intendant of commerce in France, and held office until his death. While in office he fought for free trade and the suppression of monopolies. In his economic theories he advocated government non-interference with commerce and industry. Gournay is reputed to be the originator of the term *laissez faire,* or, more fully, *laissez faire, laissez passer* ("let them act, let it pass") to describe this hands-off policy.

GOUT, a chronic disease characterized by disturbance of the uric acid metabolism, recurring arthritis, and the formation of concretions of uric acid salts, called *tophi* or *chalk stones,* in the affected joints and in the margins of the external ear. The disease has been known ever since it was first recognized by the Greek physician Hippocrates. It is associated with an increase in the uric acid concentration of the blood, but its basic cause is still unknown.

Gout affects mostly males, and is comparatively rare in persons under the age of thirty. It is most common in temperate climates, and occurs more often in the spring and fall than in summer or winter. Predisposing factors include heredity; a robust, well-nourished physique coupled with sedentary occupation; and indulgence in a diet high in malt liquors and heavy wines and high in meats, such as liver or kidney, which are rich in cell nuclei (the source of nucleoproteins which yield uric acid in the bodily metabolism).

The arthritic attack of gout may affect any of the joints, but most commonly involves the basal joint of the big toe. It may be precipitated by worry, shock, or other strong emotion, or by indulgence in rich food and drink while fatigued; it starts, often in the middle of the night, with such sharp pain and extreme tenderness in the affected joint that the patient constantly shifts about in an effort to find a comfortable position. The attack subsides after four to ten days, but may recur, at any time, in the same or another joint. Long continued recurrences may cause permanent damage to the bones, cartilages, and tendons associated with the joints involved.

In the treatment of gout colchicine is especially useful not only for the relief of the pain of the attack, but also as an aid to diagnosis, because gouty arthritis is the only form of arthritis in which it affords relief. A new drug known as phenylbutazone is highly effective in controlling acute gout attacks. According to medical reports in 1954, the use of phenylbutazone brought remission of symptoms within 48 hours, even in those cases resistant to colchicine.

GOVERNMENT, in human society, the institution invested with the regulation and control of the interrelationships of individuals within a social aggregate; of the relations of the individuals to the social aggregate; and of the relations of the social aggregate as a whole to other such aggregates. It is applied in this sense both to the governments of national states, such as the Federal government of the United States, and to the governments of subdivisions of national states, such as the State, county, and municipal governments of the United States and the governments of the provinces of Chile. The term "government" is also applied to the men comprising the supreme administrative body of a state, as in the expression "the government of Prime Minister Pitt".

Governments are classified in a great many ways and according to a wide variety of standpoints; many of the classificatory categories overlap. A familiar classification is that which distinguishes monarchic from republican governments. Scholars in modern times, especially in the 20th century, have laid stress on defining the characteristics which demarcate democratic governments from dictatorships; see DEMOCRACY; FASCISM; TOTALITARIANISM. In one classification of governments, federal states are distinguished from unitary states. Federal states, such as the United States and Switzerland, comprise unions of sovereign states, in which the authority of the central or national governments is constitutionally limited by the legally established powers of the constituent subdivisions comprising the union. In unitary states, as Great Britain and Belgium, the constituent subdivisions of the state are subordinate to the overriding authority of the national government. The degree of subordination varies from country to country. It may also vary within a country from time to time and according to circumstance; thus the central authority of the national government in Italy was greatly increased from 1922 to 1945 during the period of the Fascist dictatorship. In one classification of democratic states, parliamentary or cabinet governments are distinguished from presidential governments. Parliamentary governments, as in Great Britain and France, are distinguished by the subordination of the executive to the legislature. In presidential governments, as in the United States, the executive is independent of the legislature; see CABINET; PRESIDENT OF THE UNITED STATES. Still other classifications hinge on varying governmental forms and powers among the nations of the world. For a description of the governments of the various countries, see the articles on those countries.

In the theory of political science the function of government is to secure the common interests and desires of the members of the social aggregate over which it exercises control. In different historical epochs governments have endeavored to discharge these functions by various means. Among primitive peoples systems of social control were rudimentary; they arose directly from ideas of right and wrong common to the members of a social group, were amorphous in form, and were enforced primarily by the social pressure of the members of the group on individuals; see GENS; TRIBE; TABOO. Among more civilized peoples governments assumed organized institutional forms; they rested on defined legal bases, imposing penalties on law violators and employing force to secure their own existence and discharge their functions.

In time arose the despotic empires of the Sumerians, Egyptians, Assyrians, Persians, and Macedonians. These were followed by the rise of city-states, the first self-governing communities, in which the rule of law predominated and state officials were responsible to the citizens who chose them. The city-states of Greece (see ATHENS; CORINTH; SPARTA), and in that part of Asia Minor dominated or influenced by the Greeks, provided the material for the speculative political theories of Plato, Aristotle (qq.v.), and other philosophers. Aristotle's system of classifying states, which influenced subsequent political thought for centuries, was based on a simple criterion: those states were good which served best the general weal; those were bad which subordinated the general good to the good of the individuals in power. Aristotle distinguished three categories of governments: monarchy, government by a single individual; aristocracy, government by a select few; and democracy, government by many. The Greek philosophers, influenced by Aristotle, distinguished three perverted or degenerate forms of the classes of government defined by him. These were, respectively, tyranny, oligarchy, and ochlocracy or mob rule. Ancient Rome, which evolved from a city-republic to the seat of a despotic world empire, also greatly influenced the development of government in the Occidental world. This influence derived in part from the great achievement of the Romans in formulating clearly for the first time the principle that constitutional law, establishing the sovereignty (q.v.) of the state, is superior to ordinary law, such as that created by legislative enactments.

After the fall of Rome, the Roman conception of a universal dominion was kept alive during the Middle Ages through the formation of the Holy Roman Empire (q.v.); and also, in part, by the establishment, through canon law (q.v.) and ecclesiastical courts with jurisdiction over secular affairs, of the "world government" of the Catholic Church; see Courts. The effect of these influences was to retard the development of national territories and governments after tendencies in that direction had manifested themselves among the feudal principalities of Europe. On the other hand, the struggle of the feudal barons to limit the absolute power of their monarchs constituted a factor which eventually contributed much to the theory and institutions of representative government; see Magna Charta. During the Middle Ages arose the commercial city-states of Europe which formed the Hanseatic League (q.v.) and the powerful Italian city-republics or communes; see Genoa; Pisa; Venice.

The final emergence of national governments is attributed by historians to two principal causes. One comprised a number of underlying economic factors, including a great increase in trade and the development of manufacturing, which began to break up the feudal system, based on isolated and self-sufficient economic units (see Feudalism), and to make necessary the creation of large political units. The other cause was the Reformation, which succeeded in a number of European countries in eliminating the restraining influence of the Catholic Church in political development, as noted above.

The modern nation-state became a definite form of government in the 16th century. It was almost entirely dynastic and autocratic. The will of the reigning monarch was, in theory, and often in practice, unlimited; the famous aphorism of Louis XIV of France, *L'état, c'est moi* ("I am the state"), was not an idle boast or flight of fancy, but an expression of existing reality. However, in time, the demand of the bourgeoisie (q.v.) for constitutional and representative government made itself felt, and the power of monarchs became circumscribed. This tendency culminated in two events of historic importance, the American and French revolutions of 1776 and 1789, respectively. It is from these events that historians generally date the rise of modern democratic government. The history of government in the 19th century and in part of the 20th is largely the history of the broadening of the political base of government through extension of the suffrage and other reforms, see Electoral Reform. A tendency which became especially marked in the 20th century was the development and implementation of the concept that government is essentially an instrument for administering public and social services, including, among many others, conservation of natural resources, scientific research, education, and unemployment insurance; see New Deal. Under the Labor Party government of Great Britain, which took office in 1945, the responsibilities of government were extended to include nationalization (q.v.) of a number of basic industries as a step toward socialism. Other outstanding developments of the 20th century were the appearance of the corporative state and of fascist governments in a number of countries (see State; National Socialism), and the first so-called *proletarian* dictatorship in history (see Union of Soviet Socialist Republics). After World War II a number of eastern European countries adopted governments similar in many respects to that of the Soviet Union.

GOVERNMENT LAND. See Homestead Laws; Public Lands.

GOVERNMENT, MUNICIPAL. See Municipal Government.

GOVERNMENT PRINTING OFFICE, an agency of the legislative branch of the U.S. government, created by an act of Congress in 1860. As defined by the Printing Act of 1895 and its subsequent amendments, the functions of the Government Printing Office include the execution of all orders for printing and binding placed by Congress and the Federal executive departments and agencies; distribution of government publications as required by law; publication, for public sale, of official documents as determined by the proper authorities; compilation and distribution of catalogues of government publications; and execution of the orders of all government divisions for paper, ink, and other supplies.

The Government Printing Office is administered by the Public Printer, who is appointed by the President with the approval of the Senate. The Joint Committee on Printing, consisting of six members, three from the Senate and three from the House of Representatives, sets the standards of paper used in public printing; passes on the contracts made by the Public Printer for the purchase of paper and other supplies; passes on the wage agreements made by the Public Printer with the representatives of various employees of the Government Printing Office, pursuant to legislation enacted in 1924; and, in general, acts as the board of directors of the Government Printing Office. Initially the equipment of the Government Printing Office consisted of a commercial plant acquired by the payment of $135,000, for which purpose Congress made the requisite appropriation. In a recent year the machinery and plant of the Government Printing Office, which is regarded as the largest, best equipped, and most complete in the world, was valued at more than $20,000,000. In the same year, the Office produced 19,750,000,000 copies of printed matter at a cost of $90,000,000 for printing and binding alone; it distributed free bulletins of various types to more than 82,000,000 persons. It sold over $5,000,000 worth of printed matter, securing a profit from these sales of more than $1,700,000.

GOVERNORS ISLAND, a fortified island occupied by a U.S. military reservation, situated in New York Bay at the entrance to the East R., 500 yards off the s. tip of Manhattan, and separated from Brooklyn by Buttermilk Channel. The fortifications on the island are called Castle Williams, South Battery, and Fort Jay, headquarters of the Second Corps Area of the U.S. Army. Governors Island is served by Government ferry to the mainland.

The island was purchased from the Indians by Wouter van Twiller, second governor of New Netherlands, in 1637, and was originally known as Nutten Island. In 1698 it was officially set aside as a country residence for the colonial governors of New York, and consequently became known as Governors Island. Fort Jay was built in 1794 on a knoll dominating the island by Gen. Israel Putnam. It was reconstructed in 1806 from the designs of Lieut. Col. Jonathan Williams, who also designed Castle Williams, and the name of the fort was changed to Fort Columbus. Construction of Castle Williams was begun in 1807, and the work was completed in 1811. During the War of 1812, South Battery was built at the s. end of the island, overlooking Buttermilk Channel. Castle Williams, circular in shape, with red sandstone walls, is almost unchanged since its original construction. Confederate prisoners were confined there during the Civil War, at which time there were as many as seven regiments of Federal troops stationed on the island. Castle Williams now serves as a disciplinary barracks, and South Battery is the present-day Officers Club. Also on the island is the chapel of Saint Cornelius the Centurion, connected with Trinity Parish in New York City, and containing military relics. The original area of Governors Island, which was about 170 acres under the Dutch, was reduced to less than 70 acres in 1900 by wave erosion. In 1903 the Government commenced the reclamation of the island with filled land, and its present area is about 173 acres. Fort Columbus was renamed Fort Jay in 1904.

GOWER, JOHN (1325?–1408), English poet. The known details of his life are fragmentary. He belonged to a prosperous Kentish family, and was a landholder in Suffolk and Norwalk. He was a friend of Chaucer (q.v.), who addressed his *Troilus and Criseyde* to "moral Gower", and knew Richard II personally. Gower was married in 1398, probably for the second time. He became blind toward the end of his life. His tomb is in St. Saviour's, Southwark.

Gower is the most outstanding contemporary of Chaucer. His principal works are three long poems written in different languages. *Speculum Meditantis* (1376?), in French, is an allegory treating the nature of man, his sins and virtues, and his deliverance from sin. *Vox Clamantis* (1382?), written in Latin elegiac verse, describes the insurrection led by Wat Tyler, and deals with the faults of the various classes of society. *Confessio Amantis* (1390?), Gower's best-known work, written "in our English . . . . for England's sake" is a standard of Middle English. It is a collection of tales illustrating the vices that may accompany love, told by a lover to a priest of Venus. Besides the long poems, Gower wrote minor poems in English, French, and Latin, among which are *Traitié pour Essampler les Amantz Mariés* (1397), *Cinkante Balades* (1399), *Cronica Tripartita,* and *In Praise of Peace.*

GOWN, a long, full, sleeved garment, the distinguishing costume worn by clerics, scholars, and legal officers such as judges, and, in England, by barristers and municipal officials.

Priests of the Roman Catholic and Orthodox churches, as well as of the Anglo-Catholic and several other Protestant churches. wear gowns while officiating at mass, and in some countries wear them at all times. Certain religious orders require their members to wear a distinctive costume which includes a gown. After the Reformation in England those clergymen, principally Puritans, who had no right to the academic gown because they had no university degrees, adopted a Protestant clerical costume known as the "Geneva robe". The gowns worn by dignitaries of most religious denominations indicate by their colors and design the status of the wearer.

Judges' gowns, as worn in several European countries and in the U.S. and Canada,

Art Institute of Chicago

Above: Francisco Goya, self-portrait.
Right: "Don Isidro Maiquez," by Goya.

probably evolved from the costume worn by men of wealth and importance in the late Middle Ages. Some authorities, however, consider that they developed from ecclesiastical dress, because clergymen often acted as magistrates in the Middle Ages. The English barrister's woolen gown indicates that he has been admitted to the bar, and when an English lawyer becomes a king's counsel, or public prosecutor, he exchanges his wool gown for a silk one, and is said to have "taken silk". The mayors, aldermen, and sheriffs of London and other English cities wear gowns of office on state and civic occasions.

The academic gown developed from the costume of the Middle Ages and also from the condition that during that period all European universities were under the authority of the papal see and the student body was composed of clerics, both ordained and unordained. At Continental universities each particular faculty wears gowns of a distinctive color. At Oxford and Cambridge universities the holder of a doctor's degree has the right to wear a scarlet gown. Some English colleges, such as those at Cambridge, retain traces of their former distinctive costumes in the details and colors of their gowns. At the time of the Reformation, academic costumes were somewhat altered to suit the more sober tastes of the Protestants. In some U.S. colleges undergraduates wear a plain, full-length, long-sleeved, black woolen gown. Graduates' costumes indicate their status. The sleeves of bachelors, masters, and doctors vary in shape. Unlike bachelors, who wear worsted gowns, masters and doctors wear silk. All gowns are black, but the doctor has the right to wear on his gown three stripes of velvet, and velvet facings; these trimmings may either be black, or of a color indicating the faculty to which the wearer belongs. Some of these colors are: theology, scarlet; medicine, green; engineering, orange; philosophy, blue; law, purple; and arts and letters, white.

GOYANIA, or GOIÂNIA, capital of Goyaz State, Brazil, situated about 120 miles S.E. of the city of Goyaz. The area selected for the establishment of the proposed federal capital of Brazil, known as the Futura Districto Federal, is situated about 130 miles N.E. of Goyania. Pop. (1950) 41,584.

GOYA Y LUCIENTES, FRANCISCO JOSÉ DE (1746–1828), Spanish painter, etcher, and draftsman, born at Fuendetodos. Goya, together with El Greco and Velasquez (qq.v.), is one of the three greatest representatives of Spanish painting. He studied with José Lusan y Martínez at Saragossa, but after a series of early romantic escapades he fled to Madrid and then to Rome. In 1771 he was awarded a prize by the Academy of Parma and returned the same year to Saragossa. There he painted murals in the church of Santa Maria del Pilar and in the Cartuja

Aula Dei, a Carthusian convent. From 1775 to 1779 he was employed at Madrid by the court painter Anton Raphael Mengs (1728–79) to design cartoons for tapestries. The great originality of these designs, representing scenes from contemporary Spanish life, won him wide recognition and court honors. In 1785 he was made director of the Academy of Arts in San Fernando and in 1798 he was appointed chief court painter to Charles IV.

His series of portraits of the Spanish aristocracy belong to this period. They display remarkable psychological acumen and a broad and bold use of painting techniques. Goya slowly developed in his art a powerful sense of social satire, which was first manifest in some of his portraits of Spanish royalty. In his line and wash drawings he depicted market-place scenes, bullfights, peasants, and courtesans. His two great series of etchings include "Los Caprichos" and "Los Desastres de la Guerra". The latter group was executed in 1810 during the French occupation of Spain during the Napoleonic Wars.

Goya served the government of Joseph Bonaparte at Madrid after the overthrow of King Charles IV by the French, but was reinstated as official court painter when the Spanish throne was restored to Ferdinand VII in 1814. However, his unpopularity among Bourbon supporters subsequently forced him to seek refuge at Bordeaux, France, where he was welcomed by a colony of Spanish refugees. He turned his artistic energies to a series of macabre genre scenes, depicting man's inhumanity to man with an intensity comparable to the writings of Jonathan Swift, to whom he has often been likened. He also took up the new art of lithography, and executed a group of bullfight scenes; these prints are considered among the greatest lithographs ever made. In 1827, a year before his death, he was at last invited home to Madrid by the king to paint several portraits. Most of Goya's paintings are in the Prado, Madrid, but examples are to be found in almost every leading museum of the world. A representative group of his paintings is owned by the Metropolitan Museum of Art, New York City.

GOYAZ, or Goiás, a central State of Brazil, in the great plateau region of the Serra dos Pireneus. The greater part of the State has an average elevation of 2700 ft. above sea level. In the N., Goyaz is watered by the Tocantins and Araguaya rivers and their tributaries, and in the s. by numerous streams tributary to the Paranahiba R., a large af-

fluent of the Paraná. Forests border the rivers and streams, particularly in the N. part of the State, where they are dense and similar to those of the Amazon valley; the tablelands, however, are barren of trees, and form vast pastures. The principal agricultural industries in Goyaz are stock raising and tobacco cultivation. Although the mining industry is not fully developed at the present time, the State contains mines yielding gold, diamonds, and quartz crystal. The chief cities of the State are the capital Goyania (q.v.) and Goyaz (pop. in 1940, 5905). Goyaz, the former capital, is a mining and cattle-raising center. Area of State, 240,271 sq.m.; pop. (1950) 1,214,921.

GOYEN or **GOIJEN,** Jan van (1596–1656), Dutch landscape painter, born at Leiden. He studied in his native city and with Esaias van de Velde in Haarlem. In 1631 he settled at The Hague, where he became head of the painters' guild in 1640. His early work shows the influence of his teacher and of Pieter Brueghel the younger. Later he developed a manner of treating his subjects which emphasized perspective and lighting, suffusing his landscapes in a melancholy gray-green atmosphere. His influence on Dutch painting, exercised principally through his pupils and his younger contemporaries, was considerable. More than a thousand of his paintings have been catalogued. Many important galleries and museums contain examples of his works, including a view of The Hague painted on command of the city authorities in 1651, now in the municipal collection of that city; "View of Dordrecht" (1650, Rijks Museum, Amsterdam); "Banks of a Canal" (1653, Louvre, Paris); "Environs of Haarlem" (1656, Metropolitan Museum of Art, New York City); and "River Scene" and "Moonlight" (Pennsylvania Academy of Fine Arts in Philadelphia).

GOZZOLI, Benozzo (1420–98), Florentine painter, born at Florence. His real name was Benozzo di Lese di Sandro. He studied with the noted painter Fra Angelico, whom he assisted in some of his work. Gozzoli was one of the important masters of the Florentine school (q.v.). His paintings are noted for their realistic detail, religious feeling, and clear, bright color. Gozzoli was particularly adept at painting groups of people in processions or in dramatic action, and at depicting landscapes and architectural backgrounds. Most of his paintings were frescoes. They include a triple series from the life of St. Francis (church of San Fortunato, Montefalco);

Detail from "Procession of the Magi," fresco by Benozzo Gozzoli

"Procession of the Magi" (Riccardi Palace, Florence), which contains many portraits of eminent people of the time; a series from the life of St. Augustine (church of San Agostino, San Gimignano); twenty-four frescoes depicting scenes from the Old Testament, including "Life of Noah" and "Visit of the Queen of Sheba to Solomon" (Campo Santo, Pisa); and, attributed to Gozzoli, panels, showing four saints, of an altarpiece for a chapel of the church of Pier Maggiore, Florence (now in the Metropolitan Museum of Art, New York City). Among Gozzoli's few easel pictures are "Madonna, Saints, and Angels" (National Gallery, London) and "Apotheosis of St. Thomas Aquinas" (Louvre, Paris).

GPU, former designation of the secret political police of the Soviet government, comprising the initials of the Russian words *Gosudarstvennoe Politicheskoe Upravlenie* ("Government Political Administration"). The GPU was created in Feb., 1922, by a decree of the All Russian Central Executive Committee of the Congress of Soviets to replace the Cheka (q.v.) established several years before to combat counterrevolutionary activities. The GPU constituted a department in the People's Commissariat of the Interior of the Russian Socialist Federated Soviet Republic, and, by the terms of the decree creating it, was charged with the following functions: "suppression of open counterrevolutionary manifestations, including banditry; devising ways and means for protection from and combat of espionage; protection of railroads and waterways; political defense of the frontiers of the RSFSR; combat of smuggling and crossing of the frontiers of the republic without proper permits"; and the execution of other duties that might be assigned to it by the Council of People's Commissars. The decree also provided that, for the execution of its functions, the GPU be given direct command of "special divisions of troops" and a special staff apart from the military forces of the Soviet Union.

A constitution drafted later in 1922, which subsequently became the basic law of the Union of Soviet Socialist Republics, provided for the creation of the *Obshche Gosudarstvennoe Politichekoe Upravlenie* ("All Government Political Administration"), referred to as the OGPU, to direct the activities of the GPU organizations of the constituent republics of the Union. A decree of 1923, implementing the constitution of 1922, provided that the OGPU have its own independent budget within the general budget of the USSR. It provided further that the agents of the OGPU and its local branches "in their rights, duties, and other relations, assume the status of persons in active military service"; and that the OGPU and its local departments "have the right of active divisions of the Red

Army" with respect to transportation, communications, and equipment and supplies.

Originally, the GPU, like its predecessor the Cheka, was conceived as a temporary expedient. However, the concentration of vast powers in the OGPU, constituted as an almost independent state within a state, signified an autocratic development not contemplated at the time of the revolution of 1917. During the 1920's the OGPU broke strikes, quelled peasant opposition to government policies, persecuted political critics and opponents of the regime, made summary arrests, held secret trials in its own courts, sentenced to death and imprisonment tens of thousands of men and women, and engaged in espionage (q.v.). The OGPU also maintained penal and correctional labor camps in various parts of the Soviet Union, in which hundreds of thousands of men and women were employed in forced labor; supervision of these camps was vested in a special department of the OGPU, called GULAG after the initials of the Russian words signifying Chief Administration of Camps.

In 1934 the functions of the OGPU and the GPU organizations of the federated republics were transferred to the then newly created *Narodny Kommissariat Vnutrennikh Dyel* ("People's Commissariat for Internal Affairs"), referred to as the NKVD. In 1946, when all the commissariats of the Soviet government were renamed ministries, the NKVD became the MVD. Because of the identity in function of the GPU, OGPU, NKVD, and MVD, all these designations are used interchangeably outside the Soviet Union, irrespective of chronology, in referring to the secret police of the Soviet government. The term GPU is usually employed for a single generic designation.

GRAAF, REGNIER DE (1641–73), Dutch physician and anatomist, born at Schoonhoven, and educated at the universities of Leiden, Utrecht, and Louvain. In 1672 Graaf discovered the follicles in the ovary, which are known as Graafian follicles; see REPRODUCTIVE SYSTEM. He wrote a famous work on the nature and function of the pancreatic juice, *Disputatio Medica de Natura et Usu Succi Pancreatici* (1663).

GRAAL, HOLY. See GRAIL, THE HOLY.

GRACCHUS, in ancient Rome, the name of a distinguished plebeian family of the gens Sempronia, of whom the most famous members were the following.

1. TIBERIUS SEMPRONIUS GRACCHUS, consul in 238 B.C. He obtained a victory over the Ligurians, an aboriginal people of N.W. Italy, but is noted chiefly as the commander of the Roman fleet which took possession of the Mediterranean island of Sardinia at the end of the First Punic War with Carthage.

2. TIBERIUS SEMPRONIUS GRACCHUS (?–212 B.C.), a general during the Second Punic War. Elected consul in 215 B.C., when Hannibal, the Carthaginian general, was ravaging the Roman provinces of Campania and Apulia, Gracchus gathered a force of volunteer slaves (to whom he promised freedom if he were victorious) and recruits from the provinces, and seized the Campanian coastal city of Cumæ, which he held against the assaults of Hannibal's army. At the termination of his consulship, his *imperium,* or consular power, was continued so that he could spend the year 214 in Apulia, with headquarters at Beneventum (Benevento), from which the Carthaginian general Hanno tried in vain to dislodge him. Gracchus was consul again in 213. The following year, in Apulia, he was slain by Mago, a younger brother of Hannibal. Hannibal accorded Gracchus the honor of a public funeral.

3. TIBERIUS SEMPRONIUS GRACCHUS (210?–151?), statesman and general. He served on the staff of the consul Lucius Cornelius Scipio in Greece (190); was *tribunus plebis* (tribune of the people) in 187; prætor in Spain (181), where by his tact and justice he brought the wild Celtic tribes of the Iberian peninsula under Roman control; and consul in 177. He crushed a revolt on the island of Sardinia, returning to Rome to celebrate his triumph with large numbers of captives. He was censor in 169, and constructed the Basilica Sempronia near the Forum Romanum. In 164 he served as special envoy in Asia Minor, where he established friendly relations between a number of native rulers and the Romans. Gracchus married Cornelia, daughter of Publius Cornelius Scipio Africanus, and had twelve children by her, all dying at an early age with the exception of three: two sons (the famous Gracchi) and a daughter.

4. TIBERIUS SEMPRONIUS GRACCHUS (163–133), son of the foregoing. With his brother Gaius (see below), he was brought up under the special care of his mother, Cornelia. Gracchus took part in the capture and destruction of Carthage (146), on which occasion he is said to have been the first Roman to scale the city wall. In 137 he acted as quæstor to the army of the consul Gaius Hostilius Mancinus in Spain. There, when the people of the ancient Spanish city of Numantia would ne

gotiate with no Roman other than the son of their former benefactor, he saved from destruction an army of 20,000 Romans, who had been defeated and were at the mercy of the Numantines. Upon his return to Rome he became a champion of the cause of the common people and the impoverished farmers, and commenced an agitation for reform. He was elected tribune of the people in 133, and despite opposition from the aristocracy he obtained legislation providing for a more equitable distribution of public lands among the small farmers; a committee of three, consisting of him, his brother Gaius, and Appius Claudius, was appointed to implement the new law. When the term of his tribuneship expired, Gracchus, to strengthen his position as champion of the people, presented himself for re-election. He rebuffed with contempt the declaration of the senate that holding the office of tribune for two successive years was unlawful. A rumor then circulated to the effect that Gracchus was seeking dictatorial power. His enemies demanded his immediate death and precipitated a riot in which Gracchus was murdered and his body cast into the Tiber R.

5. GAIUS SEMPRONIUS GRACCHUS (153–121), younger brother of Tiberius. At the time of Tiberius' death, Gaius was serving with the Roman army in Spain. He returned to Rome a year or two later, but took no major part in public affairs. Upon attaining the quæstorship (126 B.C.), he accompanied the army, under the consul Lucius Aurelius Orestes, to Sardinia, then in a state of rebellion. Though the Roman senate, with uneasy recollections of Tiberius, sought to keep Gaius from Rome by extending his term as quæstor, he felt strongly the obligation of avenging his brother's murder, and accordingly returned to the capital without authorization. He became a candidate for the tribuneship, and was elected to that office in 123. He then devoted himself to the enforcement of his brother's agrarian laws, which had gradually been allowed to lapse, and carried out important new legislation in the interest of the common people as opposed to that of the senate and the aristocrats. To develop the resources of Italy, and at the same time to provide employment for the poor, he inaugurated a program of road repair and construction throughout the country. He secured passage of a law entitling every citizen resident in Rome to purchase grain at half price, and formulated measures designed to curb the power of the senate and conversely to increase that of the equites.

Gaius was re-elected tribune in 122. The aristocratic party, unable to check his reforms by open opposition, resorted to the stratagem of offering, through Marcus Livius Drusus, co-tribune with Gaius, still greater benefits, which, however, they had no intention of carrying out. Civil strife was intensified. Lucius Opimius, the implacable foe of Gaius, was elected consul. Gaius himself failed to obtain the tribuneship for the third time, was deserted by the majority of his supporters, and was forced to escape across the Tiber R. The following day, his dead body was found on the Janiculum, a hill on the west bank of the river.

GRACE, in Christian theology, divine favor freely bestowed by God upon human beings, who are thereby enabled to attain eternal salvation. The precise nature of the gift of grace, its influence upon human behavior, and the means whereby it may be secured have been subjects of dispute among theologians since the early history of the Church, but certain fundamental beliefs have found general acceptance.

Almost all Christians, with the notable exception of the Calvinists, believe that the gift of grace does not preclude the exercise of free will (q.v.); grace is viewed as a manifestation of divine mercy which assists toward salvation those who freely choose to act in accordance with God's commandments. They hold that, rather than a reward for the solicitations of the recipient, grace is a gratuitous gift, and is bestowed on the persons who utilize whatever means of obtaining grace they may possess and who interpose no action which would interfere with its efficacy in obtaining their salvation. Another point of agreement is the belief that man, as a creature born in original sin, cannot perform works meriting salvation except with the aid provided by divine grace. Calvinists contend that grace constitutes an irresistible force in the individual, eliminating the possibility of free will, and hold that grace is not freely given to all, but only to the predestined; see CALVINISM; PREDESTINATION.

Certain basic difference exists between the views regarding the means of achieving grace held by the Roman Catholic Church, on the one hand, and those held by the Protestant and Anglican churches on the other. The former declares that grace is given to mankind through the merits of Christ, and is bestowed directly upon man through the sacraments received from the Church; see SACRAMENT. In the view of most Protestant denominations, the gift of grace is granted to man directly, as a demonstration of divine love and mercy, and the sacraments constitute merely signs of grace rather than means of attaining it. Faith, prayer, scriptural study, and good works are considered by Protestant theologians to be among the chief means of attaining grace. The Anglican view differs from that of the Protestants principally in that two of the sacraments, baptism and communion, are regarded as means of attaining grace.

GRACES, in Greek mythology, originally goddesses of fertility; later, the personification of grace and charm. They were the daughters of Zeus, father of the gods, and of Eurynome, a sea divinity. At the ancient city of Orchomenus in Bœotia, the Graces had a venerable shrine, where they were worshiped in the form of three stones, said to have fallen from heaven. According to the Greek poet Hesiod, the goddesses were called Aglaia (Brightness), Euphrosyne (Joy), and Thalia (Bloom). At Sparta, the Graces were two in number, Kleta (Noise or Fame) and Phaënna (Brightness); and the same number seems to have existed originally at Athens, where the names were Auxo (Increase) and Hegemone (Queen); later, the Athenian

The Graces (painting by Sandro Botticelli)

Graces were joined by Thallo, one of the Horæ, or Seasons. The early connection of the goddesses with the fertility of nature was obscured by the conception of them as divinities of the joy of life and of beauty. They attended the feasts and celebrations of the gods on Olympus (q.v.), and were closely associated with Hera, the goddess of marriage, and above all with Aphrodite, the goddess of love. In art, the Graces appeared fully draped until the end of the 4th century B.C. In the 3rd century B.C., however, the growing connection with Aphrodite led to a change; thenceforth they appeared only scantily draped or wholly nude, and usually embracing one another or clasping hands.

GRACKLE, any New World bird of the genera *Cassidix* and *Quiscalus* in the Blackbird family, characterized by plumage with green, purple, or bronze metallic luster. Grackles average thirteen inches in over-all length; their tails are long and unusually thick. Adult males are black; female and young grackles are reddish-brown. Grackles eat all types of food; the damage they inflict on crops is offset by their destruction of insect pests, especially gypsy moths and brown-tail moths. The nest of the grackle is a huge, loosely built structure, made of small twigs, leaves, paper, and cloth, sometimes cemented with wet clay. Often grackles build these nests in portions of the larger nests of ospreys or other hawks, suffering no harm from these birds. The female grackle lays four to six bluish-green eggs heavily speckled with black or brown.

The crow blackbird, *Quiscalus quiscula,* is found throughout the U.S. east of the Rocky Mts. The eastern subspecies of crow blackbird, called the purple grackle, has glistening purplish oblongs and quarter moons on its black back. The great-tailed grackle, *Cassidix mexicanus,* found in E. Texas and Mexico is the largest of the grackles. Its tail feathers curve upward when in flight.

Grackles are often erroneously called jackdaws and starlings. In India the name "grackle" is given to the mynas, especially the hill myna.

GRADUAL PSALMS, SONGS OF DEGREES, or SONGS OF ASCENTS, a group of fifteen psalms (numbered 120 to 134 in the King James version, 119 to 133 in the Vulgate version) belonging to the fifth subdivision or "book" of the Book of Psalms. The origin of the name is uncertain. It is explained in rabbinical literature as an allusion to the fifteen steps by which the Temple was reached. Later Biblical scholars regarded these psalms as having been connected with the "going up" (migration) from Babylon to Jerusalem, or with the ascent of the Temple mound. The gradual psalms are songs of pilgrims, emphasizing either a longing for the Temple or joy at beholding it. In the Roman Catholic Church these psalms are recited on all Wednesdays of Lent except the Wednesday of Holy Week. See PSALMS, BOOK OF.

GRÆÆ, or PHORCYDES, in Greek mythology, the daughters of the sea god Phorcus. The Grææ were named Deino, Enyo, and Pephredo. Sisters and guardians of the Gorgons (see GORGON), they are described by the Greek poet Hesiod as possessing among them but a single eye and tooth. The hero Perseus stole the eye and the tooth and restored them only when the Grææ instructed him how to procure the materials by means of which he was able to behead the Gorgon Medusa.

GRAETZ, HEINRICH (1817–91), German historian and scholar, born at Xions, Posen (now Poznań), and educated at the universities of Oldenburg and Breslau. In 1853 he became a member of the faculty of the Jewish Seminary at Breslau, and in 1869 was appointed professor at the University of Breslau. He continued in both of these posts until his death. His world-wide reputation rests largely on his exhaustive eleven-volume history of the Jews, *Geschichte der Juden von den Ältesten Zeiten* (1853-75), the first authoritative and detailed work on the subject. Among his other works are critical editions of the Psalms and the Song of Solomon.

GRAFLY, CHARLES (1862–1929), American sculptor, born at Philadelphia. He studied at the Pennsylvania Academy of Fine Arts, Philadelphia, and in Paris principally under Henri Chapu. In 1892 Grafly became an instructor in sculpture at the Pennsylvania Academy of Fine Arts, and in 1917 an instructor in the school of the Boston Museum of Fine Arts. Among his works are "England and France" (New York Custom House), "General Meade Memorial" (Washington, D.C.), "Truth" (St. Louis Museum), "Pioneer Mother Monument" (San Francisco), and "In Much Learning" (Pennsylvania Academy).

GRAFTING, operation of joining the cut surfaces of plants under circumstances which will allow physiological union. The supporting plant is called the *stock;* the plant part which is grafted to it is called the *scion.* The scion may be a twig, stem, bud, or other part of a plant; grafting in which the scion used is a

The purple grackle

bud is called *budding* (q.v.). The ability of the cut surface to heal is dependent on intimate contact between the *cambium* of the scion and of the stock. The cambium layers produce a tissue, called *callus,* composed of large, undifferentiated cells, called *parenchyma cells.* Callus tissue, in a successful graft, differentiates to form food-conducting vessels, water-conducting vessels, and a cambium layer, which connect the corresponding tissues of scion and stock.

Horticultural varieties of pome fruits such as apple, drupe fruits such as cherry, and citrus fruits such as grapefruit, are now multiplied almost wholly by grafting. Trees grown from seeds often produce fruits which vary from those of the parent plant in quality and flavor. In order to maintain production of fruit of good quality, branches or buds of trees known to produce good fruit are grafted to stronger trees which produce fruit of indifferent quality. The grafted branches, once established, produce the same type of fruit as when they were joined to the parent plant. This procedure is also followed in propagating seedless fruits, such as seedless oranges and grapes.

Grafting is frequently used to combine advantageous characteristics of scion and stock. For example, high-producing scions may be grafted to dwarf stocks. The resulting trees

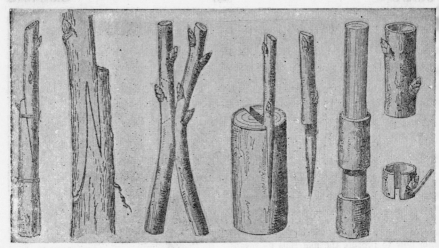

GRAFTING METHODS. *Left to right: Splice; whip; inarching; cleft; budding methods.*

produce high-quality fruit and have the advantage, from the grower's viewpoint, of being dwarf plants. Production of fruit on young trees may be hastened by grafting mature fruit-bearing branches on them.

Grafting is not a method of hybridization. The connection between a scion and a stock is merely physiological. Fertile fruits borne on scion branches will produce seeds which give rise to plants of the scion type; those produced on stock branches give rise to plants of the stock type.

Grafts are usually unsuccessful unless plants of the same or closely related kinds are used. The first successful interfamily graft, between eggplant (Nightshade family) and *Iresine* (Amaranth family), was made in 1930. More recently, in 1948, a large number of successful interfamily grafts were made; for example, white sweet clover was grafted on sunflower, tobacco, and geranium, and cowpea was grafted on tomato.

Grafting Methods. A seedling or cutting, usually chosen for hardiness and resistance to pests and diseases or for special characteristics such as dwarfing, is commonly used as the stock in grafting. When a seedling is used as a stock, it is first allowed to establish its root system; a graft is then inserted at the base of the stem. As soon as the union of scion and stock has become established, any remaining portions of the shoot of the stock are cut away; all substances absorbed by the root system are thereafter available to the scion for its development. When a cutting is used, the graft is made first, and then the cutting is

rooted. Nursery stock for rubber plantations and for many fruit orchards is produced by the seedling type of grafting.

The area surrounding the juncture of scion and stock is protected by paraffin or by grafting wax, a mixture of beeswax, beef tallow, and resin. Grafting tape is usually used to cover the waxed wound, to exclude moisture and prevent attack by diseases or pests

The most popular types of grafting used by tree and bush growers are splice grafting, whip or tongue grafting, saddle grafting, cleft grafting, and side grafting. In *splice grafting,* a simple diagonal cut is made in scion and stock. The cut surfaces are joined, and are covered with grafting wax or paraffin and bound with grafting tape. In *whip grafting,* the scion and stock are cut diagonally to provide large surfaces for union. A slit, parallel with the direction of growth, is made in both surfaces, near the apex of the diagonal cut. The thin "tongues" of wood thus formed on stock and scion are fitted into the opposing slits and the union is bound as in splice grafting. *Saddle grafting* is accomplished by cutting the uniting surface of one of the two stems to be joined, usually the stock, in the shape of a wedge, and cutting the other stem in the shape of a slot which will fit the wedge tightly. In *cleft grafting,* branches of the stock, ½ to 2 inches in diameter, are sawed straight across and the stub of the branch is split to a depth approximating the diameter of the stock. A temporary wedge, sufficient to open the slit, is inserted at the center of the split. Two scions, each having several buds, are inserted at the edges of the split, and adjusted so that the lowest bud is close to the top of the stock and facing outward. The wedge is removed without displacing the scions, and the cut is covered with grafting wax and, if necessary, bound with grafting tape. Sometimes more than two scions are used; all the scions but the strongest are removed in the following season. Cleft grafting is the most widely used method for grafting scions which produce high-quality fruit on mature trees. *Side grafting* is the method ordinarily employed in budding and is also used in stem grafting. A longitudinal cut is made through the bark layer. The scion, with its base cut in the shape of a wedge, is inserted beneath the bark, tied, and waxed. This method is useful for grafting new branches on bare spaces of tree trunks.

Branches may be grafted to adjacent plants without detaching the scions from their parent plants until the grafts have been successfully united, a procedure known as *inarching*. Another specialized type of grafting, *bridge grafting*, is used to repair injuries caused by girdling. Rodents girdle tree trunks, removing bark and the conducting tissue beneath the bark; replacement of conducting tissue is necessary to the continued life of the plant. This replacement is accomplished by inserting several shoots, slightly longer than the width of the girdled band, to bridge the gap. The edges of the wound are cut to expose healthy tissue. Slits are cut into the new upper and lower edges at four or five places around the girdled area. The scions are cut diagonally at each end, and fitted into the slots; these cut surfaces of the scions fit smoothly against the exposed wood, and the centers of the scions bow outward. The wounded area is covered with grafting wax and bound with waxed cloth.

GRAFTING, SKIN. See SKIN: *Skin Grafting*.

GRAHAM, BILLY. See GRAHAM, WILLIAM.

GRAHAM, EVARTS AMBROSE (1883–1957), American surgeon, born in Chicago, Ill., and educated at Princeton University and Rush Medical College. In 1911 he became instructor in surgery at Rush Medical College. From 1919 to 1951 he served as professor of surgery at the Washington University School of Medicine. He was elected president of the International Congress of Surgeons in 1953. Graham developed X-ray techniques for visualization of the gall bladder. He conducted extensive cancer research and was among the first to discover a relationship between cigarette smoking and lung-cancer incidence.

GRAHAM, JAMES. See MONTROSE, JAMES GRAHAM, MARQUIS OF.

GRAHAM or **GRAHAM OF CLAVERHOUSE,** JOHN, 1st VISCOUNT DUNDEE (1649?–89), Scottish soldier, educated at St. Andrews University. From 1672 to 1677 he served in Holland in the army of William of Orange, and then returned to Scotland to command the royal troops against the Covenanters (q.v.), who, in 1679, defeated his army at Drumclog. Graham then was given great powers and authority with which to suppress the Covenanters, which he did by pursuing and annihilating their leaders, and by cutting off their food supply. His success won him a grant of land and the position of sheriff of Wigtown. In 1686 he became a major general and two years later was made Viscount Dundee. Upon the flight of James II from England in 1688, Graham raised an army against the new regime of William and Mary. He was denounced as a traitor, and a price of £20,000 was placed on his head. After retreating to Blair Castle in the Highlands, he gathered a considerable force of clansmen around him. General Hugh Mackay, commanding the government forces, pursued him, and the two armies met at the pass of Killiecrankie. Graham's Highlanders won the battle, but Graham was mortally wounded. He has become a controversial figure in Scottish history. To the Covenanters and their descendants he was a monster, "Bloody Claverse"; but the Highlanders and Jacobites (q.v.) regarded him as a romantic figure, and he is the hero of the Scottish ballad "Bonny Dundee".

GRAHAM, MARTHA (?–   ), American dancer, born in Pittsburgh, Pa. She received her early training as a dancer with the Denishawn school; see ST. DENIS, RUTH. After two years (1923–25) of dancing in Broadway productions she was appointed director of the dance department at the Eastman School of Music in Rochester, N.Y., and turned to creating dances of her own. She gave her first recital in 1926.

In her earliest works the angularity and severity of her movements and the grim seriousness of her approach met with bewilderment and antagonism. As her highly individual and expressive style developed, however, she became one of the leading figures in contemporary dance. She was the first modern dancer in the U.S. to break away from small, intimate recitals to performances adjusted to modern commercial standards. She trained young dancers for her company, and formulated a teachable system of dance technique.

After 1934 she used only music specially composed for her dances, by such musicians as

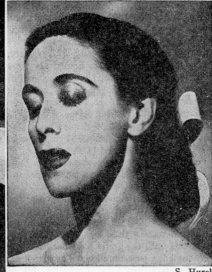

S. Hurok

Martha Graham, one of the most original of contemporary dancers in America

Aaron Copland and Paul Hindemith. In her later works she made full use of the traditional resources of the theater, including lighting, stage sets and properties, and costuming, and produced dance-dramas in both narrative and abstract forms. Her stage settings were executed by notable artists, particularly Isamu Noguchi. Outstanding among her scores of compositions are *Lamentation* (1930), *Primitive Mysteries* (1931), *American Provincials* (1934), *Frontier* (1935), *American Document* (1938), *Every Soul is a Circus* (1939), *El Penitente* (1940), *Letter to the World* (1940), *Deaths and Entrances* (1943), *Appalachian Spring* (1944), *Dark Meadow* (1946), *Innovation* (1949), and *Voyage* (1953). See DANCE.

GRAHAM, THOMAS (1805–69), Scottish chemist, born at Glasgow, and educated at the universities of Edinburgh and Glasgow. He was a professor of chemistry at Glasgow from 1830 to 1837 and at London University from 1837 to 1855. Graham is best known for his research in diffusion (q.v.) of gases and liquids and in colloid chemistry. He demonstrated that the rate of diffusion of a gas is inversely proportional to the square root of its density, a relationship now known as Graham's Law. In the field of colloid chemistry he was the earliest to distinguish between colloids and crystalloids (his term for ordinary solutes), and he discovered the method of dialysis for separating colloids from

true solutions; see COLLOIDAL DISPERSION.

GRAHAM, WILLIAM FRANKLIN, popularly BILLY GRAHAM (1918–), American evangelist, born in Charlotte, N.C., and educated at Ben Jones College, at the Florida Bible Institute, and at Wheaton (Ill.) College. He was ordained in the Southern Baptist Convention in 1939. In 1943, on his graduation from Wheaton College, he became pastor of the First Baptist Church of Western Springs, Ill. Graham turned to evangelism in 1946, embarking on a series of tours of the United States and Europe. A forceful and eloquent preacher, he attracted audiences totaling millions to his meetings during the next nine years and won many thousands of converts. He served as first vice-president of Youth for Christ International after 1946 and after 1950 conducted the weekly nationwide radio program *Hour for Decision*. He served also as president of Northwestern Schools from 1947 to 1951, when he became president of the board of directors. In 1954, during a five-month tour of Europe, Graham spoke to an estimated 2,000,000 persons; during a similar tour in 1955 he spoke to about 4,000,000 persons. His three-month New York City crusade in 1957 drew audiences totaling about 2,000,000. Among his writings are *Revival in Our Time* (1950) and *Peace With God* (1953).

GRAHAME, KENNETH (1859–1932), British author, born at Edinburgh, and educated at St. Edward's School, Oxford. In 1878 he joined the staff of the Bank of England, becoming secretary in 1898. He retired after the publication of his most successful work, *The Wind in the Willows* (1908), a fantasy about animals which has been widely popular among adults and children. His other works include *Pagan Papers* (1893) and *Dream Days* (1898).

GRAHAME-WHITE, CLAUDE (1879–   ), English aviator and aeronautical engineer, educated at Bedford Grammar School and Crondall House College. He worked as an automobile mechanic until 1909 when he became interested in aeronautics. He was the first Englishman to receive an aviator's license. Grahame-White founded a flying school at Pau, France, in 1909. During World War I he was superintendent of construction of airplanes for the British government. Among his writings are *The Aeroplane* (1911), *Learning to Fly* (1914), *Our First Airways* (1918), and *Flying, an Epitome and a Forecast* (1930).

GRAHAMITE. See ASPHALT.

GRAIL, THE HOLY (Med. Lat. *cratella*, "bowl"), in medieval legend, the Sangraal, or sacred cup, used by Jesus Christ at the Last Supper. It was preserved by Joseph of Arimathea (q.v.), who collected in it the blood from the body of Christ, either while the body was on the Cross or after it had been taken down. The vessel was then conveyed to Britain, where it was transmitted from generation to generation of Joseph's descendants. The Grail possessed many mystical properties, such as the power of furnishing food for those who were, like Joseph, without sin; of multiplying a few loaves of bread to satisfy the needs of five hundred people; and of blinding with its supernal effulgence all the impure of heart who looked upon it, or of striking dumb the irreverent who came into its presence.

The Holy Grail first makes its appearance in medieval romance united with the story of Percivale. As a youth, Percivale sets forth to achieve knighthood, at length reaching the castle of the Fisher King, a monarch renowned for his ability as an angler. The Fisher King is Percivale's uncle (though unknown to him) and is custodian of the Holy Grail and of the spear which transfixed the side of Christ while He was on the Cross. Because of his sinful ways, the Fisher King had been struck dumb on coming into the presence of the sacred chalice. When Percivale enters the castle he witnesses a procession in which the bleeding spear and the Holy Grail pass before the speechless king. In his astonishment, Percivale fails to ask any questions concerning the strange pantomime, not knowing that if he, a pure and guileless soul, had spoken, his uncle would have been healed. After many wanderings, Percivale returns to the Grail castle, welds together a broken sword or (in an alternate version) slays the enemy of the Fisher King, restores his uncle's power of speech, and succeeds him in the kingship.

In later legend, the Holy Grail has become an object of consecrated search, and the leading role in the quest is assigned to Sir Galahad (q.v.). Many other knights of King Arthur's court set out to find the sacred chalice, but the quest was realized only by Sir Bors, in addition to Percivale and Galahad.

The development of the legend of the Holy Grail was substantially as follows. Chrétien de Troyes, a French poet of the 12th century, left at his death an unfinished poem called *Perceval,* which was continued by other writers. On the same source as this romance, the 13th-century German epic poet Wolfram von Eschenbach founded his *Parzival,* one of the finest treatments of the Grail theme. Sir Thomas Malory, an English writer and translator of the 15th century, embodied the quest of the sacred chalice in his *Morte d'Arthur.* In the 19th century the legend of the Holy Grail was treated by the English poet Alfred Lord Tennyson in his *Idylls of the King* and by the German composer Richard Wagner in his music drama *Parsifal.*

Many features of the Grail story, notably the hero and the magic vessel, are now regarded as being of Celtic origin. A Celtic saga

Kenneth Grahame (from a pencil sketch)

Musical Courier

Percy Grainger

tells of a hero who journeys to the under-world and brings back three talismans: a lance which drips blood, a broken sword which only the hero can make whole, and an inexhaustible vessel of plenty and rejuvenation. Christianization of the Celtic saga was carried out by pious men who wished to make the pagan story a vehicle for moral and religious instruction.

GRAIN, a term properly applied to the edible fruits of grasses, such as corn, rice, and wheat, and of several unrelated plants, such as buckwheat; see CEREALS; FRUIT; GRASSES.

GRAINGER, PERCY (1882–), Australian-American pianist and composer, born in Melbourne. His first piano instructor was his mother, a professional teacher; later he studied with various masters in Melbourne and in Germany. Grainger first came to wide public attention as a piano virtuoso through a recital he gave in London in 1900. Subsequently he made tours of Great Britain, various Continental countries, Australia, New Zealand, South Africa, and the United States. His first appearance in the United States was in a recital in New York City, in 1915. During World War I he was an instructor in the

U.S. Army Music School; in 1919 he became a naturalized citizen of the United States. For a time he was director of the music department of the Washington Square College, New York University.

Grainger was one of the outstanding pianists of his time. His playing was known for its dash and fire and he was particularly distinguished for his playing of the works of modern composers, such as Albéniz, Debussy, and Ravel. As a composer he was self-taught. He was particularly interested in folk music and made phonograph recordings of more than five hundred examples of the playing and singing of folk music of European countries, America, Africa, and Australia. Many of his approximately four hundred compositions are based on folk music, particularly that of the British Isles.

Among Grainger's compositions are the orchestral works *Molly on the Shore* (1921), *Shepherd's Hey* (1922), *Country Gardens* (1925), and *Mock Morris;* the work for chorus *Australian Up-Country Song* (1930); the piano pieces *Handel in the Strand* (1930) and *Paraphrase of the Flower-Waltz* from Tchaikovsky's *Nutcracker Suite;* chamber music, including the octet *My Robin Is to the Greenwood Gone, La Scandinavie* (melodies for cello and piano), and *Green Rushes* (for twenty-one instruments); and songs, including *Six Dukes Went A-Fishin'* and *The Pretty Maid Milkin' Her Cow.*

GRAINING. See DACE.

GRAIN WEEVIL. See WEEVIL.

GRAIN RUST. See RUST.

GRAM. See C.G.S. SYSTEM.

GRAMA GRASS, or MESQUITE GRASS, common name for grasses of the genus *Bouteloua,* native to short-grass range lands of the Western Hemisphere. About 18 species are well represented in the Great Plains and western States of the U.S. The genus is characterized by spikelets which bear single florets. Summer is the growing season of grama grass, and the amount of growth depends on the amount of moisture available during this season. Grama grass is a valuable forage plant, and is used extensively as a soil binder in erosion control. Most of the species do not require curing as forage because standing growth from previous seasons is palatable to livestock. The important species of grama in the U.S. are side oats, *B. curtipendula,* and blue grama, *B. gracilis,* both of which are abundant in the Great Plains. Side oats is adaptable to a wide range of climatic and soil conditions. Blue grama has differentiated into strains, each of which is very successful in the region in which it has evolved but is not successful when transplanted to another region.

GRAMINEAE. See GRASSES.

GRAMMAR (Gr. *gramma,* "letter"), a branch of linguistic science dealing generally with the principles of the use of language, and specifically with the categories, functions, and interrelations of words as they are used in sentences. The study of grammar itself has several branches. *Historical grammar* is the study of the development of the words and syntax of a language. *Comparative grammar* is the study of the forms of related languages and of the influences which such languages have upon each other. *Descriptive grammar* is concerned with observing and recording the actual forms of words, pronunciations, spellings, and related details of a specific language as that language is used in a particular area. *Normative* or *prescriptive grammar* is that branch which seeks, by analyzing the characteristics and principles applying to a given language at a particular time, to establish correct linguistic usage for that period.

History of Grammar. The basic material of grammatical study is language, and grammar evolved only after the use of language had reached a fairly high stage of development. Thus, although the origins of language are prehistoric, the earliest written grammar now extant dates from so comparatively recent a period as the 4th century B.C.; this work is the eight-volume Sanskrit grammar compiled by the Hindu scholar Panini (q.v.). Panini, however, refers to sixty-four earlier grammatical works, indicating that the study of grammar had been developing for some time. Religious writings supplied the basic impetus for the work of Panini and of other Hindu grammarians; grammatical study served chiefly as an aid to the correct reading of sacred Hindu literature.

Of the other Oriental peoples, only the Arabs and Jews developed grammatical works in pre-medieval times; like the Hindus, they too were motivated by the needs of religion. Grammatical study of the Arabic language is generally believed to have begun in the 7th century A.D. The scholar Abu 'l Aswad ad-Duil (d. 688) is considered the first Arabic grammarian. Although the ancient Jews are known to have carried on some grammatical studies, not until the Jews came under the influence of the more fully developed Arabic culture did they write formal grammars. The oldest extant Hebrew grammatical work is a lexicon by David ben Abraham (10th cent.), but the work regarded by scholars as the greatest of the early Hebrew grammatical writings is the study of the language of the Old Testament written by the Rabbi Jonah (990?–1050?).

Among the ancient Greeks, the incentive for the study of grammar came from literary and philosophical rather than religious sources. The philosopher Plato, writing in the late 4th century B.C., was one of the earliest Greek writers to discuss grammar in his works; his pupil Aristotle made an important contribution to the development of the subject when he distinguished between nouns, verbs, and "connectives". Many of the technical terms still used in grammar were coined by the ancient Greek philosophers even before formal grammar was known. In the 1st century B.C., the Stoic philosopher Posidonius gave to the five cases of Greek nouns the names which are still applied to them today. In the same period the Greek grammarian Dionysius Thrax wrote the celebrated *Art of Grammar,* which served as a model not only for subsequent Greek and Latin grammars, but also for those dealing with the European languages which developed much later.

The grammatical works of the ancient Romans are generally imitative of their Greek models, but embody a few important contributions; Marcus Terentius Varro (q.v.) is especially notable for his studies of etymology. The 18-volume *Institutionis Grammaticæ,* by the 6th-century Latin scholar Priscian, was used throughout the Middle Ages as the standard authority on Latin grammar.

Very little progress in grammatical study was made during the medieval period. The few important advances were due to the spread of Christianity, which resulted in the translation of the Scriptures into the vernaculars of the peoples to whom the new religion was carried, and thereby furthered the development of nonclassical languages. The only formal grammar of this period is that written in Welsh, entitled *Desparth Edeyrn Aur,* compiled by Edeyrn the Golden-Tongued in the 13th century.

Interest in grammar was profoundly stimulated by the great revival of learning during the Renaissance. Latin and Greek exercised great influence over all grammar, and the earliest Renaissance treatises dealt with the relation of the classical languages to the vernaculars. This influence eventually proved harmful, for in their devotion to the classical forms many scholars tended to fit all languages into the rigid and totally unsuited grammatical structures of Greek and Latin. A noteworthy instance of this type of grammatical work is one of the earliest comprehensive treatises on English grammar, the *Grammatica Linguæ Anglicanæ* (1652), by John Wallis (1616–1703), which attempts to analyze and describe the English tongue in terms of Latin usage.

Although the tendency to use classical grammar as the pattern for grammatical study had begun to disappear by the opening of the 19th century, it has continued to hamper the development of scientific grammar to the present time. Many modern grammarians have, however, freed themselves of this difficulty, and base their studies on the individual characteristics of each language. Outstanding among these scholars is the Danish grammarian Jens Otto Harry Jespersen (q.v.), whose works, including *A Modern English Grammar on Historical Principles* (4 parts, 1909–31) and *Philosophy of Grammar* (1924), are regarded as monumental contributions to the science of grammar.

The Parts of Speech. The most generally accepted method of grammatical analysis is that which classifies words according to their functions in sentences. Words studied in this manner are known as *parts of speech,* and the classifications are almost identical in most of the major language groups in use today, notably the Indo-European languages and the Semitic languages (qq.v.).

For the purposes of analysis, the parts of speech are usually classified into eight categories: nouns, adjectives, pronouns, verbs, adverbs, prepositions, conjunctions, and interjections (qq.v.).

In some respects, this system of classification does not fully satisfy the demands of scientific accuracy. The English noun and adjective, for example, are so closely allied that their functions often overlap; it is thought probable that in the early history of the Indo-European languages they were both grouped in the single class of nouns, and that the custom of juxtaposing nouns, each modifying the meaning of the other, gave rise to the separate category of adjectives. Similarly, adverbs, prepositions, and conjunctions have been shown by comparative philology to be in most instances stereotyped case-forms of nouns. Pronouns are a distinct class, although in many forms they are inflected like adjectives. Verbs, particularly in the infinitive and participial forms, sometimes overlap the noun-adjective group, but in general constitute a third group. Interjections, which in their primitive forms were merely reflex emotive vocal actions, bear no direct relation to the other parts of speech, and must therefore be classed separately. Scientifically, then, the parts of speech are considered as four in number: nouns, pronouns, verbs, and interjections.

Distinctive Features of English Grammar. The grammar of the English language as it is used today avoids many of the complexities and difficulties common to most other modern languages, and hence is distinguished for its comparative simplicity; the varying relationships of English words do not require corresponding changes in the forms of the words (i.e., the words are not inflected) as often as do words in other languages, such as French, German, Spanish, Italian, and the Slavic tongues.

One of the chief means of eliminating the need for such changes in form is the complete abolition of *grammatical gender* in English. In other languages, inanimate objects and abstract terms are often classed in the masculine and feminine genders, and male and female beings are sometimes classed as neuter; but in English, males are invariably masculine, females are invariably feminine, and inanimate objects and abstractions are invariably neuter. Metaphorical usage constitutes the sole exception to this principle; for example, ships are often personified and treated as feminine objects.

The comparative absence of inflection in English is demonstrated by several additional noteworthy instances. English nouns have only three cases, namely nominative, possessive or genitive, and objective or accusative; and only two case-endings, the nominative and accusative being identical. English adjectives do not change their forms to correspond in gender, number, and case with the nouns they modify. Except for an extremely limited number of irregular verbs, the conjugation of English verbs involves relatively few changes in form. The advantage which the English language gains from these grammatical simplifications may be simply stated: they make English grammar comparatively easy to learn, and the English language extremely flexible to use.

See also ETYMOLOGY; INFLECTION; LANGUAGE; PHILOLOGY; PROSODY; SPELLING; SYNTAX.

GRAMMAR SCHOOL, a school in which the curriculum emphasizes the study of Greek and Latin grammar and related subjects. In a graded system of public elementary schools such as that of the United States, the term is, through historical derivation, sometimes applied to the grades between the primary curriculum (grades 1–3) and the high-school curriculum (grades 9–12), and less correctly to the grades of the entire elementary curriculum (grades 1–8). During the early Middle Ages, Latin grammar was almost the only subject taught in the monastic schools, the principal European educational institutions. As universities developed and education became more secular, the Latin grammar school became a college-preparatory institution.

Gradually the study of grammar, viewed as one of the seven liberal arts (q.v.), came to include all subjects relating to written language, such as style. Greek grammar was added to the curriculum during the Revival of Learning, the intellectual phase of the Renaissance in the 15th and 16th centuries. The study of vernacular languages entered the curriculum during the Reformation, but was given secondary emphasis. These subjects became and remained the major objects of study in European secondary schools, which were generically called grammar, or Latin grammar, schools, such as the British so-called "public" schools, the German *gymnasium,* and the French *lycée.* Such schools were established in America during the 17th century.

When free, State-controlled educational systems were established in the United States during the 19th century, the grammar-school curriculum was incorporated into the public-school system. Although the term "grammar school" is still used, to indicate the level of instruction next above the rudiments of reading and writing, the true grammar-school subjects have, in the U.S., been made a part of the academic branch of secondary education in public schools. Private academies, such as Philips Exeter Academy (see EXETER, N.H.), still retain aspects of the European grammar school.

See articles under the major listing EDUCATION.

GRAMMONT, ORDER OF. See GRANDMONTAINS.

GRAMPIANS, THE, or GRAMPIAN HILLS, a mountain system of Scotland, forming the natural division between the Lowlands and Highlands. They extend through the center of Scotland in a S.W. to N.E. direction, passing through the shires of Argyll, Dumbarton, Stirling, Perth, Forfar, Kincardine, Aberdeen, Banff, and Inverness. At the w. extremity of the mountain mass is Ben Nevis, the highest peak, which rises 4405 ft. above sea level. The other chief summits are Ben Macdhui (4298 ft.), Cairngorm (4084 ft.), Ben Lawers (3986 ft.), Ben More (3845 ft.), Ben Alder (3757 ft.), Ben Cruachan (3693 ft.), and Ben Lomond (3192 ft.). The principal rivers rising in the Grampians are the Findhorn, Spey, Don, Dee, South Esk, Tay, and Forth. The mountains present a generally bold aspect, but in places slope gradually, affording excellent pasturage. On the N. the mountains are more rugged and difficult to traverse. Among the famous passes through them are those of Aberfoyle, Glenshee, and Killiecrankie. The Grampians contain the finest deer forests in Scotland. The mountains derive their name from the Graupius Mons of the Roman historian Tacitus, the site of the defeat by Agricola in 84 A.D. of the Caledonians, a northern tribe of the Picts.

GRAMPUS, common name applied to two different whales in the Dolphin family: Risso's dolphin, *Grampus griseus,* and the killer whale, *Orcinus orca.* Both are world-wide in distribution. Risso's dolphin, also called cowfish, is a striped whale averaging twelve ft. in length at maturity. It has few teeth in its lower jaw and none in its upper jaw, and subsists on mollusks. The killer whale reaches a length of thirty ft. Its back is black and its underparts white. The killer whale has twenty-four permanent, conical teeth in each jaw. This animal is the only whale which habitually preys on mammals; it attacks seals, porpoises, and even larger whales, as well as large fish. It is extremely dangerous to man. The killer whales are called sea wolves by the Eskimos because of their voraciousness and because they hunt in packs. They are sometimes called swordfish.

GRAM'S STAIN, one of the most widely used methods of bacteriological staining, devised by the Danish physician Hans Christian Joachim Gram (1853–1938). Gram's method is based on the observation that most bacteria, dyed with gentian violet and Gram's solution (1 part iodine, 2 parts potassium iodide, 300 parts water), will either retain a strong blue color or be completely decolorized after washing with ethyl alcohol. In most present-day modifications of Gram's stain, a counterstain such as fuchsin or eosin is applied after the alcohol treatment to give a red color to the decolorized bacteria.

The reaction to the ethyl alcohol treatment is a basis for identifying bacteria; bacteria which retain the blue stain are known as *Gram-positive;* those which are decolorized are known as *Gram-negative.* Some organisms,

Museum model of the grampus, or killer whale

known as *Gram-variable,* sometimes retain the blue color and at other times are decolorized. Typical Gram-positive bacteria are the staphylococci which produce boils; typical Gram-negative bacteria are the bacilli which cause whooping cough; typical Gram-variable bacteria are the bacilli which cause tuberculosis.

Gram's stain is valuable as an indicator of the type of bacterium responsible for a particular infectious disease, and consequently of the medicine to be used. Penicillin and the sulfa drugs are effective against Gram-positive bacteria but generally ineffective against Gram-negative bacteria, with the notable exceptions of gonococcus and meningococcus. Antibiotics of the streptomycin group are effective against most Gram-negative bacteria and some Gram-variable organisms, particularly the tuberculosis bacillus.

GRANADA, capital of the department of the same name in Nicaragua, Central America. The city is situated on the N.W. shore of Lake Nicaragua, 36 miles S.E. of Managua, the national capital. It is served by lake steamers and by the Pacific Railroad of Nicaragua, of which it is a terminus. The city is an episcopal see, and the commercial center of an agricultural area producing sugar cane, cotton, coffee, cacao, and cattle. In addition, it is an educational center, and the site of the University of Central America, one of the three universities of Nicaragua. Granada contains many large and ornate churches, and several old mansions of the colonial period. The numerous islands in the lake resorts serve as recreational resorts for the residents of Granada. The city was founded in 1524 by Francisco Fernández de Córdoba, and it early became an important trading and political center. During the 17th century it suffered frequently from raids by pirates from the Caribbean; during one attack, in 1606, it was sacked and burned. For the greater part of its history Granada has been the headquarters of the Conservative party in Nicaragua, and as such, a bitter rival of León, 88 m. to the N.W., which has long been the center for the Liberals. The commercial and political feud between the two cities resulted in the choice of Managua as the capital of Nicaragua in 1855, although they were of greater importance at the time. In Sept., 1855, Granada was captured and partially burned by a group of revolutionaries under William Walker (q.v.), an American adventurer. The department of

Granada, lying between the Pacific Ocean on the w., Lake Nicaragua on the e., and Lake Managua on the n., has an area of 540 sq.m.; pop. (1950) 48,990. Pop. of city (1950) 21,035.

GRANADA, province of Andalusia, s. Spain, bordering the Mediterranean Sea. In 711 it was captured by the Moors, and dominated by them until 1492. In the 13th century Granada became an independent Moorish kingdom, obliged to pay tribute to the Christian king of Castile. When the vassal king of Granada refused, in 1492, to render the usual tribute, King Ferdinand and Queen Isabella of Spain conquered the kingdom, making it one of the thirteen provinces of 15th-century Spain. In 1833 old Granada was divided into the present-day provinces of Granada, Almería, and Málaga. The chief cities of modern Granada include the capital Granada (q.v.), Guadix (pop. in 1940, 18,318), Motril (15,961), Baza (14,330), Loja (11,023), Pinos-Puente (7499), Almuñécar (5258), Montefrio (4807), and Illora (4498). In the province are several mountain ranges, the chief of which is the Sierra Nevada, in the s., containing Cerro de Mulhacén (11,417 ft. above sea level), the highest mountain peak in Spain. The mountains are rich in minerals and their slopes, which receive adequate rainfall throughout the year, provide pasture for sheep and goats. The Genil and Guadiana rivers water the fertile basins of the north. In that region, one of the most fertile in Spain, are grown sugar cane, cereal grains, grapes, and cotton. Sugar refining, begun shortly after Spain lost the sugar-producing Spanish West Indies and the Philippines in the Spanish-American War, is the principal industry of Granada. Area, 4837 sq.m.; pop. (1950) 782,953.

GRANADA, capital of the province of Granada (q.v.), Andalusia, s. Spain. The city, located at the foot of the Sierra Nevada Mts., at the confluence of the Genil and Darro rivers, was founded in the 8th century by the Moors near the site of the ancient Iberian city of Iliberris. Between 1036 and 1234 Granada was a part of the kingdom of Córdoba (see CORDOVA). At the end of that period, when the Moors were deprived of most of their Spanish possessions, the city of Granada became the capital of the remaining Moorish bloc of territory, called the kingdom of Granada. The city then entered upon its most flourishing era, becoming a rich trading center and attaining a reputation as a center for art, literature, and science. Its prosperity con-

tinued for about a century after the Spanish conquest of the kingdom of Granada in 1492. The most important vestige of the splendid Moorish civilization is the Alhambra (q.v.), the fortress-palace of the Moor rulers. Other important buildings include the university, founded in 1531 by Emperor Charles V, and the cathedral, dating from 1529. Adjoining the cathedral is the *Capilla Real,* containing the tombs of Ferdinand and Isabella. During the Spanish Civil War (1936–39) the city was captured by the Nationalists, but the rest of the province of Granada was held by the Loyalists until the end of the conflict. Liqueurs, paper, woolens, and soap are manufactured in the city, and a large trade in agricultural produce is maintained. Pop. (1950) 154,378.

GRANADILLA. See PASSIONFLOWER.

Hillside houses in Granada, Spain

GRAN CANARIA. See GRAND CANARY.

GRAN CHACO. See CHACO, EL.

GRAND ALLIANCE, a coalition formed in 1689 and again in 1701 against Louis XIV of France (see FRANCE: *History*). The alliance of 1689 was entered into by the Holy Roman Empire, the Netherlands, England, and Spain to enforce upon France the conditions of the Treaty of Westphalia and the Peace of the Pyrenees. The coalition of 1701 was formed by the Holy Roman Empire, England, and the Netherlands to prevent the union of the crowns of France and Spain under the Bourbon dynasty. The second Grand Alliance was subsequently joined by Prussia, Portugal, and Savoy. See SUCCESSION WARS; SPANISH SUCCESSION, WAR OF THE.

GRAND ARMY OF THE REPUBLIC, an American patriotic organization, consisting of United States armed forces veterans of the Civil War, founded in Decatur, Illinois, during the winter of 1865–66. The G.A.R. admitted any member of the United States Army, Navy, or Marine Corps who had served between April 12, 1861, and April 9, 1865, and had been honorably discharged, and also members of State regiments who had been called into service. The organization, founded for the commemoration of dead comrades, and the practice of fraternity and mutual assistance, held its first national "encampment" in Indianapolis, on Nov. 20, 1866; two years later the G.A.R. instituted Memorial Day.

According to a rule made by the organization in 1869, the G.A.R. was intended to take no official part in politics, but the organization actually at one time wielded considerable political influence, particularly in its support of Presidential candidates between 1872 and 1904, the period during which its membership was greatest. The organization was responsible for passage of the Disability Act of 1890, which doubled the pension roll; it also established old soldiers' homes, and provided care and education for soldiers' orphans. The membership declined after 1890, when the total was 409,487. At the beginning of 1930, membership was about 21,000, and by the middle of the 20th century few Civil War veterans remained alive.

The first G.A.R. post was created in Springfield, Illinois, with Dr. Benjamin Franklin Stephenson (1823–71), one of the founders, as head of the organization. Its headquarters now are in the State House, Boston, Massachusetts. Encampments were held annually until 1949 in selected cities of the United States, but in recent years few of the delegates were physically able to march in the traditional parades celebrating the event. Auxiliary orders of the G.A.R. are the Woman's Relief Corps, the Ladies of the G.A.R., and the Sons and Daughters of Union Veterans.

GRAND BANK, a shoal, believed to be the summit of a submerged mountain range, in the Atlantic Ocean, extending for a length of 300 miles S.E. of Newfoundland (q.v.). It lies at an average depth of from 80 to 100 fathoms. The Grand Bank is one of the most famous fishing areas in the world, frequented annually by the fishing fleets of Canada, the U.S., Great Britain, and France. Marine life on the Grand Bank is unusually abundant as the result of the meeting there of the Gulf Stream and the Labrador current. Hordes of fish, especially cod, feed in the waters of the Bank.

GRAND CANAL, chief thoroughfare of the city of Venice, Italy. The canal, which follows an S-shaped course through the city, is from 30 to 60 yards wide. Along either bank stand a series of famous palaces, each one marked by a post painted with the owner's heraldic colors. The canal is crossed in the center of the city by the Rialto bridge. Two other waterways, one in China and one in Ireland, also bear the name Grand Canal (see CANAL).

GRAND CANARY, or GRAN CANARIA, island of the Canary Islands (q.v.), forming part of the Spanish province of Las Palmas. It lies in the Atlantic Ocean about 75 m. off the N.W. coast of Africa. The island, of volcanic origin, is almost circular in shape, and is mountainous, with several extinct volcanic craters. The highest peak is Los Pexos, which rises to a height of about 6400 ft. above sea level. The climate is mild and healthful. Fishing and agriculture are the principal industries. The capital and chief town is Las Palmas (q.v.). Area, 592 sq.m.; pop. (1940) 279,875.

GRAND CANYON NATIONAL MONUMENT, a national monument established in 1932 in N. Arizona, adjoining Grand Canyon National Park on the N.W. It comprises 196,-051 acres, and contains a portion of the Grand Canyon of the Colorado (q.v.). Included within the area is Toroweap Point, which affords a view of the inner gorge of the Grand Canyon at a point where it is approximately 3000 ft. deep and a mile wide.

GRAND CANYON NATIONAL PARK, a national park in N. Arizona, established in 1919. Its area of 1008 sq.m. contains the most spectacular section of the world-famous Grand Canyon of the Colorado (q.v.) River.

National Park Service

The Grand Canyon of the Colorado in Arizona, over a mile in depth

The walls of the great chasm, which has a maximum width of 18 m. within the park, rise to a height of nearly a mile. The North Rim of the canyon averages 1200 ft. higher than the South Rim, and is closed to sight-seers by heavy snows from October to May. Both rims afford excellent views of the multi-colored rock formations in the abyss. The walls and formations of the canyon, composed of many different kinds of rocks, are remark-able for their variety of hues. Within the canyon spreads a panorama of valleys and peaks, craggy cliffs, mesas, buttes, terraces, and amphitheaters.

The extreme variations in altitude from the canyon depths to the North Rim have pro-duced four distinct climatic and plant-life zones. Dense virgin stands of quaking aspen, pine, fir, and spruce grow on the North Rim, and the South Rim is forested with piñon and juniper. Among the animals in the park are deer, antelope, cougars, and mountain sheep. Prehistoric Indian tribes lived in the canyon and on its rims; the ruins of about 500 pueblos and cliff dwellings have been discovered.

Beyond the E. boundary of the park lies the Painted Desert, and on its w. boundary is Havasu Canyon, in the depths of which is the reservation of the Havasupai Indians, an agricultural people. Adjoining the park on the

N.W. is Grand Canyon National Monument (q.v.). Paved roads wind about the rims, and trails descend into the canyon, although only one, the Kaibab Trail, crosses the gorge from rim to rim. Numerous hotels and camping sites are situated along the brink of the Grand Canyon, and guides are available for trips into its depths.

GRAND CANYON OF THE COLORADO, an enormous valley in Arizona excavated by the Colorado River (q.v.). The Grand Can-yon is approximately 217 m. in length, 4 to 18 m. in width, and more than a mile in depth. The entire canyon is impressively beautiful, containing towering buttes, mesas, and val-leys within its main gorge. Approximately 56 m. of its length, together with plateau areas on either side of the canyon, were dedicated to the public use in 1919 as the Grand Canyon National Park (q.v.).

The canyon cuts steeply through an arid plateau region which lies between 5000 and 9000 feet above sea level. This region, al-though it has at present no year-round streams, is sharply eroded, showing such characteristic forms as buttes, and is inter-spersed with old lava flows, hills composed of volcanic debris, and intrusions of igneous rock. The plateau area has a general down-ward slope to the southwest, and in its upper reaches is sparsely covered with growths of such evergreens as juniper and piñon. Parts of the North Rim of the canyon are forested. The depths of the valley have very little vegetation, principally such desert plants as agave and Spanish bayonet. In general the entire canyon area has little soil. The climate of the plateau region above the canyon is severe with extremes of both heat and cold. The canyon floor, however, although it becomes extremely hot in summer, seldom experiences frost in the wintertime.

The general mechanism of the sculpturing of the canyon has been the downward cutting of the Colorado River which flows through the lowest portion of the canyon. Other factors, however, have also played their part. The Kaibab Plateau which forms the North Rim of the canyon is approximately 1200 ft. higher than the Coconino Plateau which forms the South Rim. As a result, water from the northern side has flowed into the canyon, forming tributary valleys, while the streams of the south plateau flow away in a southerly direction without carving valleys in the canyon walls. The underlying rock beds also have a southwesterly slant, with the result that ground water from the north finds its way into the canyon, but water from the south does not. The entire canyon region is one in which the rocks are much broken by jointing and faulting (see GEOLOGY), and fractures in the rocks resulting from these processes have contributed to the rapid weathering of the valley.

From the geological point of view, the Grand Canyon is of recent formation. The river apparently began its erosional work little more than a million years ago. Coupled with the downward cutting of the river has been a general rising or upwarping of the earth's surface which has added its effect to the action of the river.

Although the canyon itself is of comparatively recent origin, the rocks exposed in its walls are not. Most of the strata were originally deposited as marine sediments, indicating that for long periods of time the canyon area was the floor of a shallow sea.

In a typical section of the canyon, toward its eastern end, nine separate rock layers can be seen. The topmost layer is a limestone, the Kaibab limestone. Below this stratum is a thick deposit of sandstone, called the Coconino sandstone, and below that a layer of soft, shaly rock known as the Hermit shale. Still lower is a series of shales and sandstones interbedded with each other, collectively termed the Supai formation. The Supai and the rocks above it were probably all deposited in the Permian period, at the end of the Paleozoic era, as demonstrated by the fossils which are found in them; however, the Supai may be slightly older. Next comes a 500-ft. thick deposit of light gray-blue limestone, the Redwall limestone, which has in many places been colored red by seepage from the Supai beds above. The Redwall is easily identified because of the prominent sheer cliffs which it forms in the canyon walls. This stratum has been identified as belonging to the Mississippian period, and was laid down more than a quarter of a billion years ago. A thin layer of sandstone, the Temple Butte, beneath the Redwall, gives evidence of having its origin in Devonian times. The three next rock layers, the brown Muav limestone, the green Bright Angel shale, and the Tapeats sandstone, all belong to the Cambrian period at the dawn of the Paleozoic era. Beneath these strata, at the bottom of the canyon, are the most ancient rocks of all, Pre-Cambrian schists and gneisses, from half a billion to a billion years of age.

The Grand Canyon is of exceptional interest to students of geology in that it displays a remarkable range of strata covering a period of nearly a billion years.

History. The first white men to see the Grand Canyon were members of an expedition, headed by the Spanish explorer Francisco Vásquez Coronado, which set out from New Spain (Mexico) in February, 1540. The discovery was made later that year. Due to the inaccessibility of the canyon, it was not until more than three centuries later that it was fully explored. Beginning about 1850 a series of expeditions commanded by officers of the U.S. Army surveyed the canyon and the surrounding area. The first passage of the canyon was accomplished in 1869 by Major John W. Powell (q.v.) and five companions, who made the difficult passage through the length of the gorge in rowboats.

GRAND CAYMAN ISLAND. See CAYMAN ISLANDS.

GRAND CHARTREUSE. See CHARTREUSE.

GRANDE-COMORE. See COMORO ISLANDS.

GRAND FALLS, a cataract of the Hamilton R., Labrador, occurring about 220 m. from the mouth of the river. In a distance of 12 m. the river drops more than 760 ft., culminating in a vertical drop of 316 ft. over a rocky platform 200 ft. wide. Below the falls the river descends swiftly for another 300 ft. in a series of rapids. The narrow canyon through which the river falls is about 25 miles long and has an average depth of 400 to 500 ft. The first European to see the cataract was an official of the Hudson's Bay Company, in 1839. It was rediscovered by two separate expeditions in 1891, and officially surveyed by the Canadian Geological Survey in 1894. A recent power survey of the falls disclosed that the minimum hydroelectric energy available is 1,250,000 horsepower.

GRAND FORKS, county seat of Grand Forks Co., N.Dak., situated at the confluence of the Red R. of the North and of the Red Lake R., 78 miles N. of Fargo. It is served by two railroads, and is a railroad division point. Grand Forks is the second-largest city in the State, and is an important market and grain terminal. The city is at the center of one of the greatest wheat belts in the world. Potatoes, sugar beets, alfalfa, barley, corn, sweet clover, poultry, and livestock are also raised in the surrounding area. Among the industrial establishments in the city are a large State-owned flour mill and terminal elevator, privately-owned flour mills and elevators, meat-packing plants, sugar refineries, creameries, feed mills, bakeries, a potato-dehydration plant, printing plants, apiaries, fox fur farms, foundries, boiler works, brickyards, and factories manufacturing candy, fur clothing, and machinery. The All-American Turkey Show, the State Fair, and the State Peony Show are held annually at Grand Forks. The city is the site of the University of North Dakota (q.v.), and its affiliate, Wesley College. The North-West Fur Company established a trading post on the site of the present city in 1801, and the first permanent settlement was founded there in 1871. It became a village in 1879, and in 1881, when the Northern Pacific railroad reached Grand Forks, it was chartered as a city. Pop. (1950) 26,836.

GRANDI, DINO (1895–), Italian Fascist leader, educated at the University of Bologna. He acquired a reputation as an authority on labor problems. During the social upheaval in Italy following World War I, he became a foundation member of the Fascist movement and the leader of the Bolognese *squadristi* (see FASCISM: *Italian Fascism*). Grandi played a prominent part in the events immediately preceding the assumption of power by the Fascists in 1922, and Mussolini later made him a member of the Grand Council of Fascism, the political general staff of the Fascist Party and regime. Grandi was for a time Italy's representative in the League of Nations; he was minister of foreign affairs

from 1929 to 1932, and for the next seven years was ambassador to Great Britain. During World War II, from 1939 to 1943, he served Mussolini as minister of justice.

However, as the edifice of Italian Fascism began to crumble under the blows of successive military defeats, Grandi turned against his chief, opposing Mussolini's policy of subordinating Italian interests to German strategic plans. At a meeting of the Grand Council of Fascism in July, 1943, Grandi took the leadership of the majority which expressed its lack of confidence in Mussolini, and which caused the latter to be removed from power. After 1943 Grandi was believed to have gone into hiding in Portugal; later he entered Argentina under the assumed name Domenico Galli. In 1944 he was sentenced to death in absentia by a Fascist tribunal in Verona. Letters written by Grandi in 1934–35, while he was ambassador to Great Britain, were read in the House of Commons in 1946 and revealed that Grandi had been Mussolini's intermediary in subsidizing Sir Oswald Mosley's British Union of Fascists.

GRAND ISLAND, county seat of Hall Co., Nebr., situated near the Platte R., 85 miles w. of Lincoln. It has a municipal airport, is served by three railroads, and is a railroad division point, with extensive railroad shops. The city is the commercial, distributing, and manufacturing center of an area producing sugar beets, wheat, corn, hay, livestock, and poultry. Grand Island is one of the largest horse and mule markets in the U.S. Among its industrial establishments are beet-sugar factories, meat-packing plants, flour and feed mills, creameries, vegetable canneries, coffee-processing plants, machine shops, and factories manufacturing wire fence, iron culverts, piston rings, monuments, and serum. The city is the site of the Nebraska State Soldiers and Sailors Home, founded in 1888, and the U.S. Monitor Station, which checks the frequency of national and foreign broadcasting stations. Grand Island was laid out in 1866 following the arrival of the Union Pacific railroad at the site of the present city. The city was incorporated in 1873. Pop. (1950) 22,682.

GRAND JUNCTION, county seat of Mesa Co., Colo., situated at the confluence of the Gunnison and Colorado rivers, 274 m. by rail s.w. of Denver. It is the commercial and distributing center of an extensive irrigated area. Sugar beets, tomatoes, cantaloupes, cucumbers, peaches, alfalfa, corn, beans, wheat, and oats are grown in the surrounding area.

In the city are flour mills, fruit and vegetable canneries, beet-sugar factories, and railroad shops. Grand Junction is the site of Mesa County Junior College, established in 1925, and is the headquarters of the Grand Mesa National Forest. Colorado National Monument (q.v.) is situated 6 miles w. of the city. Grand Junction was settled in 1881 and incorporated in 1882. Pop. (1950) 14,504.

GRAND JURY, in judicial systems based on common law (q.v.), as in the United States and Great Britain, a jury (q.v.) called to hear complaints concerning the commission of crimes and to inquire by aid of testimony whether *prima facie* evidence exists for making accusations of crime, or indictments (q.v.). A grand jury functions not only to determine whether persons accused of crime shall be indicted and tried therefor, but also to inquire into such matters relating to crime as may be confided to it by a court, or which may come to its knowledge in other ways. It may, accordingly, make presentment of any matter requiring remedial action by a court or a legislature with appropriate jurisdiction, such as a widespread condition of lawlessness, inadequacy of the law to cope with various situations or conditions, inefficiency in the administration of the law, and neglect of duty by public officials.

A grand jury generally consists of twenty-four persons, of whom not more than twenty-three nor fewer than twelve are sworn, twelve being the smallest number of jurors which may make a presentment. In the United States, the number necessary to constitute a grand jury varies from State to State within the foregoing limits. In its discretion, a court may select the foreman of a grand jury from the members of the jury, or may permit the grand jurors to elect their foreman.

After being sworn and after receiving the judge's charge, the grand jurors retire to an appointed room, where the proposed indictments are laid before them. Grand-jury witnesses are sworn by an officer appointed by the court. Testimony given to a grand jury is secret and may become available for inspection by a defendant only through application to the court having jurisdiction over the grand jury.

As it is the duty of a grand jury to determine whether there is sufficient *prima facie* evidence to warrant a trial of one accused of crime, it may require the same evidence, written and oral, as may be necessary to support an indictment at a trial. However, in inquiring into a particular criminal charge, the grand jurors do not examine witnesses for the defense, for it is not their duty to find a verdict, but only to decide whether sufficient *prima facie* evidence exists to warrant a trial.

When a grand jury decides that such evidence exists, a clerk appointed by the court indorses on the indictment the words "A true bill"; should the jurors find that sufficient evidence does not exist, the clerk indorses on the indictment the words "Not a true bill". The foreman of the jury, accompanied by one or more of the grand jurors, carries the indictments into court, where they are presented to the court clerk, who states to the court the nature of the charges made in the indictments and the indorsements of the grand jury.

The institution of the grand jury has played an important role in history as a bulwark against tyranny. The crown in England long enjoyed the right of instituting criminal prosecutions by the legal process of information, and the abuse of this prerogative was one of the principal causes of the popular risings against the Stuarts in England in the 17th century and against George III in the American colonies in the 18th century. The principle established in these revolutions, that only the people should have the power to institute criminal prosecutions, was embodied in the provision in the U.S. Constitution guaranteeing the institution of the grand jury. Most of the State constitutions have similar provisions; the constitutions of approximately half the States also provide that certain indictable lesser offenses may be prosecuted by the process of information. Such offenses are generally those punishable by imprisonment for less than ten years.

GRAND MAL. See EPILEPSY.

GRANDMONTAINS or **GRANDMONTINES,** or **GRAMMONT, ORDER OF,** a religious order, founded in Auvergne, France, by St. Stephen of Muret (1026?–1124) in 1077. Returning from Italy, St. Stephen decided to follow the ascetic life led by the hermits whom he had seen in Calabria, and retired to live alone in the Glen of Muret, later gathering around him a group of disciples. The mode of life of the hermits, who became popularly known as the "Good Men", was characterized by extreme severity in fasting, silence, and mortification of the flesh. About 1150 the order, which had increased considerably in numbers, moved a few miles east to the desert of Grandmont, or Grammont, from which it derived its name. There were about sixty monasteries of the order by 1170, but it never spread outside France. During the 12th century King Louis VII founded a monastery at Vincennes, near Paris. The severe discipline of the life was relaxed by popes Innocent IV and Clement III during the 13th and 14th centuries. The order died out a short time before the French Revolution.

GRAND NATIONAL STEEPLECHASE, a classic English steeplechase, held toward the end of March every year at the Aintree track. Although founded in 1839, the race was not officially recognized by the National Hunt Committee until 1865. The course is 4 miles, 856 yards in length, and has over thirty obstacles. The Grand National is regarded as the most difficult steeplechase in the world; in one instance, only one horse out of 42 starters finished the course. The Grand National is well known in the U.S. in connection with the sweepstakes (q.v.) on the race conducted in Dublin for the benefit of Irish hospitals.

GRAND PRÉ (Fr., "great meadow"), village of Kings County, Nova Scotia, Canada, located on the Minas Basin, 15 m. by rail N.W. of Windsor. Grand Pré is celebrated as the home of the heroine in the poem *Evangeline,* by Henry Wadsworth Longfellow. The old village was founded about 1675 by the French, in what was then known as Acadia. The only extant remains are a clump of willow trees, a well, and several cellar holes, all of which lie near the site of the present village. Nearby Horton Landing, at the mouth of the Gaspereau R., marks the point of embarkation of those inhabitants of old Grand Pré who, with many other Acadians, were expelled from their homes in 1755. See ACADIA.

GRAND PRIX DE PARIS, the principal horse race on the French racing calendar, corresponding in importance to the English Derby (see EPSOM). The Grand Prix de Paris is run annually about the middle of June at the Longchamps race track near Paris, over a flat course of a mile and seven furlongs. The race first took place in 1863. It is an important social event, marking the beginning of the summer season for Parisian leisured classes, who generally do not take up their summer residences at the seashore or in the country until after the date of the race.

GRAND PRIX DE ROME, popularly known as the PRIX DE ROME, the title of an award given annually by the French government to students of the fine arts. The competition for the prize is conducted by the École des Beaux-Arts in Paris, and is open to students of painting, sculpture, architecture, music, and engraving, between the ages of fifteen and thirty.

Ten students are chosen for the final competition, and must complete within three months the entries on which they are to be judged. The prize consists of a four-year scholarship at the Académie de France in Rome, an adequate yearly allowance for expenses, and exemption from military service. During their stay in Rome, winners in the graphic arts are required to send examples of their works each year to the Salon in Paris; winners in music send their compositions to the Conservatoire.

The Grand Prix de Rome was established by Louis XIV in 1666 for painters and sculptors. It was expanded in 1720 to include architects, and again in 1803 to include musicians and engravers.

GRAND RAPIDS, county seat and port of entry of Kent Co., Mich., situated at the head of navigation on the Grand R., 30 miles E. of Lake Michigan and about 145 miles N.W. of Detroit. It is served by four railroads, and has a county airport, with regular air-line service. The surrounding agricultural area is part of the Michigan fruit belt; garden truck and tulip bulbs are extensively cultivated in the immediate vicinity of the city, and nearby are large gypsum mines.

Grand Rapids ranks second in the State in population, second in diversification of industries, and is the wholesale, shipping, and distributing center of western Michigan. The principal industries in the city are furniture manufacturing and metalworking. Because of its importance in the production and marketing of furniture, Grand Rapids is known as the "Furniture Capital of America". The products of the principal industries in the city, in addition to furniture, include machinery, sheet-metal products, metal stampings, hardware, brass goods, automobiles, automobile parts and accessories, chemicals, paper products, textiles, foods, carpet sweepers, showcases, refrigerator cabinets, flypaper, gypsum and boxboard products, hosiery, underwear, and seating for churches, theaters, and schools. Grand Rapids also contains several large printing plants. Since 1923 the city has had a zoning ordinance which limits the height of buildings and the portion of land area they may occupy, and sets aside sections to be used for residence and for industry. It ranks among the highest of the larger cities of the U.S. as to the percentage of families owning and occupying their homes. The park area of 1245 acres includes over 50 parks and playgrounds. The city is the site of Aquinas College (1923) and Mount Mercy College for

Aerial view of Grand Rapids, Michigan

women (1929), both of which are Roman Catholic institutions; Grand Rapids Junior College (1914), and the Calvin College and Seminary of the Christian Reformed Church (1876).

Grand Rapids was first settled as a Baptist mission in 1824, on the site of a village of the Ottawa Indians; in 1826 Louis Campau, a fur trader, built a post near the mission. The town was laid out in 1831 and named for the rapids in the Grand R. Grand Rapids commenced its industrial development as a lumbering center, receiving logs floated downstream on the Grand R. from the great timber stands of Michigan. The furniture industry in Grand Rapids dates from 1847; by 1876 the city was one of the most important furniture-manufacturing centers in the U.S. Grand Rapids was incorporated as a village in 1838, and chartered as a city in 1850. Pop. (1950) 176,515.

GRAND REMONSTRANCE, a manifesto presented to Charles I of England by the House of Commons on December 1, 1640. The instrument was a severe indictment of Charles for a long series of acts of alleged misgovernment. On November 22, while the king was absent in Scotland, the Commons adopted the Grand Remonstrance by a majority of eleven, 159 members having voted for, and 148 against, the measure. The document, of which the Parliamentary leader John Pym was the principal author, consisted of 204 sections. In it the forced loans and ship money, the billeting of soldiers, the imprisonment of members of Parliament, the enlargement of the royal forests, the abuse of commercial monopolies, the excesses of the courts of Star Chamber and High Commission (qq.v.), together with many other grievances, were minutely set forth. A request was made for the appointment of ministers in whom Parliament would have confidence, and it was asked that the reform of the Church be left to a "synod of the most grave, pious, learned, and judicious divines". The proposal, however, contained no suggestion of toleration for religious nonconformists.

Upon receiving the Remonstrance from the deputation of the Commons, Charles criticized and ridiculed it. On December 10 he issued a proclamation on religion, which he evidently intended as an indirect reply, and on December 23 he gave a lofty and evasive "answer" to the Petition which accompanied the manifesto. Charles seemed unaware of the grave danger of his position, and on January 3, 1642, dispatched his attorney general to impeach the leaders of the opposition before the House of Lords. (See CHARLES I; GREAT BRITAIN: *History*.)

GRAND RIVER. See HAMILTON RIVER.

GRAND RIVER, the former name of the Colorado R. (q.v.) from its source in the mountains of Colorado to its junction with the Green R. in Utah. The name was officially changed to Colorado R. by the Colorado State Assembly in 1921.

GRAND TETON NATIONAL PARK, a national park established in 1929 in Teton Co.,

N.W. Wyoming, about 11 miles S. of the southern boundary of Yellowstone National Park and adjoining Jackson Hole National Monument on the E. The park is about 150 sq.m. in area, and contains a group of scenic peaks and glaciated canyons of the Teton Mts. The highest mountains of the group are the Grand Teton, which rises to a height of 13,766 ft. above sea level, Mount Owen (12,922 ft.), Middle Teton (12,798 ft.), Mount Moran (12,594 ft.), South Teton (12,505 ft.), and Mount Teewinot (12,317 ft.). Although much of the park area is above the timber line, the lower regions are extensively forested with pine, fir, and spruce. The park also contains several lakes of glacial origin. The principal lakes are Leigh, Phelps, Taggart, Bradley, and Jenny, all of which lie along the E. border of the Teton Mts. Wildlife in the park includes moose, deer, elk, beaver, and bear; the lakes and streams abound in fish, including numerous species of trout. The Teton

Dept. of Commerce & Industry, Cheyenne, Wyoming

View of the majestic mountains in Grand Teton National Park, Wyoming

peaks, which are alpine in character, with small summit areas and sheer sides, are popular with mountain climbers, and guide service is available for scaling the peaks. Grand Teton is considered one of the most difficult peaks to climb in the U.S. A museum at Jenny Lake contains exhibits pertaining to mountain climbing and collections relative to the history, geology, flora, and fauna of the region.

GRAND TURK ISLAND. See TURKS AND CAICOS ISLANDS.

GRANGE, NATIONAL, the popular name of the NATIONAL GRANGE OF THE PATRONS OF HUSBANDRY, a secret, fraternal society founded in 1867 at Washington, D.C., by Oliver Hudson Kelley and his associates. The Grange was established to advance the social, economic, and political interests of the farmers of the United States. Its formation is historically significant in that it marked the first stage in the development of a movement of agrarian protest which arose soon after the Civil War, and which continued until the end of the 19th century; see GRANGER MOVEMENT; GREENBACK PARTY; POPULISM.

Soon after the formation of the National Grange, State, county, and local granges were set up, with membership open to farmers and their wives and children. By 1874, more than 20,000 local granges had been established in thirty-two States, chiefly in the Middle West and South. These groups attempted to alleviate the financial difficulties of their members by establishing co-operative stores, purchasing agencies, and factories for the manufacture of farm machinery. Late in the 1870's most of these undertakings collapsed as a result of inefficient management and the powerful competition of private enterprises. Membership in the Grange declined from about 860,000 in 1875 to approximately 124,000 in 1880.

Despite these setbacks, the Grange had proven successful in its program of social activities which were especially valuable as a means of relieving the isolation of farm life. In the closing years of the 19th century the Grange focused its energies on these activities. Thereafter, the membership gradually rose, and at the same time a gradual revival of other functions took place, including the establishment of co-operative ventures for the purchase and sale of commodities needed by farmers. The Grange also initiated a system of fire, windstorm, and automobile insurance for its members.

Today the Grange is active not only in these fields, but also exerts its influence to secure the passage of legislation aimed at improving both the status of farmers and of agriculture generally. In 1953 the total membership of the Grange was about 900,000.

GRANGER MOVEMENT, in United States history, the widespread agrarian movement which arose shortly after the Civil War, and which had as its aim the social, economic, and political betterment of the farmers. The movement comprised the initial stage in the development of the unrest among farmers, in many areas of the United States, which characterized the latter part of the 19th century. Among the causes of the insecurity felt by the farmers were the declining prices of farm products, the growing indebtedness of farmers to merchants and banks, the discriminatory freight rates imposed on farmers by the railroads, and the pre-emption by the railroads of public lands which formerly had served pioneer farmers as a source of new farmland.

The event which signalized the beginning of the granger movement was the formation, in 1867, of the National Grange of the "Patrons of Husbandry" (see GRANGE, NATIONAL). Although the Grange was a nonpolitical organization, its meeting places became the centers of discussion among the traditionally individualistic farmers, and out of these discussions arose an awareness of the need for concerted political action to solve mutual problems. As a result, a number of political parties, bearing such names as the Anti-Monopoly and Reform parties, were organized in several States early in the 1870's. These parties succeeded in electing several State officers and three U.S. Senators, and in a number of States, including Illinois, Iowa, Minnesota, Wisconsin, and California, contributed to the passage of laws regulating railroad rates and practices. Although most of these so-called "granger laws" were repealed or drastically modified within a few years, a number were upheld in the United States Supreme Court, and they served as the basis for much subsequently enacted legislation in the field of railroad and public-utility regulation. Other types of legislation urged by the grangers, but not enacted until later, include anti-trust laws and measures establishing the parcel post and postal savings bank systems.

Late in the 1870's, as the agrarian movement, which had formerly been conducted on a local or State scale, attained nationwide proportions, new forms of organization arose to supplant the granger movement. Among these were the Farmers' Alliances, the Greenback Party (qq.v.), and the Populist Party (see POPULISM).

GRANICUS, ancient name of a small river in Asia Minor, now known as the Bigha Chai, flowing from the northern slopes of the Ida Mts. to the western shore of the Sea of Marmara. On the banks of the Granicus, Alexander the Great (see ALEXANDER III), King of Macedonia, was victorious over the Persian army of Darius in 334 B.C. The shores of the Granicus were also the site of the victory of the Roman general Lucullus (q.v.) over Mithridates VI Eupator, ruler of Pontus, in 73 B.C.

GRANITE, igneous rock of visible crystalline formation and texture. It is composed of feldspar (usually potash feldspar and oligoclase) and quartz, with a small amount of mica (biotite or muscovite) and minor accessory minerals, such as zircon, sphene, apatite, magnetite, and ilmenite. The relative proportions of the mineral constituents of granite vary considerably. Granite is usually whitish or gray with a speckled appearance caused by the darker crystals. Potash feldspar imparts a red or flesh color to the rock.

Granite was formed by the very slow cooling of liquid-rock material beneath the earth's surface; see CRYSTAL. It constitutes the foundation of the continental masses upon which sedimentary rocks of later ages were deposited, and is the most abundant of the intrusive igneous rocks on the earth's surface.

The specific gravity of granite ranges from 2.63 to 2.75. Its crushing strength is from 15,000 to 20,000 pounds per square inch. Granite has greater strength than sandstone, limestone, and marble, and is correspondingly more difficult to quarry. It is an important building stone, the best grades being extremely resistant to weathering.

GRANITE CITY, a city of Madison Co., Ill., situated near the Mississippi R., 10 miles N.E. of St. Louis, Mo. The city is an important manufacturing center. Its industrial establishments include coke ovens, steel foundries, blast furnaces, rolling mills, brick and tile plants, and factories manufacturing graniteware, coal-tar products, creosoted timbers, and locomotive and car frames. Granite City was settled in 1892 and incorporated in 1896. Pop. (1950) 29,465.

GRAN QUIVIRA NATIONAL MONUMENT, a national monument established in 1909, situated in central New Mexico, a few miles s. of the town of Mountainair. It contains the ruins of two early Spanish missions, in addition to the remains of several Indian

pueblos. The oldest of the two missions, built about 1627, was one of the earliest missions in the Southwest, and was the place of worship for the surrounding villages of the Tompiro Indians. A few walls are all that remain of the mission. About 1659 the second mission, San Buenaventura de las Humanas, was erected. The ruins of the latter include those of a church, chapels, corrals, and a rectory. The mission was abandoned about 1672 because of drought and Apache raids. The pueblo ruins in the monument area are the source of many prehistoric Indian artifacts.

GRANT, ULYSSES SIMPSON (1822–85), American soldier and 18th President of the United States, born in Point Pleasant, Ohio. As a boy he worked on his father's farm and in his tannery at Georgetown, Ohio, to which the Grant family had moved in 1823. He attended school at Georgetown and in Maysville, Ky., and in 1839 received an appointment to the U.S. Military Academy at West Point, N.Y.; through an error in the application blank filled out by the congressman who sponsored him, Grant's given names were entered on the Academy's rolls not as Ulysses Hiram (his baptismal names in reverse order), but as Ulysses Simpson, the names which Grant continued to use thereafter.

At West Point Grant displayed proficiency in mathematics and engineering, and excelled in horsemanship. He graduated in 1843, was commissioned a second lieutenant, and was assigned to the Fourth U.S. Infantry Regiment, which was subsequently included in the army commanded by Zachary Taylor in the then newly admitted State of Texas. Following the outbreak of hostilities with Mexico in 1846, Grant fought with distinction under Taylor in the battles of Palo Alto, Resaca de la Palma, and Monterey. After being transferred to the command of General Winfield Scott, Grant took part in the campaign which resulted in Scott's capture of Mexico City in 1847; see MEXICAN WAR. In recognition of his bravery under fire, Grant was promoted, during the campaign, to first lieutenant, and at its close to captain. He remained on duty in Mexico until 1848.

Later he was assigned to garrison duty in Michigan and, in 1852, at Fort Vancouver on the Columbia River. While at the latter post, he began the first of a series of varied business enterprises which met with little financial success. A transfer to California followed in 1853. There, disheartened by barracks life and the separation from his wife, whom he had married in St. Louis in 1848, Grant became ad-

Ulysses S. Grant

dicted to drink. In 1854, offered the choice by his superiors of standing trial or of resigning, he chose the latter course.

With the aid of his father-in-law he undertook farming in the vicinity of St. Louis. After four years of toil and little success, illness forced Grant to abandon his farm. For the next two years he made a meager living in the real-estate business in St. Louis, giving that up in 1860 to move to Galena, Ill., where he worked as a clerk in his father's leather store until the outbreak of the Civil War.

In May, 1861, he offered his services to the War Department, and in June was appointed a colonel in command of a regiment of volunteers and was dispatched to suppress guerilla warfare in Missouri. On August 7, President Lincoln made Grant a brigadier general of volunteers, and in September Grant was given command of the military district comprising western Kentucky and southeastern Missouri, with headquarters in Cairo, Ill. Almost his first act in his new post was to seize the strategically situated Confederate base of Paducah, Ky., at the confluence of the Ohio and Tennessee rivers. In February, 1862, Grant won the first important Union victory of the war when, after taking Fort Henry on the Tennessee R., near the Kentucky-Tennessee border, he compelled the surrender of Fort Donelson on the Cumberland R., about 12 m. to the east of Fort Henry; see FORT DONELSON NATIONAL MILITARY PARK; FORT HENRY. The offer by the Confederate commander of Fort Donelson,

General S. B. Buckner, to negotiate an armistice, elicited from Grant the statement that he could consider only the unconditional surrender of the Confederate force. Thereafter Grant became known as "Unconditional Surrender Grant". In recognition of his signal success he was brevetted a major general.

Highly prejudicial journalistic reports of Grant's conduct of the battle of Shiloh (q.v.) in April, 1862, up to that time the bloodiest battle of the war, led to widespread demands for his removal. Lincoln, however, resisted the pressure put upon him with the explanation "I can't spare this man; he fights." In July, Grant was placed in charge of the military district of West Tennessee, and in October he was given command of the military Department of Tennessee with the specific assignment of taking Vicksburg, Miss., a primary Confederate stronghold. After a series of initial defeats in the effort to approach and invest Vicksburg, Grant finally, in May, 1863, laid siege to the city, which capitulated in July; see VICKSBURG, CAMPAIGN OF. As a result of the fall of Vicksburg, which followed soon after the victory of Gettysburg in the east, the Confederacy lost control of the Mississippi R. and was cut in two. Grant was hailed as a hero in the North and was rewarded with an appointment as major general in the U.S. regular army. Another notable success was won by Grant in November, 1863, with the capture of Chattanooga (see CHATTANOOGA, BATTLE OF), which with other corollary successes opened the way to Georgia and resulted in General William Sherman's famous eastward "March to the Sea".

Congress, in March, 1864, conferred on Grant the rank of lieutenant general, having revived the rank for that purpose in February. A few days after his promotion Grant assumed command of all U.S. army forces, under Lincoln, and established his headquarters with the Army of the Potomac in the east. He at once began planning the campaign to take Richmond, Va. There followed the long series of battles in which Grant, outmaneuvered by his great opponent, Robert E. Lee, and suffering heavier losses than Lee, nevertheless pressed his weakening opponent back toward Richmond; see WILDERNESS, BATTLE OF THE; SPOTSYLVANIA COURT HOUSE; COLD HARBOR, BATTLE OF; PETERSBURG. Finally, after the Confederate citadels of Atlanta and Savannah, Ga., had fallen to Sherman, Grant took Richmond on April 3, 1865. Six days later came the ultimate triumph for which Grant had striven, Lee's surrender at

Appomattox Court House (see APPOMATTOX COURT HOUSE NATIONAL HISTORICAL PARK); the terms of surrender imposed by Grant were generous. In 1866 he was commissioned General of the Armies of the United States, and in 1867 he was appointed secretary of war in the cabinet of President Andrew Johnson.

The Republican National Convention, meeting in Chicago in 1868, unanimously nominated Grant for President. He won an easy victory over the Democratic candidate Horatio Seymour, ex-governor of New York State. In the field of foreign policy, Grant's term of office was marked by the negotiation of a treaty (see WASHINGTON, TREATY OF) with Great Britain, providing for the solution of a number of serious disputes between the two countries, and by fruitless efforts to annex Santo Domingo. In the realm of domestic policy Grant introduced a number of civil-service reforms but evoked much criticism by favoring wealthy men in making Cabinet appointments and by showing marked favoritism to members of his and his wife's families in making other appointments. More serious dissatisfaction with his administration was caused by a series of rail and stock speculations undertaken by leading financiers and industrialists. These speculations culminated in such events as the attempt of Jay Gould and James Fisk (qq.v.) to corner the gold market, which resulted on September 24, 1869, known as Black Friday (q.v.), in financial panic.

These scandals, however, did not touch Grant personally, and in 1872 he was renominated for the Presidency. He won an even easier victory over his principal opponent, Horace Greeley (q.v.), than he had over Seymour in 1868. Upon assuming the Presidential office for the second time, in 1873, Grant had to contend with the effects of one of the greatest scandals in the history of the United States, that of the Crédit Mobilier of America (q.v.); charges of corruption involved congressmen, Federal judges, and Vice-President Henry Wilson. Another serious problem was the financial panic which began in September as a result of unsound business expansion, unfettered speculation, and currency inflation. Despite great pressure exerted on him, Grant refused to inflate the currency further. As the country continued to be shocked by scandals involving public officials, the President also began to lose public esteem; see WHISKY RING. A severe blow to the reputation of his administration was the resignation in 1876 of his secretary

of war, William Belknap, to avoid impeachment on charges of malfeasance in office.

After leaving the White House in 1877, Grant engaged in a number of unprofitable business ventures. In 1884 he became financially bankrupt. The final year of his life was spent in writing his *Personal Memoirs,* regarded as one of the great autobiographies of American literature, and in a hopeless struggle with a cancerous growth in his throat. His burial place, a mausoleum known as Grant's Tomb near the bank of the Hudson River in New York City, has become a landmark known throughout the world.

GRANVILLE, EARL. See CARTERET, JOHN, EARL GRANVILLE.

GRANVILLE-BARKER, HARLEY GRANVILLE (1877–1946), British author, actor, producer, and teacher, born in London. He began his career as an actor at the age of fourteen. In 1900 he created the part of Marchbanks in *Candida,* the first of his many successes in the plays of George Bernard Shaw. As manager of the Court Theatre, London, from 1904 to 1907, he directed and acted in many notable productions of plays by Shakespeare and Shaw. In 1915 he took a company to New York City, with a repertory which included plays by Shakespeare, Shaw, Anatole France, and himself. After World War I he turned to lecturing and writing, and was director of the British Institute of the University of Paris from 1937 to 1939. In 1940 he was visiting professor at Yale University, and from 1941 to 1943 held a similar post at Harvard University. Among the plays he wrote are *The Marrying of Anne Leete* (1901), *The Voysey Inheritance* (1905), *Waste* (1907), and *The Madras House* (1910). These plays are notable for their skillful construction and for their criticism of moral, social, and political aspects of contemporary life. His *Prefaces to Shakespeare* (2 vols., 1946–47), contain brilliant analyses of the plays from the point of view of an actor and producer.

GRAPE, common name of edible fruit of the genus *Vitis* in the family Vitaceae, and of the vines which produce the fruit. The European grape, *V. vinifera,* has been used as food since prehistoric times. Grape seeds have been found in remains of lake dwellings of the Bronze Age in Switzerland and Italy, and in tombs of ancient Egypt. Botanists believe that the Caspian Sea region was the original home of the European grape. Distribution of seeds by birds, wind, and water carried the plant westward to the Asiatic shores of the Mediter-

Brown Brothers; French Embassy, Info. Div.; French National Tourist Office

Top: Wine grapes growing on a slope in the Rhine valley, Germany. *Bottom, left:* A variety of the European grape (Vitis vinifera). *Bottom, right:* Harvesting grapes in France.

ranean. Grape culture, practiced in Palestine during Biblical times, was introduced throughout the Mediterranean region by seagoing Phenicians. The ancient Greeks cultivated grapes extensively, and use of the fruit was later adopted by Rome and its tributary territories.

The European grape is now commercially cultivated in warmer regions all over the world, particularly in western Europe, the Balkans, California, Australia, and South Africa. It was introduced to eastern U.S. during colonial times, but in those days failed in cultivation due to the attacks of diseases and pests. Successful eastern U.S. grapes, such as Concord and Delaware grapes, are strains developed from hybrids between *V. vinifera* and several native species, particularly *V. labrusca,* the northern fox grape, *V. aestivalis,* the summer grape, *V. vulpina,* the riverbank grape, and *V. rotundifolia,* the muscadine grape. Eastern American grapes are characterized by a juicy layer between the skin and pulp of the fruit which permits easy removal of the skin. Grape varieties, whether European or eastern American, are classified according to their ultimate use. Grapes used to make table wine must have high acidity and moderate sugar content; those used for dessert wines and other sweet wines must have high sugar content and moderate acidity; see WINE. Table grapes must be low in both acidity and sugar content and must conform to definite standards of size, color, and shape. Grapes used to make juices and jellies must have a pronounced flavor combined with high acidity and moderate sugar content. Raisin grapes are preferably seedless, with high sugar content and low acidity; see RAISIN. European varieties are superior to eastern American varieties for use as table grapes, dessert wines, and raisins; eastern American grapes are preferred for table wines, juices, and jellies.

Grape vines are stems which climb on walls and fences by means of specialized supporting organs, called tendrils. Palmately veined leaves arise at regular intervals along the stem. In most grape varieties, tendrils arise opposite two of every three successive leaves. Grape flowers are borne in clusters. The flowers have short sepals, five-parted corollas which fall off soon after the flower opens, five stamens, and a single pistil. The pulpy fruit which develops from the wall of the pistil is a berry, normally containing several bony seeds.

Grapevines planted in commercial vineyards are usually started in spring from year-old rooted or grafted cuttings. Roots are trimmed to three or four inches for convenience, and vines are planted eight to ten feet apart. All the shoots except the strongest one on the vine are later pruned; the remaining shoot is cut back to two or three buds. This process is repeated in the spring of the following two years. The resulting plant develops a strong main stem, resembling a small tree trunk, before it is allowed to bear fruit. Such strong stems are able to stand erect without support. During the expansion of the main stem, the vine is loosely tied to an upright support which is six or more feet tall. After the fruit-producing stage is reached, the supports are removed and the vines are carefully pruned to reduce the number of buds. Shoots that develop from the remaining buds are more prolific and bear grapes of high quality. Grapes grown in gardens are usually trained against trellises, arbors, fences, or porches.

Grapes are attacked by a great number of animal pests and plant diseases. Common pests include grape phylloxera, *Phylloxera viticola* (see PHYLLOXERA); grape rootworm, *Fidia viticida;* grape cane borer, *Amphicerus bicaudatus;* grapevine flea beetle, *Altica chalybea;* and grape-berry moth, *Polychrosis viteana.* Principal fungus diseases attacking grapes are bird's-eye rot or anthracnose (q.v.), *Gleosporium ampelophagum;* black rot, *Guignardia bidwellii,* and the grape mildews, *Plasmopara viticola* and *Uncinula necator.* Cuttings of grape varieties susceptible to these diseases and pests (but having desirable fruit) are often grafted to vines which are resistant to them. See also FUNGICIDE.

GRAPEFRUIT, common name of the fruit of a variety of *Citrus maxima;* see CITRUS. The variety probably originated in Jamaica, and was introduced to Florida by the Spaniards in the 16th century. Grapefruits are borne on small trees which rarely exceed 20 feet in height. The dense foliage consists of shiny, dark-green leaves with winged petioles. The large white flowers produce yellow, globe-shaped fruit in grapelike clusters. The fruits vary from four to six inches in diameter, and consist of a juicy, acid pulp surrounded by a leathery rind. The color of the pulp is normally light-yellow, but a few pink-pulped varieties have been developed.

More than twenty varieties of grapefruit have been propagated in the U.S. The major yellow-pulped varieties are Duncan and Marsh; the major pink-pulped varieties are Ruby and Webb. The grapefruit is readily crossed with other members of the citrus genus. The tangelo, a Florida juice fruit, was

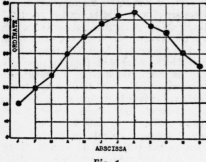

Fig. 1

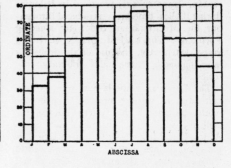

Fig. 2

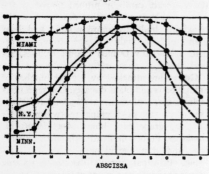

Fig. 3

produced by fertilization of grapefruit flowers with mandarin orange pollen.

Grapefruit is a low-calorie food, and is an excellent source of Vitamin C (ascorbic acid), and a good source of inositol, a member of the Vitamin-B complex. It is used extensively as a breakfast fruit or salad fruit, and its juice is very popular as a refreshment or appetizer. Practically all grapefruit in the U.S. is grown in four States: Florida produces more than half the total production, Texas produces about one third, and California and Arizona together produce about one tenth. Annual production of grapefruit in the U.S. exceeds 1,500,000 tons. Almost 100,000,000 No. 2½ cans of grapefruit pulp and almost 500,000,000 No. 2 cans of grapefruit juice are produced in the U.S. each year.

GRAPE HYACINTH, common name of herbs of the genus *Muscari,* belonging to the Lily family. Grape hyacinths, also called baby's-breath (q.v.), have small, blue, pink, or white, bell-shaped flowers borne in dense, spikelike racemes. The flowers often have a grapelike scent. The large, grasslike leaves are produced by a fleshy bulb. The genus is native to the warmer regions of Eurasia. Two popular spring-blooming species, *M. botryoides* and

M. racemosum, were introduced from Europe and grow in gardens in the U.S., occasionally spreading to orchards, thickets, and fencerows. *M. comosum* var. *monstrosum* bears sterile flowers which have shredded, fringelike petals.

GRAPE SUGAR. See GLUCOSE.

GRAPHIC METHODS, modes of representing quantitative values by means of diagrams called *graphs.* Simple graphic methods can be used for representation of the behavior of two variables; graphs of this type are commonly presented in books and periodicals. In a graph comparing the average monthly temperature for a certain year at a certain place, the two variables are (1) the average temperature for each month, and (2) the months of the year. To diagram this situation, a vertical line, called the *ordinate,* is drawn to represent the range of temperature during the year, and a horizontal line, the *abscissa,* is drawn to represent the twelve months of the year. The distances on the ordinate are calibrated to represent temperature values, and the abscissa is calibrated to represent the months of the year. If the average temperature for February is 32° F., for example, the point which represents this temperature and time is the intersection of a horizontal line drawn through the ordinate which represents 32, and a vertical line drawn through the abscissa which represents February. Fig. 1 illustrates a graph of this type.

When the points of a graph are connected by straight lines, as in Fig. 1, the graph is called a *frequency polygon.* When the points are connected by smoothly curved lines, the figure is a *frequency curve.* In Fig. 2, a form of graphic representation called a *histogram,* the data is expressed by the use of *frequency rectangles.*

When a third variable is represented on a graph, a separate curve or polygon must be drawn for each of its values. Fig. 3 illustrates such a graph.

The origin of graphic representation stems from the system of geometric co-ordinates developed by René Descartes; see GEOMETRY, ANALYTICAL. Graphic representation of mathematical functions is useful in solving many types of mathematical problems; see CALCULUS; FUNCTION. Engineering problems which involve calculation of mutual relations of external forces and inner stresses acting upon a body are solved by the methods of graphical statics; see VECTOR.

See also STATISTICS.

GRAPHITE, or PLUMBAGO or BLACK LEAD, one of the allotropic forms of carbon (q.v.). It occurs in nature as a mineral invariably containing impurities. It is widely distributed over the world; important deposits are found in Siberia, England, Madagascar, Mexico, Canada, and numerous localities in the United States. Graphite is made artificially in large amounts by heating coke to a very high temperature in an electric furnace. The coke is covered with a mixture of sand to prevent oxidation by air. Small amounts of impurities in the coke, such as iron oxide, catalyze the transformation of coke to graphite, and are then vaporized themselves, leaving pure graphite.

Although graphite is chemically the same as diamond (q.v.), it differs widely from that mineral in most of its physical properties. It is black, opaque, and metallic in luster, and has a specific gravity of 2 to 2.2. Graphite is extremely soft (hardness 1 to 2), and smudges anything with which it comes in contact; it feels greasy or slippery to the touch. It crystallizes in the hexagonal system, not as well-developed crystals but as scales or large irregular masses. It is the only nonmetal that is a good conductor of electricity; it is also, unlike other conductors of electricity, a poor conductor of heat. It does not fuse even at extremely high temperatures.

The cores of "lead" pencils contain no lead but are made of graphite mixed with clay. Graphite is used as electrodes in electrochemical industries where corrosive gases are given off, and for electric furnaces which reach extremely high temperatures. It is used as a lubricant either by itself or mixed with grease, oil (as *oildag*), or water (as *aquadag*). It is also used in stove polish, in crucibles which must withstand extremely high temperatures, and in certain paints. Graphite is an important constituent of pig iron, cast iron, and certain die steels. In recent years it has been used as a moderator in atomic piles, where enormous quantities of graphite of the highest purity obtainable slow down neutrons without capturing them. See ATOMIC ENERGY AND ATOMIC BOMB.

GRAPTOLITES (Gr. *graptos,* "written"; *lithos,* "stone"), a group of important index fossils of extinct marine animals, classed as an order, Graptolitoidea, of the coelenterates. The fossils resemble notched twigs, or notched cones, and often have many branches. They are composed of the horny, external skeletons of the animals, or sometimes only of the carbonized remains of the skeletons which, because of their resemblance to pencil markings, have given the group its name. The graptolites are found in shale and limestone rocks of the upper Cambrian, Ordovician, Silurian, and lower Devonian periods in all parts of the world.

Studies of the different forms of graptolites have indicated that the group had a rapid evolutionary cycle. Because each succeeding geological epoch was characterized by a different graptolite, these fossils are important indices used by paleontologists in determining the identity of rocks in which they are found.

GRASSE, town of the department of Alpes Maritimes, France, situated 12½ m. by rail N.N.W. of Cannes. Its parish church was built in the 12th century. Three paintings by Peter Paul Rubens hang in the chapel of the old hospital. Grasse is noted for the manufacture of perfumes and of essences, especially attar of roses. The factories of the town also produce wax, soap, and olive oil. Pop. (1946) 13,731.

GRASSES, common name of flowering plants belonging to the family Gramineae. The Grass family, which includes more than 350 genera and 4700 species, is the most important family, economically, in the plant kingdom, and includes the earliest cultivated plants. Grasses, which are distributed all over the world, grow in all land habitats capable of supporting higher forms of plant life. They vary in size from species less than an inch in height to species, such as the tropical bamboo, which may grow taller than 100 feet.

The typical organ of all grasses is the blade, which is a long, ribbonlike leaf. Leaves of most other monocotyledonous plants are similar in appearance, so that the term "grass" is applied to many unrelated plants, such as arrow grass, goose grass, and tape grass, which do not belong to the Grass family. The sedges, which comprise the family Cyperaceae (q.v.), belong to the Grass order, Graminales, and are frequently loosely termed grasses. The rushes, which comprise the family Juncaceae (q.v.), belong to the Pondweed order, but are sometimes referred to as grasses. Many true grasses which are very large or bear unique structures, such as corn, bamboo, or wheat, do not conform to the common conception of grass. Grasses bear flowers which have stamens and pistils, the essential reproductive structures, but lack petals and sepals. Grasses grow from the base, so the removal of tips of blades does not interfere with further growth. This characteristic makes grass uniquely suitable for lawns, where it may be cut frequently without interfering with growth, and for pastures, where it may be grazed extensively without deleterious effect.

Structure. Grasses are anchored to the soil by a root system composed of many slender, fibrous roots. The diameter of a fibrous root is fairly constant throughout its length. The root elongates, during the growing season, by proliferation of cells at its tip. Grass seedlings produce primary roots below their stems, but those produced after the seedling stage of development, including most of the functioning roots of the mature grass plant, are adventitious roots produced from the lower parts of the stem. In small grasses, adventitious roots serve to anchor the grass firmly to the ground, and in larger grasses, such as corn, they serve the additional function of propping up the relatively slender stems which must bear heavy seed ears and which require firm anchorage to resist uprooting by wind. In areas where the soil is shallow and relatively dry, the root system of a grass plant grows in all directions just below the surface of the ground. These lateral root systems extend for great distances, often exceeding ten feet, in order to reach as much of the available moisture as possible.

Grass leaves, regardless of size, are slender, ribbonlike structures tapering to a point at the tip. Each leaf is composed of two parts: a sheath which wraps around the stem and is attached to a node at the base, and an elongated flat blade. Each node produces a single leaf. In many grasses, the juncture of blade and sheath bears a membranous or hardened fringe or ring called a *ligule.* The veins of a grass leaf are parallel and are connected by inconspicuous veinlets.

A grass fruit is a grain; see FRUIT. A grain consists of little more than a single seed with a thin layer of ovary wall still attached to it, so that the structure which is usually called a grass seed is in reality a grass fruit.

Uses. Wild grasses in all parts of the world have long been a source of food for animals. Use as forage is still one of the most important functions of cultivated grasses. Some of the more common forage grasses found in the U.S. are *Agropyron, Andropogon,* Bermuda grass, blue grass, brome grass, buffalo grass, canary grass, fescue, gama grass, grama grass, orchard grass, redtop grass, rye grass, sorghum, Sudan grass, and timothy. Grasses used in making hay are mostly common forage grasses, including *Agropyron, Andropogon,* Bermuda grass, blue grass, brome grass, Johnson grass, orchard grass, Sudan grass, and timothy. The nutritive value of grasses commonly used as forage is illustrated by the average composition of representative species: Kentucky blue grass contains 69.8 percent water, 5.5 percent protein, 1.2 percent fat, 13.4 percent nitrogen-free extract (nonfibrous carbohydrate), 7.6 percent crude fiber, and 2.5 percent ash; timothy contains 61.6 percent water, 3.1 percent protein, 1.2 percent fat, 20.2 percent nitrogen-free extract, 11.8 percent crude fiber, and 2.1 percent ash. Forage grasses can generally meet the full mineral requirements of animals. Particular grass ranges may be lacking in sufficient quantities of certain elements, such as sodium or chlorine, especially in the winter months. These deficiencies are inherent in the soil and must be adjusted by auxiliary feeding of preparations containing minerals in which the forage is deficient. Forages are a reliable source of necessary vitamins, with the possible exception of Vitamin D. Carotene is so abundant in succulent green grass that as little as a pound of Kentucky blue grass will supply the daily Vitamin A requirement of a 600-pound steer. Significant amounts of B-complex vitamins are present in forage grasses: the amount of thiamine is equivalent to that in cereal grains, and the amounts of riboflavin, nicotinic acid, and pantothenic acid are nearly as high as those of milk products.

In temperate regions, the grasses of greatest economic importance are those used for human food. Most of these are cereals (q.v.), including barley, corn, millet, oats, rice, rye, wheat, and various sorghums, but many other grasses of warmer regions, such as sugar cane, from which most commercial sugar is manufactured, sweet sorghums, and bamboo, which is tender in the seedling stage, are used for food.

Grasses used in lawns are usually short, succulent, dark-green species; see HORTICULTURE. The most commonly used lawn grasses are bent grass, Bermuda grass, blue grass, buffalo grass, fescue, and redtop grass.

Bur. of Plant Industry, Soils, and Agricultural Engineering, U.S.D.A.

FORAGE GRASSES OF THE UNITED STATES. *Top, left: Kentucky blue grass. Top, right: Brome grass. Bottom, left: Timothy. Bottom, right: Canary grass.*

Nature Magazine

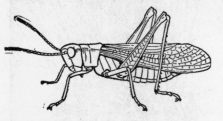

Above, left: Lubber grasshopper of south-eastern United States. Above: Long-horned grasshopper of Europe, Tettigonia viridissima. Left: Drawing showing the structural details of a short-horned grasshopper.

Grasses are used as binders in the prevention of soil erosion (see CONSERVATION), and a few, such as *Ammophila,* are used as band binders. Bamboo (q.v.) is used as construction material in the tropics. A few Asiatic grasses yield an aromatic oil known as citronella (q.v.).

Development. Most research work on grasses done in the past has been concentrated on the development of varieties useful for food, such as hardy varieties of wheat and new hybrid varieties of corn, and for forage. Current researchers continue this development, but are also attempting to develop strains for use in special situations such as lawns, playgrounds, landing fields, golf-courses, and roadside parkways. Several characteristics are sought in newly developed strains of grass: (1) resistance to disease; (2) the ability to recover quickly from injuries, such as those continually sustained by turf on landing fields; (3) tolerance of cold, heat, and sudden changes in temperature; (4) good appearance and wearing quality of the turf, which is dependent on the density and texture of the foliage; (5) ability to form a closely-knit turf; and (6) ability to withstand special conditions required of the grass, such as the very frequent and close clipping of golf-course turf, and the infrequent clipping of landing-strip turf. Species of grasses best adapted for specialized uses are mixed populations composed of many strains varying in form, structure, and physiological responses. Strains which most closely approximate the characteristics needed for a specialized use are carefully isolated and propagated as pure strains; see PLANT BREEDING.

GRASS FINCH. See VESPER SPARROW.

GRASSHOPPER, common name for any of the winged orthopterous insects in the families Tettigoniidae (long-horned grasshoppers), and Acridiidae (short-horned grasshoppers), having their hind legs especially adapted for jumping or leaping. They subsist on vegetation and are distributed throughout the world wherever vegetation grows. Grasshoppers are 1 to 5 in. long when fully grown. The young are similar in appearance to adults but are wingless. Some species undergo seasonal color changes, being green at some times and red or brown at others. Grasshoppers are closely related to crickets (q.v.), and male grasshoppers make chirping or stridulating noises similar to those produced by crickets. Females of several species also make sounds. Unlike crickets, grasshoppers chirp by rubbing their hind legs or hind wings against their fore wings. These insects have organs of hearing; their eardrums are clear, circular areas located on the abdomen at a point just behind the junction of the hind legs with the body.

The family Tettigoniidae, which is sometimes called Locustidae but which contains no true locusts (migratory grasshoppers), is characterized by antennae which extend beyond the hind end of the body. Females of this family usually lay their eggs in low bushes or in crevices in the bark of trees. Tettigoniidae includes the katydids (q.v.), the meadow grasshoppers of the genera *Orchelimum* and *Conocephalus,* which are slightly less than 1 in. long, and the so-called Mormon cricket, *Anabrus simplex,* found in w. United States, which was numerous about the early Mormon settlement in Salt Lake City and did much damage to crops there.

The family Acridiidae is characterized by short antennae. Females of this family lay their eggs in holes in the ground in the fall. The eggs hatch in spring and the young reach maturity in July or August. Acridiidae includes all the migratory grasshoppers. When a nonmigratory grasshopper reproduces too rapidly for its food supply, it becomes migratory and undergoes such extensive changes in external form that scientists have often been misled into considering the resulting locust as a distinct species. Thus the migratory form of *Melanoplus mexicanus,* a western-American grasshopper about 1 in. in length, has often been scientifically called *M. spretus.* This migratory form is popularly known as the Rocky Mountain locust. The red-legged grasshopper, *M. femur-rubrum,* is a closely related species which is common in E. United States. It reaches a length of 2 in. Another common American grasshopper is *Schistocera americana,* which is about 4 in. long. In the same genus is *S. peregrina,* a N. African locust which may have been the species described in the Biblical account of the plagues of Egypt. Other American grasshoppers in this family include the thick, almost wingless, lubber grasshoppers, *Rhomalea microptera,* of southeastern U.S., and *Brachypeplus magnus,* of southwestern U.S. These grasshoppers are 2 to 3 in. long. The European locust is *Pachytylus migratorius,* about 4 in. long. Some grasshoppers are eaten and considered delicacies in many parts of the world. See also LOCUST.

GRASSHOPPER SPARROW, QUAIL SPARROW, or YELLOW-WINGED SPARROW, a small sparrow, *Ammodramus savannarum,* characterized by a song resembling the sounds made by grasshoppers. It is found throughout the U.S., and in s. Canada and N. Mexico. This bird is 5½ in. long. Above it is ashygray blotched with brown; below it is uniformly buff. Its beak is thick and heavy, and a buff line extends from its back over the dark gray crown. Each gray wing has a yellow patch on its edge. The tail is short and stumpy. The grasshopper sparrow inhabits tall grass in dry regions and builds its nest there. When disturbed the bird flies for a short distance and then drops into another portion of the tall grass, whence it scurries along the ground to a new hiding place.

GRASSI, GIOVANNI BATTISTA (1854–1925), Italian zoologist, born at Rovellasca. He studied medicine at the University of Pavia and zoology at the universities of Heidelberg and Würzburg. He was appointed professor of zoology at the University of Catania in 1883 and professor of comparaive anatomy at the University of Rome in 1895. He was made a senator in 1908. Grassi did important research in the life history of intestinal worms, eels, ants, and termites. He also studied the sporozoan malarial parasite and the transmission of malaria by the *Anopheles* mosquito. Among his works are *I Chetognati* (1883), *Contribuzione allo Studio dei Parassiti Malarici* (with R. Faletti, 1892), and *Studi di un Zoologo sulla Malaria* (1900).

GRASSMANN, HERMANN GÜNTHER (1809–77), German mathematician and Sanskrit scholar, born at Stettin, and educated at the University of Berlin. As a mathematician he is known chiefly for his work, *Die Wissenschaft der Extensiven Grössen oder die Ausdehnungslehre* (1844), in which he formulated a theory of vector algebra which is the foundation of modern vector (q.v.) analysis.

In later life Grassmann took up the study of Sanskrit. His *Wörterbuch zum Rig-Veda* (1875), a combined dictionary and concordance, and his *Übersetzung des Rig-Veda* (1876) are still used by Sanskrit scholars. He also formulated the linguistic law known as Grassmann's law, which states that in Indo-European roots, particularly in Sanskrit and Greek, successive syllables do not begin with aspirates.

GRASS MOTH, common name for any of several small moths in the family Pyralididae which feed on grasses. Their larvae are voracious and often do considerable damage to crops such as corn and rice. The grass moths are widely distributed throughout North America. The principal genus, *Crambus,* has seventy to eighty species.

A typical grass moth, *C. vulvivagellus,* is about one inch long. Its front wings are white, long, and narrow, and taper to a point. Its hind wings are wide. During the day the adult moth rests on the stems of grasses with wings wrapped tightly about the body. The larvae builds a sheath of grass and silk an inch or more below the surface of the ground. It forages for food at night, storing grass or grain within the sheath to eat during the day.

GRASS OIL. See CITRONELLA.

GRASS SNAKE, common name for the water snake, *Natrix natrix,* the commonest snake of Europe. Grass snakes are oviparous (egg-laying) rather than viviparous (livebearing) like other water snakes. The grass

Australian News & Information Bureau

Grass trees growing in Western Australia

snake reaches a maximum length of 3½ ft. at maturity and has rough, keeled scales. Many color varieties of grass snakes exist; the most common is the ringed snake, so called because of a wide white ring around its neck. The ringed snake is greenish-olive in color, spotted with black.

The name grass snake has also been given to one of the green snakes (q.v.), and to an indistinctly striped variety of the common garter snake.

GRASS TREE, common name of small shrubs of the genus *Xanthorrhoea*, belonging to the Lily family. The genus contains about five species, which grow in Australia, Tasmania, and New Zealand. The grass tree has an upright stem which bears a tuft of long, grasslike leaves at the summit. Densely aggregated flowers are produced on long cylindrical spikes which arise from the center of the tuft of leaves. Bases of inner leaves of most species are edible. Bases of older leaves of all species produce a resinous juice which hardens when dried into a reddish-yellow substance, called *acaroid gum*. Alcoholic solutions of the gum are used as a remedy for dysentery, diarrhea, and other intestinal disorders.

Australian aborigines use the gum to unite the edges of wounds, and as a constituent of calking and cementing compounds.

The common grass tree, *X. hastilis,* grows about four feet tall. Stems of very old plants sometimes reach diameters of as much as twelve inches.

GRASS WRACK. See TAPE GRASS.

GRATIAN, full Latin name FRANCISCUS GRATIANUS (?–1160?), Italian theologian. He was a monk in the monastery of St. Felix in Bologna, and later, according to tradition, became bishop of Chiusi. He compiled the well-known body of canon law called the *Concordia Discordantium Canonum* or *Decretum Gratiani*. Although he was not critical in the use of his sources, he is regarded as the founder of canon law. A revision of the work, the *editio Romana,* was prepared by a committee of cardinals appointed at the Council of Trent. The German legal scholar Emil Friedberg included a critical edition of the work in his *Corpus Juris Canonici* (1879).

GRATIANUS or GRATIAN, FLAVIUS (359–383 A.D.), Roman emperor, born at Sirmium, in the Roman province of Pannonia. He was the eldest son of Valentinian I. In 367 he was elevated by his father to the rank of Augustus (co-emperor) at Ambiani (Amiens) in Gaul. On the death of Valentinian I eight years later, Gratianus became senior ruler of the Western Roman Empire, with his infant half brother Valentinian II as his colleague. The Roman troops in Pannonia had declared Valentinian II as emperor, and Gratianus, for his part, had received the sovereignty of Gaul, Spain, and Britain. Because of the tender age of his half brother, however, Gratianus was in effect the sole ruler of the Western Empire, while the Eastern Roman Empire continued to be ruled by his uncle, Valens. On August 9, 378, Valens was defeated and killed by the Goths, and the sovereignty of the Eastern Empire devolved upon Gratianus. Feeling himself unequal to the task of ruling both empires, he appointed Theodosius as his colleague to succeed Valens. In the reign of Gratianus, orthodox Christianity for the first time became dominant throughout the Roman Empire. But the emperor's persecution of non-Christian Romans, and afterward of heretic Christians, alienated great numbers of his subjects; and his fondness for frivolous amusements and ignoble associates earned him the contempt of the army. Consequently, when the insurgent Magnus Clemens Maximus led a revolt in Britain and was proclaimed emperor by the Roman legions there, Gratianus was deserted by his troops, who rallied to the standard of the new emperor. Gratianus was defeated by Maximus near Paris, fleeing thence to Lugdunum (Lyons), where he was overtaken and slain.

GRATIOLA, genus of herbs belonging to the figwort family, commonly known as hedge hyssop. They are small herbs which grow in meadows and on the edges of ponds and rivers. The European hedge hyssop, *Gratiola officinalis,* was formerly considered a useful medicine because of its extreme bitterness and its violent action as a purgative, diuretic, and emetic. The bitter properties result from the presence of a glucoside, *gratiolin.* Several species of hedge hyssop are native to North America. The golden hedge hyssop or goldenpert, *G. aurea,* which grows on wet ground in Eastern U.S., is an annual herb with yellow, tubular flowers.

GRATTAN, HENRY (1746–1820), Irish orator and statesman, born in Dublin, and educated at Trinity College, Dublin. In 1772 he was admitted to the Irish bar, and three years later he became a member of the Irish Parliament. The brilliance of his speeches, unequalled by any Irish contemporary except Edmund Burke, quickly brought him the leadership of the National Party. His demand for free trade for Ireland was granted by Lord Frederick North in 1779, and his petition for complete freedom of the Irish Parliament from the domination of the English privy council and for a new Irish constitution, approved by the Irish Parliament in 1782, was granted a month later by the English government.

The newly-constituted Irish Parliament had no power over the executive authorities, who were still appointed from England; moreover, elections were marred by corruption and the non-representation of the majority of the Irish people, who could not vote because they were Roman Catholics. Although Grattan was a Protestant himself, he campaigned tirelessly for the political rights of the Catholics, whose franchise was finally granted by the Irish Parliament in 1792. However, the consent of the English government was necessary before the enfranchisement of the Catholics could become Irish law, and this consent the English government refused to give. In 1794 certain other political reforms, of a mild nature, proposed by Grattan, were defeated in the Irish Parliament largely through English influence, and the following year Grattan warned the English government that its resistance to religious freedom and political reforms in Ireland was driving the people to violent measures. In 1797 he retired from Parliament, and the following year his warning to the English was fulfilled by a rebellion, which was brutally suppressed.

Grattan's popularity declined during his three-year retirement, as none of the reforms he had advocated were actually carried out. But in 1800, when the Irish Parliament met for its last session, he returned to the House, and his appearance was cheered, even by those who had been his enemies. He retired again until 1805, when he became a member of the House of Commons in London; there, despite the efforts of Henry Richard Fox and William Wyndham Grenville to make him accept office, he remained in the background, constantly fighting for Catholic emancipation. He remained in the English Parliament until his death, and although he continued to fight for Irish political reforms, his influence at home declined, as a new extremist Irish emancipation party had arisen under the leadership of Daniel O'Connell.

GRAUBÜNDEN. The easternmost canton of Switzerland. See GRISONS.

GRAUN, KARL HEINRICH (1701–59), German composer, born at Wahrenbrück, Saxony. In his early youth he sang in the choir at Dresden and composed cantatas and other pieces

Henry Grattan

for the church service. He later sang tenor roles in opera at Brunswick, where he started to compose operas. In 1741 he was appointed Kapellmeister by Frederick the Great of Prussia. Graun wrote about thirty operas, including *Semiramide* (1754) and *Merope* (1756), about fifty cantatas, many motets, and concertos. His most famous compositions are an oratorio, *Der Tod Jesu* (1755), which was regularly performed in Germany during Holy Week for a century and a half after Graun's death, and a choral work, *Te Deum* (1756).

GRAU SAN MARTÍN, RAMÓN (1887–   ), Cuban statesman, born in the town of Pinar del Río. He received a medical degree from the University of Havana and continued his studies in Europe. In 1921 he became professor of physiology at the University of Havana. In 1932, when he joined the protest against the suppression of a revolutionary organization of students by the government of President Gerardo Machado, he was imprisoned and then exiled. In August, 1933, the Machado government was overthrown by a revolution, and Carlos Manuel de Céspedes was named provisional president. Subsequently a group of rank-and-file soldiers and students overthrew the de Céspedes government and appointed Grau one of five commissioners to form a new government. Six days later (Sept. 10) Grau became president. He was unable to overcome the continuing unrest and economic chaos. The United States refused to recognize his government and he resigned in January, 1934. Grau was defeated for the presidency by Fulgencio Batista in the election of 1940 but won the election of 1944. During his four-year term of office he abolished censorship of the press and decreed tax exemption for a number of industries to promote industrialization in Cuba. Economic conditions improved somewhat. See CUBA: *History.*

GRAVES, FRANK PIERREPONT (1869–1956), American educator, born in New York City, and educated at Columbia College and Boston University, and at Heidelberg College, Ohio. He was president of the University of Wyoming from 1896 to 1898 and of the University of Washington from 1898 to 1903. Between 1904 and 1921 he served variously as professor and dean at a number of American universities, and in the latter year became commissioner of education of New York and president of the University of the State of New York. From 1937 to 1940, when he retired, he was president of the national honorary fraternity Phi Beta Kappa. His writings include *The State University Ideal* (1897), *A History of Education Before the Middle Ages* (1909), *What Did Jesus Teach?* (1919), and *Administration of American Education* (1932).

GRAVES, ROBERT RANKE (1895–   ), English poet and novelist, son of the poet Alfred Perceval Graves, born in London, and educated at Charterhouse School and Oxford University. He served during World War I as an officer in the Royal Welch Fusiliers; his first volume of poems, *Fairies and Fusiliers,* appeared in 1918. In 1926 he was appointed professor of English literature at the Egyptian University, Cairo; later in collaboration with his wife Laura Riding, Graves conducted the Seizin Press at Deya, Majorca, Spain. His first book to achieve success was *Goodbye to All That, an Autobiography* (1929), a frank and satiric account of military life during World War I. Graves was particularly noted for historical novels characterized by color, drama, and accuracy of historical detail. His novels include *I, Claudius* (1934), *Claudius the God* (1934), *Count Belisarius* (1938), *Sergeant Lamb of the Ninth* (1940), *Proceed, Sergeant Lamb* (1941), *Wife to Mr. Milton* (1943), *Hercules, My Shipmate* (1944), *King Jesus* (1946), *Homer's Daughter* (1955), and *They Hanged My Saintly Billy* (1957). His early poetry was simple and lyrical; later he treated mythological subjects in the manner of the Symbolists (q.v.). Collected editions of his poems were published in 1926, 1938, 1947, and 1955. Among Graves' critical and historical works are *The White Goddess, a Historical Grammar of Poetic Myth* (1948), *The Greek Myths* (2 vols., 1955), and *Crowning Privilege; Collected Essays on Poetry* (1956).

GRAVESEND, municipal borough of Kent County, England, and part of the Port of London, situated on the Thames R., 22 m. by rail S.E. of London. In the 11th-century *Domesday Book* (q.v.), "Gravesham", a part of the lands of the bishop of Bayeux, is mentioned as having a *hythe,* or landing-place; "Gravesham" was probably the site of Gravesend. The town was incorporated in 1562, during the reign of Queen Elizabeth, who established Gravesend as the point at which distinguished foreign visitors to the realm should be received and thence conveyed in state to London. In the 17th century Gravesend became known as a station for pilots and East Indiamen. Vessels from foreign countries are detained for health inspection at present-day Gravesend. The Royal Thames Yacht Club maintains headquarters in the town. The American Indian princess

Pocahontas is buried in the cemetery adjoining the church of St. George. Industries include commercial fishing, boat-building, truck farming, and the manufacture of earthenware and iron castings. Pop. (1951 prelim.) 45,043.

GRAVITATION, the property of mutual attraction possessed by all bodies of matter. The term "gravity" is sometimes used synonymously, but properly refers only to the gravitational force between the earth and objects on or near it.

The law of gravitation, discovered by Sir Isaac Newton (q.v.) in 1684, states that the gravitational attraction between two bodies is directly proportional to the product of the masses of the two bodies and inversely proportional to the square of the distance between them. In algebraic form the law is stated $F = G \dfrac{m_1 m_2}{d^2}$, where F is the gravitational force, m_1 and m_2 the masses of the two bodies, d the distance between the bodies, and G a constant, the gravitational or Newtonian constant. The value of this constant was first measured by Henry Cavendish (q.v.) in 1798 by means of the torsion balance. The best modern value for this constant is .0000000666 dynes centimeter squared per gram squared (6.66 $\times$ 10^{-8} dyne cm.^{2}/gm.^{2}). The force of gravitation between two spherical bodies each having a mass of 1 gram and having a distance of 1 centimeter between their centers is .0000000666 of a dyne, or about one thirty-billionth of a gram.

The force of gravity for objects on the surface of the earth is less than the earth's gravitational attraction for such objects because the centrifugal force caused by the earth's rotation tends to counteract the gravitational effect. For the same reason the acceleration of gravity is greater at the poles than it is at the equator, as the centrifugal force is large at the equator and zero at the poles. The bulging of the center of the earth and the flattening of the poles, caused by centrifugal force, has the opposite effect but is not large enough to counteract the effect of centrifugal force. The force of gravity decreases slightly with increasing altitude. To escape from the gravitational force of the earth, an object traveling upward from the earth's surface requires a velocity of about seven miles per second.

Gravity is commonly measured in terms of the amount of acceleration which the force gives to an object on the surface of the earth. At the equator the acceleration of gravity is 977.99 centimeters per second per second, and at the poles it is more than 983 centimeters per second per second. The generally accepted international value for the acceleration of gravity used in calculations is 980.665 centimeters (in the English system, 32.17 feet) per second per second. Thus, neglecting air resistance, any body falling freely will increase its speed at the rate of 980.665 centimeters (or 32.17 feet) per second each second of its fall.

The orbits of the planets around the sun and of the moon around the earth are controlled by the gravitational forces existing between the various bodies of the solar system. Because of its great mass the gravitational pull of the sun is by far the largest factor in the orbit of each of the planets, but the attraction between the planets themselves produces small *perturbations* in their regular paths. Observation of these perturbations, and calculations based on them, resulted in the discovery of the previously unobserved planets Neptune and Pluto. See CELESTIAL MECHANICS; PLANET; SOLAR SYSTEM; STARS.

Before the 20th century various theories were advanced to account for the fact of gravitational attraction, but none of the theories were satisfactory. As a part of his general theory of relativity (q.v.), however, Albert Einstein showed that gravitation exists as a consequence of inertial force acting on bodies in curved space. This statement of the identity of momentum and gravitational force is known as the *Einstein equivalence principle*.

GRAVITY, SPECIFIC. See DENSITY.

GRAVURE. See PHOTOMECHANICAL PROCESSES: *Photogravure*.

GRAY, ASA (1810–88), American botanist born at Sauquoit, near Paris, N.Y. He received the degree of M.D. from a medical school at Fairfield, New York, but never practiced medicine. Gray's first position as a professional botanist was as curator of the New York Lyceum of Natural History, a position secured for him in 1835 by John Torrey. Gray was appointed professor of natural history at Harvard University in 1842. The flora of North America was at that time being studied, discovered, and scientifically systematized, and his work in taxonomy accorded Gray the position of the foremost botanist of his day. Cambridge became the leading center of botanical investigation in the United States, and the herbarium at Cambridge, established by Gray, grew to be the largest and most valuable in the country.

From 1835 until his death Gray wrote copiously and his books and papers were not only of great importance in establishing a scientific

Asa Gray

system of taxonomy for plants, but they encouraged and popularized the study of botany. He was one of Darwin's earliest supporters. Gray's most important work, *Manual of the Botany of Northern United States* (1848), has been through many revisions. It was the most widely used manual for many generations of botanists, and the 8th edition, entitled *Gray's Manual of Botany* (1950), is still a standard work of reference. Some of his other books are *Elements of Botany* (1836), *Botanical Textbook* (1842) *First Lessons in Botany and Vegetable Physiology* (1857), *How Plants Grow* (1858), *How Plants Behave* (1872), and *Darwiniana* (1876).

GRAY, ELISHA (1835–1901), American inventor, born at Barnesville, Ohio, and educated at Oberlin College. He invented and patented many electrical devices, including a facsimile telegraph (q.v.). He filed a *caveat* claiming invention of the telephone in 1876 a few hours after Alexander Graham Bell (q.v.) had registered his final patent. Bell's right to the patent was sustained by the U.S. Supreme Court. Gray organized a manufacturing concern which later developed into the Western Electric Company. He wrote *Experimental Researches in Electro-Harmonic Telegraphy and Telephony* (1878).

GRAY, HENRY PETERS (1819–77), American genre, historical, and portrait painter, born in

New York City. He studied painting principally in Italy and his style is closely modeled on the styles of the Italian masters, particularly those of the Venetian school. Toward the end of his career he devoted himself mainly to the painting of portraits, of which he executed about 250. Among his paintings are "Greek Lovers" (Metropolitan Museum of Art, New York City), "Judgment of Paris" (Corcoran Gallery, Washington, D.C.), "Cupid Begging his Arrow" (Pennsylvania Academy of Fine Arts, Philadelphia), and a portrait of William Cullen Bryant (Historical Society, New York City).

GRAY, ROBERT (1755–1806), American sea captain and explorer, born at Tiverton, R.I. During the American Revolution he served in the navy, and in 1787 he was made commander of the *Lady Washington,* one of a fleet subsidized by Boston merchants who wished to procure furs from the Northwest for trade with the Orient. After the expedition had procured a load of furs from the Indians on the Pacific coast, Gray was made head of the expedition and placed in command of the ship *Columbia.* He sailed to China and thence eastward, completing the first voyage around the world by an American vessel; he arrived in Boston on Aug. 10, 1790. Shortly after his return he undertook a second voyage to the Northwest on the *Columbia,* and in 1792 discovered the mouth of the Columbia River, which he named after his ship. He completed the trip around the world a second time and arrived in Boston in July, 1793. The explorations and discoveries of Gray in the Pacific Northwest gave America a basis for claim to the Oregon country.

GRAY, THOMAS (1716–71), English poet, born in Cornhill, London, and educated at Eton College and Peterhouse, Cambridge University. In 1750 he finished the poem by which he is best known, the *Elegy Written in a Country Churchyard,* and sent it to his friend Horace Walpole, at whose insistence it was published in the following year. Since that time the work has remained a favorite. Before 1751 Gray had written other poems, but these were not collected until the publication of his *Poems* (1753), a volume including the *Ode on a Distant Prospect of Eton College* and the *Ode on the Death of a Favourite Cat* (both written in 1747). The poems are possibly the last expression in English verse of the classicism of John Dryden and Alexander Pope (qq.v.). Living at Cambridge, Gray wrote *The Progress of Poesy* in 1757 and in the same year refused to accept an appointment as poet laureate. He became professor of history and modern languages at Cambridge University in 1768, and, in the intervals of his scholastic duties, traveled widely throughout Great Britain in search of picturesque scenery and ancient monuments, recording his impressions in his *Journal* (1775). An interest in Celtic and Norse mythology, which was later to distinguish the English Romantic poets, was expressed in such of his poems as *The Bard* (1757) and *The Descent of Odin* (1761). See ENGLISH LITERATURE.

GRAYLING, common name for any fish of the family Thymallidae, in the same suborder as the herrings and trout. They are freshwater fish, prized for food and sport. Three species are found in the lakes and streams of N. North America. The Michigan grayling, *Thymallus tricolor,* found in Michigan, is a large-scaled fish, about eleven inches long, with a long, broad, dorsal fin. Its mouth is small and contains few teeth. The Montana grayling, *T. montanus,* is found in some of the headstreams of the Missouri River. The Alaska grayling, *T. signifer,* is found in Alaska and Canada.

Graylings are also found in the frigid lakes and streams of Europe and Siberia. The common European species, *T. thymallus,* is a favorite game fish of British sportsmen; it is often found together with trout.

GRAYSON, DAVID. See BAKER, RAY STANNARD.

GRAY'S PEAK, mountain in Clear Creek and Summit counties, N. central Colorado. It is one of the loftiest peaks in the Rocky Mountains, rising 14,274 ft. above sea level. The peak was named for the American botanist Asa Gray.

GRAY WHALE, a whale, *Rhachianectes glaucus,* found in the N. Pacific Ocean, especially in shallow water near the coasts of North America, Japan, and Korea. The gray whale is mottled gray and black in color. It is 35 to 45 ft. long; its head is comparatively small, taking up less than 10 ft. of the body length. Long hairs cover the head and lower jaw. The mouth of this whale contains whalebone plates acting as sieves, through which the animal filters small marine organisms from the water. The gray whale is active and difficult to capture. Other names sometimes applied to the gray whale are: devilfish, grayback, hardhead, and mussel digger. See WHALE.

GRAZ, capital of the Austrian province of Styria, about 140 m. by rail s.w. of Vienna, located on both sides of the Mur R., and sur-

rounded on three sides by the Styrian Alps. Graz is known to have existed in the 9th century A.D., and is thought to occupy the site of an earlier Roman town. In the 15th century it was a residence of the Holy Roman emperors. In the 16th century it became one of the important centers of resistance to the Turks. The town was occupied by the French in 1797, 1805, and 1809, during the Napoleonic Wars. The old town, on the left bank of the river, is connected with the new town, on the right bank, by seven bridges. The old town is built around the Schlossberg park, which until 1809 was a strongly fortified hill. The buildings of Graz include an 11th-century castle, the 13th-century church of the Teutonic Knights, a 15th-century cathedral, and a 16th-century parish church with an altarpiece by the Venetian painter Tintoretto. Graz contains, in addition to the University of Graz, founded in 1573, a technical school, industrial and trade schools, and several Gymnasia. Paper, cloth, steel, and precision instruments are among the products manufactured in the city; a considerable trade in wine, fruit, and cereal grains is carried on. Following World War II Graz was included in the British zone of occupation of Austria. Pop. (1951) 226,453.

GRAZIANI, RODOLFO, MARCHESE DI NEGHELLI (1882–1955), Italian Fascist soldier and administrator. From 1930 to 1934 he commanded the Italian forces in Libya, and the following year became governor of Italian Somaliland. In 1936 he was appointed viceroy of Ethiopia, under the Italian domination of the country, and in 1938 was honorary governor of Italian East Africa. Graziani commanded the Italian forces in Libya at the beginning of World War II, suffered crushing defeats in the early months of 1941, and resigned his command. He returned to Mussolini's favor in 1943, when Marshal Pietro Badoglio's government had accepted the peace terms of unconditional surrender offered by the Allies. Graziani retreated to the north of

The Montana grayling

Italy with Mussolini, became minister of defense in the new Fascist government organized there under German domination, and commanded the remnants of the Italian armies in Liguria. His armies surrendered to the Allies early in the spring of 1945, and Graziani was captured near Lake Como by anti-Fascist Italian forces in April, 1945. He was indicted for treason, tried, and imprisoned in May, 1950, but released in August because of ill-health.

GREASE. See FATS AND FIXED OILS; LUBRICANTS; PETROLEUM.

GREASEWOOD, common name of plants belonging to the Goosefoot family which grow in salty, alkaline soils in arid areas of w. United States, and including members of the genera *Sarcobatus*, *Atriplex*, *Grayia*, and *Allenrolfia*. Greasewoods are shrubs which grow two to eight feet tall and bear small, fleshy, stalkless leaves. The stems are covered with mealy scales, making the surfaces greasy to the touch. Cattle and sheep eat the leaves and tender portions of the stem. From the depths of the soil the deep roots of greasewood bring considerable quantities of alkali to the surface. See SALTBUSH.

GREAT AWAKENING. See EDWARDS, JONATHAN.

GREAT BARRIER REEF. See BARRIER REEF, THE GREAT.

GREAT BASIN, an area of inland drainage in w. United States, situated between the Wasatch Mountains on the east and the Sierra Nevada and Cascade ranges on the west. It comprises most of Nevada and portions of Utah, Oregon, Idaho, and California, and has a total area of about 210,000 sq. m. The basin has a gradual slope from the north, where the elevation is 4000 feet above the sea, toward the south. The Humboldt River is the only perennial stream of any size rising in the interior, but on the borders there are numerous short streams which act as feeders to a number of lakes, including Winnemucca, Carson, Owens, Mono, Pyramid, Sevier, Utah, and Great Salt Lake. There are several arid wastes within the basin, such as Great Salt Lake Desert, Carson Desert, and Mojave Desert. The climate is dry. In Pleistocene times the climate was damp and much of the northern and eastern portions of the Basin were occupied by two large lakes, Bonneville Lake (q.v.) and Lahontan Lake. See GREAT SALT LAKE.

GREAT BEAR LAKE, an extensive fresh water lake in the Mackenzie District of the Northwest Territories of Canada, lying on the Arctic Circle. The lake is irregular in shape and has a total area of approximately 11,660 sq.m. and a depth of 270 ft. The surface is approximately 200 ft. above sea level. At its western extremity Great Bear Lake empties into the Mackenzie River. The lake is fed in part from Great Slave Lake (q.v.) through the Marian River which flows into the lake at the southeast through a chain of smaller lakes. The only important settlement on Great Bear Lake is Port Radium on the eastern shore. The discovery of pitchblende and other radium and uranium ores on the shores and on islands in the lake in 1930 led to a "radium rush". The uranium deposits in the neighborhood of the lake are among the most important in the world and achieved great importance following the discovery of practical methods of atomic fission.

GREAT BRITAIN, the largest island of Europe, one of the British Isles, and since 1603 a kingdom consisting of England, Scotland, and Wales. In popular usage, the name was formerly often employed to designate the expanded kingdom of Great Britain, known officially as the Kingdom of Great Britain and Ireland; the name is often applied, in contemporary times, to the United Kingdom of Great Britain and Northern Ireland. Great Britain is separated from the continental mainland by the North Sea, the Strait of Dover, and the English Channel, and from Ireland by North Channel, the Irish Sea, and St. George's Channel. For information regarding the topography, climate, flora, fauna, and the social, economic, and political features of Great Britain, see ENGLAND; SCOTLAND; WALES; UNITED KINGDOM. See also BRITAIN. Area of the island, 88,745 sq.m.; pop. (1955 est.) 49,574,000.

History. The following account concerns the history of England, Scotland, and Wales as a national unit, dating from 1603, when James VI of Scotland (as James I of England) succeeded Elizabeth I as ruler of England, to 1801, when the legislative union of these countries and Ireland created the United Kingdom of Great Britain and Ireland. From 1603 the entire island of Great Britain was ruled by one sovereign, although legislative union with Scotland was not accomplished until more than a century later. For the history of England and Scotland prior to 1603, and the history of Wales before 1536, when the latter country was formally united with England, see articles on the separate countries; for their history after 1801, see UNITED KINGDOM.

The England which, in 1603, received James

I (q.v.) as its first Stuart king was a peaceful and prosperous country. The great political problems of the 16th century, such as the succession to the throne, religious strife between Catholics and Protestants, and fear of foreign invasion, had been resolved during the reign of the Tudors. A major part of this resolution had resulted, however, from the firm, almost autocratic control of the Tudors over the English government, a necessary centralization in the troubled 16th century. With the emergence of England as a great world power, the English population, particularly the increasingly important middle class, began strongly to resent the royal autocracy. During the last years of Elizabeth's reign, Parliament had opposed her will on several occasions, and only the queen's personal popularity had prevented open conflict. The death of Elizabeth removed the obligation of loyalty, and Parliament was ready to assert its rights when her successor, James, came to the throne.

James I, believing in the divine right of kings, the theory by which kings were responsible for their actions only to God (see DIVINE RIGHT), had no intention of submitting to Parliament. James I stood also for the divine right of bishops and a strong episcopacy which, acknowledged as the spiritual power by the ruler, would support his own claims to absolute temporal power (see BISHOP). The religious temper of Reformation England, with the developing influence of Presbyterianism (q.v.) and tendencies to church self-government, was opposed to episcopacy. Thus, in both politics and religion, James inevitably clashed with his subjects.

The differences between the king and his people became obvious immediately after James's entry into London. In 1603 and again in 1604 demands were made by the Puritan clergy (see PURITANS) for reforms in ecclesiastical affairs. These demands brought about the unsuccessful Hampton Court Conference of 1604. James, reiterating his support of episcopacy, refused to relax his views, and the Conference resulted only in the decision to make the translation of the Bible, known as the King James version (see BIBLE, ENGLISH TRANSLATIONS OF). On the other hand, the monarch maintained a vacillating policy toward Catholics, sometimes being lenient and at other times strictly enforcing anti-Catholic laws. This perversity resulted, in 1605, in the unsuccessful Gunpowder Plot (q.v.), a scheme of English Catholics to blow up the houses of Parliament when the king and members were present.

James I, first Stuart king of Great Britain

Conflict between king and Parliament began with the Parliament of 1604. When James claimed his divine right on major issues, Parliament disabused him and informed him that the authority of the people was above that of the king (see SOCIAL CONTRACT); moreover, Parliament refused to act on the king's demand that the union with Scotland be formalized. In 1611, when the legislators began to debate the royal right to collect import duties in a discussion concerning an annual fixed grant to the king (the Great Contract), James considered that they had gone too far and dissolved Parliament. Financial difficulties proving too much for him three years later, he was forced to recall Parliament, which alone had the power to grant money; but the body, which became known as the Addled Parliament devoted so much time to discussing abuses of royal power that it enacted no legislation and James dissolved it. For the next seven years he ruled without a Parliament, obtaining money by levying taxes without other authority than that of his royal prerogative. Added grievance resulted from his interference in the court system, James hold-

Charles I, king of Great Britain, 1625–49

ing that he could set aside judgments of common law (see COKE, SIR EDWARD; STAR CHAMBER). Moreover, popular indignation increased against the king's favorites, notably Robert Carr, Earl of Somerset, and George Villiers, Duke of Buckingham (see VILLIERS). These men, by flattering the king, had maneuvered themselves into the positions of important counselors of state. The Spanish ambassador, Diego Sarmiento de Acuña, Count of Gondomar, also ingratiated himself with James by flattery. The leading Catholic state in Europe, Spain was preparing for war with the Protestant German states (see THIRTY YEARS' WAR), and hoped to prevent England from joining a German alliance, even proposing a marriage between a Spanish princess and Charles, the British crown prince. However, when Spain in 1620 invaded the Palatinate, ruled by James's son-in-law, the English king broke off negotiations with Spain. In order to get the money for a Spanish war, he was compelled to recall Parliament. Soon after convening, Parliament began to voice its grievances; the second session framed a petition, called the Great Protestation, reasserting the right of Parliament to debate on state affairs and to advise the king concerning them. James, enraged, dissolved Parliament. Still influenced by the Spanish ambassador, James decided to pursue the issue of the Spanish mar-

riage and hold off war; but, after an unsuccessful courting in Spain by Charles in 1623, the king reconvened Parliament in 1624 to declare war. In the same year a treaty with France, against Spain, was bound by the marriage of Charles to Henrietta Maria, the sister of the French monarch Louis XIII.

At the death of James in 1625 and the accession of Charles I (q.v.), Parliament was in a strong position, having declared its rights and taken a firm position on them. Charles was personally popular when he became king and, had he been willing to co-operate with his legislature, the great conflict between king and Parliament might well have been resolved. The new king was, however, as firm a believer in the theory of divine right as his father had been. He could get little money from a recalcitrant Parliament. On his own initiative, he mismanaged the Spanish war and, by not fulfilling the terms of the French marriage treaty, alienated France to such an extent that Louis XIII declared war on England in 1626. Unable to obtain funds without first redressing the grievances of Parliament, Charles forced the taxpayers to "lend" him five times the amount of an ordinary Parliament grant, imprisoning those who refused to contribute. He called Parliament in 1628 to enact a money grant and immediately received the Petition of Right (q.v.), a statement of Parliamentary grievances. Charles was obliged to grant the petition, but a later remonstrance against his unauthorized levying of a royal duty on exports and imports of wine and other merchandise led him to end that session of Parliament. After another turbulent session in 1629, Charles dissolved the legislature and, for the next eleven years, ruled without it, raising money by unlawful methods. Lack of sufficient funds compelled him to make peace with France and Spain in 1630, severely damaging the international prestige of England. The king was supported in his despotism by his ministers, notably Thomas Wentworth, Earl of Strafford (see STRAFFORD), an able but intolerant man, and William Laud (q.v.), Archbishop of Canterbury, who attempted to institute throughout England a High Church ritual similar to the Catholic. An attempt to force the Anglican prayer book on Scotland, in 1637, resulted in an armed rebellion there with which the moneyless king was unable to cope. The Scottish Presbyterians bound themselves to repulse any attempt on their religion; they brought Charles to terms in the so-called Bishops' War of 1639 (see COVENANTERS). At length, the Scottish situation and his financial straits forced Charles to call for Parliamentary elections in England.

The Parliament which convened in 1640 insisted first upon a redress of grievances, and Charles dissolved it after a session of only three weeks. The Scots then invaded England and, in order to halt them, Charles had to guarantee them an indemnity, forcing him to convoke Parliament again. Known as the Long Parliament (q.v.), because it sat continuously from 1640 to 1653, the body was in a position to dictate to the king, the Scottish army being a threat until the indemnity was paid. Led by John Hampden and John Pym (qq.v.), it passed a bill of attainder against the Earl of Strafford, who was executed, and abolished the Star Chamber and the ecclesiastical court known as the Court of High Commission (see HIGH COMMISSION, COURT OF). Another act forbade the king to dissolve Parliament without its own consent. In 1641 the legislators framed the Grand Remonstrance (q.v.), a summarization of grievances against Charles. Religious matters, however, divided Parliament, some members, chiefly Puritans, demanding the abolition of episcopacy "root and branch", and others, the Episcopalian group, favoring the continuance of the ecclesiastical organization then in effect. These religious differences were reflected in the English population, and many sects, such as the Society of Friends, began to worship as they pleased (see FRIENDS, SOCIETY OF).

Charles refused to accept the Grand Remonstrance and, in 1642, attempted unsuccessfully to seize the leaders of the House of Commons. Parliament then attempted to have the militia put under its control and, as a final measure, submitted the Nineteen Propositions to Charles, who rejected them. The struggle between the king and Parliament inevitably divided England into two formidable factions. The civil war, known as the Great Rebellion, began with the indecisive battle of Edgehill in 1642. (For a detailed account of the first and second civil wars, which comprised the Great Rebellion, see CROMWELL, OLIVER; GREAT REBELLION.) The Solemn League and Covenant, guaranteeing uniformity of religion in England, Scotland, and Ireland, was signed by the English and Scottish Parliaments in 1643, and the Scots became allies of the Parliamentary party, the so-called Roundheads. Reorganized by Oliver Cromwell, the New Model army of Parliament decisively defeated the Royalist, or Cavalier, forces, in the battle of Naseby in 1645. A year later, Charles gave himself up to the Scottish army, ending the first civil war. The Scots surrendered Charles to the English Parliament in 1647. In 1648, however, believing that the English government was too tolerant of what they considered heretical religious sects, the Scots signed a secret treaty with the captive Charles, and, with the Irish, rose in support of the king, beginning the second civil war. Cromwell's army crushed the rebellions in Scotland and Ireland. As a result, the army became the supreme power in Great Britain. When the army, which supported toleration for all religious sects, conflicted with Parliament, consisting chiefly of Presbyterians, the military leaders expelled those who disagreed with them from the House of Commons (see PRIDE, THOMAS; RUMP PARLIAMENT). Charles was brought to trial and beheaded in 1649; in the same year, the Rump Parliament abolished the title and office of king, and the House of Lords. England was proclaimed a Commonwealth (q.v.).

The English Commonwealth represented the triumph of the middle classes and, particularly, the Puritans. It pursued a vigorous colonial policy, notably in co-operation with the Puritans, and an aggressive commercial policy, which resulted in a successful war with the Netherlands (1652–54). The domestic policies of the unrepresentative Rump Parliament were, however, unpopular, and friction between Parliament and the powerful army resulted in the dissolution of Parliament in 1653. The army set up a new Parliament, the so-called Barebone's Parliament (q.v.), but the new legislature was so intolerant in matters of religion that the army dissolved it in less than six months. At length the army, in the first modern written constitution, known as the Instrument of Government, established a Protectorate, with all the governmental power being given to Cromwell, named Lord Protector. Cromwell's policies included the improvement of the English navy, which in alliance with the French won a great victory over Spain (1656–59) and restored the international prestige of England. Domestically, he established religious toleration for all Protestant sects; repeated rebellion, however, forced him to withdraw toleration from the Episcopalians. He ruled absolutely, but used his power for the advancement of England. On his death, in 1658, his son Richard was named Lord Protector. Richard lacked his father's strength, however, and the army acquired control once again, forcing the Protector to resign (1658), and recalling the Rump Parliament. Shortly afterward, the

Oliver Cromwell, Lord Protector of England

English population, angered now by military despotism, began to agitate for a return of the Stuarts. In 1659 General George Monck (q.v.), the Parliamentary governor of Scotland, led an army to London; he ordered Parliament to dissolve itself and initiated negotiations with Charles II (q.v.), then in France. A convention Parliament, so-called because it was not summoned by royal writ, proclaimed Charles king in 1660, and Charles entered London shortly afterward.

The Restoration of the Stuarts released a wave of reaction against the austere morality of the Puritan Commonwealth; the theater, dancing, and games, all forbidden under Cromwell, again became a prominent part of social life (see DRAMA: *British Drama;* ENGLISH LITERATURE: *The Seventeenth Century*). So pronounced was anti-Puritan feeling that the bodies of Oliver Cromwell and others who had participated in the trial of Charles I were disinterred from Westminster Abbey and displayed on scaffolds. In Scotland a Royalist Parliament disavowed the Solemn League and Covenant and repealed all acts passed during the preceding twenty-eight years.

Though Charles was an able ruler when he wished to exert himself, he was not much interested in the affairs of government. His first chief adviser, Edward Hyde, Earl of Clarendon (see HYDE), was an excellent and scrupulous minister, but Hyde and the king soon differed on religious matters. The Parliament

of 1661 had enacted intolerant religious legislation. These acts, known as the Clarendon Code, compelled magistrates, municipal officials, clergymen, fellows of universities, and schoolmasters to conform with the Anglican Church; ministers who refused to conform were forbidden to come within five miles of an incorporated town or their former parishes. Charles, however, was pro-Catholic and a cousin and friend of Louis XIV of France, the most powerful Catholic monarch in Europe. His differences with Hyde concerning toleration for Catholics led to the minister's impeachment and exile in 1667. From that time forward, Charles appointed as his ministers men who were more obedient to the royal will.

During the period directly following the Restoration, English affairs, domestic and foreign, declined under a succession of blows. The city of London was visited by two great disasters during an eighteen-month period: an epidemic of plague swept the city in April, 1665, and it was devastated by a great fire in Sept., 1666. A naval war with the Netherlands (1665–67) was a ruinous drain on the treasury, and the English navy was severely damaged. In order to get money and, as well, to manifest his Catholic tendencies, Charles indicated to Louis XIV that England could be bought as an ally. Negotiations with France being unsatisfactory, the English king entered the Triple Alliance with Sweden and the Netherlands against French aggression in the Netherlands. However, in 1670, by the secret Treaty of Dover with France, Charles agreed not to intervene in return for a large annual grant; moreover, the Treaty of Dover included a clause by which Charles promised to join the Catholic Church and further the cause of Catholicism in England.

Charles declared war on the Netherlands in 1672. The war was exceedingly unpopular in England and, when Parliament refused to grant money, the king was forced to withdraw from the Dutch war in 1674. The sympathy of the Stuarts for Catholicism was even less popular; the king's brother, James, Duke of York, had openly professed Catholicism in 1670. Factions were again evident, the most prominent being the supporters of the royal prerogative and strict Anglicanism, who became the forerunners of the Tories, and the supporters of toleration of all Protestant sects and the supremacy of Parliament, the forerunners of the Whigs (see TORY; WHIG). Animosity toward Catholicism was heightened by rumors of a Catholic plot in 1673, and widespread persecution resulted from the perjured testimony of one of the supposed organizers of the so-called Popish Plot, Titus Oates (q.v.). As a result, the Test Act was passed in 1673, excluding Catholics and Nonconformists (to the Anglican Church) from public office. Parliament made several attempts to exclude the Catholic Duke of York, heir to the throne, from the succession, but Charles successfully opposed them. To prevent future attempts to pass an exclusion act, Charles went so far as to remodel the borough charters so that he could control elections to the legislature. He died, however, before the results of the new charters could be brought into force.

Except for an abortive rebellion by James Scott, Duke of Monmouth (see MONMOUTH), the illegitimate son of Charles II, little opposition was aroused by the accession of the Duke of York as James II (q.v.) in 1685; England wanted no more civil war. The new king began working at once to restore the Roman Catholic religion. He set aside the Test Act and caused Catholics to be accepted into the universities, the army, and even into the royal council. Gathering a standing army to support his plans, he tried to form an alliance with the Protestant Dissenters, who suffered discrimination equal to that against Catholics, but his efforts were only partially successful. His unlawful proclamation of religious liberty in 1687 was resisted by seven Anglican bishops, whom he tried vainly to convict of libel for refusing to read the declaration of indulgence toward dissenters. The birth of a male heir, in 1687, with the resultant prospect of a perpetuation of Stuart despotism and a Catholic ruler, caused even the Tories to turn against the king. Seven of the most influential men in England invited Protestant Mary Stuart, daughter of James II, and her husband William, Stadtholder of Holland (see WILLIAM III), to rule the country. Soon after they had landed and the so-called Glorious Revolution (q.v.) had begun, James fled from London and escaped to France. A convention Parliament in 1689, which was assembled to determine the succession, offered the crown of Great Britain conjointly to William and Mary. The offer was dependent upon the acceptance of the Declaration of Rights. This document, also called the Bill of Rights (q.v.), ended the dispensing power (for Catholics) used by James, barred Roman Catholics from the throne, and established the supremacy of statute law over royal proclamations. These conditions being acceptable to them, William and Mary ascended the throne in 1689. They

also accepted the Scottish crown which the Scottish Parliament offered on condition of agreement to the Claim of Right abolishing episcopacy in Scotland. The supporters of James, however, refused to be quiescent; rebellions, aided by France, broke out in Scotland and Ireland (1689–90). James led the Irish revolt in person, but his forces were defeated at the Battle of the Boyne (July 1, 1690). Sporadic rebellions, notably in the Scottish Highlands, attested the continuance of Stuart support until late into the 18th century (see JACOBITES; ORANGEMEN).

The accession of William and Mary marked the complete disappearance of the divine-right theory from the British government. The political theory of the Restoration had been that Parliament and the king held equal power and could act harmoniously, but the reign of James II effectively disproved this principle. Until about 1689 the king's advisers had been his personal choices, acting only as counsellors. The modern British cabinet system began in the reign of William III, when the king, desiring to forestall conflict between himself and Parliament, chose his advisers from leaders of the Whigs, the influential party in the House of Commons. Thus, the king's ministers became accountable for their actions to Parliament and, during the succeeding two decades, the cabinet system developed until the ministers were changed in accordance with the political complexion of the House of Commons. Parliament limited its own power in 1694 with the passage of a bill providing for triennial Parliamentary elections. The king's complete dependence upon Parliament was effectuated by his need for money in the war with France, which had begun in 1689 as a result of French aid to the Stuarts. The large sums needed were not available and the permanent national debt began in 1693, when Parliament enacted legislation to borrow £1,000,000. The securities were not easily sold to the public, however, and when a second loan was authorized in 1694, a group of merchants founded the Bank of England, largely to assist the raising of public funds for the prosecution of the French war.

Though the war, with its heavy costs, was unpopular in England, it succeeded in quelling fear of invasion by France; by 1697, Louis XIV agreed to negotiate terms and the Peace of Ryswick (see RYSWICK, PEACE OF) was signed in that year. Four years later, English relations with France again became strained. At the death of the childless Charles II of Spain, Louis XIV proclaimed his grandson,

William and Mary, joint rulers of Great Britain

Philip, Duke of Anjou (see PHILIP V), king of Spain. Counterclaims to the Spanish throne were advanced by Austria. William, leading opponent of France, brought England into the Grand Alliance with the Holy Roman Empire and the Netherlands, but the Tories, then in control of Parliament, demurred at war. Their objections were overcome when James II died (1701) in France, and Louis XIV proclaimed the exiled king's son, James, king of Great Britain and Ireland. The succession to the British throne had been fixed earlier in the year, following the death of the Duke of Gloucester, son of Princess Anne, second daughter of James II and heir to the throne. By the terms of the Act of Settlement (see SETTLEMENT, ACT OF), the succession to the throne, after Anne, was given to the Protestant Electress Sophia of Hanover, granddaughter of James I, and to her heirs, in order to forestall claims by the Catholic Stuarts. The action of Louis XIV therefore precipitated popular indignation throughout England, and a new Whig-controlled Parliament, in 1702, was preparing for war when William died.

War against France was declared several months after the accession of Queen Anne (see SPANISH SUCCESSION, WAR OF THE). Led by John Churchill, Earl of Marlborough (see CHURCHILL), who was created a duke for his generalship, the English forces won a series of brilliant victories, climaxed by the battle of Blenheim in 1704. Marlborough became the greatest figure in England, and his position at court was bolstered by the influence of his wife, Sarah, who had for many years been the intimate of Anne. The queen had little executive ability and was easily swayed in her political judgments by her personal likes and dislikes. She favored the Tories because of her fervent Anglicanism; Marlborough and her first minister, Sidney, 1st Earl of Godolphin, were both Tories in name, at least. Both men were, however, against the extreme Tories, who opposed the prosecution of the war, and when the Whigs won control of Parliament in 1705, Godolphin and Marlborough allied themselves with that party. Anne was then persuaded to replace all her Tory ministers with Whigs, thus furthering the development of the cabinet system which had begun under William and Mary. Because of the queen's dependence on their advice, members of the cabinet began the custom of agreeing on policies before they were presented to the sovereign. In 1707, under the Godolphin ministry, legislative union with Scotland was finally accomplished. Forty-five Scottish members were added to the English House of Commons, and sixteen to the House of Lords; Scotland retained its own local political, legal, and religious institutions.

The bitterness of strife between Whigs and Tories persisted unabated throughout Anne's reign. This strife was reflected in a literary development that made the early 18th century famous for its prose. Political pamphlets, newspapers, and essays became widely used as an important means of influencing public opinion, and leaders of both parties subsidized political writers. Daniel Defoe and Jonathan Swift, both writing for the Tories, became famous for their pamphlets, and the essays of Sir Richard Steele and Joseph Addison are notable for their polished delineation of the contemporary middle-class morality influenced by Queen Anne's sober court (see ENGLISH LITERATURE: *The Eighteenth Century*). During the first ten years of the 18th century the Whigs held their place. By 1710, however, the political tide turned.

Despite continued English victories, the heavy costs of war made it increasingly unpopular, to the detriment of the Whigs, who supported a war policy. Moreover, the Duchess of Marlborough had lost her place as Anne's confidante to Lady Abigail Masham, who served the Tory opposition. With both the queen and the country disapproving them, the Whigs lost their support and little was needed to overthrow them. That little was supplied by the trial of Henry Sacheverell, a Tory clergyman who was impeached by the Whig House of Commons for preaching against the principles of the Glorious Revolution. Anne, taking advantage of anti-Whig feeling, dismissed Godolphin and his cabinet and gave their places to Tories under Robert Harley, Earl of Oxford, and Henry St. John, Viscount Bolingbroke (see HARLEY; BOLINGBROKE). In the ensuing elections, the Tories won an overwhelming victory.

Though they had ostensibly been elected to bring the war to an end, the Tories, instead, busied themselves with enacting legislation designed to prevent a return to power by the Whigs. Acts were passed to disqualify townsmen and Dissenters, among whom were found many Whigs, from holding public office. Some Tory leaders went so far as to treat with James Stuart, the so-called Old Pretender, for a restoration of the Stuarts in order to prevent the Whigs from returning to power. The creation of twelve new peers in 1711 gave the Tories a majority in the House of Lords and became an important constitutional precedent, demonstrating that, in case of disagreement between the two houses of Parliament, the Commons could always prevail by the creation of enough new peers to constitute a majority of the party in power. The War of the Spanish Succession was terminated in 1713 by the Peace of Utrecht (see UTRECHT, PEACE

OF), which gave Great Britain permanent possession of Gibraltar and Minorca (occupied during the war) as well as the French colonies of Nova Scotia, Newfoundland, and Hudson Bay. Further Tory plans against the Whigs were thwarted by the death of Anne in 1714, and the end of the Stuart dynasty.

The accession of George I (q.v.), first ruler of the House of Hanover, or Brunswick, brought about a return of the Whigs and an undisputed Whig supremacy for the next half century. An unsuccessful rebellion by the Jacobites, the partisans of James Stuart, occurred in Scotland in 1715–16. Because the Tories favored the House of Stuart, the first Hanoverians chose their ministers from among the Whigs in order to make their dynasty secure. They were more interested, however, in their German than in their British realms, and the first two Georges did not even trouble themselves to learn the English language. As long as Great Britain supported his policies on the Continent, George I gave British leaders control of home affairs. The cabinet ceased holding sessions in the king's presence and, by degrees, his place at the head of the council came to be filled by one of its members, usually the most influential man in the cabinet and eventually designated as the prime minister. During the first years of George I's reign, this power was shared by the two leading

Robert Walpole, first British prime minister

Whigs, Lord James Stanhope and Lord Charles Townshend (q.v.).

The first act of the Whig Parliament of 1715 was the impeachment of Tory leaders for treasonable correspondence with the exiled House of Stuart; Harley was imprisoned and Bolingbroke fled to France. As a result of the Jacobite rebellion in 1715, Parliament, in 1716, passed the Septennial Act, prolonging its life for seven years in order to make Whig power secure. Three years later the Tory legislation against Dissenters was repealed. In foreign affairs, Stanhope, as foreign secretary, was confronted by a series of European conflicts arising from the terms of the Treaty of Utrecht. According to the treaty, Philip V was permitted to ascend the Spanish throne provided that he agreed to relinquish all claims to the crown of his grandfather, Louis XIV of France. However, at the death of Louis in 1715, Philip, coveting the French throne, began to conspire against Louis XV, then a minor. Great Britain, the Netherlands, and the French regency therefore formed the Triple Alliance against a Spanish offensive in 1717. When Spanish forces attacked Austrian possessions in Italy, Austria joined the three countries in 1718, forming the Quadruple Alliance. Philip's aspirations were blocked, and a series of treaties in 1721 finally brought peace to Europe.

In 1720 a financial crisis caused political repercussions in Great Britain. Wild speculation had begun in shares of the South Sea Company, which had been incorporated in 1711 as a trading monopoly dealing with the Spanish colonies in South America. The government allowed holders of government bonds to convert their securities into South Sea stock, and, with the government seemingly behind the scheme, shares rose from £128 to more than £1000 (see SOUTH SEA BUBBLE). The prospectus of the company, which had promised returns of as much as 60%, was soon proved fraudulent, and the inevitable crash caused a financial panic. The cabinet was forced to resign and the Whigs became the target of widespread condemnation. Complete financial and political disaster was averted, however, by Sir Robert Walpole (q.v.), one of the principal opponents to the South Sea Scheme. Walpole, appointed First Lord of the Treasury, reorganized the cabinet and became its head.

Walpole became the first British prime minister in every sense of that term, controlling the cabinet, Parliament, and the Whig Party, as well as dispensing patronage formerly the province of the king. For the next twenty-one years (1721–42), he was the most influential man in Great Britain. The accession of George II (q.v.) in 1727 did not affect Walpole's policies; the new queen, Caroline of Anspach, was one of the minister's staunchest supporters. Through his astute statecraft and maneuvering of the Whig Party machine, the efficacy of Parliamentary government was permanently established; the cabinet system became an efficient mechanism, and the House of Commons acquired its lasting position as the center of political action. One of the greatest financiers in modern British history, Walpole strengthened the prosperity of Great Britain and encouraged commerce, particularly with the American colonies. To effectuate this prosperity, the prime minister determined to keep England out of war, refusing to intervene in the European wars of the period. Though France and Spain were the greatest colonial and commercial rivals of Great Britain, Walpole negotiated treaties with them in order to protect the internal development of his own country. He was, however, extremely conscious of public opinion and its weight in politics, even withdrawing wise measures when the public was against them. Despite Walpole's nonintervention policy, his sensitivity to public opinion led him to support the so-called War of Jenkins's Ear. Robert Jenkins, an English mariner, claimed, in 1731, that his ear had been cut off by a Spanish pirate. The ear became a *cause célèbre* and during the next eight years public sentiment, fanned by the Tory opposition, caused such a clamor against Spain that Walpole reluctantly assented to a declaration of war in 1739. The war went well, but it threatened to merge with the War of the Austrian Succession which broke out in 1740 (see SUCCESSION WARS: *War of the Austrian Succession*). George II, fearing for the safety of Hanover, declared Great Britain neutral in the new conflict, but public opinion was against him. The Whig majority was so small in 1741 that Walpole resigned a year later. His place as leader of the cabinet was taken by John Carteret (q.v.), Earl Granville.

The War of the Austrian Succession, in which Great Britain fought with Austria against France and Spain, was an aimless struggle. Though the English army vanquished the French at Dettingen (Bavaria) in 1743, it was defeated by the French two years later at Fontenoy (Flanders). Encouraged by the French victory at Fontenoy, Charles Edward Stuart (q.v.), the so-called Young Pretender and grandson of James II, landed in Scotland

and, leading an army of Scottish Highlanders, defeated the British forces at Prestonpans. He invaded England but, deciding to winter in Scotland, returned there and was defeated in 1746 at Culloden. The rebellion of 1745–46 was the last concerted attempt by the Jacobites to seize power; the chiefs of the Scottish clans, strongholds of Stuart sentiment, were relieved of their hereditary jurisdictions with monetary compensation for their loss of title. The Austrian war ended two years later with the Treaty of Aix-la-Chapelle, in which the prewar status of the belligerents (except for Prussia, which kept Silesia) was re-effected.

Though the Whigs held their leadership, dissension began to grow within the party itself. Carteret was a leader of a faction which had been opposed to Walpole, but he was unable to control the House of Commons and resigned in 1743. His place was taken by Henry Pelham, a partisan of Walpole, who headed a coalition cabinet made up of representatives of both Whig factions and several Tories. Pelham, though a weak executive, was able to control the House of Commons for the next eleven years, largely through the efforts of his brother, Sir Thomas Pelham-Holles, Duke of Newcastle, who controlled many of the English boroughs. At Pelham's death in 1754 the Duke took over the administration, but his incompetency was particularly marked at a time when European rivalries were tending to war.

Colonial rivalry between France and Great Britain in America resulted in hostilities in 1754 (see FRENCH AND INDIAN WAR). A reversal, meanwhile, had taken place in the diplomatic relations of the early 18th century. Casting about for allies against France, and to protect Hanover, George II made a treaty with Prussia; France concluded an alliance with its traditional foe, Austria, and was joined by Russia and by the German states which supported the Austrian Hapsburgs. Europe, thus, was divided into two armed camps when war began on the Continent in 1756 (see SEVEN YEARS' WAR). Defeats for the British army and navy disheartened the British public, which began to clamor for the removal of Newcastle and the appointment of the elder William Pitt (q.v.), long a popular figure and an influential member of the House of Commons. George II, who disliked Pitt intensely because the statesman had criticized the subordination of England to Hanover, was forced to appoint Pitt prime minister in 1757.

Though Pitt was nominally a Whig, he had

The younger William Pitt

consistently opposed Walpole and the corrupt methods of the Whig political machine. The middle class trusted him and was his strongest support. In 1757 the country united behind Pitt and, with powerful oratory, the minister was able to control the House of Commons. He reorganized the army and planned the campaigns himself; using two great principles of strategy, command of the sea and concentration of land forces in vital areas, he brought the Seven Years' War to a triumphant conclusion in America and Europe. In India, under the leadership of Robert Clive (q.v.), British forces gained a supremacy over the French which eventually resulted in the establishment of India as a British colony. Pitt resigned in 1761 because of policy differences with his cabinet, but the prime minister's work had already been done. By the terms of the Treaty of Paris, in 1763, Great Britain became the foremost colonial power in the world, receiving Canada, Florida, Cape Breton Island, Grenada, all land east of the Mississippi R. on the North American continent and the French Senegalese possessions in Africa.

King George III of Great Britain

Meanwhile, the death of George II in 1760 had brought George III to the throne, with the fixed ambition of restoring as far as possible the royal prerogatives which his two predecessors had, in their disinterest, allowed to be taken from them. He was determined to break up the party system as it then existed, to destroy the Whig oligarchy, and, by selecting his own ministers, to exert the controlling influence on British politics. Taking back the royal patronage, which had been distributed by the prime ministers under the first two Georges, he soon formed a party of adherents, the so-called "king's friends", who were guided by George's political ideas. Dissensions in the Whig cabinet were already evident and, taking advantage of the fact, the king forced John Stuart, Earl of Bute, his favorite and a Tory, into the cabinet as prime minister. Lord Bute negotiated the Treaty of Paris, but the English public felt that England could have received even more than was granted it in the treaty, and Bute was forced to resign. Several ministries followed that of Bute, including a return of Pitt (1766–67), but the king was dissatisfied with them. His efforts to make Parliament submissive to the crown aroused public indignation, which found a rallying point in the case of John Wilkes (q.v.). Wilkes' scurrilous newspaper articles concerning the king caused the writer's arrest and imprisonment; but he was everywhere praised as a champion of liberty, and condemnation of the king was voiced both by the public and Parliament. George, however, could not be swayed from his theories of absolutism, and in 1770 he found a minister through whom he could carry out his ideas in Lord Frederick North (q.v.); the Tories supported North and, for the first time in fifty years, with the advantage of Whig factional strife, procured a majority in the House of Commons. George was then able to carry out his plans of personal government.

One of the king's primary concerns was the North American colonies. Throughout most of the 18th century, these colonies had been allowed a large measure of political autonomy, supervised by British officials. The autocratic treatment of the thirteen colonies by George III inevitably resulted in their rebellion (see REVOLUTION, THE AMERICAN). During the first years of the Revolution, the colonists rapidly gained the military advantage, and the British situation became desperate after France entered the conflict against Great Britain in 1778; Spain became an ally of France a year later. After the surrender of Lord Burgoyne at Saratoga in 1777, British sentiment turned against the disastrous war in America, and only the will of the king prolonged the struggle. George knew that the resignation of North, for which the public agitated, would end his personal government because it would be interpreted as an admission of the king's blunders. Well aware of this fact, Whig leaders led a concerted campaign in the House of Commons against the king's influence. After the surrender of Lord Cornwallis at Yorktown, in 1781, George could no longer withstand the pressure against him and against the continuance of the American war, and he even contemplated abdication. With the greatest reluctance, in 1782, he called on Charles Watson-Wentworth, Marquis of Rockingham (see ROCKINGHAM), a leading Whig, to form a coalition cabinet. After Rockingham's death, a few weeks later, Sir William Petty, Marquis of Shelburne, became prime minister and, in 1783, concluded the Treaty of Paris which gave the American colonies their independence and underlined the defeat of Great Britain. France received several West Indian islands, a majority of trading posts in Africa, and various positions in India given up by the 1763 treaty; Spain acquired Florida and the island of Minorca.

During the treaty negotiations, the Whig Party resumed its internal dissension, dividing into factions led by Shelburne and Charles James Fox (q.v.), the secretary of state for foreign affairs. The king was quick to take advantage of the strife in an attempt to reassert his personal power by setting the dissidents against each other. Fox resigned, but immediately joined forces with the Tory opposition led by Lord North. The coalition defeated Shelburne, and North and Fox formed a ministry, to the anger of the king, who now considered North a traitor to him. George defeated Fox's bill for the reform of the colonial government of India by informing the House of Lords that he would consider supporters of the bill as his enemies. Then, using the defeat as a pretext, George dismissed the cabinet. In the face of a hostile majority, he asked the younger William Pitt (q.v.), whose sentiments were Tory, to form a cabinet. Pitt, then only twenty-five years old, faced heavy opposition led by Fox and North, but in three months he succeeded in acquiring a majority to support him in the House of Commons.

Pitt took office at a time when powerful social, political, and economic forces were changing every aspect of western civilization. The Industrial Revolution (q.v.) was creating a new class of society, the wealth of which lay primarily in industry rather than in land; and the growth of the factory system resulted in new theories of economics and international trade (see FACTORIES AND THE FACTORY SYSTEM; ECONOMICS). In politics, the lower classes, which had rarely been taken into account in government until that time, were beginning to make themselves heard, and a new religious movement, Methodism (q.v.), had become firmly established in opposition to the aristocratic Anglican Church. The young prime minister set himself to reconstructing Great Britain and to working out policies based on the new movements that would strengthen the country.

Although the king did not always approve the measures proposed by Pitt, the two agreed on the general policy to be pursued, an agreement facilitated by the liking which George had for his prime minister. When they differed, however, Pitt won; the king's efforts to rule personally were definitely at an end. Considered one of the greatest prime ministers in British history, Pitt proved his value soon after he took office by reorganizing British finances. The American war had severely damaged public credit and the treasury was dangerously low. Pitt simplified the revenue system, lowered tariffs sufficiently to make smuggling unprofitable, and instituted an auditing commission for government funds. long a source of income for corrupt officials. Tak-

ing cognizance of the growth of industrialization, he negotiated a treaty with France, in 1786, which reduced tariffs in both countries and facilitated trade. An India Bill, in 1784, reduced the power of the East India Company by compelling it to submit its political measures for approval to a royal commission. In 1785 he introduced a bill to reform the corrupt electoral system and to give more of the population a voice in government by redistributing Parliamentary representatives; though the bill was not passed, Pitt managed to carry out several reforms to reduce corruption.

When the French Revolution began, public sentiment in England at first favored it, but as the Revolutionary government became terroristic, the British public and political leaders turned against it. The British attitude of distrust was considerably stimulated by the writings of the influential Whig leader Edmund Burke (q.v.), who effectively defended the "old order" in a famous pamphlet, *Reflections on the French Revolution*. Pitt opposed the Revolution and was soon joined by a majority of the Whigs, though Fox led a Whig faction which argued that revolutionary feeling should be countered by democratic reforms in Great Britain. This party dissension resulted in a Tory majority in the 1790 elections. Seizing this advantage, Pitt refused to consider any attempts at reform in England and, instead, worked to stimulate an anti-French sentiment. War was declared against France in 1793, and the government at once moved to put down any internal revolutionary agitation, interpreting demands for reform as seditious, and going so far as to suspend the act of habeas corpus. Great Britain formed a European coalition against France, paying subsidies to Spain, Austria, Prussia, and Sardinia.

The French armies were overwhelmingly successful, and particularly so when the French command was given to Napoleon Bonaparte. By 1796 the participants in the coalition had been defeated, and only Great Britain was left to oppose France. As a result, economic conditions in Great Britain began to verge on the disastrous; prices rose, a financial crisis resulted, and the population began to complain against the excessive taxation necessary to prosecute the war. The situation was aggravated by a revolt in Ireland in 1798, when the Irish, aided by French troops, began to fight for their independence from Great Britain. Although the rebellion was suppressed, Pitt was convinced that the solution to Irish agitation resided in Parliamentary union be-tween the two countries. After prolonged negotiations with the Irish Parliament, the Act of Union was passed by both the British and Irish legislatures in 1800. Pitt, however, was compelled to resign in 1801 because the king refused to grant concessions to Catholics, one of the terms which Pitt had proposed to make union satisfactory to all of Ireland. After the Act of Union, the British Isles were governed by one Parliament as the United Kingdom (q.v.) of Great Britain and Ireland.

RULERS OF GREAT BRITAIN

(for rulers of England, Scotland, and United Kingdom, see tables in respective articles)

Name	Dynasty	Reign
James I (James VI of Scotland)	Stuart	1603-1625
Charles I	Stuart	1625–1649
Commonwealth	(no king)	1649–1660
Oliver Cromwell, Lord Protector		1653–1658
Richard Cromwell, Lord Protector		1658–1659
Charles II	Stuart	1660–1685
James II	Stuart	1685–1688*
William III and Mary	Stuart	1689–1702
Anne	Stuart	1702–1714
George I	Hanover	1714–1727
George II	Hanover	1727–1760
George III	Hanover	1760–1820**

*Interregnum, 1688–89.
**After 1801, ruler of the United Kingdom.

GREAT CRESTED FLYCATCHER, a bird, *Myiarchus crinitus,* in the American flycatcher (q.v.) group, characterized by a slight eleva-tion of the crown. The great crested flycatcher is 9 in. long. Its back is greenish-tan; its head is slightly darker. Its wings are banded with yellow. The tail is reddish-brown; the throat and chest are gray; and the abdomen is bright yellow. This bird is found in North America from s. Canada to Florida, and w. to Texas and the Great Plains. It is found in open country containing tall trees, and has a loud, discordant note. The great crested flycatcher is famous for its unusual nesting habits. Whenever possible, it lines its nest with a soft, dry, recently moulted snakeskin. The female lays as many as eight white eggs, blotched with various other colors.

The Arizona flycatcher, *M. tyrannulus,* found in s. Arizona and w. Mexico, is also called crested flycatcher.

New York State Museum

The great crested flycatcher

GREAT DANE, a breed of working dog of unusually large size, which supposedly origi-nated in Germany about the middle of th 16th century, probably from an interbreed-ing of the Irish wolfhound and the old Eng-lish mastiff. The origin of the name "Great Dane" is not known; the breed neither origi-nated nor was developed in Denmark, and a more fitting name would be German mastiff, from the term *Deutsche Dogge* by which the breed is known in Germany. The dog was once a hunting dog, used particularly to hunt the wild boar; in modern times it is used chiefly as a draft animal or as a pet. The dog has a smooth, glossy coat of short, thick hair; the chief colors are brindle, fawn, blue, black, or harlequin (black on a white ground). It has a long, narrow head; medium-sized, dark eyes; medium-sized ears, set high on its head; a broad chest; strong, muscular legs; and a tail of medium length. The male meas-ures at least thirty inches high at the shoul-ders; the bitch, twenty-eight inches. The Great Dane is statuesque in appearance, and placid and affectionate in disposition.

GREAT DIVIDE, the popular name in the United States for the Rocky Mountain water-shed.

GREAT EASTERN, the world's largest steamship for about half a century, from the time it was launched in 1858, to 1901. The vessel was constructed for the Eastern Steam Navigation Co., an English corporation which was formed in 1852 to maintain an ocean steam route from England to Australia around the Cape of Good Hope. In 1853 the corpora-tion's directors came to the conclusion that, owing to the cost of maintaining coaling stations on the way, such a route would not pay unless the carrier could carry enough coal for the voyage out and home, besides a large number of passengers and a sizable cargo. The result was the construction of the *Great Eastern,* which took four years to build. Its gross tonnage was 18,914; length, 680 feet between perpendiculars (or 692 along upper deck); breadth, 83 feet (or 118 over paddle boxes); depth of hull, 60 feet (or 70 to top of bulwarks). Its iron hull was propelled by both paddle and screw, with auxiliary sail-power consisting of 7000 yards of sail on six masts, five of iron and one of wood. It had five funnels, each 100 feet high and six feet in diameter. The paddle wheels were 56 feet in diameter.

Despite the elaborate planning for the *Great Eastern* and the fame of its size, the vessel was financially a failure. In 1860 and 1861 it made many transatlantic crossings carrying passengers and cargo at a loss. Aside from its size, it is remembered chiefly as the vessel which laid the Atlantic cable. It was scrapped in 1888.

GREAT ELECTOR. See FREDERICK WILLIAM, Elector of Brandenburg (1640–88).

GREATER ANTILLES. See ANTILLES.

GREAT FALLS, county seat of Cascade Co., Mont., situated on the Missouri R., 94 m. by rail N.E. of Helena. The vicinity is rich in minerals, including copper, zinc, lead, iron, gypsum, hematite, bituminous coal, and sandstone. Four dams and power houses on the Missouri R., at a point just below Great Falls, provide hydroelectric power for the manufacturing establishments of the city, the chief of

Great Dane

which are copper and zinc refineries, flour mills, an oil refinery, and railroad shops. Although the city is principally an industrial one, it also serves as a shipping point for wool and is the distributing center for a large agricultural region. The locality of Great Falls presents many scenic attractions. The Missouri there, in a distance of 7 miles, has a fall of 526 feet. The most notable of its waterfalls are Rainbow and Great Falls, from the latter of which the city derives its name. Giant Springs, situated 4½ miles N.E. of the city on the S. bank of the Missouri, is one of the largest fresh-water springs in the world, having a flow of 388,000,000 gallons a day. Adjacent to the springs is a fish hatchery. In Great Falls are located the State Deaf and Blind Institute, Great Falls College of Education, and St. Mary's Institute, a junior college for women founded in 1929. Lewis and Clark (see LEWIS AND CLARK EXPEDITION) visited the site of the city in 1805 and there conducted the first Fourth of July celebration held west of Lake Superior. Great Falls was founded in 1883 and incorporated in 1888. Pop. (1950) 39,006.

GREAT FISH RIVER, properly called BACKS RIVER, a river of the Northwest Territories, Canada, rising in Sussex Lake, Mackenzie District, and flowing generally N.E. through Keewatin District, emptying into an inlet of the Arctic Ocean. It has a total length of about 605 m., and passes through several large lakes, including lakes Pelly, Garry, MacDougall, and Franklin. The name of the river was changed to Backs R. in honor of Sir George Back (q.v.), who first explored the region and traced the river to its mouth.

GREAT HORNED OWL, an enormous owl, *Bubo virginianus,* with a wingspread, in the largest specimens, of about sixty inches. Its average body length is about twenty-two inches. It differs from other true owls in having more conspicuous ear tufts. Great horned owls are generally light in color, light brown to yellow, with about six heavy, irregular, black lines on the upper part of the breast. Like other true owls, their habits are nocturnal, and their food consists principally of fish, reptiles, and mammals such as hares. They also prey on porcupines, dogs, and even on the powerful bald eagle. When driven by extreme hunger, they have been known to attack human beings. Great horned owls are found in most parts of North and South America, but chiefly in E. North America. They settle in isolated areas, such as deep woods, swamps, and mountains. They are

Great horned owl

among the owls colloquially known in the U.S. as "hoot owls" because of the deep, booming monotone of their call. They occasionally emit an eerie, penetrating scream. Their eggs, usually two or three in number, are white.

GREAT KANAWHA. See KANAWHA.

GREAT LAKES, a chain of five large lakes, located generally along the boundary of the U.S. and Canada between 75° and 92° w. longitude. The five lakes are, from east to west, Ontario, Erie, Huron, Michigan, and Superior. The total area of the Great Lakes is 94,700 sq.m., making them collectively the largest body of fresh water in the world. The U.S.-Canada international boundary runs through all of the Great Lakes except Lake Michigan, which lies wholly in U.S. territory. Use of all the waters of all the lakes is free to citizens and shipping of both countries as a result of a treaty, called the Boundary Waters Treaty, signed by the U.S. and Great Britain in 1909. In this article only lake shipping and

the geological formation of the lakes are discussed. For other details see articles on the individual lakes.

Shipping. The Great Lakes and the rivers and canals that join them form one of the great shipping arteries of the world. To the east the lakes are connected to the Atlantic Ocean via the St. Lawrence River, to the west they communicate with the Gulf of Mexico via the Illinois and Mississippi Rivers. Eight states front on the five lakes and the lakes themselves form an important avenue of communications between the agricultural, lumbering, and mining areas of the middle west and the industrial cities of the east. The Great Lakes were an important factor in the industrial development of the U.S. and particularly in the development of the steel industry. Much of the steel-producing capacity of the country relies on iron ore from the Mesabi mines in Minnesota which is shipped via the lakes to steel plants located in and near the coal fields of Pennsylvania, West Virginia, Ohio, Indiana, and Illinois.

Special types of vessels have been built for freight-carrying on the lakes, among them tankers, grain boats, and ore boats, each arranged for the swift and economical handling of its particular type of cargo. Loading by means of chutes from overhead bins, an ore boat can leave the dock within forty minutes of its arrival, carrying a full cargo of 11,000 long tons of ore.

In 1951 the combined receipts and shipments at Great Lakes ports amounted to 389,641,000 short tons of cargo, or slightly more than the entire commerce, coastwise and foreign, of all the ports of the Atlantic, Pacific, and Gulf coasts during the same year.

Geological Formation. Geologically, the Great Lakes are the result of glacial action during the comparatively recent Pleistocene period. Before the glacial age the area occupied by Lake Superior was a broad valley and the area occupied by the other lakes was a spreading plane. As the ice advanced southward, it deepened the bed of Lake Superior and gouged deep depressions in the low plains to form the beds of the other lakes. When the ice sheet retreated, fingers of ice were left in these depressions, and, as the ice melted further, lakes were formed. During successive advances and retreats of the ice caps, the drainage pattern of the lake region was altered until finally, approximately 10,000 years ago, an upwarping of the northern part of the area caused the lakes to empty into the St. Lawrence through what is now the Niagara River.

Ewing Galloway

GREAT LAKES. *Entrance to system of locks which join Lake Superior with Lake Huron.*

GREAT MOTHER. See CYBELE.

GREAT PYRENEES DOG, a breed of working dog which is believed to have originated in Central Asia or Siberia and to have first come to Europe between 1800 and 1000 B.C. In Europe the breed is indigenous chiefly to the Pyrenees Mountains. Its particular function was and still is to guard sheep from wild animals, such as wolves; from the 15th century the dog was also used for protecting estates and castles in France; and in the 17th century, during the reign of King Louis XIV

Ewing Galloway

GREAT LAKES. *Steamers at the ore yards in Cleveland, Ohio, on the shore of Lake Erie.*

Great Pyrenees dog

of France, the breed was in great favor as a pet at the royal court and among the French nobility. In modern times it is widely used by French peasants for tasks about the farm, including the drawing of carts. The dog was first introduced into the United States in 1824.

The great Pyrenees dog is of unusually large size. The male is from 27 to 32 inches high at the shoulder and the bitch from 25 to 29 inches; the male weighs from 100 to 125 pounds and the bitch from 90 to 115. The great Pyrenees dog has a large, wedge-shaped head; V-shaped ears which are rounded at the tip; medium-sized, dark-brown, well-pigmented eyes set slightly obliquely in the head; and a double coat, consisting of a heavy undercoat of fine white hair and an outercoat of thick, coarse, straight or slightly wavy hair. The dog is either all white in color or white with markings of gray, tan, or badger. The great Pyrenees is unusually intelligent, extremely sensitive to its master's moods and desires, and faithful to its master's interests to the point of self-sacrifice.

GREAT REBELLION, the name applied to the civil wars in England and Scotland fought between Charles I (q.v.) of England and his Royalist supporters on the one hand, and Parliament (q.v.) and its Puritan sympathizers (see PURITANS) on the other. These wars are generally divided into the First Civil War (1642–46) and the Second Civil War (1648–49). The Royalists, including most of the nobility and their peasant retainers, the Roman Catholics, and the Episcopalians (see ANGLICAN CHURCH), were referred to as Cavaliers; the Parliamentarians, including the middle classes, the prosperous merchants, the Presbyterians (q.v.), the navy, and the nucleus of

a powerful new army, were called Roundheads, because they wore their hair closely cropped in scorn of the Royalist fashion of wearing ringlets.

The issues involved in the struggle were both political and religious. The Parliamentarians objected to the highhanded, arbitrary policies of Charles I's absolutist reign. In such instruments as the Petition of Right and the Grand Remonstrance (qq.v.) they had appealed to the crown for the redress of public grievances and the correction of such abuses of royal power as the levying of unjust and oppressive taxes, unwarranted arrest and imprisonment, and the invocation of martial law in time of peace. In the matter of religion, Puritan and Presbyterian elements in England and Scotland were outraged by the attempt of William Laud (q.v.), Archbishop of Canterbury and influential adviser of Charles I, to enforce a semi-Catholic or "High Church" worship throughout the realm. The Scottish Presbyterians responded with the Solemn League and Covenant for the preservation and protection of the reformed religion (see COVENANTERS; REFORMATION), abolished episcopacy (see BISHOP), and raised an army against Charles I. The king, in 1640, requiring funds for a campaign against the Scots, was obliged to convene the Short Parliament, so called from the brevity of its duration. Parliament, however, refused to vote money for the king's war until its demands for the redress of public grievances were satisfied, whereupon Charles promptly dissolved the assembly. The Scottish army then invaded N. England, and the king, in desperation, called the Long Parliament (q.v.) into being. Although hostile to Charles, the Long Parliament was divided along religious lines, some members supporting the Root and Branch Bill, which called for the complete eradication of episcopacy from the English church, and others taking a more conservative position. A leader among those advocating the Root and Branch Bill was Oliver Cromwell (q.v.), who also proposed that Parliament should assume control of the nation's military establishment.

Shortly thereafter, the king ordered the impeachment of five members of Parliament on the charge of their having entered into a treasonable conspiracy with the Scottish Presbyterians to overthrow him. The House of Commons refused to authorize the arrest. Charles personally set out at the head of a small Royalist contingent to take the men by force, but being turned back by the aroused Parliamentary partisans of London, with whom the accused had taken refuge, he retired to York, where he was joined by thirty-two sympathizers from the House of Lords and sixty-five from the House of Commons. The lines of the impending conflict thus were drawn. As the king had taken the Great Seal with him, Parliament was compelled to pass measures without royal endorsement. The Parliamentarians made their last attempt to reach a basis of understanding with Charles in the Nineteen Propositions, submitted to him on June 2, 1642. The king rejected the propositions, whereupon Parliament issued a call to arms. Charles, terming the mobilization an act of rebellion, called upon his loyal subjects to quell the revolt, and raised his standard at Nottingham on August 22, thus precipitating the military phase of the Great Rebellion.

The battle of Edge Hill (q.v.), the opening engagement of the First Civil War, produced no decisive results. Oliver Cromwell, commanding the Ironsides, an efficient fighting force raised by the associated English counties of Essex, Norfolk, Suffolk, Cambridge, and Hertfordshire, kept the Royalists at bay in a series of subsequent encounters, and on July 2, 1644, won a major victory in the crucial battle of Marston Moor (q.v.). Meanwhile, in return for Scottish military assistance, the Parliamentarians pledged themselves to adopt in England and Ireland the provisions of the Solemn League and Covenant, thereby making for a uniform Presbyterian Church. It was in Scotland itself, however, that the Roundheads suffered a temporary setback when James Graham, Marquis of Montrose (q.v.), rallied the Highland Clans to the Royalist cause, and won a series of notable victories.

About this time, a serious split developed among the Puritans. The Presbyterians, who held the majority in Parliament, were alarmed at the growth of a number of independent religious sects within the Roundhead army. They therefore came to desire a reconciliation with Charles I in order to be free to suppress the Independents. The army, on the other hand, had become the stronghold of Independency, and stood for a prosecution of the war to the end. Oliver Cromwell was the chief spokesman of the party of religious toleration. He charged Edward Montagu, second Earl of Manchester, the nominal commander of the Parliamentary forces at Marston Moor, with apathy and incompetence in the prosecution of the war. Cromwell was sustained in his charge by the Commons but opposed by the Lords. In a triumph for the Independents, however, Montagu resigned; the leadership of the army was reorganized, and Cromwell was appointed lieutenant general of the cavalry. On June 14, 1645, at the battle of Naseby, Cromwell led a victorious charge which resulted in the decisive defeat of the Royalists. Three months later, at Philiphaugh, Scotland, the king's Highland partisans were overcome by the Roundhead general David Leslie, and the Marquis of Montrose made his escape to the Continent. The final engagement of the First Civil War ended with the rout of the remaining Cavalier forces at Stowe-on-the-Wold on March 26, 1646. Charles surrendered himself to the Scots, by whom he was turned over to Parliament.

The antagonism between the Presbyterian Parliament and the Independent army flared up once more when Parliament not only proposed to disband the army without giving the troops their back pay, but made conciliatory overtures to Charles. Cromwell, who had become the recognized leader of the military establishment, sought to mediate between the two parties, but failing in his efforts, took his stand on the side of the army. Charles, hoping to advance his own interests by precipitating strife between the opposing factions, negotiated secretly and in bad faith with both. At length he consented to abolish Episcopacy and establish Presbyterianism as the official religion, whereupon the Scots, who saw the opportunity of arresting the spread of religious toleration in England, pledged to restore Charles to the throne by force of arms. Parliament then broke off all negotiations with the king (who had meanwhile escaped to the Isle of Wight), and the Second Civil War began.

The second military phase of the Great Rebellion was brief but many-sided, being at once a struggle between England and Scotland, between the Roundheads and the Cavaliers, and between the Independents and the Presbyterians. A Scottish army under William, Duke of Hamilton, invaded England, but was defeated by Oliver Cromwell in the three-day battle of Preston Pans (August 17–19, 1648). Other Royalist opposition was quickly put down. The army now clamored for the life of the king, who had been responsible for the resumption of the war. Charles accordingly was taken into custody, and Presbyterian objections to his execution were overcome by Pride's Purge, in which Colonel Thomas Pride (q.v.), by the forcible exclusion from Parliament of its pro-Royalist Presbyterian mem-

Library of Congress

Great seal of the United States, obverse side

bers, established the so-called Rump Parliament (q.v.), which proclaimed itself the supreme power of the nation and voted that the king be brought to trial. Found guilty of treason, Charles was beheaded at Whitehall on January 30, 1649. For the establishment of the Commonwealth and the Protectorate, see the article GREAT BRITAIN.

GREAT SALT LAKE, a large body of salt water in the northern part of the State of Utah (q.v.). The lake is irregular in shape and is approximately 75 m. long from north to south and 30 to 50 m. in width. The average depth of the lake is about 20 ft. but is subject to a seasonal variation of more than a foot, being greatest in the spring when the lake is fed by the melting snows from the Wasatch Mountains to the east. The area of the lake has diminished markedly since the 1860's, partly because of the diversion of water for irrigation. The present area is about 1500 sq.m. The surface of the lake is at an altitude of about 4200 ft. above sea level.

Great Salt Lake occupies a portion of what was, in Pleistocene times, the bed of the great Bonneville Lake (q.v.). The present lake has no outlets and loses water naturally only by evaporation. Evaporation is also the cause of the salinity of the lake, serving to concentrate the dissolved salts carried into the lake by its tributaries. The lake is fed from Utah Lake to the south through the Jordan River, by the Weber River to the east, and by Bear River to the northeast.

The salinity of Great Salt Lake has increased as its area has diminished, and is now about 23 percent. The chief constituent of

the dissolved salts is sodium chloride, which is recovered from the lake in commercial quantities. The lake has been estimated to contain 400,000,000 tons of sodium chloride. A few species of marine life occur in the lake, including certain algae, the larvae of two types of fly, and a species of brine shrimp.

The first white man to visit the Great Salt Lake was a Franciscan priest, Father Escalante, who traveled in the area in 1776. The American soldier John C. Fremont explored the lake region thoroughly in 1843, and six years later the area was surveyed by a party of U.S. Army engineers.

GREAT SAND DUNES NATIONAL MONUMENT, a national monument established in 1932, in the San Luis Valley of s. central Colorado. The reservation lies about 38 miles N.E. of Alamosa, at the foot of the w. slope of the Sangre de Cristo Mountains. Its area of 35,908 acres embraces several of the largest and highest sand dunes in the U.S., including some rising to a height of 1000 ft.

GREAT SCHISM. See SCHISM, WESTERN.

GREAT SEAL OF THE UNITED STATES, the official seal of the United States government. It is a two-sided seal, having both an obverse and a reverse side. Only the obverse side has been cut in brass, but the design of the reverse side has been copied and appears, for example, on the U.S. one-dollar bill. The dominant figure on the obverse side of the seal is an American eagle, shown with wings spread. On its breast the eagle bears a shield having thirteen narrow vertical stripes, seven white alternating with six red, which are surmounted by a broad horizontal stripe of blue. The eagle holds an olive branch in its right talon, a cluster of thirteen arrows in its left, and in its beak a scroll on which appears the motto *E Pluribus Unum* ("Out of Many, One"). A cluster of thirteen five-pointed stars, surrounded by a glory, appears immediately above the eagle. A pyramid, truncated near the top, is the central figure of the reverse side. The base of the pyramid is inscribed with the date "1776" in Roman numerals: *MDCCLXXVI*. At the zenith of the pyramid, within a triangle surrounded by a glory, appears the all-seeing eye of Divine Providence. Above the eye is inscribed the motto *Annuit Cœptis* ("He Has Smiled on Our Undertakings"). Below the pyramid appears a scroll bearing the motto *Novus Ordo Seclorum* ("New Order of the Ages").

The designing of a seal of the United States was first commissioned by the Continental Congress immediately after the signing of the

Declaration of Independence on July 4, 1776; a committee, consisting of Benjamin Franklin, John Adams, and Thomas Jefferson, submitted a design which was deemed unacceptable, as were designs submitted by two succeeding committees. In 1782 these designs were turned over to Charles Thomson, secretary to the Congress, who was charged with the preparation of a new seal. Using many of the features already suggested, particularly those of Will Barton, Thomson prepared a design which, with some alterations, was adopted by the Congress on June 20, 1782. The obverse of the seal was cut in brass soon after the adoption of Thomson's design.

In 1789 the custody of the seal was entrusted to the Secretary of State, in accordance with a law which further provided that the impression of the obverse side of the seal should be affixed to all civil commissions given to officers of the United States appointed by the President. Use of the impression was later expanded, and it now appears on a wide variety of documents, including Presidential proclamations, instruments of ratification of treaties, and the commissions of Cabinet officers, ambassadors, and other Foreign Service officers.

The seal used by the President of the United States is in most respects similar to the Great Seal, differing from it in certain details and in the fact that it is bordered by the inscription "The Seal of the President of the United States". Each of the States and territorial possessions of the United States has a seal of its own.

GREAT SLAVE LAKE, a large fresh-water lake located in the Mackenzie District of the Northwest Territories of Canada. The lake is irregular in shape, being roughly 325 m. in length from west to east and from 15 to 50 m. in width, with a total area of 11,170 sq. m. The surface of the lake is 390 ft. above sea level. The lake is fed from the south by the Great Slave River, which rises in Lake Athabaska and has a course approximately 300 m. in length, and by the smaller Hay River. Water from Great Slave Lake flows to the Arctic Ocean through the Mackenzie River which rises at the western end of the lake. Great Slave Lake also drains into Great Bear Lake (q.v.) through the Marian River which rises at the end of a northwesterly arm of the lake. The chief settlements on the lake are Reliance at the eastern end, Fort Resolution at the mouth of the Great Slave River, Fort Providence at the western end of the lake, and Rae at the head of the Marian River.

The waters of Great Slave Lake are navigable from the middle of June to the middle of October, but are frozen during the remainder of the year. The Great Slave River, except for a stretch of about 15 m. of rapids, is also navigable during a portion of the year. Great Slave Lake was discovered in 1771 by the English explorer Samuel Hearne (1745-92) during a mineral-prospecting expedition for the Hudson's Bay Company.

GREAT SMOKY MOUNTAINS NATIONAL PARK, a national park established in 1930, comprising 461,004 acres in western North Carolina and eastern Tennessee. The Great Smoky Mountains, one of the most massive ranges of the Appalachian (q.v.) system, runs the entire length of the park, and contains some of the highest peaks in eastern North America. Sixteen of the peaks rise to an elevation of more than 6000 ft. above sea level, including Clingman's Dome (6642 ft.), Mount Guyot (6621 ft.), Mount Le Conte (6593 ft.), Mount Chapman (6430 ft.), and Mount Kephart (6150 ft.). The name of the range is derived from the dense bluish haze which rises from the valleys to the summits of the mountains. The region is noted for its rich variety of plant life. Approximately 40% of the park area is covered with virgin forest, and a total of 130 native tree species have been found in the region. Canada hemlock, red spruce, silverbell, yellow buckeye, mountain ash, and other trees grow to a record size there. The mountain peaks themselves are covered with forests of spruce and fir. Rhododendron, dogwood, laurel, and flame azaleas are among the flowering plants which grow in abundance throughout the park. The area is a wildlife sanctuary, containing black bears, deer, red and gray foxes, raccoons, bobcats, wild turkey, and ruffled grouse. The many streams which flow through the park are noted for rainbow and brook trout, and smallmouthed black bass. The park was formally dedicated on Sept. 2, 1940, and is the eighth-largest national park in the U.S. Its western boundary is within 35 miles of Knoxville, Tennessee, and its eastern boundary is 50 miles distant from Asheville, North Carolina. Adjoining the park on the s.e. is the Cherokee Indian Reservation, on which live the descendants of those Cherokee Indians who hid in the Great Smoky Mountains when, in 1838, most of the Cherokees were removed to Oklahoma.

GREAT WALL, fortification along the northern and northwestern frontier of China proper, the first and largest portion of which

*The horned grebe, showing differences in its
winter (left) and summer plumage*

was erected by Emperor Shih Huang Ti as a
symbol of the unity of the Chinese empire
and as a defense against barbarian hordes.
Systematic work on the first segment of the
wall was begun about 228 B.C., after Emperor
Shih Huang Ti had united the different parts
of China into an empire under his rule, and
was finished about 204 B.C. Small sections of
the wall were probably already in existence
but Shih Huang Ti is supposed to have had
nearly 1200 miles of the wall erected during
his reign. In succeeding centuries, chiefly during the period of the Ming dynasty (1368–
1644 A.D.), the Great Wall was repaired and
extended. The fortification finally reached a
length of about 1500 miles, following the
course of rivers instead of bridging them and
conforming to the contours of the mountains
and valleys in its path. Surmounting the
wall, which is 18 to 30 feet wide, is a passage-
way 10 feet wide, running between crenellated
parapets. At intervals of above 100 yards are
large watchtowers. Hundreds of miles of the
Great Wall of China are still intact at the
present time.

GREAT YARMOUTH, municipal, county,
and parliamentary borough, and seaport of
Norfolk, England, on the North Sea, 121 m.
by rail N.E. of London. Nearby is the site
of the ancient Roman camp *Garianonum,*
on a peninsula bounded on the w. by the rivers Yare and Waveney, and on the E. by the
North Sea. Great Yarmouth is a popular resort town of E. England. The principal industries are herring fishing, shipbuilding, and
the production of smoked fish (Yarmouth
bloaters), cordage, net, silk, and foundings.
Pop. (1953 est.) 51,300.

GREAVES. See ARMOR.

GREBE, common name for any of the water
birds of the order Colymbiformes. Grebes resemble ducks and loons, but are entirely unrelated to either; the feet of grebes, unlike

those of ducks and loons, have three uncon-
nected, individually webbed toes, the fourth
toe being separate and very small. Their legs
are placed far back on their bodies and are
not efficient for walking but enable the birds
to swim powerfully. Grebes walk erect like
penguins. The plumage, especially on the
breast, is dense and silky. The color of all
species is dull gray, brown, or black; a few
species have blue or red-brown markings on
the neck and head. Grebes measure about
eighteen inches in length. The majority nest
in swamps and on the edges of ponds. Some
birds nest on plant matter floating near the
water's edge. The nests of all species are made
of vegetation such as grass and reeds, and
lined with softer material. The eggs, usually
from three to five in number, are dull white
in color.

Grebes have a feeding custom of which the
explanation is not known. When a grebe's
stomach is opened it is generally found to
contain more than 50% feathers. Grebes not
only eat feathers—apparently their own—but
also feed them to their young. Ornithologists
have speculated that the feathers have some
special nutritive or digestive function, or that
they perform a straining function for fish
bones and other hard substances which are
ingested.

North America has six species of grebes,
among the most important of which are the
horned grebe, *Colymbus auritus,* which has
a black ruff around the head, and the dab-
chick or pied-billed grebe, which is bigger
than the horned grebe and has no ruff.
Both species are known colloquially as "hell-
divers". These birds generally nest in summer
in Canada and winter in the U.S.

The dipper (q.v.) is also sometimes called
a grebe, and the finfoot (see GRUIFORMES)
is known as the sun grebe.

GRECHANINOV, or GRETCHANINOV, ALEK-
SANDR TIKHONOVICH (1864–1956), Russian
composer, born at Moscow. He attended the
Moscow Conservatory and the St. Petersburg
Conservatory, where he studied with Nikolai
Rimski-Korsakov. He was a professor at the
St. Petersburg Conservatory until 1922. In
1929 he made a tour of the United States, appearing as guest conductor with leading symphonies. Grechaninov is especially known for
his sacred music, which includes two complete
liturgies and a *Laudate Deum* for chorus and
orchestra. Among his other works are symphonies, string quartets, songs, piano pieces,
and two operas, *Dobrinya Nikititch* (1903)
and *Sœur Beatrice* (1912).

GRECIAN GAMES. See Games, Ancient; Isthmian Games; Nemean Games; Olympian Games; Pythian Games.

GRECO, EL (Sp., "the Greek"), pseudonym of Kyriakos Theotokopoulos, called also (in Sp.) Domenico (1541–1614), Spanish painter, born at Phodele, near Candia, Crete. About 1560 he went to Venice, where for about ten years he worked in the studio of the painter Titian. He subsequently went to Rome, and worked under the patronage of Cardinal Alessandro Farnese, later Pope Paul III. About 1576 he settled in Toledo, Spain, where he designed and painted, for the church of Santo Domingo el Antigua, an altarpiece considered one of the great masterpieces of Spanish painting. The panels containing the paintings of St. John the Baptist and St. John the Evangelist, "The Adoration of the Shepherds", and "The Resurrection" still remain in their original positions; the centerpiece, "The Assumption of the Virgin", is in the Chicago Art Institute; and the "Dead Christ in the arms of God the Father" is in the Prado, Madrid. In 1577 El Greco was commissioned to paint a picture for the sacristy of the Toledo cathedral and chose as his subject "The Stripping of Christ before the Crucifixion" (known as *El Espolio*). This painting is outstanding among the early works he painted in Spain, and he made several versions of the subject; two of these later paintings are in the Barnes Foundation, Merion, Pa., and the Institute of Art, Minneapolis.

In 1580 he painted, for King Philip II, "The Martyrdom of St. Maurice" (Escorial, Madrid), noted for its spiritual quality. His next important work, showing his power in composing a large number of figures within the limits of his canvas, is "The Burial of Conde de Orgaz" (Santo Tomé, Toledo). His altarpiece depicting the life of Christ was completed in 1590 for the church of Dona Maria de Aragon, in Madrid; three of the pictures that survive are "The Crucifixion", "The Resurrection", and "The Baptism" (all in the Prado). In these paintings he elongated the figures, for purposes of emotional expression, to such an extent that many of his contemporaries asserted that his eyesight had developed defects, while others declared that he had become mad. Other important paintings are "The Coronation of the Virgin", "St. Joseph and the Infant Christ" (chapel of San José, Toledo), "St. Martin and the Beggar", and "The Virgin with Saints" (both in the Widener Collection, Elkins Park, Pa.). Outstanding among his portraits is "The Cardinal Inquisitor Don Fernando Niño de Guevara" (Metropolitan Museum of Art, New York City).

El Greco is considered one of the great masters of all time. though his works were neglected for nearly three hundred years. His technique of distortion for purposes of expression foreshadowed the use of the same technique in modern Expressionism (q.v.). In the "View of Toledo under Storm" (Metropolitan Museum), one of the earliest of European landscapes, he was a forerunner of the later Romantic landscape painters.

GREECE (Gr. *Hellas*), a kingdom of S.E. Europe, occupying the southern prolongation of the Balkan Peninsula, extending into the Mediterranean Sea between the Ægean Sea on the E. and the Ionian Sea on the W. The kingdom includes many islands, the largest of which is Crete (q.v.). Greece is bordered on the N.W. by Albania, on the N. by Yugoslavia

Art Institute of Chicago

"The Assumption of the Virgin," by El Greco

and Bulgaria, and on the N.E. by Turkey. The geographical divisions of Greece, each of which contains a number of prefectures (*nomoi*), are Central Greece and Eubœa, Thessaly, the Ionian Islands, the Cyclades, the Peloponnesus, Macedonia, Epirus, the Ægean Islands, Crete, and Thrace. The Dodecanese (q.v.), a group of islands in the S.E. Ægean Sea, under Italian rule after the Turko-Italian War of 1912, were ceded to Greece following World War II at the Paris Conference of Foreign Ministers held in June, 1946. Formal transfer to Greece by the British Military Administration, which governed the Dodecanese from May, 1945, was made on March 31, 1947. The capital and chief city of Greece is Athens (q.v.). Other important cities are Peiræus, Salonika, Patras, and Kavalla (qq.v.). The area of Greece, including islands, is 51,246 sq.m.; pop. (1956 est.) 8,400,000.

The coastal waters of Greece are shallow and penetrate far inland. The deep gulfs of Corinth and Ægina, separated by the isthmus of Corinth, divide the Peloponnesus from central and N. Greece. The country, despite its indented coasts, has few good harbors. The best facilities are found in the Gulf of Ægina, where the fine natural harbor of Peiræus is located, serving as the port of Athens, 6 m. inland.

The topography of Greece is predominantly mountainous, with the ranges of the Balkan Peninsula extending into and through the country. The rugged chain of the Pindus Mts., extending from the Albanian frontier S.E. to the head of the Gulf of Corinth, forms the principal watershed of the country. West of the Pindus Mts., the ranges of the Dinaric Alps (q.v.) extend through Greece to the S. end of the Peloponnesus. Generally the mountains of Greece are of medium elevation, although Parnassus (q.v.), the best-known summit of the eastern ranges, rises to a height of 8065 ft. above sea level, and Mount Hagios Elias (anc. *Taygetus*), the culminating point of the Dinaric system in the Peloponnesus, is 7904 ft. above sea level. The only great plains are those of Thessaly in eastern Greece. There the soil is fertile and the vegetation luxuriant. Other arable plains, considerably smaller, are found in Bœotia, Messenia, Argolis, and along portions of the coast. Macedonia contains many fertile, hill-girdled regions, yielding grain, tobacco, and, on the coast, olives.

All the islands of Greece are mountainous. They were once a part of the mainland, and the largest one in the Ægean Sea, Eubœa, is still so regarded, as it is separated from central Greece only by the narrow Strait of Euripos, which at Chalkis, the capital of Eubœa, is little more than 100 ft. wide. A chain of volcanic islands bounds the Cyclades on the S. The rivers of Greece, which are of little economic importance, flow generally s. or w., both in the Peloponnesus and on the mainland.

The climate of Greece is generally similar to that of other Mediterranean countries. The lowlands have hot, dry summers with rains in autumn and winter. The mountain areas, on the other hand, are much cooler, with considerable rain in the summer months. Frost and snow are rare in the lowlands, but the mountains are covered with snow in the winter. The mean temperature at Athens is 63° F., with a minimum of 31.5° F. in January and a maximum of 99° F. in July.

About 18% of the total land area of Greece is covered with forests, the principal trees being oak, pine, and fir. A tabulation of the country's livestock in 1952 showed 7,906,-633 sheep, 4,302,202 goats, 885,971 cattle, 476,975 asses, 297,024 horses, 189,581 mules, and 64,000 pigs. Mineral resources include iron ore, iron pyrites, silver, copper, nickel, lead, zinc, chromite, aluminum, magnesite, antimony, manganese, bauxite, emery, lignite, bitumen, sulfur, marine salt, ochre, and marble (white and colored). Great quantities of sponges are taken from the sea.

Although more than one half of the population of Greece is engaged in agricultural activities, only a fifth of the total land area is cultivable, due to soil erosion and the insufficient use of fertilizers. Scientific methods of farming are being introduced. The two chief export crops, currants and tobacco, are raised for their high market value abroad, so that the country can pay for much-needed imports such as wheat, flour, and meat. The principal crops of Greece, in addition to the two mentioned above, are wheat, barley, corn, cotton, and olives. Fruits widely cultivated are oranges, apples, lemons, figs, grapes, pears, and tangerines. Rice also is grown. Olive oil, wine and other alcoholic beverages, cheese, chemicals, rugs, textiles, leather, cigarettes, and building materials are among the products of Greece's industry, operated mostly on a small-scale basis.

Prior to World War II, Greece's imports averaged about $100,000,000 annually; exports, $75,000,000. In 1952 imports were valued at about $346,000,000; the chief imports were foodstuffs, clothing and piece goods, machinery, and coal. Exports in the same year were valued at about $120,000,000; the chief exports were tobacco (44%), currants and raisins (18%), olives, and wines and liquors. Until 1939 the bulk of Greece's trade was with Germany. In 1952 the principal sources of the country's imports were the United States (21%); West Germany (12%), and Italy (12%); exports went chiefly to West Germany (30%), the United Kingdom (16%), and the United States (12%).

School attendance in Greece is compulsory for all children between the ages of six and fourteen. Educational facilities include (1951–52) 980 kindergartens, 9331 primary schools, 511 high schools, and two universities, one in Athens and one in Salonika. Schools for specialized study are the School of Fine Arts and the Polytechnic, both located at Athens. The state religion is that of the Greek Orthodox Church (see ORTHODOX CHURCH), but complete freedom of worship is guaranteed to all denominations. Nearly the entire population is Orthodox; about 2% is Mohammedan. Of the 67,591 Jews in Greece in 1940, only about 8500 survived the German occupation. An autonomous monastic community is located on Mount Athos (see ATHOS).

Greece maintains (1951) 13,706 m. of roads and (1950) 1555 m. of railway. A canal, opened in 1893, cuts across the Isthmus of Corinth. Severely damaged during the German occupation, the canal was restored to use in 1948. In 1939 the merchant marine had 589 steam and motor vessels with a total tonnage of 1,812,723; about 25% remained after the war. Gross tonnage in 1953 had risen to 1,139,-609. A Greek domestic air service and thirty foreign air lines provide air transportation.

The Republic of Greece was established by a plebiscite on April 13, 1924. The Republic lasted until the restoration of the monarchy was voted in a plebiscite, and George II (q.v.) returned to power as king of the Hellenes on November 25, 1935. At that time, the monarchial constitution of 1911 was revised and once more put into force (see *Modern Greece*, below). Upon the death of George II in 1947, his brother, Prince Paul, succeeded to the throne. Greece is at present a constitutional hereditary monarchy with executive power nominally vested in the king. Actual administration of the government, however, is in the hands of a council of ministers, or cabinet, headed by the premier; the council must enjoy the confidence of the legislative assembly.

HISTORY OF ANCIENT GREECE. Historically and culturally, the peninsula of Greece, since the Neolithic age, has been linked with the w. coast of Asia Minor and the islands which stud the Ægean Sea between the two land masses. The convolutions of both coasts, with their many harbors, and the multiplicity of closelying islands inevitably led to the development of a homogeneous, maritime civilization. Cultural homogeneity did not, however, induce political unity. At no time during its ancient history was Greece a single, independent political entity. Mountain ranges and deep valleys cut the country into small economic and political units, each little larger than a city with its surrounding territory. For a detailed history of the most famous city-states, see ATHENS; SPARTA.

Prehistoric. Archeological evidence indicates that a primitive Mediterranean people, closely akin to the races of North Africa, inhabited the s. Ægean area as far back as the Neolithic age, before 4000 B.C. Such evidence shows a cultural progression from the Stone Age to the Bronze Age, which, in the Near East, began about 3500 B.C. Beginning with the latter period, the prehistoric Ægean civilization (q.v.) progressed to an extremely high level. The Ægean Bronze Age civilization was divided into three main phases. On the mainland, particularly the Peloponnesus, arose the *Helladic* culture, centered in such cities as Mycenæ and Tiryns (qq.v.); this culture was largely indigenous and, according to archeological opinion, was produced by the assimilation of the aborigines, a people akin to those of the Danubian area, with a southern people which had migrated to the peninsula in very early times. Related to the Helladic was the *Cycladic* culture of the adjacent Cyclades Islands (q.v.). On the islands, however, probably because of the development of seagoing commerce, the budding civilization was considerably influenced by earlier civilizations of the E. Mediterranean, notably that of Egypt. Thus, the greatest center of Ægean civilization became, after 3000 B.C., the island of Crete (q.v.), only 400 m. northwest of Egypt and directly on the sea routes to the great ancient countries of the Middle East; the *Minoan* (from *Minos,* the generic name for the Cretan kings) culture was, it is thought, engendered by Egyptians who migrated to the island before 2500 B.C. By the 17th century B.C., Crete and its Minoan culture dominated the Ægean.

About this time began a series of invasions by tribes from the north, speaking an Indo-European language which was the ancestor of the Greek (see GREEK LANGUAGE). Evidence exists that the northerners were an Aryan race who originally inhabited the basin of the Danube R. in s.E. Europe. The most prominent of the early invaders were the Achæans (q.v.), a Thessalian tribe which had, in all probability, been forced to migrate by other invaders. They overran s. Greece and established themselves on the Peloponnesus to such an extent that for centuries thereafter the name of the tribe was used to mean all Greeks. A second tribe, the Ionians (q.v.), settled chiefly in Attica, E. central Greece, and the Cyclades, where they were assimilated with the Helladic people to a greater degree than the other tribes. The Æolians (q.v.), a third, rather vaguely defined tribe, settled across the peninsula from s.w. to N.E.

Gradually, in the last period (1600–1100 B.C.) of Bronze Age Greece, the mainland absorbed the civilization of Crete. By 1250 B.C. the Achæans were in possession of the island itself, and dominance of the Ægean passed to the mainland, notably to the region of which Mycenæ was the center. Although this city has given its name to the Achæan ascendancy because of extensive archeological investigations of its ruins (see ARCHEOLOGY), other city-kingdoms were of great, if not equal, importance. The names of many kings, such as Œdipus of Thebes and Creon of Corinth as well as Agamemnon of Mycenæ (qq.v.) have been preserved in legends which, denuded of their fabulous quality, are the only records of the time. This era of Achæan supremacy has become known as the Heroic Age, when heroes later celebrated as semidivine performed the exploits associated with such names as Hercules, Perseus, and Theseus (qq.v.). An alternate name for the period is the Homeric Age, the time of the events described by Homer (q.v.) in the *Iliad* and the *Odyssey* (qq.v.). The Trojan War (q.v.), described in these epics, occurred about 1194 B.C., and was probably one of a series of wars waged by the warlike Achæans during the 13th and 12th centuries B.C.

The last and most important of the invasions from the north occurred about 1100 B.C. and brought the Iron Age to Greece. The Dorians (q.v.) left their mountainous home in Epirus (N.W. Greece) and pushed their way down to the Peloponnesus and Crete, using iron weapons to conquer or expel the previous inhabitants of those regions. The invading Dorians overthrew the Achæan kings and settled, principally, in the districts of Messenia, Argolis, and Laconia; Sparta and Corinth became the chief Dorian cities. Many of the Achæans took refuge in the N. Peloponnesus, a district afterward called Achaia; others resisted the Dorians bitterly and, after being

subjugated, were made slaves, called *helots* (q.v.). The Ionians of the Peloponnesus fled to their kinsmen in Attica and the island of Eubœa, but later migrated, as did the Æolians, to the coast of Asia Minor. In the two or three centuries after 1100 B.C., the growth of colonization, first by refugees from the Dorians, and then by the Dorians themselves, made this coast a political and cultural, if not geographical, part of Greece. Three great confederacies were established by the three Greek ethnic divisions. In Æolis, the northern part of the coast of Asia Minor, and on the island of Lesbos (q.v.), was situated the Æolian confederacy. The Ionian confederacy occupied the middle district, called Ionia (q.v.), and the islands of Chios and Samos; Ephesus, Miletus (qq.v.), and Phocæa became the greatest Ionian cities. A Doric confederacy was established in Doris, in the south, and the islands of Rhodes and Cos (qq.v.). Several centuries later (800–600 B.C.), because of internal difficulties, mainly a shortage of food, another great colonization impulse spread from Greece proper, this time to places as widely separated as the E. coast of the Black Sea and Marseille (q.v.) in s. France. These colonies included settlements in Sicily; in s. Italy, which was so thickly settled by Greeks that it became known as *Magna Græcia* (Lat., "Greater Greece"); and in Africa. Thus was fixed the geographical extent of Greek influence during the greatest period of Greek civilization.

Hellenic Period. After the conclusion of the great migrations in the Ægean, the Greeks developed a proud racial consciousness. They called themselves Hellenes, originally the name, according to Homer, only of a small tribe living south of Thessaly. The term "Greeks" was used by later foreign peoples, and derived from *Græci*, the Latin name for a small Hellenic tribe of Epirus, presumably the Hellenes with whom Italians first had dealings. As Hellenic race pride developed, the pre-Hellenic inhabitants of Greece, called the Pelasgians (q.v.), came to be considered an inferior race, with the exception only of two tribes, the Carians (see CARIA) and the Leleges. Out of the web of mythology which became the basis of an intricate religion (see GREEK RELIGIOUS MYTHOLOGY), the Hellenes developed a genealogy for themselves which gave them aspects of divinity. The three most important branches considered themselves descendants of Hellēn, son of Deucalion (q.v.) and grandson of Prometheus, through Hellēn's sons Ion, Dorus, and Æolus. In time, the Dorians and Ionians became the foremost

Greek Govt. Office of Information

Street along the quay in the city of Salonika, seaport in northeastern Greece

branches, the name of Æolians being the general term for all other Hellenes. The question of race was of great importance during the Hellenic period; the rivalry between Dorians and Ionians for domination of Greece developed into mutual antipathy, each branch claiming the other to be less purely Hellenic.

Although the small Hellenic states maintained their autonomy, they pursued a common course of political development. In the pre-Hellenic period the tribal chiefs of invading tribes became the kings of the territories they conquered. These monarchies were slowly replaced (800–650 B.C.) by oligarchies of aristocrats, as the noble families acquired land, the measure of wealth and power. About 650 B.C. many of the Hellenic oligarchies were themselves overthrown by wealthy commoners, called tyrants. Only in Sparta and in some cities within Sparta's orbit of influence did the aristocracy maintain its position. The rise of the tyrants was due, mainly, to economic reasons. Popular discontent, under the oligarchies, had become a major political factor because of the increasing enslavement of landless peasants; the introduction of coin money, about 680 B.C., hastened the development of the landless, wealthy class, which took advantage of the mounting discontent to make themselves political masters of the city-states.

The age of the Greek tyrants (about 650–500 B.C.) was notable for advances made in Hellenic civilization. The title of tyrant connoted that political power had been illegally seized, rather than that it was abused. Generally, the tyrants, such as Periander of Corinth, Gelon (q.v.) of Syracuse, and Polycrates of Samos, were wise and popular rulers. Trade and industry flourished. In the wake of political and economic strength came a flowering of Hellenic culture (see EDUCATION: *History;* GREEK ART AND ARCHITECTURE; GREEK LITERATURE). Greek philosophy began with the speculation of Anaximander, Thales (qq.v.), and Anaximenes (see GREEK PHILOSOPHY). The development of cultural pursuits common to all the Hellenic cities was one of the factors which united ancient Greece, despite the political separation of the various states. Another factor was the Greek language, the many dialects of which were readily understandable in any part of the country or any colony. Thirdly, the Greek religion held the Hellenes together, and the sanctuary of Delphi (q.v.), with its oracle, became the greatest national shrine. As a corollary to their religion, the Greeks held four national festivals, called games, and distinguished as the Olympian, Isthmian, Pythian, and Nemean (qq.v.); see also GAMES, ANCIENT. The Olympian games were considered so important that the Greeks dated their own historical reckoning from the first Olympiad (the four-year period between sessions at the Olympian games) held in 776 B.C. Related to religion, at least in origin, was the Amphictyonic League (q.v.), an organization of Hellenic tribes which was established for the protection and administration of shrines.

Politically, too, some unification of the city-states took place. Between the 8th and 6th centuries B.C., the two dominant cities of Greece became Athens and Sparta, or Lacedæmon; each of these great states united its weaker neighbors into a league or confederacy under its control. Sparta, a completely militarized and aristocratic state, established its leadership mainly by conquest, and kept its subject states under strict rule. The Spartans pursued a policy of expelling the tyrants of cities they dominated and influencing the cities to maintain the aristocratic forms the Dorians preferred. The unification of Attica was, however, carried on by mutual and peaceful agreement under the leadership of Athens, and the smaller cities were given Athenian citizenship. The hereditary kingship of Athens was abolished in 683 B.C. by the nobles, or Eupatridæ, who ruled Athens until late in the 6th century B.C. The Eupatridæ retained complete authority by their supreme power to dispense justice, often in an arbitrary fashion. In 621 B.C., however, the statesman Draco codified and published the Athenian law, thereby limiting the judiciary power of the nobles. A second major blow at the hereditary power of the Eupatridæ was the code of Solon (q.v.) in 594 B.C., which reformed the Draconian code and gave citizenship to the lower classes. During the wise and enlightened rule (561–527 B.C.) of the tyrant Pisistratus (q.v.), the forms of government remained democratic, and in time became more so. Hippias and Hipparchus (see HIPPIAS), sons of Pisistratus, inherited their father's power, but they were considerably more despotic, and were expelled by a popular uprising in 510 B.C. In the resulting political strife, the supporters of democracy, under the great statesman Cleisthenes (q.v.), won a complete victory, and a new constitution, based on democratic principles, took effect in 502 B.C. The beginning of democratic rule was the dawn of the greatest period of Athenian history. Agriculture and commerce flourished. Moreover, the center of artistic and intellectual endeavor, until that time situated in the cities of the Asia Minor coast, was transferred to Athens as a result of the Persian invasions.

The Greek colonies in Asia Minor had been conquered by Crœsus, King of Lydia, in the early part of his reign (560–46 B.C.) and brought into the Lydian Empire. Crœsus was a mild ruler, sympathetic to the Hellenes, and an ally of Sparta; the economic, political, and intellectual life of the colonies was considerably stimulated by Lydian domination. In 546 B.C., however, Crœsus was overthrown by Cyrus the Great, King of Persia; except for the island of Samos, which ably defended itself, the Greek cities in Asia and the coastal islands became part of the Persian Empire.

In 499 B.C. the district of Ionia, assisted by Athens and Eretria revolted against Persia. The rebels were, at first, successful, and Darius, the Persian king, swore to avenge himself both on them and the two cities which had aided them. He put down the revolt in 493 B.C. and, after sacking Miletus, re-established his absolute control over Ionia. A year later Mardonius, the king's son-in-law, led a great Persian fleet to exact vengeance from Greece, but most of the ships were wrecked off Mt. Athos. At the same time, Darius sent heralds to Greece, requiring tokens of submission from all the Greek city-states. Though most of the smaller states acquiesced, Sparta and Athens refused, and slew the Persian heralds as a gesture of defiance. Darius, enraged by the Greek insult as well as by the fate of his fleet, prepared a second expedition, which set sail in 490 B.C. After destroying Eretria, the Persian army proceeded to the plain of Marathon (q.v.), near Athens. The Athenian leaders sent to Sparta for aid, but the message arrived during a religious festival which prevented the Spartans from leaving. Nevertheless, the Athenian army, under Miltiades, won an overwhelming victory over a Persian force ten times as large, and the Persians withdrew. Darius immediately began to make ready a third expedition; his son Xerxes, who succeeded him in 486 B.C., brought together one of the largest armies in ancient history. In 481 B.C. the Persians crossed the Hellespont strait over a bridge of boats and marched southward. The Greeks made their first stand in 480 B.C. at Thermopylæ (q.v.), where the Spartan leader Leonidas (q.v.) and several thousand soldiers heroically defended the narrow pass. A treacherous Greek showed the Persians another path which enabled the invaders to enter the pass from the rear. Leonidas permitted most of his men to withdraw, but he and a force of 300 Spartans and 700 Thespians resisted to the end and were annihilated. The Persians then proceeded to Athens, capturing and burning the city, which

An old walled village on the island of Santorin, Greece

Greek Govt. Office of Information

ANCIENT RUINS IN GREECE. *Top: The Acropolis. Bottom: The Parthenon.*

had been abandoned. Meanwhile, the Persian fleet pursued the Greek fleet to Salamis, an island in the Gulf of Ægina near Athens. In the naval battle which ensued, less than 400 Greek vessels, under Themistocles (q.v.), defeated 1200 Persian vessels. Xerxes, who had watched the battle from a golden throne on a hill overlooking the harbor of Salamis, fled to Asia. In the following year, 479 B.C., the remainder of the Persian forces in Greece were overwhelmed at Platæa (q.v.) and the invaders were finally driven out.

As a result of its brilliant leadership in the Persian wars, Athens became the most influential state in Greece. Moreover, the wars had demonstrated the increasing importance of seapower, for the naval battle of Salamis had been the decisive engagement; Sparta, hitherto the greatest military power in Greece because of its army, lost its prestige to the Athenian fleet. In 478 B.C. a large number of Greek states formed a voluntary alliance, the Delian League (q.v.), to drive the Persians from the Greek cities and coastal islands of Asia Minor; Athens, as a matter of course, headed the alliance. The victories of the League, then under the Athenian general Cimon (q.v.), resulted (476–66 B.C.) in the restored independence of the colonies. Athens, however, began to exert its power over the other members of the League to such an extent that they became its subjects rather than its allies. The Athenians exacted tribute from their erstwhile confederates and, when Naxos attempted to withdraw from the League, the fortifications of that city were razed.

The period of Athenian domination during the 5th century B.C. has become known as the "golden age" of Athens. Under Pericles (q.v.), who became leader of the popular party and head of the state in 460 B.C., the city attained its greatest splendor. The constitution, reformed to further internal democracy, contained provisions such as payment for jury service, thereby permitting even the poorest citizens to serve. Pericles, determined to make Athens the most beautiful city in the world, commissioned the sculptor Phidias to design and supervise the erection of the Parthenon (q.v.), the Propylæa, and other great buildings. Greek drama reached its greatest expression with the plays of such dramatists as Euripides and Sophocles. Thucydides and Herodotus became famous historians, and the cultivation of intellect in Periclean Athens made the city famous as an artistic and cultural center.

Despite the excellent internal condition of the city, the foreign policy of Athens proved its undoing. The members of the Delian League were discontented and chafed under Athenian rule. Sparta, moreover, was envious of Athenian prosperity. A league between the cities of the Peloponnesus had existed since about 560 B.C., under the leadership of Sparta, and the Peloponnesian League began to oppose Athens actively. In 431 B.C. the inevitable clash between Athens and Sparta occurred, precipitated over Athenian aid to Corcyra during a dissent between Corcyra and Corinth, an ally of Sparta. Known as the Peloponnesian War, the struggle between the two great confederacies lasted until 404 B.C., and resulted in the complete abasement of Athenian pride and the establishment of Spartan supremacy in Greece. At the conclusion of the war, Sparta set up an oligarchy, known as the Thirty Tyrants, to rule Athens; similar ruling bodies were established in the cities and islands of Asia Minor. Spartan rule, however, soon evinced itself as more harsh and oppressive than that of democratic Athens. In 403 B.C. the Athenians, under Thrasybulus, revolted and overthrew the Spartan oligarchy, though the city of Athens remained under Dorian domination. Revolts in other Greek cities, moreover, consistently opposed the hegemony of Sparta.

The Greek states began, individually, to seek aid from their traditional enemy, Persia. In 399 B.C. the marauding activities of Persia on the Asia Minor coast led Sparta to send an army there. Though the Spartan army met with some success, it was forced to return in 394 B.C. to oppose a coalition of Argos, Athens, Corinth, and Thebes. The resulting conflict, known as the Corinthian War, continued, mainly as small-scale warfare, until 387 B.C., when Sparta, allying itself with Persia, imposed the Peace of Antalcidas (see ANTALCIDAS) on its unwilling subject states. By the terms of the Persian-Spartan settlement, the entire west coast of Asia Minor was ceded to the Asiatic power, and the city-states of Greece were made autonomous. Despite this agreement, Sparta, in 382 B.C., invaded Thebes and captured the city of Olynthus in the north. The Theban general Pelopidas (q.v.), supported by Athens, led an uprising three years later and expelled the Spartan occupation force. War between Sparta and Athens, in alliance with Thebes, was resumed, ending with the battle of Leuctra, in 371 B.C., in which the Thebans, led by Epaminondas (q.v.), so completely defeated their enemies that Spartan domination came to an end. Thebes, by virtue of its victory, became the leading Grecian state. The other states resented its leadership, however, and the ascendancy of Thebes inaugurated an unhappy period of civil unrest and economic misery resulting from internecine strife. Athens, in particular, refused to submit to Theban supremacy and, in 369 B.C., became an ally of Sparta. At best insecure, the Theban hegemony was dependent, principally, on the brilliant leadership of Epaminondas, and when he was killed in the battle of Mantinea in 362 B.C., Thebes again became only one state among many.

During this period of strife in Greece, Macedon (see MACEDONIA), its neighbor to the north, was initiating a policy of expansion that was destined to make it one of the greatest world powers in ancient history. The Macedonians, a people akin to the Hellenes, had been consistently sympathetic to Greece. Philip II, who became ruler of Macedon in 359 B.C., was a great admirer of Greek civilization, but he was well aware of its greatest weakness: the lack of political unity. Directly after he came to the throne, Philip annexed the Greek colonies on the coast of Macedon and Thrace, and determined to make himself master of the peninsula (see PHILIP OF MACEDON). He gained his first foothold in Greece by invitation of the city-states themselves, which twice called upon Macedon for military aid in their internal dissensions. Astute political craft and the force of Macedonian arms helped Philip to realize his ambitions (see DEMOSTHENES). By 338 B.C., he was sufficiently powerful to call a congress of the Greek states which acknowledged Macedonian supremacy in the peninsula and appointed Philip commander in chief of the Greek forces. A year later, a second congress declared war on Persia, the traditional enemy. The king began at once to prepare for an Asiatic campaign, but he was assassinated in 336 B.C. His son, Alexander, who was then twenty years old, succeeded him.

At Philip's death, several large Greek cities rose in revolt against Macedon, but Alexander quickly suppressed the rebellion and razed Thebes as a warning to other cities. In 334 B.C. he set out to invade Persia. During the next ten years, the conquests of Alexander in the Far and Middle East extended Greek influence as well as the Greek civilization and language throughout a Macedonian empire which ranged as far as northern India to the east and Egypt to the south. By the time of Alexander's death, in 323 B.C., the culture of Greece had become the greatest influence in the an-

cient world of the 4th century B.C. See ALEXANDER THE GREAT.

Hellenistic Period. Following Alexander's death, the Macedonian generals, notably Antigonus, Lysimachus, Ptolemy, and Seleucus, began to partition Alexander's vast empire among themselves. The disagreements arising from this division resulted in a series of wars (322–275 B.C.), many of which took place in Greece. Thus, one of the characteristics of the Hellenistic period, which lasted from the death of Alexander to the acquisition of Greece as a Roman province in 146 B.C., was the deterioration of the Greek city-states as political entities and the gradual decline of Greek political independence as a whole. Economically, too, Greece suffered. Lacking in natural resources and opportunities for wealth, it began to lose its vigor as its citizenry emigrated to the East in search of new opportunities.

On the other hand, the Hellenistic period was marked by the triumph of Greece as the fountainhead of a culture and way of life adopted, as a result of Alexander's conquests, throughout most of the ancient world. The Greek-speaking imitators of Grecian ways were termed Hellenists.

Of the kingdoms established by Alexander's generals, called the Diadochi (Gr. *diadochos,* "successor"), the most important were the kingdom of Syria (q.v.), under the Seleucid dynasty, and the kingdom of Egypt (q.v.), the realm of the Ptolemies; see also PTOLEMY; SELEUCIDAE. The capital of Ptolemaic Egypt, Alexandria, which had been founded by Alexander in 332 B.C., developed into a center of Greek learning rivaling and, occasionally, surpassing Athens. Every part of the Hellenistic world devoted itself to the cultivation of art and intellect, and such men as the mathematicians Euclid and Archimedes, the philosophers Epicurus and Zeno, and the poets Apollonius of Rhodes and Theocritus were characteristic of the age. So strongly was Hellenistic culture implanted that it became one of the most important elements in early Christianity. Indeed, the firm hold of Greek culture on the eastern Mediterranean as opposed to its dispossession by Roman culture in the west was an important factor in the great schism (see SCHISM, GREAT) between the eastern and western Catholic churches.

The widespread adulation for Greek civilization, however, was insufficient satisfaction to the Greeks for the inglorious state in which they found themselves in the 3rd century. They made two more attempts to assert them-

Greek Govt. Office of Information

Canal cutting across the Isthmus of Corinth, south central Greece

selves. In 290 B.C. the city-states of central Greece began to join the Ætolian League, a powerful military confederation which had originally been organized during the reign of Philip II of Macedon by the cities of Ætolia (q.v.) for their mutual benefit and protection. A second, and similar, organization, known as the Achæan League and nominally an ancient alliance of cities in Achaia, became, in 280 B.C., the supreme confederation of the cities in the N. Peloponnesus; later other cities, including Athens and Corinth, joined. Both alliances dedicated themselves to serving Greece from the kingdom of Macedon; both acted as political confederations, maintaining armies, levying taxes, and holding regular assemblies. The Achæan League, however, became much more powerful than its rival, and tried to acquire control of all of Greece for itself. Led by Aratus, the League began to conflict with Sparta, which had joined neither alliance. In the war between the Achæans and the Dorian city, the League was at first defeated, and putting aside its primary purpose, called on Macedon for military aid, which was granted. The alliance then defeated Sparta, but from that time on it was dominated by Macedon. Under the leadership of Philopœmen, called "the last of the Greeks" for his efforts in behalf of Greek independence, the League

was restored to some measure of militant activity, but it never regained its earlier power.

In 215 B.C. Rome (q.v.) began to interfere in Greek affairs. Philip V of Macedon allied himself with Carthage against Rome, but the Latins, acquiring the support of the Ætolian League, overcame the Macedonian forces in 206 B.C., and obtained a firm foothold in Greece. Rome, aided by both leagues, again defeated Philip in 197 B.C., and Macedon, completely subjugated, agreed to a peace with Rome which recognized the independence of Greece. The Greeks, however, found they had exchanged one master for another. In a last desperate attempt to free themselves, the members of the Achæan League resisted demands which Rome made on it in 149 B.C. The resulting war ended with the destruction of Corinth by Roman legions in 146 B.C. The leagues were abolished and Greece passed completely into the power of Rome, later becoming a Roman province under the name of Achaia.

ROMAN AND MEDIEVAL GREECE. For sixty years following 146 B.C., Greece was competently administered by Rome, some cities, such as Athens and Sparta, even retaining their free status. However, in 88 B.C., when Mithridates (q.v.), the king of Pontus, began a campaign of conquest in Roman-controlled territories, many cities of Greece supported the Asiatic monarch because he had promised to help them regain their independence. Roman legions under Lucius Cornelius Sulla forced Mithridates out of Greece and crushed the rebellion; they sacked Athens in 86 B.C., and Thebes a year later. Roman punishment was heavy on all the rebellious cities, and the campaigns fought on Greek soil left central Greece in ruins. As a result, the country began to disintegrate economically, and its cities were reduced to contemplation of their splendid past and to trading on the respect with which the Romans regarded their ancient culture. Athens, for example, remained a center of philosophy and learning, but its commerce, once the greatest in the Ægean, became almost nonexistent.

Under the Roman Empire, in the first centuries of the Christian era, a Greek renaissance took place, particularly during the reign (117–38 A.D.) of the emperor Hadrian. With his contemporary, the wealthy Greek scholar Atticus Herodes, Hadrian beautified Athens and restored many of the ruined cities. In the middle of the 3rd century A.D., however, this rebirth was checked by the Gothic hordes which in 267–68 A.D. overran the peninsula, captured Athens, and laid waste the cities of Argos, Corinth, and Sparta (see GOTHS). The first Gothic foray finally was repulsed by the Romans. Athens recovered its stature as an intellectual center and, despite the spread of Christianity in Greece, became the seat of non-Christian culture. In 395–96, a Gothic army again devastated Greece, virtually destroying the revival.

When the world empire founded by the Romans was halved in 395 A.D., the eastern half, including all of Greece and the Ægean region, became the Byzantine Empire (q.v.), also known, because of the influence of Hellenism, as the Greek Empire. The civilization of the Byzantine Empire, however, was an Oriental version of Greek culture rather than classic Hellenism. Greece itself became a neglected and obscure province. From the 6th to the 8th centuries, Slavonic tribes from the north crowded into the peninsula. The invaders were, to some extent, assimilated by the ancient Hellenic peoples. Though a Byzantine army conquered them in 783, the Slavs continued to occupy Thrace and Illyria (now Yugoslavia and part of Bulgaria).

In the 13th century the ambition of the Frankish leaders of the Fourth Crusade (1202–04) interrupted the continuity of Byzantine rule. Constantinople fell to the Crusaders in 1204, and the conquerors, after sacking the Byzantine capital, established the Latin Empire of the East. They divided the Greek peninsula into feudal fiefs, of which the most prominent was the Duchy of Athens. The Latin Empire fell in 1261, when Constantinople was reconquered by Michael VIII, the Byzantine emperor. The Duchy of Athens, however, outlasted the Empire, and, for the next two centuries, was controlled successively by French, Spanish, and Italian rulers; in the 14th century, the court of Athens was one of the most brilliant feudal courts of Europe.

In 1453 the sultan of Turkey, Mohammed II, captured Constantinople and then turned his attention to the Morea (the Peloponnesus) and Attica; by 1460 these parts of Greece had been incorporated into the Ottoman or Turkish Empire. The Turkish conquest, sending thousands of Greeks into exile, spread Greek learning through w. Europe and was a considerable factor in the revival of learning (see RENAISSANCE).

MODERN GREECE. For the next three centuries the Christian powers, particularly Venice, Austria, and Russia, warred intermittently with the Turks, and Greece changed hands several times. In 1718, by the terms of the treaty of Passarowitz between Turkey, Venice, and Austria, the Turkish Empire was given full possession of Greece. Under Turkish rule, Greece was partitioned into districts, each ruled by an autocratic governor. The Turkish administration of Greece was rigid. Except for the *klephts* (q.v.), brigands who lived in the mountains and waged unceasing guerrilla warfare against the Turks, the Greek population was prostrated under the alien tyranny. Only the *klephts,* together with some few Greek pirates on the Ægean Sea, kept the spirit of Greek independence alive.

In the latter 18th century, Greek nationalism began to revive. The sentiment was considerably aided by Russia, which continually incited the Greek Christians, Russian coreligionists, to revolt. In 1769 the Russian count Aleksei Orlov landed a Russian fleet in the Morea and led an unsuccessful Greek revolt. Later, the influence of the French Revolution found a ready acceptance by Greek patriots, who began to plan for a major rebellion. A literary revival heralded the spread of nationalism; particularly notable was the philological work of the Greek scholar Adamantios Coray who created modern written Greek and gave to modern Greece its method of literary expression. A great secret society, the

Greek Govt. Office of Information

Above: A Greek farmer ploughing on a farm in the plains of Thessaly, eastern Greece.
Right: A woman spinning thread on a street in one of the older sections of Athens.

Philikê Hetæria (Gr., "Friendly Association"), was founded in 1815 to prepare for the coming revolution, and collected funds and arms through its centers in the Balkan and E. Mediterranean regions. In 1821 Alexander Ypsilanti, an aide-de-camp of the Russian czar Alexander I, and head of the Hetæria, entered Jassy, the capital of Moldavia (then Turkish territory), with a small force and proclaimed the independence of Greece. Ypsilanti's revolt ended in disaster a few months later, because the czar refused to aid a revolutionary movement. However, following Ypsilanti's abortive attempt, a general uprising occurred in the Morea under the leadership of Archbishop Germanos of Patras.

In the first phase, 1821 to 1824, of the war for Greek independence, the Greeks fought alone, aided by money and volunteers from other European countries, where the Greek cause had aroused a great deal of sympathy. Notable among the volunteers was the English poet, Lord Byron, who died in Greece. Among the leaders of the Greeks were Marco Bozzaris, Theodoros Koloktrones, Alexandros Mavrokordatos, and Andreas Vokos Miaoules. The Turkish sultan Mahmud II, at last, in 1824, asked for aid from Mehemet

Ali (q.v.), the pasha of Egypt, who agreed to help Turkey in return for the grant of control of Crete and other Turkish possessions should he quell the rebellion. The Egyptian troops pushed their way up the Morea and, by 1826, the entire southern peninsula was in their hands. The Greeks suffered from political as well as military weakness because of factional strife among their leaders. A temporary conciliation was effected in 1827 and a new republican constitution was approved in that year by the national assembly, which elected the Russian-Greek statesman Count Ioannes Kapodistrias the first president of the Greek republic. Party quarrels, however, began again almost immediately after this short-lived truce.

In 1827, conscious of the strategic position of Greece in the continent of Europe, the great European powers agreed, after several conferences, on military intervention in behalf of the Greeks; they were, moreover, fearful of Mehemet Ali's potential menace to them should he receive further Mediterranean territory. France, Great Britain, and Russia first demanded an armistice, which the Porte, the Turkish government, refused. The powers then sent naval forces to Greece. The presence of the naval forces, and the efforts of Russia, in particular, forced the Porte to accept a settlement. In 1829, by the Treaty of Adrianople, ending the Russo-Turkish War (1828–29), which had grown out of the Greek revolution and Russia's own aspirations in southeastern Europe, the defeated Porte consented to whatever arrangements the European powers would make for Greece. In 1830, however, France, Great Britain, and Russia issued the London Protocol, negating the Greek republic and constitution, and declaring Greece an autonomous kingdom under their united protection. The territory of the kingdom was defined as considerably less than the Greeks had expected, the northern frontier being set only slightly north of the Gulf of Corinth.

A period of great civil unrest followed the end of the War of Independence. Factional strife persisted, and the Greeks, who envisioned their renascent country as commensurate with their ancient Hellas, objected strenuously to the diminution of their territory. Prince Leopold of Saxe-Coburg (later Leopold I of Belgium) declined the throne of so small and poor a kingdom, and Kapodistrias governed in so dictatorial a fashion that he was assassinated in 1831; civil war then broke out. At length, in 1832, Otho, the second son of King Louis I of Bavaria, accepted the throne offered him by the European powers and in the following year was crowned as Otto I, King of the Hellenes.

Fully as complicated as the political situation was the economic condition of Greece, poverty-stricken to the point of financial collapse. The public treasury in 1832 contained about $300. The three powers therefore jointly lent the new country 60 million francs

(about $12,000,000), and the loan became one of the pre-eminent factors in the relations of Greece to the great powers; indeed, Britain had refused to contribute its third of the loan unless the British nomination of Otho as king were acceptable. The kingdom was never able fully to repay its foreign loans and was forced to borrow increasing sums, thus giving its creditors a reason for interfering in Greek internal affairs. By the end of the 19th century, Greece was forced to agree to complete foreign control over all its financial affairs.

The political reorganization of Greece was undertaken by a Bavarian regency, Otto being only seventeen years of age at his accession to the throne. The Bavarian regents denied the Greeks a constitution, burdened them with excessive taxation, and tried to set up a centralized bureaucracy. Greek resentment culminated in a bloodless revolution in 1843; the king was compelled to dismiss his Bavarian advisers and grant the country a constitution which established a bicameral legislature, although it did not restore the local self-government which was a tradition in Greece. Popular discontent with Otto increased in 1854, when the king, against the will of his people, approved the British and French occupation of the Peiræus (the seaport of Athens) to prevent a Greco-Russian alliance during the Crimean War (1854–56). In 1862 part of the Greek army revolted against Otto, and he was deposed by a national assembly in the same year with the approval of the powers. A national plebiscite chose Prince Alfred, second son of Queen Victoria of England, as king, but the British government rejected the offer and nominated Prince William George, the second son of King Christian IX of Denmark. The prince being acceptable to the Greeks, he was crowned George I (q.v.) in 1863. To demonstrate its approval, the British ceded the Ionian Islands, a British protectorate since 1815, to the reconstituted monarchy. In the following year, a new, more democratic constitution granted universal male suffrage and a unicameral legislature, the Boule.

During the last decades of the 19th century, the major portion of Greek foreign policy was devoted to expanding the territory of the kingdom. Following the defeat of Turkey in the Russo-Turkish War (1877–78), the Congress of Berlin, in 1878, recommended that Turkey readjust the northern frontier of Greece. Turkey refused, and Greece declared war (1878). The great powers, however, intervened again before major hostilities began,

Greek Govt. Office of Information

Girls in southern Greece carrying baskets of grapes at harvest time

and recommended that Turkey award Thessaly and part of Epirus to Greece. Turkey refused, however, to give up all the stipulated territory. In 1885 Eastern Rumelia revolted against Turkish rule and it was incorporated into Bulgaria. Greece was at once aroused into militant activity, demanding that Turkey adhere to the territorial recommendations of 1878. Again, the powers forced Greece to disarm, this time by blockading the main Greek ports until Greece complied. The annexation of Macedonia and Crete then became the object of Greek agitation for territorial expansion. A secret military society, the *Ethniké Hetæria,* was founded in 1894 to foment insurrection in these Turkish provinces. In 1896 the Cretans revolted against their rulers and Greece came to their aid. Though the powers requested the withdrawal of Greek forces from Crete and declared the island autonomous, the military party of Greece, then in control of the government, refused. Some months later (1897), members of the *Ethniké Hetæria* attacked Turkish posts in Macedonia, inciting Turkey to declare war, a conflict for which Greece was in no way prepared. After several weeks

of fighting, the Greek army became a panic-stricken mob, fleeing before the Turkish troops. Total disaster was prevented by action of the powers, and Russia demanded that the Turks cease fighting. Greece, following this episode, was required to pay Turkey a large indemnity, adding to the precarious state of Greek finances and giving the European powers added control as the Greek foreign debt increased. In 1898 Turkey was compelled by the powers to withdraw all its forces from Crete; Prince George, the second son of George I, was appointed high commissioner of Crete under the protection of the powers. For the next ten years, Crete was shaken by internal disputes based, mainly, on the refusal of the powers to permit union with Greece. Disagreements between Prince George and Eleutherios Venizelos (q.v.), the pro-Greek political leader of Crete, led the Prince to resign in 1906. Two years later the Cretan assembly proclaimed the long-desired union. The powers reluctantly withdrew their forces of occupation from the island and, in 1912, Cretan representatives sat for the first time in the Greek legislature.

Meanwhile, the question of Macedonia was

becoming more complicated, for Greece was not the only Balkan country desiring that region. Rising currents of nationalism in the Balkans, particularly in Serbia, Bulgaria, and Romania, were considerably stimulated by the gradual disintegration of the Turkish Empire, now so decadent and weak that it was called the "Sick Man of Europe". During most of the 19th century, the emerging Balkan states maintained friendly relations with each other because of their mutual offensive against Turkey. They formed alliances, and a Balkan Confederation was in prospect. The disposition of Macedonia, however, aroused bitter disagreement. Conflicting political ambitions began to emphasize religious differences between Moslems and Christians and disputes among the various Balkan peoples (see BALKAN PENINSULA). A series of violent, internecine battles took place throughout Macedonia. In 1903 a Bulgarian insurrection in Macedonia broke out, the rebels declaring for union with Bulgaria. Greece resolved covertly to aid Turkey, encouraging Greek guerrillas to cross the border and attack Bulgarians and Romanians in Macedonia. Turkey determined to quash the revolt in 1912, and Turkish troops marched against the armed partisans of Macedonia. At this move, Greece, Bulgaria, Serbia, and Montenegro laid aside their quarrels and, forming military alliances, declared war on Turkey (see BALKAN WARS). Turkey was completely defeated in the first Balkan War (1912-13). By the terms of the Treaty of London, Turkey relinquished all claims to Crete and all its European territory, except for a small area including Istanbul. Dissension between the Balkan allies concerning the disposition of the former Turkish territory, however, led to the second Balkan War, with Greece and Serbia fighting Bulgaria. Bulgaria was defeated in a month. By the Treaty of Bucharest (1913), Greece almost doubled its area and population, being awarded the most valuable regions of Macedonia and Thrace, including Salonika.

Exhausted by the Balkan Wars, Greece proclaimed its neutrality when World War I began in 1914. Strict neutrality, however, was impossible. King Constantine I (q.v.), who had succeeded his father George I in 1913, favored Germany. The leader of the pro-Allied faction was the prime minister Eleutherios Venizelos, the Cretan leader who, after the union with Greece, had become head of the Liberal Party and one of the foremost political figures in Greece. Twice, in 1915, the Venizelos government voted to aid the Allies,

and each time the king ordered new elections. During successive ministries, Constantine treated with both the Allies and the Central Powers, refusing to commit himself openly. In 1916 Venizelos went to Salonika, where he established a Greek government in opposition to Constantine, and was recognized by Great Britain and France. A year later, the Allies forced the king to abdicate in favor of his second son, Alexander. Venizelos returned in triumph, and Greece formally entered the war on the Allied side.

In the postwar territorial settlements, Greece received eastern Thrace from Turkey and the Ægean islands then occupied by Italy. Greece also claimed Smyrna in Asia Minor. Greek troops landed in Smyrna in 1919 and engaged in violent hostilities against the Turkish population and, later, Turkish troops; the Greek and Turkish armies both committed atrocities.

King Alexander died in 1920; his younger brother, Paul, having refused the throne, a plebiscite returned King Constantine despite the disapproval of the Allies. With the resultant loss of Allied support, the Smyrna expedition ended in a complete Greek rout in 1922. The Greek government ordered demobilization, but the army revolted and set up a military dictatorship under Gen. Nicholas Plastiras. Constantine was forced to abdicate and was sent into exile, his eldest son becoming king as George II (q.v.). The king, however, was virtually a puppet in the hands of the army. In 1923, by the terms of the Treaty of Lausanne, Smyrna reverted to Turkey and more than a million Greek residents of Asia Minor were repatriated, as were the Turks resident in Greece.

The Greek refugees as well as the powerful military faction were strongly antiroyalist. Their mutual agitation reached a climax in early 1924, and, after the king had been requested to leave the country, the Boule proclaimed a republic which was ratified by a national plebiscite. Venizelos, though a Liberal, was loyal to the monarchy, and he left Greece. Political dissension and strife followed the proclamation of the republic. In 1925 Gen. Theodoros Pangalos seized control of the government; a year later, as the sole candidate, he was elected president and became dictator of the country. Some months later, Pangalos was overthrown in a *coup d'état* engineered by General Georgios Kondyles, who acted briefly as military dictator. In the general elections a few months later, the Republican majority was so small that a coalition government had to be formed, including the royalist Populist Party. Though the coalition government finished drafting and, in 1927, promulgated the republican constitution begun in 1925, it passed through successive crises and was beginning to lose its control when, in 1928, Venizelos returned to Greek politics. After being appointed prime minister by the president, Admiral Pavlos Koundouriotes, Venizelos reorganized the system of national elections and his party (Liberal Party) won an overwhelming victory in the 1928 general elections.

For the next four years, the prime minister worked to stabilize Greece, both domestically and in its foreign relations. In 1928 Greece signed a friendship pact with Italy and, a year later, a pact with Yugoslavia. A treaty with Turkey was signed in 1930, and in the same year negotiations for a Balkan pact (concluded, 1934, between Greece, Turkey, Yugoslavia, and Romania), were begun. Domestically, however, Venizelos met with less success. Though he was a convinced supporter of constitutional monarchy, his patriotism compelled him to support the national republic; thus, both the royalists and the more radical republicans resented him. A grave financial crisis was precipitated in 1932 by the abandonment of the gold standard in Great Britain, for Greece was committed, despite the world monetary crisis of that time, to paying its foreign debts in gold. The desperate financial situation was reflected in the diminished prestige of the Venizelos government and its defeat in the 1932 elections. For the next three years the increasingly strong royalist faction, led by Panages Tsaldares (1868–1936), and the Venizelists struggled for control of the government. A large part of the army, strongly republican, revolted in 1935 against the rising current of royalism. The rebellion was quelled by Gen. Kondyles, the leader of the rival military faction, and he assumed dictatorial powers for the second time. Royalist military leaders forced the resignation of Prime Minister Tsaldares who, though a royalist, had promised to defend the republic. Kondyles then influenced the Boule to vote for a restoration of the monarchy, and a plebiscite, organized and directed by the Kondyles government, sustained the vote. The republican constitution of 1927 was set aside, and a revised version of the monarchical constitution framed in 1911 was declared in force. George II was restored to the throne in late 1935. The political scene was further complicated by the deaths of Kondyles, Venizelos, and Tsaldares during the ensuing six months. In 1936 General Joannes Metaxas, who led the Free Opinion Party and had the support of the army, took the situation in hand. By means of a *coup d'état* (August), he made himself dictator and proclaimed a state of martial law. The Metaxas dictatorship imposed a rigid press censorship, abolished political parties, and countenanced no opposition.

In 1939, as a result of the Italian occupation of Albania, the safety of Greece against Italian aggression was guaranteed by France and Great Britain. Despite these assurances, Greece was attacked by Italian troops advancing from Albania soon after the beginning of World War II. The Greek army, however, was unexpectedly successful against the Italian troops. By December, 1940, the Greeks had driven the invaders from Greece and were in possession of a fourth of Albania. A complete Italian rout was averted by the arrival, in April, 1941, of German troops, which overcame Greek resistance. Greece was forced to sign an armistice on April 23 and the Germans entered Athens four days later. The Greek government was in a state of collapse, Metaxas having died in January and his successor, Alexander Korizis, having committed suicide at the advent of the Germans. A Nazi-controlled government was established at Athens, under Gen. Georgios Tsolakoglou. King George fled to Crete and, after the German occupation of that island, established a government-in-exile first in Cairo and, later, in London.

Greece suffered enormously from the German occupation; famine and inflation were rife by late 1943. An intense guerrilla warfare was waged by many organized resistance groups throughout the country. Of these groups, the largest, estimated at from 60 to 90% of the population, was the leftist E.A.M. (Gr. *Ethniko Apeleftherotiko Metopo,* "National Liberation Front"), a combination of many political and other organizations, notably trade unions. The E.A.M. had its own army, the E.L.A.S. (Gr. *Ethnikos Laikos Apeleftherotikos Stratos,* "National Popular Liberation Army"). Less effective was the E.D.E.S. (Gr. *Ethnikos Dimokratikos Ellinikos Syndesmos,* "National Democratic Greek Union"), a resistance organization with a more conservative political program. In late 1943, following the Allied invasion of Italy and the prospect of the liberation of Greece, the E.A.M. and E.D.E.S. began to fight each other for the eventual control of the country.

The British first gave their support to the dominant E.A.M., but later, fearful of the Communist domination of that organization, they strongly supported the E.D.E.S. The strife was only partially lessened by a conference in Lebanon, in May, 1944, during which a coalition government for Greece was agreed upon.

In October, 1944, the German army withdrew from Greece, and the new government, which had been temporarily located in Italy, entered Athens on October 18 to resolve the vast problems which awaited it. Georgios Papandreou, the prime minister, then ordered the E.L.A.S. to disband and disarm. The E.L.A.S. leaders refused to do so. Tension increased, and the British brought in reinforcements for their own troops in Athens. Civil war between the E.L.A.S. and the government forces began in Athens in December, following an E.L.A.S. demonstration in which the Athenian police fired on the demonstrators. The E.L.A.S. controlled all of Greece except for a British-patrolled sector of Athens; the British aided the government forces, which gained military superiority. In December, 1944, Archbishop Damaskinos was installed as regent of Greece pending a plebiscite to determine the state of the monarchy.

In February, 1945, the E.L.A.S. finally agreed to a truce, which was signed at Varkiza, near Athens. In return for the dissolution of its army, the E.A.M. was promised freedom to engage in political activity and a nonpolitical Greek army. In October, 1945, Greece became a charter member of the United Nations. The nominal cessation of the civil war had little effect on the desperate economic situation.

The first Greek postwar general elections were held in March, 1946. The result of the elections, a victory for the royalist Populist Party, was bitterly contested by the E.A.M., which claimed that the election proceedings had been irregular. The plebiscite on Sept. 1, 1946, again returned George II to the throne. A few months later (April, 1947) George died and was succeeded by his brother, Paul I.

The increasing strength of the insurgent Communist forces in N. Greece became a source of concern to the Greek government, which claimed that the guerrillas were receiving aid from Albania, Bulgaria, and Yugoslavia, three countries within the sphere of influence of the Soviet Union. The differences between these three countries and Greece were aggravated by their respective claims to territory lying along their common borders. By

the terms of the peace treaties drafted at the Paris Peace Conference of 1946, Greece received the Dodecanese Islands from Italy and reparations of $62,500,000 from Bulgaria.

In February, 1947, Great Britain, unable because of economic difficulties to extend further aid to Greece, asked the United States to assume British obligations to the beleaguered Greek regime. U.S. President Harry S. Truman approved the British appeal and, enunciating the so-called Truman Doctrine of stopping the advance of communism, obtained in May a large appropriation to subsidize Greece. American aid, however, did not alleviate the political disharmony and economic helplessness of Greece. Meanwhile, the Greek parliament, backing the "Enosis" (union with Greece) movement on Cyprus, requested that Great Britain relinquish control over the island.

In January, 1948, a group of American army officers arrived in Greece to advise the government forces. Throughout 1948 a stream of military supplies and relief supplies for Greek civilians was poured into Greece by the United States. Nearly a half-billion dollars was expended by the beginning of 1949, and additional funds were furnished the government through the European Recovery Program (q.v.) for reconstruction of housing, roads, and bridges, and for food and clothing supplies for the indigent Greek population. Government forces conducted a strong offensive against rebel positions during the spring and summer of 1948. However, the rebels succeeded in holding their chief strongholds, especially those in the mountainous areas along the N. frontier. Several of the rebels' major defense bastions in the Grammos Mts. were captured by government troops in the summer of 1949. In August President Truman, reporting on results of the Truman Doctrine, declared that Greek rebel casualties had exceeded 7000 in the period since the program was instituted. The rebel leadership proclaimed on October 16 that military operations against the government had been halted "to avoid the total destruction of Greece".

Rehabilitation of the Greek economy progressed steadily following the civil war. By the end of 1950 funds allocated to Greece under the European Recovery Program totaled almost $400 million and the country's rate of industrial production was nearly 90 percent of the rate prevailing in 1939. Restoration of diplomatic relations with Yugoslavia, which had previously withdrawn from the Soviet bloc of states, was one of the main developments in the realm of foreign affairs during 1950. Toward the close of the year the Greek government assigned an infantry battalion to duty with the U.N. forces in Korea. The Council of the North Atlantic Treaty Organization (q.v.) voted in October, 1951, to allow Greece and Turkey to become signatories of the treaty.

Governmental instability, resulting largely from the multiplicity of political parties, dominated the Greek domestic scene until late in 1952. In the November election of that year the Greek Rally Party, a right-wing group headed by Field Marshal Alexander Papagos, won a parliamentary majority (238 out of 300 seats). A new cabinet, with Papagos as premier, assumed office on Nov. 19.

On Feb. 28, 1953, Greece, Turkey, and Yugoslavia signed a five-year treaty of "friendship and collaboration". The treaty contained provisions for mutual-defense measures. In April the government, in an effort to lessen inflationary pressures in the economy, devaluated the currency by 50 percent.

Taking steps to strengthen further the ties established under the 1953 treaty, Greece, Turkey, and Yugoslavia signed (Aug. 9, 1954) a twenty-year mutual-defense pact patterned after the North Atlantic Treaty. On Aug. 20 the Greek government formally requested the United Nations to arrange for a plebiscite in Cyprus on the issue of union with Greece. Strongly opposed by Great Britain, the Greek request was tabled by the Political Committee of the U.N. General Assembly on Dec. 14. On Aug. 29, 1955, Greece, Great Britain, and Turkey opened talks on the Cyprus issue. Greece demanded self-determination for the Cyprians, Turkey insisted on retention of the status quo as the best guarantee of the future interests of the large Turkish minority on Cyprus, and Great Britain offered to institute a program leading to Cyprian self-rule. The resultant deadlock was attended (Sept. 6) by an anti-Turkish incident in Greece and violent anti-Greek riots in Turkey. In protest, Greece subsequently refused to participate in N.A.T.O. defense maneuvers. Premier Papagos died in October. He was succeeded by Constantin Karamanlis, minister of public works.

On Jan. 4, 1956, Premier Karamanlis announced the formation of a new right-wing party, called the National Radical Union. The latter replaced the Greek Rally Party, which had disintegrated after Papagos' death. In parliamentary elections held on Feb. 19 the National Radical Union won 161 out of 300 seats, though the Democratic Union, a coalition of seven opposition parties, received a majority of the votes cast.

Greek resentment at British policy in Cyprus was climaxed (May 9) by anti-British rioting in Salonika and Athens. Three persons were killed and 124 were injured in the disorders. Foreign Minister Spyros Theotokis was forced to resign on May 28 because his Cyprus policy was regarded as too moderate. He was replaced by Agriculture Minister Evangelos Averoff. In December Premier Karamanlis visited Yugoslavia and reaffirmed the Greek-Yugoslav defensive alliance.

GREEK ART AND ARCHITECTURE, the art and architecture produced in Greece and the Greek provinces from about 900 B.C. until sometime after the destruction of Corinth, in 146 B.C., when Greece became a Roman province. The Greek was the first integrated national art to appear in Europe, and has influenced the whole development of art and architecture in the Western world and, to a lesser degree, in the Orient. Few original Greek art works and buildings were known to the modern world until the liberation of Greece from Turkey, between 1821 and 1831, stimulated extensive archeological research. Before that time Greek art was known principally from statues found in Italy, the majority of which were Roman copies of lost Greek originals; Greek architecture was known only from a few ruins, the majority of which were in territory controlled by the Turks and not easily accessible to Europeans. Some gems engraved with copies of earlier Greek works also existed, but in these the representations were altered to suit the shape of the stone. From these two sources, artists of the Renaissance (q.v.) and of the Greek revival period of the 18th and 19th centuries drew inspirations for their attempts to recapture the classical spirit.

The Archaic Period. Beginning about 900 B.C., when the Ægean civilization fell before the successive waves of Dorian invaders, this period lasted until the Persian Wars of 490 B.C. The culture of the Dorians was considerably less developed than that of the older Ægean civilization. In place of the elaborate golden cups found in the tombs of Mycenæ in Argolis (see ÆGEAN CIVILIZATION), and the highly developed frescoes and sculptures of Knossos (q.v.), the earliest Archaic Greek works are stiff and unanimated, derived from the Egyptian sculpture of the Pharaohs, which were carved from hard stone and were therefore rigid in form (see EGYPTIAN ARCHITECTURE AND ART). Typical of such early work is the "Apollo of Tenea" (Glyptothek, Munich), which resembles the Old Kingdom statues of the Nile valley but has a grace which is lacking in their massiveness and formalization. Another early work is the columnlike "Hera of Samos" (Louvre, Paris), which, although primitive and static, conveys an impression of power and dignity. Decoration on the pottery of the Ægean civilization had displayed highly organized forms, based upon marine and plant life, but the earliest Greek vases, known as "Dipylon" ware from the name of Athenian cemetery where they were found, employ a simple use of geometric decoration.

The faces represented in sculptures of this period display only one expression, a stereotyped smile, but the artists of the 6th century portrayed differences of feeling in the faces of their statues, particularly in the series of statuettes of girls, known as *Korai* (National Museum, Athens). These statuettes were colored and sometimes gilded and encrusted with precious stones. In a bronze figure of a girl (British Museum, London) by Antenor, the pupils of the eyes are represented by diamond chips.

The first typically Greek religious architecture appeared in the 6th century B.C., as the Dorian civilization became well-established. Some of the survivors of the earlier civilization, the Ionians, apparently migrated toward the east and came under Phenician and other Oriental influences. Ionic architecture of the 6th century B.C. is exemplified by the treasury of Cnidus, restored by French archeologists at Delphi, where the capitals of the caryatids, figures of women used as supporting columns, are carved with elaborate reliefs. The Ionic capital (see COLUMN), developed slowly and in its beginnings showed typical Assyrian motives.

The Doric style, which derived from the remnants of Ægean architecture, may be seen in its earliest form in the Heræum at Olympia. This temple originally had columns of wood which were later replaced by stone. The combination of the Ionic and Doric styles, as in the Propylæa or gateway of the Acropolis (q.v.) at Athens, did not develop until after the Persian Wars, when the two peoples had intermingled.

The sculpture on the early Doric temples was usually of crude workmanship, cut in soft stone and painted with bright colors. The muscular development of the heroes who appear upon these temples is exaggerated probably because the Dorians identified themselves with the legendary figure of Hercules. Not until fairly late in the Archaic period did sculptors start to make use of hard marble in place of the softer limestone previously employed. About the same time, bronze, which had been used for small sculptures from an early date, was first employed for life-size and heroic figures. An outstanding example of such late Archaic work is the "Charioteer of Delphi" (Delphi Museum), the only figure surviving from a lost group. In this work, stylization had not yet been subordinated to a more realistic treatment.

Most of the paintings of the Archaic period have been destroyed. Walls were apparently decorated with murals in broad horizontal bands, depicting such traditional scenes as the Trojan War and battles between Amazons and giants. Vase paintings, from which most modern knowledge of Archaic painting is derived, were also divided into horizontal bands. Outstanding among such vases is the "François Vase" (Archaeological Museum, Florence) by Clitias, circumscribed by five bands with representations of more than two hundred and fifty figures in a series of ten legendary processional scenes; the figures are formalized and their attitudes are governed by the shape of the vessel. One of the supreme artistic survivals of the period is an unbanded vase painting on the inside of a *cylix,* or shallow drinking vessel. This work, "Dionysus Sailing the Sea" (Alte Pinakothek, Munich) by the painter Execias, shows Dionysus in a dolphin-prowed sailing boat around which seven dolphins play; a vine grows up the mast of the boat, filling the top of the composition with leaves and grapes. The figures in this cylix are as severely formalized as those of the "François Vase", but none are distorted. In such ceramics the background was always the pinkish-yellow of the clay, and the enamel used to outline the figures was black. Notable among ceramic painters of the Archaic period are Amasis, a contemporary of Execias, and Epicetetus, who worked toward the beginning of the 5th century B.C.

The Attic Period. Sometimes called the Periclean Age, from Pericles (q.v.), who ruled from about 460 until 429 B.C. (see GREECE: *History*), this period dates from the Persian Wars of 480 and 470 B.C. until about 320 B.C. In the earlier part of the period the making of painted vases increased rapidly, chiefly in Athens. The black-figured vases of the Archaic period were replaced by vases carrying figures in red against a black background. The great master of the period was Euphronius,

Metropolitan Museum of Art

GREEK ART. *Left: Copy of a statuette of the "Koraï" series, 6th century B.C. Right: Roman copy of the "Diadumenus" of Polyclitus, the famous sculptor of Sicyon.*

two of whose works are the cylix showing "The Cattle of Geryon" (Alte Pinakothek, Munich) and the "Theseus Cylix" (Louvre, Paris). Other vase painters competed with this master, and one of them, Euthymides, went so far as to inscribe upon one of his works "This outdoes Euphronius".

Some of the vases of the Attic period are generally accepted as copies of the paintings of Polygnotus (q.v.) and his school. Such is the vase (National Museum, Athens) showing Hercules delivering Theseus from Hades, a copy of a fresco by Micon, one of the pupils of Polygnotus. According to the accounts of the ancient writers, Polygnotus employed deep, pure colors in his painting, and the makers of some of the later vases, in trying to achieve the brilliance of his colors, used an enamel base beneath their colors, which were mostly blue, carmine, and ochre. An Etruscan copy of his "Combat between Athenians and Amazons" (Archaeological Museum, Florence), from a sarcophagus, gives some indication of his formal manner of composition.

By the end of the Attic period Greek artists in all mediums had accepted the dictum of Aristotle that all art is imitation. As a result the more closely a work resembled the model, the more highly it was valued. Cimon of Cleonæ is said to have made the first attempts at perspective drawing, and the view that art should copy nature found expression in the legend that a painting by Zeuxis (q.v.) depicted a plate of grapes with such fidelity that birds attempted to peck at them.

Because the sculptors of the Periclean Age became famous through the writings of later historians, their true stature as artists is problematical. No original exists of the masterpiece of Myron (q.v.), the "Discobolus" (q.v.). Three Roman copies are extant in the Vatican Museum, the Palazzio Lancelotti, Rome, and the British Museum, London; the copies differ in quality, and no one knows which is closest to the original. The modern reconstruction of the Discobolus (Terme Museum, Rome), is said to combine the best points of all three copies. Copies of the work of Polyclitus (q.v.) of Sicyon indicate that he, like Myron, intended his works to be cast in bronze; both artists employed the same clustering of curls close to the head, and a marble copy of the "Diadumenus" of Polyclitus (Museum of Madrid) was evidently intended to include a ribbon carried between the figure's hands, a device which could be cast in metal but which could not easily be carved in stone.

The "Athena Lemnia" (body in Dresden Museum, head in Bologna Museum) is generally supposed to be a marble copy of a bronze original by Phidias (q.v.), who supervised the construction of the Parthenon (q.v.) at Athens. The sculptures from the pediment, the Elgin marbles (q.v.) now in the British Museum, were probably not of his designing. Phidias' most celebrated sculptures, the colossal statues of Athena in the Parthenon and Zeus in the temple at Olympia (q.v.), made of gold and ivory and brightly colored, have disappeared; these works probably did not

have the simple dignity and massive quality which distinguish the pediment figures of the Parthenon.

The masterpiece of Attic architecture is the Parthenon itself. Its Doric columns, originally designed to be made of wood, were adapted to marble and could be made slender without loss of strength. The entasis or swelling of the columns was only one of the minute perfections of the architecture, for the proportions of the various parts were calculated with a nicety far above that of the better preserved Theseum. Another outstanding temple of the Acropolis is the Erechtheum (q.v.), which employed refined Ionic columns and also made use of the earlier architectural design (as in the treasury of Cnidus) of six caryatids as supports for the entablature (q.v.) of the south porch. The common practice of the period was to paint all stone buildings, chiefly in red and blue. The colors were originally a method of clarifying the relationship between the various structural masses, but later became purely decorative.

In the 4th century B.C. a considerable amount of building continued throughout Greece and in Asia Minor, especially in the Ionic temples at Miletus and Ephesus. At about the same time, the Corinthian order first appeared on columns, but did not reach its full expression until the Roman architects adopted it.

The Mausoleum (q.v.), a memorial to

GREEK ART. *Left: The "François Vase," from which we have learned much concerning forms in Archaic painting. Right: The head of the "Athena Lemnia," in the Bologna Museum.*

Metropolitan Museum of Art

GREEK SCULPTURE

Above: A Niobid, 4th century B.C., in the Vatican Museum, Rome. Above, right: Sculpture of faun by Praxiteles, about 350 B.C. Right: "Old Market Woman," 100 B.C.

Mausolus, King of Caria, and one of the Seven Wonders of the World (q.v.), was erected at Halicarnassus in 353 B.C., and was decorated with sculpture by the most popular artists of the day. The best known of these was Scopas (q.v.), the sculptor of the carvings on the eastern façade (British Museum, London). Carved in high relief, his work shows a vigor of action very different from the static dignity of the sculptures on the pediment of the Parthenon.

Scopas and his followers are said to have originated the figures known as *Niobids,* depicting the children of Niobe fleeing from the arrows of Apollo and Diana. A damaged copy **of** a single Niobid (Vatican Museum, Rome),

Metropolitan Museum of Art

GREEK ARCHITECTURE

Top: A model of the Parthenon, which stood on the Acropolis at Athens, an outstanding example of Attic architecture. Left: Drawing of the Mausoleum at Halicarnassus, one of the Seven Wonders of the World. Above: A section of molding from the Erechtheum.

with the sculptured robe of the fleeing child billowing as if made of cloth, indicates the realistic trend of Greek art of the late Attic period.

The sculptor Praxiteles (q.v.) flourished toward the end of the Attic period, about 350 B.C. His influence as a maker of prettified nude statues was to last for the remainder of the time that Greek art was a national expression and was to be carried on as an ideal by the Romans. Unlike the majority of the famous Greek sculptors, Praxiteles is known by at least three original works, including "Mercury and Bacchus" (Olympia Museum), discovered in the Old Temple of Juno in 1877. The overpretty face of Mercury, the weak-

ness of composition evident in the placing of the figure of the infant, and the lack of vigor in the whole, are indications of the decadence which was overtaking Greek art.

The Hellenistic Period. Continuing until shortly after the subjection of Greece by the Romans in the 2nd century B.C., this period was dominated in sculpture by the pupils and successors of Praxiteles who, although possessing great technical mastery, tried to obtain effects of realism for which their materials, marble and bronze, were unsuited. The court sculptor of Alexander the Great, Lysippus (q.v.), is credited with having carved many likenesses of the king, although no original work by him is known. He probably introduced the late Greek practice of placing a small and sensitive head upon a heavily developed muscular body. One of the pupils of Praxiteles, Euphranor of Corinth, is supposed to have carved the lost original of the "Apollo Belvedere", a copy which was admired as one of the greatest of Greek statues by the artists of the Renaissance and of the later Greek revival. This marble copy is in the Vatican Museum, Rome; it has been much restored and a marble cloak has been added.

The influence of Praxiteles, and particularly of his "Cnidian Aphrodite" (copy in the Vatican Museum), did not immediately become apparent, and for a while Venus continued to be represented in draperies, generally falling from the waist, as in the "Venus de Milo" (Louvre, Paris). This statue was found on the Island of Melos, in 1822, in a fragmentary condition. A portion of the pediment bore the name of the sculptor, Alexandros, but this fragment, together with the arms of the statue, found at the same time, later was lost. Other similar statues indicate that the goddess was represented holding up her drapery with one hand and extending the other to clasp the apple awarded to her by Paris.

The "Victory of Samothrace" or "Winged Victory" (Louvre, Paris), carved by an unnamed artist at the beginning of the 2nd century B.C., may be more beautiful in its present mutilated condition than it was originally. It now possesses a vigor of movement, derived from the loose robes streaming backward as if blown by the wind, but, judging from Roman copies of similar works and other "Victories" engraved on gems, it was probably originally encumbered by wreaths and torches and lacked its present dignity.

In the 2nd century the manufacture of copies of earlier works was a flourishing industry in Athens, and such reproductions were exported widely. An example of such journeyman work is the "Venus de Medici" (Uffizi Gallery, Florence), which was founded upon the "Cnidian Aphrodite" of Praxiteles but instead of having the goddess coming from her bath depicted her rising from the sea. Works of this character were extremely popular, and their success was judged primarily by their naturalism.

A typically realistic work of this century is the "Old Market Woman" (Metropolitan Museum of Art, New York), a genre work which depicted an everyday character rather than an idealized portrait of a god or hero.

Attention was concentrated upon the subject rather than upon use of the medium, as in the torso of the "Cyrenean Venus" (Terme Museum, Rome), which is a minutely accurate presentation of the body of a beautiful young woman. Even in imaginative works the aim of the artist became purely representational, and 2nd-century works such as the twin statues of centaurs (Capitoline Museum, Rome), lacked the severe simplicity of such Archaic works as the 8th-century horse (Metropolitan Museum of Art, New York).

In the Hellenistic era art became purely illustrative. Lysistratus, the brother of Lysippus, was famed for his skill in making casts of the faces of prominent men, and acquired his artistic reputation for an ability which was purely mechanical. Portraits in marble, such as that of Sophocles (Lateran Museum, Rome), and sculptured story-telling groups became popular. Examples of the anecdotal work of the period are "Hercules with the Stag" (Museum of Palermo), "Boy Strangling a Goose" (Vatican Museum, Rome), and "Cupid and Psyche" (Capitoline Museum, Rome).

The "Allegorical Group of the Nile" (Capitoline Museum, Rome) consisted of sixteen small children, each representing a stage of the river's annual flood, clustered about the body of a recumbent old man; this work set a standard for later Roman work, in which the theme was borrowed for allegorical representations of the Tiber and other rivers.

Under the successors of Alexander the Great and in the early days of the Roman conquest, the art of Greece became separated into various schools, especially those at Alexandria, Pergamum (now Bergama), and Rhodes. The Alexandrian school was responsible for two distinct types of sculpture: statues of Venus carved in a style derived from that of Praxiteles, with increased emphasis upon the sensual qualities of the model; and small, grotesque bronzes depicting the everyday life of the city, and musicians, dancers, and actors. The Pergamene school was not concerned with such small sculpture, preferring larger and more heroic subjects. After the defeat of the Gauls about 230 B.C. the sculptors of Pergamum carved many figures of the courageous barbarian warriors. The most famous of these statues, the "Dying Gaul" (Capitoline Museum, Rome), was formerly believed to represent a dying gladiator. Other examples of Pergamene sculpture which survive, in a mutilated condition, are the reliefs from the Altar of Jupiter (Kaiser Friedrich Museum, Berlin) in the Acropolis of Pergamum; these reliefs are melodramatic and vigorous representations of battles between gods and giants, and are among the finest works of the late Greek period. The sculpture of Rhodes tended to be involved and pretentious and produced typically exaggerated works such as the "Laocoön" (q.v.), in the Vatican Museum, and the copy of the "Farnese Bull" (see FARNESE ART). The Laocoön was carved by Agesander and his sons Polydorus and Athenodorus. The group, greatly admired by Michelangelo, had an immense effect upon later esthetic criticism, particularly in 19th-century Germany.

Among the most pleasing works of the Hellenistic period are the terra-cotta figurines (q.v.), usually associated with Tanagra. Their attraction lies in their unpretentious realism. Examples of these figurines are to be found in many museums.

Very little painting of the Hellenistic period has survived, but copies, either in fresco or transferred to the medium of mosaic, convey an approximate impression of the originals. Outstanding among these copies is the mosaic of "The Battle of Issus" (National Museum, Naples), found in Pompeii. This picture makes no use of perspective, and in it the illusion of distance is contrived by the arrangement of the soldiers' spears, which point at Alexander the Great at different angles.

The architecture of the Hellenistic period is less distinguished than that of the earlier Greeks, and is generally a repetition of motives which had already been used. The Corinthian capital became popular in such Greco-Roman buildings as the Temple of the Olympian Zeus, at Athens, which was begun in 174 B.C. This temple illustrates the difference between the grandiose conceptions of the Romans and the simple Greek ideals which produced the Parthenon.

From coins and gems of the period some idea of various lost works of art can be obtained, and from the gems the art of cameo (q.v.) cutting was developed. This art in turn had an effect upon the makers of ceramics, in such works as the Portland Vase (British Museum, London), in which glassy white figures stand in low relief against a blue background.

The Greek Revival. The excavations at Pompeii which began in 1763 encouraged archeological research throughout the countries once occupied by the Romans, and stimulated the artists of the 18th and 19th centuries to employ classic themes. When the Portland Vase was found near Rome about 1770 and was taken to England, the potter Josiah

Wedgwood (q.v.) obtained permission to copy it, and set a fashion for Hellenistic work. Outstanding among the sculptors whom he employed was John Flaxman (q.v.), whose outline designs illustrating the *Iliad* and the *Odyssey* were based upon the designs in Greek vase-paintings. In Italy, Antonio Canova (q.v.) imitated Praxiteles with such success that his contemporaries acclaimed him as the equal of the ancients. During the 19th century, the English sculptor John Gibson, not content with copying the works of the Greeks, tried to return to their fashion of painting works of sculpture, producing tinted statues of Venus and Queen Victoria. In architecture, the style of Greek temples became the accepted design for public buildings, with sculptured façades carved by journeymen after the designs of neo-Grecian sculptors. In more recent times connoisseurs have preferred the works of the Archaic period to those of the Attic and Hellenistic periods which served as models for the artists of the Greek Revival. See REVIVAL.

GREEK CHURCH. See ORTHODOX CHURCH.

GREEK EMPIRE. See BYZANTINE EMPIRE.

GREEK FESTIVALS. See FESTIVALS AND FEASTS: *Ancient Greek Festivals.*

GREEK FIRE, WET FIRE, or SEA FIRE, an inflammable mixture formerly used in warfare which ignited on contact with water. Other liquid incendiaries had long been in use, but the secret of Greek fire was held for many centuries only by the Byzantine Greeks of Constantinople. The composition of Greek fire is not known with certainty, but it was probably composed of easily inflammable materials together with a substance such as lime which evolved enough heat upon reacting with water to ignite the inflammable ingredients.

GREEK GAMES. See GAMES, ANCIENT; ISTHMIAN GAMES; NEMEAN GAMES; OLYMPIAN GAMES; PYTHIAN GAMES.

GREEK LANGUAGE, the language of the people of Greece, embracing the epic, classical, Alexandrine, Roman Byzantine, and modern periods of literature; see GREEK LITERATURE. It is the only known branch of the Hellenic subfamily of the Western division of the Indo-European languages (q.v.; see also LANGUAGE), and is related to the Italic subfamily of languages, including Latin, Oscan, and Umbrian (see ITALIC LANGUAGES). The language spoken by the people of ancient Greece differs in several respects from the language spoken by present-day Greeks, which is known as "Modern Greek". However, both ancient and modern Greek employ the same alphabet, derived from the Phenicians and comprising the twenty-four letters which are listed with their English equivalents in the following table.

Greek		Greek Names	English
A	α	Alpha	a
B	β	Beta	b
Γ	γ	Gamma	g
Δ	δ	Delta	d
E	ε	Epsilon	ĕ
Z	ζ	Zeta	z
H	η	Eta	ē
Θ	θ	Theta	th
I	ι	Iota	i
K	κ	Kappa	k
Λ	λ	Lambda	l
M	μ	Mu	m
N	ν	Nu	n
Ξ	ξ	Xi	x
O	ο	Omicron	ŏ
Π	π	Pi	p
P	ρ	Rho	r
Σ	σ ς	Sigma	s
T	τ	Tau	t
Υ	υ	Upsilon	u, y
Φ	φ	Phi	ph
X	χ	Chi	ch
Ψ	ψ	Psi	ps
Ω	ω	Omega	ō

Ancient Greek. Researches conducted by scholars over several centuries, and based chiefly on the examination of ancient documents and inscriptions, as well as on comments in ancient literary works, indicate that the various dialects which today are known collectively as the Ancient Greek language were in use for some centuries before the era of recorded history. The ancient peoples who migrated from central and northern Asia, to the more fertile lands to the south, settled in various sections of Greece, in each of which a distinct dialect arose; the three main dialects were the Doric, the Æolic, and the Ionic.

The Doric dialect, in some respects the most primitive of the three, was spoken in N. Greece, in the Peloponnesus, on the island of Crete, and also in the Greek colonies in Asia Minor, Sicily, and Italy. The poems of Pindar and most of the works of Theocritus (qq.v.) were written in this dialect. Æolic was spoken principally in the districts of Æolis, Thessaly, and Bœotia. It was the language of the poets Alcæus and Sappho (qq.v.), and three of the idyls of Theocritus. The Ionic dialect was spoken on many of the islands of the Ægean and on the Mediterranean shores of Asia Minor. It had two branches: Old Ionic, or

epic, the literary, highly stylized language known chiefly from its use in the Homeric poems (see HOMER); and New Ionic, the tongue spoken in the Ionic cities of Asia and some islands, and employed in various literary works of the 5th century B.C., notably the writings of Hippocrates and Herodotus.

From the Ionic dialect developed the Attic, the standard form of classical Greek. It was the language of Athens and the surrounding district of Attica, and differed from the other Ionic forms chiefly in its contraction of vowels. Because of the political supremacy of Athens during and after the 4th century B.C., and the dominant role of Athenian art, philosophy, and drama, the Attic dialect superseded all others and became the chief literary language. Its influence was enhanced through its use by the greatest contemporary intellects, including Plato, Æschylus, Euripides, Sophocles, Demosthenes, Xenophon, and Thucydides.

With the conquests of Alexander the Great and the extension of Macedonian rule in the 4th century B.C., there was a shift of population from Greece proper to the new Greek colonies in Asia Minor. In this period, known as the Hellenistic, the Attic dialect, spoken by the educated as well as by the merchants and the mass of emigrants, became the language common to all Asia Minor. As the Greeks mixed with other peoples, certain inevitable linguistic changes took place; Attic became the foundation of a new form of Greek—the *Koinē,* which spread throughout all areas of Greek influence. *Koinē* was the language of the court, and of literature and commerce throughout the Hellenistic empire.

Koinē soon became differentiated into two groups, the literary *Koinē* and the vernacular, or popular tongue. The literary language was spoken and used by the educated upper classes, who until the Roman Conquest were greatly influenced by the philosophers, writers, and orators of the Athenian Golden Age (see GREECE: *Ancient History*), and who sought to keep the language as close as possible to the pure Attic. Nevertheless, their own erudition and usage wrought changes upon the Attic. The musical quality of pure Athenian Attic was lost; vowel values began to be leveled out, and diphthongs to have a single sound.

The vernacular tongue, on the other hand, existed among the masses of the people, who were for the most part culturally undeveloped, and whose speech was uninfluenced by the oratory, theater, and literature of Athens. This popular speech was still crude, and possessed a limited vocabulary, incapable of expressing complex ideas; it was not used by contemporary writers. The Evangelists provided the best existing record of the vernacular, the Greek version of the New Testament. Later followers of the Christian Church, especially those from the upper classes, wrote in the literary language, whch became the official instrument of the Church Fathers; churchmen wrote their theological disputations and carried on their complex, religio-philosophical controversies with the heretics in the richer literary tongue.

During the 2nd century A.D. a group of ultra-conservative scholars advocated an artificial return to the pure Athenian dialect of the 5th and 4th centuries B.C. Despite a few vigorous advocates, notably Galen (q.v.) of Pergamum and Phrynicus of Bithynia, the so-called Atticist movement made no progress; the 600-year-old language of Sophocles and Plato was not revived. The great writers of the 2nd century, including Plutarch, Pausanias, and Lucian, used the literary *Koinē*. Later, with the closing of the Athenian schools of philosophy and the University of Athens (529 A.D.), and the burning of the Alexandrian libraries by the Arabs, even the literary language, which was deviating more and more from the spoken and living vernacular, became confined to the Church, to a few scholars, and the hack writers of the time.

As the Empire suffered further from internal crises, and the central power broke up, Byzantium became divided into small independent states. The literary *Koinē,* which was confined to the great cultural centers, remained static, but the vernacular *Koinē* broke up into many local dialects throughout the Empire, developing further as it was influenced by the migrating peoples in the Near East—the Venetians, Turks, and Romans, among others. The Balkans meanwhile gradually became isolated from the great naval and commercial enterprises of western Europe, which was becoming concerned with the New World.

Modern Greek. During the period following the collapse of the Eastern Roman Empire, and throughout the Byzantine period and the years of Turkish domination, the Greek language remained largely static; the main literature produced was hagiography, theological works, and religious poetry. Toward the end of the 18th century, a rising Greek bourgeoisie, with the beginnings of a national consciousness, began to develop. However, until about 1880 the leaders of this bourgeoisie were mainly shipowners and roving merchants who lived in Greek colonies outside Greece and

based their linguistic as well as their cultural standards on an idealized Athenian heritage. In Greece proper, which remained under Turkish rule, the energies of the people were absorbed by revolutionary activities aimed at national independence. In the 19th century, after freedom had been achieved, the Greeks faced more immediate problems than the linguistic, with the result that no uniform, established language was spoken throughout the new nation.

Late in the 19th century, Greek scholars and writers concerned themselves with a systematization of the popular tongue for purposes of education and communication. The leaders of this widespread movement were known as the "Demotikists", the vernacular language which they propagated being known as the *Demotike*. Prominent among such advocates were the poet Dionysios Solomos (q.v.), the dramatist Ioannis Kambisis (1872–1902), and the philologist Jean Psichari (1854–1929). The principal result of the movement was the creation of a vernacular grammar, and the production of a large body of literary works, based on the achievements, life, and customs of the people. In present-day Greece the vernacular is the chief medium of most Greek novelists and poets.

Opposed to the Demotikists were the advocates of a purified Greek (*Katharevousa*), called the "Purists". These scholars aimed primarily at reawakening the Greek people to a consciousness of their ancient cultural heritage. The Purists disregarded the widespread use of the written and spoken vernacular, espousing an elegant, scholarly, artificial language based on Ancient Greek, and remote from the speech of everyday life. They counseled study of the ancient authors, with emphasis on the traditional stylists and poets. The leading scholars of this movement were various academicians, including several professors of philology at Athens University. Through the campaigns waged by the Purists the government adopted the Purist Greek for all official speeches, correspondence, and publications, and made its use compulsory in all the schools. Purist Greek is also the language of the Greek courts and of most newspapers, excepting certain republican journals.

The Purist and vernacular forms of Modern Greek differ chiefly in that the grammar, orthography, and vocabulary of the former are much closer to Ancient Greek. Phonetically the two are identical, both varying from the Ancient principally in the substitution of stress for pitch in accented syllables, and in the altered pronunciation of diphthongs. In the word *anthropoi* ("men"), for example, the final diphthong *oi* is pronounced in Modern Greek as a single sound, the English long *e;* whereas in Ancient Greek the two letters of the diphthong were pronounced separately.

The principal grammatical differences between Modern and Ancient Greek are in declension and verbal conjugation. In declension, Modern Greek (Purist and vernacular) has abandoned two basic forms used in Ancient Greek: the dual, a form indicating that a noun, pronoun, or adjective refers to two persons or things; and the dative case, which is used only in a few idiomatic expressions. The dual form has also been abolished from verbal conjugation, as have the optative mood, or mood of desire or wish, and the infinitive. In place of the specific verb forms used to denote the various tenses in Ancient Greek, Modern Greek makes extensive use of auxiliary verbs. The Ancient Greek imperative forms have been largely supplanted by the use of an auxiliary with the subjunctive form of the verb.

In vocabulary, Modern Greek vernacular is characterized by the use of a large number of words borrowed directly from foreign languages, especially from Italian, Turkish, and French, and by a great facility for combining with other words. The Purists on the other hand, avoid the use of foreign words, preferring to meet the demand for new words to express new concepts by coining words based on analogous ancient Greek expressions, striving at all times to preserve the ancient Greek forms and idioms.

GREEK LETTER FRATERNITY or SO-CIETY. See Fraternities, Sororities, and Societies.

GREEK LITERATURE, the literature of the Greek-speaking peoples (see Greek Language) from about the second millennium B.C. until the present. This literature developed as a national expression with little outside influence until the Hellenistic period (see below), and had a formative effect upon all succeeding European literature. For additional information on writers whose influence and works are discussed below, see individual biographies on names not followed by dates.

The Early Period. The early inhabitants of Greece, the people of the Ægean and Mycenæan civilizations, possessed an oral literature largely composed of songs about wars, harvests, and funerals, which was taken over by the Hellenes (q.v.) in the second millennium B.C. Comparatively few fragments of these songs exist, but the art of the ballad

singers who celebrated the actions of heroes must have developed from them. Subsequently these folk ballads became the basis of the Greek school of epic poetry. The Greek epic reached its height in the *Iliad* and *Odyssey* (qq.v.) of Homer, composed probably during the 10th century B.C. and written in the dialect of the Greek language later called Ionic. The perfection of the hexameter, the meter in which the epics of Homer were written, indicates that the poems are the culmination rather than the beginning of a literary tradition. The Homeric epics were disseminated by the recitations of professional poets who, in succeeding generations, made alterations in the original text, substituting current phrases for those which had become obsolete. Mythical and heroic events not celebrated in the Homeric works are recounted in extant fragments written by various later anonymous poets.

Not much later than Homer is the contrasting work of the poet Hesiod, whose *Works and Days,* written in the Ionic dialect of Homer with some admixture of Æolic, is the first Greek poem to forsake mythological subject matter in favor of a theme drawn from everyday life, the experiences and thoughts of a Bœotian farmer. The *Theogony,* which is probably later than Hesiod although it has sometimes been attributed to him, is an account of the establishment of order from chaos, and the birth of the gods.

The elegiac couplet or distich became popular throughout Greece during the 7th century B.C., and was used for compositions of all kinds, ranging from dirges to love songs. In the same century occurred the first known use of iambic verse, in which the fables of Æsop were originally written, although the surviving texts are all of a much later date (see Fable).

The lyric (q.v.), which was originally a song to be sung to the accompaniment of the lyre, was developed on the Island of Lesbos where its greatest exponents were Sappho, the only great woman poet of ancient Greece, and the musician Terpander. The lyric reached its height about the middle of the 5th century B.C., in the works of Anacreon and Pindar.

Toward the end of the 5th century B.C. some of the earliest Greek prose works now surviving were produced, the most notable being those on medicine attributed to Hippocrates.

The Attic Period. Overlapping the early period the establishment of tragedy (see Drama: *Greek Drama*) took place in Athens during the 6th century B.C. Æschylus, the first great writer of tragedies, is supposed to have written about ninety plays, of which seven have survived, including the trilogy dealing with the story of Orestes, the *Oresteia.* The second great Greek tragedian was Sophocles, who was noted for his studies of human emotions, particularly in *Œdipus Rex.* The playwright Euripides, a younger contemporary of Sophocles, was recognized as an opponent of the established order in politics and religion.

The greatest of the comic dramatists was Aristophanes, a conservative in politics and religion, whose first comedy, *Daitaleis,* now lost, was produced in 427 B.C. He employed drama as a medium of satire, ridiculing Euripides in the *Frogs* and the philosopher Socrates in the *Clouds.* Later Greek comedy was less satirical; the chief writer of comedies was Menander, whose witty plays exist today only in fragmentary form, although they had a strong influence upon the Latin dramatists of the 3rd and 2nd centuries, notably Plautus and Terence.

One of the earliest historians, Herodotus, writing in the Ionic dialect, gave an account of Greek history from the time of Crœsus to that of Xerxes, explaining historical events in terms of divine justice. Thucydides was the first great Attic prose writer; in his account of the Peloponnesian War he commented on history in political terms. The chief literary works of the soldier-historian Xenophon, *Anabasis* and *Memorabilia,* took up Greek history where Thucydides left off, but lack his power of argument. A later historian, Timæus, wrote a history of Sicily, and is supposed to have introduced the method of reckoning time by the Olympiads (see OLYMPIAD).

Attic prose reached its supreme expression in the works of the Athenian orators. The earliest of those whose works have survived was Antiphon (about 408–411 B.C.), a teacher of rhetoric; he was celebrated for his dignified style as a pleader of murder cases. A simple, forthright style devoid of rhetorical devices was also used by the orator Lysias, who is said to have written a speech for Socrates to use at his trial. The speeches of Isocrates are literary works intended to be read rather than spoken. The full perfection of Greek oratory was achieved in the works of Demosthenes, who employed all the resources of the language in his speeches, which became models for subsequent orators.

Of Greek philosophical writers in the Attic period, the greatest is Plato, who elaborated on the philosophy of Socrates, and expressed the idealism (q.v.) of the ancient world (see

GREEK PHILOSOPHY), in writings acclaimed as stylistically perfect. The philosopher Aristotle, a pupil of Plato, wrote a large number of works concerning logic, metaphysics, ethics, rhetoric, and politics, and consisting mostly of lectures prepared for delivery in his school at Athens. Of his literary criticism only sections on tragedy and poetry have been preserved. Theophrastus, a pupil and successor of Aristotle, is notable as one of the earliest scientists to attempt the classification of plants, although his *Characters,* a minor writing, is better known today than his botanical work.

The Hellenistic Period. Following the conquests of Alexander the Great in the 4th century B.C., Greek culture spread throughout the Near Eastern empire which he established. The most outstanding of the many literary schools which came into being was the Alexandrian school (q.v.), centering at Alexandria where, under the Ptolemies (see PTOLEMY) the greatest library of antiquity was founded; see ALEXANDRIAN AGE. The best Alexandrian poetry was that of Callimachus and his followers, who made many improvements in the use of meter, wrote short stories in verse, and perfected the epigram, which was later adopted by their Roman disciples. Theocritus wrote pastoral poems and was much imitated by his successors. Possibly the most important work of the Hellenistic period was that of the scientific and scholarly writers, particularly the physician Herophilus, the anatomist Erasistratus, and the astronomers Hipparchus and Ptolemy.

Following the conquest of Greece by Rome, in 146 B.C., the Greek historian Polybius wrote the history of that conquest, and a century later Plutarch produced his famous *Parallel Lives,* in which a biography of a celebrated Greek is matched with that of a notable Roman. At about the same time the geographer Strabo compiled his *Geographica,* a systematic account of places, animals, and objects of interest. In the 2nd century A.D., Galen, the greatest of the ancient anatomists, wrote works which laid the foundations of modern medicine.

The early Christian writers who transcribed and compiled the New Testament made use of a Hebraic Greek, a tongue distinct from that employed by the classical Greek writers and their imitators.

The 2nd century A.D. witnessed the beginnings of the Greek novel, notably in the work of the satirist Lucian, author of *Dialogues of the Dead* and *Dialogues of the Gods,* to whom

GREEK LITERATURE

Above: Homer reciting the "Iliad." Above, right: A portrait bust of Thucydides, the first great Attic prose writer. Right: A portrait bust of the orator Demosthenes.

also was credited a narrative work on which the Roman author Apuleius based his work *The Golden Ass.*

Stoic philosophy was represented in the writings of Epictetus and Marcus Aurelius. The Neoplatonists (see NEOPLATONISM) found their chief exponent in Plotinus, whose works in six books were edited by his pupil Porphyry toward the end of the 3rd century.

The finest verse of the Hellenistic period consisted of the epigrams, largely anonymous, contained in the *Greek Anthology* (see ANTHOLOGY), a collection composed of two books compiled in the 10th and 14th centuries A.D. and known respectively as the *Palatine Anthology* and the *Anthologia Planudea.*

The Byzantine Period. From 323 A.D., the beginning of the reign of Constantine the Great, until the disruption of the Eastern Empire in 1453 (see BYZANTINE EMPIRE), Greek literature lacked the homogeneous character of that written in earlier periods, and was strongly influenced by both Latin and Oriental elements. The greater part of the writings are theological, and attack the various heresies (see HERESY) which arose during the first millennium of the Christian Era. Thus St. Athanasius in the 4th century assailed Arianism

(see ARIUS), and later Anastasius of Antioch and Leontius of Byzantium (both fl. 6th century) attacked the Monophysites (q.v.). In the 8th century the last of the great Greek theologians, St. John of Damascus, wrote polemics against the Iconoclasts (see ICONOCLASM); he also wrote one of the earliest books on Christian dogma, *The Fountain of Knowledge.* Symeon Metaphrastes (fl. 10th century) is important as the editor of the *Acts of the Martyrs,* which revised and compared older accounts. Numerous hymns were composed by the early Christian Fathers, particularly by St. Gregory of Nazianzus in the 4th century, and Cosmas of Jerusalem (fl. 8th century). Under religious auspices the writing of secular verse declined but some epigrams written in this period appear in the *Greek Anthology.*

In the 12th century Eustathius of Thessalonica wrote a commentary on the works of Homer. In the following two centuries many commentaries were prepared on the works of classical authors including Hesiod, Pindar, and the Greek tragedians.

The greatest of the Byzantine critics was Photius, whose summaries and extracts of 280 classical works still extant in the 9th century preserved much that might otherwise have been lost.

The Modern Period. With the gradual dissolution of the Eastern Empire following the capture of Constantinople by the forces of the Fourth Crusade (see CRUSADES) in 1204, Greece was invaded by Frankish barons; in turn these Frankish rulers of parts of Greece were conquered by the Turks, and after 1460 Greece became a part of the Ottoman Empire. Little literary work of importance was produced during the years of subjection; all of it is of two types, that in the vernacular, and that written in a literary language based on ancient models. One of the early vernacular works, the anonymous *Chronicle of the Morea,* dating from the 14th century, shows the influence of the Frankish invaders.

Crete was the literary center of Greece during the 16th and 17th centuries, under the Venetians, until the capture of the island by the Turks in 1669. Dramas, such as the *Erophile* of Georgios Hortatzis (fl. early 17th century), were largely formed upon Italian models. The beginning of the 17th century saw the production of two of the greatest Cretan vernacular works, the romantic poem *Erotokritos* by Vincentios Kornaros, which is ranked with the Homeric epics; and *The Sacrifice of Abraham,* by an anonymous author, which is a mystery play (q.v.) in structure and a psychological study of family relationships. There were also written a large number of popular songs, including the pastoral poem *The Fair Shepherdess,* a well-known version of which was published in 1627. The making of such songs also flourished in Cyprus and the Ægean islands. The ballads of the *klephts* (q.v.), of the 18th century, are the songs of the brigands who, from the mountains of Greece, carried on guerrilla warfare against the Turks.

Outstanding among advocates of the classi-

cal tradition was Adamantios Coray, who, living in Paris, issued annotated editions of ancient Greek authors. Poems in the classical manner were written by Constantine Rhigas (1754–98) and Jacobos Rizos Neroulos (1778–1850). The classical tradition was carried on through the 19th century by the poet Alexander Rizos Rangabé or Rhangavis (1810–92), who also wrote several prose works, novels, and histories.

The beginning of the 19th century witnessed a revival of interest in the use of the vernacular for literary purposes, such as the love poems and drinking songs of Athanasios Christopoulos (1772–1847), in his *Lirika* (1811). The most important name in the history of the renaissance of popular language is that of Dionysios Solomos, who made use of the dialect of the Ionian islands of which he was a native. His most famous poem, *E Odi tis Elephtherias* ("Ode to Liberty", 1824), published during the Greek War of Liberation from Turkey, has become the national anthem of Greece. Other vernacular poets of the Ionian school were Andreas Kalvos (1796–1869), Andreas Lascaratos (1811–1901), and Julius Typaldos (1814–83). The language of the klephtic ballads was employed by Aristotle Valaoritis (1824–79), in his poems praising the patriotic revolutionaries.

Among the French symbolist poets of the 19th century was the Greek, Ioannis Papadiamantopoulos, writing under the name of Jean Moréas (q.v.). He had a considerable influence upon Greek poets, among whom are Konstantinos Hadzopoulos (1868–1921), author of *To Phthinoporo* ("Autumn", 1917), and Miltiadis Malakassis (1870–   ). Educated in Paris, John Psichari (1854–1929) started his career as a French author, but soon turned to modern Greek as a form of expression; his prose work *To Taxidi Mou* ("My Journey", 1888) was effective in converting many other Greek authors to the use of the vernacular.

Although many 19th-century Greek authors imitated the works of their contemporaries in other European countries, the stories of Alexandros Papadiamandis (1851–1911), collected in *Ta Rodina Akroyalia* ("The Happy Shores", 1913), are free from outside influences. Also Greek in their subject matter and treatment are the Ionian stories written by Argyris Eftaliotis (1849–1923), in *Nisiotikes Istories* ("Stories from the Islands", 1897).

The first important Greek dramatists of the 19th century, Demetrios Vernadakis (1834–1907) and Spyridon Vasiliadis (1845–

74), wrote in the classical manner. Plays in the vernacular were later written by Ioannis Kambisis (1872–1902), who depicted the life of Athens in realistic and satirical dramas. The novelist and playwright Spyros Melas (1883–   ) was influenced by the realism of the Russians. His dramas include *Ios tou Iskyou* ("Son of Shadow", 1907) and *Kokkino Poukamiso* ("Red Shirt", 1908). The plays of Gregorios Xenopoulos (1867–1951), particularly *Stella Violanti* (1909), show an interest in the works of the Norwegian dramatist Henrik Ibsen. The Greek symbolist movement found its expression in plays such as *Zontani ke Pethameni* ("The Living and the Dead", 1905), by Demetrios Tangopoulos (1867–1926).

One of the most popular poets in the early part of the 20th century was Georgios Drossinis (1859–   ). He started by writing in the "purist", literary language, but later adopted and propagated the vernacular. His work includes the volumes of poems *Photera Skotadia* ("Light Shadows", 1903–14) and *Klista Vlephara* ("Closed Eyes", 1914–17). Ranked by critics as one of the most important poets in Europe was his contemporary, Kostes Palamas, some of whose best poetry is contained in *Assalephti Zoi* ("Immutable Life", 1904); his long poem *Phloyera tou Vasilia* ("The King's Flute", 1910) presents a pageant of Byzantine history, and his epic poem and masterpiece *Dodekalogos tou Yiphtou* ("The Gypsy's Dodecalogue," 1907) expresses the hopes and aspirations of the Greek people. One of the first Greek poets to use free verse (q.v.) was Angelos Sikelianos, among whose finest works are the poems *Aphierosi* ("Consecration", 1922), and *Hristos sti Romi* ("Christ in Rome", 1946), and the poetical drama *Thanatos tou Digeni* ("Death of Digenes", 1948); the collection of poems *Lirikos Vios* ("Lyric Life"; 3 vols., 1947) confirmed his position as the poet laureate of Greece.

Among Greek men of letters one of the most important was Kostas Varnalis, whose outstanding works are the novel *Penelope* (1945), the collected poems in the volume *To Fos Pou Keï* ("The Light which Burns", 1922), and the satire *I Alithini Apoloyia rou Sokrati* ("The True Apology of Socrates", 1931). Another distinguished novelist was Kosmas Politis, whose masterpiece is *Eroica* (1912), a novel of youth, and whose other works, including *Hecate* (1946), were popular successes. Also well known are the novels of Elias Venezis (1904–   ), among which

are *Galini* ("Calm", 1939) and *Æoliki Ge* ("Æolian Earth", 1943).

During and following World War II, because of their participation in the struggle of the Greek people for survival, many writers were prompted to a new kind of literary activity. Themos Kornaros (1906–   ), whose account of the monks of Mount Athos, *To Agion Oros* ("Holy Mountain", 1931) was popular, vividly described in *Haidari* (1946) the attempts of the Nazis to break the morale of Greek prisoners in a concentration camp in Athens. Other documentary works possessing literary merit were written about the Greek Resistance movement, and several patriotic poems dealt with the Resistance and the events of the civil war of December, 1944.

GREEK MUSIC, the music of the ancient Greeks. The term "music" was applied in ancient Greece not only to vocal and instrumental music but also to dancing and oratory; music, comprising these four forms of art, was one of the two main branches of learning taught in Greek schools. The following discussion, however, relates to Greek music in the sense only of music for voice or instrument.

Although music was an important part of the festivals of ancient Greece, and of the Greek drama (see DRAMA: *Greek Drama*), in which the chorus sang and danced, virtually no music of ancient Greece is extant. A few fragments of musical notation recorded on papyrus and stone, and three complete compositions in manuscript, are all that remain of what must have been a considerable body of music. However, accounts of the theoretical basis of Greek music were set down by a number of Greek poets, including Sappho and Terpander, and by Greek philosophers, including Pythagoras, Aristotle, and Plato. These accounts of the scales, intervals, and modes (qq.v.) of ancient Greek music became the basis for the modes of medieval times, which in turn formed the foundation for the theory of modern European music.

Greek music was monodic in form; i.e., it was composed of melody, which was rarely harmonized or combined with another melody. Early Greek music was usually sung, sometimes accompanied by an instrument such as the aulos, or flute, or the lyre (qq.v.); the aulos and lyre were also used for solo performances. Two schools of music existed: the *kitharoedic*, which used the lyre or harp; and the *auletic*, which used the aulos.

The national musical instrument of ancient Greece was the lyre. The lyre originally had

Metropolitan Museum of Art

GREEK MUSICAL INSTRUMENTS. *Left: Orpheus playing the lyre. Right: Girl playing a double flute. (From paintings on ancient Greek vases.)*

four strings from which was derived the tetrachord (q.v.), the series of four notes which formed the basis for all Greek music. The four notes of the tetrachord, reckoning downward from the first and not upward as in modern times, covered together the interval of the perfect fourth. Two tetrachords comprised a scale; the tone between the two tetrachords was known as the diazeutic tone. Three types of tetrachord existed in Greek music, namely the Dorian, Phrygian, and Lydian, each named from the particular region of ancient Greece or Asia Minor where it originated; from each tetrachord a separate scale was developed, and named after its tetrachord. To these three original scales were added three more, the hypodorian or æolian, the hypophrygian, and the hypolydian; the first note of each of the last-named group is a fifth below the first note of the scale from which it was developed. Still later, three ad-

ditional scales were added to Greek music, the hyperdorian, the hyperphrygian, and the hyperlydian; the first note of each of these scales was a fifth above the first note of the scale from which it was derived.

GREEK PHILOSOPHY. The philosophical concepts developed by the Greeks, particularly during the flowering of Greek civilization between the years 600 and 200 B.C., lie at the root of all later philosophical speculation in the western world. The intuitive hypotheses of the ancient Greeks foreshadowed many of the theories of modern science, and many of the moral ideas of pagan Greek philosophers have been incorporated into the body of Christian moral doctrine. The political ideas set forth by such Greek thinkers as Plato influenced the framers of the American Constitution and the founders of various twentieth-century totalitarian states.

The Ionian School. The founder of Greek

philosophy was Thales (640–546), a native of the flourishing Greek city of Miletus in Ionia on the shores of Asia Minor. He was noted as an astronomer and geometer and was also the first of his race to speculate on the ultimate nature of the physical world. None of his writings survive, and little is known of his theories except that he believed water to be the basic substance out of which all matter is created.

The next important figure in the Ionian school which Thales founded was Anaximander (611–547?). Anaximander rejected Thales' statement that water is the primal substance. He held instead that the raw material of all matter is an unknown substance which he called the "Indeterminate", which is eternal and which changes into the forms of matter that men know. These forms in turn change and merge into one another according to the rule of "justice", i.e. balance and proportion. In his belief in the transformation of matter from one form to another Anaximander expressed in primitive form the doctrine of the conservation of matter. He argued that the world could not be composed of any one of what he regarded as the primitive elements, air, earth, fire, and water, because if any one element were dominant the others would cease to be.

Anaximenes, a younger contemporary of Anaximander, believed that all matter is composed of air and that the differences between different forms of matter depend only on the amount of condensation or rarefaction of the air of which they are made.

The earlier disciples of the Ionian school approached philosophy from the scientific point of view. Their successor Heraclitus, who lived about 500 B.C., wove mysticism and theology into his account of the material world. Heraclitus taught that fire is the primordial source of matter, but laid even greater stress on the beliefs that the entire world is in a constant state of change or flux and that most objects and substances are produced by a union of opposite principles. For example he regarded the soul as a mixture of fire and water. In this unity of opposites Heraclitus saw a harmonious universal principle which is the reflection of an unchanging "universal reason", a god who governs the changes of the physical world in an orderly manner. Heraclitus' universal change is echoed by the equivalence of matter and energy in modern physics.

Later Ionian philosophers included Anaxagoras who carried the ideas of his school into Athens at the time of Pericles. Anaxagoras introduced the concept of *nous* (mind), an infinite and unchanging substance which enters into and controls every living object. Inanimate objects and living objects alike, according to his belief, are composed of a fusion of all possible opposites (such as wet and dry, hot and cold), but only the living contain mind. Anaxagoras' followers included Diogenes of Appolonia who rejected the pluralism of his predecessor and believed that all matter is created from air, which he regarded as eternal, intelligent, and infinite in extent.

The Pythagorean School. One of the most important of the earlier schools of Greek philosophy was that founded at Croton in southern Italy by Pythagoras (582?–507?). Pythagoras was at once a scientist and a mystic. He made many important mathematical discoveries. His experiments with musical instruments led him to the discovery of the numerical basis of musical harmony and to the belief that number relationships are the basis of the structure of the world. This doctrine stresses the importance of form rather than matter in explaining material structure. Pythagoras also believed that after death the soul is translated into another body, and held "that whatever comes into existence is born again in the revolutions of a certain cycle, nothing being absolutely new; and that all things that are born with life in them ought to be treated as kindred." The Pythagorean school laid great stress on the importance of the soul, regarding the body only as the soul's "tomb".

The Eleatic School. This philosophical school, like that of Pythagoras, was located in southern Italy; it was founded about 540 B.C. by refugees who fled from Ionia following the capture of the Ionian cities by the Persians under Darius. The first leader of the school was Xenophanes, who affirmed the existence of a single god but believed that there is no possible way for man to arrive at theological truth except by guessing. He ridiculed the gods of the Greek pantheon, saying that they had been created in the image of the men who worshipped them, ". . . yes, and if oxen and horses or lions had hands, and could paint with their hands, and produce works of art as men do, horses would paint the forms of gods like horses, and oxen like oxen, and make their bodies in the image of their several kinds." The Pythagorean theory of the transmigration of souls also served as a target for Xenophanes' scorn.

Parmenides, a disciple of Xenophanes, held

beliefs that were the direct antithesis of those of Heraclitus. He stated that change is impossible, reasoning that it is not possible to think or speak of something that has no existence, and therefore anything that has once existed must continue to exist because it can still be thought or spoken of. The real universe, according to Parmenides, is a motionless, unchanging sphere in which the appearance of movement and of separate objects are mere illusions. His view of the universe, often called *monism* to distinguish it from the pluralism of the Ionians, was supported by two subsequent philosophers of the Eleatic school, Zeno and Melissus. Zeno invented a famous series of logical paradoxes to prove the impossibility of motion, and Melissus extended Parmenides' finite sphere of reality to infinity.

Another Greek philosopher living in Italy was Empedocles (500?–430?), who accepted the belief that reality is eternal, but declared that it is composed of the four primal substances: fire, air, earth, and water. These elements combine and separate through the action of two primal forces, Love and Strife, which are continually at war, the temporary ascendancy of one or the other being governed entirely by chance.

The Atomists. The philosophical endeavor of the early Greeks to determine the ultimate substance or substances from which the real world is made reached its climax in the doctrines of the Atomists Leucippus and his disciple Democritus. Little is known of the former, except that he lived about 440 B.C., and maintained the existence of "non-being" or empty space in the universe in addition to matter. He is also said to have foreshadowed the teachings of Democritus in regard to the atomic nature of matter.

Democritus (460?–362?) was the first philosopher to give a connected account of reality which purports to explain the manner in which material objects are formed. The universe, according to Democritus, is made up of empty space and an infinite number of indestructible, indivisible atoms which differ from each other in size, shape, and, perhaps, weight. The atoms move at random in infinite space, striking and deflecting each other and sometimes joining together in definite forms if their shapes are such that they can interlock. He explained the various forms which matter assumes by the differences in shape, size, position, and arrangement of the component atoms. Democritus did not attempt to account for the original motion of his atoms and did not postulate any guiding

intelligence or master plan which govern their motion. This doctrine, which resembles in many ways the attitude of modern scientists, was repugnant to most of Democritus' contemporaries, who believed that it is possible to discover the ultimate nature of the world by a process of deductive reasoning. One of Democritus' most famous successors, the Roman philosopher and poet Lucretius, attempted to explain the original motion of atoms by saying that all the atoms of the universe are falling freely through space and that, as heavier atoms fall faster than light ones, collisions occur. This account, however, still leaves the ultimate cause (i.e. the fall of the atoms) unexplained.

The Sophists. In the rich, democratic city of Athens in the middle of the 5th century B.C. a new school of philosophers arose, differing sharply from those that had preceded them. This was the school of the Sophists, the "men of wisdom", whose chief concern was to teach wealthy young Athenians the arts of grammar, rhetoric, and argument, useful to them in the practice of politics and law. In keeping with the practical nature of their teaching, the Sophists developed a philosophy of skepticism. They doubted that men would ever be able to reach objective truth through reason, and taught that material success rather than truth should be the purpose of men's lives.

The first and one of the most typical Sophists was Protagoras, who stated, "man is the measure of all things, of things that are that they are, and of things that are not that they are not." Because he believed that the only truth which the individual man can know comes through his own imperfect perceptions and that the perceptions of different men are invariably different, Protagoras declared that it is necessary to believe what the majority believe. He carried this argument to the point of saying that everyone should worship the gods because the majority of men worship them, and for no other reason. As a result of his book *Of the Gods,* he was tried for impiety and exiled.

Among the other members of the Sophist group was Gorgias, who defended three propositions: that nothing exists; that if anything does exist, it is unknowable; and that if anything does exist and is knowable, it is still not possible to communicate this knowledge. The Sophists frequently substituted clever playing with words for logical reasoning and invented an entire science of *eristic,* the science of winning an argument. Their attitude is

Left: Heraclitus. Right: Socrates.

well illustrated by a story told of Protagoras who is said to have taught a young man rhetoric with the understanding that his teaching fees would be paid only if the young man won his first lawsuit. The first suit that the young man defended was a suit by Protagoras for the recovery of his fees. In the teaching of grammar and rhetoric, however, Sophists laid the foundation for classic Greek prose and had a strong influence on such writers as Plato and Demosthenes; see GREEK LITERATURE.

Socrates. Although he dedicated his life to teaching, Socrates differed widely from the Sophists who were his contemporaries in Athens. He did not teach for pay, and his chief concern was not rhetoric or even the ultimate nature of the world but rather the discovery of what constituted ethical conduct in the individual and in society. His method of teaching was by discussions in which, after a proposition had been stated, the philosopher asked a series of questions designed to test and refine the proposition by examining its consequences and discovering whether it was consistent with the known facts. Often this method of questioning, usually called the Socratic method, resulted in reducing the original proposition to absurdity.

As a deeply religious man, Socrates conceived that God had ordered him "to fulfil the philosopher's mission of searching into myself and other men." The good life, he believed, consists not in caring for the needs and desires of the body but in making one's soul as good as possible. Socrates described the soul not in terms of mysticism but as "that in virtue of which we are called wise or foolish, good or bad," in other words as a combination of an individual's intelligence, personality, and character. In his politics Socrates stressed the need for the same virtues as in his individual ethics: the knowledge of good, and the endeavor to make one's own soul and one's fellow-citizens' souls as good as possible. In his philosophy and his life Socrates foreshadowed in some particulars the Stoics and the Cynics discussed below. Like the Stoics, he believed that virtue is the ultimate good; and like the Cynics, he despised bodily comforts. Socrates left no books and the only existing accounts of his philosophy are in the works of later writers, particularly those of his pupil Plato. Even in Plato's dialogues, in which Socrates is the leading character, it is uncertain which of the ideas belong to Socrates and which to Plato.

Plato. The idealism of Socrates was organized by Plato into a complete philosophical system. Plato, who studied with Socrates for the last eight years of the latter's life, was profoundly influenced by the older philoso-

Aristotle

pher, although he also drew inspiration from the doctrines of Pythagoras, Parmenides, and Heraclitus. From his own lifetime to the present day Plato has been, with Aristotle, the most important and influential thinker in western civilization. In this article only four of his contributions to philosophy are mentioned: the Republic (the theory of the perfect state); the theory of ideas; the theory of immortality; and the theory of knowledge.

Plato's Republic, described in a work of that name consisting of an imaginary dialogue, was an attempt to create a perfect state or Utopia, a task which has occupied many other writers and philosophers since Plato's time. In his commonwealth, which Plato defines as a "just" state, Plato borrowed many details from the government of the contemporary city-state of Sparta.

Plato, in his theory of ideas, regards the objects of the real world as being merely shadows of eternal "forms" or "ideas". Only these changeless, eternal forms can be the sub-

ject of true knowledge; the perception of their shadows, i.e. the real world as heard, seen, and felt, is merely opinion. The goal of the philosopher, he said, is to learn to know the eternal forms and to instruct others in that knowledge.

In his theory of immortality Plato extended the dualism of his theory of ideas. The knowledge of ideas, he said, is a property of the soul and opinion is a property of the body. Freed by death from the body, the soul becomes purified and can know true wisdom. Plato also argued that the soul must be immortal because it has certain concepts, such as the concept of absolute equality, which cannot be derived from ordinary experience. Such ideas, he said, are the result of the soul's memory and prove that the soul must exist before birth.

Plato's theory of knowledge also is implicit in his theory of ideas. Plato stated that both the material objects perceived and the men perceiving them are constantly changing; but, since knowledge must be concerned only with unchangeable and universal objects, knowledge and perception are fundamentally different.

Aristotle. In 387 B.C., twelve years after the death of Socrates, Plato founded a philosophical school, the Academy, in Athens, which flourished until it was closed by the Byzantine emperor Justinian in 529 A.D. One of the earliest pupils of the Academy was Aristotle who studied there for twenty years beginning at the age of seventeen. Aristotle was a natural scientist as well as a philosopher; in the former field his ideas were a dominant factor for two millenniums, while in the latter his ideas are still influential. His philosophical studies covered an extremely wide range and in this article only his contributions to metaphysics, logic, and natural science are discussed.

In the field of metaphysics Aristotle has been described by the modern British philosopher Bertrand Russell as "Plato diluted with common sense." In place of Plato's doctrine of ideas which have a separate and eternal existence of their own, Aristotle proposed a group of "universals" which represent the common properties of any group of real objects. The universals, unlike Plato's ideas, have no existence outside of the objects they describe. In addition to the universals, Aristotle defined two other properties of objects, "form" and "matter". The form of an object is the property that sets it off from other objects and makes it an individual entity. The matter is the raw material to which the form gives shape and individuality. In Aristotle's view, form is not a universal and has an existence of its own, independent of the objects in which it is found. This idea is reminiscent of Plato, as also is his further statement that the "actuality" of an object is dependent on the amount of form it possesses and that only God is pure form and pure actuality.

Probably the most important contribution that Aristotle made to philosophy was in the field of logic, particularly in the reduction of logical reasoning to the form of syllogisms. The syllogism was a valuable tool which enabled philosophers to test the validity of certain arguments and reasoning processes by reference to a set of simple, fixed rules. Aristotle and his successors set down all the forms of valid syllogisms and worked out a technique for recasting any argument in the form of a set of syllogisms so that the truth of its reasoning could be determined according to the rules. For more than two thousand years all strictly logical reasoning was carried on according to the Aristotelian system, and not until the 19th century did mathematicians and philosophers develop other and more useful forms of deductive reasoning; see Logic.

Aristotle's biological researches, particularly in the growth of plants and animals, led him to the doctrine that all living things have an ideal form or "nature" which they strive to attain. This form, which inheres in their matter, represents the perfection of the purpose for which the animal or plant was created. Describing the universe, Aristotle stated that it consists in matter of the four elements, fire, air, earth, and water, plus a fifth element which exists everywhere and is the sole constituent of the heavenly bodies "above" the moon. The earth is the center of the universe and only "beneath" the moon (i.e. at points which are closer to the earth than is the moon) do the living processes of generation and decay occur. Above the moon are only the heavenly bodies, composed of the fifth element, set in spheres which revolve around the earth.

Hellenistic Philosophers. The Hellenistic age, which began with the conquests of Philip and Alexander of Macedon about 335 B.C. and endured for more than a century until the Roman conquests, was a period of wars, civil unrest, and individual insecurity. Because of these circumstances, the philosophers of the period generally created systems of thought that offered rules for individual conduct and consolation in adversity. The preoccupation with the nature of the world and with political organization which characterized Greek philosophy of earlier ages was replaced in Hellenistic times with concern for the individual human being. During this period four major schools of "individual" philosophy arose: the Cynics, the Skeptics, the Epicureans, and the Stoics.

Antisthenes, a pupil of Socrates, was the forerunner of the Cynic school. After Socrates' death he turned from the abstruse and aristocratic discussions of the Athenian schools to the doctrine of the simple life. Forswearing formal philosophy, he declared that the only knowledge worth having is the knowledge available to all. Antisthenes dressed simply and preached in simple language to ordinary working men rather than to aristocrats. He advocated the abolition of all institutions, including government, property, marriage, religion, and slavery.

The most famous of the Cynic philosophers was Diogenes, another Athenian. He also lived with great simplicity, "like a dog" (Gr. *cynos,* dog), and despised all material possessions. Diogenes taught that the only enduring and satisfactory good lies within the individual, in such qualities as moral virtue and resignation.

Epicurus

The school of the Skeptics was founded by Pyrrho, a soldier in the armies of Alexander the Great. He carried the doctrines of the Sophists one step farther, saying that there is no rational reason to select one type of conduct rather than another, and that all actions can properly be governed by expediency. Pyrrho's successor Timon (the protagonist of Shakespeare's *Timon of Athens*) claimed that philosophical speculation is useless because it is impossible to find any valid premises from which to make deductions. He taught that real knowledge is impossible, but that inferences can be made on the basis of observed phenomena.

The attitude of the Skeptics was adopted in the middle of the 3rd century B.C. by Arcesilaus, the head of the Athenian Academy, and for about two centuries thereafter Skepticism was the official doctrine of the Academy, despite the complete antithesis between this philosophy and the teachings of Plato.

The most influential of the Hellenistic schools were those of Epicurus (342?–270) and the Stoics, both of which exerted a strong influence not only on their contemporaries but also on the writers and thinkers of Roman times. The central doctrine of Epicurus and his followers is hedonism, the belief that bodily pleasure is the primary good. Even mental pleasure he regarded as secondary to the pleasures of the senses. Carrying his thesis further, Epicurus maintained that passive pleasures are more to be desired than active ones, and that the prudent man should seek an absence of pain rather than active happiness. In his view of the physical world, Epicurus followed Democritus' theory of atoms. He taught that fear of the gods and of punishment after death is needless, because the gods, although they exist, pay no attention to human beings, and because the soul after death is broken down into the individual atoms that compose it. "Death is nothing to us; for that which is dissolved is without sensation, and that which lacks sensation is nothing to us". Epicurus' doctrines of hedonism and of the atomic nature of the world were adopted by Lucretius, mentioned above.

The Stoic school of philosophy came into being about the beginning of the 3rd century, and was roughly contemporary with Epicureanism. Zeno of Citium, the founder of the school, laid his chief stress on virtue, which in his view consists of "willing' to live in harmony with nature. Zeno believed that the entire world is constructed according to a fixed plan in which everything has its place. Even evil men live according to their places in the natural plan, but they do so unwillingly and hence are not virtuous. Although the plan of nature is inflexible, according to Zeno, men are free because they are free to be virtuous. He condemned all worldly desires and passions because they make it more difficult to achieve virtue. Likewise he declared that pains and tribulations have no effect on virtue and therefore the individual need not suffer if he be virtuous. In his description of nature Zeno adopted the belief of Heraclitus that the world is ultimately composed of fire. He believed that the world was born of fire and will be consumed by fire and that this cycle will repeat itself forever. Thus the plan of nature is eternal and all past and future events will repeat themselves an infinite number of times.

Zeno's beliefs about the nature of the world were somewhat modified by later followers such as Cleanthes of Assos, Chrysippus, and Posidonius, but his ethical beliefs were adopted unchanged by these men and by such later stoics as the Romans Lucius Anneus Seneca, Epictetus, and Marcus Aurelius.

See articles on most of the philosophers, schools, and writers, and also ESTHETICS; ETHICS; GREECE: *History of Ancient Greece*; GREEK LITERATURE; NEOPLATONISM.

GREEK RELIGIOUS MYTHOLOGY, the more or less integrated body of myths and legends, constituting an allegorical explanation of the creation of the universe, the operation of natural laws, and the genealogy and functions of the gods, which formed the religion of the ancient Greeks. The salient features of this religion were a hierarchy of individualistic divinities having human form and feelings (anthropomorphic polytheism), the absence of any established canon or authoritative revelation such as the Holy Scriptures, a strong ritualism, and complete subordination of religious life to the state. Apart from the mystery cults of Eleusis, Samothrace, and Andania (see MYSTERIES, CLASSIC), the element of asceticism and mystical rapture, an Asiatic importation so conspicuous in the Hellenistic period (about 300–100 B.C.), is almost completely lacking in the early religion of Greece.

At its first appearance in classical literature, the Greek religious system had already received its definitive form. Some divinities were either introduced or developed more fully at a later date, but Homer's *Iliad* and *Odyssey* exhibit the hierarchy of the gods in

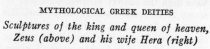

MYTHOLOGICAL GREEK DEITIES

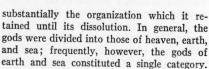

Sculptures of the king and queen of heaven, Zeus (above) and his wife Hera (right)

substantially the organization which it retained until its dissolution. In general, the gods were divided into those of heaven, earth, and sea; frequently, however, the gods of earth and sea constituted a single category.

The celestial gods dwell in the sky, or on a lofty mountain, usually Mt. Olympus (see OLYMPUS) in Thessaly. The earth, or chthonian, deities are conceived of as dwelling on or under the earth, and often include the heroes and the dead. The lines separating these divine orders are very indefinite, and the deities of one order are not infrequently found in another. The gods are held to be immortal; yet they have a beginning. They are represented as exercising control over the world and the forces of nature. This control, however, is limited by Ananke (Necessity), to which even the gods must bow.

At the head of the divine hierarchy was Zeus, the spiritual "father of gods and men", His wife was Hera, queen of heaven, and the special guardian of the sanctity of marriage. Associated with them as the chief divinities of heaven were Hephæstus, god of fire and the patron of metalworkers; Athena, the virgin daughter of Zeus, and pre-eminent as a civic

goddess; Apollo, deity of light, poetry, and music, and his sister Artemis, goddess of the moon and of wild life; Ares, the god of war, and his consort Aphrodite, the goddess of love; Hermes, the divine messenger and the god of science and invention; and Hestia, goddess of the hearth. Around these greater gods and goddesses were grouped a host of lesser deities, some of whom enjoyed particular distinction in certain localities. Among them were Helios, the sun; Selene, the moon (antedating Artemis); the attendants of the Olympians, such as the Horæ, or Seasons, the Charites, or Graces, the nine Muses, and Iris, goddess of the rainbow, Hebe, goddess of youth and the cupbearer of the gods, and Ganymede, the male counterpart of Hebe. The sea was ruled by Poseidon, the worship of whom was often accompanied by worship of his wife, Amphitrite. In their train were the Nereids, the Tritons, and other minor sea divinities.

The chief chthonian deities were Hades, ruler of the underworld, and his wife, Persephone, the daughter of Demeter. Demeter herself was usually accounted an Olympian, but as the bestower of grain and the knowledge of agriculture, she was more closely connected with the earth. Another Olympian whose tutelary functions were likewise of an earthly character was Dionysus, god of the grape and of wine. He was accompanied by bands of satyrs, the horse-tailed sylvan demigods; sileni, the plump, bald-headed woodland deities, occasionally represented as having goat's legs; and mænads, nymphs who celebrated the orgiastic rites of Dionysus. Gæa, the earth mother; Asclepius, the god of healing; and Pan, the great Arcadian god of flocks, pastures, and forests, were also among the more important divinities of the Greek pantheon.

The ancient Greek was a deeply religious person. He had a strong sense of his weakness before the grand and terrifying powers of nature, and acknowledged his dependence upon the divine beings by whom he believed those powers to be controlled. In general, the relations between gods and men were cordial, divine wrath being reserved for those who transgressed the limits assigned to human activities, and who, by overweening pride, reckless ambition, or even immoderate prosperity, provoked the divine displeasure and brought upon themselves Nemesis, the personification of retributive justice. The saying of the historian Herodotus, "the god suffers none but himself to be proud", epitomizes a philosophy which pervades the whole of classical Greek literature. The sense of human limitation was thus an integral feature of the Greek religion, and the gods, as the sole source of the good or evil that befell men, were approached with invocation and sacrifice, either in thanksgiving for past blessings or in supplication for future favors.

In front of every street door stood the conical stone of Apollo Agyieus (Apollo of the Thoroughfare); in the courtyard was placed the altar of Zeus Herkeios (Zeus as the patron of family ties); at the hearth Hestia was worshiped; and bedchamber, kitchen, and storeroom each had its appropriate divinity. From birth to death, the ancient Greek invoked the gods on every memorable occasion. And since the very existence of the state was believed to depend upon the divine favor, the festivals of the gods were celebrated with devout regularity under the supervision of high officials, and public gratitude for unexpected deliverance or unusual prosperity was marked by rich votive offerings.

Despite its central position in both private and public life, however, the Greek religion was notably lacking in an organized professional priesthood. At the sites of the mysteries or the oracles (Eleusis or Delphi), the priests did of course exercise a great authority; but in general they were merely official representatives of the community, chosen as other officers were, or sometimes permitted to buy their position. Even when the office was hereditary or confined to a certain family, it was not regarded as conferring upon its possessor any peculiar knowledge of the will of the gods, or any special power to constrain them. The need of an intermediary between the Greek worshiper and his god was not recognized.

Greek ideas about the soul and the afterlife were indefinite, but it was apparently the popular belief that the soul survived the body and either hovered about the tomb or departed to a shadowy region, where it led a melancholy existence in need of the offerings brought by living relatives. The soul was also presumed to have the power of inflicting injury beyond the grave, and proper funeral rites for the dead were held necessary to insure its peace and good will.

The origins of the ancient Greek religion have been the subject of speculation and research from classic times to the present. Herodotus believed that the names of many of the gods had been derived from the Egyptians. Prodicus of Ceos, a Sophist of the 5th century B.C., seems to have taught that the gods were simply personifications of natural phenomena, such as the sun, moon, wind, and water; and Euhemerus, a mythographer of the 4th century B.C., in his *Sacred History,* gave expression to ideas long prevalent when he interpreted the myths as distortions of history, and the gods as idealized heroes of the past. In modern times, studies along etymological and anthropological lines have produced the theory that Greek religion resulted from the synthesis of Indo-Germanic beliefs with ideas and customs native to the Mediterranean countries, the original inhabitants of those lands having been conquered by Indo-Germanic invaders.

Within the framework of Greek anthropomorphic polytheism there are vestiges of primitive animism, the belief that all natural objects are endowed with spirits. Fetishism, the belief in the magical efficacy of objects (either natural or artificial) employed as talismans against evil, was another feature of early Greek religion. Examples of fetishes are the sacred stones, sometimes regarded as images of specific deities, such as the pyramidal Zeus at Phlius, or the rough stones called

Charites at the ruined city of Orchomenus in Bœotia.

GREELEY, county seat of Weld Co., Colo., situated on the Cache la Poudre R., 52 miles N.N.E. of Denver, at an altitude of 4637 ft. above sea level. It is served by two railroads, and is the center and shipping point of a farming and coal-mining region. The principal industries in the city are flour milling and the refining of beet sugar. Greeley is the site of the Colorado State College of Education, established in 1889. The city was founded in 1870 by a group of settlers from New England and New York under the leadership of Nathan Cook Meeker; known as the Union Colonists, they organized for the purpose of establishing a colony in Colorado, and were sponsored by Horace Greeley (q.v.), for whom the city is named. Greeley was incorporated as a city in 1886. Pop. (1950) 20,354.

GREELEY, HORACE (1811–72), American journalist and political leader, born in Amherst, New Hampshire. He was apprenticed in 1825 to a printer in East Poultney, Vermont, and became an itinerant journeyman printer four years later.

In 1831 he settled in New York City, where he became editor, successively of the *New Yorker,* the *Jeffersonian,* and the *Log Cabin,* rapidly gaining a reputation as an influential political writer. He also became associated with the Whig leaders Governor William Seward (q.v.) of New York and the journalist Thurlow Weed, with whom he worked in behalf of progressive governmental policies.

In order to serve the Whig cause with a low-priced newspaper which would avoid the sensationalism of the New York *Herald* and academic detachment of the New York *Evening Post,* Greeley founded in 1841 the New York *Tribune,* which met with immediate success and which he edited for thirty-one years. During this period he opposed unequal distribution of wealth, denounced monopoly, and attacked the pre-emption of public lands by the railroads and speculators. He advocated a protective tariff, the development of agriculture, and migration to the West; his advice to a Congregational clergyman who had lost his voice and had to leave the ministry, "Go west, young man, go west", has become a familiar phrase. For a time he was sympathetic to the ideas of the utopian socialists François Fourier and Robert Owen (qq.v.) and the English Chartists (see CHARTISM). For several years Greeley employed the revolutionist Karl Marx as a European cor-

respondent, publishing dispatches which later became famous as classics of Marxian Socialism.

Although opposed to the Abolitionists, who denounced him as a conservative, Greeley was unequivocally opposed to slavery. He opposed the Mexican War because he saw it as a slave owner's plot, and for the same reason he urged rejection of the Kansas-Nebraska Bill (q.v.). His increasing preoccupation with these issues led him, in 1854, to break his ties with Seward and Weed.

In 1856 and again in 1860 Greeley attended the Republican Party national conventions; in the latter year he was influential in bringing about the nomination of Abraham Lincoln. Believing at first that the South should be allowed to secede if a majority of its inhabitants voted to do so, Greeley later urged that the Southern States be compelled by force to abide by the decision of the national electorate and its government under Lincoln. He urged vigorous prosecution of the Civil War and frequently criticized Lincoln's hesitation to free the slaves.

After the Civil War he urged a general amnesty, thus antagonizing the Republican Party; and his proposal of unrestricted universal suffrage to form a basis of reconstruction in the South pleased neither side; see RECONSTRUCTION. Greeley also evoked great anger in the North and alienated many erstwhile admirers when he signed a bail bond for Jefferson Davis, leader of the defeated Confederacy, whose long imprisonment he held to be a violation of constitutionally guaranteed rights.

Later holding that the administration of President Ulysses S. Grant was corrupt, Greeley, in 1872, accepted the nomination for President by the dissident Liberal Republican Party. He was subsequently endorsed by the Democrats, but was defeated by Grant in the election. Thereafter his health failed and he took little part in the editorship of the *Tribune.*

Greeley's published works are chiefly collections of his editorials, speeches, and lectures. They include *Hints toward Reforms* (1850), *A History of the Struggle for Slavery Extension or Restriction* (1856), *The Overland Journey to California* (1859), *American Conflict* (2 vols., 1864 and 1867), and his autobiography *Recollections of a Busy Life* (1869).

GREELY, ADOLPHUS WASHINGTON (1844–1935), American army officer and Arctic explorer, born in Newburyport, Mass. After participating as a volunteer with the Union forces during the Civil War he entered the regular army in 1867. He was subsequently appointed to the signal service and from 1876 until 1879 supervised the erection of 2000 miles of telegraph line in Texas, North and South Dakota, and Montana. In 1881 he became commander of a United States expedition to establish one of a chain of thirteen circumpolar meteorological stations recommended by the International Geographical Congress in 1879. His expedition discovered new territories north of Greenland and several members of the group reached 83° 24', the northernmost point attained to that date. Because relief parties sent out during 1882 and 1883 failed to reach Greely and his men, all but the leader and six of his party died as a result of cold and famine during the winter of 1883. In the spring of 1884 Greely and the other survivors were rescued by Commander Winfield Scott Schley. For his service in the Arctic Greely was awarded the Founder's Medal of the Royal Geographical Society. In 1887 he was made chief signal officer and brigadier general, becoming the first volunteer and enlisted man in the U.S. Army to attain that rank. During the Spanish-American War he was in charge of constructing telegraph lines and establishing communications in Puerto Rico, China, Cuba, and the Philippines. He was later given a similar commission in Alaska, establishing the first wireless stations in that territory. Greely supervised relief operations in San Francisco after the earthquake of 1906. In 1908 he retired from the army, having become a major general. He wrote *Three Years of Arctic Service* (2 vols., 1885), *Handbook of Alaska* (1912), and *Polar Regions in the Twentieth Century* (1928).

GREEN, BARTHOLOMEW (1666–1732), American printer and publisher, born in Cambridge, Mass. He succeeded to the printing business of his father, Samuel Green (1615–1702) in 1692, and moved the business from Cambridge to Boston. He subsequently became the foremost printer in New England. He printed the first American newspaper, the *Boston News Letter* (q.v.), from 1704 until his death, except for a four-year period. In 1723 he became the publisher as well as the printer of the paper, which became known for its independent and original thinking on politics and religion.

GREEN, HENRIETTA HOWLAND, known as HETTY GREEN (1834–1916), American financier, born in New Bedford, Mass. She was reputed to be the richest woman in America,

as well as the cleverest woman financier of her time. She inherited a large fortune from her father Edward Mott Robinson (1800–65) and, by shrewd manipulation of her worldwide holdings, increased them greatly. Her wealth was said to have totaled $100,000,000.

GREEN, JULIAN (1900–   ), French novelist, born in Paris of American parents. After serving in the French army at the end of World War I, he was educated in the U.S. at the University of Virginia. He became for a time a painter in Paris. His first novel, *Le Voyageur sur la Terre,* appeared in 1924. His novels, influenced by the works of Edgar Allan Poe and William Faulkner, among other American writers, show an interest in the forces of evil and in abnormal psychology. During World War II Green lived in the United States, producing a volume of reminiscences, *Memories of Happy Days* (1942), and some translations into English of the poems of Charles Péguy (q.v.). His novels include *Adrienne Mesurat* (1927), *Léviathan* (1929), *Le Visionnaire* (1934), *Minuit* (1936), *Varouna* (1940), *Si J'Étais Vous . . .* (1947), *Moira* (1950), *Sud* (1953), and *L'Ombre* (1956).

GREEN, PAUL ELIOT (1894–   ), American writer, born at Lillington, North Carolina, and educated at the University of North Carolina and Cornell University. He began his career as a playwright with the Carolina Playmakers, a group for which he wrote a number of one-act plays dealing with conditions among Southern Negroes. In 1927 he was awarded a Pulitzer Prize for his play *In Abraham's Bosom.* His full-length plays about Southern life include *The Field God* (1927), *Tread the Green Grass* (1929), and *The House of Connelly* (1932). *The Lost Colony* (1937), a pageant concerning the colonial life of Roanoke Island, is produced there annually. He also wrote *Wide Fields* (1928) and *Dog on the Sun* (1949), books of short stories; *This Body the Earth* (1935), a novel; and *Dramatic Heritage* (1953), essays.

GREEN, THOMAS HILL (1836–82), British educator and philosopher, born in Birkin, and educated at Rugby and at Oxford University. He taught at Oxford from 1860 until his death, initially as a fellow and after 1878 as Whyte Professor of Moral Philosophy.

A disciple of the German philosopher Georg Wilhelm Hegel, Green led the revolt against empiricism, the dominant school of thought in Great Britain during the latter part of the 19th century. Whereas the empiricists reasoned that knowledge is impossible to achieve and conduct has no ethical significance, he insisted that consciousness provides the necessary basis for both knowledge and morality. He argued that man's highest good is self-realization and that the individual can achieve self-realization only in society. Society has an obligation in turn, he held, to provide for the good of all its members. The political implications of his philosophy laid the basis for sweeping social-reform legislation in Great Britain. Besides being the most influential British philosopher of his time, Green was a vigorous champion of popular education, the temperance movement, and political liberalism. His writings include *Prolegomena to Ethics* (posthumously published, 1883) and *Lectures on the Principles of Political Obligation* (posthumously published, 1895).

GREEN, WILLIAM (1873–1952), American labor leader, born in Coshocton, Ohio. After receiving a public-school education, he worked in the bituminous coal mines of Ohio. He became a member of the United Mine Workers of America in 1890. From 1900 to 1906 he was president of one of the subdistricts of the UMW, and for the following four years was president of the Ohio district. From 1912 to 1924 he was secretary-treasurer of the entire union. In the latter year Green succeeded Samuel Gompers as president of the American Federation of Labor, to the Executive Council of which he had been appointed in 1913. Thereafter he was re-elected for many successive terms at the annual conventions of the AFL. He also served as editor of the *American Federationist*, official organ of the AFL.

During the schismatic struggle in the AFL in 1935–36 over the organization of the unorganized workers in the basic industries of the United States, Green opposed the Committee on Industrial Organization, established in the AFL by a number of labor leaders, including John L. Lewis, president of the United Mine Workers; see AMERICAN FEDERATION OF LABOR; CONGRESS OF INDUSTRIAL ORGANIZATIONS. In the course of the bitter feud which ensued between Green and Lewis, the latter had the former expelled from the UMW.

While still an official of the mine workers' union, Green had twice been elected, as a Democratic candidate, to the Ohio State senate; during both terms he was the Democratic floor leader. In the State senate he secured passage of the Ohio Workmen's Compensation Law, subsequently used as a model in other States by legislators friendly to labor, and was successful in achieving the enactment of other measures beneficial to labor.

American Federation of Labor
William Green

He was a delegate to the Democratic National Conventions of 1912, 1920, and 1924. He was frequently consulted on labor and other matters by the Presidents, Secretaries of Labor, and other high-ranking Federal officials of several administrations, and was a member of numerous government bodies, including the Labor Advisory Council of the National Recovery Administration, in 1935–37. During those years he was also a member of the governing board of the International Labor Office sponsored by the League of Nations.

GREEN ALGAE. See CHLOROPHYCEAE.

GREENAWAY, KATE (1846–1901), English artist, born in London and educated at the Slade School. She exhibited her water-color drawings at the Dudley Gallery, London, in 1868. She drew the illustrations for the children's book, *Little Folks,* in 1873, and began to draw for the *Illustrated London News* in 1877. In the following years she illustrated *Mother Goose, Under the Window, The Birthday Book,* and *Little Ann.* These books had a large sale. Kate Greenaway's work featured a revival of the fashions in children's clothes dating from the beginning of the 19th century and had great influence on the style of children's clothes in her own day.

GREENBACK, the popular name given to the paper currency issued by the U.S. Federal government during the Civil War to facilitate the payment of war expenses; it was so called because the reverse side of each note was printed in green ink. This action by the government constituted the first issue of legal-tender notes since the adoption of the Constitution in 1787. The law authorizing this currency, passed in February, 1862, provided for an issue in the amount of $150,000,000. Further issues totaling $300,000,000 were authorized in July, 1862, and March, 1863.

The market value of the greenbacks, which were not backed by gold reserves, began to depreciate almost immediately after their issuance, contributing to a sharp inflation of the entire economy. An act passed in 1866, providing for the gradual retirement of the greenbacks, was repealed two years later, and the notes continued to circulate without gold-reserve backing until 1879. In that year, when the amount of greenback currency in circulation was about $347,000,000, the greenbacks were made redeemable in gold; thereafter they circulated on the same basis as all other forms of legal tender. See GREENBACK-LABOR PARTY; GREENBACK PARTY.

GREENBACK-LABOR PARTY, in United States history, the popular name for the National Party, a political party organized in 1878, by workers and farmers, as a means of relieving their economic difficulties resulting from the depression of the 1870's. The party was formed by the members of the defunct Greenback Party (q.v.), who were called "greenbackers", and the members of a number of labor organizations. The greenbackers sought to obtain labor support for their program, which called for the issuance of paper currency and the initiation of a monetary policy based on bimetallism (q.v.); the labor groups desired greenbacker support for their demands, which included a reduction in working hours, the establishment of a labor bureau in the Federal government, and the curtailment of Chinese immigration, which was viewed as a cause of lowered wages. At the first national convention of the party, held at Toledo, Ohio, in February, 1878, each of the two major elements within the party pledged its support to the demands of the other.

In the Congressional elections of 1878 the Greenback-Labor Party polled a total of about one million votes, and elected fourteen Representatives to Congress. This election marked the height of the party's power. In the following year, economic conditions in the nation improved, and interest in politics among the workers and farmers decreased. The 1880 convention of the party, held at Chicago, Ill., nominated James Baird Weaver for the Presidency. He received only about 309,000 votes, but eight Greenback-Labor candidates were elected to Congress. In ensuing years the party continued to decline. Its last national campaign was that conducted in 1884, when its Presidential candidate, Benjamin F. Butler (q.v.), won about 175,000 votes. Soon afterward the Greenback-Labor Party passed out of existence; it was succeeded in the 1890's by the Populist Party (see POPULISM).

GREENBACK PARTY, in United States history, a political party formed in 1875, chiefly by Middle Western and Southern farmers. The primary aims of the party were the adoption of a national monetary policy based on bimetallism (q.v.), and the issuance by the Federal government of paper currency, not backed by gold. The name of the party was derived from the popular name for this currency, "greenback" (q.v.).

The party was organized as a result of the economic depression of the early 1870's, when the indebtedness of farmers to merchants and banks was rising and the prices of farm products were declining. The farmers believed that the adoption of the measure advocated by them would result in general prosperity for the nation, and would at the same time enable them to pay off their debts and raise the prices of their products.

The "greenbackers" determined on the formation of an independent party late in 1874, after their efforts to persuade the Democratic Party to adopt their views failed and that party nominated Samuel Jones Tilden (q.v.) as its Presidential candidate. The first national convention of the Greenback Party was held at Indianapolis in 1876, and the philanthropist Peter Cooper was nominated for the Presidency. Cooper received about 82,000 popular votes, but no electoral votes, in the election held that year. Two years later the Greenback Party dissolved; its members united with the members of a number of labor organizations to form the Greenback-Labor Party (q.v.).

GREEN BAY, county seat and port of entry of Brown Co., Wis., situated at the s. tip of Green Bay, an arm of Lake Michigan, and at the mouth of the Fox R., 114 miles N. of Milwaukee. The surrounding area is noted for lumbering, farming, and dairying. Green Bay is served by three railroads and by lake and river steamers; a county airport is on the outskirts of the city. The Green Bay harbor is one of the finest on the Great Lakes, with extensive dock facilities for accommodating a large trade in coal and paper pulp. The city ranks second only to Milwaukee in importance as a distributing, wholesale, and jobbing center in Wisconsin, and is the largest U.S. cheese processing and shipping center. It is also noted for the manufacture of paper. Additional products include canned foodstuffs, paper-mill machinery, lumber and woodwork, brick and tile, precision machinery, power shovels, cranes, and automobile parts. The city also contains steel plants, railroad shops, cold-storage plants, warehouses, breweries, fisheries, and a shipyard. Within Green Bay are eighteen municipal parks, covering a total area of 400 acres. Among the interesting buildings in the city are Tank Cottage, built about 1775 and said to be the oldest house still standing in the State, and the Neville Public Museum, which contains exhibits pertaining to the early history of the region.

Green Bay is the oldest permanent settlement in the State. Its site was first visited in 1634 by Jean Nicolet, a French explorer, and in 1671 Claude Jean Allouez, a Jesuit missionary, built a mission there which was destroyed by fire in 1687. The French commenced the construction of Fort St. Francis on the site in 1717, and in 1745 Augustin de Langlade established a permanent settlement near the fort. In 1760 the fort was surrendered to the British, who named it Fort Edward Augustus, and occupied it intermittently until 1816, when it was officially possessed by American troops, and named Fort Howard. The old hospital building of the fort has been preserved. In 1839 the two fur-trading centers, Navarino and Astor, which had been established within the limits of the present city, were united as the town of Green Bay; in 1854 Green Bay was chartered as a city. Fort Howard, a separate city on the w. bank of the Fox R., was consolidated with Green Bay in 1893. Pop. (1950) 52,735.

GREENBONE. See GARFISH.

GREENBRIER. See SMILAX.

GREENE, GRAHAM (1904–), English author, educated at Berkhamsted School and Balliol College, Oxford University. He worked on the staff of the London *Times* from 1926 to 1930. Greene was motion-picture critic from 1935 to 1939 and literary editor in 1940–41 of the English weekly the *Spectator*. From 1941 to 1944 he held a post in the British Foreign Office, spending 1942 and 1943 on

Viking Press

Graham Greene

special duties in West Africa. Although his works are written in the idiom of adventure stories, Greene was concerned with the moral and social problems of his time and dealt with them from the Roman Catholic point of view. Among his works are *The Man Within* (1929), *The Name of Action* (1930), *Stamboul Train* (1932), *It's a Battlefield* (1934), *England Made Me* (1935), *A Gun for Sale* (1936), *Brighton Rock* (1938), *The Confidential Agent* (1939), *The Power and Glory* (1940), *The Ministry of Fear* (1943), *The Heart of the Matter* (1948), *The End of the Affair* (1951), *Lost Childhood and Other Essays* (1952), and *Quiet American* (1956). Greene is the author also of children's books and of the plays *The Living Room* (1953) and *The Potting Shed* (1957).

GREENE, NATHANAEL (1742–86), American Revolutionary soldier, born in Potowomut, R.I. He was brought up in the Quaker faith of his father, a preacher, and was self-educated. In 1770 he was elected a member of the General Assembly of Rhode Island. As the conflict between the American colonies and England increased, Greene prepared himself for war, which he foresaw as inevitable, by engaging in military exercises. In 1775 he was appointed brigadier general of the Rhode Island forces sent by the General Assembly to join the Continental army besieging the British in Boston. Later, after winning the esteem of George Washington for his service in battles in the vicinity of New York City, Greene was made a major general and was assigned to the command of the Revolutionary troops in New Jersey. Subsequently he fought in the battles of Trenton, Princeton, Brandywine, and Germantown. In 1778 he was appointed quartermaster general of the Revolutionary Army, occupying that post until 1780. In the latter year he sat as president of the military court which tried Major John André, the accomplice of Benedict Arnold (qq.v.) in espionage and treachery. Greene was then given command of the southern Revolutionary army and in 1781–82 conducted a notably successful campaign against the British in Georgia and the Carolinas, forcing the enemy to retreat to three coastal bases where they were subsequently bottled up. North and South Carolina and Georgia honored Greene with gifts of valuable estates, to one of which, Mulberry Grove on the Savannah R. in Georgia, he retired after the war was won.

GREENE, ROBERT (1560?–92), English dramatist and prose writer, born at Norwich, and educated at Oxford and Cambridge universities. After traveling in Europe between 1578 and 1583 he settled in London, where he spent the rest of his short and debauched life. Greene was a prolific and popular prose writer. Some of his prose romances were *Mamillia* (1583), written in imitation of John Lyly's *Euphues; The Myrrour of Modestie* (1584); *Perimedes the Blacke-Smith* (1588); and *Menaphon* (1589), written in imitation of Philip Sidney's *Arcadia*. Greene's verse and songs are scattered throughout his prose. He wrote many pamphlets, including a series on the London underworld. The autobiographical *Greene's Groat's-Worth of Wit Bought with a Million of Repentance* which contains an alleged allusion to William Shakespeare, *The Repentance of Robert Greene, Master of Arts,* and *Greene's Vision* were all written in 1592. His most outstanding dramatic works are *The Honorable History of Friar Bacon and Friar Bungay* (1592) and *The Scottish History of James IV* (1592).

GREENFINCH, common name for any of a number of birds of the Finch family, often classified as a genus, *Chloris*. The most common species is the European greenfinch, *Chloris chloris*. Its plumage is green, mixed with gray and brown. The male, generally yellowish-green in color, is more brightly tinted than the female. The greenfinch is a poor singer in its native state, but readily mimics the songs of other cage birds when confined

with them. Its nest is cup-shaped, and four to six eggs are laid in one setting. Greenfinches are found throughout Europe and in w. Asia and N. Africa. They are among the commonest birds in England, and are found there in all seasons of the year. Greenfinches are also sometimes called green linnets.

An entirely different bird, the Texas sparrow, *Arremonops rufivirgatus,* is sometimes called greenfinch in the U.S. Its plumage is olive-green in the upper parts and dull white below. It frequents bushes and thickets from S.E. Texas to the E. part of Mexico, and is about 6½ in. long.

GREENGAGE. See PLUM.

GREENHEART, or BEBEERU, a timber tree, *Nectandra rodioei,* belonging to the Laurel family, native to Guiana. It has thick, shiny leaves, pale-yellow flowers borne in clusters, and a bitter, one-seeded fruit. The greenish wood, called greenheart, is extremely strong and hard and takes a high polish. It is very resistant to water-soaking and insect attack, and is extensively used in the building of ships, wharves, docks, and canal locks. The bark, called bebeeru, contains the alkaloid *bebeerine,* a drug used as a substitute for quinine.

GREENHOUSE, a glass building used for cultivation and protection of tender plants and of plants grown out of season. Several specialized types of greenhouses are named according to their function. A conservatory is a greenhouse used primarily for displaying plants, particularly cultivated ornamental plants. A hothouse, or stove, is a greenhouse in which the temperature is sufficient to maintain normal growth rates of tropical plants. A dry stove is a greenhouse in which humidity and soil moisture are controlled to aid the growth of plants, such as cactus, which require a dry environment.

Modern greenhouses are adapted to any greenhouse use by suitable control of temperature, moisture, and lighting. Small greenhouses are frequently of the lean-to type. A lean-to house is built against an existing wall, and consists of a glass-paned sloping roof and three supporting glass-paned sides. Larger greenhouses have roofs which slope toward two sides; the roof is supported by two sidewalls and two endwalls. When more than one greenhouse is built on the same site, the buildings are arranged in a row so that two adjacent buildings share the same inside wall. Another extensively used type of greenhouse, the ridge-and-furrow house, has no walls between adjacent units, so that a row of structures comprises a single large house. Posts supporting greenhouse walls and roofs are usually steel pipe or structural steel in the form of I-beams. The frames of the walls and roofs are usually made of a combination of wood and steel. A frame must be strong enough to hold panes of glass in severe weather and still be so narrow that a minimum of shade is cast. The upper row of panes on each side of the roof may be opened partially or completely, for ventilation. All wooden and metal parts are painted prior to the erection of a greenhouse, and must be repainted frequently to protect them from extremes of moisture and temperature.

Light. Natural sunlight, in temperate regions, is usually sufficient to meet the light requirements of plants during spring and fall. In winter, natural light is sometimes supplemented by artificial light to assist plants which are in active growth. The amount of sunlight is sometimes too great in summer, and so the glass panes of greenhouses are often covered with slat shades or whitewashed to reduce the light.

Temperature. Proper temperature conditions in greenhouses are maintained through much of the year by heat derived from the sun's rays. Energy given off by the sun is transmitted by short waves, which pass freely through the atmosphere and glass. Short-wave energy falling on objects in greenhouses is transformed to long-wave energy (see FLUORESCENCE) which cannot pass through glass, but is absorbed or reflected by the glass walls and roof. Most of this energy is retained within the greenhouse. During the winter months it is often necessary to supplement natural heat. During the hotter months, greenhouse heat is reduced by whitewashing the panes, by opening ventilators, and sometimes by use of artificial cooling systems.

Moisture. Humidity is primarily controlled by the quantity of water used in the greenhouse. The humidity of houses containing plants which are adapted to arid environments is controlled by watering the plants sparsely. Humidity necessary to plants which are adapted to moderately moist situations is supplied by evaporation from thoroughly-watered soils. When greater humidity is required, extra moisture is supplied by watering the floor of the greenhouse. Humidity may also be raised by opening the ventilators when outside air is more humid than greenhouse air, and may be lowered by the same means when outside air is less humid than greenhouse air. Pot-grown plants, such as orchids, are often humidified by setting them on racks above beds of moistened cinders.

GREENLAND, largest island in the world (Australia considered as a continent), belonging to Denmark and situated between the North Atlantic and Arctic oceans. Greenland lies mostly within the Arctic circle, and is separated from the American Arctic Archipelago chiefly by Davis Strait and Baffin Bay, and from Iceland, on the E., by the Strait of Denmark. From Cape Farewell (59° 45′ N.) to Cape Morris Jesup (83° 39′ N.), the extreme s. to N. distance is about 1650 m. The maximum distance from east to west is nearly 800 m. (near the 70th parallel). The entire coast, lined with fiords, is roughly estimated at 3600 m. The total area is about 840,000 sq.m., of which about 710,000 sq.m. is icecap and 130,000 sq.m. is ice-free land. The population (1953) is 25,302, including 1443 Europeans.

The capital, Godthaab (pop., about 1300), on the southwestern coast, is the oldest Danish settlement on the island, having been founded in 1721. Julianehaab (about 3000), on the southern coast, is the largest settlement. Other settlements include Godhavn (about 300), on Disko Island, off the western coast; Etah, a point of departure for Polar expeditions, on the northwestern coast; Jakobshavn, on the west coast; Ivigtut, about 100 m. west of Julianehaab; and Angmagssalik and Scoresbysund (about 1000), on the eastern coast.

The interior of Greenland is a lofty plateau, 4000 to 9000 ft. or more in altitude, composed chiefly of granite and gneissose rocks, and covered with ice. Only a few isolated peaks, such as Tiningertok (7340 ft.) near Cape Farewell, emerge above the icecap, which has a maximum depth, near the center of the island, of 6200 ft. Drainage is afforded mainly by the so-called ice-fiords, in which thousands of icebergs are formed each year. The mammals of Greenland are more American than European, and include the musk-ox, polar wolf, lemming, and reindeer. The varieties of seal and whale, and most of the species of fish and sea birds, are also American rather than European. The polar bear, Arctic fox, Arctic hare, and stoat are circumpolar forms.

Whaling, sealing, fishing, and fur trapping are the principal industries. Cattle, sheep, and goats are raised in small numbers in some portions of the southwestern coast; and hardy vegetables are grown. Greenland is the main source of natural cryolite, used in the manufacture of aluminum. Marble is quarried, graphite is abundant, and some coal, of poor

Keystone

IN GREENLAND

Above: An inlet at the settlement of God-havn, on Disko Island, off the west coast. Left: An Eskimo hunter and his daughter.

are cryolite (to Denmark and the U.S.), fish, hides and skins, whale and fish oil, marble, and graphite.

History and Exploration. Greenland was discovered by Eric the Red, father of Leif Ericson, toward the end of the 10th century, and Norse settlements, which later vanished, were established in the extreme southern portions. In the course of the search for the Northwest Passage, Greenland was rediscovered. John Davis (q.v.) visited the island in 1585, and his explorative work, together with that of Henry Hudson and William Baffin (qq.v.), afforded knowledge of the west coast. The foundation of Danish Greenland was laid by the establishment by Hans Egede of a Danish mission at Godthaab in 1721. In the 19th century the exploration of the west coast was continued by E. A. Ingelfield, E. K. Kane, C. F. Hall, G. S. Nares, A. W. Greely, and R. E. Peary. The exploration of the east coast was conducted by the Scoresbys, father and son, and by W. A. Graah, G. K. Amdrup, G. F. Holm, T. V. Garde, C. Ryder, A. G. Nathorst, K. C. Koldeway, M. Erichsen, J. P. Koch, A. Wegener, and E. Mikkelsen. L. A.

quality, is mined in the Disko Bay region. The climate is extremely cold, but during the short summer in the south the mean temperature is 48° F. Only a small part of the narrow coastal fringe is inhabited, chiefly the southwestern portion. The trade of Greenland, except in cryolite, is a government monopoly. Exports

Beaumont, J. B. Lockwood, and R. E. Peary made the first explorations of northern Greenland. Explorations of inner Greenland were made by Peary, Fridtjof Nansen, Garde, Erichsen, Mikkelsen, A. de Quervain, K. Rasmussen, Koch, Wegener, and W. H. Hobbs. In 1930-31, British and German expeditions made weather observations on the inland ice north of the Arctic circle. In 1933 an American expedition fostered by the University of Michigan and Pan-American Airways made meteorological researches more than 340 m. north of the Arctic circle. See ARCTIC EXPLORATION.

The United States relinquished its claim to land in northern Greenland, based on Peary's discoveries, when it purchased the Virgin Islands from Denmark in 1916. In May, 1921, Denmark declared the entire island of Greenland to be Danish territory. The questioning by Norway of Denmark's exclusive jurisdiction over Greenland led to an agreement in 1924 whereby hunting and fishing rights on the northeast coast were granted to Norway. Germany's occupation of Denmark in 1940, during World War II, brought the status of Greenland again into question. Negotiations between the U.S. government and the Danish minister at Washington resulted in an agreement on April 9, 1941, granting the United States the right "to construct, maintain and operate such landing fields, seaplane facilities and radio and meteorological installations as may be necessary" to protect the status quo in the Western Hemisphere; at the same time the United States assumed protective custody over Greenland for the duration of World War II, although recognizing Danish sovereignty.

Greenland is the source of many of the weather changes in the northern hemisphere, and knowledge of Greenland weather is of prime importance for the prediction of conditions in the North Atlantic and in western Europe. Weather and radio stations are of inestimable value for Atlantic aerial traffic. In 1944, during World War II, a German radioweather station on the northeast coast was destroyed by U.S. Coast Guardsmen, and various German attempts to establish weather bases on Greenland were dispersed by Coast Guard vessels. Three American bases were established, one above the Arctic circle on the west coast, one at Julianehaab, and one on the east coast at Angmagssalik. In May, 1947, Denmark requested that the United States end the 1941 agreement. The U.S. reply stressed the importance of Greenland "in the defensive system of the . . . Western Hemisphere" and requested a "new agreement in keeping with the

letter and spirit of the Charter of the United Nations . . .". Protracted negotiations between the two countries culminated (April, 1951) in a twenty-year pact providing for Danish control of the chief U.S. naval station in Greenland and for the establishment of jointly operated defense areas. By the terms of other provisions the armed forces of the members of the North Atlantic Treaty Organization (q.v.) were authorized to use all naval, air, and military bases on the island. Later in 1951 the United States began construction of a vast strategic air base at Thule, an Eskimo settlement on the N.W. coast, about 930 m. from the North Pole.

In June, 1952, the Danish government and private Danish, Swedish, and Canadian interests formed a company to exploit recently discovered deposits of lead, zinc, and wolfram in eastern Greenland. Under the provisions of the new Danish constitution, adopted in May, 1953, Greenland became an integral part of the Danish Commonwealth and obtained representation in the national parliament. The U.S. Air Force base at Thule was completed in 1953. Greenland's new political status was formally recognized by the U.N. General Assembly on Nov. 22, 1954.

GREENLET. See VIREO.

GREENLING. See ROCK TROUT.

GREEN LINNET. See GREENFINCH.

GREEN MOUNTAIN BOYS, the name applied to the soldiers of Vermont in the American Revolution. They were originally organized in 1775 by Ethan Allen (q.v.) to oppose the claims of New York to Vermont territory. At the outbreak of the Revolutionary War, the Green Mountain Boys, with reinforcements from Massachusetts and Connecticut, seized British-held Fort Ticonderoga, at the head of Lake Champlain.

GREEN MOUNTAINS, a range of the northern section of the Appalachian Mountains (q.v.), extending northward through the center of Vermont to the Canadian boundary and southward, under the names of Berkshire Hills and Taconic and Hoosac mountains, through w. Massachusetts and Connecticut into E. New York. The greater part of Vermont, called the Green Mountain State, is covered by the forested peaks of the Green Mountains. Erosion and weathering have worn and rounded the peaks of the Green Mountains, one of the oldest ranges in North America. The highest elevations reached are in Vermont, where five of the peaks exceed 4000 ft. above sea level. Mount Mansfield is the highest, rising to 4393 ft. above sea level, and the others are Killington Peak (4241 ft.), Lincoln (4135 ft.), Camel's Hump (4083 ft.), and Jay Peak (4018 ft.). The valley of the Connecticut R. lies to the E. of the range and on the W. are the Lake Champlain and Hudson R. basins. The mountains are heavily wooded with pine, spruce, and other evergreens, to which fact they owe their name; in addition they contain forests of sugar maple, beech, and birch. Several streams flowing into the Connecticut and Hudson rivers rise in the mountains, where they furnish abundant water power to communities in the region. The area is rich in deposits of granite, marble, and slate. Farming and dairying are important industries in the fertile valleys.

The Green Mountains are a popular summer and winter resort area. Smuggler's Notch, a wooded gorge more than 1000 ft. deep, lying just N. of Mount Mansfield, is frequently visited. The many lakes and streams in the mountains abound in fish, and the mountain slopes afford many miles of ski trails. The Long Trail, a path for hikers built by the Green Mountain Club, extends along the ridge of the mountains.

GREENOCK, a seaport and parliamentary burgh of Renfrewshire, Scotland, situated on the S. shore of the Firth of Clyde, 23 m. by rail N.W. of Glasgow. It has a fine harbor, which has been continuously enlarged and improved since 1710. The chief import of the port is raw sugar, and the principal exports are machinery and ships. Greenock has been a shipbuilding and sugar-refining center since 1765; other important industries in the burgh include fishing, distilling, and the manufacture of aluminum, engines, woolens and worsteds, sailcloth, cordage, and paper. The burgh fronts on the firth for a distance of about 4 m., rising gradually to a series of hills in the S. Among its interesting buildings are the museum and lecture hall, dating from 1876, and the Watt Institution, founded in 1837 in memory of James Watt, the noted mechanical engineer and inventor, who was born in Greenock in 1736. The institution contains the public library, a scientific library, and a marble statue of James Watt by Sir Francis Chantrey. In addition, Greenock contains the grave of Mary Campbell, the "Highland Mary" celebrated by Robert Burns in his poetry, and the subject of his poem *To Mary in Heaven*. Greenock became a burgh of barony in 1635 under a charter granted by Charles I, and early in the 18th century, with the increase of trade between Great Britain and the American possessions, it began its development from a small fishing village into an important seaport. It became a parliamentary burgh in 1832. Pop. (1953 est.) 77,600.

GREENOUGH, HORATIO (1805–52), American sculptor, born in Boston, and educated at Harvard University. He executed busts of John Quincy Adams and other leading citizens in Boston in 1826. He then went to live in Florence, Italy, where he received a commission to sculpture some figures for James Fenimore Cooper. The U.S. government appointed him to make a large statue of George Washington. The statue was unveiled in 1843, and is now in the Smithsonian Institution in Washington, D.C. The government then commissioned him to do a large group sculpture, the "Rescue", representing the conflict between the Indians and the Anglo-Saxons, which was also placed in Washington. Among his other works are the "Venus Victrix", the "Medora", and "Lafayette", all in the gallery of the Boston Athenaeum.

GREEN RIVER, a river of Wyoming and Utah, rising in western Wyoming, and flowing S. and E. through the N.W. corner of Colorado into Utah where, after a southerly course, it unites with the Colorado R. in San Juan County. It has a total length of about 750 m., and is one of the principal headstreams of the Colorado R. The river flows through the Dinosaur National Monument in N.E. Utah and N.W. Colorado, and is there noted for the scenic beauty of its canyons.

GREENSBORO, county seat of Guilford Co., N.C., situated 80 miles N.W. of Raleigh, in the Piedmont region. It is served by two railroads, and maintains a municipal airport. The city is the commercial and manufacturing center of a cotton-growing region. The principal industry in Greensboro is the manufacture of cotton textiles, especially blue denim; the city contains a denim mill said to be the largest of its kind in the world. Other important industries in the city are the manufacture of chemicals, automobile bodies, sheet metal, machine tools, stoves, fertilizer, and cigars. Greensboro is the site of the Woman's College of the University of North Carolina, established in 1892; Greensboro College for women (Methodist, 1838); and three educational institutions for Negroes, the Negro Agricultural and Technical College (1891), Bennett College for women (1873), and Emanuel Lutheran College (1903). Guilford College, founded in 1837 by the Society of Friends, is situated about 5 miles W. of the city, in a Friends settlement dating from the colonial period. William Sydney Porter (O. Henry), the famous American short-story writer, was born in Greensboro; the Masonic Temple Museum in the city stands on the site of his birthplace. Guilford Courthouse National Military Park, commemorating a Revolutionary battle fought on March 15, 1781, is 6 miles N.W. of the city.

Greensboro was founded as the county seat in 1808, and named in honor of General Nathanael Greene, the American hero of the Battle of Guilford Courthouse. The Confederate general, Joseph E. Johnston, disbanded his army at Greensboro after his surrender to General William T. Sherman on April 26, 1865. Pop. (1950) 74,389.

GREEN SNAKE, name commonly applied to several different snakes which are predominantly green in color. In the U.S., the term refers to either of two harmless, colubrine snakes, which subsist solely on insects. Both are oviparous (egg-laying). The smooth green snake, or grass snake, *Liopeltis vernalis,* is found E. of the Rocky Mts. from S. Canada to Mexico. This slender, smooth-scaled snake attains a maximum length of two feet. Its back is bright green, and its lower parts white. The smooth green snake is often found in heaps of stones at the edges of moist meadows. The newly hatched young snakes are bluish-black in color.

The rough green snake, *Opheodrys aestivus* is common in the S.E. States, and is occasionally found as far north as central New Jersey. This snake attains a maximum length of three feet, and is slender, with rough, keeled scales. Its back is bright green and its lower parts yellow.

The name green snake has also been applied to several African snakes, especially those in the genus *Chlorophis.*

GREEN TURTLE, an edible sea turtle, *Chelonia mydas,* used in the preparation of such table delicacies as turtle soup and turtle steak. It derives its name from the green color of its fat. The eggs of the green turtle are also valued as food. The green turtle is common in all warm seas and may sometimes be found, in summertime, along the N. Atlantic coasts of the U.S. and Europe. Adult green turtles reach a shell length of over 3½ ft. The body weight of a turtle this size is over 400 lbs. Commercial specimens usually weigh from 50 to 150 lbs. The smooth shell on the green turtle's back is olive-green blotched with yellow. The head and the seal-like flippers are dark-brown. They are covered with rough, horny plates, each plate bordered with white or brilliant yellow. The shell covering the chest and abdomen of the green turtle is soft and yielding,

Green turtle, about 3½ feet in length

and cannot long support the weight of the animal out of water; specimens that are to be kept alive and fresh in market are turned on their backs. The male green turtle never leaves the sea; the female leaves it only to lay her eggs. The eggs, 200 to 300 in number, are laid at night, in sand above the reach of the sea. The young are hatched by the sun's heat and soon crawl into the sea in search of food. Green turtles are omnivorous but subsist chiefly on marine vegetation.

GREENVILLE, county seat of Washington Co., Miss., situated on the Mississippi R., 95 miles N. of Vicksburg. It is served by two railroads, and by river steamers and barges. A bridge at Greenville spans the Mississippi R. to Lake Village, Arkansas. The city is the center and shipping point of an agricultural region producing large quantities of long-staple cotton, and also corn, oats, alfalfa, hogs, and beef cattle. Greenville contains extensive stockyards, warehouses, cotton compresses, cotton-oil mills, woodworking plants, and a pulp mill manufacturing wallboard and insulating material. A yacht harbor at Greenville serves pleasure craft on the river.

The city was established after the end of the Civil War just north of the site of its first settlement, known as Old Greenville, which was burned by Federal troops following the capture of Memphis. It was incorporated as a town in 1870 and as a city in 1886. Pop. (1950) 29,936.

GREENVILLE, county seat of Pitt Co., N.C., situated on the Tar R., 84 miles E.S.E. of Raleigh. It is served by two railroads, shipping on the Tar R. and the Inland Waterway, and has a city-county airport. The city is the commercial center of a rich agricultural area producing bright-leaf tobacco, cotton, corn, potatoes and sweet potatoes, peanuts, cucumbers, vegetables, livestock, and poultry. It is one of the largest tobacco markets in the U.S., and contains many tobacco warehouses and processing plants. Greenville is also a market for cattle and hogs. Among the industrial establishments in the city are lumber mills, a chick hatchery, a feed mill, marble works, brickworks, a hosiery mill, printing plants, sheet-metal works, machine shops, a potato-processing plant, a meat-packing plant, and factories manufacturing fertilizer, soft drinks, plastics, cotton yarns, and drugs. Greenville is the site of East Carolina Teachers College, established in 1907. The town was founded as Martinborough in 1774, and the name was changed to Greenville in 1786 in honor of Gen. Nathanael Greene, a hero of the Revolution. Pop. (1950) 16,724.

GREENVILLE, county seat of Greenville Co., S.C., situated on the Reedy R., about 30 miles s.w. of Spartanburg. It is served by three railroads, and has a municipal airport. The city lies near the foot of the Blue Ridge mountains, at an altitude of 1040 ft. above sea level. It is one of the leading textile centers of the South, and a large cotton market. Products manufactured by the textile plants in Greenville and the surrounding region range from heavy duck to fine silks. Among the textile plants in the city are a worsted mill, a yarn-dyeing plant, and two of the largest bleaching, printing, and finishing plants in the South. Other important industries in Greenville are meat packing, the processing of peanuts, and the manufacture of dresses, shirts, underwear, concrete pipe, leather belting, foundings, machine-shop products, and textile equipment. Greenville is the site of Furman University (Baptist), organized in 1826, Bob Jones University (1927), and the Shriners Hospital for Crippled Children. The site was laid out for the county seat in 1797 as Pleasantburg and in 1831 the name of the town was changed to Greenville. In 1868 it was incorporated as a city. Pop. (1950) 58,161.

GREENWEED. See DYER'S-BROOM.

GREENWICH, a town of Fairfield Co., Conn., situated on Long Island Sound, 28 miles N.E. of New York City, of which it is a residential suburb. It is served by a railroad, with railroad stations at four of the nine sections of which the town is constituted. Greenwich has about 6 miles of coastline containing numerous public and private beaches, beach clubs, and yacht clubs. The town occupies an area of 48 sq.m., and is noted for the beauty of its homes and estates, and for its many recreational facilities. The latter include 330 miles of bridle paths and six golf courses. Among the interesting buildings in Greenwich is Putnam Cottage, built in 1731,

from which Revolutionary general Israel Putnam fled when surprised by a British force in February, 1779. The cottage contains relics of the colonial and Revolutionary periods. Greenwich was settled in 1640 by Captain Daniel Patrick and Robert Feaks under the auspices of the New Haven Colony. However, from 1642 to 1650 it was a part of the Dutch province of New Amsterdam. In 1656 the settlement again became a part of the New Haven Colony, and was united with Stamford. In 1662, as part of Stamford, it came under the jurisdiction of Connecticut. Greenwich became a separate town in 1665. Pop. (1950) 40,835.

GREENWICH, a metropolitan borough of London, England, situated on the s. bank of the Thames R., and connected with the part of London on the N. bank by the Greenwich and Blackwell tunnels. The main street, extending through the borough from west to east, is Woolwich Road, part of the old Roman highway through Kent. The Royal Naval College in Greenwich, established in 1873, occupies the famous Greenwich Hospital building. Begun at the end of the 17th century, on the site of the earlier Greenwich House, the building was opened as a hospital for seamen in 1705. One of its designers was Sir Christopher Wren. At one time 2700 retired sailors were boarded at Greenwich Hospital and 6000 outpensioners received aid from the institution's funds. In 1869 an act was passed compelling the seamen in residence to leave, after provisions had been made for the granting of liberal pensions to them in lieu of board. Historic Greenwich House, which stood on the site before the construction of the present buildings, was a royal palace in 1300, when it was granted by Henry V to Thomas Beaufort, Duke of Exeter. In 1447 it reverted to the crown, and was the birthplace of Henry VIII, Queen Mary, and Queen Elizabeth. It was destroyed by order of Charles II during the Restoration, and the construction of the present buildings commenced. Another celebrated structure in Greenwich is the Greenwich Observatory (q.v.). The National Maritime Museum is attached to the Royal Naval College. The borough was once famous for the annual whitebait dinners held by the members of the British cabinet at the ancient Ship Tavern from the early 19th century until 1894, when the custom was discontinued. The tavern was closed in 1908. Greenwich is first mentioned as a port for the Danes in the early 11th century. Present-day Greenwich contains ship-

British Information Services

Original buildings of the Greenwich Observatory at Greenwich in London, England

building yards, machine shops, and cordage factories. Pop. (1951 prelim.) 91,492.

GREENWICH OBSERVATORY, astronomical observatory situated at Hurstmonceux Castle in East Sussex, England, about 60 miles S.E. of its original site in Greenwich (q.v.). The former location of the observatory was arbitrarily established as longitude 0°. A plaque in the original structure marks the zero point from which longitude is calculated. Because the London haze had made accurate astronomical observations almost impossible, the observatory's equipment was gradually moved, beginning in 1946, from its original site to Hurstmonceux Castle. The move to East Sussex was completed late in 1953.

The observatory was founded in 1675 by King Charles II to keep accurate tables of the moon's position for the calculation of longitude by English ships. In 1750 publication of the tables was begun in the *Astronomical Observations,* which were published annually after 1838. Meridian observations of the sun, stars, and planets also proceeded at the observatory. Photographs of the sun were taken daily, conditions permitting, and a continuous photographic record of sunspots was kept, starting in 1873. The satellites of the planets Neptune and Uranus were discovered through the observatory's 24-inch Newtonian reflector telescope by the English astronomer William Lassell in 1846 and 1851 respectively. The eighth satellite of Jupiter was another discovery made at the observatory. The Greenwich Observatory, properly termed the Royal Greenwich Observatory, was under the jurisdiction of the Admiralty,

and its director was the Astronomer Royal. Among famed astronomers royal who worked at the observatory were Edmund Halley (q.v.) and Nevil Maskelyne.

GREENWICH VILLAGE, a residential section of the borough of Manhattan, New York City, usually regarded as comprising the area within West 14th Street on the N., Broadway on the E., West Houston Street on the S., and West Street on the W. The history of Greenwich Village dates from colonial times, when a number of wealthy residents of the city, then confined to the region S. of Wall Street, constructed country homes in the area. At the close of the 18th century, the Village still retained its rural character, but subsequent events, particularly a series of yellow-fever epidemics which forced hundreds of New Yorkers to take refuge beyond the city limits, speeded the growth of the community. By the middle of the 19th century the Village, largely inhabited by well-to-do families, had become an integral part of the metropolis. Large numbers of immigrants, mainly Irish and Italians, found homes in the Village during the final quarter of the 19th century. The neighborhood then developed distinctive characteristics, including sidewalk markets, inexpensive cafes, numerous saloons, and an Old-World character.

Shortly after the turn of the century Greenwich Village became the mecca of artistic, literary, and political rebels from all parts of the country. They transformed the community into a stronghold of the cultural renaissance then burgeoning in America. As the center of the "Bohemian" movement, which the rebellion against conventionalism was popularly termed, Greenwich Village rapidly and justifiably gained wide renown. Such Village publications as *The Seven Arts* and *The Masses* became the focus of liberal-radical thought in art and politics. The "A" Club, led by Frances Perkins, Mary Heaton Vorse, and other prominent feminists, substantially advanced the struggle for women's suffrage and social reforms. The Washington Square Players, nucleus of the present-day Theater Guild, and the Provincetown Players provided opportunity and scope for the fresh and genuinely creative talents of such distinguished figures of the American theater as the dramatist Eugene O'Neill, the impresario-playwright George Cram Cook, the novelist and playwright Susan Glaspell, the lyric and dramatic poetess Edna St. Vincent Millay, the stage designer Robert Edmond Jones, and a host of others.

After the United States entered World War I, stringent wartime curbs on radical activity and strong pressure for social conformity tended to disperse the Bohemian community in Greenwich Village. Except for the prevalence of night clubs and nondescript buildings, the contemporary Village differs little outwardly from other residential districts of Manhattan. Artists, sculptors, writers, and poets, professional as well as neophyte, still gravitate toward the section, however, and periodic open-air exhibits of their paintings, sculptures, and other works are one of the notable features of the neighborhood.

The Village contains numerous historic landmarks, including the site of the house in which Tom Paine, the pamphleteer of the American Revolution, passed the final years of his life; Washington Square, the traditional center of the community and formerly the site of a potter's field; MacDougal Alley, a blind lane fronted by rows of converted century-old mews; and St. Luke's Chapel, dating from 1822. Among the well-known cultural and educational institutions situated in Greenwich Village are the Salmagundi Club, the New School for Social Research, and several of the schools which comprise New York University.

GREENWOOD, county seat of Leflore Co., Miss., situated on the Yazoo R., 135 miles s.s.w. of Memphis, Tenn., in the heart of the Mississippi Delta. It is served by two railroads, and is an important market and shipping point for long staple cotton. Among its industrial establishments are cotton compresses and gins, cottonseed-oil mills, canneries, sawmills, woodworking shops, and factories manufacturing furniture, drugs, agricultural implements, and radio-testing machines. Greenwood was settled in 1834, incorporated in 1844, and named for Greenwood Leflore, the Choctaw chief, whose home "Malmaison", built in 1854, is situated 10 miles E. of the city. Greenwood was chartered as a city in 1915. Pop. (1950) 18,-061.

GREGARINE, any parasitic, single-celled animal in the order Gregarinida. Gregarines attack invertebrate animals, especially beetles, cockroaches, earthworms, flies, and lobsters. They are world-wide in distribution. Typical adult gregarines are shaped like the figure 8, and are less than 1/100 in. long. The largest gregarine, *Gregarina gigantea,* which attacks the European lobster, reaches a length of over ½ in. The gregarines are sporeformers; their young are produced within hard, round capsules, or spores, which protect them until the spore is eaten by a specific host. The spore is dissolved by the intestinal juices of the host and the young enter the lining cells of the intestine, where they mature. When the gregarines have outgrown their host cells, they pass into the intestinal cavity and mate, producing new spores, each containing several young. The new spores are eliminated in the feces of the host. See SPOROZOA.

GREGG, JOHN ROBERT (1867–1948), inventor of a shorthand system of writing, born in Rockcorry, Ireland. He attended public school, and at the age of ten took up the study of "speed writing". After studying the shorthand methods already devised, Gregg, in 1888, wrote a pamphlet *Light Line Phonography, the Phonetic System of Writing,* containing a shorthand system of his own invention. He emigrated to the United States in 1893, and his shorthand system became very popular soon thereafter. The system was adapted to thirteen languages, and by the time Gregg died eighteen million people throughout the world had studied his system of shorthand. Gregg received many awards for his work. The basic book on Gregg shorthand is *The Gregg Shorthand Manual;* some of Gregg's other books are *The Gregg Phrase Book, Gregg Speed Practice, The Gregg Reporter,* and *The Private Secretary.* See SHORTHAND.

GREGORIAN CHANT, a variety of plain song which has been used for liturgical purposes by the Roman Catholic Church since early Christian times, and which has taken its name from a notable collection of over six hundred examples of such music assembled by Pope Gregory the Great (see GREGORY) in the 6th century and known as *Antiphonarius Cento*. The Gregorian chant consists of melody sung in unison; the melody is not combined with any other melody as in counterpoint (q.v.), nor does it have any harmonic accompaniment. The Gregorian chant is not divided into bars in the manner of modern music, and its rhythm is not indicated by time signatures, such as 4/4 and 6/8; the chant has a flexible and irregular rhythm closely following that of the texts, usually Biblical, for which it is composed. It employs any one of the eight church modes (see GREEK MUSIC).

The Gregorian chant was standardized and further developed by the *Schola Cantorum*, a school of music established by Pope Gregory at Rome. St. Augustine introduced the chant into England toward the end of the 6th century, and subsequently it spread from Rome to France, Spain, and other European countries. It was the chief form of music in Europe during the 11th century, but began to decline in popularity during the 13th century when contrapuntal church music came into use; its use declined further in the 14th century when secular musical forms such as madrigals and folksongs became popular, and by the 16th century it had fallen into almost complete disuse. Several attempts to revive the Gregorian chant were subsequently made, but not until the second half of the 19th century and the early part of the 20th were they successful. Under popes Pius IX, Leo XIII, and Pius X many original manuscripts of the chants were collected, and extensive research was made as to their proper delivery, which by that time had become virtually a lost art. In 1904 Pope Pius X decreed that the Church use the Gregorian chant thenceforth, and in 1908 a large collection of the chants, edited by the Benedictine monks of Solesmes, France, and known as the *Vatican Gradual,* was made obligatory for the Church.

GREGORY, name of sixteen popes and two antipopes of whom the most important were the following.

1. GREGORY I, THE GREAT (540?-604), Saint, Pope of Rome, born in Rome. His father was Gordianus, a wealthy patrician, and his mother was Saint Silvia. When about thirty years of age he was made Prefect of Rome by the Emperor Justin II. At the death of his father Gregory inherited considerable wealth, which he used for religious purposes.

Pope Gregory I (early-manuscript miniature)

He founded six monasteries in Sicily and one (St. Andrew's) in Rome. He resigned his civil office, gave all his money, jewels, robes, and furniture to the poor, and retired to St. Andrew's as an ordinary monk. Pelagius II appointed Gregory as ambassador to the imperial court of Constantinople in 579. Several years later Gregory was appointed abbot of St. Andrew's, and there completed an exposition of the Book of Job (the *Moralia*) and delivered lectures on other Old Testament books. During this period, according to the Venerable Bede, he saw a group of handsome Anglo-Saxon youths in the slave market and, learning that they came from a pagan land, resolved to devote himself to the conversion of England to Christianity. Gregory is said to have set out on this journey, but was intercepted by direction of the papacy and compelled to return to Rome, where he served as regionary deacon.

Pelagius II died of plague in 590, and Gregory was unanimously chosen to succeed him. Over his own earnest protest, Gregory was consecrated Pope in September, 590. His pontificate was marked by zeal in propagating Christianity. His most important missionary endeavor was the conversion of Britain, which was begun, under his direction, by Augustine in 597. Gregory vigorously opposed paganism and the Christian heresies, such as Arianism, Donatism, and Manichæanism, of Italy, Spain, and Gaul, but protected the Jews from persecution and loss of legal privilege. The organization of the medieval papacy was patterned after his administration. He introduced several changes into the liturgy of the mass, such as the inclusion of the Pater Noster prior to the division of the Host, and of the Gloria after the Gradual. Gregorian chant is traditionally considered to have been his revision of the system of church music. He exerted great influence in matters of doctrine, and became the Fourth Doctor of the (Latin) Church. He died in 604, and was buried in the basilica of St. Peter. His feast is celebrated on March 12.

2. GREGORY II, Saint (d. 731), Pope of Rome, born in Rome. He was elected to the papacy in 715, succeeding Constantine I. During the early part of his pontificate he supported the Eastern Roman Empire in preference to the Lombard invaders of Italy. He later broke off with the eastern Emperor, Leo the Isaurian, because of the excessive taxation of Italian imperial subjects. Leo attempted to subdue Gregory by violence, but the pope, with the support of the Lombards and the people of Rome, succeeded in evading the Emperor. Gregory supported St. Boniface, an English Benedictine monk, in his missionary work in Bavaria, Thuringia, Hesse, and Friesland. His feast is celebrated on February 13.

3. GREGORY III, Saint (d. 741), Pope of Rome, born in Syria. He became pope in 731, and excommunicated the Iconoclasts at a council held at Rome in the same year. The retaliations of the emperor, Leo the Isaurian, weakened the tenuous tie between the eastern empire and the papacy. The encroachment of the Lombards in Italy during his pontificate became so formidable that Gregory sent three papal missions to Charles Martel, the mayor of the Frankish palace, offering him a protectorate over Rome in return for assistance against the Lombards. The missions yielded no results during the lifetime of Gregory, but an alliance was later concluded with Martel's son, Pepin the Short, during the pontificate of his successor, Stephen II. The feast of St. Gregory III is celebrated on November 28.

4. GREGORY VII, Saint (1020?–85), Pope of Rome, born at Siena, Tuscany, and educated at the convent of St. Mary on the Aventine in Rome. He was known as Hildebrand before his election to the papacy. As a

Benedictine monk he became chaplain to Gregory VI, and shared a year of exile with that pontiff at Cologne, where he gained a thorough knowledge of ecclesiastical and political conditions in Germany. He accompanied the succeeding pope, Leo IX, to Rome in 1049. Leo appointed Hildebrand administrator of the patrimony of St. Peter. Hildebrand became a dominant personality in the papacy during the pontificates of Leo IX, Stephen IX, Nicholas II, and Alexander II. Under Nicholas, Hildebrand was instrumental in bringing about an alliance with the Normans of s. Italy and in instituting necessary legislation for the future election of pontiffs by the College of Cardinals.

Hildebrand was unanimously elected pontiff at Rome, three days after the death of Alexander II, and was consecrated as Gregory VII on June 30, 1073. His pontificate was a series of attempts to bring about a state of affairs which he considered to be ordained by God; he believed that the divine will should be the force governing a unified society comprising all mankind, and as a result was continually in conflict with civil governments.

Controversy over the right of investiture supplied the motive for the battle which Gregory carried on until his death. The Holy Roman Emperor, Henry IV, declared Gregory deposed from the pontificate in 1076. Gregory excommunicated Henry the following day. The nobles of Germany threatened to use the excommunication as a pretext for deposing the emperor, and so Henry followed Gregory to Canossa in January, 1077, and submitted himself to a humiliating three-day penance to gain absolution from the pontiff. When his political position had again become secure, Henry resumed his attitude of hostility toward Gregory and, in 1080, again declared the pontiff deposed. Henry then influenced the German and N. Italian bishops to elect an antipope, Guibert, the excommunicated Archbishop of Ravenna, as Clement III.

Henry besieged Rome until 1084, when the city finally fell. Gregory shut himself up in the Roman castle of St. Angelo. As he was on the point of falling into imperial hands, Gregory was rescued by Robert Guiscard, the Norman duke of Apulia and Calabria, who sacked the city and forced Henry to return to Germany. Guibert was still antipope, however, and Gregory was taken to Monte Cassino by his Norman allies. He sent out appeals for help and held a reforming synod at Salerno, where he uttered his famous dying words: "I have loved justice and hated iniquity, therefore I die an exile". His feast is celebrated on May 25.

5. GREGORY XIII, UGO BUONCOMPAGNO (1502–85), Pope of Rome, born at Bologna, Italy. He was one of the prominent theologians at the Council of Trent (1562–63) and was created Cardinal by Pius IV in 1564. He was elected pontiff in 1572, on the death of Pius V. The reform of the calendar to the system currently in use and called the Gregorian calendar (see CALENDAR) was carried out under his direction. He issued a new edition of the *Corpus Juris Canonici* (1582), expended large sums for education and the building of colleges, and constructed many great public works, such as the Quirinal palace. He was vigorous in anti-Protestant propaganda, attempted to form a coalition against the Protestants, and aided Philip II in his attack on the largely Protestant Netherlands.

GREGORY, LADY AUGUSTA, *nee* PERSSE (about 1859–1932), Irish dramatist, born in Roxborough, County Galway. In 1881 she married Sir William Gregory (1817–92), a noted member of Parliament from Galway and governor of Ceylon She worked with William Butler Yeats to found the Irish National Theatre Society, and became director of the Abbey Theatre, Dublin, where many of her plays were produced. Much of her work concerns Irish folklore, and she was instrumental in making popular the dialect of the English language spoken in the west of Ireland. Many of her own plays were written in this dialect; she also translated into the Anglo-Irish idiom several of the dramas of Molière, collected and published as *The Kiltartan Molière* (1910). She provided help and encouragement to such modern Irish writers as John Millington Synge, George Moore, and Sean O'Casey, and is said by Moore to have collaborated with Yeats in the writing of *Kathleen ni Houlihan* and *A Pot of Broth*. In 1911 and in 1913 she visited the United States with the Irish Players.

Lady Gregory also wrote sketches, stories, and translations of Gaelic sagas. Her plays, mostly one-act comedies of modern Irish life, include *The Full Moon; Coats; The White Cockade; Macdaragh's Wife; The Dragon;* and *The Golden Apple.* Her other works include *Poets and Dreamers* (1903), *The Kiltartan History Book* (1909), *Our Irish Theatre* (1914), and *Coole* (1931).

GREGORY OF ARMENIA, SAINT (257?–332?), called THE ILLUMINATOR, first patriarch and patron saint of the Armenian Church.

Gregory was reputedly the son of a Parthian chieftain; he was born at Valarshapat in the Armenian province of Ararat. According to legend his father was killed by soldiers of the Armenian king and Gregory was taken to Cæsarea in Cappadocia where he was educated as a Christian. He then entered the service of Tiradates III, the king of Armenia, but was persecuted for his refusal to participate in pagan rites. According to tradition Gregory was confined in a pit for fourteen years and was released as the result of a mystical revelation granted to the king's sister. Historically, Gregory was ordained at Cæsarea in 290 and was made vicar-general for Armenia. Toward the end of his life, Gregory forsook his position as head of the Armenian Church and became a hermit. Although Gregory is frequently called the founder of the Armenian Church, he did not in fact bring Christianity to that country. He is, however, responsible for organizing the church in that country, for stamping out paganism, and for allying the Armenian Christians to the Catholic Church.

GREGORY OF NAZIANZUS, SAINT, called THEOLOGUS (329?–89?), one of the four Fathers of the Eastern Church, born near Nazianzus, in Cappadocia, and educated in Alexandria and Athens. He was baptized in 360 by his father, who was bishop of Nazianzus. Gregory then decided to pursue a life of devotion and went to Pontus, where he lived in the desert near the Iris River with Basil the Great. The two men compiled an anthology of the writings of Origen, called the *Philocalia.* Basil later became bishop of Cæsarea and, in 371 or 372, prevailed upon Gregory to accept the see of Sasima, a small town in Cappadocia. Gregory disliked public life, however, and retiring, moved to Nazianzus, where he remained until the death of his father in 374. He then returned to Seleucia in Isauria, where he remained until 378 or 379, when he left to take charge of the Nicene congregation of Constantinople. There he delivered five discourses on the Trinity, which earned him his fame as the Theologian. He was appointed bishop, but retired in the face of resistance from the Arians, and returned to Nazianzus, where he remained until his death. His feast day is celebrated on May 9 in the Roman Catholic Church and on January 25 in the Orthodox Church. His surviving works comprise about 45 sermons, 243 letters, and 407 dogmatic and moral poems.

GREGORY OF NYSSA, SAINT (331?–96?), bishop of Nyssa and one of the fathers of the Eastern Catholic Church. He was born in

Neocæsarea, a younger brother of St. Basil the Great. About the year 371, Gregory was ordained by his brother and made bishop of the town of Nyssa in Cappadocia. Prior to his ordination Gregory had been married, but on assuming orders he renounced his wife Theosebia, who then took vows as a deaconess. Gregory's religious position was strictly orthodox and he was particularly zealous in combatting the doctrine of Arianism (see ARIUS). The Arians charged Gregory with fraud in his election to the bishopric and with mishandling the funds of his office. Convicted of these charges, he was exiled from Nyssa during the years 376–378. After his return Gregory was a strong supporter of the orthodox position against the Arians at the first Council of Constantinople in 381. In the next year he was sent by the Church to reorganize the churches of Arabia.

Gregory's chief fame is as a theologian. Among his important theological treatises are: *Against Eunomius,* a defense of the Nicene Creed; *Oratio Catechetica,* a defense of the Christian faith against Jews and pagans; *On Faith,* a treatise against the Arians; and *Ten Syllogisms,* directed against the Manichæans.

GREGORY OF TOURS, SAINT (538–94), Catholic bishop and historian whose real name was Georgius Florentius, born at Arverni (now Clermont-Ferrand). He took the name Gregory in memory of a great-grandfather who had been bishop of Langres. Gregory was educated by an uncle and received instruction in the classic literature and religious principles, but did not study theology or the writings of the fathers of the church. He was ordained a deacon in 563 and shortly thereafter journeyed to Tours to seek a cure for an illness by visiting the tomb of St. Martin. In Tours he became a protégé of the bishop Euphronius, and after the latter's death in 573 Gregory was elected bishop by the people of Tours. During his bishopric, Gregory resisted the power of the Frankish king Chilperic, who held the city of Tours in the years 575–585. He was accused of vilifying Chilperic's wife Fredegond, and was tried, but he was acquitted.

Gregory wrote, edited, and translated a number of books, including accounts of the lives and miracles of St. Julian and St. Martin. His most important work, however, is his *Historia Francorum,* the History of the Franks, which deals with the history of the Frankish people from the creation to the year 591. The earlier parts of this history are mere compilations from earlier chroniclers.

The last six of the ten books of the history, however, deal with events of which Gregory had first-hand, or at worst second-hand, knowledge. These books are the most valuable source of historical information on Merovingian times.

GREIFSWALD, a city of Mecklenburg, Germany, situated on the navigable Ryck R., 3 miles w. of the Baltic Sea and 19 miles S.E. of Stralsund. Greifswald was founded in 1240 by Dutch traders, and received municipal rights ten years later from the duke of Pomerania. In the latter part of the 13th century it joined the Hanseatic League. It was taken by Sweden in 1631, and was ceded to Prussia in 1815. The University of Greifswald was founded in 1456; it contains an art collection, a display of antiquities dating from before Christ, a botanical garden, and a zoological museum. The famous 16th-century Croy tapestry, representing Martin Luther preaching, is shown every tenth year at the university. The town is the site also of a gymnasium, a dairy school, and a geographical and scientific museum. The chief manufacturing establishments of Greifswald are machine shops, foundries, electrical works, chicory factories, and shipbuilding yards. The principal trade is in wood and cereal grains. Pop. (1946) 43,590.

GRENADA, southernmost of the Windward Islands, British West Indies, lying in the Caribbean Sea, 90 miles N. of the island of Trinidad. Grenada is of volcanic origin, and is traversed by a mountain range, the highest point of which is Mt. Catherine, 2749 ft. above sea level. The mountains contain deposits of sulfur and fuller's earth; the valleys lying between their spurs are picturesque and fertile, producing cacao, bananas, spices, cotton, and limes. The island is watered by several streams, and contains many hot springs. It is a popular health and pleasure resort. Near one of two mountain lakes occupying the site of extinct volcanic craters is a large sanatorium. Excellent bathing beaches extend along the coast. The principal exports of Grenada are cacao, nutmegs, mace, raw cotton, lime oil, and bananas. St. George's (pop. about 6500), the capital, is situated on the s.w. coast and has a fine landlocked harbor. The town is the residence of the governor of the Windward Islands; however, it is not the capital of the group, as each island of the Windwards is administrated separately, except for the Grenadines (q.v.).

Columbus discovered the island of Grenada in 1498, but it was not colonized by the Spanish. In 1627 the Spanish granted it to the

British, from whom it was bought by the French in 1650. The French settled there and established cacao, coffee, and cotton plantations, eventually exterminating the Caribs, the island's aboriginal inhabitants. Granada became a British possession permanently in 1783.

Area (including that of the island of Carriacou), 133 sq.m. Area of Grenada alone, 120 sq.m.; pop. (1950 est.) 80,056.

GRENADE, name applied to a group of diversified military missiles used by infantry troops as antipersonnel or antitank weapons or for the production of smoke screens or signals. The grenade consists of a metal shell containing a fuze (q.v.) and a charge of high explosives, gas, or chemicals, depending on its function. Grenades may be classified according to their function, e.g., antipersonnel, antitank, or smoke grenades, or according to the method of delivery. Those designed to be thrown by hand are known as hand grenades and those for longer-range delivery are known as rifle grenades.

Grenades were first used in the wars of the 17th century. The original type contained gunpowder and had a primitive protruding fuze. After the fuze was lighted, the grenade was hurled by hand into the midst of enemy troops; the flying fragments of iron caused serious wounds. The term *grenadiers* was applied originally to special companies of tall men equipped with hand grenades. Rifle grenades were first introduced in World War I. During World War II many advances were made in the design of both hand and rifle grenades, widely extending the efficiency and the applications of the weapon.

There are two types of hand grenades for use against enemy personnel. One is the fragmentation type, which bursts into lethal fragments, and the other is the concussion type, which kills by the force of its blast. The fragmentation type consists of a lemon-shaped, cast-steel case filled with TNT. Fitted close to the case is a curved lever arm, held against a spring-driven striker by a safety pin. To operate the grenade the pin is removed and the lever is held in place by the hand. When the grenade is thrown, the lever is released and the striker is driven against a primer which ignites the delay fuze. The main charge explodes 4 or 5 seconds after it is thrown. The concussion type has a thin case made of tin and explodes only upon impact with its target after the safety pin has been removed. Concussion grenades are used at short range in open-field fighting when fragmentation

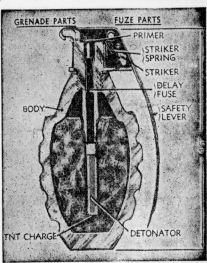

Diagram of a fragmentation hand grenade

grenades might prove dangerous to the thrower as well as to his target.

Rifle grenades which are used against enemy troops are similar in principle to the fragmentation hand grenade. Rifle grenades used against tanks and armoured vehicles are a special type designed to have much greater penetrating power.

Smoke grenades, incendiary grenades, and those containing irritant chemicals are usually similar in construction to the concussion hand grenade.

GRENADIER, or RATTAIL, common names for any of the large-eyed, deep-sea fishes in the family Macrouridae, characterized by long, pointed tails without tail fins. The fins on their backs and undersides are prolonged and reach the tip of the tail. These fishes are called grenadiers because of their resemblance to old-fashioned hand grenades. They are not valued as food. Grenadiers are found on the ocean bottoms of the N. Atlantic and Pacific oceans, and feed on sea invertebrates.

GRENADINES, a group of about 600 islets of the Windward Islands, British West Indies, extending N.E. and S.W. between the islands of Grenada and St. Vincent (qq.v.) for a distance of 60 m. Only a few of the islets are inhabited. The N. section of the group is administered at St. Vincent, and the S. portion at Grenada. The largest of the Grenadines is Carriacou (area, 13 sq.m.; pop. in 1946, 6769), which is administratively attached to Grenada. Bequia (area, 6 sq.m.) is the chief is-

French National Tourist Office

Aerial view showing the Isère River in the city of Grenoble, France

land of the northern group. Cotton and cattle are raised by the inhabitants of the Grenadines. Total area, about 30 sq.m.; pop., about 13,000.

GRENFELL, Sir Wilfred Thomason (1865–1940), English physician and missionary, born at Parkgate, Cheshire, and educated at Oxford University and London Hospital. In 1889 he joined the Royal National Mission for Deep Sea Fishermen, and organized in the North Sea the first hospital ship to serve fishermen. In 1892 he began his famous work as a medical missionary among the fishermen and Eskimos in Labrador, where he established homes, missions, hospitals, stores, schools, and orphanages, and helped organize industries. Grenfell lectured in Canada, America, and England to raise funds for his missions, and, in 1912, branches in those countries united to form the International Grenfell Association. In the same year Grenfell organized the Seaman's Institute at St. John's, Newfoundland. Grenfell received many awards, and was knighted in 1927. He wrote many books about his experiences, including *Adrift on an Icepan* (1909), *Down North on the Labrador* (1911), *The Adventures of Life* (1912), *Northern Neighbors* (1923), and *Forty Years for Labrador* (1932).

GRENOBLE, capital of the department of Isère, S.E. France, situated on the Isère R., in a mountainous region, 75 m. by rail S.E. of Lyons. A group of fortresses guard the city from strategic points on the slopes of Mont Rachais, which rises to the N. Grenoble is the seat of a bishopric dating from the 4th century, and the city contains several old churches, notably the 11th-century church of St. Laurent, with a crypt constructed about the 8th century; the 11th-century cathedral of Notre Dame; and the 13th-century church of St. André. The Palais de Justice, of Renaissance architecture, is the principal public building. The city library is noted for its collection of early manuscripts and books. The University of Grenoble, founded in 1339, has faculties of law, letters, and science. Grenoble is noted for the manufacture of kid gloves, and the city contains about eighty glove factories. Other industrial products of Grenoble are cement, linen and leather goods, furniture, copper products, liqueurs, and straw hats.

Grenoble is the ancient *Cularo* of the Allobroges, a tribe of Gaul. After the 4th century it was known, in honor of the Roman emperor Gratian, as *Gratianopolis*, the name eventually being corrupted to Grenoble. The city was a part of the kingdom of Provence from the 9th to the 11th century, and later was made the capital of the old province of Dauphiné, becoming the capital of Isère upon the formation of that department in 1790. Pop. (1946) 102,161.

GRENVILLE, GEORGE (1712–70), British statesman, educated at Christ Church College, Oxford University. In 1741 he became a member of Parliament, where he served for the rest of his life. Except for a brief period in 1757, he held office as treasurer of the navy from 1754 until 1762. Grenville was leader of the House of Commons and a member of the cabinet in 1761. In 1762–63 he occupied the post of first lord of the admiralty. In the following year he was named prime minister, first lord of the treasury, and chancellor of the exchequer. During his administration libel proceedings were started against John Wilkes (q.v.), and the Stamp Act, one of the chief causes of friction between Great Britain and the American colonies, was enacted. He was unpopular with King George III, who dismissed him in 1765. Grenville was known in Parliament as "the Gentle Shepherd" after the Elder Pitt recited the ditty "Gentle Shepherd, tell me where!" in reply to Grenville's fretful request that Parliament direct him *where* to impose new taxes.

GRENVILLE or GREYNVILE, SIR RICHARD (1541–91), English naval officer. As a young man, he is reported to have served under the Emperor Maximilian II against the Turks. After returning to England, he became a member of Parliament. He headed the fleet of seven ships in which colonists organized by his cousin, Sir Walter Raleigh, sailed to Roanoke Island, North Carolina, in 1585. Grenville was second in command of the fleet which went to the Azores in 1591 to capture a Spanish treasure fleet. On this expedition he was captain of the *Revenge,* a ship which had been commanded by Sir Francis Drake against the Spanish Armada in 1588. The *Revenge* was cut off from the rest of the British fleet and engaged fifteen Spanish vessels. The battle lasted for fifteen hours and ended with the capture of the *Revenge* and the loss of Grenville's life. The battle is described in Alfred Tennyson's poem *Revenge.*

GRENVILLE, WILLIAM WYNDHAM, BARON GRENVILLE (1759–1834), British statesman, educated at Oxford University. He became a member of Parliament in 1782. In 1782–83 he was chief secretary for Ireland and between that time and 1789 held several other government posts. He was made speaker of the House of Commons in 1789 but resigned in the same year to become secretary of state for the Home Department. In the following year he was elevated to the peerage, being created Baron Grenville. Although not always in accord with the prime minister, William Pitt (q.v.) the Younger, Grenville supported Pitt's protest against the refusal of King George III to consent to legislation providing relief for Roman Catholics, and Grenville resigned with Pitt in 1801 over that issue. When offered a place in the new Pitt ministry in 1804, Grenville rejected it because his political ally, Charles James Fox (q.v.), was excluded from the cabinet by the king. After the death of Pitt in 1806 Grenville became nominal head of a coalition government, called the "All-the-Talents Administration". That administration secured the passage in 1807 of a law abolishing the slave trade. However, the "All-the-Talents Administration" was considered generally incapable in its handling of foreign affairs. Unwilling to comply with the request of King George III that no more measures proposing relief for Roman Catholics be presented to the king, Grenville and his ministry resigned in 1807. Grenville did not again hold an administrative office although many times asked to do so. However, he continued to sit in Parliament, where he consistently supported Roman Catholic emancipation bills.

GRESHAM, SIR THOMAS (1519?–79), English financier and founder of the Royal Exchange, notable in the history of economics as the formulator of Gresham's law (q.v.).

Sir Thomas Gresham

After attending Cambridge University he was apprenticed to his uncle, a merchant, in whose service he displayed unusual business ability. In later years he became one of the wealthiest men in England.

In 1551 he was appointed a royal agent or factor by Edward VI and charged with the management of the royal debt abroad, which he virtually liquidated subsequently by the use of adroit financial manipulations on the bourse, or stock exchange, of Antwerp.

He was knighted by Queen Elizabeth I in 1559. While serving as her financial agent abroad, Gresham found that his tasks were difficult to execute because of the lower value of English currency in relation to the currencies of other countries; this condition he attributed to the previous debasement of the English currency in the reign of Henry VIII. In attempting to persuade Elizabeth to restore the currency of England, Gresham formulated the observation "bad money drives out good", which three centuries later became known as Gresham's law. He financed the construction of the Royal Exchange, which was opened in 1571; see EXCHANGE; STOCK EXCHANGE. His will made provision for the establishment of an institution of higher learning, which became known as Gresham College.

GRESHAM, WALTER QUINTIN (1832–95), American soldier, jurist, and statesman, born near Lanesville in Indiana, and educated at Indiana State University. In 1854 Gresham was admitted to the bar. In 1860 he was elected to the Indiana House of Representatives and became chairman of the committee on military affairs. In 1861 he was commissioned colonel of the 53rd Indiana Infantry which participated in the siege of Vicksburg in 1863. After Vicksburg Gresham was made brigadier general in command of the Union forces at Natchez. In 1864 he received a wound in the Atlanta campaign which lamed him for life. The following year he was awarded the honorary rank of major general. Gresham returned to law practice and Republican politics and was made U.S. District Judge for Indiana in 1869. He was postmaster general and later Secretary of the Treasury in the cabinet of Chester Alan Arthur, but resigned this post in 1884 to accept appointment as judge in the Circuit Court of Appeals. Gresham sought the Republican presidential nomination unsuccessfully in 1884 and 1888, after which, disagreeing with Republican tariff policies, he became a Democrat. In 1892 he supported Grover Cleveland's campaign, and became Cleveland's Secretary of State from 1893 until his death.

GRESHAM'S LAW, in economics, the principle that the concurrent circulation of debased or depreciated currency with coins of full value in terms of precious metal will result in the withdrawal of the latter from circulation. According to Gresham's law the good coins, those of full value, are either exported or melted down in order to realize their higher market value in foreign exchange or as bullion (see EXCHANGE, FOREIGN).

The phenomena described by Gresham's law were noted by merchants, financiers, and statesmen long before the 16th century. However, when the English financier and founder of the Royal Exchange, Sir Thomas Gresham (q.v.), formulated the thought that "bad money drives out good", he made no theoretical exposition of his formulation, and not until the latter part of the 19th century did his principle become known as Gresham's law.

As originally conceived, Gresham's law applied exclusively to the effect of the circulation of depreciated, debased, mutilated, or worn coins of full value. After the use of paper money became widespread, Gresham's law was also applied to the similar effect of the circulation of depreciated paper money on metallic money.

GRETNA GREEN, village of the civil parish of Gretna, in Dumfries County, Scotland, 9 miles N.N.W. of Carlisle and ¾ m. from the Sark R. boundary between England and Scotland. After the proscription in 1754 of Fleet Marriages, the village of Gretna Green became the scene of many clandestine marriages between English people; the Scottish law required only that a couple assent to marriage vows before witnesses. Anyone could officiate at a wedding ceremony, and the village blacksmith usually read the Anglican wedding service at a runaway marriage. The practice of performing such marriages for English couples in Gretna Green ended in 1856 with the passage of a statute requiring that at least one of the contracting parties should be a resident of Scotland of at least twenty-one days' standing. During World War I Gretna Green was the site of a temporary manufacturing center, covering a tract of land 10 m. long and about 1½ m. wide, established for the production of munitions. Pop. of parish (1951 prelim.) 2057.

GRÉTRY, ANDRÉ ERNEST MODESTE (1741–1813), Belgian composer, born at Liége, and educated at the Collège de Liége in Rome Grétry was a popular composer of comic opera. Of his more than fifty operas, some of the most notable are *Zémire et Azor* (1771), *L'Amant Jaloux* (1778), *L'Épreuve Villageoise* (1784), and *Richard Cœur de Lion* (1784). In his *Mémoires* (1789) he clearly stated his theories about dramatic composition.

GREUZE, JEAN BAPTISTE (1725–1805), French genre and portrait painter, born at Tournus, Burgundy. He studied in Lyon and Paris. The subject of the first picture he exhibited, "A Father Explaining the Bible to His Children", was in marked contrast to the rococo (q.v.) type of painting then prevailing in France, and attracted wide attention. Greuze went on to paint a great number of moralistic genre works, including "The Village Bride", "The Wicked Son Punished", "The Broken Pitcher", "The Father's Curse", and "The Milkmaid" (all in the Louvre, Paris); "The Broken Mirror" (Wallace Collection, London); "The Dead Canary" (National Gallery, Edinburgh); and "Girl Winding Wool" (Metropolitan Museum of Art, New York City). Greuze was also an eminent portraitist; among his portraits are those of the Dauphin, the son of Louis XVI, Robespierre, and Napoleon (all in the Versailles Museum); of Armand Gensonne, the French revolutionary politician (Louvre); and of Sophie Arnould, the noted French opera singer (Wallace Collection).

GREVILLE, SIR FULKE, 1st LORD BROOKE (1554–1628), English poet, born at Beauchamp Court, Warwickshire, and educated at Shrewsbury School and Jesus College, Cambridge. At Shrewsbury he met Sir Philip Sidney. The two became and remained close friends until Sidney's death in 1586. Greville went to the court of Queen Elizabeth with Sidney in 1577, and soon became a prominent courtier there. He saw active military service under Henry IV in Normandy about 1591, and was a member of Parliament four times between 1592 and 1620. In 1598 he became Treasurer of the Navy, and from 1614 to 1621 he was Chancellor of the Exchequer. He was created Baron Brooke in 1621. He was murdered by a disgruntled servant. His writings include *The Tragedie of Mustapha* (1609), *A Treatie of Humane Learning* (1633), and *The Life of the Renowned Sir Philip Sidney* (1652).

GREVILLEA, large genus of trees and shrubs belonging to the family Proteaceae. The genus native to Australia. The silk oak, *G. robusta,* contains about 150 species, all of which are which is especially valuable because of its

Detail from "The Broken Pitcher," by Greuze

resistance to drought, is cultivated in desert areas of Australia. Its wood, used for barrel staves, is elastic and durable. The silk oak is used as a cultivated shade tree in the warmer parts of the U.S., particularly in California. Young silk oaks, which are easily propagated from seed, are used as ornamental plants in greenhouses and on lawns. They bear graceful, orange-yellow flowers and have delicate, fern-like foliage. The wood of *G. linearis,* which is harder and closer-grained than that of silk oak, is used extensively in the manufacture of furniture and cabinets. Another grevillea, *G. thelemanniana,* is a spreading shrub, cultivated in the U.S., which bears unusual, green-tipped, red flowers.

GRÉVY, FRANÇOIS PAUL JULES (1907–91), French lawyer and statesman, third president of the French Republic, born at Mont-sous-Vaudrey, near Dôle, Jura. He was educated in law at Paris and became an advocate. A strong republican, he was elected to the constituent assembly in 1848–49. When it became apparent in 1852 that Louis Napoleon would become the next president of the republic, Grévy proposed making the president of the council, instead of the president of the republic, the highest public officer in France. For that act Grévy was compelled to withdraw from politics. He was subsequently made president of the Paris bar. In 1868 he reentered politics, and was chosen president of the national assembly in 1871, in which capacity he served for two years. From 1876 until 1879 he was president of the chamber of deputies. When Marshal MacMahon resigned from the presidency of the republic in 1879, Grévy was elected president. On the completion of his first term of office in 1885, he was re-elected. However, because his son-in-law, Daniel Wilson, was trafficking in decorations of the Legion of Honor, Grévy, although in no way implicated in the ensuing scandal, was forced to resign in 1887.

GREW, NEHEMIAH (1641–1712), English plant physiologist, born at Warwickshire, and educated at Cambridge and Leiden universities. He is known as one of the first investigators of the morphology and physiology of plants, and his books are among the earliest on those subjects. Linnaeus named a genus of trees *Grewia* (q.v.) in his honor. Some of his writings are *The Anatomy of Vegetables Begun* (1672), *The Comparative Anatomy of Trunks* (1675), *A Discourse of the Colors of Plants* (1677), and *Cosmologia Sacra, or a Discourse of the Universe* (1701).

GREWIA, genus of Old-World shrubs and trees belonging to the Linden family, named after Nehemiah Grew (q.v.). Plants of the genus have simple, alternate leaves, flowers borne in cymose clusters, and drupaceous fruits. Most grewias are native to tropical or subtropical Africa, Asia, and Australia. Several species which grow in India, such as *G. sapida* and *G. asiatica,* bear cherrylike fruits which are used in the manufacture of beverages. Fibers of the inner bark of *G. oppositifolia* are used by Himalayan tribes to make rope, and leaves of *G. laevigata* are fed to their cattle.

Several shrubby species have been introduced into the U.S. as cultivated ornamental plants. *G. parviflora,* native to China, is a hardy shrub which bears large, toothed leaves and small clusters of light-yellow flowers. It is grown in all but the coldest parts of the U.S. *G. caffra,* a South African shrub or small tree, which bears purple flowers, can be grown outdoors only in the warmer parts of the United States.

GREY, CHARLES, 2nd EARL GREY (1764–1845), English statesman, born at Fallodon, Northumberland, and educated at Cambridge University. In 1786 he became a Whig member of the House of Commons, and soon associated himself with Charles James Fox (q.v.), the leader of the opposition. Grey was one of the leaders of the prosecution in the trial of Warren Hastings (q.v.), governor general of India, and later promoted the unsuccessful Whig secession from Parliament when his electoral reforms were not adopted. After the deaths of Fox and of Prime Minister William Pitt the Younger, in 1806, Grey became foreign secretary in the coalition government of William Wyndham Grenville and leader of the House of Commons. In 1807 he helped carry through Parliament the act introduced by William Wilberforce (q.v.) abolishing the African slave trade. The cabinet lost power in less than a year, and from 1812 to 1830 Grey was the leader of the opposition. He broke with Grenville in 1815, when he opposed the ministry's decision to renew the war with France upon the escape of Napoleon from Elba. During the Tory reaction after 1815, his support in Parliament became very small, but in 1830, when the agitation for reform (see REFORM BILLS) had developed into a dangerous crisis, William IV summoned Grey to form a new government. By making William threaten to create enough new peers to defeat the strong opposition in the House of Lords, Grey was able to pass the Reform Bill through Parliament in 1832. He resigned two years later and spent his last years in retirement.

GREY, SIR EDWARD, 1st VISCOUNT GREY OF FALLODON (1862–1933), English statesman, born at Oxford, and educated at Winchester College, and at Balliol College, Oxford University. At the age of twenty he succeeded to the baronetcy on the death of his grandfather, Sir George Grey. In 1885 he entered Parliament, and became undersecretary of state for foreign affairs in 1892. He was a member of the Privy Council in 1902. In 1905 he was appointed secretary of state for foreign affairs, and in the two years following he conducted negotiations with France and Russia which led to the formation of the Triple Entente (q.v.).

In 1908 he tried to organize an international conference to deal with the annexation of Bosnia and Herzegovina by Austria-Hungary, but failed because of the readiness of Germany to use arms in support of the annexation. When the German cruiser *Panther* arrived at Agadir, in 1911, as a sharp protest against the spread of French influence in Morocco (q.v.), the warning issued by Grey that Great Britain intended to stand by the French, with whom Great Britain was united in an alliance known as the *Entente Cordiale* (q.v.), served to lessen German belligerency in the situation. Grey's attitude was one of the factors in averting the European war that threatened to result from this "Agadir incident". He was created a knight of the Garter in 1912. Sir Edward attempted to mediate in the Balkan Wars of 1912–13, presiding over the negotiations of European ambassadors at the London Peace Conference.

On the outbreak of World War I, he made one of his most famous speeches, including the phrase "The lights are going out all over Europe; I doubt if we shall see some of them again in our time." He spent the early years of the war working for closer co-operation between the Allies, resigning in 1916 because of ill health. He was created viscount the same year. In 1919 he acted as temporary ambassador to the United States in connection with the peace negotiations. In 1928 he was chancellor of Oxford University. He left all his private correspondence as secretary of state for foreign affairs to the Foreign Office. Among his writings are *Twenty-Five Years, 1892–1916* (1925), *Fallodon Papers* (1926), and *The Charm of Birds* (1927).

GREY, Sir George (1812–98), English colonial governor, born in Lisbon, Portugal, and educated at Sandhurst Royal Military College. He was an army officer from 1829 to 1839, when he left the service with the rank of captain. Grey explored the northwest area of West Australia, under the auspices of the Royal Geographical Society, beginning in 1837. From 1840 to 1867 Grey served successively as governor of New Zealand, Cape Colony, and again of New Zealand. His books include *Journals of Discovery in Australia* (1841), *Polynesian Mythology* (1855), and *Proverbial Sayings of the Ancestors of the New Zealand Race* (1858).

GREY, Lady Jane (1537–54), Queen of England for nine days, born at Bradgate, Leicestershire, the great-granddaughter of King Henry VII and daughter of Henry Grey, Duke of Suffolk and 3rd Marquis of Dorset, and of Lady Frances Brandon. When she was sixteen, a marriage was arranged for Lady Jane with Lord Guildford Dudley by the latter's father, John Dudley, Duke of Northumberland and Earl of Warwick, who was plotting to change the royal succession on the death of the ailing young king, Edward VI, to the Dudley family through Lady Jane. Before his death a short time later, Edward VI gave his approval of the marriage and through coercion secured the witnessing signatures of all but one of the judges in the council to a deed declaring Lady Jane his successor. On the death of the king, Lady Jane was proclaimed queen, but Mary Tudor (see Mary I), half sister of Edward, contested the succession.

When the army of Mary defeated that of the Duke of Northumberland, Lady Jane, after a nine-day reign, agreed to relinquish the throne to Mary. Lady Jane was subsequently imprisoned in the Tower with her father, who was soon released. The former queen and her husband were later accused of treason, and sentenced to death. Although the execution was delayed, when Lady Jane's father became a participant in Wyatt's Rebellion protesting the marriage of Queen Mary to Philip II of Spain, both Jane and her husband were beheaded.

GREY, Zane (1875–1939), American novelist, born at Zanesville, Ohio. He studied dentistry at the University of Pennsylvania, and practiced in New York City from 1898 to 1904, when he turned to writing. He wrote about forty books, most of them tales of adventure with a western setting, including *Riders of the Purple Sage* (1912), *The Lone Star Ranger* (1915), *The Wanderer of the Wasteland* (1923), *The Thundering Herd* (1925), *Code of the West* (1934), and *West of the Pecos* (1937). Most of his novels were best sellers and several of them were adapted to the motion-picture screen. He also wrote several books on his hobby, fishing, including *Tales of Swordfish and Tuna* (1927) and *Tales of the Angler's Eldorado, New Zealand* (1926).

GREYHOUND, a breed of hunting dog noted for its speed and keen sight. Carvings on Egyptian tombs prove that the greyhound was known in the third millennium B.C. The first complete description of the dog was written by the Roman poet Ovid in his *Metamorphoses,* about the beginning of the Christian era; the dog was known in England as early as the 9th century A.D. The deriva-

Greyhound

Musical America

Edvard Grieg at the piano

tion of its name is not certain; some authorities claim the term "greyhound" is derived from Graius or Grecian, others that it comes from the British word *grech* or *greg* ("dog"), and still others that the term came into being because the prevailing color of the breed once was gray. The dog has been used for hunting goats, foxes, deer, and other game, particularly the hare. In England for the past two hundred years the greyhound has been used in the popular sport of coursing (q.v.), in which the quarry, generally a hare, is started from its hiding place in sight of the greyhounds, who thereupon pursue the quarry by sight, and not by scent as is the usual case with hunting dogs. In recent years the greyhound has been used as a racing dog in England and United States; on race tracks built for the purpose, the dogs pursue an electrically propelled replica of a rabbit.

The greyhound is a large dog; the male weighs from 65 to 70 pounds, the bitch from 60 to 65 pounds. The breed is characterized by a long and narrow head; small, pointed ears; bright, intelligent eyes; a broad, muscular, and well-arched back; a deep, wide chest; thin, well-muscled loins; and a long tapering tail with a slight upward curve. It has a coat of smooth, short hair which is white, black, gray, or a combination of these colors. The greyhound is slender and graceful in appearance, and gentle and lovable in disposition.

GREYHOUND, ITALIAN. See ITALIAN GREYHOUND.

GRIBBLE, a small, oval, marine crustacean, *Limnoria lignorum,* in the order containing the wood louse. This animal eats the submerged portions of harbor timber, often causing serious destruction. It is common in the seas of Europe and North America, especially off the coasts of California. The gribble is flattened and has no shell. It is about ½ in. long. See BORER.

GRIEG, EDVARD HAGERUP (1843–1907), Norwegian composer, born in Bergen. He was taught the piano by his mother, a professional pianist, and from 1858 to 1860 studied piano, harmony, and theory at the Leipzig Conservatory. Subsequently Grieg was encouraged to become a composer by the Danish composer Niels Gade; his interest in Norwegian folk music was awakened by the Norwegian composer Richard Nordraak. From 1866 to 1874 Grieg lived in Christiania (now Oslo), where he taught music and became conductor of the Philharmonic Society; he also composed a number of his best-known works there, including the *Piano Concerto in A Minor* (1868).

Grieg's advocacy of a school of music based on Norwegian folk music met with opposition from conservative musicians and critics, and his own works were at first slow in gaining recognition. The famous composer Franz Liszt, whom Grieg met at Rome in 1870 at Liszt's invitation, encouraged Grieg in his work; and in 1874 the Norwegian government granted Grieg an annual stipend that enabled him thenceforth to devote all his time to composition. He became world-famous for his incidental music (1874–75) to the poetic drama *Peer Gynt* by Henrik Ibsen; two orchestral suites drawn from this music are among the most popular of modern orchestral works.

Grieg was the most important of Norwegian composers. Although his music was greatly influenced by that of the German Romantic school, particularly that of Robert Schumann, and also by the works of Frédéric Chopin, Grieg fashioned his melodies in the style of Norwegian folk music, and was a master of a harmonic style that has the power to evoke the atmosphere of his native land. Among his compositions are the works for string orchestra *Heart Wounds* and *The Last Spring* (melodies after a Norwegian poem), and *Holberg Suite;* the works for chorus and orchestra *Landsighting* and *Olaf Trygvason;* chamber music, including three sonatas for violin and piano and a string quartet; and numerous piano pieces, including ten books of *Lyric Pieces,* and *Ballade in G Minor.* He was particularly distinguished as a writer of songs; among the 150 songs he composed are *I Love Thee, Solvejg's Song,* and *The Odalisque.*

GRIERSON, Sir George Abraham (1851–1941), Irish Orientalist, born at Glenageary, County Dublin, and educated at Trinity College, Dublin, at the universities of Dublin and Halle, and at Calcutta University. He joined the Indian Civil Service in 1873, and from 1898 to 1902 was head of the linguistic survey of India, the result of which was published in 9 volumes (1903–08). Much of his writing was on the Indian vernacular languages; among these works are *Introduction to the Maithili Language of North Bihar* (1882) and *Manual of the Kashmiri Language* (1911). His other writings include *Hatim's Tales: Kashmiri Stories and Songs* (1923) and a translation of *Lalla-Vakyani* (1920).

GRIFFIN, or Griffon, a mythical creature, half bird, half animal, usually represented in literature and art as having the head, beak, and wings of an eagle, and the body and legs of a lion. In variant forms it appears with a horned head, of either a leopard or tiger, or with the head of a cock and all four legs like those of an eagle; occasionally it has a serpent for a tail. The griffin seems to have originated in the East, as it is found in the paintings and sculptures of the ancient Babylonians, Assyrians, and Persians. Thence the mythical figure passed to the Ægean peoples and to the Greeks. It is depicted on the great bronze Phenician shields from Mount Ida in Crete, on Corinthian vases, and on imported Greek objects found in early Italian graves. The griffin motif also decorates the helmet of the famous statue of the goddess Athena by the Greek sculptor Phidias. It is particularly associated with the sun god Apollo, whose chariot the griffin is frequently represented as drawing. To the Greeks, the griffin symbolized vigilance, swiftness, and strength. Among its functions were the protection of man and the treasures of the earth, and the guardianship of the dead. In the latter capacity griffins often appeared on the limestone sarcophagi of the Greeks. The Romans used the griffin merely for decorative purposes in friezes and on table legs, altars, and candelabra. The griffin motif continued to appear in early Christian times in the Bestiaries, or beast allegories, of St. Basil and St. Ambrose; and stone replicas of griffins frequently served as gargoyles in the Gothic architecture of the late Middle Ages. The griffin is still a familiar device in heraldry.

GRIFFIS, William Elliot (1843–1928), American minister, educator, and author, born in Philadelphia, and educated at Rutgers University, the Dutch Reformed Theological Seminary at New Brunswick, and the Union Theological Seminary in New York City. In 1870 he accepted an appointment to organize Japanese schools on the American model. While in Japan he was appointed professor of physical sciences at the Imperial University in Tokyo. He returned to the U.S. in 1874 and was pastor of several churches until 1903,

Relief carving of a griffin

when he began to devote the major portion of his time to writing and lecturing. His books include: *The Mikado's Empire* (1876) ; *Corea, the Hermit Nation* (1882) ; *Japan, in History, Folk-lore, and Art* (1892) ; *The Religions of Japan* (1895) ; *The Japanese Nation in Evolution* (1907) ; and *The Mikado, Institution and Person* (1915).

GRIFFITH, ARTHUR (1872–1922), Irish political leader and journalist, born at Dublin. After several years of working as a printer and newspaperman, he founded, in 1899, the weekly *United Irishman,* to which such well-known Irish writers as W. B. Yeats and "A.E." (George William Russell) contributed. Griffith himself wrote eloquent editorials urging the Irish to work for self-government within their own country, rather than to strive for representation in the British Parliament. He founded a group in 1902 which later became the nucleus of the Sinn Fein (q.v.), whose policy was to refuse to pay taxes to the British government, and to form a separate Irish Parliament whose only link with Britain would be a formal submission to the crown. Griffith, who was against any partition of Ireland, supported the Irish Volunteers, a group which was vigorously opposed to the Home Rule Bill of 1912 because it excluded Ulster from the future state of Ireland.

Although Griffith took no overt part in the "Easter Revolution" of 1916, the British imprisoned him as a Nationalist leader. He was released the following year, but again imprisoned in 1918. After the Armistice of 1918, a general election put the Sinn Fein in power, and the new members of Parliament, meeting as the Dail Eireann, or "Irish Assembly", elected Griffith vice-preisdent of an Irish republic, under Eamon de Valera. Months after his election Griffith was still in prison, but after his release, while De Valera was in the United States in 1919–20, he served as head of the new republic, and in 1921 he accepted the responsibility of leading the delegation to Great Britain to negotiate the treaty of recognition for the Irish Free State. Griffith was elected first president of the duly constituted Dail Eireann in January of 1922, but died the following August, shortly after the outbreak of the Irish civil war. His newspaper, always a powerful force in the Irish Nationalist movement, was several times compelled, by political or economic pressure, to cease publication and to reappear under a different name. See IRELAND: *History;* IRELAND, REPUBLIC OF: *History.*

GRIFFITH, DAVID (LEWELYN) WARK (1880–1948), American motion-picture producer, born at La Grange, Ky., and educated at the University of Kentucky. Griffith was an actor in stock and road companies before he became a motion-picture actor for the Biograph Company in 1907. He subsequently became a director for the company in New York City and in California, and in 1913 became an independent producer. His pictures *Judith of Bethulia* (1913), *Birth of a Nation* (1915), and *Intolerance* (1916) established him as the leading motion-picture producer of the time. With these and other pictures Griffith established a new high standard for motion-picture production.

Up to his time motion pictures had been short, rarely exceeding one reel; episodic rather than dramatic; and poorly produced and acted. Griffith's motion pictures contained powerful dramatic situations and vivid characters, were produced with new technical devices, and frequently were several hours in length. He originated some of the best-known devices in motion-picture production, such as the "close-up", a close view of a character's face or figure, or of an object, shown for dramatic emphasis; the "fade-out", a transition from one scene to another by the gradual disappearance of the first scene from the screen; and the "cutback" or "flashback", the introduction, for purposes of clarification of plot or characterization, of scenes antedating those already shown.

In 1919, with Douglas Fairbanks, Mary Pickford, and Charles Chaplin, Griffith formed the United Artists Corporation for the production of feature pictures. Among the pictures he directed for this company were *Broken Blossoms* (1919), *Way Down East* (1920), *The Orphans of the Storm* (1922), the *Battle of the Sexes* (1928), and *Lady of the Pavement* (1928). All the abovementioned productions were silent pictures, with the exception of the last, in which there was some singing. Griffith made a number of talking pictures, the best of which was *Abraham Lincoln* (1930). He retired as a motion-picture director in 1932 and as a member of United Artists in 1933.

GRIFFON, a breed of dog which supposedly resembles the griffin (q.v.), a mythological animal, whence the name. Two principal types of griffon exist: a hunting dog known as the wire-haired pointing griffon; and a toy dog known as the Brussels griffon.

The wire-haired pointing griffon was first bred in the last quarter of the 19th century by the Dutch breeder E. K. Korthals, near Haarlem, the Netherlands; the breed was subsequently developed, by him and by others, in France, and was imported into England in the last quarter of the 19th century and into the United States in 1900. The wire-haired pointing griffon has a keen scent and great ability both in pointing and retrieving game. It is a medium-sized, vigorous animal, the male standing 21½ to 23½ inches at the shoulder and the bitch 19½ to 21½. It has a hard, stiff and bristly coat which makes the dog well adapted to swimming and to hunting in marshy country. Its color is steel gray or gray white, with chestnut splashes, or entirely chestnut. The dog has a long head; a square muzzle; brown nose; flat ears set high; and long, sloping shoulders.

The Brussels griffon is a tiny dog valued as a pet. There are two types: the small, which weighs seven pounds or less; and the large, which weighs no more than eleven (males) or twelve (bitches). The dog has a wiry, dense, reddish-brown coat; a large, round head; a short nose; unusually large and prominent eyes, black in color; and an undershot chin.

GRIGNARD, VICTOR (1871–1934), French chemist, born at Cherbourg, and educated at the University of Lyon. He taught organic chemistry at Lyon from 1906 until 1909 and then at the University of Nancy, where he was a full professor from 1910. Grignard's fame rests upon his discovery, first disclosed in his doctoral thesis written in 1900, of the so-called Grignard reagents, which are of great value in synthesizing complex organic compounds. He received half of the Nobel Prize in chemistry in 1912. See GRIGNARD REACTIONS.

GRIGNARD REACTIONS, syntheses of many types of organic compounds, in which organometallic reagents containing magnesium are used. The reagents, named after their discoverer, Victor Grignard (q.v.), are made by combining magnesium turnings with an organic halide dissolved in anhydrous ether. Thus, ethyl bromide treated with magnesium yields a typical Grignard reagent, ethyl magnesium bromide. Grignard reagents react with water, alcohols, aldehydes, ketones, amines, phenols, and a wide variety of other organic compounds. For example, when ethyl magnesium bromide reacts with formaldehyde, the ethyl group of the reagent attaches to the carbon atom of formaldehyde and, after further simple treatment, the end product of the reaction is propyl alcohol. By

Brussels griffon

reacting Grignard reagents with different compounds, a wide variety of compounds including alcohols, hydrocarbons, and acids, can be easily synthesized. In preparing Grignard reagents all air and moisture must be excluded. Grignard reactions are therefore not adaptable to large-scale industrial work, but they are among the most versatile and valuable reagents in synthetic organic chemistry.

GRILLAGE. See FOUNDATION.

GRILLPARZER, FRANZ (1791–1872), Austrian playwright, born in Vienna. He studied law at the University of Vienna, but for financial reasons was forced to terminate his studies after two years. Starting in 1813 as a clerk in the government revenue administration, he had a successful career in the civil service, but he regarded his official career merely as a means of income. Grillparzer was one of the outstanding dramatists of the nineteenth century. He wrote many plays of dramatic and poetic beauty, particularly notable for their psychological insight into character, and was an influence on later dramatists, including Gerhardt Hauptmann and Maurice Maeterlinck. Some of Grillparzer's most notable dramas are *Die Ahnfrau* (1817), *Sappho* (1810), *Das Goldene Vlies* (a trilogy, 1822), *Des Meeres und der Liebe Wellen* (1831), *Der Traum ein Leben* (1834), and *Die Jüdin von Toledo* and *Libussa,* published posthumously. His outstanding prose work is a short story, *Der Arme Spielmann* (1848). His verse includes a cycle of poems, *Tristia ex Ponto* (1835).

GRILSE. See SALMON.

GRIMALDI. See MONACO.

GRIMALDI, JOSEPH (1779–1837), English clown and pantomimist, born in London, the

Wilhelm (left) and Jacob Grimm

son of an Italian actor. He made his stage debut at the age of two at Sadler's Wells Theatre, London, and appeared at that theater every season but one from that time on until his retirement from the stage. His best-known role was that of the clown in the pantomime (q.v.) *Mother Goose*, first produced in 1806 and frequently revived. Grimaldi was the most famous clown in the history of pantomime; his nickname "Joey" came into colloquial use in England as a synonym for "clown". He retired in 1828, worn out by hard work. His last appearance was as "Harlequin Hoax" in a benefit (1828) given for him at the Drury Lane Theatre, London. His *Memoirs of Joseph Grimaldi* (1838) were edited by Charles Dickens.

GRIMM, BARON (FRIEDRICH) MELCHIOR VON (1723–1807), French author, born at Ratisbon, Germany, and educated at Leipzig. In 1748 he traveled to Paris as the tutor of a young German nobleman. He remained in France, becoming friendly with Jean Jacques Rousseau, Madame Louise d'Épinay, Denis Diderot, and other members of the group known as the Encyclopedists (qq.v.). Following the example of the French historian and philosopher Guillaume Thomas François Raynal (1713–96), he began a correspondence with several European monarchs, including Catherine II of Russia and Stanislas II Augustus of Poland. His literary fame is based on these letters, covering the period from 1750 to 1790; they dealt extensively with the ideas circulating in contemporary Parisian literary and philosophical circles and were first published between 1812 and 1814, in 17 volumes,

as *Correspondence Littéraire, Philosophique et Critique*. Grimm was aided by both Diderot and Mme. d'Épinay, and by his secretary, Jakob Heinrich Meister, in this work. In 1775 he was made a baron of the Holy Roman Empire. He gained the favor of Catherine II, and lived in St. Petersburg from 1792 to 1795, after the French Revolution had driven him out of France. In 1796 Catherine sent him as minister to Hamburg, but upon her death the same year, he retired to Gotha, where he spent his last years.

GRIMM, JACOB LUDWIG KARL (1785–1863), German philologist and mythologist, born at Hanau in Hesse-Kassel. He studied law at the University of Marburg, where, under the guidance of Friedrich Karl von Savigny, he became deeply interested in medieval literature and the scientific investigation of ancient and modern language. He was librarian to Jérôme Bonaparte, King of Westphalia, in 1808, and held the post of secretary to the Hessian legation from 1813 to 1816. He was librarian and professor at the University of Göttingen from 1817 to 1837, where he lectured on ancient law, literary history, and philology. In 1841, at the invitation of Frederick William IV of Prussia, Grimm settled in Berlin, where he received a professorship at the university and was elected a member of the Academy of Sciences.

Grimm's greatest scientific work is *Deutsche Grammatik* (1819–37), a work which is generally considered the foundation of Germanic philology. It contains Grimm's formulation of the philological law known as Grimm's law (q.v.). Some of his other works on language, and also on German literature, are *Geschichte der Deutschen Sprache* (1848), *Über den Altdeutschen Meistergesang* (1811), *Rechtsaltertümer* (1828), and *Deutsche Mythologie* (1835).

Jacob Grimm and his brother, Wilhelm Grimm (q.v.), were attracted to folk tales, and collected folklore material from popular stories as well as from ancient books and manuscripts. The Brothers Grimm, as they are known all over the world, wrote *Kinder- und Hausmärchen* (1812), known in English as *Grimm's Fairy Tales*. Some of the other works on which the brothers collaborated are *Deutsche Sagen* (1816) and *Deutsches Wörterbuch* (1854).

GRIMM, WILHELM KARL (1786–1859), German philologist and mythologist, brother of Jacob Grimm, born at Hanau in Hesse-Kassel. His interests and career followed closely along the lines of those of his brother.

He attended the University of Marburg, was assistant librarian and professor at the University of Göttingen, and was professor at the University of Berlin and a member of the Academy of Sciences. Some of his works, other than those written in collaboration with his brother, are *Altdänische Heldenlieder* (1811), *Die Deutsche Heldensage* (1829), *Ruolandslied* (1838), *Altdeutsche Gespräche* (1851), and *Kleinere Schriften* (1881). See GRIMM, JACOB.

GRIMMELSHAUSEN, HANS JAKOB CHRISTOFFEL VON (about 1620–76), German writer, born reputedly at Gelnhausen. He was a soldier in the Thirty Years' War; in the latter part of his life he was converted from Protestantism to Catholicism, entered the employ of the bishop of Strasbourg, and finally became a magistrate at Renchen. Grimmelshausen was the author of a number of picaresque novels (see PICARESQUE NOVEL), including *Der Abenteuerliche Simplicissimus* (1669), one of the outstanding German novels of the 17th century. In this work, dealing with the adventures of a naïve youth who is in turn soldier, jester, robber, slave, and hermit, a realistic picture is given of the social and economic conditions created in Germany by the Thirty Years' War. Among other novels by Grimmelshausen, all of the picaresque type, are *Der Seltsame Springinsfeld* (1670), *Das Wunderbarliche Vogelnest* (1672), *Der Teutsche Michel* (1673), and *Das Vortrefflich Keuschen Josephs in Aegypten Erbauliche Lebensbeschreibung* (1670).

GRIMM'S LAW, a phonetic law concerning the changes undergone by the mutes or explosives of the Indo-European consonant system in Teutonic languages, such as High Germanic, and Low Germanic (including Gothic and English). The law, which was developed by Jacob Grimm (q.v.) in 1820, is one of the most important of phonetic laws. The basic principles of the law are: (1) Indo-European *tenues* (voiceless stops such as *k, t,* and *p*) become the corresponding *aspirates* (voiced stops followed by audible emission of breath such as *h,* or *gh, dh,* and *bh* respectively) in Low and High Germanic; for example, the *c* in Lat. *capere* becomes h in Goth. *hafjian,* Eng. *heave,* and Ger. *heben.* (2) Indo-European *mediæ* (voiced stops intermediate between tenues and aspirates, such as *g, d,* and *b*) become the corresponding tenues in Low Germanic and become fricatives (such as *k* and *z*) in High Germanic; for example, Lat. *genu,* Goth. *kniu,* Eng. *knee,* Ger. *knie.* (3) Indo-European aspirates (such as *gh, dh,* and

bh) become mediæ in Low Germanic and tenues in High Germanic; for example, Sanskrit *bhrater,* Lat. *frater,* Goth. *brothar,* Eng. *brother,* Ger. *bruder.* These changes are illustrated in the following table:

IE	LG	HG
Tenues		
k	h	h
t	th	th(d)
p	f	f
Mediæ		
g	k	ch(k)
d	t	z
b	p	pf
Aspirates		
gh	g	k(g)
dh	d	t
bh	b	p(b)

Medieval Gothic and modern English and Dutch are Low Germanic languages which have undergone the first change only; Old High German and modern High German have undergone the final shift. There are exceptions to Grimm's law, but these have been categorized in the laws of Verner and Grassman; See ETYMOLOGY; PHONETIC LAW; LANGUAGE; PHILOLOGY.

GRIMSBY or **GREAT GRIMSBY,** a seaport and county borough of Lincolnshire, England, situated on the coast near the mouth of the Humber R., 15 miles S.E. of Hull and 155 m. by rail N. of London. It is the major fishing port of Great Britain, and one of the greatest fishing centers in the world. Steam trawlers operating out of Grimsby range from the Arctic to the Mediterranean seas. In addition to fish docks, the harbor facilities of Grimsby include dry docks, and docks accommodating steamship lines with regular passenger service to Dutch, Danish, and s. Swedish ports. Other leading industries are shipbuilding, brewing, and the manufacture of rope. Large quantities of coal are exported from the port, and timber is a principal import. Among the notable buildings in Grimsby are the church of St. James, of Early English architecture, the Exchange, and the structure containing the town hall and the grammar school (founded in 1547). Grimsby is the traditional site of the Danish invasion landings in Britain in the 8th century. It was granted a charter and an annual fair by King John in 1201. During the 14th century Grimsby was a noted seaport, but it declined in importance as its harbor became blocked by silt from the Humber R. In the 19th century the harbor was improved by a company of landowners incorporated for that purpose. Pop. (1953 est.) 93,300.

GRINDAL, EDMUND (about 1519–83), English Protestant churchman, born near St. Bees, Cumberland, and educated at Cambridge University. Nicholas Ridley (q.v.), when he became bishop of London in 1850, appointed Grindal one of his chaplains and precentor of St. Paul's. Upon the accession of Queen Mary I in 1553, Grindal, who was an active opponent of the Roman Catholic Church, fled to Germany. He returned to London in 1559 and succeeded Edmund Bonner (q.v.) as bishop of London. Grindal's laxity in forcing Puritans to conform with the Anglican Church caused him to be criticized, and in 1570 he was transferred to the archbishopric of York, where most of the non-conformists were Catholics. Six years later he became archbishop of Canterbury. He opposed Queen Elizabeth's demand that he suppress the discussion meetings of the Puritans, and in 1577 he was deprived of his jurisdictional powers. He was reinstated in 1582.

GRINDELIA, genus of herbs belonging to the Thistle family, named after the Russian botanist David Hieronymus Grindel (1776–1836). The genus comprises about fifty species, found in the temperate and tropical regions of North America. The yellow-flowered plants are coarse biennials or perennials, many of which exude a sticky resin. Leaves and flowers of three species, *G. robusta, G. squarrosa,* and *G. cuneifolia,* commonly called gum plants or tarweeds, are used in preparing *fluid extract of grindelia,* a medicine administered internally in the treatment of asthma, whooping cough, and bronchitis, and applied externally in cases of ivy poisoning. Grindelias, although not usually cultivated, are sometimes transplanted to poor garden soils for ornament.

GRINNELL COLLEGE, a coeducational institution of higher learning, founded as Iowa College in Grinnell, Iowa, in 1846 under the auspices of the Congregational Church; it is now nonsectarian. In 1909 its name was changed to Grinnell College, in honor of Josiah Bushnell Grinnell, its president for many years. It offers a course in the liberal arts, leading to the MUS.B. and A.B. degrees. In a recent year its student body numbered 1125 and its faculty 88.

GRIPPE or **GRIP.** See INFLUENZA.

GRIQUALAND EAST, district of the Transkeian Territories, Cape Province, Union of South Africa. The capital, Kokstad, is named after Adam Kok, a Griqua chief who settled in the district in 1862 with 15,000 Griquas (q.v.), a hybrid race of Dutch and native origin. Area, 6602 sq.m.; pop. (1946) 360,775.

GRIQUALAND WEST, district of N. Cape Province, Union of South Africa. Kimberley (q.v.) is the capital. The famous diamond fields of the district were discovered in 1867, when the area belonged to Andries Waterboer, a native chief (see GRIQUAS). The disturbances caused by boundary disputes with the former Orange Free State and the Transvaal Republic resulted in Waterboer's consent to the annexation of Griqualand West by Great Britain in 1871. The region was incorporated into the Cape Colony in 1880. Area, 15,077 sq.m.; pop. (1946) 144,725.

GRIQUAS, the name applied to descendants of Dutch farmers and Hottentot women, now inhabiting Griqualand East and Griqualand West (qq.v.), Cape Province, Union of South Africa; they were formerly known as Bastaards (q.v.). The Griquas, who once lived further s. in the present Cape Province, migrated N., in the middle of the 19th century, under the leadership of two chiefs, Andries Waterboer and Adam Kok. Subsequently the latter's son, also Adam Kok, with some 15,000 followers, moved E. to the region now known as Griqualand East.

GRIS, JUAN (1887–1927), Spanish-French Cubist painter, born José Vittoriano Gonzalez at Madrid, and educated there at the Escuela de Artes y Manufacturas (now the Escuela Industrial). He left Madrid in 1906 and went to Paris, making the acquaintance of Pablo Picasso and Georges Braque (qq.v.). His first Cubist paintings appeared in 1912. He spent the next summer at Céret with Picasso, and while there adopted the use of *papier collé,* shapes cut from paper and glued to the canvas. During World War I he worked in Paris, where he had his first one-man exhibition in 1919. From 1922 to 1924 he designed settings for the ballets of Sergei Pavlovich Diaghilev, *Les Tentations de la Bergère, La Colombe,* and *L'Éducation Manquée,* as well as continuing work upon his own paintings; at this time, also, he wrote a series of notes upon the problems of the contemporary artist. After 1925 he worked mainly on gouaches, watercolors, and illustrations for books. Typical of his cut-paper technique is "Glasses and Newspaper" (1914, Smith College Museum of Art, Northampton, Mass.). Typical of his Cubist paintings are "Guitar and Bottle" (1917,

Philadelphia Museum of Art), "The Chessboard" (1917, Museum of Modern Art, New York), and "Guitar and Fruit Dish" (1919, Albright Art Gallery, Buffalo, N.Y.).

GRISON, or HURON (Fr. "gray-haired", from *gris,* "gray"), a genus of carnivorous mammals of the Weasel family. The common grison, *Grison vittatus,* is found in South and Central America. Its upper parts are light in color, gray or gray-blue on the top of the head, back, and tail. Underneath it is black or dark brown, and the face, legs, and tail are coal-black. Its hair is long, and its tail, which measures about 12 in., is bushy. The body is from one to two feet in length. The diet includes small mammals and birds. Grisons make their homes in hollow trees, holes in the ground, and crevices in rocks. When attacked, they give off a disagreeable, pungent odor, similar to that of the skunk. They are gregarious, and hunt in packs. Their call is a squealing bark.

GRISONS or (Ger.) **GRAUBÜNDEN,** most easterly and most sparsely populated canton of Switzerland, bounded on the E. by Austria and on the S. by Italy. Chur (q.v.) is the capital of Grisons. The Alps Mountains completely cover the canton. Numerous rivers, including the upper Rhine and upper Inn (qq.v.), or Engadine, both of which rise in Grisons, flow through lofty, narrow valleys between the mountain peaks. Some of the inner valleys are among the highest in central Europe, and in one of them is located the small village of Juf (6998 ft. above sea level), at an altitude greater than that of any other permanently inhabited village in the Alps. A number of famous glaciers are found high on the mountain slopes. St. Moritz, Davos (qq.v.), and other resort towns, established near mineral springs, attract many foreign tourists. Abundant forests provide timber for export. Sheep and cattle are raised on the mountain slopes, and agriculture is carried on in the valleys, where the climate is temperate throughout most of the year. The prevailing language comprises two dialects, Romansch and Latin, of the Rhæto-Romanic tongues in the Romance language group. German-speaking inhabitants are scattered throughout the canton but are concentrated chiefly around Chur. Italian is spoken in the valleys of Mesocco, Bregaglia, and Poschiavo.

In 15 B.C. nearly all of Grisons was conquered by the Romans and included in the S. part of the province of Rhætia. Southern Rhætia was conquered by the Ostrogoths in the 5th century and in the following century

by the Franks. In the 9th century the area was ruled by bishops, whose power was absorbed by the Hapsburg rulers of the Holy Roman Empire. After a protracted struggle with the Hapsburgs, the Rhætians gained practical independence from the Holy Roman Empire in the 16th century. The territory that is now Grisons became a canton in the Swiss Confederation in 1803 (see SWITZERLAND: *History*). Area, 2746 sq.m.; pop. (1950) 137,100.

GRISWOLD, A(LFRED) WHITNEY (1906–), American educator, born in Morristown, N.J., and educated at Yale University. In 1933 he joined the Yale faculty as an instructor in history. He was a research assistant in international relations at the university from 1936 to 1938, assistant professor of government and international relations from 1938 to 1942, and associate professor of history from 1942 to 1947. Appointed full professor of history in 1947, he served in that capacity until 1950, when he was elected president of Yale University. His writings include *The Far Eastern Policy of the United States* (1938), *Farming and Democracy* (1948), and *Essays on Education* (1954).

GROCYN, WILLIAM (1446?–1519), English scholar and humanist, born in Wiltshire, and educated at Winchester College and Oxford University. He became a fellow at Oxford University in 1467, and is believed to have been the first teacher of Greek at Oxford. He traveled and studied in Italy between 1488 and 1491, and after his return lectured at Exeter College on the classics.

GRODNO, city in the province of Bialystok (Belostok), Byelorussian S.S.R., the Soviet Union, located on the Niemen R., 160 m. by rail N.E. of Warsaw, Poland. Among the important industrial plants in the city are tobacco factories, distilleries, and machine shops. Grodno was part of Poland from 1919 until 1939, when it was occupied by Soviet troops. In 1941 Grodno was taken by Germany, which held it until 1945. Following the defeat of Germany in World War II, Grodno was included, by the terms of the Potsdam agreement (see POTSDAM CONFERENCE), within the Polish territory incorporated into the Soviet Union. Pop. (1931) 49,818.

GROETE, GERHARD. See GROOTE, GERHARD.

GROFÉ, FERDE (1892–), American composer and orchestrator, born at New York City. He studied violin, piano, and harmony with his mother, and viola with his grandfather. Subsequently he studied orchestration with Pietro Floridia (1860–1932), and became a member of symphonic, theater, and jazz orchestras. About 1920 he became pianist and orchestrator with the noted jazz band conducted by Paul Whiteman. Grofé is particularly known for his orchestration of *Rhapsody in Blue* (1924) by George Gershwin, a pioneer composition in "symphonic jazz", i.e., jazz written in large musical form. Subsequently Grofé conducted his own orchestra on radio programs, and wrote a number of compositions in symphonic jazz, including *Mississippi Suite* (1925) and *Grand Canyon* (1932).

GROMWELL, or PUCCOON, common name of plants belonging to the genus *Lithospermum* of the family Boraginaceae. The genus contains about forty species, native to north temperate lands, including about ten species which grow in the U.S. The common gromwell, *L. officinale,* was formerly incorrectly considered a cure for bladder stones. It is a native of dry, gravelly places in Eurasia and grows in similar places in the U.S. It has an erect, many-branched stem which bears small, lance-shaped leaves, small pale-green or pale-yellow flowers, and shiny white, stony nutlets. The corn gromwell, *L. arvense,* has similar leaves, small dull-white flowers, and dull-gray, wrinkled nutlets. The roots of both species yield a red dye, called *puccoon,* formerly used for coloring beverages and foods.

GRONCHI, GIOVANNI (1887–   ), Italian statesman, born in Pontedera, and educated at the University of Pisa. He became active in the Roman Catholic trade union movement at the age of fifteen, served with distinction in World War I, and in 1919 was elected to Parliament as a candidate of the Populari Party. As a leader of that group, the forerunner of the Christian Democratic Party, he held an undersecretaryship in the government formed (October, 1922) by the Italian Fascist chief Benito Mussolini. Gronchi joined the anti-Fascist opposition in August, 1923, whereupon he was expelled from the government and Parliament. He was prominent in the anti-Fascist underground movement during World War II, serving as a representative of the Christian Democratic Party on the leading committee of the National Liberation Front, and held cabinet positions in several postwar governments. Widely respected for his liberalism, militant Roman Catholicism, and oratorical ability, he was elected speaker of the Chamber of Deputies in May, 1948. He held that post until April, 1955, when he was elected president of Italy.

GRONINGEN, capital of the province of the same name, the Netherlands. The city is located at the junction of the canalized rivers Drentsche Aa and Hunse, 16 m. north of Assen and 33 m. by rail E. of Leeuwarden. It is the focus of a number of canals, and is an important port. The principal industries are the manufacture or processing of beet sugar, beer, flax, furniture, pianos, and tobacco; a large trade is carried on in oil-seed, cattle, and lumber. In addition, many goldsmith, silversmith, and book-printing shops are located in the city. In 1040 Groningen was granted to the bishop of Utrecht by Emperor Henry III. The town was fortified in 1255 and prior to 1284 it joined the Hanseatic League (q.v.). By the end of the 14th century power was wrested from the bishop by the rich burghers. Noteworthy architectural features of the city are the 15th-century Aa and Martini churches. In the library of the University of Groningen (est. 1614) is the New Testament of Erasmus, annotated by Martin Luther.

The province of Groningen is the northernmost in the Netherlands, and is bounded on the north and northeast by the North Sea and the mouth of the Ems River, and on the southeast by Germany. Included in the province are two of the Frisian Islands (q.v.), Boschplaat and Rottumeroog. The railways of the province form a part of the northern division of the State railway system and provide access to Germany. Land along the seacoast and along what was formerly a morass between Holland and Germany has gradually been reclaimed during the past century for use in agriculture, which is the chief occupation in the province. Barley, oats, flax, and wheat are raised in areas of the lowest altitude. In the more elevated areas, horses and cattle are bred and dairy products are processed. Area of province, 867 sq.m.; pop. (1952) 463,722. Pop. of city (1953 est.) 139,114.

GROOTE, GROOT, or **GROETE,** GERHARD (Lat. GERARDUS MAGNUS) (1340–84), Dutch preacher, born in Deventer, and educated at the University of Paris, where he studied theology, medicine, and astronomy. Groote, as a traveling deacon, preached against the barriers which Greek and Latin presented to the masses and advocated translation of the Scriptures into everyday language so that they could be widely read. Groote himself translated the Psalms into Dutch and in 1376 gathered together a group of men to do further translations. These men put their goods into common trust, and called themselves the

"Bonaparte Before the Battle of the Pyramids," painting by Baron Antoine Jean Gros

Brothers of the Common Life. Groote taught these men the monastic principles of St. Augustine and, after his death, many of them broke with the original order to found the Augustinian Order of Canons Regular at Windesheim which, in the 15th century, brought about moral reforms in the way of life of clerics in numerous monasteries (see AUGUSTINIANS).

GROPIUS, WALTER ADOLF (1883–   ), German-American architect, born at Berlin, and educated at the Technische Hochschule, Munich, and the Technische Hochschule, Berlin. In 1910, he began to practice as an architect, but his career was interrupted by the outbreak of World War I, in which he served in a German Hussar Regiment. At Weimar, in 1918, he founded the Bauhaus, a school for the study of the relation of art and architecture to modern technology and the functional use of new materials. The Bauhaus moved to Dessau in 1925, and Gropius continued as director until 1928, when he returned to architectural practice in Berlin. When Adolf Hitler became chancellor of Germany in 1933, Gropius, who was opposed to the Nazi idea of art, left Berlin, settling in London in the next year. He came to the U.S. in 1937 and became professor and chairman

of the School of Architecture at Harvard University a year later. In 1952 he became professor emeritus. Gropius was one of the foremost teachers of contemporary architecture, and influenced modern architecture in all countries. The most famous of his writings is *The New Architecture and the Bauhaus* (1935).

GROS, BARON ANTOINE JEAN (1771–1835), French painter, born at Paris. He studied art with his father, a painter of miniatures, and with Jacques Louis David, the leading figure in the French classical school of painting. Gros painted mainly portraits and historical scenes; his works of the latter category were the foremost among French historical paintings of the time of Napoleon and the Bourbon restoration. In 1816 he became a member of the French Institute and professor at the École des Beaux-Arts; and in 1824, for his painting in the cupola of the Panthéon, Paris, representing the dynasties of France offering homage to St. Geneviève, patron saint of Paris, he received the title of Baron. The work of Gros marks the transition from the classicism of David to the Romantic school. Although trained in the methods of the classical school, Gros was the first French historical painter of the period to abandon subjects

Rose-breasted grosbeak

taken from the history of ancient Greece and Rome for subjects from contemporary history; and the rich color, dramatic action, and depth of feeling of his paintings foreshadowed the Romantic school. Among his historical paintings are "Bonaparte at the Bridge of Arcole" (1796), "Plague at Jaffa", and "Napoleon at Eylau" (the latter two in the Louvre, Paris). Among his most famous portraits are those of the Napoleonic marshal André Masséna, and Eugène de Beauharnais, son of Napoleon's wife Josephine by her first marriage.

GROSBEAK (Fr. *gros*, "large"; *bec*, "beak"), common name for any of a number of species of large-billed birds, especially of the Finch family. Among the true grosbeaks is the evening grosbeak, *Hesperiphona vespertina*, so named because of the false belief that it sings only in the evening. The male is more brightly colored than the female, its upper portions being a mixture of yellow and olive-brown. Evening grosbeaks are about eight inches long. They nest in the summer in w. Canada, and winter in w. United States, occasionally being seen as far east as New England.

The strength of the bills of grosbeaks is illustrated by the habits of the pine grosbeak, *Pinicola enucleator*, which breaks open pine cones with its beak and eats the seeds. The North American pine grosbeak measures about nine inches; it breeds in the far N. part of the continent. It is also found in Asia and Europe. Other important species are the cardinal grosbeak or cardinal bird (q.v.), and the rose-breasted grosbeak, *Hedymeles ludovicanus*, a North American bird which measures about eight inches, breeds from Maine to Manitoba and winters in Central and South America; the breast plumage of the male

of the latter species is rose-red in color.

The genus *Geospiza* was studied in the Galápagos Islands by Charles Darwin in 1835; the study furnished considerable data for his *Origin of Species.*

GROSSETO, town, commune, and capital of the province of the same name, Tuscany, Italy. The town is located 90 m. by rail s.s.e. of Pisa. Grosseto became an episcopal see of the Roman Catholic Church in 1138. In 1224 the town came under the control of the Sienese, who built a citadel there in 1311. Grosseto was included in the dominions of Cosimo I of Tuscany in 1559. The Gothic cathedral, completed in 1294, is constructed of red and white marble. The fortified walls of the town were built in the late 16th century. Among the principal occupations in the town are trade in the cattle, timber, grain, and horses of the surrounding area, and the manufacture of agricultural implements. Pop. of town (1936) 15,988; of commune (1951) 38,224.

GROSSULARIACEAE, family of dicotyledonous plants belonging to the Rose order, commonly called the Gooseberry family. It contains two genera, *Ribes*, the currant (q.v.), and *Grossularia*, the gooseberry (q.v.). About 100 species, distributed throughout the north temperate zone, are included in the two genera. The family consists of shrubs with alternate, palmately lobed leaves and small flowers borne in clusters. In older classifications, the Gooseberry family was a subfamily of the Saxifragaceae, but differs from the saxifrages, which have capsules or follicles as fruits, in producing berries.

GROSSULARITE. See GARNET.

GROS VENTRES (Fr., "great bellies"), the name given by early French traders to two unrelated tribes of North American Plains Indians, the Hidatsa, or Minitari, of Siouan stock, and the Algonquin Atsina, an offshoot of the Arapaho Indians. The home of the former is the Missouri R. region of North Dakota; the latter tribe, to whom the name is now generally confined, are settled in Montana. The two tribes are sometimes distinguished from one another by the terms Gros Ventres of the Missouri and Gros Ventres of the Prairie.

GROSZ, GEORGE (1893–), German-American painter and illustrator, born in Berlin. He studied art at the Royal Academy, Dresden, the Kungstgewerbe Museum, Berlin, and the Académie Calarossi, Paris. His first successful works were expressionist paintings (see EXPRESSIONISM), but later he turned to the fiercely satirical drawings upon which his world-wide reputation rests. Collections of these drawings, concerned with conditions in Germany at the end of World War I, appeared in *Ecce Homo* (1922) and *Geschichte die Herrschenden Klasse* (1922). An uncompromising opponent of militarism and fascism, Grosz was one of the first German artists to attack Adolf Hitler. He emigrated to the U.S. in 1932. Recognized as one of the most brilliant draftsmen of his time, Grosz was also well known as a teacher. His work is represented in many permanent collections in the U.S. and Europe. An account of his experiences as an artist appears in his autobiography, *A Little Yes and a Long No* (1946). He was elected to the National Institute of Arts and Letters (q.v.) in 1954.

GROTE, GEORGE (1794–1871), British banker, historian of Greece, and politician, born at Clay Hill, Kent. When he was sixteen he entered the banking business. Between 1826 and 1830 he aided John Stuart Mill (q.v.) and Henry Peter Brougham in founding London University, serving for a time as a member of the council that organized the faculties and curriculum of University College. Between 1832 and 1841 he was a member of the House of Commons. He retired from the banking business in 1843 and devoted much of his time thereafter to the study of Greek history and philosophy and to writing. In 1849, on his re-election to the council of University College, he resumed his activities in connection with London University. He was made vice-chancellor of the university in 1862 and six years later president of the University College council. Grote established an endowment for a chair in philosophy of mind and logic in University College. His greatest work is the *History of Greece* (8 vols., 1846–56). Among his other writings are *Plato and Other Companions of Socrates* (3 vols., 1865) and the *Organon* (2nd ed., 1880).

GROTIUS, HUGO, or GROOT, HUIG DE (1583–1645), Dutch jurist, theologian, and statesman, born in Delft, and educated in law at the University of Leiden, where his father was curator. Grotius distinguished himself by editing, at the age of fifteen, the works of Martianus Capella. In 1603 he was commissioned by the States-General to write the history of the Dutch, a task to which he devoted himself until his death; the work, published in 1657, is known as *Annals of the Low Countries*. In 1604, as lawyer for the Dutch East India Company, he followed with interest a controversy over the capture of a

Associated American Artists Galleries
"He Is Taken Care Of," a wash drawing by the German-American illustrator, George Grosz

rich Portuguese ship by a sea captain of the company. As a result of his observations he composed *De Jure Prædæ* (On the Laws of Booty), an unpublished work which served as the basis of his *De Jure Belli et Pacis* (On the Laws of War and Peace), written 21 years later, and considered one of the foundations of modern international law (q.v.). In 1613 Grotius was made chief magistrate of Rotterdam, serving until 1619, when he was jailed and condemned to life imprisonment for leading the Arminians, a group of religious dissenters. See DORT, SYNOD OF. He escaped in 1621 to France, where he remained for thirteen years. From 1634 until his death Grotius was Swedish ambassador to France.

GROTON, a town of New London Co., Conn., situated on the Thames R., opposite the city of New London. Among the industrial establishments in Groton are a chemical plant, a thread mill, and one of the largest submarine-building yards in the world. The town is the site of a U.S. Submarine Base and a U.S. Coast Guard Academy. The first settlement of Groton was made from New London in 1649, and in 1705 it was incorporated as a separate town, receiving its present name. From the early days of settlement it has been a shipbuilding center; among the other early industries were whaling and deep-sea fishing. On Sept. 6, 1781, during the Revolutionary War, occurred the attack on Fort Griswold at

Ground hornbill (Bucorvus cafer)

Groton called the "Massacre of Fort Griswold". The fort was garrisoned at the time by a force of 150 colonial militiamen under the command of Lieut. Col. William Ledyard. The small garrison attempted to beat off an attack by about 800 British regulars and Tories under Benedict Arnold. The prolonged resistance of the militiamen infuriated the British and Tories, and when the Americans surrendered, the greater part of them were massacred, and Col. Ledyard killed by his own surrendered sword. The site of the massacre is now a State reservation, and contains the ruins of Fort Griswold and a monument commemorating the fort's defenders. Near the monument is a memorial library containing the sword of Col. Ledyard. Pop. (1950) 21,896.

GROUND ALMOND. See CHUFA.

GROUND BEETLE, common name for any of the swift-running, carnivorous beetles in the family Carabidae. More than 17,000 species are known, of which more than 2000 are found in North America. The carabids are world-wide in distribution, and live under rocks, or in moist or sandy soil, from which they get their name. Ground beetles rarely fly; the hind wings are generally atrophied and the wing covers fused along the midline. The slender legs are well developed for swift running. These beetles are most often unmarked black or brown; several species have wing cases striped or bordered with metallic blue, green, or bronze. The head of a ground bettle is narrower than its body; long, thin, threadlike antennae jut out from the sides of the head. The mouth parts are adapted for crushing and eating insects, worms, and snails. Members of *Carabus,* the type genus, are about 1 in. long. The larvae of the ground beetles have

well-developed legs, antennae, and mouth parts, and are also carnivorous. They live underground and pupate within the earth.

Ground beetles are agriculturally important and valuable because they destroy such harmful insects as the potato beetle, brown-tail moth, gypsy moth, cutworm, cankerworm, June beetle, and plum curculio. Few ground beetles are considered harmful; species in the genus *Harpalus* feed on seeds, corn, and strawberries. For representative members of the Ground Beetle family see BOMBARDIER BEETLE; CATERPILLAR HUNTER; FIDDLE BEETLE.

GROUND CHERRY. See PHYSALIS.

GROUND DOVE, common name for several land birds of the Pigeon family. Most species differ from typical pigeons in having inferior flying power, because of their short, rounded wings, and in having longer legs. The plumage of most species, except for that of the bronzewings, is dull in color. Among the important North American species is *Columbagallina passerina,* which is common throughout southern U.S. These ground doves are about 7 inches in length. They live mostly on the ground, nesting in the trees only at night. They are generally seen in pairs. See COLUMBIFORMES.

GROUND HOG or **WOODCHUCK,** name in the U.S. for a marmot (q.v.). In South Africa the aardvark (q.v.) is sometimes called ground hog.

GROUND-HOG DAY or **WOODCHUCK DAY,** February 2 of each year when, according to rural American tradition, the ground hog (see MARMOT) leaves the burrow where it has been hibernating to discover whether cold winter weather will continue. If the ground hog cannot see its shadow, it remains above ground, ending its hibernation, but if its shadow is visible (i.e., if the sun is shining), six more weeks of cold weather are in store and the animal returns to its burrow. Ground-hog day falls on Candlemas (q.v.). An old church tradition maintains that a pleasant Candlemas means a cold spring; this belief has probably given rise to the legend.

GROUND HORNBILL, either of two species of African birds, the Abyssinian ground hornbill, *Bucorvus abyssinicus,* of N. Africa; and *B. cafer,* called "bromvogel" by the Boers, native to S. Africa. Like other hornbills, ground hornbills have large bills with a hollow, bony ridge, or casque, on the upper surface of the bill. The casque of the Abyssinian bird is open at the front. The plumage of both species is black, except for the quills of the wings, which are white. Both species are large birds; the Abyssinian species measures about 3½ ft. in length.

Ground hornbills are gregarious and live in small flocks on the ground and in trees. They generally nest in trees. The diet is varied, and includes fruit, insects, mice, and snakes. They are famous for their ability to attack and kill poisonous snakes. Several ground hornbills work together, closing in on a snake and flapping their wings until the snake strikes. Then all the birds attack at once and peck the snake to death. Ground hornbills are a source of superstitious stories among the African natives, who believe that the birds can foretell storms.

GROUND IVY, common name of *Nepeta hederacea,* a small creeping herb of the Mint family, also known as gill-over-ground. Native to Eurasia, the ground ivy was introduced to the U.S. where it grows near hedges and forests and in waste places. It has kidney-shaped, crenate leaves, and pale purple flowers which are borne in clusters of three. The aromatic leaves were formerly used as a stimulant, usually as an herb tea. The leaves were also used to clarify and flavor ale, but have been supplanted by the flowers of hops.

GROUND LAUREL. See ARBUTUS.

GROUNDNUT. See EARTHNUT.

GROUND PINE. See CLUB MOSS.

GROUND ROBIN. See CHEWINK.

GROUNDSEL. See SENECIO.

GROUND SLOTH, common name for the extinct, massive, New-World edentate mammals which lived in the Pliocene and early Pleistocene epochs. The ground sloths developed from the common ancestor of the armadillos and present-day sloths.

The most important group of these animals, typified by the genus *Megatherium,* consisted of gigantic individuals 18 to 19 ft. in average length. The skull, which was about 2 ft. long, had heavy protruding jaws and resembled the skull of the present-day sloth. The hips were broad and rested on large, three-toed hind limbs, the third toe of which had a large claw. The long forelimbs had four toes, three of them with claws. These animals, the remains of which have been found in Pleistocene deposits of South America and s. United States, subsisted on vegetation.

Another group, typified by the genus *Mylodon,* consisted of smaller individuals, with skulls 1½ ft. long, and with short jaws. The hind limbs were four-toed, and the forelimbs five-toed. These animals lived in the Pleistocene epoch in both North and South America.

Remains of species within this group indicate that some of them had hinged bones, just below their hides, somewhat resembling the telescoping armor of the Armadillo. Compare GANODONTA.

GROUND SNAKE, common name of any of several small colubrine snakes, especially the brown snakes of the genus *Storeria* and the worm snakes. See BROWN SNAKE; WORM SNAKE.

GROUND SQUIRREL or SPERMOPHILE, any of the medium-sized, burrowing, terrestrial, western American rodents of the genus *Citellus* in the Squirrel family, characterized by large cheek pouches opening inside their mouths; they are often erroneously called gophers. Like the true gophers, they are agricultural menaces, destroying grass and grain. The name spermophile (Gr., "seed lover"), is derived from their usual diet. The ground squirrels resemble both the prairie dogs and the chipmunks. Most of the ground squirrels have longitudinal stripes along their backs. All of these animals hibernate during the winter; the duration of hibernation varies with the environment. Ground squirrels are found in open country, often in arid regions.

The Great Plains ground squirrel, *C. elegans,* found west of the Rocky Mountains, is typical of most of the spermophiles. This rough-haired ground squirrel has a length of eleven inches, including a three-inch bushy tail. Its back is brown and its lower parts yellowish-gray; it has a white chin and a white ring around each eye. The head is stubby, with round, wide ears. The legs are short. These animals seek their food close to their burrows. They mate after they emerge from hibernation in the spring; the female gives birth to about five offspring at a time. The thirteen-striped spermophile, *C. tridecemlineatus,* found near the Mississippi River, has seven grayish-yellow stripes running down its back, interspersed with six stripes composed of spots. Its lower parts are pale fawn in color. This ground squirrel subsists on mice and small insects as well as grain.

GROUPER or GROPER, common name for any of several large, carnivorous, tropical fish, constituting the family Epinephelidae, but sometimes included in the Sea Bass family. They are characterized by a large mouth, and projecting lower jaw. Eight of the grouper's teeth are remarkably similar in location and appearance to the canine teeth of mammals. The teeth of the lower jaw fit tightly into those of the upper jaw when the mouth is closed, so that the small fish which constitute

The hamlet, a grouper

the grouper's prey cannot wriggle free. Many groupers are important table fish; most of them are sought after by anglers. Groupers are most common between S.E. United States, the West Indies, and Central and South America; several species are found off S. Europe and Africa, and in the Pacific Ocean.

The most common grouper is the red grouper, or cherna, *Epinephelus morio,* found from Virginia to Brazil. This valuable food fish attains a maximum length of 3 ft.; it gradually changes color during its lifetime from gray to flesh pink. Other groupers in this genus include the hamlet, *E. striatus,* found from Key West to Brazil, and averaging 2 ft. in length; the cabrilla; and several varieties of hinds. Several groupers, found in the Caribbean Sea, are called bonacis; they include *Mycteroperca bonaci* and *M. apua.* Other species in this genus are the gag, *M. microlepis,* found off the Atlantic coasts of southern U.S., and the garlopa, *M. venadorum,* found off the Pacific coasts of Mexico. The largest grouper is the black jewfish. Local names indiscriminately used for several groupers include mero and aguaji. The name grouper is sometimes applied to several rockfish. See JEWFISH; NIGGERFISH.

GROUSE, common name for any of several species of galliform birds of the family Tetraonidae. Grouse resemble small domestic fowl in appearance, but have thick, strong legs which make it possible for the birds to jump quickly into flight when surprised. The plumage of grouse is thick and soft. In most species, the color of the plumage is somber, generally brown, speckled and barred with black. A few species have a more brilliant plumage of dark greens and purples. All species have short, thick bills with the upper portion of the bill rounded. The nest, built in slight hollows in the ground, consists of sticks, leaves, grasses, and a few feathers of the parent birds. The young are covered with a fine, heavy down. The diet is varied, and includes

snails, worms, insects, berries, seeds, and buds. Most species frequent woods, but a few species, such as ptarmigans (q.v.), grouse which generally inhabit northern regions, are found in open country. All grouse, except ptarmigans, are polygamous. The males of polygamous species fight for possession of the harem, and the males of some species gather at certain fixed "fighting fields" in the spring.

Of the forty-six species of grouse found in North America, the most important are the blue or dusky grouse, *Dendragapus obscurus,* an inhabitant of western U.S., noted as an easy bird to hunt because it has no fear of man, and the sage grouse *Centrocercus urophasianus,* the largest grouse in North America, native to western U.S. The ruffed grouse, *Bonasa umbellus,* sometimes called "partridge" and "pheasant", is well known for the "drumming" sound produced by the males in spring. The noise is a part of the bird's mating behavior, like the gestures of some other birds in the mating season. The mechanism which the bird uses to produce this noise has long been a subject of controversy. Recent high-speed photographs have proved that the noise comes from a quick beating of the wings in the air in rising tempo. The cock often stands on a log during the drumming.

The red grouse, *Lagopus scoticus,* is a bird found only in the British Isles. It frequents Scotland and N. England. The red grouse is bred on the moors of Scotland as a game bird. Extensive regions in Scotland, called grousemoors, are owned and rented for grouse shooting only. The season traditionally opens on August 12 of each year, and sportsmen from all over the world go to Scotland at that time. The birds are

Male ruffed grouse

"flushed", or frightened into the air, either by beaters or by game dogs such as pointers and setters.

For descriptions of various species of grouse, see BLACKCOCK; CAPERCAILLIE; PRAIRIE CHICKEN; PTARMIGAN.

GROVE, SIR GEORGE (1820–1900), English music critic, born at Clapham. As a young boy he was apprenticed to a civil engineer, and he worked as an engineer for several years. Grove was appointed secretary of the Society of Arts in 1849, and resigned from this position in 1852 to become secretary of the Crystal Palace at Sydenham. Grove wrote excellent evaluations of the works performed at the Crystal Palace, particularly of the Beethoven symphonies. He was editor of *Macmillan's Magazine* from 1868 to 1883. Grove is best known for his *Dictionary of Music and Musicians* (1878), a work which has been revised and enlarged several times and is still used as a standard reference source in music. In 1883 he was knighted and appointed the first director of the Royal College of Music. Among his other books is *Beethoven's Nine Symphonies* (1884).

GROVE, ROBERT MOSES, popularly known as "LEFTY" GROVE (1900–), American professional baseball player, born in Lonaconing, Md. Grove was one of the best left-handed pitchers in the history of baseball. He began his career in 1920, as a member of the Baltimore team of the International League. In five years with the Baltimore team he won 108 games and lost 36, for a percentage of .750. From 1925 to 1934 he was a member of the Philadelphia team ("Athletics") of the American League, and from 1935 to 1941 of the Boston team ("Red Sox") of the American League. His pitching record for his sixteen years in the American League was 300 games won and 141 lost, for a percentage of .680. He was the sixth pitcher in modern baseball to win 300 or more games in a major league. During his career he struck out 2217 batsmen, becoming the eighth pitcher in baseball history to strike out more than 2000. Grove was elected to the Baseball Hall of Fame in 1947.

GROWLER, the largemouthed black bass. See BASS.

GROWTH, increase in total volume of any animate or inanimate object. Growth is one of the primary characteristics of living things; see LIFE. Normal growth is carried on by all living organisms during all or part of their lifetimes. All plants grow until they die.

Growth in unicellular plants is accomplished by expansion of the protoplasmic content of the cell; growth in more complex plants usually takes place in definite areas which are known as *meristems* (embryonic regions). In animals, growth may continue throughout life, but most higher animals, such as insects and vertebrates, arrive at a fixed adult size. Many segmented animals, such as tapeworms and earthworms, have special growth zones which periodically produce additional segments. In both animal and plant forms, growth rates may be high during certain seasons and greatly reduced or arrested during the remainder of the year. Both animals and plants are vulnerable to pathological conditions which lead to abnormal rates of entire growth (see DWARF; GIGANTISM), or to uncontrolled growth of specific tissues or organs (see NEOPLASM).

Normal growth in higher organisms is accompanied by differentiation of new organic matter into tissues and organs. This phenomenon is strikingly demonstrated in the early growth of organisms; see EMBRYOLOGY. However, differentiation is not a necessary concomitant of growth, inasmuch as normal growth in lower organisms, and abnormal growth in most organisms, may proceed without differentiation.

The absolute rate at which growth takes place varies widely between organisms and between parts of a single organism. It is governed by a fundamental mathematical law which states that the rate of growth is proportional to the absolute size, so that an organism, as it increases in size, accelerates its rate of growth in direct proportion. The same law applies to inanimate growth (as in the growth of crystals), social growth (as in the growth of populations), and negative growth or decay (as in decomposition of radioactive substances). All such phenomena are governed by a simple but all-important mathematical equation: $y = e^x$; see E (in mathematics). A newly-formed cell, for example, undergoes a brief initial "lag" period, followed by a long middle period of accelerated growth, which eventually ceases altogether. This pattern of growth is called *the normal growth curve*. The accelerated growth of the middle period is slowed down by gradual aging and by normal size limitations.

The proportions of various parts of the body are relatively uniform within a single species, but there is considerable variation in these proportions during the course of the lifetime of the body. The human infant, for example, has a larger head and shorter limbs in proportion to its body size than does an adult. The proportionate growth of organs in closely related species is not always uniform. In the Deer family, for example, the smallest species have the smallest antlers in proportion to their body size, and the largest deer have the largest antlers in proportion to their body size. This type of growth is called *allometric* or *heterogonic* growth.

The upper and lower limits of effective growth are governed by a mathematical law which states that if growth is symmetrical, doubling of all linear dimensions increases volume by a factor of eight, but increases area by a factor of only four. For example, if a man were to grow to twelve feet in height, he would be eight times as heavy as a normal six-foot man, but the arches of his feet would be only four times as great in area, so that he would have insufficient support for his body. At the other extreme, a tiny mammal such as a shrew has an enormous surface area in proportion to its weight, and must eat an enormous quantity of food to compensate for the loss of heat through its skin. A smaller mammal could not eat fast enough to keep alive.

Growth must be supported by the accumulation of organic matter necessary to build new protoplasm. This process is governed by the effect of two classes of substance, hormones and vitamins. The presence of small quantities of vitamins permits considerable growth, but growth is severely restricted or arrested when vitamins are absent. Hormones act directly on the metabolism of an organism, which, in turn, determines the rate of growth; see METABOLISM.

GROZNY, administrative center of Grozny Region, Soviet Russia, located in the N. Caucasus, about 110 miles N.N.E. of Tbilisi, Georgia. The city lies in the rich Grozny oil field, and is one of the largest oil-producing centers in the U.S.S.R. Oil-well supplies and equipment, chemicals, and by-products of the oil refineries also are produced in the city. Pipe lines run from Grozny to the Caspian Sea on the E. and to the Black Sea on the W. Pop. (1939) 172,468.

GRUB, a name applied to certain legless insect larvae, particularly those of beetles. See LARVA.

GRUDZIADZ (Ger. *Graudenz*), a town of N. central Poland, situated on the Vistula R., about 60 miles S. of Gdansk (Danzig). It is the commercial and manufacturing center of a farming and stock-raising area. The town contains a citadel erected between 1772 and 1776 by Frederick the Great. Grudziadz was founded as Grodek by the Teutonic Knights in the 13th century. By the treaty of Thorn, in 1466, it came into the possession of Poland; between 1655 and 1659 it was occupied by the Swedes, and it was annexed to Prussia in 1772 at the first partition of Poland. After World War I Grudziadz was returned to Poland by the Treaty of Versailles. Pop. (1946) 36,805.

GRUENTHER, ALFRED MAXIMILIAN (1899–), American soldier, born in Platte Center, Nebr., and educated at the United States Military Academy. Between 1918, when he was commissioned a 2nd lieutenant in the Field Artillery, and 1940 he filled various routine posts, graduated from the Field Artillery School, the Command and General Staff School, and the Army War College, and rose to the rank of major. After the entry of the United States into World War II he served in the European Theater of Operations in leading staff positions, notably as chief of staff of the Fifth Army (1943–44) and of the Fifteenth Army Group (1944–45), and received successive promotions, advancing to the permanent rank of lieutenant general in 1944. He was successively deputy commandant of the National War College, director of the Joint Staff of the Joint Chiefs of Staff, and army deputy chief of staff for plans from 1945 to 1950. In December, 1950, he was made chief of staff to General of the Army Dwight David Eisenhower, newly appointed supreme commander, Allied Powers in Europe (S.C.A.P.E.), and he subsequently served in that capacity under Gen. Matthew Bunker Ridgway. Gruenther rose to the rank of full general in July, 1951. In May, 1953, he succeeded General Ridgway as S.C.A.P.E. He relinquished this post in November, 1956, and resigned from the U.S. Army the following month.

GRUIFORMES, an order of birds including the bustards (Otididae), the cranes (Gruidae), the limpkins or courlans (Aramidae), the rails, coots, and gallinules (Rallidae), and the trumpeters (Psophiidae). Several uncommon species of uncertain classification are included in Gruiformes. They include the kagu, the finfoot or sun grebe, and the sun bittern.

The kagu, *Rhinochetos jubatus,* found only on New Caledonia, is a large bird, ashy above, white below, with a movable crest of feathers on its crown. The male and female both participate in the courtship ceremony, which involves lifting the crest and spreading and dropping the wings.

The sun grebe, *Heliornis fulica,* found in

Detail from a painting of Christ, in oil on wood, by Matthias Grünewald

South and Central America, is an aquatic, grebelike bird about 18 in. in length, and, like the grebes (q.v.), has individually webbed toes. Related species occur in Africa.

The sun bittern, *Eurypyga helias,* found in South and Central America, is a many-colored bird about 17 in. long. Its body is a patchwork of black, brown, white, gray, and tan, colors which are especially striking when the bird spreads its wings and tail.

All gruiform birds are characterized by long legs and large, powerful feet; most of them have elongated necks and short bodies, and are found in reed-filled, marshy areas. See separate articles on the common birds mentioned above.

GRÜN, ANASTASIUS. See AUERSPERG.

GRÜNEWALD, MATTHIAS or MATHÄUS (fl. 1500–30), German painter. He is considered the supreme painter of the late German Gothic period (see GERMAN ART AND ARCHITECTURE). Grünewald is particularly celebrated for his paintings of the agony of Christ during the Crucifixion, and has been ranked by many experts as the equal of such painters as Lucas Cranach and Albrecht Dürer. Little is known of the facts of his life, although it is possible that he was born at Aschaffenburg, where, in 1517, he painted an altarpiece for the Maria Schnee chapel. The right wing of the altarpiece, showing the "Foundation of St. Maria Maggiore", is now in the Freiburg Museum, and the centerpiece, representing the Virgin Mary, is in the church of Stuppach near Mergentheim. Grünewald was appointed court painter to the cardinal and elector of Mainz, Albert of Brandenburg. His early works show the influence of Martin Schongauer (q.v.), but his mature productions are expressions of his own personality. Collections of his drawings are in the Ashmolean Museum, Oxford, the Albertina Museum, Vienna, and many other places; and a sketchbook is in the Kaiser Friedrich Museum, Berlin.

GRUNION, a small, silvery, marine fish, *Leuresthes tenuis,* closely related to the mullets, and found only along the s. California

coast. Male grunions are about 5 to 7 in. long; females are about 6 to 8 in. long. The grunions have gray backs and silver sides with a longitudinal stripe of black along each side. They are the only North American fish which come out of the water to mate and lay their eggs. Their spawning season begins in March and ends in August. The spawning of these fish is punctiliously regulated by the tides; they always breed on the first four nights after the highest tide of the full moon or the new moon. They are so prompt and predictable in their spawning time that the California State Fisheries Laboratory yearly publishes a timetable indicating when they will appear. Thousands of the fish appear at a time on the long, gently sloping beaches and are netted by sportsmen; they are excellent food fish. The grunions come in on high waves about 15 minutes after the peak of high tide. The females dig holes 2 in. deep in the sand and deposit about 2000 eggs each; the accompanying males fertilize the eggs. The entire process of deposition and fertilization takes about 25 seconds; the fish return to sea on the ebb of the wave after the one which carried them in. The eggs remain in the sand for two weeks, till the next high tide, when the young hatch and are washed out to sea.

GRUNT, common name for any of several fishes of different families which make loud grunting, rasping, grating, or humming sounds. These sounds have achieved military importance since World I, because they interfere with underwater detection apparatus (see SONAR). Typical grunts include the gurnards, the sea robins (qq.v.), certain triggerfish, and the tropical fish belonging to the genus *Haemulon.* The glistening-white margaret grunt, *H. album,* found from Brazil to Florida, is a typical fish of the last-named group.

Grunts utilize several mechanisms of sound production. The gurnards make loud, rasping noises by gnashing their pharyngeal teeth. Sea robins grunt by means of muscles which contract the air bladder, and force air out into the mouth. In some fish the air is forced into the alimentary tract, and the sound is pro-

Infantida Palace court, Guadalajara, Spain

duced when it escapes through the anus. Certain triggerfish rub their pharyngeal teeth together to produce a grating sound; others have a tight membrane, located above the air bladder just behind the pectoral fins, which acts as a drumhead when struck by the fins. Margaret grunts produce their noises by a combined action of the pharyngeal teeth and the air bladder.

Compare DRUM (fish).

GRUYÈRE, district in the S.E. part of the canton of Fribourg, Switzerland, noted for its cattle and its cheese. The district is watered by the Sarine R. and its tributaries the Hongrin, Jogne, and Trême. French is spoken by most of the inhabitants. Bulle (Ger. *Boll*) is the administrative center of the district, but the town of Gruyères (Ger. *Greyerz*), on the Sarine R., is the historical center. The counts of Gruyère were known to have resided in the district in 1073. In 1555 their domains were divided and sold to the cantons of Bern and Fribourg. The portion purchased by Fribourg was enlarged by the addition of Bulle,

Albeuve, and the lordship of Jaun to form the district of Gruyère as it is now constituted. Area, 192 sq.m.; pop. (1941) 26,107. Pop. of Gruyères (1941) 1356.

GRYLLIDAE (Lat. *grillus,* "cricket"), scientific name for a family of orthopterous insects commonly known as crickets (q.v.).

GUACHARO, FATBIRD, or OILBIRD, a bird, *Steatornis caripensis,* the only surviving species of a family in the Goatsucker order. Young guacharos are valued as food and for their fat, which is extracted and used as a butter substitute. The guacharo resembles the goatsuckers but has a stronger beak and eats fruit rather than insects. It is about 16 in. long. The mottled plumage is reddish-brown and gray, barred with black and dotted with white. The guacharo is found in deep caverns in N. South America and Trinidad, and is especially abundant near Cumaná, Venezuela. The bird emerges from these caverns at night to seek its food.

GUADALAJARA, capital of the state of Jalisco, Mexico, situated 275 m. by rail W.N.W. of Mexico City, in the Antemarac Valley, near the Río Grande de Santiago. The city was founded in 1531 and became an episcopal see in 1549. The cathedral, constructed between 1571 and 1618, is noted for its size and for the magnificence of its decoration. Among the principal educational institutions in the city are the university (1792), a normal school, a law school, an episcopal seminary, and an academy of fine arts. Guadalajara is located in a rich farming region, and is an important commercial center. Hydroelectric power from the nearby Juanacatlán Falls is used to operate the factories of the city. Among the important products manufactured in Guadalajara are textiles, leather goods, furniture, hats, paper products, and cordage. The Indians of Guadalajara and its environs are noted for the pottery they make from the clay found in large deposits in the neighborhood. Pop. (1950) 377,928.

GUADALAJARA (Ar. *Wad-al-hajarah,* "Valley of Stones"), capital of the Spanish province of the same name. The town is located on the Henares R., 35 m. by rail E.N.E. of Madrid. It contains factories producing woolens, bricks, soap, and leather, and has a considerable trade in salt and agricultural products. Guadalajara was a town in Roman times, and was known as *Arriaca* or *Caraca.* Between 714 and 1081 it was in the possession of the Moors The province of Guadalajara is located in central Spain. The Guadarrama

Mts. and the Sierra de Albarracin cover a large part of the area, and the soil of the province is rocky and comparatively unproductive. It is watered by small tributaries of the Tagus R. Goats and sheep are raised in the highlands, and olives, grapes, grains, saffron, and flax are raised in the lowlands of the province. Silver and salt are mined. The industries of Guadalajara Province include also the making of olive oil, wine, coarse cloth, and pottery. The capital is the only city of importance in the province. Area of province, 4709 sq.m.; pop. (1950) 203,278. Pop. of town (1940) 21,466.

GUADALCANAL or **GUADALCANAR,** a mountainous island in the s.w. Pacific, the largest of the British Solomon Islands, having an area of about 2500 sq.m. Guadalcanal was the site of heavy fighting between United States and Japanese forces during World War II. On Aug. 7, 1942, American Marines, under the command of Gen. Alexander A. Vandergrift, landed on the island in the first of the amphibious assaults against Japanese-held positions in the Pacific. The Marines obtained and held Henderson airfield on the island in face of bitter ground, sea, and air attacks by the Japanese. On Oct. 13, 1942, American Army reinforcements began to arrive on Guadalcanal, and on Dec. 9 the command of the area was assumed by the Army under the direction of Gen. Alexander M. Patch. Fighting continued in the jungles of Guadalcanal until Feb. 9, 1943, when the Army and Marine forces secured the island against Japanese resistance. Continual naval engagements between the Japanese and the Americans were fought off Guadalcanal. American naval forces, under the command of Adm. William F. Halsey (q.v.), were dispatched to the battle area and the so-called naval battle of Guadalcanal was fought on Nov. 13, 14, and 15, 1942. Japanese losses in the engagement were at least twenty-eight naval craft sunk; American losses were considerably lighter. See SOLOMON ISLANDS; SOLOMON ISLANDS, BATTLE OF.

GUADALQUIVIR (anc. *Bætis*), river of s. Spain, rising in the E. part of the province of Jaén and flowing 374 m., generally s.w., to Sanlúcar de Barrameda, where it empties into the Gulf of Cádiz. After coursing through the provinces of Jaén, Córdoba, and Seville, the Guadalquivir, for 10 m. above its mouth, forms the boundary between the provinces of Huelva and Cádiz. Below the city of Seville the river flows around the Isla Mayor and the Isla Menor. In the region between the town of Coria del Río and the mouth of the river,

the Guadalquivir traverses a region of tidal marshes called *Las Marismas*. Supplied by rain water in the winter and by the melting snows of the Sierra Nevadas in the summer, the river maintains a full stream throughout the year. During the Moorish occupation of Spain in the Middle Ages the river (*Wad el Kebir*, "Great River") was navigable as far as Córdoba; now, as a result of silt accumulation, it is navigable no farther upstream than Seville, a distance of about 50 m.

GUADALUPE HIDALGO, former town, now part of Villa Gustavo A. Madero, the Federal District of Mexico, 2.5 miles N. of Mexico City. The town was named for Our Lady of Guadalupe, the patron saint of the Mexican Indians, and for Miguel Hidalgo y Costilla (q.v.), who, under the banner of Our Lady of Guadalupe, began the War for Mexican Independence in 1810. A shrine to Our Lady of Guadalupe, the principal Roman Catholic shrine in the Western Hemisphere, now stands on the Hill of Tepeyacac, where an Indian, Juan Diego, had miraculous visions of the Virgin in 1531. The town was also noted as the place where the Treaty of Guadalupe Hidalgo, ending the Mexican War, was signed on Feb. 2, 1848.

GUADALUPE MOUNTAINS or **SIERRA DE GUADALUPE,** a branch of the Rocky Mts., extending from southern New Mexico to western Texas. Its highest peak, El Capitan (8,078 ft. above sea level), is the highest point in Texas.

GUADELOUPE, an overseas department of France, situated in the Lesser Antilles, French West Indies. It comprises two islands, separated by the Rivière Salée (Salt River), a narrow arm of the Caribbean Sea, about 4 m. long and varying in width from 100 to 400 ft. The island on the w. is called Guadeloupe (area, 364 sq.m.; pop. in 1954, 99,736); that on the E., Grande Terre (area, 255 sq.m.; pop., 103,-718). Five smaller islands, Marie-Galante (pop., 16,037), Saint-Martin (3366, northern portion only, the southern portion belonging to the Netherlands), Les Saintes (2574), Saint-Barthélemy (2079), and Désirade (1610), are dependencies of the department. The town of Basse-Terre on the island of Guadeloupe is the capital. The chief town of Grande Terre, and the principal port of the department, is Pointe-à-Pitre (q.v.). The total area of Guadeloupe and dependencies is 688 sq.m.; total pop. (1954) 229,120.

The climate of the islands, though hot and

moist, is not on the whole unhealthful. The mean annual temperature is 78° F. Over 30% of the total land area is under cultivation; of this figure almost 50% is planted with sugar cane. The chief products are sugar, bananas, cacao, coffee, vanilla, and rum. The population of the department is composed predominantly of Negroes and mulattoes, with some white planters and government officials and a number of East Indian immigrants from French colonies in India. On the island dependencies dwell the descendants of the original Breton and Norman colonists who settled there three centuries ago. These folk, engaged for the most part in shipbuilding, fishing, and small-scale farming, maintain a patriarchal family organization and have little or no contact with the outside world.

The department of Guadeloupe is governed by a prefect and a 36-member elected general council, and is represented in the Assembly of the French Union by one delegate, in the Council of the French Republic by two councillors, and in the French National Assembly by three deputies.

Guadeloupe Island was discovered by Christopher Columbus on November 3, 1493, and named for the monastery of Santa Maria de Guadalupe in the old province of Estremadura, Spain. Colonists of the French Company of the Islands of America established settlements in 1635, and inaugurated a policy of extreme cruelty toward the native Carib Indians, resulting in the virtual extinction of the aborigines. After the failure of four chartered companies to colonize the island permanently, it was annexed by the French crown in 1674 and made a dependency of Martinique. During the latter half of the 17th century the French colonists resisted a series of attacks by the British, who finally captured the island in 1759, retaining it until 1763, when it again passed to France. In 1775 Guadeloupe and Martinique became separate colonies. The British repossessed Guadeloupe in 1794 and again in 1810, the latter occupation lasting for six years. Slavery was abolished in 1848. See FRENCH WEST INDIES.

GUADIANA (anc. *Anas;* Ar. *Wadi Ana*), river of Spain and Portugal, rising as the Upper Guadiana, in the Campo de Montiel lowland, Spain. After flowing from its source through a series of small lakes, called the Lagunas de Ruidera, the Upper Guadiana turns N.W. and, 3 m. from the Zancara R., disappears underground, re-emerging when it reaches the Zancara R. At Cuidad Real the combined streams form the Guadiana, which

thence flows circuitously s.w. to Badajoz. Past Badajoz, the river forms the boundary between Spain and Portugal as far as a point near Mournao, Portugal, where it enters the latter country. The Guadiana again becomes the Spanish-Portuguese boundary near Mertola, Portugal, and remains a frontier stream until it empties into the Gulf of Cádiz between the Portuguese town of Villa Real de Santo Antonio and the Spanish town of Ayamonte, where it forms an estuary 25 m. long. In its total course of 515 m., the river is navigable for a distance of 42 m. from its mouth. It drains an area of 31,940 sq.m.

GUALBERT or **GALBERT,** JOHN. See VALLOMBROSA, CONGREGATION OF.

GUALEGUAYCHÚ, commercial city of Entre Ríos Province, E. Argentina, located on the river of the same name, 12 miles N. of its junction with the Uruguay R. Gualeguaychú is served by a railroad and by river steamers, and is the center of a cattle-raising section. The chief industry of the city is the processing and shipping of meat. Among the other industries of the city are tanning and the manufacturing of shoes. Pop. (1947) 36,911.

GUAM or **GUAHAN,** largest and southernmost island of the Marianas, and an unincorporated Territory of the United States, situated in the w. Pacific Ocean, about 1590 miles E. of Manila. The length of Guam, in a N. and s. direction, is 32 m.; its width varies from 4 to 10 m. A thickly wooded upland, with an average elevation of about 500 ft., occupies the N. half of the island. The s. half is a region of barren hills and fertile valleys. Due to off-lying shoals, Guam has few good harbors. Apra Harbor, on the w. coast, is the best anchorage. One of the chief U.S. defense bastions in the w. Pacific, Guam is the site of extensive naval, military, and air-force installations. Farming, livestock raising, and fishing are the principal native occupations. Crops include coconuts, cacao, tropical fruits, sugar cane, corn, and sweet potatoes. The native Guamians are mainly Chamorros, a people of Malaysian origin. Roman Catholicism is the predominant religion.

Guam is governed according to the Organic Act of Guam, legislation enacted by the U.S. Congress in 1950. By the terms of this law, which conferred U.S. citizenship on the native Guamians and placed the island under the jurisdiction of the Department of the Interior, executive power is vested in a governor, who is appointed by the President of the United States. Legislative authority is vested in a unicameral congress consisting of a maximum of 21 members and elected biennially by universal adult suffrage. Judicial power is exercised by a Federal district court, an island court, and various minor courts. Agaña (q.v.) is the capital and largest town of the Territory.

The island was discovered in 1521 by the Portuguese navigator Ferdinand Magellan, who claimed it for his patron Charles V, Holy Roman Emperor and King of Spain. Guamian resistance to Spanish rule, which was instituted in 1565, continued for more than a hundred years. By the terms of the peace treaty ending the Spanish-American War, Spain ceded (1898) Guam to the United States. As a U.S. possession it was administered by the Department of the Navy until implementation of the Organic Act of 1950. The Japanese captured Guam in December, 1941, during World War II. American forces recaptured the island between July 20 and Aug. 10, 1944. Area, 203 sq.m.; pop. (1950) 59,498.

GUANACO, common name of a species of wild South American ruminant, *Lama huanacos,* from which the domesticated alpaca and llama (qq.v.) are derived. The guanaco is one of the two wild, humpless species of the Camel family found in South America, the other being the vicuña. It is found on mountains and plains from Peru to Tierra del Fuego. The guanaco takes to water readily and has often been seen swimming from one island to another. A full-grown male stands about 4 ft. high at the shoulder and is covered with a thick coat of long, soft, reddish-tan hair. Its head is small, with pointed ears; its neck is long, with a graceful curve; its legs are long and slender. The fur on its belly is pure white. Guanacos are fast-running animals but are often destroyed through their curiosity; an entire herd, containing an average of eighteen animals, will be attracted to the antics of a performing human and will remain in the vicinity after shots are fired, accepting gunfire as part of the performance. This characteristic is utilized by South American natives who value the guanaco's flesh and skin. These animals are also unusual in that, before dying a natural death, they seek out places where other guanacos have died. Heaps of guanaco bones are often found in one spot.

GUANAJUATO, inland state of Mexico, contained within the limits of the central plateau of Mexico and having an average eleva-

The guanaco

tion of 6000 ft. above sea level. In the mountains of the N. and central portions of the state are found deposits of silver, gold, mercury, lead, copper, tin, and opals. Mining is the principal industry of the state. A fertile plain, called El Bajío, watered by the Lerma R. and its tributaries, is found in the s. part of Guanajuato. On that plain and in the arable mountain valleys of the s. and w., corn, barley, wheat, beans, and livestock are raised. Other industries include the milling of flour, tanning, distilling, and the manufacture of leather goods and textiles. The state is served by two railroads. Among the important cities are the capital, Guanajuato, and Léon, Celaya, Irapuato, and Silao. Area of state, 11,804 sq.m.; pop. (1950) 1,328,712.

GUANO (Peruvian, *huanu,* "dung"), the dried excrement of certain vertebrates, particularly sea birds, valued as fertilizer. The Peruvians have used guano since before the Spanish Conquest. One of their sources of supply was the Chincha Islands, off the coast of Peru. These islands were breeding grounds for sea birds, whose accumulated droppings resulted in piles of guano often 100 feet high. In 1804 a visitor to Peru took some guano to Europe. Its value as a fertilizer became widely known and by 1850 the Peruvians had begun to export it in large quantities. Other sources of guano, such as Bolivia, Mexico, Chile, and various Pacific islands, were used as the Peruvian supply dwindled. The dried feces of other creatures also came into use as guano, particularly bat guano, found in caves in New Zealand. The term "guano" is sometimes applied to other organic fertilizers; for example, the dried and powdered bodies of certain fish are often called fish guano.

GUANTÁNAMO, municipality and town of the province of Oriente, s.e. Cuba, located near the head of Guantánamo Bay, 41 m. east of Santiago. French refugees from Haiti founded the town in 1822, and for many years it was a popular summer resort for inhabitants of Havana. The development by the U.S. of Guantánamo Bay (q.v.) infused the town with industrial activity, and it became a sugar-exporting center. Pop. (1943) of municipality, 91,737; of town, 42,423.

GUANTÁNAMO BAY, harbor of Oriente Province, s.e. Cuba, located on the Caribbean Sea, about 20 m. by rail s. of the town of Guantánamo. Caimanera (pop., about 1000) is the port of the bay. The bay is landlocked and is composed of two basins; the total area is 30 sq.m. After fortifying much of the outer harbor of Guantánamo Bay and using it as an anchorage for American warships during the Spanish-American War, the United States, by a treaty in 1903 with Cuba, obtained the right to establish and maintain a naval base on both sides of the entrance to the harbor. Because of its position near the Windward Passage route from the Central American mainland to the east coast of the United States, and because of the protection from storm or attack afforded by the narrow entrance to the harbor, the Guantánamo Bay station has become the chief U.S. naval base in the West Indies.

GUAPORÉ, the largest of the federal territories of Brazil (q.v.) created in October, 1943, from portions of n.w. Mato Grosso and s. Amazonas. The territory borders s. Peru and Bolivia. Pôrto Velho is the capital. Area, 98,107 sq.m.; pop. (1950) 1,844,655.

GUAPORÉ or **ITÉNEZ,** a river of South America, rising in the state of Mato Grosso, s.w. Brazil, and flowing n.w. between Brazil and Bolivia to the Mamoré R., a tributary of the Madeira. The Guaporé is navigable for the greater part of its course of about 950 m.

GUARANI, a group of aboriginal Indian tribes of South America, constituting a linguistic subdivision of the Tupis (q.v.). They were once widely diffused through central and southern Brazil, Paraguay, Bolivia, Argentina, and Uruguay. The present population of Paraguay and Uruguay is largely Guarani, or of Guarani extraction. Descendants of the Guarani in Brazil dwell in villages surrounded with a double line of palisades; family life is communal. The Indians are industrious, and engage in farming, hunting, and fishing. Their weapons are the bow and arrow and the club. Netted hammocks are made on prim-

itive upright looms. The Guarani are short in stature, their average height not exceeding 5' 4". They are long-headed and have a light pigmentation.

GUARANTY or **GUARANTEE,** in law, an obligation undertaken by one party to answer for the default of another. It is an agreement by one person to answer to another for the debt, or the performance of some contract or duty in case of default, of a third person who is originally liable for such payment or performance. The party who promises that the obligation of the principal or debtor will be paid or performed is called the guarantor. A guaranty is similar in principle to a suretyship (q.v.), but differs in that the promise of the guarantor is distinct from and collateral to that of the principal debtor, whereas a surety, although an accessory, is bound with the principal debtor as a copromissor. In common law a guaranty was equally enforceable whether made in writing or orally. Under existing statutes in the United States, a guaranty must be in writing.

GUARAUNO, a tribe of South American Indians, dwelling for the most part in the delta of the Orinoco R. in e. Venezuela. They are dark in color and of a well-developed physique. Their subsistence is derived principally from hunting and fishing, and to a lesser extent from agriculture. The Guaraunos are skillful laborers, building their houses upon piles to safeguard them against the overflowing of the river.

GUARDAFUI, CAPE (Lat. *Aromatum promontorium*), next to Ras Hafun, the most easterly point of the African continent. Cape Guardafui is situated on a promontory of Italian Somaliland extending between the Gulf of Aden and the Indian Ocean.

GUARD CELLS. See STOMATA.

GUARDI, FRANCESCO (1712–93), landscape painter, born in Venice, Italy. He studied under Antonio Canaletto, and his work so closely resembles his master's that their paintings are sometimes confused. Both artists painted Venetian scenes, but Guardi introduced processions of figures in brilliant colors and animated groups in brightly hued costumes. Among his most important works are "Procession of the Doge", "Fête of Corpus Domini", "Grand Hall of the Palazzo Ducale" (Louvre, Paris), "Church and Piazza of San Marco" (National Gallery, London), and "The Rialto" (Metropolitan Museum of Art, New York City).

GUARDIAN, in United States law, the individual to whom is entrusted the care of a person, or of his property, or of both, when such person, by statutory definition or judicial finding, is incapable of administering his own affairs, whether because of age, lack of understanding, or lack of self-control. The usual form of guardianship is that of infants, individuals considered as minors under State statutes.

Three types of guardianship with respect to infants were distinguished at common law: *guardianship by nature; guardianship by nurture;* and *guardianship by socage. Guardianship by nature* was that possessed by a father, or by his widow, with respect to the person of the heir apparent or oldest son. *Guardianship by nurture* was that possessed by the father or by his widow, with respect to the persons of children other than the heir apparent. *Guardianship by socage* was that vested in the next of kin of a tenant by socage (see TENURE) under fourteen years of age. This guardianship could be claimed only by relatives other than the heirs of the infant.

In the United States *guardianship by nature* is the prevailing form of guardianship, and is the right of the father, mother, and next of kin, in the order named, to the custody of the person of a minor child. *Guardianship by nurture* does not exist in the United States; and *guardianship by socage* is practically unknown, except in the State of New York, where it obtains only when a minor has acquired realty.

In most States the appointment of guardians and their duties to their wards are regulated by statute. In general such statutes vest jurisdiction over appointment and control of guardians in the courts, usually in courts of probate in the case of the death of the paternal parent. The legal right to guardianship of minor children, as at common law, normally belongs to the surviving parent, since the statutes generally provide that a married woman is, with her husband, a joint guardian of her children, with equal powers, rights, and duties in regard to them. However, whether such surviving parent will be appointed guardian by a court depends on the court's determination that such action will best promote the child's welfare under all circumstances. The laws of most States authorize the surviving parent to designate a guardian for minors in his or her will. Such a guardian is termed a *testamentary guardian.* A guardian may be appointed by a probate court when the parents of a minor child are still living, if the parents appear unfit for control of the minor or have interests adverse to it.

Guardians appointed by a court, or by will, have control both of the ward's person and of his entire property. It is the duty of the guardian to take possession and control of his ward's personal property and of the rents and profits of his real estate; to keep, invest, and protect the same; and to render a just and true account on the ward's coming of age.

When a cause of action exists directly in favor of an infant, or when an action or law suit is brought against an infant, the court of appropriate jurisdiction will appoint a *guardian ad litem* to protect the interests of the infant in such action; the guardian ad litem may or may not be the same as the infant's general guardian. In estate-administration proceedings in which a minor is involved, the probate courts appoint special guardians for the purpose of protecting the interests of said minor. A special guardian is usually an attorney, rather than the infant's general guardian.

GUARDIAN ANGELS. See ANGEL.

GUARIBA. See HOWLING MONKEY.

GUARINI, GIOVANNI BATTISTA (1538–1612), Italian poet, born at Ferrara, and educated at Pisa and Padua. After fourteen years in the diplomatic service of Alphonso II, Duke of Ferrara, he became the duke's court poet in 1581. A year later he resigned and withdrew to his family estate, the Villa Guarina, where he wrote his most notable work, *Pastor Fido* (produced 1585; published 1590). This play, a pastoral tragicomedy, polished in style, was translated into many languages and became popular during the 17th century. It set the pattern for a code of refinement and gallantry that lasted in Europe until the time of the French Revolution. Guarini's work has been compared to that of Torquato Tasso (q.v.), but it lacks the deep feeling and sentiment of Tasso.

GUARNIERI, the name of a family of Italian violin makers, all of whom were born in Cremona and whose activities for the most part were carried on in that city. The family is often known by the Latinized form of its name, Guarnerius. Its principal members were the following. **1.** ANDREA (1626–98). He learned the art of violin making in the workshop of the noted violin maker Nicolò Amati (see AMATI) in Cremona. The violins made by Andrea Guarnieri were patterned after the Amati violins. **2.** PIETRO

GIOVANNI (1655–1728), elder son of Andrea. From the fact that he settled in Mantua he is known as "Peter of Mantua". He made a number of technical improvements in the type of violin made by his father; instruments made by Peter of Mantua are highly valued today. **3.** GIUSEPPE GIOVANNI BATTISTA (1666–1739), younger son of Andrea. He also made a number of changes in the violin model created by his father; some of Giuseppe's innovations had influence on the work of the most outstanding member of the family, Giuseppe Antonio (see below). **4.** PIETRO (1695–1765), son of the preceding, and known as "Peter of Venice" because he utilized in his work some of the features of the work of Venetian violin makers. **5.** GIUSEPPE ANTONIO (1683–1745), nephew of Andrea. He was known as *Giuseppe del Gesù* ("Giuseppe of Jesus") from the Greek sacred monogram *I.H.S.* ("Jesus Christ Savior"), which he added to his name on the labels which he placed on his violins. As a maker of violins Giuseppe del Gesù is regarded as second only to the greatest of all violin makers, Antonio Stradivari (q.v.). The violins made by Giuseppe del Gesù are particularly noted for their rich tone. One of his best instruments was played by the great violin virtuoso Niccolò Paganini; this instrument, now the sole violin made by Giuseppe which remains in Italy, is today in the Municipal Palace, Genoa.

GUATEMALA, a republic of Central America, bounded on the w. by the Pacific Ocean, on the E. by British Honduras and the Caribbean Sea, on the N. by Mexico, and on the S. by El Salvador and Honduras. The capital is the city of Guatemala (q.v.). Other important towns are Quezaltenango (q.v.), Cobán, and Zacapa. Puerto Barrios, Guatemala's chief Atlantic coast port, is some 200 m. from the city of Guatemala, and receives 75 percent of the country's import trade. The United Fruit Company maintains regular sailings between Puerto Barrios and Atlantic seaboard ports in the United States. The chief Pacific port of Guatemala is San José. The country has an area of 42,042 sq.m. The population (1955 est.) is about 3,258,000, of whom more than half are pure Indian, descendants of the ancient Mayas (q.v.), the remainder being for the most part mixed Spanish and Indian.

Physical Features and Climate. Roughly two thirds of Guatemala's total land area is covered by mountains, of which many are volcanic. The Sierra Madre system, traversing Guatemala from N. to S., divides the country into two drainage areas of unequal extent. The Pacific slope, relatively narrow, is abundantly watered and fertile in its mid-region, in which the greatest density of population occurs. The Atlantic slope, and notably the broad hilly plain of Petén in the N., ranges from grazing land to forest, and is thinly populated. Most of the volcanoes of Guatemala are extinct; severe eruptions have been recorded, however, for Tacaná, Fuego, and Pacaya. Other volcanic summits are Agua, Atitlán, Tajumulco, Acatenango, and Santa María. Earthquakes are frequent in the vicinity of the S. volcanic belt, where many towns have been destroyed.

The climate of Guatemala is, for the most part, equable, although temperatures vary considerably according to altitude. Between 3000 and 8000 ft. above sea level, where most of the country's population is concentrated, the days are warm and the nights cool; the temperature ranges from 45° F. in December and January to 85° F. in March and April. The weather in the low-lying coastal regions is more tropical in character, with an average annual temperature of around 80° F. The period of greatest rainfall occurs between May and October, with a corresponding dry season from November to April.

Industry. The principal industry of Guatemala is agriculture, for which the country is well adapted because of its exceptionally fertile soil. The chief commercial crop is coffee, to which 20% of the land under cultivation is devoted, and which comprised over 75% of the total exports in 1952. Upward of 30% of all coffee plantations in Guatemala, located high on the mountainsides, were formerly owned by German interests, but these holdings were taken over by the Guatemalan government in 1942, and are now nationally owned and operated. Bananas, grown by the most modern methods in the Atlantic coastal areas under the auspices of the United Fruit Company, are second in importance to coffee as an export crop. Most of the laborers on the low-lying banana plantations are Negroes brought in principally from the British West Indies. Other agricultural products of Guatemala are sugar cane, corn, potatoes, wheat, beans, rice, and oranges. The corn, potatoes, and other temperate products are produced on the sides and in the valley of the mountains by the Indians, who use primitive farming methods. Honey also is produced in considerable quantity. Livestock includes cattle, sheep, goats, asses. mules, and horses. Guatemala, next

United Fruit Co.

Street scene in the town of Santiago de Atitlán, southern Guatemala

to Mexico, is the world's largest source of chicle, employed in the manufacture of chewing gum. The country's forests are rich also in pine, dyewoods, and such cabinet woods as mahogany and cedar. Mineral resources comprise gold, chromite, silver, copper, iron, lead, mercury, tin, salt, and sulfur, although with the exception of gold, chromite, and salt, the deposits are not sufficiently large to warrant commercial exploitation. Manufacturing, on a small scale and exclusively for domestic use, includes sugar refining, flour milling, distilling, brewing, tanning, and the making of shoes. Handicraft products are produced by the Indians.

Commerce. Guatemala's imports in 1952 were valued at about $69,700,000; exports were valued at $94,700,000. In the same year the United States absorbed almost 85% of the country's exports, and furnished about 63% of the imports. The principal exports are coffee, bananas and other fruits, chicle, essential oils, vegetable fiber, and timber; imports are chiefly textiles, motor vehicles, machinery, and foodstuffs.

Communications. The total mileage of all railroads in Guatemala is 720 m., of which about 90% is controlled by the American-owned International Railways of Central America. A railway link between North and

South America was established in 1942 with the opening of a railroad bridge across the Suchiate R. from Mexico to Guatemala. In 1952 there were 2316 m. of highways, and 3277 m. of secondary roads suitable for automobile traffic during nine months of the year, giving access to most parts of the country. The unfinished Pan-American Highway traverses Guatemala from Mexico to El Salvador. A local air service provides communication between Guatemala City, Quezaltenango, Puerto Barrios, and Coban.

People. The Indians of Guatemala, constituting the largest single element of the population, steadfastly maintain the ancient customs and institutions of their Mayan ancestors. Some eighteen different Indian dialects are said to be spoken by the various tribes inhabiting the uplands of the interior, and tribal distinctions are further emphasized by individual dress. In physical appearance, however, the Indians vary but little, having in common the squat build, coarse black hair, coppery skin, and high cheekbones of their ethnic group. So great is the village and tribal solidarity among the Indians of Guatemala that they have an unofficial or shadow government within the frame of the Guatemalan state. Local officials are rarely if ever appointed until there is a consultation with the *principales,* or elders of the Indian community.

Education and Religion. The rate of illiteracy in Guatemala in 1950 was about 72%. In 1952 there were 3640 primary schools and a number of secondary schools with an aggregate of 264,000 pupils. The University of Guatemala (established in 1678 as the University of San Carlos de Borromeo) was reorganized in 1910 with seven schools and faculties; it has over 150 instructors and an average annual enrollment of nearly 700. Teacher-training schools are located at Guatemala City, Chiquimula, and Quezaltenango. Education is free and compulsory at the primary level. Roman Catholicism is the prevailing religion, but the members of all other denominations enjoy absolute freedom of faith. The worship of ancient tribal deities is still widely practiced among the Indian population.

Government. Under the Guatemalan constitution of 1945, executive power is vested in the president, who is elected by popular vote for six years, and who may not run for re-election during the twelve years subsequent to the expiration of his term of office. The legislative branch of the government is a unicameral national assembly, elected by universal suffrage every four years, one half of the body being renewed biennially. Administratively, Guatemala is divided into twenty-two departments, each under a governor who is appointed by the president. Mayors of municipalities are elected directly by the people. A seven-member council of state, advisory in function, is composed of four men appointed by the president and three elected by the national assembly. Men and women who have passed their eighteenth year are entitled to vote. Males need not satisfy the literacy requirement; females must be able to read and write. Voting, compulsory for literate males, is optional for illiterates and women.

History. Guatemala, site of the ancient civilization of the Mayas, was conquered by a Spanish force under Pedro de Alvarado (q.v.) in 1524. After three centuries of Spanish domination, Guatemala, virtually coextensive with all that is now known as Central America, proclaimed its independence on September 15, 1821. Almost at once, Augustín de Iturbide (q.v.), Emperor of Mexico, incorporated the territory into the Mexican Empire. Guatemala did not regain its autonomy until 1823, when a revolution in Mexico forced Emperor Iturbide to abdicate, and a Mexican republic was proclaimed. In the same year, the Confederation of Central America was established, com-

prehending present-day Guatemala, Honduras, El Salvador, Nicaragua, and Costa Rica. The confederation was maintained only with the greatest difficulty, however, and finally collapsed upon the secession of Guatemala in 1839.

The government of Guatemala has been in the hands of military men virtually from the beginning of the republican era. These military leaders were often self-appointed and had come up through the ranks in the process of frequent revolutions. In 1854 Rafael Carrera (q.v.), who fourteen years earlier had made himself dictator of Guatemala and a large portion of Central America, became president for life. In 1873, eight years after Carrera's death, Justo Rufino Barrios was elected to the presidency. Barrios, seeking to revive the Central American federation by military means, invaded El Salvador, and was killed in the ensuing battle between the two countries. His successor, General Manuel Barillas, re-established peaceful relations with El Salvador and the other countries of Central America. José María Reina Barrios, elected president in 1892, and re-elected five years later, was assassinated in 1898.

For the next twenty-two years, Manuel Estrada Caberera was dictator of Guatemala. In 1906, ex-president Barillas organized a revolt against the Caberera regime which soon involved all Central America in war, Nicaragua alone excepted. Further hostilities were averted by the intervention of presidents Theodore Roosevelt of the United States and Porfirio Díaz of Mexico, who arranged an armistice. The following year, representatives of the five Central American nations attended a peace conference in Washington, D.C., at which provision was made for the establishment of a Central American Court of Justice to settle all future disputes.

Guatemala severed diplomatic relations with Germany on April 27, 1917, during World War I. In 1920 the dictatorship of President Estrada Caberera came to an end with a revolution of liberal elements which forced the dictator's resignation. Dr. Carlos Herrera was appointed provisional president, taking the oath for the unexpired term (1916–23). On December 7, 1921, Herrera was overthrown and General José María Orellana, Guatemalan chief of staff, succeeded to the presidency, serving until his death in 1926. Unrest resulting from economic depression and charges of corruption leveled against the dictatorship of the new president, Lazaro Chacón, culminated in a revolutionary out-

R. R. Rowe, from Black Star

IN GUATEMALA

*Above: A church in Huehue-
tenango. Right: An Indian
woman in Chichicastenango,
weaving cloth on hand loom.
Hand-woven cloth produced
by the natives of this Central American country is famous for its bright-colored
beauty.*

break in December, 1930. On December 16, a coup d'état in Guatemala City led by General Manuel Orellana overthrew the government. Orellana in turn was soon forced out, his place being taken by Dr. José María Reina Andrade, who served until the election of General Jorge Ubico as president in February, 1931.

The growing economic disturbance compelled Ubico to give his attention primarily to measures aimed at relieving the crisis. His policies were arbitrary and aroused widespread dissatisfaction, but little political disorder. In 1934, however, a revolutionary conspiracy against his life was put down with great severity. Throughout the following year, Ubico tightened his absolutist control of the government, inaugurating a stringent program of militarization. In 1937 he nullified the presidential non-re-election clause of the 1928 Guatemalan constitution by maintaining himself in office beyond the expiration of his term. Despite opposition to this act by Guatemalan political exiles, who denounced Ubico's retention of power without even the formality of a vote, the president encountered no serious threat to his dictatorial regime within Guatemala itself. The country's foreign pol-

icy under Ubico manifested a spirit of amity and co-operation toward the Axis powers (Germany, Italy, and Japan), although government circles issued a vigorous denial of the charge. Trade with Germany prospered, however, and the Guatemalan envoy in Berlin was raised to the rank of minister.

With the outbreak of World War II in September, 1939, Guatemala, however, declared itself strictly neutral. All foreign political organizations were outlawed and their activities banned, an action particularly detrimental to the Nazis and Fascists. Ubico's progressive reorientation of Guatemalan economy toward the United States culminated in declarations of war on Japan, Italy, and Germany in December, 1941. Guatemala secured membership in the United Nations on January 1, 1942, and throughout the year collaboration with the United States was strengthened. The progress of modern war made it necessary that Guatemala send to the United States and elsewhere a number of its younger army officers to be trained in new military techniques. When these young men returned to Guatemala, however, they found themselves under the command of the more or less illiterate colonels and generals of the

United Fruit Co.

An Indian village in the mountains of Guatemala

Lake Atitlán in southern Guatemala. Atitlán volcano is seen in the background.

old regime. Discontent among the technically-trained junior officers, who had also come into contact abroad with democratic concepts and institutions, spread throughout the army, and on July 1, 1944, President Ubico resigned in consequence of rising revolutionary opposition to his dictatorial regime. In December, after a period of general strife, the Guatemalan educator Juan José Arévalo Bermejo (1904–   ), who had the support of the National Renovation and Popular Front Liberation parties, was elected president. Arévalo Bermejo's administration was plagued by recurrent political crises in which the government charged that reactionary forces were plotting its overthrow. The government moved to meet the alleged threat by the suspension of constitutional guarantees, and the arrest and deportation of suspects. In January, 1945, the government severed diplomatic relations with the fascist regime in Spain. A new constitution was promulgated in March.

In September, 1945, Guatemala renewed its claim, outstanding since the republic was formed, to British Honduras (q.v.). A treaty negotiated with Great Britain in 1859 had laid down the southern boundary between Guatemala and British Honduras; claiming that Great Britain had not complied with all

the terms of the boundary agreement, Guatemala reopened the entire dispute in the late 1930's. In January, 1946, Great Britain proposed that the border dispute be submitted for arbitration to the United Nations International Court of Justice. On September 2, 1947, Guatemala became a signatory to the Inter-American Treaty of Reciprocal Assistance, known also as the Treaty of Rio de Janeiro, serving notice, however, that it did not recognize the United Kingdom's sovereignty over British Honduras. The dispute was aggravated in 1948 when units of the British Caribbean navy were dispatched to the port of Belize, British Honduras, to avert an alleged Guatemalan move to take over the colony. Guatemala issued a protest to the United Nations, the Pan-American Union, and all American countries. The republic then sealed off its frontier with British Honduras.

Minor rightist uprisings occurred during the first half of 1949, but the principal political development of the year was the government's intervention in a long-standing dispute between the United Fruit Co. and its workers. As a result of official pressure the company capitulated to the workers' demands. In August, 1949, Guatemala was accused by the Dominican Republic of aiding Dominican revolutionaries. The Council of the Organization of American States confirmed the charge in April, 1950, and threatened Guatemala with sanctions. The same month Guatemala requested the recall of the U.S. ambassador, accusing him of meddling in its domestic affairs. The request and accusation were promptly rejected by the United States.

General elections were held in November, 1950. Supported by a coalition of left-wing parties, presidential candidate Jacobo Arbenz Guzmán (1913–), minister of national defense in the Arévalo cabinet, won a decisive victory. The new administration assumed office in March, 1951, and during the remainder of the year President Arbenz Guzmán generally perpetuated the centrist domestic policies of his predecessor. Foreign-affairs developments included the reopening (May) of the frontier with British Honduras and participation (October) in the creation of the Organization of Central American States.

The administration moved steadily leftward during 1952. Among numerous indications of the growing influence of Guatemalan communists were a government order (January) forbidding anticommunist demonstrations and enactment of a radical social-security bill. During the early part of the year the government intervened in another dispute between the United Fruit Co. and its employees. The company again capitulated (March), making substantial concessions.

In May President Arbenz Guzmán vetoed the social-security bill, which he termed a threat to the national economy. The national assembly enacted (June) an agrarian-reform law providing for the distribution of uncultivated estates of more than 225 acres to landless workers. Early in February, 1953, the assembly removed from office four supreme court justices who had ruled against the law. Despite strong right-wing protests, government supporters were named to the vacancies.

The agrarian-reform program went into effect on Feb. 17, and several days later the government approved expropriation of 225,000 acres of United Fruit Co. lands on the Guatemalan west coast. By the middle of June expropriated private property, paid for with nonnegotiable government bonds, totaled 300,-000 acres; over 400,000 acres of government-owned lands had been distributed to landless workers.

Opposition to the Arbenz Guzmán regime mounted on both the international and domestic fronts during the first half of 1954. At the 10th Inter-American Conference, held in March, the United States secured approval of an anticommunist resolution implicitly condemning the Guatemalan government. In April the Roman Catholic archbishop of Guatemala, in a pastoral letter to his charge, appealed for an uprising against communism. Claiming discovery of a plot aimed at its overthrow, the government began on May 31 a wholesale roundup of opposition leaders; on June 8 civil rights were suspended.

On June 18 a "liberating" army of political exiles, led by Colonel Carlos Castillo Armas (1914?–57), invaded Guatemala from headquarters in Honduras. The rebels' ground forces quickly captured key supply points and their planes bombed the capital and other cities. Troops of the regular army offered only token resistance to the invaders. Arbenz Guzmán resigned on June 27 and two days later an anticommunist military junta, accepting the terms laid down by Castillo Armas for a cease-fire, dissolved the legislature, ordered the arrest of prominent Reds, and released 600 political prisoners. Various differences between the rebels and the junta were mediated by foreign diplomats, including the U.S. ambassador to Guatemala, and the civil war was formally ended on July 2. A new junta with representatives of both factions assumed supreme governmental authority pending nationwide elections and adoption of a new constitution.

Castillo Armas was named provisional president on July 8. On Oct. 10 a national plebiscite resulted in an overwhelming victory for Castillo Armas; he was formally installed as president for a 5-year term on Nov. 6. Meanwhile a constituent assembly convened to draft a new constitution. Among the provisions of the new basic law, work on which continued throughout 1955, are guarantees of freedom of worship and extension of the franchise to illiterates. In November, 1955, the government authorized the formation of political parties. Elections for a new national assembly were held in December. The government party won all 66 seats. On Dec. 31, 1955, Guatemalan security police uncovered a conspiracy aimed at overthrowing the government. A number of army officers implicated in the plot subsequently were imprisoned or deported. President Castillo Armas signed the new constitution on Feb. 2, 1956, and the new assembly took office on March 1. On June 24 security forces dispersed an allegedly procommunist student rally staged in the city of Guatemala in honor of the 1944 revolution, killing four of the demonstrators. The government proclaimed a state of siege on June 26. The unrest pervading the country subsided in the following weeks, and the state of siege was lifted on Aug. 26. During the remainder of 1956 and well into 1957 the political opposition remained relatively quiescent. President Castillo Armas was assassinated in the Presidential Palace by a member of the palace guard on July 26; he was succeeded by Vice-President Luis Arturo Gonzalez Lopez (1901–   ).

GUATEMALA, capital city of Guatemala, and largest city of Central America, situated 75 m. by rail N.E. of the Pacific Coast port of San José and 198 m. by rail S.W. of the Caribbean port of Puerto Barrios, on a plateau 4850 ft. above sea level. The present city is the third capital in the history of the country. The first capital, also called Guatemala, founded in 1524, was destroyed by a volcanic eruption in 1556. The second capital, founded in the 16th century, was almost completely destroyed by an earthquake in 1773; it is located 25 miles w. of the present city and is now known as Antigua (pop. in 1950, 10,691). The present city was founded in 1773. Guatemala is the commercial center of the country. Its principal article of trade is coffee. A considerable trade is carried on also in lumber, hides, and gold. Furniture, cigars, soap, and shoes are manufactured. The city is the seat of an episcopal see; its great cathedral is noted as an excellent example of Spanish colonial architecture. Pop. (1950) 293,998.

GUATEMOTZIN, GUATEMOC, or CU-AUHTEMOC (1495?–1525), last Aztec emperor of Mexico and nephew of Emperor Montezuma II. Guatemotzin was leader of the political party opposed to Montezuma's policy of appeasing the Spanish invaders. He organized the attack, known as "la Noche Triste", which drove Hernando Cortes (q.v.) from Mexico City on June 3, 1520. Upon the death of his uncle, Guatemotzin was chosen emperor of the Aztecs. As emperor, he succeeded in defending the capital city throughout the spring and summer of 1521. When he was finally captured by the Spanish, he refused to reveal the location of the Aztec gold treasury. He was taken as a hostage by Cortes and his party on their march through Honduras. During this march the emperor was tortured and killed by the Spanish. A commemorative statue of Mexico's last Aztec emperor stands in Mexico City.

GUATOS, a South American Indian tribe, dwelling on the Brazilian-Bolivian border, in the vicinity of lakes Uberaba and Gaiba and the Paraguay R. They live in small, thatched huts, isolated rather than communal, and derive their subsistence principally from fishing.

GUAVA, common name of shrubs or small trees of the genus *Psidium,* belonging to the Myrtle family, and of the fruits which they produce. Guavas are native to the tropics of America and Asia. The most common cultivated guava is the fruit of a small tree, *P. guajava* variety *pyriferum,* the white guava. The tree, which attains a height of 15 to 20 feet, is native to tropical America and is cultivated in Florida. The yellow, pear-shaped fruits are about the size of hen's eggs. The rind is thin and brittle, and the light-yellow, soft pulp is sweet and somewhat acid. Red guava, *P. guajava* variety *pomiferum,* bears a globular red fruit with sour red pulp. Strawberry guava, *P. cattleyanum,* is a Brazilian species producing a large, spherical, claret-colored fruit with soft pulp which has a flavor similar to that of strawberry. Strawberry guava has been cultivated in tropical America since the pre-Columbian period. Jellies, preserves, and pastes made from guavas are considered delicacies.

GUAYAQUIL, capital of the province of Guayas, Ecuador, and the chief seaport of the country, located on the w. bank of the estuary of the Guayas R. at the Gulf of Guayaquil. The harbor is large and contains many quays and shipyards. The chief exports from Guayaquil are cacao, rubber, coffee, quinine, gold, silver, and hides. The city is the site of one of the six universities in Ecuador and of a government aviation school. See ECUADOR. Pop. (1950) 258,966.

GUAYCURUAN, a distinct stock of South American Indians living in the Gran Chaco (see CHACO, EL). The Guaycuruan family comprises about twenty tribes, of which the Guaycurus is the most prominent.

GUAYULE, common name of a shrubby perennial herb, *Parthenium argentatum,* belonging to the Thistle family, yielding guayule rubber. Guayule is native to the dry regions of s.w Texas and N. Mexico. The plant grows about two feet tall, bearing gray, silvery leaves. The dry weight of five-year-old plants is about twenty percent guayule rubber. Crude guayule rubber contains a large amount of resin, which must be removed, at considerable expense, to obtain good quality rubber. Guayule rubber, in small quantities, was formerly obtained from wild Mexican plants of this species. Because of the shortage

The Diana monkey, a guenon

of *Hevea* rubber during World War II, scientists of the United States Forest Service carried on experimental cultivation of 30,000 acres of guayule in s. California. They found that two-year-old guayules yield about 600 pounds of rubber per acre, five-year-olds yield about 1600 pounds per acre, and six-year-olds yield about 2200 pounds per acre. See RUBBER.

GUBBIO (anc. *Iguvium*), town, commune, and episcopal see of the province of Perugia, Umbria, Italy. The town is located on the s. slopes of the Apennines, 1735 ft. above sea level, 23 miles N.N.E. of the city of Perugia and 13 m. by rail N.W. of Fossato di Vico. Gubbio dates from pre-Roman times. In 552 A.D. the Goths destroyed the town. Later it was rebuilt by order of the Byzantine general Narses. After its reconstruction the town was subject to the Lombard kingdom. In 774, following the fall of the Lombards, Gubbio was included in the donation of Charlemagne to the pope. St. Francis of Assisi is thought to have begun his life of religious teaching in Gubbio, about 1206. The principal buildings are the 12th-century cathedral of S.S. Mariano e Jacopo, containing Gothic sculpture and Umbrian painting; The Residenza Municipale, containing ancient and modern majolicas, for which the town is noted, and the Eugubine Tables; and the 15th-century ducal palace. Gubbio is a market for the cattle, grain, wine, olive oil, linen, silk, and lumber produced in the vicinity. The manufacture of majolica is the principal industry in the town. Pop. of commune (1936) 32,727; of town (1936) 7432.

GUELDER-ROSE. See VIBURNUM.

GUELDERS. See GELDERLAND.

GUELPHS and **GHIBELLINES,** the names of two great political factions existing in N. and central Italy from about the 12th to the 15th centuries. These factions originated in the early 12th century in Germany as the partisans of a struggle between two princely houses, the Welfs, who were the dukes of Saxony and Bavaria, and the Hohenstaufens, then the ruling house of the Holy Roman Empire. (For the most famous Welf ruler, see HENRY THE LION.) During the course of the 12th century, the struggle between the German factions was transferred to Italy. The name "Guelph" was a corruption of Welf; "Ghibelline" was a corruption of Waiblingen, an estate belonging to the Hohenstaufen emperors.

By the beginning of the 13th century, the names of the two groups had lost their original German significance. The Guelphs became the party opposing the authority of the Holy Roman emperors in Italy and supporting the power of the papacy. The Ghibellines supported the Imperial authority, particularly the rule of Frederick I (Barbarossa) (q.v.). The Guelph party, moreover, became a nationalist party in a sense, for it enlisted itself in support of the Italian principalities and city republics which were demanding provincial or municipal rights and liberties.

Medieval Italy was disrupted by the violent political and military conflicts between the partisans of the two great factions. In general, the great noble families adhered to the Ghibellines, and the great cities supported the Guelphs. Eventually, the division became more geographical. The nobles in the more northern districts inclined toward the Ghibellines, those in the central district toward the Guelphs. Pisa, Verona, and Arezzo were Ghibelline strongholds; Bologna, Milan, and, particularly, Florence supported the Guelphs. In Florence, struggles between the parties resulted in a civil war which raged for more than ten years until, in 1266, the Ghibellines were expelled from the city.

About the 14th century, after the German emperors had ceased to be a major power in Italy, the contest degenerated into a mere struggle of local political factions availing themselves of the prestige of ancient names and traditional or hereditary prejudices. In

1334 Pope Benedict XII forbade, under pain of the censures of the Church, the further use of the Guelph and Ghibelline names. After the 14th century, they were rarely used as the names of factions actually existing.

GUENON, common name for any long-tailed African monkey in the genus *Cercopithecus,* the largest genus of monkeys. Many guenons have been domesticated and trained; they comprise the majority of organ-grinder monkeys and are valued as pets throughout the world because of their intelligence and gentleness. Guenons were the monkeys best-known in ancient Egypt, Greece, and Rome. The small, slender guenons are characterized by large cheek pouches. Many species are multicolored, their fur showing brilliant, contrasting tints. These monkeys live in the trees of forests in the wild state, subsisting on fruits and leaves. Among the species found in w. Africa are the mustache monkey, *C. cephus,* which has a white band under its nose, the malbrouck, *C. cynosurus,* and the mona, *C. mona.*

GUERCINO (It., "squint-eyed"), common name of GIOVANNI FRANCESCO BARBIERI (1591–1666), Italian painter of the Bolognese School, born at Cento and educated there and in Bologna. He studied with various painters, including Lodovico Carracci. From 1621 to 1623, the year of the death of his patron, Pope Gregory XV, Guercino was in Rome, where he painted several well-known canvases and the "Aurora" fresco on the walls of the Villa Ludovisi. He lived in Cento from 1623 until 1642, when he went to Bologna to fill the place vacated by the death of Guido Reni (q.v.), head of the Eclectics. In attempting to imitate Reni's style, Guercino lost much of the force which previously characterized his own.

Guercino is famous for over 250 still-existing paintings and for numerous frescoes. Among his best-known works are the fresco "Capture of St. Roch", and the paintings, "St. Bruno and His Companions in the Desert" and "Raising of St. Petronella".

GUEREBA. See HOWLING MONKEY.

GUEREZA, common name for any long-tailed African monkey in the genus *Colobus,* closely related to the langur and proboscis monkey (qq.v.). The guerezas are characterized by vestigial thumbs, which cannot be used in grasping, and by a large stomach specially adapted for the digestion of leaves, which constitute their principal food. The best-known guereza, *C. guereza,* found in Ethiopia, reaches a maximum length of 26 in. from head to rump. The tail is 22 in. long. The slender, long-legged monkeys of this genus have beautiful fur, satiny black in color, with long white fringes on the head, sides, and back; they are hunted for their skins, which are used to decorate the shields of Ethiopian and Kaffir tribesmen. *C. caudatus,* a white-tailed species, is protected from extinction in the Kilimanjaro game reserve of Tanganyika.

GUERICKE, OTTO VON (1602–86), German physicist, born at Magdeburg. He studied law at the universities of Leipzig and Jena and mathematics at the University of Leiden. In 1627 he was elected alderman of Magdeburg and in 1646 was elected burgomaster of that city. Von Guericke was interested in natural science, and having heard of the experiments of Galileo, Pascal, and Torricelli in connection with atmospheric pressure, he became interested in the properties of air and the creation of a vacuum. His first attempt to create a vacuum by pumping water out of a barrel failed, because when the water was pumped out of the barrel air permeated the wood and

Otto von Guericke's famous demonstration of the Magdeburg hemispheres (early drawing)

replaced the water. He then fitted a globe of copper with a stopcock and pump, and found that he could pump the air out of the globe. He thus invented the first air pump in 1650. In 1654 he carried out before the Imperial Diet at Ratisbon the famous demonstration of the Magdeburg hemispheres. Two hollow bronze hemispheres were carefully fitted together and the air removed from the resulting sphere by means of a pump. Two eight-horse teams could not pull the two halves apart. When the air was readmitted the hemispheres fell apart. Similar evacuated hemispheres are used today in laboratory demonstrations of atmospheric pressure.

Von Guericke investigated fields of natural science other than pneumatics. In 1672 he developed the first machine for producing an electric charge; see ELECTRICAL MACHINE. His observations and studies are recorded in his *Experimenta Nova, ut Vocant, Magdeburgica de Vacuo Spatio* (1672).

GUERILLAS. See GUERRILLAS.

GUERNSEY, the second-largest island of the Channel Islands (q.v.), 69 miles S.E. from England and 46 miles S.W. of France. Its greatest length, from E. to W., is 9 m., and its greatest width is 5 m. The N. part of the island is flat, and the S. part rises to about 300 ft. above sea level. About two thirds of the soil is arable. There is evidence of early Celtic and Norse habitation on Guernsey. By the 11th century, the Normans were in control of the island. Agriculture is the principal industry. Tomatoes and grapes, two of the leading crops, are grown in glasshouses because of the exposed location of the island. Guernsey is particularly noted for its breed of cattle (see GUERNSEY CATTLE). St. Peter Port is the capital and principal seaport. Area, 25 sq.m.; pop. (1952) 43,667.

GUERNSEY CATTLE, sometimes called Alderney cattle, a breed of dairy cattle developed on the island of Guernsey. Guernsey, like its sister Channel Island, Jersey, where Jersey cattle are developed, has for more than 100 years prohibited the introduction of any other breed of live cattle except for slaughter. The purity of the Guernsey breed is thus assured. Guernseys were first brought to the U.S. in 1833, and after 1874 were imported in considerable numbers. The breed is also common in England and Canada. Guernseys are famed for the richness of their milk. On the island, the average cow is expected to produce 5000 pounds of milk and 300 pounds of butterfat a year. In the U.S., individual cows have produced over 18,000 pounds of milk and 1000 pounds of butterfat a year. The standard size for mature Guernsey bulls is about 1500 pounds; for cows, about 1000. See CATTLE.

GUERRAZZI, FRANCESCO DOMENICO, known also as ANSELMO GUALANDI (1804–73), Italian patriot and writer, born in Leghorn, and educated for a legal career at Pisa. He returned to his native city and began the practice of law. Soon he met the nationalist revolutionary Giuseppe Mazzini, and in 1829 they founded the *Indicatore,* a paper advocating the unification of a free Italy. The Austrian authorities suppressed the publication, and Guerrazzi served several terms in prison for his espousal of the cause of Italian unification. He wrote the novel *Assidio di Firenzi* (1834) while he was in jail. He became the foremost Liberal leader in Leghorn, and in 1848 accepted a post in the ministry of Grand Duke Leopold II of Tuscany. The revolution of 1848 caused Leopold to flee, and in 1849 Guerrazzi became dictator. Upon the restoration of the grand duke a few months later, Guerrazzi was imprisoned on the charge of failing to repress the revolution. Three years later he was banished to Corsica. The triumph of the Italian nationalist movement in Tuscany caused Guerrazzi to be restored to liberty, and from 1862 to 1870 he sat in the Parliament of Turin. Among his works are the novels *Isabella Orsini* (1845) and *Beatrice Cenci* (1854).

GUERRERO, a state of Mexico, bordering the Pacific Ocean. The state is mountainous, the N. portion containing spurs of the Mexico and Morelos ranges, and the S. portions containing the Sierra Madre del Sur range. The Balsas R., the principal river, connects the E. and W. portions of the state. Coffee, tobacco, cereal grains, vanilla, cotton, and rubber are the principal agricultural products, and gold, silver, lead, iron, and coal are mined. The principal cities are Acapulco (q.v.), the capital Chilpancingo (pop. in 1940, 8834), and Iguala (12,756). Area, 24,885 sq.m.; pop. (1950) 919,386.

GUERRERO, MARÍA (1868–1928), Spanish actress, born in Madrid. She studied drama in Paris and acted with Jean Coquelin and Sarah Bernhardt. From 1894 until 1909 she produced and appeared in plays at the Teatro Español, Madrid. Her most notable roles were in *Mancha que Limpia* and *El Loco Diós,* by José Echegaray y Eizaguirre; and *La Estrella de Sevilla,* by Lope de Vega.

GUERRILLAS or **GUERILLAS** (Sp., diminutive of *guerra,* "war"), bands of combat personnel engaged in irregular warfare. Since ancient times, guerrilla warfare has been conducted principally by peoples unable to oppose their enemies with regular armies, for example, the war carried on in the 2nd century B.C. by the Israelites, under the leadership of the Maccabees, against the Greek armies occupying Palestine. Revolutionary movements have often resorted to guerrilla warfare; one of the earliest of these movements was the slave insurrection of the 1st century B.C., led by the Roman gladiator Spartacus (q.v.), who conducted successful guerrilla warfare against the armies of Rome for many years. In more recent times, guerrilla bands have also been employed as an adjunct to regular armies, as in the cavalry incursions led by the Confederate general J. E. B. Stuart (q.v.) against the Union armies in the American Civil War.

The strategic aim of guerrilla warfare is to harass the enemy, while avoiding pitched battles. In effectuating this strategy, guerrillas almost invariably operate from bases in mountainous or forested terrain difficult of access to regular armies. Guerrilla tactics usually involve the execution of sudden, swift raids on exposed enemy units, and on installations and lines of communication and supply, followed by equally swift withdrawals to the base of operations.

History affords a number of outstanding examples of guerrilla operations, in addition to those cited above. Among these are the struggle of the Spanish irregulars against the French armies occupying Spain during the Napoleonic Wars early in the 19th century, and the Filipino resistance led by Emilo Aguinaldo (q.v.) against the American forces in the Philippines immediately after the Spanish-American War.

During World War II guerrilla operations were carried on in many parts of the world on a scale previously unknown in history. Hundreds of thousands of men and women, called "Partisans", were deployed by the Soviet government behind the German lines, their activities being closely co-ordinated with the operations of the Soviet armies. In France guerrillas known as "Maquis", operating from remote mountain bases and forest retreats, comprised a part of the national resistance movement to the Nazi occupation army and civil authorities; their activities were correlated with those of the underground resistance movement in the cities.

After the war, the republican revolutionary movement of the Indonesians, who were seeking freedom from Dutch rule, employed guerrilla warfare to achieve its aims. In the civil war which broke out in Greece soon after the defeat of the Axis Powers, the communist-led opposition to the government also employed guerrilla tactics.

GUESCLIN, BERTRAND DU. See DU GUESCLIN, BERTRAND.

GUESDE, JULES (1845–1922), French socialist leader, sometimes called the founder of modern French socialism, born in Paris. His real name was Mathieu Basile. After working for a time in the press department of the French ministry of the interior, he became editor of the periodical *Les Droits de L'Homme* ("Rights of Man") in 1870. To avoid imprisonment for his articles in defense of the Paris Commune (see COMMUNE OF 1871) Guesde fled into exile, eventually settling in Switzerland. There he came into contact with the ideas and proponents of the International Workingmen's Association (q.v.) or First International, led by Karl Marx.

After his return to France in 1876 Guesde was at first a supporter of the anarchist Mikhail Bakunin (q.v.), Marx's principal opponent in the struggle for control of the First International. Later, Guesde became the leading French exponent of Marxian revolutionary doctrines. In the publication *L'Égalité* ("Equality"), which he founded in 1877, Guesde advocated "collective appropriation of the soil and of the instruments of labor", and the organization of an independent political party of workingmen, with the aim of taking power by revolutionary means.

Guesde played a leading role in the organization of the Federation of Socialist Workingmen of France in 1879, and in the following year, in collaboration with Marx, formulated the program which the party adopted at its congress in Le Havre. In 1882 the party split into a moderate wing, which advocated reforms as the means of achieving socialism, and a revolutionary wing, led by Guesde, which constituted itself the *Parti Ouvrier Français* ("French Worker's Party"). Guesde's party, which had considerable strength among the textile workers in northern France, held that power could be won only during a revolution and that socialism would thereupon be instituted through the socialization of industry.

In the elections of 1892 a number of Guesdists won seats in municipal councils in working-class communities, and in 1893 Guesde was one of more than fifty socialists elected to the Chamber of Deputies. He failed of re-election in 1902, but was returned to the Chamber four years later and retained his seat until 1921.

From the time of their first electoral successes, the Guesdists, including their leader, adopted a change in doctrine, emphasizing reforms and laying stress on revolution only as an ultimate and temporally distant solution of social problems. In the Chamber, Guesde played a prominent role in advocating social-reform legislation. By 1896 the Guesdists had embraced the moderate democratic view that universal suffrage was the key to social progress.

Guesde's political evolution to the right, however, was a contradictory process. While becoming more moderate, he nevertheless fought, in the Socialist and Labor International (see SECOND INTERNATIONAL) which he had helped found in 1899, against those who advocated support of capitalist parties. Guesde bitterly denounced, as a betrayal of principle and the working class, the acceptance, in 1899, of a cabinet post by the socialist leader Alexandre Millerand (q.v.), later president of France.

In 1914, in violation of earlier decisions of the Second International calling for irreconcilable opposition to war, Guesde supported his country's entry into World War I; in 1914–15 he served as minister without portfolio in the *Union Sacrée,* the coalition government of the former socialist Premier René Viviani. For these actions Guesde was denounced as a traitor to socialism by the Bolshevik leader Nikolai Lenin. In 1920, during the struggle for control of the *Parti Ouvrier Socialiste* ("Socialist Worker's Party", founded in 1905 by Guesde and others), Guesde supported the minority which was defeated at the Congress of Tours by followers of the Communist International.

After Guesde's death, his name became involved in sensational charges made in the French parliament by Deputy Paul Faure in 1928, and amplified by him in the press. Faure alleged that Guesde had been a principal in the successful intrigue conducted by the French cabinet in 1914 to subsidize the then relatively unknown Italian, Benito Mussolini, to found a paper (*Popolo d'Italia*) urging abandonment of Italy's neutrality in World War I and its entry into the conflict on the side of France. These charges buttressed previous allegations made in the press and also during the course of a celebrated political murder trial in 1926 by Henry Torrès, an outstanding leader of the French bar. According to these earlier allegations Guesde's political emissary to Mussolini had been Marcel Cachin, later leader of the French Communist Party, and the actual

bearer of the money had been Guesde's secretary Charles Dumas.

GUESS, GEORGE. See SEQUOYA.

GUEST, EDGAR ALBERT (1881–   ), American writer, born in Birmingham, England. He came to the United States in 1891, and attended grammar and high school in Detroit, Mich. Starting in 1895 Guest wrote a column in the Detroit Free Press, and his verse and sketches of a simple, colloquial quality won him a wide audience. The verse, *Home,* beginning with "It takes a heap o' livin' in a house t' make it home" was one of his earliest successes, and provided the title for the collection of verse, *A Heap o' Livin'* (1916). Some of his other collections are *Over Here* (1918), *When Day Is Done* (1921), *Rhymes of Childhood* (1924), *The Friendly Way* (1931), *All in a Lifetime* (1938), and *Today and Tomorrow* (1942).

GUEVARA Y DE NOROÑA, ANTONIO DE (about 1480–1545), Spanish writer, born at Treceño, Santander. He became a Franciscan monk, and in 1518 was made court preacher and historiographer by Charles V of Spain. In 1523 he was appointed inquisitor, in 1527 bishop of Guadix, and in 1537 bishop of Mondoñedo. Most of his writings were didactic in content and artificial in style. His *Relox de Príncipes con el Libro de Marco Aurelio* (1529) purported to be a biography of the Roman emperor Marcus Aurelius, based on historical documents; actually the documents were nonexistent, and the work was merely an idealized characterization of a perfect prince. It was translated into English by Sir Thomas North under the title of *The Diall of Princes* (1557). Guevara's affected style was developed in England by John Lyly (q.v.) as euphuism.

GUEVEI. See DUIKER.

GUGGENHEIM, the name of a family of industrialists and philanthropists.

1. MEYER GUGGENHEIM (1828–1905), born in Langnau, Switzerland. He emigrated to the United States at the age of nineteen, and established a flourishing business in Philadelphia, Pa., as a retailer and importer of Swiss embroidery. Guggenheim purchased mining property in Colorado, and believing that processing minerals rather than mining them was the more profitable enterprise, built large smelters in Colorado and Mexico and a refinery in New Jersey. The firm of Guggenheim Brothers was organized in 1881 by Guggenheim and his seven sons. In 1901 the Guggenheims gained control of the American Smelting and Refining Company.

2. DANIEL GUGGENHEIM (1856–1930), son of Meyer Guggenheim, born in Philadelphia, Pa. As a member of the firm of Guggenheim Brothers he became a leading figure in the copper industry of the United States and extended the activities of the firm to include gold mines in Alaska, rubber plantations in Africa, tin mines in Bolivia, and nitrate deposits in Chile. He negotiated the merger of Guggenheim Brothers with the American Smelting and Refining Company and was president and chairman of the board of directors of the American Smelting and Refining Company from 1901 to 1919. Daniel Guggenheim's philanthropic activities included the establishment of the Daniel and Florence Guggenheim Foundation to promote "through charitable and benevolent activities the well-being of mankind throughout the world" in 1924, the school of aeronautics at New York University in 1925, and the Daniel Guggenheim Foundation for the Promotion of Aeronautics in 1926.

3. SIMON GUGGENHEIM (1867–1941), son of Meyer Guggenheim, born in Philadelphia, Pa., and educated in Philadelphia public schools and in Europe. He was a member of Guggenheim Brothers, and from 1919 until his death was president of the American Smelting and Refining Company. He was elected U.S. senator from Colorado for the term 1907 to 1913, but declined to be a candidate for re-election. In 1925 he established, with his wife, the John Simon Guggenheim Memorial Foundation in memory of a son; see GUGGENHEIM MEMORIAL FOUNDATION.

4. HARRY F. GUGGENHEIM (1890–   ), son of Daniel Guggenheim, born at West End, N.J., and educated at Yale University, Pembroke College, Cambridge University, and Georgia School of Technology. He began his association with the American Smelting and Refining Company in Mexico in 1907, and was a member of Guggenheim Brothers from 1916 to 1923. He was instrumental in the development of the Chile Copper Company, which became the largest low-grade copper producer in the world. Harry Guggenheim was the U.S. delegate on commercial aviation to the Third Pan-American Conference in Washington in 1927 and to the International Conference on Civil Aeronautics in Washington in 1928. During World War II he was a naval aviator, advancing to the rank of captain in 1945. He wrote *The Seven Skies* (1930) and *The United States and Cuba* (1934), and published *Newsday,* a Long Island, N.Y., newspaper.

GUGGENHEIM MEMORIAL FOUNDATION, JOHN SIMON, a fund established in 1925 by Simon Guggenheim, former U.S. senator from Colorado, in memory of his son, John Simon Guggenheim, who died in 1922. The initial endowment was $3,000,000, but through additional gifts the Foundation's assets in a recent year reached a total of over $25,000,000. The purpose of the fund is "the advancement and diffusion of knowledge and understanding and the appreciation of beauty, by aiding without distinction on account of race, color or creed, scholars, scientists, and artists of either sex in the prosecution of their labors". Fellowships are granted to citizens and permanent residents of the United States for work in all fields of knowledge or the fine arts. A limited number of fellowships are also offered to Puerto Ricans and to citizens of Canada, Argentina, Bolivia, Brazil, Chile, Colombia, Cuba, Ecuador, Mexico, Panama, Paraguay, Peru, Uruguay, and Venezuela. The stipends are usually $2500 a year, and are granted for varying periods of time. Fellows may go to any part of the world where their work can best be done. The Foundation has headquarters in New York City.

GUIANA, a region in the N.E. part of South America, bordering the Atlantic Ocean and extending between the Orinoco, Negro, and Amazon rivers. Its area of 690,000 sq.m. embraces British Guiana, Surinam (Dutch Guiana), French Guiana (qq.v.), and part of Venezuela and Brazil.

The coast of Guiana was first visited in 1499–1500 by the Italian navigator Amerigo Vespucci, and by the Spanish explorers Alonso de Ojeda and Vicente Yáñez Pinzón. During the 16th century, the interior of the region was traveled by missionaries. Sir Walter Raleigh, inspired by legends of gold (see EL DORADO), ascended the Orinoco R. in 1595, and in succeeding years his sailing masters carefully explored the coast to the east. After the formation of the Dutch West India Company in 1621, the Dutch gained a permanent foothold at the head of the Essequebo delta in s.w. Guiana. In 1648, the Treaty of Westphalia confirmed the Dutch West India Company in possession of the territory. Meanwhile, the French had settled in the east and the English near the mouth of the Surinam R. in the north. In 1667, by the Treaty of Breda, England gave its Guiana settlement to Holland in exchange for the Dutch colony of New Netherlands on the Hudson R., including its capital, New Amsterdam (New York). In 1814 the Dutch formally surrendered the colonies of Demerara, Berbice, and Essequebo to the British. The boundary between British Guiana and Venezuela, long a subject of dispute, was finally laid down by an arbitration treaty in 1897. The boundary between French Guiana and Brazil was determined in 1900, between British Guiana and Brazil in 1904, and between French Guiana and Surinam in 1905.

GUIB. See BOSCHBOK.

GUICCIARDINI, FRANCESCO (1483–1540), Italian statesman and historian, born at Florence, and educated at the universities of Ferrara and Padua. He contemplated entering the church, but turned to law and in 1506 became professor of law at Florence. Six years later he gained his first experience in diplomacy when he was sent to the court of King Ferdinand V of Spain as Florentine ambassador. In 1515 he entered the service of Pope Leo X, and was made governor of the papal states of Reggio and Modena, Parma being added to his domain six years later. Pope Clement VII appointed him vice-regent of Romagna in 1523 and lieutenant general of the papal states in 1526. Five years later he became governor of Bologna, but he resigned in 1534, in order to serve the Medici family in Florence.

A cynical mercenary, Guicciardini is known to have hated bitterly the despotic princes whom he served. He spent his last years writing *La Storia d'Italia,* the greatest historical work of the 16th century. Though it is overcrowded with detail, the book is remarkable because of its scientific impartiality, and because it treats Italy as a whole rather than as a group of separate sovereignties.

GUIDED MISSILES, designation applied to pilotless military projectiles which can be steered, either by remote control or by self-contained mechanisms, toward a target during flight. The term came into use toward the end of World War II, but the steerable projectile is much older. In its simplest form the guided missile is an ordinary airplane loaded with explosives and controlled by radio signals from the ground or from another airplane. Such planes, commonly called "drones", were used soon after World War I, chiefly as targets. The devices had little military value, being moderate in speed and hence vulnerable to attack; in addition their radio controls could be jammed by the enemy.

Guided missiles were made possible and militarily important by three technical advances of World War II: rocket and jet propulsion, which permitted much greater speed; radar and associated improvements in electronics, which ensured more accurate control; and nuclear explosives, which made expensive, long-range missiles a profitable military investment. See ROCKET.

Contrary to popular belief, the German V-1 and V-2, projectiles used against London and Antwerp toward the end of World War II, were not guided missiles. Neither the V-1, a pulse-jet pilotless airplane, nor the V-2, a 14-ton rocket, could be steered in flight. Both were inaccurate, and the effect of their explosive charge was hardly sufficient to justify the cost of manufacture. Nonetheless, it became obvious that these missiles had great possibilities. The V-2 was especially promising. Its range of more than 150 miles was enough for many tactical purposes, and its speed of about 3500 m.p.h. made it invulnerable to any kind of counteraction. If the V-2's had carried atomic bombs, their inaccuracy would have been outweighed by their destructiveness. See ROCKETS, MILITARY.

Among the guided missiles used in World War II were the German antiaircraft rockets, devices launched from the ground and controlled by radio, and the German and U.S. steerable bombs, which were dropped from aircraft. None of these early weapons reached full effectiveness in wartime, but all were sufficiently successful to justify further development. See ANTIAIRCRAFT WEAPONS.

Modern guided missiles are generally classified according to the use for which they are intended.

Surface-to-surface missiles are launched from the ground or a ship toward a surface target. Such projectiles may be large rockets, on the general pattern of the V-2, or steerable airplanes presumably fast enough to defy most kinds of defensive action. The American "Corporal" series are typical surface-to-surface rockets. The Matador, also American, is an "uninhabited" jet airplane that is launched by a booster rocket. Experimental work on both types was recently in progress in Great Britain and the Soviet Union.

Surface-to-air missiles are steerable rockets launched against attacking bombers. The American Nike, which is being produced in large numbers, is typical. Its horizontal range is short, totaling only about 30 miles, but it can climb well above airplane ceilings, its speed (more than 1300 m.p.h.) is much greater than that of any operational bomber, and its accuracy is said to be notable. Batteries of Nikes are an integral part of the defense system of U.S. cities.

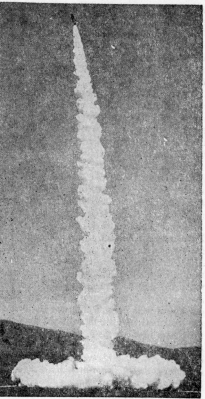

Nat. Adv. Comm. for Aero.; U.S. Air Force Official

GUIDED MISSILES

Above: The "Tiamat," 14-foot experimental two-stage rocket. Stage one (rear section) launches the missile and then drops off. Right: A U.S. Air Force test model of the "Ground-to-Air Pilotless Aircraft" seen as it is being launched. This extremely fast rocket is used against enemy aircraft.

Air-to-surface missiles are steerable bombs launched by bombers in flight. These weapons may be powered partly by gravity, but are equipped with jet engines for the longer ranges. Consequently the air-to-surface missile amounts to a small, expendable, very fast airplane. Bombers armed with it may attack while still well out of range of the target's defensive cordon. Missiles of this type are under intensive development, but none has been described officially.

Air-to-air missiles are used by aircraft against other aircraft. The device is necessarily small, and its range need not be great. Equipped with such missiles, which are steered from the aircraft or by self-contained mechanisms, interceptors become high-altitude launching platforms capable of attacking a bomber while still out of range of its defensive weapons. An atomic air-to-air missile tested by the United States in 1955 was reported capable of destroying aircraft within a range of a half mile from the blast.

A great variety of control systems are employed in guided missiles. The missile may be a "beam rider", keeping to the center of a radio beam, or may follow "command signals" directing it toward a visible target. Often it has a "homing" feature; on the approach to a target, a small radar measures its speed, direction, and distance, and then a computer works out a course that will bring the missile to the target. A missile may be guided by means of infrared waves. In this type, an electronic device tracks the heat emanating from the target's metal. According to reports in 1955, such missiles had been tested by the United States and Great Britain.

Long-range missiles cannot depend on direct radio controls because high-frequency waves are ineffective beyond the horizon. In one proposed method of overcoming this difficulty, the missile would be equipped with apparatus designed to steer by the stars or by variations in the earth's magnetic field. Another proposed method involves a sensitive, self-contained device designed to measure accurately all forces, such as winds, that tend to deflect the missile from the proper course. Other possibilities include mechanisms which could "read a map" and make comparisons with the terrain below as seen by its own radar. An alternative apparatus would "report" from the missile over a chain of flying relays what its radar or television "eyes" are seeing. Then human operators could direct the missile to its target.

Military authorities believe that many kinds of guided missiles will be used in any future major war. There is no known dependable defense against such weapons, and all except the smallest types will be capable of delivering nuclear explosives.

GUIDI, TOMMASO. See MASACCIO.

GUIDO D'AREZZO or **GUIDO ARETINO** (about 995–about 1050), Benedictine monk and reformer of music, born either near Paris or in Arezzo, Italy. He is also known as Fra Guittone. As a monk in the monastery of Pomposa, near Ferrara, he made a number of innovations in regard to musical notation. About 1030 he went to Rome on the invitation of Pope John XIX to explain his innovations. Later he returned to Pomposa and also worked in the monastery of St. Maur des Fossés near Paris. Guido was the first to use systematically the lines of the staff and the spaces between them, and to give to the notes of the scale the names which are still used today. Among his writings on music are *Micrologus de Disciplina Artis Musicæ* (about 1025) and *Antiphonarium.*

GUIDO DELLE COLONNE or **DA COLONNA,** Italian poet of the 13th century, born probably in Sicily. His chief work was the *Historia Troiana* (1282), which was later translated from the Latin into nearly all the languages of western Europe, and was used by Giovanni Boccaccio, Geoffrey Chaucer, and William Shakespeare as a source for their works pertaining to the Trojan War. William Caxton's English version of the *Historia* was the first book printed in the English language. Guido also wrote poems in Italian patterned after Provençal models.

GUIDO RENI. See RENI, GUIDO.

GUILD or **GILD,** an association of persons who have similar interests in a craft, business, or profession; the purpose of the association is mutual aid and protection. The term is particularly applied to two types of such association which flourished in continental Europe and England in medieval times: the merchant guild or guild merchant; and the craft guild, sometimes known as the trade guild or trade corporation.

The merchant guild came into existence on the European continent in the 11th century,

and in England after the Norman Conquest (1066). The guild arose as a consequence of the growth in that century both of commerce and of urban communities. Merchants traveled from market to market in foreign countries, and, for the sake of mutual protection from attacks by brigands and other enemies during such journeys, a group of merchants from the same city often banded together in a caravan. The members of a caravan elected a leader and made rules which they were pledged to obey. The rules did more than prescribe duties for defense against physical attack; the members of the caravan were obliged to stand by each other in legal disputes in which any might engage. The name for such a caravan was *gilde* or *hansa* in the Germanic countries of Europe; in the countries speaking languages derived from Latin the term was *caritas* or *fraternitas.* Frequently the members of a *hansa* or *fraternitas* remained in close association after they had made the return journey to their city. Such an association then began to assume, and later to obtain from the feudal lord of the city or sometimes from the city itself, if it were free of feudal control, rights and privileges in regard to the trade of the municipality. In time the merchant guild came to possess a monopoly over the entire industry and commerce of the city, supervising the various crafts, and selling, both at wholesale and retail, all the commodities manufactured there. Individual merchants who were not members of such a guild were also permitted to sell goods, but only at wholesale, and were subject, in business transactions, to many special restrictions from which the members of the guild were free; for example, the nonmember was forced to pay special dues to the feudal lord or to the city, whereas the guild paid the dues annually for all its members, who also enjoyed freedom from other municipal taxes. The merchant guild was usually composed of the richest merchants of the city and acquired considerable political influence, often becoming vested with the power of administration of some of the municipal functions. A merchant guild sometimes admitted to membership merchants of other cities; as a result, particularly on the Continent, merchant guilds occasionally developed which monopolized the commerce of several cities.

Toward the end of the medieval era the merchant guilds declined and by the 14th century had almost completely disappeared. The principal cause of their elimination from economic life was the rise of craft guilds, which included in their membership all those engaged in any particular craft, and which monopolized the making and selling of a particular commodity within the cities in which they were organized. As the various craftsmen of a city organized into craft guilds, the merchant guild of that city was little by little deprived of its power to regulate the commerce of that municipality and in time ceased to function altogether. Where the merchant guilds were strongly intrenched in the municipal governments, they came into conflict with the strong national governments which came into being toward the end of the medieval period, and frequently yielded their powers to these governments.

The craft guild, known by that name in England and parts of the Continent, and as *corporation de métier* in France, *arte* in Italy, and *Zünft* or *Innung* in Germany, came into existence about the beginning of the 12th century. In general, the craft guild arose when a group of artisans, imitating the example of the merchants of the city, decided to unite for mutual benefit. In some instances a group organized originally for religious purposes, and which had drawn its membership entirely from the artisans of one craft, began to stress aid for the economic rather than the religious needs of its members, and in time became a full-fledged craft guild. By the middle of the 12th century, craft guilds had been established in all parts of western Europe. In some cities the individual worker was permitted the right to join or remain out of the guild in his craft; in others, a guild would purchase from the municipality or the royal government the right to control its branch of industry, and in such instances everyone who desired to follow his trade in that particular city was compelled to join the guild. The members of a craft guild were divided into three classes: masters, apprentices, and journeymen. The master, who was a small-scale proprietor, owned the raw material and the tools, and sold the goods manufactured in his shop for his own profit. The apprentices and journeymen lived in the master's house; the apprentices, who were beginners in the trade and learned it under the master's direction, as a rule received only their board in return for the work they did. After an apprentice had completed his training, he became a journeyman and was paid a fixed wage for his labor; in time a journeyman might become a master. However, since it was to the advantage of those who were already masters not to increase their own number, the conditions under which a journeyman might become a master were always made difficult; after the 14th century the requirements became so severe that it was virtually impossible for a journeyman to become a master. In the 14th, 15th, and 16th centuries journeymen organized into associations of their own, the object of which was to obtain better wages and working conditions from the masters. In England such associations were known as journeyman or yeoman guilds, and in France as *compagnonnages*. They succeeded to some extent in improving working conditions and pay, sometimes forcing changes by means of strikes, but on the whole did not greatly improve the economic status of their class. However, because of their defense of the rights of labor, their strong control over their members, and the financial and other benefits they extended to their members, the journeyman guilds are considered the forerunners of the modern trade union.

The craft guild was the most prominent feature of the economic life of the medieval city, closely affecting the economic welfare of both the artisan and the consumer. It sought to aid the artisan in two principal ways: by protecting him against the competition of artisans in the same trade in other cities, and by protecting him from possible competition of fellow citizens working in other shops belonging to the same trade. The guild accomplished the first aim by monopolizing its trade in the city, thus permitting no goods from other cities to be imported for sale. It fulfilled the second by establishing uniform hours for all shops making the same commodity, and uniform wages for workers in the same industry. To prevent any one master from obtaining an advantage over another, the guild decreed how many people were to be employed in each shop, the number of tools to be used, the hours of labor, and the prices the master could charge for his finished goods. The guild enforced its rules by constant and close supervision of the shops. No master was permitted to advertise his goods, lest he attract more business than another master; any improvement in the technique of production, which might enable one shop to produce goods more quickly and cheaply than another, was likewise prohibited. The aim of the craft guild was to create a complete equality among the members of each of the three classes into which it was divided. The consumer benefited from the existence of the craft guild chiefly because of the high standards the guild set up for finished work;

"Chiefs of the Guild of Goldsmiths in Amsterdam," painting by Bartholomeus van der Helst

at the same time the consumer was deprived by the guild of possible lower prices from improved methods of production and from competition in selling.

The craft guilds were a large force in the economic life of Europe from the 12th to the 15th century. In France and Flanders in the 12th and 13th centuries they frequently threatened to seize control of municipal governments, and in order to weaken them, various municipalities took from the guilds the right to regulate industries, and also deprived them of other privileges. Nevertheless, in the 14th century the guilds began to compete with the rich merchants of the cities for the right to govern. In some cities the guilds actually succeeded in taking over the municipal government completely, as in Liége, where in 1384 the municipal council was composed entirely of representatives from the thirty-two craft guilds of that city.

In the 15th century, however, the power of the craft guilds began to decline. They became subject to much internal tension because of the antagonism, described above, between masters and journeymen; and they were subjected to much criticism and sometimes to action by public authorities because of the restrictions they placed upon industrial activity and freedom of labor. The chief cause, how-

ever, of the decline and eventual disappearance of the craft guilds was the rise in the 16th century of a new system for producing and distributing commodities, capitalism. This new economic system stressed large-scale production of goods, competition for markets between producers, and wide distribution of goods. Inasmuch as the craft guild was inclined against all three principles, the capitalist generally established his shops in centers where no craft guilds existed. The latter, unable to produce goods even for their own local markets as quickly or cheaply as did the capitalistic enterprises, were little by little forced out of existence. In France, Jacques Turgot, controller general of finance for Louis XVI, in 1776 abolished all but four of the craft guilds in order to permit workers freely to offer their services to employers, and during the French Revolution all guilds were abolished. Prussia and other German states abolished the German craft guilds at the beginning of the 19th century, and those craft guilds that still remained in England were abolished by acts of Parliament in 1814 and 1835.

The term "guild" is still in considerable use today. It is applied to associations of various kinds, for example, associations for charitable work and organizations formed to promote various cultural activities, such as music and the drama (see THEATRE GUILD); to certain labor organizations, for example, the American Newspaper Guild; and to a type of modern socialism (see GUILD SOCIALISM).

GUILDFORD, municipal borough and county seat of Surrey County, England, located on the Wey R., 30 m. by rail s.w. of London. Originally Guildford was a possession of King Alfred. During the Middle Ages the town became known as a center for the cloth trade, owning market rights and holding several fairs a year. According to the Arthurian legend as rendered by Thomas Malory in the *Morte d'Arthur,* Elaine's home, Astolat, was located on the site of Guildford. Guildford was incorporated as a borough in 1486. Near the town are located the ruins of a Norman castle. The grammar school dates from 1509 and the guild hall from 1683. Sheep and cattle fairs are held regularly at Guildford, and there is an active trade in grain. The borough contains flour mills, knitting mills, and iron foundries. Previously a bishopric suffraganate, Guildford was made a diocese in 1927. Pop. (1951 prelim.) 47,484.

GUILD SOCIALISM, a variety of socialism (q.v.), advocated in England early in the 20th century as a substitute for capitalism. The outstanding leader of the short-lived movement organized to propagate guild socialism was the economist George Douglas Howard Cole (1889–   ).

The social system advocated by the guild socialists centered on the ownership and operation of the means of production, distribution, and exchange by nation-wide industrial guilds, which were to differ radically from the guilds (q.v.) of medieval times. Each of these modern guilds was to have the following characteristics: it would include all of the workers, managerial and technical as well as clerical and manual, in the industry, trade, or profession over which it had jurisdiction; it would have autonomy within its spheres of production; and it would democratically elect its officers. Even managerial officials were to be elected by the workers whose operations they supervised, and were to be subject to recall by those workers.

The nature of the state under the proposed society was a subject of disagreement among the guild socialists. Some believed that the state should carry out only the functions of preserving public order, and conducting foreign relations and national defense. Others, particularly Cole, advocated a system of government by communes, which would comprise organizations representing consumers and producers, and which would be charged with the responsibility for national economic planning, the enactment and interpretation of legislation, the management of finances, and the conduct of foreign relations and national defense.

Most guild socialists believed that the change from capitalism to socialism was basically economic rather than political, and therefore regarded political action solely as a means of propagating their ideas. In preference to political action, they put forth the principle of "encroaching control", whereby the workers, through trade-union activity, would gradually take over the administration of industrial enterprises and eventually drive out the private owners.

The first organized body to advance the principles of guild socialism was the Guilds Restoration Movement, which was formed in 1906 and was superseded in 1915 by the National Guilds League. The membership of the League began to decline in the mid-1920's, as the Labor Party (q.v.) grew in numbers and influence, and by 1930 the League had passed out of existence.

GUILFORD COURTHOUSE, formerly a small village in Guilford Co., N.C., now a national military park, situated 5 miles N.W. of Greensboro. It is the site of a five-hour battle of the American Revolution (see REVOLUTION, THE AMERICAN), fought on March 15, 1781, between 4400 Americans under General Nathanael Greene, and 2200 British under General Charles Cornwallis. The Americans lost 400, the British 600, in dead, wounded, and captured. Although neither side gained a decisive advantage, the battle is considered to have been a strategic victory for Greene, as the depletion of Cornwallis' troops compelled him to abandon the Carolinas, the loss of which contributed materially to the final defeat of the British.

GUILLAUME, CHARLES ÉDOUARD (1861–1938), French physicist, born at Fleurier, Switzerland, and educated at the universities of Neuchâtel and Zurich. Most of his research was done in connection with the work of the Bureau of International Weights and Measures at Sèvres, where he worked from 1883, becoming director in 1915. Guillaume is best known for his invention of the nickel-steel alloy, invar. He was awarded the 1920 Nobel Prize for physics. His writings include *Traité Pratique de la Thermométrie de Précision* (1889), *Les Applications des Aciers au Nickel* (1904), and *Les Récents Progrès du Système Métrique* (1921).

GUILLAUME DE LORRIS (d. about 1235), French poet. His name is derived from a township in the department of Loiret. He is the author of the first 4000 lines of the 22,-000-line verse romance the *Roman de la Rose*, (see FRENCH LITERATURE), the second part of which was written by the French poet Jean de Meung. Nothing is known of Guillaume's life. His section of the poem is distinguished by the beauty of the imagery and the allegorical setting.

GUILLAUME D'ORANGE (about 750–812), a leader of Charlemagne's armies and the hero of a group of southern French *chansons de geste*, born in what is now northern France. He was known also as Fierabrace, Saint Guillaume de Gellone, and the *Marquis au Court Nez* ("Marquis Short-Nose"). His prowess as a soldier led Charlemagne to charge him, in 790, with the training of the emperor's eldest son, Louis the Pious. D'Orange led Charlemagne's forces against the Saracens at the battle of Villedaigne in 793. Although his forces were defeated, he avenged this defeat ten years later when he commanded an army which invaded Spain and captured Barcelona. In 804 he founded a monastery at Gellone (now St. Guilhem-le-Désert) to which he retired in 806, and where he died six years later.

The *chansons de geste* in which D'Orange appears as a principal character often incorporate the exploits of other historical personages in their descriptions of his feats. They include *Fierabras* and *Aliscans*, considered to be among the finest examples of early French epic poetry.

GUILLEMOT, common name for a narrowbilled seabird of the Auk family. Guillemots are swimming and diving birds, found chiefly in the Arctic. Their legs are set far back on the body, and are highly efficient for swimming, but cause the birds to waddle awkwardly, with the body upright, when on land. The feet, which are fully webbed, each have three long toes. The bill is straight. Guillemots, like some other birds such as dippers (q.v.), are remarkable for their capacity for "subaqueous flight"; after diving they appear to fly under water, beating their short wings in the same manner as in flight, instead of paddling with their legs.

A common North American species, the pigeon guillemot, *Cepphus columba,* is found along the Pacific Coast, from Alaska to California. Pigeon guillemots are about 13 inches long. The plumage is black, except for a large white patch on the wings, and the legs are a bright red. Similar in color and size to the pigeon guillemot is the black guillemot, *C. grylle,* which is known also as the dovekie (q.v.).

Guillemots of the genus *Uria* are called murres, because of the sound of their guttural note. They are 16 to 18 in. long. *U. aalge* is also called "foolish" guillemot because, during the breeding season, it will stand still and allow a human to capture it by hand. It summers in Arctic areas and winters as far south as the Mediterranean and off N.E. and W. United States. It is black or dark-brown on the back and whitish underneath, with streaks of these colors on the sides. It lays only one egg and makes no nest. When incubating the egg, murres place their webbed toes beneath the egg and warm it beneath and between their legs and thighs.

The murrelets are similar in appearance to the murres, but are only 9 or 10 in. long. Three genera and five species are found on the Pacific coasts of North America. The most widely distributed species is the marbled murrelet, *Brachyramphus marmoratus,* found from Alaska to s. California.

GUILLOTIN, JOSEPH IGNACE (1738–1814), French physician, born at Saintes, and educated at a Jesuit college. He taught at the Jesuit College at Bordeaux for several years. As a deputy to the National Assembly in 1789, Guillotin proposed that decapitation be adopted as the method of capital punishment, in order to make execution as swift and painless as possible. His proposal was accepted by the National Assembly, and the beheading machine adopted for use, similar to that described by Guillotin, was called the guillotine (q.v.). The legend that Guillotin died by the instrument that bears his name is not based on fact; he survived the French Revolution and died a natural death.

GUILLOTINE, a decapitating machine, named after the French physician Joseph Guillotin (q.v.), who proposed its use in 1789. It consists of two upright posts, grooved on the inside and connected at the top by a crossbeam. A sharp, oblique-edged, iron blade, placed between the grooves, is held at the top of the machine by a rope. On release of the rope, the blade drops onto the neck of the victim strapped to a board at the base of the machine. Similar devices were used for executions from early times. The Italian *mannaia,* used from the 13th century, the Scottish *maiden,* used from 1581 to 1685, and the German *dolabra* of the 16th century, were similar to the guillotine, but had horizontal blades. The guillotine received its most extensive use during the French Revolution (q.v.).

GUILT, in criminal law, the quality which imparts criminality to a motive or act and thereby renders an individual liable to punishment. It may be expressed in an overt act or revealed in a state of mind. A person charged with a crime is said to have a "guilty mind" or "consciousness of guilt" when he possesses sufficient mental capacity to understand the nature and the quality of the overt criminal act which he is alleged to have committed.

In most cases a criminal intent is requisite to constitute guilt on the part of the person committing an act which results in harm to the person or property of another. In certain cases, however, the commission of a forbidden act in itself constitutes legal guilt; and there are other acts, innocent in themselves, which become criminal when performed with a guilty intent (see CRIME).

A person accused of crime is presumed to be innocent until his guilt has been established by the verdict of a jury. What is meant by this principle, is not that the jury is to hold the opinion, as a matter of fact, that a person presented by a grand jury for trial is probably innocent, but only that the burden rests upon the prosecution of establishing all the elements of conduct and intention which constitute the crime charged, and, further, of satisfying the jury beyond a reasonable doubt of the guilt of the accused. In the United States and in England there are only two general verdicts which can be given in criminal cases: "guilty" or "not guilty".

GUINEA, a geographical term formerly designating the West African coast region between the Senegal R. on the N. and the Orange R. on the S., but now restricted to the littoral extending from the Liberian border to the mouth of the Gabon R. The region lying between the enclave of Portuguese Sierra Leone in French West Africa and the Gabon estuary in French Equatorial Africa was generally termed Upper Guinea, and the region S., Lower Guinea. The four Guinea islands were Fernando Po, Annobón, Principe, and São Tomé. The names applied by traders of early times to the different portions of the Guinea coast were based upon the characteristic commodities of the respective regions (i.e., the Grain coast, the Gold coast, the Ivory coast, and the Slave coast). The first systematic explorers of the Guinea

N.Y. Zoological Society
Guinea fowl (Acryllium vulturinum)

coast, the Portuguese, were largely impelled by the prospect of gold, and later by the opportunities of slave trading. See FRENCH GUINEA; PORTUGUESE GUINEA; SPANISH GUINEA.

GUINEA FOWL, common name for any fowl of the family Numididae, order Galliformes, native to Africa and Madagascar. The plumage is alike in both sexes, jet-black in most species, dotted with small, light-colored spots; the neck is surrounded by a ruff of feathers, and except in the crested guinea fowl of the genus *Guttera* the skin of the head is completely bare. Guinea fowl nest on the ground and roost in trees. Minor differences mark the sexes, such as larger wattles in the males. The call of the female normally has two syllables, and sounds like "buckwheat", although it is occasionally monosyllabic. The call of the male always sounds like "quit" Because of their shrill cries, guinea fowl are rarely raised domestically on small farms; they are sometimes kept in chicken houses on relatively large farms where they serve as watchmen, raising a clamor when the chickens are endangered.

Of the twenty species of guinea fowl known, the common "helmeted" guinea fowl, *Numida meleagris,* is most important. Its head is covered with a bony cap, or "casque", rising into a hard crest. A similar species, *N. mitrata,* is noted for its red crown. The best-known species of crested guinea fowl is *Guttera cristata;* which has a large tuft of feathers on its crown. The handsomest species of guinea fowl is *Acryllium vulturinum,* of Somaliland, which has bright-blue plumage.

N.Y. Zoological Society

Guinea pig (Cavia porcellus)

Guinea fowl are cooked and eaten like other poultry, and are considered a delicacy. See POULTRY.

GUINEA, GULF OF, that portion of the Atlantic Ocean which washes the w. coast of Africa between Cape Palmas at the s.e. tip of Liberia and Cape Lopez in French Equatorial Africa. The gulf forms two open bays, the Bight of Benin and the Bight of Biafra.

GUINEA PIG, common name for any rodent of the genus *Cavia* (see CAVY); guinea pigs are properly domesticated cavies, but in popular usage the term is applied to all species, domesticated or wild. Guinea pigs resemble rabbits, but have short, rounded ears and no tails. They are small, stout-bodied animals, measuring about six or seven inches in length. The hair in some species is long, and varies in texture from rough to smooth. Some guinea pigs are solidly white, black, or tawny; others are white, streaked, or blotched with darker colors. In the wild state guinea pigs live in burrows. The diet consists of vegetation. Wild guinea pigs breed only annually and produce litters of one or two young. The young are born in an advanced stage of development, and are able to feed themselves by nibbling foliage the day after birth. Wild guinea pigs are native to South America. Among the most important species are *Cavia porcellus,* a native of Brazil; *C. boliviensis,* found in the higher ranges of the Andes; and *C. cutleri,* a Peruvian species.

Some authorities believe the domestic guinea pig was developed from the Peruvian animal; others believe that it was developed from the Brazilian. Domestic guinea pigs resemble wild guinea pigs in the rapidity of their early maturity. They develop so quickly during gestation that they shed their lacteal teeth in the womb, being born with their definitive teeth already in place. Domesticated guinea pigs begin to breed at the age of two months. They breed five or six times a year, and

the litters comprise from four to twelve animals. Because of this breeding capacity, guinea pigs have been valuable as experimental laboratory animals, especially in bacteriology for research on the effects of pathogenic microorganisms. Guinea pigs have been largely replaced in the laboratory by smaller animals, such as mice, rats, and hamsters. They are useful in diagnostic tests for tuberculosis, however, because of their low resistance to the tubercle bacillus, which kills them in from four to eight weeks.

The origin of the term "guinea pig" is an unsolved etymological problem. Some authorities believe the name may come from "Guineamen", who were in the slave trade, and may have been the first to bring the animals from South America to England. Others believe it is a corruption of "cony", basing this theory on evidence that guinea pigs were called pig conies in 1607.

GUINEA WORM. See FILARIA.

GUINEVERE (Welsh *Gwenhwyfar*), wife of King Arthur of Britain. She appears in the 12th century *Historia* cycle of Arthurian romances by Geoffrey of Monmouth as Gwanhumara, a lady of a noble Roman family who surpassed all the women of Britain in beauty, and who became a nun after the defeat of King Arthur by Mordred. With the introduction of Lancelot to the Arthurian legend in the 12th century romance, *Le Chevalier à la Charette,* by Chrétien de Troyes, Guinevere became "the first perfectly human woman in English literature" by her sinful but romantic love for Lancelot. The story was similarly treated by Dante in his *Divine Comedy* (canto V of *Inferno*), by Thomas Malory in *Le Morte d'Arthur* (1485), by William Morris in the *Defense of Guinevere* (1858), and by Alfred Tennyson in the *Idylls of the King* (1859–85). See ARTHURIAN CYCLE; LANCELOT DU LAC.

GUIPURE. See LACE.

GUIPÚZCOA, a maritime Basque province of Spain, bounded on the N. by the Bay of Biscay, and on the N.E. by the Bidassoa R., which there forms the French frontier. The province occupies the northern slopes of the Cantabrian Mountains; its surface is rugged and unsuitable for farming. Forests of oak, pine, and chestnut cover a large part of the province, and there are numerous apple orchards and vineyards. It is watered by the Deva, Urola, Oria, Bidassoa, and Urumea rivers, none of which are navigable. Extensive deposits of lead, copper, iron, zinc, cement rock, and lignite are found in Guipúzcoa, and mineral springs abound. The coastline is high and rocky, with few natural harbors. Fishing is an important industry in the province; oysters, sardines, cod, and tunny are the principal catch. Other important industries in the province are lumbering, gold-working, and the manufacture of paper, baskets, chemicals, arms, cotton and linen goods, wines, and liqueurs. The capital and chief town of Guipúzcoa is San Sebastian (q.v.); among the other leading towns, with population figures for 1940, are Eibar (10,607), Tolosa (10,114), Pasajes (9656), Rentería (8237), Irún (7790), Azpeita (6082), Vergora (4081), Beasaín (3553), Placencia (2319), Andoain (2179), and Fuenterrabia (1193). Guipúzcoa is the smallest province of Spain. Area, 770 sq.m.; pop. (1950) 374,040.

GUISCARD, ROBERT (1015?–85), Norman adventurer, son of Tancred of Hauteville, born near Coutances in Normandy. He went to Italy about 1046 and, after serving in the forces of the prince of Capua, organized an army to secure possessions for himself in Calabria. When Pope Leo IX attempted to expel the Normans from Italy, in 1053, Robert played an important role in defeating the papal forces at Civitate. In 1057, after the death of his older brother Humphrey, Robert became Count of Apulia. The pope, anticipating difficulty with the Holy Roman emperor over the right of investiture, decided to enlist the Normans as allies. In 1059 Pope Nicholas II created Robert "by the Grace of God and St. Peter duke of Apulia and Calabria and, with their help, hereafter of Sicily". Sicily was in Greek hands at the time, and so Robert and his brother Roger embarked on a series of campaigns, capturing Messina in 1061 and Palermo in 1072. In 1081 Robert gained a great victory over the Byzantine emperor Alexius I Comnenus at Durazzo, and captured the city. His campaigns in Macedonia and Thessaly were being carried on, meanwhile, by his son Bohemund. Robert was recalled from his victorious campaigns in 1085 to go to the aid of Pope Gregory VII, who was besieged in the castle of St. Angelo by King Henry IV. Robert drove Henry IV from Rome, and reduced one third of the city to ashes. Because of the unpopularity of Gregory VII with the Roman populace, Robert took the pope to Monte Cassino. Robert then went to the support of Bohemund in the Greek campaign, but died at Cephalonia a few weeks later.

GUISE, name of a ducal family of Lorraine (q.v.), important as rivals to the power of the French kings, especially in the 16th century. The principal members of the family are the following.

1. CLAUDE I, DUC D'AUMALE (1496–1550), 1st Duc de Guise, son of René II, Duc de Lorraine. In 1513 he married Antoinette de Bourbon, a princess of the French royal house. He subsequently entered the service of King Francis I in the French wars in Italy, distinguishing himself in the battle of Marignano in 1515. As governor of Champagne, beginning in 1523, Claude fought against the army of the Holy Roman Empire in that same year and against the Anabaptists (q.v.) in 1525. In 1527 King Francis I transformed the countship of Guise into a duchy, making Claude a duke, a dignity theretofore reserved for princes of the royal family. Although Francis continued to favor the Guise family, he became increasingly jealous of its growing power and ambition. Mary, daughter of Claude, became the wife of King James V of Scotland, and their daughter was Mary Stuart (q.v.).

2. FRANÇOIS DE LORRAINE (1519–63), 2nd Duc de Guise, soldier and statesman, known as LE BALAFRE, ("the Scarred") because of wounds received at the siege of Boulogne in 1545. The son of Claude I, he was born at Barcastle, Provence. He participated in the various battles of the wars of France against the Emperor Charles V, rendering outstanding service, especially at Metz in 1552. In

François de Lorraine, 2nd Duc de Guise

Henri I de Lorraine, 3rd Duc de Guise

1557 he fought against the Spanish in Italy and in the following year took Calais from the English, allies of Spain against France. François and his brother Charles de Lorraine gained great influence over King Francis II, the husband of their niece Mary Stuart, and in that way almost completely controlled the French government during the short reign of Francis. In that period the Guises directed the persecution of the Huguenots, becoming widely disliked for their violent suppression of the Huguenot conspiracy of Amboise in 1560. After the death of Francis II in 1560, Catherine de Médicis, mother and regent for the new king, Charles IX, ousted François and his brother from their position of influence. François subsequently joined Duc Anne de Montmorency in the leadership of the Catholic party, opposing both the Huguenots and the tolerance of the regency. The massacre of Huguenots at Vassy by the soldiers of François in 1562 caused a civil war to break out in that year between the Catholics and the Protestants. In the following year François was assassinated by a Protestant, Jean de Poltrot, Seigneur de Méré. Despite allegations of cruelty imputed to François, he was considered by his soldiers to be a generous man and he was respected for his military skill.

3. CHARLES DE LORRAINE (1524–74), Roman Catholic prelate and politician, brother of François de Lorraine. He became Arch-bishop of Reims in 1538 and was made Cardinal of Guise in 1547 and three years later Cardinal of Lorraine. With his brother François he held control of the French government during the reign of King Francis II. After the exclusion of the Guises from power at court the Cardinal entered into intrigue with King Philip II of Spain, promising at one point to acknowledge Philip as king of France should the French king die without direct heirs. The Cardinal of Lorraine is considered responsible for most of the acts which brought opprobrium upon the name of Guise during his lifetime.

4. HENRI I DE LORRAINE (1550–88), 3rd Duc de Guise, politician and soldier, leader of the Catholic party, son of François de Lorraine. He was possessed with a desire to avenge the assassination of his father and in 1567 entered the struggle against the Huguenots. In 1569 he defeated the Huguenot leader Gaspard II de Coligny, then besieging Poitiers. He took a leading part in the Massacre of St. Bartholomew (see SAINT BARTHOLOMEW, MASSACRE OF) in 1672, personally supervising the murder of Coligny, whom he believed to have been one of the chief instigators of his father's assassination. Unwilling to recognize the peace established in 1576, Henri formed in that year an alliance of Catholic nobles, known as the Holy League, for the resumption of war against the Huguenots. It is possible that Henri's aim in establishing the League was to secure the French kingship for himself. However, King Henry III assumed nominal leadership of the League and disbanded it on the conclusion of peace in 1577 (see HUGUENOTS; FRANCE: *History*). The League was revived in 1584, when, on the death of Francis, Duke of Anjou, the succession to the throne was assigned to the Huguenot Henry of Navarre, later King Henry IV. In the ensuing civil war against the government, as champion of the Catholic interest, Henri de Lorraine attained great popularity with the people, at the expense of the king's prestige. In 1588, leading the people of Paris on the Day of Barricades in revolt against the king, Henri de Lorraine was in a position to seize the kingship, but he allowed the king to escape the mob. About a month later the king made an agreement with the League and appointed Henri lieutenant general of the royal armies. Henri de Lorraine was assassinated a short time later by the king's guard.

5. CHARLES DE LORRAINE, DUC DE MAYENNE (1554–1611), brother of Henri I de Lorraine.

He participated in the Huguenot wars with his brother Henri. After the assassination of the latter he became commander of the forces of the Holy League, renewing war against the combined forces of King Henry III and Henry of Navarre. On the death of King Henry III in 1589, the League refused to recognize King Henry IV, and proclaimed Charles, Cardinal of Bourbon, as King Charles X. The forces of Charles de Lorraine suffered several defeats at the hands of King Henry IV, notably at Arques in 1589 and Ivry in 1590. The death of the Cardinal of Bourbon in 1590, the lack of popular support for Charles as leader of the League, and Charles's own moderate views caused the Catholic chief in 1596 to recognize the kingship of Henry, who became a Catholic convert. For the rest of his life Charles remained loyal to Henry IV.

6. FRANÇOIS JOSEPH (d. 1675), last Duc de Guise. After his death and the death of his successor, his great-aunt Marie, the titles and lands of the Guise family were absorbed by the Bourbon-Orléans family.

GUITAR, a stringed instrument of the lute family, with a long fretted neck along which are stretched six strings, three of catgut and three of silk wound with wire. The strings are tuned upward from E (one line below the bass clef) as follows: E, A, D, G, B, and E (first line of the treble clef); the guitar has a range of three octaves. The instrument is played by plucking the strings with the fingers of the right hand while those of the left hand stop the strings at the various frets to produce the different tones or chords. Its soft tone makes it a particularly suitable instrument for the accompaniment of voices, but it is also used for playing music independently and has been played in solo recitals by such virtuosos as the Spanish musician Andrés Segovia.

Forms of the guitar existed in ancient times. In the 12th or 13th century the instrument, then made with four strings, was introduced into Spain by the Moors. A fifth string was later added and in this new form the guitar became the national instrument of Spain (about 17th century) and was known there and elsewhere as the Spanish guitar. The guitar became popular throughout Europe in the 19th century and is in considerable use in Europe, the United States, and Latin America today.

GUITAR FISH or **FIDDLER FISH,** common name for any of the sharklike rays of the family Rhinobatidae. About twenty species are known, inhabiting tropical and subtrop-

ical waters throughout the world. These rough-skinned, olive-gray rays have long bodies which are narrowed anteriorly and prolonged into a flat snout, and widened like a guitar behind. They feed on small, benthonic invertebrates. Their eggs are hatched within the body of the female, whereas eggs of rays in the related family. Rajidae are hatched in the water. The best-known species is the California guitar fish, *Rhinobatos productus;* other common forms are the West Indian fiddler fish, *R. percellens,* and the Australian fiddler fish, *Trygonorrhina fasciata.* See RAY.

GUITEAU, CHARLES. See GARFIELD, JAMES.

GUITRY, SACHA (1885–1957), French actor and playwright, born in St. Petersburg, Russia. He wrote many plays for his father, Lucien Guitry (1860–1925), and for his wife, Yvonne Printemps, from whom he was divorced in 1934. His later plays include *Jean de la Fontaine* (1916), *Un Sujet de Roman* (1923), *Mozart* (1925), *On ne Joue pas pour s'Amuser* (1925), *Le Miracle* (1927), *Mariette* (1928), *Desiré* (1932), and *Mon Double et Ma Moitié* (1935). He wrote, directed, and acted in many motion pictures, including *Le Roman d'un Tricheur* (1937); *Les Perles de la Couronne* (1938); and *Royal Affair in Versailles* (1957), which he also produced.

GUIZOT, FRANÇOIS PIERRE GUILLAUME (1787–1874), French statesman and historian, born at Nîmes, and educated in Geneva and Paris. During the time of the Empire, he devoted himself to writing and teaching. In 1809 he wrote the *Nouveau Dictionnaire des*

Woman in Spain playing the guitar

François Guizot

Synonymes, and two years later his translation of Edward Gibbon's *Decline and Fall of the Roman Empire* appeared. In 1812 he became professor of modern history at the University of Paris; though he stayed aloof from politics at the time, he associated himself with a number of Liberals. Upon the Restoration of 1814, he was appointed secretary-general of the Ministry of the Interior, and after Napoleon's final defeat became secretary-general of the Ministry of Justice.

From 1820 to 1830 he was a member of the Doctrinaires and one of the foremost opponents of the government of Charles X. Among his writings of this period are *Histoire des Origines du Gouvernement Représentatif* (2 vols., 1821–22), *Histoire de la Civilisation en Europe* (1828), and *Histoire de la Civilisation en France* (4 vols., 1830). In 1830 he was elected to the Chamber of Deputies, and was called upon to frame the Liberal protest to the July ordinances of the Prince de Polignac, the minister of foreign affairs for Charles X. During the July Revolution (q.v.) Guizot supported Louis Philippe, who succeeded Charles X in August, 1830. From 1832 to 1840 Guizot was a member of the Conservative cabinet, working in close co-operation with Louis Thiers. After a cabinet crisis in 1840, he was sent as ambassador to Great Britain, but he returned the same year to take over the government; Thiers' belligerent policy in Syria had lost favor with the peaceful Louis Philippe.

At first foreign minister and later prime minister, Guizot controlled the government for the next eight years. His policies were completely conservative. He supported monarchy limited by a comparatively few members of the bourgeoisie, and did not allow electoral or other reforms. It was a time of peace and prosperity; but it was also a time of moral and political corruption, extraordinary scandals, and careless hypocrisy. The upshot of this regime was the proletarian revolution of 1848. Guizot escaped to Belgium, and thence to England, where he stayed for one year. He returned to France, but his political career was over; he spent his remaining twenty-six years on his estate in Normandy, living simply and supporting himself largely through his writing. He was active otherwise only in supporting the independence of the Institute of France, and in defending the literary profession. Among his writings of this period are *Histoire de la République d'Angleterre et de Cromwell* (2 vols., 1854) and *Histoire Parlementaire de la France* (5 vols., 1863).

GUJARAT, a geographical division of Western India, formerly a N. division of the Bombay Presidency. The region is in the N.E. portion of the Kathiawar Peninsula, N. of the Narbada R. The surface is generally level. The area is watered principally by the Narbada and the Tapti rivers. Agricultural products grown in Gujarat are cotton, rice, wheat, barley, corn, tobacco, sugar cane, and fruits. Area, 7352 sq.m.; pop. (1941) 1,458,702.

GUJARĀTĪ LANGUAGE AND LITERATURE. The Gujarātī language is spoken by some 11,000,000 people in the Gujarat States, in Baroda, and in the neighboring provinces of Bombay, in Western India. To the east it merges gradually into Rājasthānī. It belongs in the Sanskritic group of Indo-Iranian languages, and is derived from the medieval dialect group called Prakrit, principally the Apabhramśa form of the Saurasēnī dialect. Gujarātī contains many words borrowed from Sanskrit, Arabic, and Persian. It is written in a vernacular alphabet of the type of the western group of Nagari alphabets, derived from the ancient Sanskrit script Devanagari. The manner in which the language is pronounced varies greatly from the speech of the illiterates to the speech of the educated classes.

Early Gujarātī literature includes many bardic chronicles. Two of the most distinguished poets who wrote in this language are Narsingh Mēta (1413–79), who composed short religious poems, and Rēwa Shankar, who translated the great epic *Mahābhārata* (q.v.) into the vernacular. Present-day Gujarātī literature is based for the most part on translations from the English.

GUJRANWALA, city and capital of the district of the same name, Lahore Division, Punjab Province, Pakistan, situated 40 miles N.W. of Lahore. It was once the center of Sikh power. The district is served by the North-Western Railway, and exports wheat and cotton. Area of district, 2311 sq.m.; pop. (1951) 1,044,000. Pop. of town (1951) 120,860.

GULBARGA, capital of the district of the same name, Hyderabad, India, situated 70 miles S.E. of Sholapur and about 110 m. by rail W. of the city of Hyderabad. It is the trading center of an extensive agricultural area. The principal industrial establishments in the city are flour mills, cotton and cotton-seed-oil mills, cotton compresses and gins, and factories manufacturing cotton textiles and paints. Among the buildings in Gulbarga is the Jama Masjid, a mosque dating from the 13th century, and built after the design of that of Cordova in Spain. Gulbarga also contains the ruins of palaces, fortifications, mosques, and tombs of the Bahmani kings, who ruled in Gulbarga from 1347 to 1422. The present industrial importance of the city dates from the opening there of a station on the Great Indian Peninsula Railway. The district of Gulbarga has an area of 6975 sq.m.; pop. (1951) 1,448,944. Pop. of city (1941) 53,551.

GÜLEK BOGAZ. See CILICIAN GATES.

GULFPORT, county seat and port of entry of Harrison Co., Miss., situated on Mississippi Sound on the Gulf of Mexico, 13 miles W. of Biloxi and about midway between Mobile, Ala., and New Orleans, La. It is served by two railroads and by ocean steamers. The city has a fine harbor, with a deepwater channel to the Gulf, and excellent dock and storage facilities. It has a frontage of 6 miles on the Gulf, and is protected by a sea wall extending along the shore for a distance of 27 miles. The principal exports of the port are lumber, creosoted piling, staves and headings, cotton and cottonseed products, rosin, glucose, and sea food. Industrial establishments in the city include railroad shops, lumber mills, cotton compresses, bottling works, a shrimp and oyster packing plant, a creosoting plant, and factories manufacturing shirts, concrete, fertilizer, and naval stores. Gulfport is a popular resort, with bathing beaches, golf courses, yacht clubs, and waterfront bridle paths included among its recreational facilities. It is the site of Gulf Park College, a junior college for women, established in 1921; the Gulf Coast Military Academy, maintained by the War Department; and a U.S. veterans hospital. The city was founded in 1898. Pop. (1950) 22,659.

GULF STREAM, a warm current of the North Atlantic Ocean flowing in a general northeasterly direction from the Straits of Florida to the Newfoundland Banks. The term is often extended to include the North Atlantic Drift which flows from the Newfoundland Banks to the shores of western Europe, Scandinavia, and the Arctic islands as far north as Novaya Zemlya. The Gulf Stream is of great climatological importance because of its effects on the climate of western Europe. This great body of warm water gives France, the Low Countries, and the British Isles a comparatively temperate climate, despite the fact that they lie in latitudes comparable to those of Newfoundland and Labrador in the western hemisphere.

The sources of the Gulf Stream are the two west-flowing equatorial currents: the North Equatorial Current which flows roughly along the Tropic of Cancer; and the South Equatorial Current which flows from the coasts of S.W. Africa to South America and thence north along the coasts of N. Brazil and the Guianas into the Caribbean. The result of these two currents is a concentration of warm water in the Caribbean Sea and in the Atlantic Ocean north of Cuba and the Greater Antilles. The fusion of these two currents and a certain amount of water from the Gulf of Mexico forms the Gulf Stream.

In the straits that separate Florida from the Bahamas and Cuba, the Stream has a maximum width of about 50 m. and a depth of about 2100 ft. The surface temperature is about 25°C. (77°F.) and the surface current about 2.7 to 3.8 m. per hour. At a depth of 670 ft. the temperature is 10° to 18°C. (50° to 64°F.), and the current flow between 0.9 and 1.7 m. per hour. Farther north the Stream widens and is approximately 150 m. wide off the coast of South Carolina, and 300 m. wide off New York. Between the Stream and the coast of the U.S. lies an area of colder water, sometimes called the Cold Wall.

South of the Newfoundland Banks the Stream meets and mixes with the Labrador Current (q.v.) which flows southward from Baffin Bay, forming numerous whirlpools. From this point the Stream, or properly the North Atlantic Drift, moves northeastward across the ocean, driven at a rate of about 4 to 5 m. per day by the prevailing south-

Ring-billed gull. Top, the adult in summer; bottom, the immature bird.

westerly winds. The drift then splits into several branches, of which the most important are: the central flow which reaches the coasts of Europe and then turns northward; a northerly tongue, the Irminger Current which reaches the southern and western shores of Iceland; and a southerly tongue which flows past the Azores and the Canary Islands.

From its source to the region of the Newfoundland Banks, the Gulf Stream has special physical characteristics including a markedly blue color and strong salinity. After mixing with the Labrador Current the characteristic color is lost, but the water of the North Atlantic Drift is markedly salty. Because of this salt concentration, the water of the Drift sinks below the surface as it cools and is found as a warm underwater current when it reaches the Arctic regions.

See OCEAN AND OCEANOGRAPHY: *Ocean Currents.*

GULFWEED. See PHAEOPHYCEAE.

GULICK, CHARLOTTE VETTER (1865–1928), American sociologist, born at Oberlin, Ohio, educated at Washburn College, Drury College, and Wellesley College. She was the wife of Luther Halsey Gulick and was associated with him in several movements. Her most prominent activity was the establishment and direction of the Camp Fire Girls of America, an organization similar to the Girl Scouts.

During World War I she and her husband served in France as Y.M.C.A. workers. She was a pioneer in the advocacy of sex instruction for children and wrote numerous articles for women's and child-study magazines. See CAMP FIRE GIRLS, INC.

GULICK, LUTHER HALSEY (1865–1918), American specialist in physical education, born at Honolulu, Hawaiian Islands, and educated at Sargent Normal School of Physical Training and New York University. He was director of the physical training course in the Y.M.C.A college at Springfield, Mass., until 1903. While at Springfield, he co-operated with James Naismith (q.v.) in the invention of basketball. He served as president of the American Physical Education Association from 1903 to 1906, as director of the child hygiene department of Russell Sage Foundation from 1907 to 1913, and as president of the Camp Fire Girls of America after 1913. His publications include *Physical Education by Muscular Exercise* (1904); *The Efficient Life* (1907); *Mind and Work* (1908); and *The Healthful Art of Dancing* (1910).

GULL, common name for any of a number of water birds in the same family as the tern (q.v.). They are similar in appearance to terns, but are larger and have heavier bodies and bills more sharply hooked at the tip. The plumage of most species is white, mixed with gray, black, or brown. The majority nest on cliffs or beaches; some species make their nests in trees. The nests of all species are characteristically lined with grass, moss, and feathers. The diet is varied and includes small fish, small mammals, shellfish, and garbage. Some species drop shellfish from a height onto rocks, and even on cement and macadam roads, to break the shells. A number of species are migratory, nesting in the summer in Maine and wintering along the coasts of the southern States.

About twenty species of gulls are found in the United States. See HERRING GULL; LAUGHING GULL.

GULLET, a term properly meaning the esophagus, but often applied to the throat.

GULLIVER'S TRAVELS, popular title of a satire by the English writer Jonathan Swift (q.v.), published in 1726 as a picaresque novel under the title *Travels into Several Remote Nations of the World*. Swift's satire was originally intended as an allegorical and acid attack on the vanity and hypocrisy of contemporary courts, statesmen, and political parties; but in the writing of his book, which is presumed to have taken more than six years,

Swift embodied his ripest reflections on man and society, making of *Gulliver's Travels* a savagely bitter and misanthropic mockery of all mankind. Nonetheless, it is so imaginatively, wittily, and simply written that it became and has remained a favorite travel tale, akin to fairy tales, of children in many countries.

GULLSTRAND, ALLVAR (1862–1930), Swedish ophthalmologist, born at Landskrona, and educated at the universities of Uppsala, Vienna, and Stockholm. He was professor of ophthalmology at Uppsala University from 1894 to 1913 and then professor of physiological and physical optics. Gullstrand investigated the nature of refraction of the human eye and developed a new approach to the theory of optical images. He was awarded the Nobel Prize for physiology and medicine in 1911, and became a member of the Nobel committee on physics. His most important writings include *Allgemeine Theorie der Monochromatischen Aberrationen* (1900) and *Einführung in die Methoden der Dioptrik des Auges des Menschen* (1911).

GUM, a colloidal substance exuded by plants. Gums are composed of complex organic acids, called *gum acids,* or the salts of these acids. When hydrolyzed, gum acids, such as *arabin,* yield sugars, such as arabinose, galactose, and xylose, and simple acids. Gums have a consistency similar to glue when moist, but are hard when dry. They are colorless and odorless and will not dissolve in organic solvents, though readily soluble in water. Gums are used as a base for mucilage, in cloth finishing and calico printing, or as emulsifying or soothing constituents of medicines.

Gum arabic, an exudate of several species of acacia, is typical of gums which contain arabin. Finest quality gum arabic is obtained from *Acacia senegal* and *A. arabica,* found in w. and N. Africa. The gum forms a clear, viscid solution in water. When ethyl alcohol is added to an aqueous solution of gum arabic which has been slightly acidified with hydrochloric acid, arabin is precipitated. A similar gum, cherry-tree gum, is exuded from the bark of several species of *Prunus,* such as common cherry and plum trees.

Tragacanth, which is obtained from various Anatolian and Iranian species of *Astragalus,* particularly *A. gummifer,* is typical of gums which contain bassorin. Tragacanth, like gelatin, absorbs water readily, and will take up as much as fifty times its weight in water, forming a thick mucilage. Tragacanth, also

known as gum dragon, is a type of dragon's blood (q.v.).

Many gum resins and other plant exudates are commonly called gums; see GUM TREE. Gum resins are substances which contain both gum and resin, so that both water and alcohol are required to dissolve them. The principal gum resins are the "gums" of ammoniac, asafetida, benzoin, galbanum, gamboge, myrrh, and sandarac. Latex (q.v.), from which chicle, rubber, and gutta-percha are derived, is composed of gum resins, waxes, and fats. Chewing gum is usually made from chicle. See also RESINS.

GUMBO, a vegetable. See OKRA.

GUMMATA. See SYPHILIS.

GUM PLANT. See GRINDELIA.

GUMTI, a river of N. India, rising in the Pilibhit district of the United Provinces, and flowing generally S.E. for 500 m., emptying into the Ganges R. about 20 m. below Benares. The principal towns on its banks are Lucknow and Jaunpur. A bridge across the river at Jaunpur dates from the 16th century.

GUM TREE, common name of many trees that exude gum or resin. The sapodilla, *Sapota achras,* yields chicle, used as the base for chewing gum. In the U.S., the name is applied to *Liquidambar styraciflua,* the sweet or red gum (see LIQUIDAMBAR), and to *Nyssa sylvatica,* the tupelo (q.v.), also called black or sour gum. Species of *Eucalyptus* (q.v.) are called gum trees in Australia, and *Styrax benzoin,* which produces benzoin (q.v.) is called the gum tree in the East Indies. Many other trees throughout the world which exude gums or resins are called gum trees in their native localities.

GUNNEL. See BUTTERFISH.

GUNNISON RIVER, a river of Colorado, formed at Gunnison by the confluence of the Tomichi and Taylor rivers, and flowing generally w.N.w. for about 200 m., emptying into the Colorado R. at Grand Junction. It falls a distance of 6477 ft. through a series of deep canyons, and is particularly famous for its Black Canyon (see BLACK CANYON OF THE GUNNISON), which is now contained within a national monument. The river abounds in fish.

GUNPOWDER, an explosive powder used in ballistics, specifically black powder, an explosive mixture of about 75% potassium nitrate, 15% charcoal, and 10% sulfur. Gunpowder was the first explosive known. It was probably discovered by the English monk Roger Bacon in the middle of the 13th century, although the Chinese had previously used pyrotechnics which may have been similar to gunpowder. Berthold Schwartz, a German monk of the early 14th century, was probably the first person to employ gunpowder for propelling a projectile. Whatever the precise dates and identities of its first discoverers and users, it is certain that gunpowder was manufactured in England in 1334, and that there were powder manufacturing plants in Germany in 1340. In the time of Queen Elizabeth the manufacture of gunpowder was conducted as a monopoly of the crown. Regulations relating to gunpowder in England date from about 1623. It was the only explosive known to man until the first preparation of fulminates in 1798. For historical and modern uses of gunpowder, see EXPLOSIVES.

GUNPOWDER PLOT, a conspiracy to destroy the King of England, the Lords, and the Commons at the opening of Parliament on November 5, 1605. The plot was fomented by a group of prominent Roman Catholics in retaliation for the oppressive anti-Catholic laws being applied by James I. The originator of the scheme was Robert Catesby. First he took his cousin Robert Winter, and John Wright into his confidence. Later, Thomas Percy, Robert Keyes, Francis Tresham, John Grant, Thomas Bates, Ambrose Rokewood, and Robert Winter's brother, Thomas, were included. They in turn drew Guy Fawkes (q.v.), a soldier of fortune, into the plot. The conspirators discovered a vault directly beneath the House of Lords. They rented this cellar, and stored in it thirty-six barrels of gunpowder.

In the final arrangement for the execution of their design on November 5, Fawkes was to set fire to the gunpowder in the cellar and then flee to Flanders. Through a combination of circumstances, the plot was exposed. Fawkes was arrested early on November 5 as he emerged from the cellar. On his person were found fuzes, and in the cellar a lighted lantern and the barrels of gunpowder. Examined under torture, Fawkes confessed his own guilt and after long obstinacy revealed the names of his associates, nearly all of whom were killed on being taken, or died with Fawkes on the scaffold. The Gunpowder Plot is commemorated by an annual celebration on November 5, in which it was formerly the custom to burn Guy Fawkes in effigy.

GUNTER, EDMUND (1581–1626), English mathematician, born at Hertfordshire, and educated at Westminster College and at Christ Church, Oxford. He was professor of astronomy at Gresham College, London, from 1619 until his death. He introduced the words cosine and cotangent into trigonometry, and is credited with the discovery of the magnetic variation of the compass; see MAGNETISM, TERRESTRIAL. Among his many practical inventions are the surveying instrument known as Gunter's chain (see SURVEYING INSTRUMENTS), a portable quadrant, and a measuring device, called Gunter's scale, graduated in trigonometric functions and logarithms. His most important writings are *New Projection of the Sphere* (1623) and *Canon Triangulorum, or Table of Artificial Sines and Tangents* (1620).

GUNTHER, in the *Nibelungenlied* (q.v.), a king of Burgundy. He was the brother of Kriemhild and husband of Brunhild, whom he won with the assistance of Siegfried. Gunther was slain by his sister Kriemhild.

GUNTHER, JOHN (1901–), American journalist, born in Chicago, and educated at the University of Chicago. He became a reporter on the Chicago *Daily News* in 1922, and after 1924 was European correspondent for various American newspapers. In 1939 he became a radio commentator on international affairs. Gunther wrote, on the basis of his travels and experience in many parts of the world, *Inside Europe* (1936), *Inside Asia* (1939), *Inside Latin America* (1941), *Inside U.S.A.* (1947), and *Inside Africa* (1955); in *Inside Europe Today* (1949) he started on a new series, bringing his former works up to date. Other works are *The High Cost of Hitler* (1940), *The Troubled Midnight* (1945), *Death Be Not Proud* (1948), *Roosevelt in Retrospect* (1950), *Riddle of MacArthur* (1951), *Eisenhower, the Man and the Symbol* (1952), and *Days to Remember: America 1945–1955* (with Bernard Quint, 1956).

GUPPY, a small, active, carnivorous freshwater fish, *Lebistes reticulatus*, belonging to the Killifish family, found in Venezuela, the Guianas, and the West Indies. It was named after the Trinidadian ichthyologist R. J. Lechmere Guppy, who first sent specimens to the British Museum. The guppy is often kept in aquaria because of the brilliant coloration of the male, which is about 1 in. long, tinted with combinations of yellow, red, orange, green, blue, and purple, and spotted with black. No two individuals show the same color pattern. The female, which is about 2 in. long, is dull in color. Male guppies go through an elaborate courtship ceremony, spreading their fins before the female much in the manner of certain birds. The female produces a new litter every four weeks, the number of young varying from 2 to 126 at a time; as many as

five litters are produced as a result of a single
mating. The young, which are frequently de-
voured by the parents, survive in their native
surroundings by staying in the bottom vegetation; in aquaria, separate tanks or thick
vegetation must be provided to insure segrega-
tion of the young from other guppies. The
aquaria must be kept at about 75° to 85° F.
for the fish to thrive. Guppies are valued in
the West Indies because they destroy the
larvae of mosquitoes which carry malaria.

GURKHAS (Skr. *gōraksa,* "cowherd"), a
Hindu people of Rajput origin (see RAJASTHAN
UNION), inhabiting Nepal, a state situated on
the southern slope of the Himalayas, between
Tibet and India. The Gurkhas first invaded
Nepal in the 12th century. An attempt to extend their power farther south brought them
into conflict with the British in the Gurkha
War of 1814. By the Treaty of Segauli (1816),
the territorial limits of the Gurkhas were
clearly defined. In physique the Gurkhas are
short and stout. They are excellent fighters,
and carry a large, broad-bladed knife, called
the *kukri,* which they use at close quarters in
preference to the bayonet.

GURNARD (Fr. *grogner,* "to grunt"), common name for any of several species of spiny-
rayed marine fish of the family Triglidae.
Their name comes from the grunting sound
certain species make when taken from the
water; see GRUNT. Gurnards attain a length
of only 18 inches in the largest specimens.
Gurnards, like the sculpin (q.v.), have rough,
spiny skull bones; their bodies are covered
with bony scales, and their heads are angular
and wholly covered with bony plates. The
body is elongated, nearly round, and tapering.
There are two dorsal fins. The lower three
rays of the large pectoral fins are detached
and elongated into long feelers, which are used
in the search for food, and for locomotion.
Gurnards live on the bottom of the sea generally along the coast. They often frequent
depths of several hundred fathoms. Several
gurnards are known as sea robins (q.v.).

GUSTAVUS, or (Swed.) GUSTAF, name of
five kings of Sweden. **1.** GUSTAVUS I, known
as GUSTAVUS VASA, also GUSTAVUS ERIKSSON
(1496–1560), king from 1523 until 1560, first
ruler of the house of Vasa, born in Lind-
holmen, the son of Eric Johansson. He was
educated at the University of Uppsala and in
1514 entered the service of the regent Sten
Sture the Younger (1493?–1520). In 1518–19
he participated in the war waged against Denmark in protest of the Union of Kalmar, which
placed Sweden and Norway under the Danish

King Gustavus II of Sweden

crown. Gustavus was sent as a hostage to the
Danes during the war but escaped from his
prison to Lübeck, whence he returned to
Dalecarlia, Sweden, and while living in se-
clusion there became a miner. On the coronation of the Danish king, Christian II, at Stockholm in 1520, leaders of the Swedish party, including the father of Gustavus, were killed.
The following year Gustavus successfully led
a revolt of Dalecarlians against the Danes, and
in 1521 he was named administrator of the
Swedish kingdom by an assembly at Wads-
tena. He served two years in that capacity and
in 1523 was elected king. More for political
than spiritual reasons, Gustavus introduced
the Reformation movement in his country. In
1527 he made Swedish bishops subject to
royal power, and in 1528 he was crowned by
the Protestant archbishop of Uppsala. Luther-
anism was proclaimed the state religion in
1529. Four uprisings occurred between 1525
and 1542, but Gustavus suppressed them. He
was constantly menaced by the threat of Danish intervention. In 1544 he made the Swedish
kingship hereditary in his family.

2. GUSTAVUS II, known as GUSTAVUS
ADOLPHUS (1594–1632), and called the "Snow
King" and "Lion of the North", king from
1611 to 1632, son of King Charles IX and
grandson of Gustavus I, born at Stockholm
and raised in the Lutheran religion. He was

noted as a leader of the Protestants in the Thirty Years' War. From a very early age he was trained in statesmanship and military affairs. When he was sixteen, Gustavus Adolphus succeeded to the throne. Sweden was at that time at war with Denmark, and the young king assumed command of the army, securing the support of the nobles by granting them extensive concessions. By 1613 he regained the s. districts of Sweden from Denmark and in that year concluded peace with Denmark. From 1613 until 1617 he waged a war against Russia, winning territories in Livonia and Estonia. Gustavus Adolphus fought from 1621 until 1629 against the Polish king, Sigismund III, who maintained a claim to the Swedish crown. The truce of Altmark in 1629 confirmed Gustavus Adolphus in the kingship and granted Sweden possession of the delta of the Vistula R. and of several commercial cities. A religious interest in the Protestant cause and a fear of Catholic encroachment upon the Baltic provinces impelled Gustavus Adolphus to enter the Thirty Years' War, leaving his chancellor Count Axel Gustafsson Oxenstierna (q.v.) to administer Sweden. After making alliances with France, Pomerania, and Brandenburg, Gustavus Adolphus led his troops in the defeat of the army of the Holy Roman emperor, driving the Imperial forces from Pomerania in 1630. In 1631, when Saxony also joined the alliance led by the Swedish king, the latter was victorious against Johan Tserclaes, Count of Tilly (q.v.), at Leipzig. Following a second successful engagement against Tilly, Adolphus was confronted by Albrecht Eusebius Wenzel von Wallenstein (q.v.). At the battle of Lützen in the fall of 1632, Wallenstein was defeated, but the Swedish leader was fatally wounded. Gustavus Adolphus was not only noted as a great general, but also as a capable administrator. With the aid of Count Oxenstierna, he developed a sound and centralized system of government and laid plans for colonial expansion. He left his only child, Christina, as his successor.

3. Gustavus III (1746–92), king from 1771 until 1792, son of King Adolphus Frederick, born in Stockholm. When he succeeded to the throne on the death of his father, Sweden was in a state of near anarchy as a result of strife between two factions of nobles, the aristocratic Francophile Hats and the more conservative pro-Russian Caps (see SWEDEN: *History*). When the Caps continued attempts to further limit the royal prerogative, Gustavus finally secured the support of army officers in 1772 in a plot to suppress the diet and

constitution. After staging a mock revolt, he massed troops, ostensibly to put down the revolt, but used them instead to force the assembly to accept a new constitution, which firmly established the prerogative of the king. During an inconclusive war with Russia in 1788 the nobles influenced the assembly not to provide the king with needed military supplies. Accordingly, in the following year the king exacted further powers from the assembly in order to counteract the rebelliousness of the nobles. In 1789–90 war with Russia was resumed and Sweden offset military defeats by destroying a third of the Russian navy at Svensksund. By the peace of Värälä Sweden agreed to an eight-year defensive alliance with Russia. While preparing, in 1792, to intervene in the French Revolution, the king was assassinated in a plot conceived by hostile nobles. Gustavus was a devotee of French culture and has often been accused of being whimsical and extravagant. However, he reformed and improved the administrative and judicial systems and gave salutary encouragement to art and literature. In his own right he was an accomplished author, having composed historical essays, poetry, and dramatic pieces.

4. Gustavus IV, or Gustavus Adolphus (1778–1837), king from 1792 to 1809, son of King Gustavus III, born at Stockholm. He was king under the regency of his uncle the duke of Södermanland from 1792 until 1800, when he was crowned. From his father Gustavus inherited a dislike for the principles of the French Revolution, and from 1805 until 1807 he participated in a coalition against Napoleon, losing Pomerania and Stralsund when Napoleon was victorious over the allies. Although aided by England, the Swedish king was defeated by Russia in 1808 and was forced to cede Finland. Because he was believed insane, the king was captured by nobles and compelled to abdicate in 1809. He subsequently traveled through Europe, dying in poverty in Switzerland.

5. Gustavus V, better known as Gustaf (1858–1950), king from 1907, son of King Oscar II, of the Bernadotte dynasty, born at Drottningholm and educated at the University of Uppsala. By marrying Princess Victoria, daughter of Frederick William Louis, Grand Duke of Baden, he joined the house of Bernadotte with that of the traditional Swedish ruling dynasty of Vasa, from which his wife was descended. In 1892 he was made a lieutenant general, with the status of commander of the army. After serving a number of times as regent for his father when the latter was ill or absent from the kingdom, Gustavus became king in 1907. During his reign much progressive social legislation, such as paid vacations for housewives, health insurance, and public child welfare, was enacted. Gustavus was noted for his physical activity, especially his tennis-playing, which he finally relinquished in 1946 at the age of eighty-eight. A very popular king, he was presented with a gift of $1,000,000 by the Swedish people on his eightieth birthday.

6. Gustavus VI (1882–   ), king from 1950, son of King Gustavus V, born in Stockholm. He was married in 1905 to Princess Margaret, daughter of the British prince Arthur, Duke of Connaught. In 1923, three years after Margaret's death, he married Princess Louise of Battenberg. On his father's death in 1950, he became king.

GUSTAVUS ADOLPHUS, or Gustaf Adolf. See Gustavus II and IV of Sweden.

GUSTAVUS ADOLPHUS COLLEGE, a co-educational institution of higher learning, founded in St. Peter, Minnesota, in 1862. The college, which is operated under the auspices of the Lutheran Church, offers a four-year course in the liberal arts, leading to a B.A. degree. In a recent year it comprised a student body of about 1250 and faculty of 70.

GUSTAVUS VASA. See Gustavus I.

GUTENBERG, Johann (1400?–68?), German printer, and pioneer in the use of movable type, born probably in Mainz. His family later settled in Strasbourg, where in 1438 Gutenberg entered into a partnership with three others to conduct experiments in printing. In Mainz, about 1450, Gutenberg formed a partnership with a goldsmith, Johann Fust, and set up a press on which he started printing a large Latin Bible and some smaller books and leaflets. Fust's demands for the repayment of money he had invested led to a law-suit in 1455, and Gutenberg surrendered his share of the firm. The famous Bible known as the "Gutenberg Bible" (q.v.) was finished before the middle of 1456, but was actually printed by Peter Schöffer, who was Fust's partner. Following the split with Fust, Gutenberg continued printing, either at Mainz or the nearby town of Eltville. In 1465 Archbishop Adolph of Nassau, Elector of Mainz, became his patron.

GUTENBERG BIBLE, known also as the "Mazarin Bible" and the "Bible of 42 Lines", a Latin edition of the Bible, printed at Mainz, Germany, sometime between 1450 and 1456. Although German bibliographers claim that

King Gustavus V of Sweden

it was printed by Johann Gutenberg (q.v.), perhaps in co-operation with Conrad Humery, the edition probably was the work of Peter Schöffer and Johann Fust, who at one time had been associated with Gutenberg. The book is the first volume known to have been printed with movable metal type. The first copy that attracted attention was discovered about 1760 among the books of Cardinal Jules Mazarin. The finest known copy was acquired by the Library of Congress, Washington, D.C., in 1930. Only two other perfect copies of the Gutenberg Bible are known to be in existence.

GUTHRIE, Samuel (1782–1848), American chemist, born at Brimfield, Mass. He studied medicine with his father, and later attended the University of Pennsylvania. He was an army surgeon during the War of 1812. In 1831 Guthrie discovered "chloric ether", or chloroform (q.v.). He also succeeded in producing percussion priming powder (fulminating powder) for firearms, and invented a punch lock for exploding the powder in place of the flintlock used in muskets.

GUTTA-PERCHA, a rubberlike substance obtained from the latex found in the stems and leaves of several Malayan trees of the genera *Payena* and *Palaquium*. It is a pale-brown, somewhat elastic solid that becomes plastic upon heating. It contains a white amorphous hydrocarbon, gutta. Gutta-percha is very resistant to water, and is a poor conductor of electricity; because of these properties it is used as insulation for marine cable and other electrical equipment. It is also used as temporary fillings in dentistry, as the outer covering of golfballs, in making surgical splints, and, with chicle, in chewing gum.

GUYON, MADAME, name used by JEANNE MARIE BOUVIER DE LA MOTTE-GUYON (1648–1717), French mystic, born at Montargis. Left a rich widow at the age of twenty-eight, she came under the influence of Père Lacombe (d. 1715), a Barnabite monk, and with him started spreading her religion of mysticism in southeastern France. She introduced into France the doctrine of quietism (q.v.), which stressed the religious value of contemplation. Her ideas aroused the severe criticism of the archbishop of Paris, and in 1688 she was imprisoned; she was released the next year through the influence of Madame la Marquise Françoise de Maintenon, who was influential at the court of Louis XIV. During the next four years she was often present at the court, and formed a friendship with the writer and prelate François Fénelon, to whom she imparted many of her views. Imprisoned again for her quietist writings in 1695, she remained in the Bastille until 1703, when she obtained her release on condition that she leave Paris and live in retirement with her son near Blois. She spent her last years performing charitable deeds, and died professing absolute belief in the Roman Catholic Church. Her writings include *Le Cantique des Cantiques Interprété selon le Sens Mystique* (1685) and *Discours Chrétiens et Spirituels* (1716).

GUYOT, ARNOLD HENRY (1807–84), Swiss-American geographer and geologist, born at Boudevilliers, Switzerland, and educated at Neuchâtel College and the University of Berlin. He was professor of history and physical geography at Neuchâtel from 1839 to 1848, at which date he emigrated to the United States. He was professor of geology and physical geography at Princeon University from 1854 until his death. Guyot studied and collected important data concerning glaciers. He also made extensive meteorological observations which led to the establishment of the U.S. Weather Bureau; his *Meteorological and Physical Tables* (1852) was a

standard reference work for many years. He wrote many textbooks which were important in popularizing the study of geology in the United States. Some of his other writings are *A Memoir of Louis Agassiz* (1883) and *Creation, or the Biblical Cosmogony in the Light of Modern Science* (1884).

GUZMÁN BLANCO, ANTONIO (1829–99), Venezuelan statesman and soldier, born at Caracas, and educated at the Central University in that city. He traveled for several years in the United States, returning in 1859 to Venezuela, where he took part in the successful revolution of which Gen. Juan Falcón was the leader. Guzmán Blanco was vice-president from 1863 to 1868, when a revolution caused the overthrow of the government. In 1870 he headed a counterrevolutionary movement and seized control. Although he was out of the country frequently, he retained absolute control of the government until 1889, when another revolution overthrew his regime. He was in Europe when this happened, and never returned to Venezuela. During his administration many reforms were enacted, including the establishment of primary education, the construction of railroads and highways, and the stabilization of finances.

GWALIOR, former princely state of India, now forming part of Madhya Bharat State, Union of India. Gwalior (q.v.) was the capital. Cotton, pulse, millet, wheat, rice, corn, sugar cane, tobacco, garlic, ginger, and turmeric are the leading agricultural crops of the region; the processing of cotton is the leading industry. Hindus predominate among the people.

The ruling house of the princely state was founded by a Maratha (q.v.) chieftain in the middle of the 18th century; at one time Gwalior controlled much of central India. In 1948, following the termination of British paramountcy in India, Gwalior acceded to Madhya Bharat State. Area of former princely state, 26,008 sq.m.; pop. (1941) 4,006,159.

GWALIOR, city and winter capital of Madhya Bharat State, Union of India, situated 65 m. by rail s. of Agra. Its nucleus is a citadel crowning an isolated rock about 300 ft. in height, nearly 2 miles in length, and 900 yards in width. The rock is said to have been occupied as a stronghold for more than ten centuries. On the E. base of the rock is the old city of Gwalior. The old city contains a noted white-sandstone mosque, palaces, rock temples, and statues of archeological and archi-

tectural interest. In the new city, extending
s.w. of the old, are industrial establishments
producing cotton yarn, leather products,
paint, ceramics, glass, chemicals, and pharmaceutical products. Pop. (1951) 241,577.

GWINNETT, BUTTON (about 1735-77),
American patriot, born in Gloucester, England. He emigrated to Charleston, S.C.,
and about 1770 bought a plantation on St.
Catherines Island, Ga. He was politically active early in the Revolutionary movement in
Georgia, became a member of the Continental
Congress, and was one of the signers of the
Declaration of Independence. From 1776 to
1777 he was a member of the convention that
met to frame the Georgia Constitution. He
was killed in a duel with General Lachlan
McIntosh, his successful rival for the brigadier generalship of the Georgia troops. Gwinnett's autograph is rare, and highly valued by
collectors of the signatures of the signers of
the Declaration.

GWYN or **GWYNNE,** ELEANOR, known as
NELL (1650-87), English actress, and mistress of Charles II, born either in London or
Hereford. As a child she sold oranges outside
the Drury Lane Theater in London; she became an actress at the age of fifteen. Her
first known appearance was in Dryden's *Indian Emperor*. She was well suited to the gay
feminine roles common in Restoration comedies, and Dryden wrote several plays with
roles especially for her. She became the mistress of the king about 1669, and retained her
affection for him until his death in 1685. Although almost completely illiterate, she was
a favorite in London society, and the diarist
Samuel Pepys described her as "pretty, witty
Nell." She bore Charles II two sons, Charles
Beauclerk (1670-1726), Duke of St. Albans,
and James Beauclerk (1671-80).

GYMNASIUM, type of classical secondary
school in Germany. The term "Gymnasium"
was derived from the gymnasia of ancient
Greece, where youths met for exercise (*gymnos*, "naked"), conversation, and discussion.
German Gymnasia arose during the humanistic movement of the early part of the 16th
century. Schools existing at that time were
either owned by the Church or staffed by
clergy These schools were devoted to the
study, in Latin, of the traditional liberal arts
which consisted of the trivium (grammar,
rhetoric, and logic) and quadrivium (arithmetic, astronomy, geometry, and music). The
influence of the humanistic movement resulted in emancipation of schools from the
teaching of the Church. Meanwhile the Prot-

Nell Gwyn

estant Reformation, which favored seculariza-
tion and uniformity of education, had begun.

The first Protestant school of the humanistic type was established at Magdeburg in
1524. The first general system of schools
which provided for Gymnasia was that of
Saxony, initiated in 1528. The most influential Gymnasium, that of Strasbourg, was
placed under the leadership of Johannes
Sturm (q.v.) in 1538. In 1540 the Jesuit
Order established the first of numerous schools
which differed from Gymnasia only in being
under religious control. Rivalry between the
Gymnasia and Jesuit schools, together with
a decline in emphasis on humanism, was responsible for a decline in character of the
Gymnasia. Instruction became very formal,
with little attention given to the meaningful
content of the literature studied. Members
of the Pietistic movement substituted a more
vital interest in the content of the classics,
and were largely responsible for the formation of new nonclassical schools, for students
who did not intend to enter the learned professions. The Prussian monarchy exerted a
stimulating influence on education throughout the 18th century, especially under Frederick the Great, but not until the latter part
of that century did a new humanistic spirit
become infused into the German Gymnasia,
under the influence of such men as Herder,
Kant, Lessing, Goethe, and Schiller. During
the 19th century, the rapid rise in importance of mathematics and natural science influenced the curriculum of the Gymnasium,

but the study of classical antiquity continued to be the chief object of Gymnasial teaching.

During the period just prior to World War I, the curriculum of the Gymnasium was extensively modernized. Latin remained the basic subject, but Greek had been put on an elective basis, and a considerable part of the language instruction was devoted to French. The study of German included instruction in mythology, grammar, rhetoric, poetics, and reading of the *Nibelungenlied,* the more important works of Walther von der Vogelweide, Lessing, Schiller, and Goethe, and German translations of Shakespeare. Mathematical subjects included arithmetic, algebra, geometry, trigonometry, and analytical geometry. Instruction in natural sciences included descriptive natural history, botany, zoology, anthropology, mineralogy, physics, astronomy, chemistry, and physical geography. The history curriculum was so organized that each period was covered twice, once in the lower school and once in the upper school. Geography, religion, singing, drawing, and gymnastics comprised the remainder of the curriculum.

Since the close of World War I, the Gymnasia have become less important in the general structure of German education. German universities, which formerly accepted only Gymnasium graduates, now accept graduates of semiclassical and nonclassical secondary schools. Gymnasia have, however, retained considerable social prestige because of their classical curricula and, during the educational reorganization in the western zones of occupation following World War II, have maintained their position as the "keystone" of German secondary education.

GYMNASTICS, a system of physical exercises designed wholly or chiefly for the purpose of improving health and developing the body. The term, which was created by the Greeks, originally signified all forms of athletics; but in modern times it does not include those sports in which the idea of competition or of mere recreation has become dominant. Originally in Greek gymnastics, each youth would try to perform whatever feat he could, but soon the games were reduced to formal contests, including such events as running and javelin and discus throwing. Greek youths spent a large part of the day in the gymnasium, where space was set aside for the philosophers to teach. The Spartans had the most rigid system of gymnastics, compulsory for girls as well as for men. It included war dances, climbing ropes, and the keeping of

balance while jumping on slippery wine-filled skins.

Although the Romans adopted the Greek forms of gymnastics, these exercises were soon abandoned, and did not reappear in any similar form until the latter part of the 18th century. With the Industrial Revolution, however, the movement of population into crowded cities and the introduction of machinery lessened the demand upon the body and increased that made on the nervous system and the mind. The provision of some sort of physical activity soon became a necessity to the individual and a subject of major importance to the nation at large. The impetus for the revival in gymnastics came from Germany and the Scandinavian countries, spreading to the rest of Europe; the great German migration to the United States immediately following the revolutionary uprisings in Germany in 1848 brought the institution of the Turnverein, or gymnastic club, with it.

At present, gymnastics constitutes an integral part of the educational system of continental Europe, where in several countries an hour each day of this exercise is compulsory by state law. Gymnastics forms a part of the curriculum of most schools and colleges in the United States but has never attracted the popular attention accorded to such competitive sports as football. Nevertheless, in the United States gymnastics forms an essential part in the training of firemen, soldiers, policemen, and others whose occupation demands the greatest possible physical co-ordination. Joint meetings of gymnastic teams form an important feature of indoor sport during the winter. Championships are awarded, notably in the contests between members of the A.A.U., Y.M.C.A., and various colleges and preparatory schools.

Exercises in modern gymnastics can be divided into two main categories: light gymnastics or calisthenics, consisting of rhythmic exercises, frequently with the use of such equipment as dumbbells, bar-bells, or Indian clubs; and heavy gymnastics, consisting of exercises using fixed gymnasium equipment, such as horizontal bars, parallel bars, the trapeze, ladders, and ropes. Gymnastics was developed greatly by the Swedes, notably Pehr Henrik Ling (1776–1839), who brought fencing with the foil, sabre, and bayonet to a high degree of perfection, and concentrated on the training of physical education teachers for the army.

The simplest and one of the oldest of gymnastic apparatuses is the dumbbell, which was

International Committee of the Y.M.C.A.

GYMNASTICS

Above: Performing a difficult handstand on parallel bars. Above, right: An athlete working out on a vaulting horse. Right: Boys doing exercises in a high-school gymnasium.

in use in England as early as the 16th century. By means of a few exercises with the dumbbell, all parts of the body can be developed. Another apparatus widely used in the U.S. is the pulley weight machine. It is fixed against one wall of the gymnasium, and by varying the weight, the height of the handle, or the exerciser's position at the apparatus, the effects can be applied to any desired group of muscles. Most of the other fixed equipment to be found in gymnasiums is designed either for jumping and vaulting exercises, or for hanging, swinging, and climbing exercises. Such equipment includes the vaulting horse, flying rings, climbing ropes, floor mats, wrestling and tumbling mats, and horizontal and vertical ladders. Gymnasiums also frequently have specialized equipment for strengthening the chest, lungs, and other parts of the body.

GYMNOCLADUS, genus of trees belonging to the leguminous family Caesalpiniaceae. The only native North American representative is *G. dioica,* the Kentucky coffee tree, or chicot,

found in deep woods in Ontario and N. United States. It is a deciduous tree which attains a height of 50 to 100 feet, and is frequently cultivated as a lawn or park tree. It has large, compound leaves composed of dark-green ovate leaflets. The greenish-white, irregular flowers are borne in terminal clusters. The fruit is a brown, leathery pod, about ten inches long, containing a sweet, dark-red pulp and large brown seeds. The seeds were used by American settlers as a substitute for coffee beans.

GYMNOPHIONA. See CAECILIA.

GYMNOSPERMS (Gr. *gymnos,* "naked"; *sperma,* "seed"), or Gymnospermae, one of the two great subdivisions of the phylum Spermatophyta (seed-bearing plants), the other being the angiosperms (q.v.). Gymnosperms differ from angiosperms in having seeds which are not (excepting in two genera of Gnetaceae) covered by a carpel or ovary wall. There are about 60 living genera and 700 living species of gymnosperms. Gymnosperms are divided into seven orders: (1) Cycadofilicales, the seed ferns, now extinct; (2) Cycadales, represented by the family Cycadaceae (q.v.); (3) Bennettitales, an extinct group which bore reproductive organs protected by a thick covering; (4) Cordaitales, an extinct group represented by the fossil genus *Cordaites*; (5) Ginkgoales, represented by a single living genus, *Ginkgo* (q.v.); (6) Coniferales, the cone-bearing, needle-leaved conifers (q.v.), which comprise the bulk of living gymnosperms; and (7) Gnetales, represented by the single family Gnetaceae, the Joint-Fir Family. See SPERMATOPHYTES.

GYMNOTIDAE, family of South American deep-sea fish, closely related to the electric fish of the family Electrophoridae, containing one species, the carapo, *Gymnotus fasciatus*. The eel-like carapo has a long tail with a rudimentary caudal fin; the anal fin is extremely long and the dorsal and pelvic fins are absent. The electric fish were formerly included in the Gymnotidae; the present distinction between the two families is based on the fact that the carapo has no electric organs. See ELECTRIC FISH.

GYNECOLOGY, the specialized branch of medicine which deals with the study and therapy of the diseases of women, especially of the genitourinary system. Until modern times, gynecology included the problems of pregnancy and childbirth, but today the specialty obstetrics (q.v.) largely covers that field. Another specialty which is further narrowing gynecological practice is urology, which deals with problems of the urinary system. These various fields overlap, but the tendency is toward greater specialization.

An important part of gynecological practice consists of diagnosis and treatment of disturbances of menstruation (q.v.). Gynecologists also treat the large number of diseases and malformations affecting the uterus. vagina, Fallopian tubes, and other parts of the reproductive system. Among the urinary disturbances, cystitis and other diseases of the bladder may require gynecological treatment. Surgery constitutes a large part of gynecological practice, and includes such im-

portant operations as hysterectomy, removal of the uterus. See REPRODUCTIVE SYSTEM; URINE AND THE URINARY SYSTEM.

GYÖR (Ger. *Raab*), a city of Hungary, 67 miles W.N.W. of Budapest, at the confluence of the Raab R. with a tributary of the Danube. Györ is a market for the cereal grains, hogs, and horses of the surrounding agricultural area, and contains industrial establishments producing textiles, alcoholic beverages, brick, matches, chemicals, and agricultural implements. The city is a Roman Catholic bishopric. Györ was built on the ruins of the Roman *Arabona*. It was captured by the Turks in 1594, but held by them only until 1598. The city has served throughout history as a gateway to both the east and west. Pop. (1941) 57,192.

GYPAËTUS. See LAMMERGEIER.

GYPSIES, a nomadic people, found in every part of Europe, most of w. Asia, N. Africa, the Americas, and Australia. The origin of the Gypsies is obscure, but it is now generally believed that they came from southeastern or central India, migrating by way of the foothills of the Himalayas and reaching Persia about the beginning of the 10th century A.D. There they divided into two groups, the Bhen or Bheni, who gave rise to the north African and Asiatic Gypsies, and the Phen, who gave rise to the Bosa of Armenia and the south Caucasian regions, and to the Byzantine Gypsies, from whom are descended all the groups of Gypsies in Europe and America. The first Gypsies appeared in Europe at the beginning of the 14th century, and became peddlers and smiths.

The names by which the Gypsies are known in the various countries in which many of them have settled reflect the popular confusion about their origins. The Balkan groups are known by variations of the name *Atsinkanoi* ("touch-me-not's"), given by early Byzantine writers. This name developed into *Atsigan* or *Atzigan*, which becomes in German, *Zigeuner;* in Italian, *Zingari;* and *Tshingian* in Turkey and Greece. The other tribes are called by variants of the word *Egyptian* (ethnologists believe that the original Gypsies confused Armenia with Egypt, and considered themselves natives of the latter country). The English *Gypsy*, and *Gitano* in Spanish and *Gyphtos* in modern Greek, are some of the variants. Similar terms are the Hungarian *Pharao Nephka* and the Romanian *Faraon,* meaning Pharaoh's people. Other names by which they are known include *Bohemiens* (in France), Tartars, Saracens, Nubians, and heathens. In speaking of themselves, the European Gypsies use the word *Rom,* the Syrian use *Dom,* and the Armenian use *Lom.*

The Gypsies have been persecuted wherever they have wandered, and have been accused of crimes ranging from petty thievery to witchcraft and cannibalism. Following an Act of 1531, during the reign of Henry VIII, Gypsies in England lived in the fear of having their goods seized by any sheriff or justice, who kept half for himself and gave half to the king's exchequer. They were also condemned to banishment unless they were willing to settle down. In Poland, Hungary, Lithuania, Venice, and probably Scotland, they were placed under the rule of a local nobleman who, in return for his protection, had the right to tax them twice a year. This form of slavery was abolished in Hungary in 1781 and in Romania in 1866. In modern times in Germany the Gypsies have been subjected to much suffering; measures were enacted against them in 1906 and 1907, and during the Nazi regime (1933–45) many male Gypsies were sterilized and both sexes were set to forced labor.

The Gypsies accept the religion of the peoples among whom they move, mixing with it the mythologies which they have picked up in their wanderings. Their acceptance of the local religion does not, however, extend to all the practices of that religion, for example, to a church wedding. Their social customs do not prohibit the marriage of near relatives, but there have been no signs of degeneration from such marriages, possibly because only a virile male is likely to be allowed to purchase a desirable bride. While in England and America there is some male ascendancy, on the continent of Europe the organization of the family remains matriarchal; the woman plays the larger part in the support of the group, principally by means of her fortune-telling, in which she employs various forms of prediction, ranging from tea leaves to the tarot pack of cards. The Gypsy chief, however, is almost always a male, who is chosen for his ability as a leader, though often he inherits the position in direct line of descent. In America the head of the Kris, or Gypsy court, deals with all major questions affecting tribal matters.

The Gypsies of Central Europe are skillful craftsmen, and do much work in copper. They are said to have introduced the violin into Europe and are famous as performers

upon it; however, the statement of Franz von Liszt that they originated all Hungarian music is without foundation.

As a persecuted group the Gypsies have always remained isolated. Under present-day conditions it seems likely that increasing numbers, freed from persecution, will forsake their nomadic habits and that they may gradually disappear as a separate ethnic group. At the present time ethnologists estimate their total numbers to be about 2,000,000.

Language. The language of the Gypsies, called by them Romany, belongs to the Indo-European family; it is one of the clearest indications of the origins of the Gypsies, for all its dialects are clearly connected with Sanskrit, the oldest-known written language of the Indo-European family. The fact, also, that it shows grammatical and phonetic changes which the other Indian languages exhibited about the beginning of the Christian Era, demonstrates that the Gypsies did not leave the country of their origin before then. As it is not known whether all the Gypsies left India at the same time or in separate migrations, it is impossible to say by what means the three major dialects developed. These dialects, the Asiatic, the Armenian, and the European, show marked differences in the treatment of the voiced aspirates. Thus the Sanskrit *gh* becomes *g* in the Asiatic Romany, while in Armenian and European forms it is *kh,* shortened to *k'.* Within these groups there is such vast diversity of minor dialects that one may find, as in Wales, a practically pure Indian idiom, although a comparatively short distance away the dialect consists of the English language merely sprinkled with Romany words.

In the course of their wanderings the Gypsies have adopted words from each country through which they have passed, so that, for example, among the Gypsies of Wales, the dialect contains words originating in Persia, Armenia, Greece, Bulgaria, Serbia, Germany, Romania, France, and England. Some indication of the time spent in each place can be gained from a count of the number of words of each language that appear in Romany. Such a count indicates that the greatest number of words so introduced are of Greek origin.

While the Gypsies do not possess an alphabet or a written literature, they possess a vast body of folklore, largely Indo-European in its origins and probably connected with the fertility and protective rituals which still survive among them.

GYPSOPHILA. See BABY'S-BREATH.

GYPSUM, a common mineral consisting of hydrated calcium sulfate; $CaSO_4 \cdot 2H_2O$. It is a widely distributed form of sedimentary rock, formed by the precipitation of calcium sulfate from sea water, and is frequently associated with other saline deposits, such as halite and anhydrite, as well as with limestone and shale. Gypsum is produced in volcanic regions by the action of sulfuric acid on calcium-containing minerals, and it is also found in most clays as a product of the action of sulfuric acid on limestone. It occurs in all parts of the world; some of the best workable deposits are in France, Switzerland, and Mexico, and in California, Ohio, Michigan, and Utah in the United States. Alabaster, selenite (qq.v.), and satin spar are varieties of gypsum.

Artificial gypsum is obtained as a by-product in an old method for the manufacture of phosphoric acid. Phosphate rock, the essential constituent of which is tricalcium phosphate, is treated with sulfuric acid, producing phosphoric acid and gypsum. The gypsum is compacted into blocks and used for construction of nonsupporting walls in buildings. By properly controlling the concentration and temperature of sulfuric acid added to phosphate rock, a mixture of monocalcium phosphate, dicalcium phosphate, and gypsum may be obtained. This mixture is the valuable fertilizer, superphosphate (q.v.).

Gypsum crystallizes in the monoclinic system in white or colorless crystals, massive or foliated in formation. Many specimens of gypsum are colored green, yellow, or black by impurities. It is soft enough to scratch with a fingernail (hardness ranges from 1.5 to 2), and has a specific gravity of 2.3. When heated to 128° C. (262.4° F.), gypsum loses part of its water of hydration and is converted into plaster of Paris, $CaSO_4 \cdot \frac{1}{2}H_2O$. Finely ground plaster of Paris, when moistened with water, sets in a short time into a hard mass of gypsum, the rehydrated crystals forming and interlocking in such a way that there is expansion in volume.

In a recent postwar year over five and a half million tons of mineral gypsum were produced in this country and one and a half million tons were imported. By far the greatest amount of gypsum is used in the calcined state, known as plaster of Paris, by the building industry.

Because of its property of swelling and filling all interstices upon drying, plaster of Paris is used extensively in making casts for statuary, ceramics, dental plates, fine metal parts for precision instruments, and surgical splints. Uncalcined gypsum is used as a fertilizer in the form of land plaster for arid, alkaline soil. It is also used as a bed for polishing plate glass and as a basis for paint pigments. Large amounts of gypsum are used as a retarder in Portland cement (q.v.).

GYPSY MOTH, a large Old World moth, *Porthetria dispar,* of the family Liparidae, accidentally introduced about 1868 into New England, where the ravenous, orchard-destroying larvae became a serious economic menace. Initially confined to the New England area, the gypsy moth recently invaded other northeastern States. The spread of the insect is ascribed to hurricanes which struck the Atlantic seaboard in the 1950's. It is believed that the heavy winds carried debris laden with gypsy-moth eggs southward and westward of their original habitat.

The gypsy moth is closely related to the brown-tail moth and the tussock moth, both of which are similarly destructive. The adult female gypsy moth is white with dark wing markings. The wing span is about two and one-half inches. The female has a heavy body and rarely flies, despite well-developed wings. Throughout her adult life span, the female gypsy moth remains near the pupal shell from which she emerged. The adult male is olive brown with dark wing markings, and, though a powerful flier, has much smaller wings than the female.

The yellow eggs, which measure a twentieth of an inch in diameter, are deposited in masses numbering from less than 200 to more than 1000, and are covered with buff-colored scales from the abdomen of the adult female. The larvae occasionally appear within a few weeks, but more often they hatch in the following spring. The larvae are yellow, with long hairs, and have four longitudinal rows of colored tubercles. One tubercle from each row appears on each of the larval segments, those on the anterior segments being blue and those behind being red. The caterpillars devour the foliage of numerous trees, especially of oaks and birches.

Because repeated defoliation kills the trees, State authorities in infested areas have instituted intensive control measures, including the use of airplanes to spray the trees with D.D.T. in May, when the eggs hatch. The Department of Agriculture directs its efforts toward preventing the spread of the gypsy moth into other areas. See ENTOMOLOGY, ECONOMIC.

GYROMANCY. See SUPERSTITION.

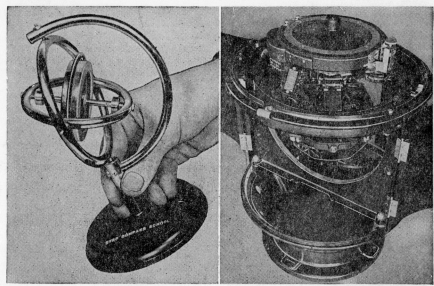

Sperry Gyroscope **Co.**

Left: A simple model which illustrates the principles of the gyroscope. Right: Complex gyrocompass of the type used aboard a ship, with casing opened to show the inner parts.

GYROSCOPE, any rotating body which exhibits two fundamental properties: *gyroscopic inertia,* or rigidity in space, and *precession,* the tilting of the axis at right angles to any force tending to alter the plane of rotation. These properties actually are inherent in all rotating bodies, including the earth itself. The term "gyroscope" is commonly applied to spherical, wheel-shaped, or disk-shaped bodies which are universally mounted so that they are free to rotate in any direction. Such bodies can be used either to demonstrate these properties or to serve the important purpose of enabling man to sense his movements in space. A gyroscope which is constrained from moving around one axis other than the axis of rotation is sometimes referred to as a *gyrostat.* Actually, however, in nearly all of its practical applications, the gyroscope is so constrained or controlled, and it is customary to prefix the word "gyro" to the name of the particular application, as, for instance, gyrocompass, gyrostabilizer, gyropilot, and gyrosyn compass.

Gyroscopic Inertia. The "rigidity in space" of a gyroscope is a consequence of Newton's first law of motion, which states that a body tends to continue in its state of rest or uniform motion unless subject to outside forces. Thus, the wheel of a gyroscope, when started spinning, tends to continue to rotate in the same plane about the same axis in space. An

example of this tendency is a spinning top which has freedom about two axes in addition to the spinning axis. Another example is a rifle bullet which, because it spins or revolves in flight, exhibits gyroscopic inertia, tending to maintain a straighter line of flight than it would if not rotating. Rigidity in space can best be demonstrated, however, by means of a model gyroscope consisting of a flywheel supported in rings in such a way that the axle of the flywheel can assume any angle in space. When the flywheel is spinning, the model can be moved about, tipped or turned, at the will of the demonstrator; but the flywheel will maintain its original plane of rotation as long as it continues to spin with sufficient velocity to overcome the friction between itself and its supporting bearings.

Precession. When a force applied to a gyroscope tends to change the direction of the axis of rotation, the axis will move in a direction at right angles to the direction in which the force is applied. This motion is the resultant of the force produced by the angular momentum of the rotating body and the applied force. A simple example of precession can be seen in the rolling hoop: to cause the hoop to turn a corner, guiding pressure is not applied to the front or rear of the hoop as might be expected, but against the top. This pressure, though applied about a horizontal axis, does not cause the hoop to fall over, but causes it to precess about the vertical axis at right angles to the applied pressure, with the result that it turns and proceeds in a new direction.

Applications of the Gyroscope. By utilizing the characteristic of gyroscopic inertia and applying the force of gravity to cause precession, the gyroscope can be made use of as a directional indicator or compass. Briefly, if we consider a gyroscope as mounted at the earth's equator with its spinning axis lying in the east-west plane, the gyro will continue to point along this line as the earth rotates, because of "rigidity in space". For the same reason, the east end will rise (in relation to the earth) although it continues to point the same way in space. By attaching a tube partially filled with mercury to the frame of the gyro assembly in such a way that the tube tilts as the gyro axle tilts, we can take advantage of the effect of gravity about the horizontal axis of the gyro. In other words, the weight of the mercury on the west or low side applies a force about the horizontal axis of the gyro. The gyro resists this force and *precesses* about the vertical axis toward the meridian. In the gyrocompass the controlling forces are applied automatically in just the right direction and proportion to cause the gyro axle to seek and hold the true meridian, i.e., to point north and south.

Gyrocompasses are used in naval vessels and merchant fleets all over the world. They are free from the vagaries of the magnetic compass; they indicate true, geographic north rather than magnetic north, and they have sufficient directive force to make practicable the operation of accessory equipment such as course recorders, gyropilots, and repeater compasses. The marine gyropilot has no gyroscope, but picks up electrically any divergence from the set course reference supplied by the gyrocompass; these signals are amplified and applied to the ship's steering engine to cause the rudder to return the ship to its proper course.

Aircraft automatic pilots or gyropilots generally employ two gyroscopes, one of which supplies the directional reference, the other

the pitch and bank reference (longitudinal and lateral). A sensitive pick-off system (see SERVOMECHANISMS) detects the angular divergencies of the airplane from the gyro references and converts them into corrective movements of the rudder, ailerons, and elevators.

Flight instruments such as the artificial horizon, the directional gyro, the gyrosyn compass, and the turn-and-bank indicator employ single gyroscopes. The artificial horizon spins with its axis vertical and supplies the pilot with a pitch-and-bank reference in the form of a gyro-actuated horizon bar observed in relation to a miniature airplane on the dial of the instrument. The directional gyro spins about a horizontal axis. This is one of the few gyroscopic instruments that functions on the principle of rigidity in space alone, i.e., like a free, unconstrained gyroscope. For this reason it is subject to wander or drift, and must be checked, and reset if necessary, at frequent intervals. The gyrosyn compass, unlike the directional gyro, is north *seeking*. It is in effect a gyro-stabilized magnetic compass. The turn-and-bank indicator is a primary flight instrument used in every airplane. This instrument employs the precessional forces of the gyroscope to actuate an indicator that shows the pilot his rate of turn.

During World War II, a successful gunsight was developed for antiaircraft guns in naval vessels. Two gyroscopes are used, one for tracking in azimuth, the other for elevation. As the gun pointer swings his gun to keep the target in the sight, the gyros precess and control the sighting mechanism in such a way that the gun is automatically set ahead with the proper amount of lead to cause the projectile to intercept the target.

A supersensitive gyroscope, many times more accurate than conventional instruments, was recently developed for use in automatic flight of supersonic aircraft and guided missiles. According to reports issued in 1954, the new instrument is capable of detecting very slow motion through angles as small as .00003°.

H, aitch, the eighth letter in the English and Latin alphabets. Originally the letter derived from the Semitic Ⱶ , *cheth,* which was adopted into the Phenician alphabet as Ⱶ In Greek in the form of H, *eta,* the letter corresponded to the sound of a long *e,* but in the Semitic, eastern Greek, and Latin alphabets it represented the sound of aspiration or rough breathing which is the sound value which it usually retains in modern English. In some English words, such as honor, the H is silent. The letter also combines into digraphs with other consonants to form various consonant sounds: *gh* as in laugh; *ph* as in telegraph; *rh* as in Rhine; *th* as in then or thin; *sh* as in should; *ch* as chorus, chill, or chauvinism; and *wh* as in where. In the Romance languages, Italian, French, Spanish, and Portuguese, H is silent. This difference in English and Romance pronunciation is reflected in such forms of uncultured English speech as the cockney in which the H is pronounced in words like *hour* and *heir* and is dropped from words like *habit* and *home.*

In music H is used in orchestral scores as an abbreviation for *horns.* German musical notation employs H as a symbol for *B natural.* This usage dates back to a time when a rounded capital B was used to indicate *B flat* and a square B, ⏢, to indicate *B natural.* The German use of H is a corruption of the latter form.

In medieval Latin H was employed as the symbol for 200 in the Roman numeral system. The form H̄ was also used for 200,000.

The letter, usually in the form of a qualifying noun, also denotes an object having the shape of a capital H, as in *H-beam* or *H-frame.*

As an abbreviation H is used to denote the element hydrogen in chemistry; the *henry,* the magnetic unit of flux intensity, in physics; the horizontal component of the earth's magnetism in terrestrial magnetism; and a particular Fraunhofer line in the calcium spectrum in spectroscopy. In military usage H. or Hq. are employed as abbreviations for *headquarters.* The capital H is also an abbreviation for various Christian names, such as Henry and Helen. The small or lower case h is used in the metric system as an abbreviation for *hecto-* (hundred) and in modern physics as the symbol for Planck's constant. For H-hour, see D-DAY.

HAAKON, name of seven kings of Norway, most important of whom are the following.

1. HAAKON I, called THE GOOD (914?-61), king from 935, the natural son of Harold Haarfager. He was raised in the Christian religion by King Athelstan of England. On the death of his father in 933 Haakon sailed with a fleet provided by King Athelstan to Norway to depose his half brother Eric Bloodaxe, who had seized the Norwegian throne. Gaining the aid of the landowners by granting them tax concessions on inherited property, Haakon drove Eric from Norway and established himself as king in 935. He consistently suppressed the attempts of Eric's sons to dethrone him, but was killed during the final battle which established his victory over them. Although he introduced Christian influences into his country, he was unable to install Christianity as the official religion of Norway.

2. HAAKON IV HAAKONSSON, called THE OLD (1204-63), king from 1217, believed to be the

Norwegian Official Photo

King Haakon VII of Norway

natural son of King Haakon III. He remained under the protection of his predecessor King Inge from the age of one until the death of Inge in 1217. His illegitimate birth delayed papal recognition of his kingship and his coronation until 1247. During part of the period between his accession and coronation Earl Skule acted as regent for Haakon, but the latter had his regent killed in 1240 for plotting against him. Haakon acquired Iceland and Greenland in 1262, and in 1263 conducted a successful war with the Scots, confirming Norwegian possession of disputed territory in w. Scotland.

3. HAAKON VI MAGNUSSON (1339–80), king from 1355, the son of King Magnus VII. During the regency of his father, between 1343 and 1355, he was nominal king, and in 1355 he was crowned. He also ruled Sweden for a year after the dethronement of his father in 1362. From 1363 until 1371 he conducted a war with Sweden. In 1363 he married Margaret, daughter of King Waldemar IV of Denmark, and their son Olaf became king of both Denmark and Norway, providing a basis for the Union of Kalmar (see DENMARK: *History*).

4. HAAKON VII, originally CARL (1872–), king from 1905, the son of King Frederick VIII of Denmark. He was unanimously chosen king of Norway by the Storting, or

Norwegian parliament, and confirmed in the kingship by a plebiscite of the Norwegian people. In the following year, 1906, he was crowned at Trondheim. When Germany invaded Norway in 1940, during World War II, King Haakon led the resistance to the Nazis for two months and then went to England to continue resistance operations (see NORWAY: *History*). He conducted the affairs of the Norwegian government-in-exile until the defeat of the Nazis in the spring of 1945, when he returned to Norway to resume his royal duties.

HAARLEM, capital of the province of North Holland, Netherlands, situated on the Spaarne R., 12 miles w. of Amsterdam. A notable building in the city is St. Bravo's Church, or the Groote, built in the 15th century, and containing an organ with 5000 pipes, one of the largest instruments of its kind in the world. Before the church stands a statue of Laurens Janszoon Coster, to whom his countrymen ascribe the invention of printing. The town hall, formerly the residence of the counts of Holland, contains canvases by the celebrated Dutch painter Frans Hals, and a valuable collection of early printed works. Other buildings of note are the Dutch Society of Sciences, and the Pavilion, a château in Italian style containing an industrial art museum.

The chief industries in Haarlem are printing, type casting, brewing, bleaching, dyeing, and the manufacture of cotton goods, paint, and railway cars. In addition, extensive horticultural activity makes Haarlem the center of a prosperous trade in bulbs, notably tulips and hyacinths. Haarlem took a prominent part in the revolt of the Netherlands against Spanish rule. In 1572 the city was besieged by a Spanish army of 30,000 men, and after a resistance of seven months, was compelled to capitulate. Four years later William of Orange delivered Haarlem from the Spanish tyranny, and incorporated the city into the United Netherlands. Pop. (1953 est.) 164,974.

HÁBA, ALOIS (1893–), Czech composer, born in Vyzovice. He is known as one of the world's foremost exponents of the fractional-tone systems. Hába studied composition with Vítězslev Novák at the Prague Conservatoire and continued his musical education in Vienna and Berlin. While still a boy, his interests in Moravian folk music and his attempts to duplicate the melodic nuances of the peasant musicians led to his studies in quarter-tones and his development of the sixth and twelfth tones. He composed many works, some of the best known being the operas *The Mother, The Unemployed,* and *New Earth.* In 1924 he was appointed teacher at the Prague Conservatoire.

HABAKKUK, one of the twelve minor prophets of the Old Testament. He appears as a prophet of Judah, announcing the divine chastisement which is to come upon his nation at the hands of the Chaldeans. He was the first of the prophets who saw in the victory of Carchemish (Circesium), in the fourth year of Jehoiakim, the fall of the Egyptian supremacy before Babylon. His period is thus fixed in the last decade of the 7th century B.C. The keynote of the whole prophecy is the sentence in 2:4: "the just shall live by his faith", quoted by St. Paul in Rom. 1:17 and Gal. 3:11.

HABANA. See HAVANA.

HABANERA (Sp., "of Havana"), Cuban dance in duple time characterized by the insistent rhythmic phrase of a dotted eighth note followed by a sixteenth and two eighth notes. The dance is also known as the *contradanza criolla* (Creole country dance). It is commonly assumed by musicologists to have been introduced into Cuba by the African Negroes and later to have become popular in Spain. The Habanera was made world-famous by the French composer Georges Bizet, who utilized this dance in the first act of his opera *Carmen.*

HABEAS CORPUS (Lat., "[that] you have the body"), in U.S. and English law, a writ issued by a court commanding a person having custody of another under the claim of law to produce the detained person for the purpose of determining the legality of his detention. The writ of habeas corpus is of ancient English origin, and its original purpose was to liberate illegally detained persons. The earliest use of the writ as a constitutional remedy against the tyranny of the crown took place in the latter part of the 16th century, when it was applied in behalf of persons committed to prison by the Privy Council.

Many ways of avoiding the effectiveness of the writ were subsequently developed. In a case in 1627 the judges decided that a return to a writ of habeas corpus which set forth that the prisoner was detained by warrant of the Privy Council was a sufficient answer to the writ. In 1641 Parliament, by legislation abolishing the Star Chamber (q.v.), endeavored to increase the effectiveness of the writ. This law provided that persons imprisoned by a court exercising jurisdiction similar to the Star Chamber, or by command of the king or of his privy council, should be granted a writ of habeas corpus without delay; and that the court was to determine within three days after the return of the writ the legality of such commitment. The subsequent refusal of judges

to issue writs of habeas corpus during vacation periods resulted in the passage by Parliament of the Habeas Corpus Act of 1679. That statute imposed severe penalties on any judge who refused without good cause to entertain the writ, and upon any officer or other person who failed to comply with it. After this date the authority of the court was paramount to any order of the sovereign, and the writ became a powerful weapon for the protection of the liberty of the king's subjects. The statute, however, dealt only with imprisonment for criminal offenses, and it was not until 1816 that its benefits were extended to persons detained in England on other grounds.

In the United States the remedy of habeas corpus is established by both Federal and State constitutions. The Constitution of the United States provides that the privilege of the writ of habeas corpus shall not be suspended except in cases of rebellion or invasion, when the public safety may require it. The constitutions of most States contain similar provisions, and in some States suspension of the writ is forbidden in any case. The State of Massachusetts suspended the privilege of the writ from November, 1786, to July, 1787, on the occasion of Shays' Rebellion (q.v.). The outstanding instance in the United States of the suspension of the right of habeas corpus occurred in 1861 during the Civil War, when Abraham Lincoln suspended it by Presidential proclamation. In 1863 Congress explicitly empowered Lincoln to suspend the privilege of

Amsterdam Gate in Haarlem, the Netherlands

the writ during the war. In recent years the courts in several States have suspended the privilege when State executives have declared martial law during strikes. See MARTIAL LAW.

In the United States the writ was originally limited to cases of illegal imprisonment but its use was subsequently extended, and it now is also applicable to controversies in divorce and adoption proceedings involving the custody of infants. The basis for such applications of the writ is the assumption of a right in the State, paramount to any parental or other claims, to dispose of children as their best interests require.

Both the Federal and State courts issue writs of habeas corpus. The Federal courts, however, can issue such writs only under given conditions, as when a prisoner is detained by order of the Federal government, or has been committed for trial before a Federal court. They can also issue writs of habeas corpus when a charge against a prisoner is in respect of an act done in pursuance of a Federal law or order of a Federal court, or when his detention is alleged to be in violation of the Federal Constitution or of a law or treaty of the United States. The jurisdiction of the Federal courts in this regard extends to a foreigner, if he has acted under the authority of his own government, so that his guilt or liability must be determined by international law. The State courts may issue the writ in all cases which do not fall exclusively under the jurisdiction of the United States courts.

Protection against arbitrary imprisonment by the right of habeas corpus is not found in continental Europe. It has been adopted in many Latin American countries, either by constitutional provision or statutory enactment, but has frequently been abrogated in practice during the many political and social upheavals which have occurred in those countries.

HABER, FRITZ (1868–1934), German chemist, born at Breslau, and educated at the universities of Berlin, Heidelberg, and Charlottenburg. He taught chemistry at the Hochschule at Karlsruhe from 1896 to 1911; thereafter he served as director of the Kaiser Wilhelm Institute for Physical Chemistry at Berlin. He did research in electrochemistry and on thermodynamic gas reactions. He is best known for his invention of a process, called the Haber process, for synthesizing ammonia directly from nitrogen and hydrogen; see NITROGEN FIXATION. He was awarded the 1918 Nobel prize for chemistry.

HABIMA THEATRE, Hebrew-language theatrical group, organized in Moscow, Russia, soon after the revolution of 1905. The noted Russian actor and producer Stanislavski (1863–1938) was adviser to the new troupe. In 1911 persecutions by the Czarist regime forced the Habima to suspend public performances. After the collapse (1917) of the Czarist government, the company again appeared publicly. In 1926, while on a world tour, the Habima troupe presented several plays in repertory at the Jolson Theatre in New York City. One of its best-known productions was *The Dybbuk,* a drama based on an old Jewish folk tale. The company removed to Tel-Aviv, Palestine (now Israel) in 1929, and there it became the leading theatrical group in the country.

HABINGTON, WILLIAM (1605–54), British poet, born in Worcestershire, and educated at the college at St. Omer. His most celebrated works are the collection of lyrical poems, *Castara* (1634), addressed to his wife, and *The Queene of Arragon,* (1640) a tragicomedy. Habington also wrote *Historie of Edward the Fourth* (1640) and *Observations upon History* (1641).

HABIT, in psychology, a fixed tendency acquired by an organism during its lifetime. Formerly, academic and philosophical psychologists drew a broad distinction between habit, which is acquired after birth, and instincts and reflexes (qq.v.), which are congenital. With the development of the dynamic point of view in psychology and the dramatic presentation by Ivan Pavlov (q.v.) of the conditioned-reflex mechanisms, in the early part of the 20th century, psychologists have tended to limit use of the term "habit", replacing it in specific applications by more exact terminology. In describing what they once termed the "accident habit", for example, they have come to speak of "accident proneness". Medical psychologists have tended to replace the term "habit spasm", an involuntary twitching of a part of the body, by the term "tic". Such phenomena as tics and stuttering, sometimes described as habits, are now regarded as neuroses or as symptoms of neuroses. See PSYCHOLOGY, ABNORMAL.

HABITATION. See HOUSE.

HABITUAL CRIMINAL, in criminal law, an individual subject to increased punishment for the commission of a crime because of previous conviction for a criminal offense or offenses. The number of offenses that must have been committed before an individual is subject to such increased punishment is regulated by State statutes. In some States the statutes fix three convictions as the minimum number required to constitute one a habitual criminal or offender. In other States, one previous conviction of a felony or five convictions of a misdemeanor warrant a judgment of habitual criminality. The statutes of a particular jurisdiction fix the punishment to be inflicted on a convicted defendant who is adjudged to be an habitual criminal. In general, such statutes provide for a penalty equal to double or treble that imposed for a first offense.

HABSBURG. See HAPSBURG.

HACHIOJI, a city in Tokyo Prefecture, central Honshu Island, Japan, 23 miles s.w. of Tokyo. Hachioji is an important center of the silk industry. Pop. (1947) 72,947.

HACKBERRY. See CELTIDACEAE.

HACKEE, a name for the chipmunk (q.v.).

HACKENSACK, county seat of Bergen Co., N.J., situated on the Hackensack R., 13 miles N. of Jersey City. It is served by two railroads, and maintains a municipal airport. Although the city is principally a residential community, it contains factories manufacturing chemicals, paperboard, and airplane parts, and is the business center of an area with a population of more than 400,000. Hackensack was first settled by the Dutch about 1640, and the Huguenots settled there in 1678. It was occupied alternately by the British and Americans during the Revolutionary War. Hackensack was incorporated in 1868 and chartered as a city in 1933. Pop. (1950) 29,219.

HACKETT, JAMES HENRY (1800–71), American actor, born in New York City. He started his career on the stage in 1826, and soon became popular in eccentric comedy roles. His best-known role was that of the Shakespearean character Falstaff. He toured the United States and England, and managed several theaters in addition to acting. He was the author of *Notes and Comments on Shakespeare* (1863).

HACKETT, JAMES KETELTAS (1869–1926), American actor and manager, born at Wolfe Island, Ontario, and educated at the College of the City of New York. He was leading man at the Lyceum Theatre in New York City from 1896 to 1899. Afterwards he became an independent theatrical manager. Plays in which he appeared include *The Prisoner of Zenda* (1896), *Rupert of Hentzau* (1898). *The Pride of Jennico* (1900), *Don Caesar's Return* (1901), *The Crisis* (1902), *The Walls of Jericho* (1906), *Samson* (1909), and *The Grain of Dust* (1912).

HACKMATACK. See LARCH.

HADDINGTONSHIRE. See EAST LOTHIAN.

HADDO, the humpbacked salmon. See DOG SALMON.

HADDOCK, a marine gadid fish, *Gadus aeglefinus*, in the genus containing the cod, differing from the cod in its smaller mouth, longer anterior dorsal fin, and in the black line which runs along its side. It is about 2 ft. long and has a brown back and silvery underside; a black spot is located on each side, behind the gills. It feeds on shellfish, and is abundant in the North Atlantic Ocean from Iceland to Cape Hatteras. The haddock is an important food fish; it is frequently sold smoked, when it is known as *finnan haddie*, or dried.

HADEN, SIR FRANCIS SEYMOUR (1818–1910), British etcher, writer, and surgeon, born in London, and educated at University College, London, the medical school at the Sorbonne, and at Grenoble. He became a member of the Royal College of Surgeons in 1852 and a fellow in 1857. He developed the operation of ovariotomy, and founded a hospital for incurables in London. He is best known, however, as an artist, and he is considered one of the most important masters of the art of etching. His landscapes reveal poetic expression and are noteworthy for their broad freedom of style. In addition to more than two hundred etchings, Haden also produced mezzotint engravings and watercolor paintings. Among his best-known writings are *About Etching* (1879) and *The Etched Work of Rembrandt True and False* (1895). He was also founder and president of the Royal Society of Painters, Etchers, and Engravers. The finest collections of Haden's works are in the British Museum, the Metropolitan Museum, New York City, and the New York Public Library. He was knighted in 1894.

HADENDOA, an African people of Hamitic stock (see HAMITES), dwelling between the Red Sea and the Nile R. An important division of the Beja (q.v.), the Hadendoa speak a Beja dialect, and include the Ashraf, Amarar, Artega, and Nurab tribes.

HADES, in Greek mythology, the god of the underworld, the son of Cronus and Rhea, and brother of Zeus and Poseidon. Hades, also named Pluto (q.v., "giver of wealth"), possibly through confusion with a fertility god, was represented as grim, gloomy, and devoid of compassion. A magic helmet, which he received from the huge, one-eyed Cyclops, made him invisible. Out of fear, he was customarily referred to by such respectful titles as Eubulus (the bestower of good counsel), Polydectes (the taker of many), and Clymenus (the distinguished one). In writers after Homer, Hades is employed to denote the realm of the divinity, called by the earlier poets "House of Hades". The Greek conceptions of this region varied greatly. According to general belief, it was in the depths of the earth. Another view, however, notably that expressed in Homer's *Odyssey*, placed the home of the dead in the far west, the region of sunset and night. Wherever situated, Hades was depicted as a melancholy region, with its wide gates ever open to receive the shades, but closely guarded by the hideous three-headed dog Cerberus, who kept all from returning to the upper world. In the joyless meadow of asphodels in Hades the shades wandered forlornly. In this realm of the dead flowed with a mournful thunder the rivers Styx (Cold), Acheron (Woe), Cocytus (Lamentation), and Phlegethon (Blazing). In the Septuagint, the Greek version of the Old Testament, Hades is the translation of the Hebrew *Sheol*, the abode of the dead, in which sense it occurs frequently in the New Testament. See HELL.

HADFIELD, SIR ROBERT ABBOTT (1858–1940), English metallurgist, born in Sheffield, and educated at Sheffield Collegiate School. He became interested in metallurgy at an early age, and developed many important metallurgical processes. He is best known for his invention in 1883 of a method for manufacturing manganese steel, the first steel alloy to be both hard and ductile. Hadfield was director of several large metallurgical companies. He was knighted in 1908, became a fellow of the Royal Society in 1909, and was created a baronet in 1917. His book, *Metallurgy and Its Influence on Modern Progress* (1925), is a standard reference work.

HADHRAMAUT, coastal district of eastern Aden (q.v.) Protectorate, s. Arabia, extending along the Gulf of Aden, and comprising the Kathiri State of Seiyun and the Qu'aiti State of Shihr and Mukalla. In addition to the coastal plain, about 30 m. wide, the Hadhramaut contains an interior plateau. Though the Hadhramaut is for the most part barren, a number of its valleys yield a luxuriant vegetation. The main crops are dates, millet, wheat, coffee, and a fine tobacco called *hummi*. Mukalla (pop. in 1946, 20,000) is the capital of the Qu'aiti State; Seiyun (pop. in 1946, 9707) is the capital of the Kathiri State.

Exports include tobacco, coffee, and salt; the chief imports are cotton goods, coal, fuel oil, and foodstuffs. Archeological researches disclose that the Hadhramaut was the site of a highly developed civilization in ancient times. Area, about 60,000 sq.m.

HADLEY, ARTHUR TWINING (1856–1930), American economist and educator, son of James Hadley, born at New Haven, Conn., and educated at Yale University and the University of Berlin. He taught at Yale, starting as a tutor in 1879 and becoming a professor of political science in 1886. He was commissioner of labor statistics for the state of Connecticut between 1885 and 1887. From 1899 to 1921 Hadley was president of Yale University. He wrote *Railroad Transportation* (1885), *Economics* (1896), *Standards of Political Morality* (1907), *Some Influences in Modern Philosophic Thought* (1913), and *The Conflict between Liberty and Equality*.

HADLEY, HENRY KIMBALL (1871–1937), American conductor and composer, born at Somerville, Mass. He received his early musical training from his father and later entered the New England Conservatory, where he studied with George Whitefield Chadwick. At the age of twenty-two he toured the U.S. as conductor of the Schirmer-Mapleson Opera Company. In 1909 he became the conductor of the Seattle Symphony Orchestra, and from 1911 to 1916 he conducted the San Francisco Symphony Orchestra. He was appointed associate conductor of the N.Y. Philharmonic Orchestra in 1920 and formed the Manhattan Symphony Orchestra in 1929. Among his best-known works are the symphony *The Four Seasons;* an orchestral rhapsody, *The Culprit Fay;* and the opera *Cleopatra's Night,* produced at the Metropolitan Opera House in 1920 and again in 1921.

HADRIAN, or ADRIAN (76–138 A.D.), Roman Emperor from 117. Under the emperors Nerva and Trajan he filled high offices of state. When Trajan died, Hadrian was proclaimed emperor both by the army and by the Roman senate. The Empire at the time was in an extremely critical state as a result of barbarian invasions and the revolts of subject peoples. Hadrian, realizing the necessity of consolidation, resolved to limit the boundaries of the Roman Empire in the E. and the W., and established the series of defensive fortifications (*limites*) which historically marked the end of Roman expansion. The emperor then strengthened his position at Rome by liberality toward the people, by generous support of poor children, and by his considerate attitude toward the senate. In 119 Hadrian set out on a grand tour of the Roman Empire, visiting Gaul, Germany, Britain (where he built the famous wall extending from Solway Firth to the mouth of the Tyne R.), Spain, Mauretania, Egypt, Asia Minor, and Greece. He returned to Rome in 126 or 127, where he received the title of *pater patriæ* (father of the country). Resuming his travels, he went to Athens, where he spent the years 132 and 133. He then went to Palestine to put down an insurrection of the Jews under Bar Cocheba. After visiting Syria, Hadrian returned to Italy and spent the last years of his life partly at Rome and partly at Tibur, the site of his palatial villa. He appointed Titus Aurelius Fulvus Boionius Arrius (afterward Emperor Antoninus Pius) as his successor.

HADRIAN'S WALL, an ancient Roman wall, 74 m. in length, traversing Britain from Solway Firth to the estuary of the Tyne River. Constructed about 120 A.D. by the Emperor Hadrian to protect the northern boundary of Roman Britain against the invasions of hostile tribes, the wall linked a series of heavily garrisoned forts and fortified sentry posts. It served also to demarcate the frontier of Roman civil jurisdiction. A military road ran alongside the fortifications. Vestiges of Hadrian's Wall are still extant.

HADROSAURUS, a genus of dinosaurs in the order Ornithischia, found fossil in Cretaceous rocks of the Laramie epoch in Wyoming. These large dinosaurs, which reached 35 ft. in length, were characterized by a flattened bill, resembling that of a duck, with which they grasped the marsh grass and other vegetation comprising their food. The bill, unlike that of a duck, contained many small teeth. Their hides were thick, but not covered by armor. Their heads were large, and their tails were thick and heavy. The hadrosaurs moved about on their thick, three-toed hind limbs; their forelimbs, which were five-toed, were small and weak.

HADRUMETUM, a city of ancient times, in N.E. Tunisia, North Africa, situated on the Gulf of Hammamet. A Phenician colony of even greater antiquity than Carthage, Hadrumetum in time became subservient to Carthage and fell together with that city under the sway of Rome. On the subdivision of the Roman province of Africa Propria, Hadrumetum became the capital of Byzacium, or Africa Byzacena. The Roman emperor Trajan made it a colony, called *Colonia Concordia Ulpia Traiana Augusta Frugifera Hadrume-*

Ernst Haeckel

tina. Following the devastation inflicted upon the city by the Vandals in 434, it was restored by the emperor Justinian, being known thereafter as Justinianopolis. The site of Hadrumetum is occupied in part by the modern town of Susa. Archeological excavations have disclosed extensive remains dating from the Carthaginian and the Roman periods.

HAECKEL, ERNST HEINRICH (1834–1919), German biologist and philosopher, born at Potsdam. He studied medicine and natural science at the universities of Berlin, Würzburg, and Vienna, and after practicing medicine for one year he turned to biology. Starting in 1861 he taught comparative anatomy and zoology as the University of Jena, where a chair in zoology was created especially for him in 1865. Haeckel made many expeditions for scientific study, and gathered material for a great number of monographs on descriptive and systematic zoology, including *Calcareous Sponges* (1872), *Siphonophora* (1869), and *Radiolaria* (1887). He was the first German biologist who wholeheartedly supported Darwin's doctrine of organic evolution, and his many books and lectures helped popularize Darwin's theories in Germany. In his *General Morphology* (1866) and *Natural History of Creation* (1868) Haeckel attempted to work out the practical applications of organic evolution. He stressed the biogenetic law (q.v.) that ontogeny recapitulates phylogeny, and from the biogenetic law he evolved the gastrea theory. Haeckel also made the first attempt to apply the doctrine of organic evolution to the whole field of morphology, and formulated a genealogical classification of the various orders of animals.

Haeckel attempted to apply the doctrine of evolution to philosophy and religion in *Die Welträtsel* (1899). Some of Haeckel's other books are *Die Systematische Phylogenie* (1894), *Anthropogenie* (1874), and *Der Kampf um den Entwickelungsgedanken* (1905).

HAEMANTHUS, genus of South African plants belonging to the Amaryllis family, commonly called blood lilies. *H. coccineus,* the common blood lily, has blood-red flowers in dense, globular clusters. *H. katherinae,* a closely related species with similar flowers, has leaves more than a foot long and more than six inches broad. Blood lilies are cultivated as potted house plants in the northern part of the United States.

HAEMODORACEAE, family of herbs, having fibrous roots and sword-shaped leaves, belonging to the Lily order. It contains about 50 species, most of which are native to the tropical regions of the Southern Hemisphere. Two genera, *Lachnanthes* and *Lophiola,* are native to the U.S. The common redroot (q.v.) is *Lachnanthes tinctoria.* The golden crest, *Lophiola aureus,* is a slender perennial bog plant which grows in eastern U.S. Its yellow, panicled flowers have perianth-lobes which are clothed at the base by woolly tufts or crests.

HAFIZ, pen name of SHAMS UD-DIN MO-HAMMED (d. about 1388), Persian lyric poet, born at Shiraz. At an early age he began the study of poetry and mystic philosophy, and joined an order of dervishes (q.v.). His studies won him the title of Hafiz ("one who remembers") applied to those who knew the Koran by heart. His most famous work was the *Divan,* a collection of short odes called *gazels.* Like most of his writings, its form is that of the rigid, artificial poetry of the period, but it is in content passionate and richly sensuous, dealing with love, wine, and the transitory quality of life. While some critics attribute to Hafiz's poetry only gaiety and surface luxuriance, comparing it to that of the Greek poet Anacreon (q.v.), others see a mystical, esoteric significance in his work. Hafiz wrote numerous other poems, including verses satirizing those of his associates who accused him of departing from the dervish's life of monastic asceticism and leading a dissipated existence. His tomb at Shiraz, which is adorned with one of his odes, is

visited by Persian pilgrims and by many foreign lovers of poetry.

HAFNIUM (Lat., "Copenhagen"), sometimes called celtium, an element, symbol Hf, atomic number 72, atomic weight 178.6, valence 4, m.p. 1700°C. (3092°F.), b.p. above 3200°C. (5792°F.), specific gravity 13. It was discovered in Copenhagen in 1923 by the Hungarian chemist Georg von Hevesy and the Dutch physicist Dirk Coster who, on the basis of Niels Bohr's prediction that element 72 would resemble zirconium in structure, looked for the element in zirconium ores. Hafnium is found in nearly all ores of zirconium, and is 47th in order of abundance of the elements in the earth's crust. It resembles zirconium so closely in chemical properties and crystal structure that separation of the two elements is extremely difficult. Separation is obtained most efficiently by means of the ion-exchange (q.v.) technique. Hafnium is used in the manufacture of tungsten filaments. In combination with zirconium it is under investigation (1954) as a possible structural material for atomic-power plants because of its high resistance to heat.

HAG, common name for a cyclostome, the hagfish (q.v.), or for a bird, the hagdon or shearwater (q.v.).

HAGAR, concubine of Abraham and mother of Ishmael. She was the handmaid of Sarah, Abraham's wife, but the latter remaining barren up to an advanced age, she consented to Hagar becoming her husband's concubine in the hope of establishing a family. She soon regretted her action and began to treat Hagar cruelly. To escape from Sarah's persecution, Hagar fled into the desert, but returned on being comforted by an angel, and bore Abraham a son who was called Ishmael. After the birth of Isaac Sarah urged Abraham to drive Hagar and Ishmael away, and, though reluctant to do so, the patriarch at God's command complied. The bondwoman and her son went again into the desert, where they were almost spent with famine when an angel appeared and prophesied greatness for Ishmael, and God showed Hagar a well of water.

The story of Hagar has been interpreted in various ways. Some commentators think that Hagar personifies a tribe that at one time stood in close relationship to some of the Hebrew clans. Rivalry ensued, and the result was a separation, which is pictured as a dismissal on the part of the clan regarding itself as the superior. The opposition between Israelites and Ishmaelites leads the Hebrew writers so to construct genealogical traditions as to make Ishmael the son of the "hand-maid", whereas Isaac is the offspring of the real wife, Sarah. As a justification for the separation of two nations having so much in common as Israel and Ishmael, it is represented that Hagar, though the inferior, attempted to gain the supremacy, and that Ishmael, the "inferior" offspring, failed to recognize the superiority of Isaac. The separation, which no doubt was voluntary on the part of the Ishmaelites, is therefore portrayed as a deliberate act of dismissal on the part of Abraham, in whom the genealogical traditions of Hebrews and Arabs are thus made to unite.

The story of Hagar and Ishmael is introduced in the New Testament and in rabbinical literature. Hagar is contrasted with Sarah allegorically by St. Paul (Gal. 4:22 et seq.), who makes Hagar, the bondwoman, represent the earthly Jerusalem, Sarah, who is free, the heavenly; Paul also contrasts Ishmael and Isaac in a similar way. A Jewish tradition identifies Hagar with Abraham's second wife, Keturah (Gen. 25:1), and another makes her the daughter of Pharaoh. The Mohammedans look upon Hagar as Abraham's true wife and upon Ishmael as the favorite son.

HAGDON. See SHEARWATER.

HAGEN, city of North Rhine-Westphalia, Germany, located at the confluence of the Ennepe and Volme rivers, 15 m. by rail N.E. of Elberfeld. The city has large iron and steel works. Among other important industries are cotton printing, sugar refining, brewing, distilling, and the manufacture of tobacco products, leather, and paper. Alabaster and limestone are quarried nearby. The city was included in the British Zone of Occupation following World War II. Pop. (1950) 146,099.

HAGEN, WALTER (1892–), American professional golf player, born at Rochester, N.Y. Among the numerous championships he won are the United States Open (1914 and 1919), the Professional Golfers' Association championship (1921, 1924, 1925, 1926, and 1927); and the British Open (1922, 1924, 1928, and 1929). One of his noteworthy feats was his defeat (1926) of the great American golfer Robert T. Jones, Jr. ("Bobby" Jones) in a challenge match in Florida. Hagen was a member of the United States Ryder Cup team in 1935; its captain (1927, 1929, 1931, and 1933); and its honorary captain (1937, 1941, and 1947). He retired from active competition in 1940. He is the author of *The Walter Hagen Story* (autobiography, 1956).

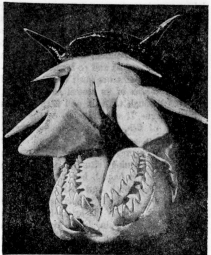

American Museum of Natural History
The mouth of a hagfish

HAGERSTOWN, county seat of Washington Co., Md., situated on Antietam Creek, 6 miles N. of its confluence with the Potomac R., and 72 miles W.N.W. of Baltimore. It is served by four railroads, and maintains a municipal airport. The city is the center of a fertile agricultural area, and is especially noted for its manufacturing industries. Among the industrial establishments in Hagerstown are a pipe-organ factory and a plant producing sand-blast-cleaning and dust-control equipment. Other industries in the city are the manufacture of aircraft, hosiery, shoes, dresses, furniture, fertilizers, leather and rubber goods, paper, farm implements, flour, dairy products, machine-shop products, cold-storage doors, and cement. Hagerstown is the site of the annual Washington County Fair. The Antietam National Battlefield Site, marking the site of one of the most sanguinary battles of the Civil War, fought on Sept. 16 and 17, 1862, covers an area of 195 acres 11 miles S. of Hagerstown. It contains several monuments and a national cemetery. The site of the present city was first settled about 1740, and in 1762 the town was laid out by Jonathan Hager, an early settler. Pop. (1950) 36,260.

HAGFISH, common name for any of several eel-like, parasitic, marine cyclostomes in the order Myxinoidea, the most primitive of the craniate vertebrates. The hagfishes, which attain a maximum length of 3 ft., are extremely slimy, boneless animals, with vestigial eyes, a single large nostril, and a circular sucking mouth surrounded by four pairs of tentacles. The roof of the mouth contains a single tooth; the muscular tongue has two rows of strong, pointed, horny teeth which are periodically shed and re-formed. The voracious hagfish attaches itself to the body of a fish by means of its mouth and tentacles, and files through the skin and flesh with its rasping tongue. It subsists solely on the blood and flesh of fish, and can consume several times its own weight in a few hours. While attached to its prey it breathes through two external gill openings situated on each side of its body. The hagfish has a single gonad which produces both eggs and sperm. Hagfishes are found in all temperate seas. The best-known hagfish is the bright-red *Myxine glutinosa,* about 15 in. long, found in the North Atlantic Ocean. The common Pacific species belong to the genus *Polistotrema.* See CYCLOSTOMATA; compare LAMPREY.

HAGGADA (Heb. *haggādāh,* fr. *higgīd,* "to relate"), in Judaism, the body of rabbinical lore comprising legends, anecdotes, and parables illustrating the religious and ethical principles of the traditional law compiled in the Talmud (q.v.) during the first five centuries of the Christian era. The Haggada is a complement to the Halakah (q.v.), which includes the legal sections themselves. The two types of interpretations were set down concomitantly. Although the Haggadic sections of the Talmud are still considerable, the great bulk of Haggadic lore was extracted by Jewish scholars during the Middle Ages and set down in separate compilations known as *Midrashim* (see MIDRASH), homiletic interpretations of the Old Testament. The oldest of these collections, in which the commentaries run parallel with the text, are the *Mechilta,* a Haggadic interpretation of the Book of Exodus; the *Siphra,* commentaries on Leviticus; and the *Siphre,* commentaries on Numbers and Deuteronomy. The greatest of the *Midrashim* is the *Midrash Rabbah,* or Great Midrash, a Haggadic interpretation of the entire Pentateuch (q.v.) and of the five scrolls (Esther, Ruth, Lamentations, Ecclesiastes, and Song of Songs) which are read on the various holidays of the Jewish calendar. On the basis of this Midrashic literature, a great number of interpretative works on Judaism were written during the Middle Ages, and others are still being produced which, in addition to selections from earlier compilations, contain additions and amplifications. An extract from Haggadic liter-

ature, entitled *Haggada shel Pesach* and written partly in Hebrew and partly in Aramaic, is read as part of the ritual observed on the first two evenings of the Passover (q.v.).

HAGGAI, tenth of the minor prophets of the Israelites, active after the return of his people from the Babylonian captivity. According to the Book of Haggai in the Old Testament, Haggai, in 520 B.C., a year of drought, blight, and general dissatisfaction, attributed the misfortunes of the Israelites to their failure to finish reconstruction of the old temple, which was destroyed in 586 B.C. He declared that the Lord was punishing the Israelites for decorating their own houses instead of completing the work begun on the temple after the return from exile fifteen years before. The Book of Haggai records that the people set to work on the temple again in the year of Haggai's prophecy.

HAGGARD, SIR HENRY RIDER (1856–1925), English novelist, colonial administrator, and agriculturist, born at Bradenham Hall, Norfolk. At the age of nineteen he went to Natal, South Africa, and later served in the Transvaal as a master of the High Court. When the Transvaal was ceded to the Boers in 1881, Rider Haggard returned to London. He was admitted to the bar at Lincoln's Inn in 1884, but did not practice law, devoting most of his time to agriculture and to the writing of novels. His *King Solomon's Mines* (1886) was an immediate success; its story, suggested by the Zimbabwe ruins in Mashonaland, Southern Rhodesia, dealt with the adventures of an English explorer among fabulous, lost white tribes. The characters who appeared in this book were featured in several others, including *She* (1887), *Allan Quartermain* (1888), and *Ayesha, or the Return of She* (1905). Rider Haggard also wrote a number of books on agriculture, the most important being *Rural England* (2 vols., 1902), *The Poor and the Land* (1905), and *Rural Denmark and Its Lessons* (1911). He was knighted in 1912.

HAGGIS, an ancient Scottish dish, made of the stomach of a sheep (or, less commonly, of a calf) turned inside out and filled with a mixture of chopped meat and vegetables. The ingredients of the stuffing include the liver, heart, lungs, intestines, and suet of the sheep, and oatmeal, seasoned with pepper, salt, and onions. The haggis is boiled for about three hours. It is the national dish of Scotland, and is served on St. Andrew's day, the 30th of November, and on Robert Burns' night, the 25th of January.

HAGIA SOPHIA. See SAINT SOPHIA; IsTANBUL.

HAGIOLOGY. See SAINT.

HAGUE CONFERENCES, the term generally applied to two international peace conferences, one of which took place near the end of the 19th and the other at the beginning of the 20th century at The Hague, capital of the Netherlands.

The first Conference was called on the initiative of Czar Nicholas II of Russia for the purpose of discussion and possible agreement among the principal nations of the world concerning the problems of maintaining universal peace, reducing armaments, and ameliorating the conditions of warfare. Twenty-six states accepted the invitation to the conference issued by the minister of foreign affairs of the Netherlands, and on May 18, 1899, one hundred and one delegates, including jurists, diplomats, and high army and naval officers, held their first meeting, at a building in The Hague known as "House in the Woods". The last meeting took place on July 29, 1899. The president of the Conference was Baron de Staal of the Russian delegation. The chairman of the American delegation was Andrew D. White, ambassador to Germany; among the members of the delegation were Alfred Thayer Mahan, the naval officer and noted historian, and Seth Low, president of Columbia University.

The delegates to the first Conference entered into three formal conventions or treaties. The first and most important treaty set up permanent machinery for the optional arbitration of controversial issues between nations (see ARBITRATION, INTERNATIONAL); this machinery took the form of the Permanent Court of Arbitration (q.v.), popularly known as the Hague Court or Tribunal. The second and third conventions revised some of the customs and laws of warfare to eliminate unnecessary suffering during a war on the part of all concerned, whether combatants, noncombatants, or neutrals. These two conventions were supplemented by three declarations, to stay in force five years, forbidding the use of poison gas, expanding (or "dumdum") bullets, and bombardment from the air.

The conventions and declarations represented the positive results of the first Conference. Its failures included its inability to carry out any limitation in armament and to provide for compulsory arbitration of international disputes. The great nations refused to adopt compulsory arbitration because it involved giving up a certain measure of national sovereignty. However, because it was the first multilateral international conference on general issues since the Congress of Vienna (1815), and because it set up the Permanent Court of Arbitration, the Conference is considered to have been one of the most significant international conferences of modern times.

The idea of holding the Second International Peace Conference was first promulgated by the U.S. secretary of state John Milton Hay in 1904, and it was called three years later on the direct initiative of the Russian government. The Conference took place at The Hague from June 15 to October 18, 1907, and was attended by representatives from forty-four states. The Second Conference resulted in thirteen conventions, which were concerned principally with clarifying and amplifying the understandings which had been arrived at in the first Conference. In particular, new principles were established in regard to various aspects of warfare, including the rights and duties of neutrals, naval bombardment, the laying of automatic submarine contact mines, and the conditions under which merchant ships might be converted into warships. The Second Conference recommended that a third conference be held within eight years. The government of the Netherlands actually began preparations for such a conference, to be held in 1915 or 1916; the outbreak of World War I, however, put an end to the preparations. After 1919 and until the formation of the United Nations in 1945, the functions of the Hague conferences were largely carried on by the League of Nations (q.v.).

HAGUE, THE, (Du. *'s Gravenhage*), administrative center of the Netherlands, and capital of the province of South Holland, situated within 3 miles of the North Sea and 33 miles s.w. of Amsterdam. In addition to its railroad facilities, the city, the third largest in population in the country, is served by a branch of the canal from Rotterdam to Amsterdam. The Hague is the official residence of the court and diplomatic groups, and the seat of the states-general, the ministry, the council of state, and the high court of the Netherlands. The general government buildings are situated in the center of the city around the Vyver, a small artificial lake. The royal palace dates from the 16th century, and was enlarged early in the 19th century. An equestrian statue of William I of Orange stands in front of the building. The Binnenhof ("inner

Netherlands Information Bureau

The Mauritshuis, a museum containing many fine examples of Dutch art, in The Hague

court") and Buitenhof ("outer court"), comprising a group of government structures dating in part from the 13th century, include the palace of the states-general, the Treveshall, the courts of justice, and the Ridderzaal ("Hall of the Knights"), built in 1252, in which the states of the Netherlands repudiated the sovereignty of Philip II of Spain on July 26, 1581. Ancient towers and gateways surround the group. Nearby is the Mauritshuis, completed in 1644, containing the renowned gallery of Dutch paintings, including several by Rembrandt. Among the other notable buildings in The Hague are the Royal Library, founded in 1798, which contains early illuminated manuscripts and a collection of medals, coins, and antique gems; the town hall, dating from 1565; the municipal museum; the provincial government building; and the Palace of Peace, designed by the French architect L. M. Cordonnier and dedicated in 1913, which houses the International Court of Justice and an extensive international law library. A monument in memory of the Dutch philosopher Baruch Spinoza stands opposite the house in which he died in 1677. His tomb, together with the tombs of Jan and Cornelis De Witt, 17th-century Dutch statesman, is contained in the Nieuwe Kerk ("New Church"), a building dating from the early 17th century. The Groote Kerk ("Great

Church") of St. James, built in the 15th and 16th centuries, is another of the notable buildings in the city.

Canals intersect The Hague and lindens shade several of the avenues. The city is known for the beauty of its suburbs, and is connected with the seaside resort of Scheveningen, 3 miles distant, by a broad, tree-lined highway. A forested park, called the Haagsche Bosch ("The Wood"), surrounds a 17th-century royal villa, the Huis ten Bosch ("The House in the Wood"). The villa is richly decorated and contains valuable collections of art; its Orange Hall, in 1899, was the site of the Hague Peace Conference.

The Hague is mainly residential, and commerce and industry are comparatively unimportant. The principal industries are lithographing, printing, distilling, copper and lead smelting, and the manufacture of iron castings, furniture, and jewelry.

The Hague was originally a hunting seat of the counts of Holland. It became a princely residence in 1250 and subsequently developed into the administrative center of Holland, serving as the seat of the states-general in the 16th century. In the 17th and 18th centuries The Hague was the diplomatic capital of Europe. The Triple Alliance of England, Sweden, and the Netherlands against France (1688), and the Triple Alliance of

England, France, and Holland (1717) for the preservation of the Treaty of Utrecht, were among the European agreements concluded there during that period. Between May 18 and July 29, 1899, the city was the site of the Hague Peace Conference. One of the results of the conference was the establishment of the International Court of Arbitration, or the Hague Tribunal, with its seat at The Hague. To house this court the Palace of Peace was erected; Andrew Carnegie, the American industrialist, contributed $1,500,000 toward the expenses of its construction. After World War I the Permanent Court of International Justice, created by the League of Nations and often called the World Court, sat in the Palace of Peace. The present occupant, the International Court of Justice, is based upon the Permanent Court and was created by the United Nations at the San Francisco Conference in 1945. The greater part of The Hague was undamaged by the German invasion and occupation of the Netherlands during World War II. Pop. (1953 est.) 584,435.

HAGUE TRIBUNAL. See PERMANENT COURT OF ARBITRATION.

HAHN, OTTO (1879–   ), German physical chemist, born in Frankfort on the Main, and educated at the universities of Marburg and Munich. He became a member of the Kaiser Wilhelm Institute for Physical Chemistry in 1911 and served as director of the institute from 1928 to 1945, when it was taken into Allied custody. Hahn's greatest contributions were in the field of radioactivity. In 1918 he discovered, with Lise Meitner (q.v.), the element protoactinium. Hahn, with his co-workers, Lise Meitner and Fritz Strassman, continued the research started by Enrico Fermi (q.v.) in bombarding uranium with neutrons. Until 1939 scientists believed that elements with atomic numbers higher than 92 (transuranic elements) were formed when uranium was bombarded with neutrons. In 1939, however, Hahn and Strassman, while looking for transuranic elements in a sample of uranium that had been irradiated with neutrons, found traces of the element barium. This discovery was irrefutable evidence, confirmed by calculations of the energies involved in the reaction, that the uranium had undergone fission, splitting into smaller fragments consisting of lighter elements in the periodic table; see ATOMIC ENERGY. Hahn was awarded the 1944 Nobel Prize in chemistry for his work in nuclear fission.

During World War II, Hahn was one of the important German scientists who worked on the problem of utilizing atomic energy for military purposes. When his laboratories at the Kaiser Wilhelm Institute for Physical Chemistry in Berlin were bombed, he and his staff were evacuated to a small village in s. Germany, where he was later found by the American scientific mission under Samuel Goudsmit (q.v.) and interned. After a short internment in England he settled in Göttingen; there he became president of the Max Planck Society for Advancement of Science. His works include *Applied Radiochemistry* (1936).

HAHNEMANN, (CHRISTIAN FRIEDRICH) SAMUEL (1755–1843), German physician, born in Meissen, Saxony, and educated at the universities of Leipzig, Vienna, and Erlangen. He practiced medicine in various cities, finally settling in Leipzig. In 1790, while translating William Cullen's *Materia Medica* into German, he was struck by the fact that the symptoms of disease that were cured by the use of quinine were the same as those produced in a healthy person who was treated with quinine. This observation led Hahnemann to formulate the "law of similars", *similia similibus curantur;* i.e., a disease can be cured by those drugs which produce symptoms of the same disease in a healthy person. In 1800 Hahnemann asserted further that drugs were more efficacious when used in small doses and that the greater the dilution of the medicine, the more potent is its effect. He called his new treatment homeo-

Samuel Hahnemann

Douglas Haig

pathy (q.v.), in opposition to the general practice of medicine, which he called allopathy, and he organized a school of homeopathy in Leipzig. Hahnemann administered a large number of drugs to healthy subjects, including himself, and studied the symptoms produced; he was thus one of the first investigators of pharmacology to put that science on a systematic, experimental basis. Hahnemann's beliefs were met with hostility in Leipzig, particularly by the apothecaries, and he was forced to leave the city in 1821. He lived in Cöthen until 1835, and then moved to Paris where he practiced and had a large following until his death. Hahnemann's chief work was *Organon der Rationellen Heilkunde* (1810); among his other important writings were *Reine Arzneimittellehre* (1811) and *Die Chronischen Krankheiten* (1828).

HAIDA, a group of tribes native to the Queen Charlotte Islands, British Columbia. Their languages constitute the Skittagetan linguistic family, which is related to the Athapascan and Tlingit stocks, and is itself a member of a proposed larger family, the NADENE. The Haida represent one of the most advanced of the typical Indian cultures of the North Pacific region. They are skillful carvers, producing miniature totems and utilitarian articles in black slate, large wooden family totems, and decorated canoes. These canoes are used for both traveling and fishing, and the economic organization of the tribes, which is largely maritime, centers around them. Contact with the civilization of white men has decimated their numbers: from a peak population of considerably more than 8000 (the number recorded in the first census in 1841) and a territory which extended, in raids, as far south as the mouth of the Columbia River, they have been reduced to a group of about 500 people inhabiting only two villages.

HAIDARABAD. See HYDERABAD.

HAIFA (anc. *Sycaminum*), city and chief seaport of the republic of Israel, located at the base of Mt. Carmel, on the s. shore of the Bay of Acre. Haifa is a terminal for three railroads and a British-owned pipe line carrying oil from Iraq to the Mediterranean Sea. The city is the most important oil-refining center in the Middle East, and both crude and refined oil are exported from the port. In recent years many Jewish immigrants have established modern colonies in and around the city. They have also founded textile plants, cement factories, soap factories, and flour mills. The industrial establishments of Haifa are the largest in Palestine. The city figured prominently in the armed struggle between the Arab League and the Jews of Palestine following the 1947 United Nations partition resolution for the division of Palestine into Arab and Jewish states (see ISRAEL; PALESTINE). In accordance with that resolution Haifa was included in Israel. Pop. (1950 est.) 130,000.

HAIG, DOUGLAS, 1st EARL HAIG (1861–1928), British soldier, born in Edinburgh, and educated at Clifton College and at Brasenose College, Oxford University. He joined the 7th Hussars in 1885, and served in the South African War of 1899–1902; at the end of the war he was made a colonel and given command of the 17th Lancers. He subsequently served in India as inspector general of cavalry, was promoted to major general in 1904, and was later recalled to London to serve as a director of the War Office. In 1909 he again returned to India as chief of the general staff, becoming lieutenant general in the following year. He was ordered home in 1912 to take command of the troops stationed at Aldershot, and was knighted the next year.

When World War I broke out, in 1914, Haig was made commander of the 1st Army Corps of the British Expeditionary Force in France and in Flanders. He became a full general later in the year. When the British

Expeditionary Force was divided into two armies, he was given command of one; the troops under his command took part in the battles of Neuve-Chapelle, Festubert, and Loos during 1915. He became commander in chief of the British Expeditionary Force in December, 1915, and was appointed field marshal in 1917.

In 1919 he was created Earl Haig and Baron Haig of Bemersyde. He remained commander in chief of the Home Forces in Great Britain until 1921, but after the position was abolished he devoted his energies to the welfare of ex-servicemen. He was one of the founders and first president of the British Legion, formed to unite the many small ex-servicemen's associations in Britain, and he also organized, for the benefit of disabled ex-servicemen, the sale of poppies, commemorating Armistice Day, on November 11 each year.

HAIL, a form of precipitation consisting of roughly spherical pellets of ice and snow combined in alternating layers. True hailstorms occur only at the beginning of thunderstorms in hot weather. Raindrops formed in cumulo-nimbus clouds are swept upward and downward many times in the turbulent air currents characteristic of thunderstorms. In the upper portion of the cloud the raindrops freeze into ice and collect a layer of snow; as they descend to the lower portion of the cloud the ice pellets receive a coat of moisture which freezes and collects another layer of snow as it is drawn upward again. This process continues until the pellets are too heavy to be supported by the air currents, and fall to the earth. Particles of hail range in diameter from one sixteenth of an inch to five inches; large particles, called hailstones, are sometimes very destructive. Often several hailstones freeze together into a large, shapeless, heavy mass of ice and snow. The so-called "hail" that occurs in the winter consists of frozen raindrops. See CLOUD; METEOROLOGY.

HAILE SELASSIE, RAS TAFFARI or TAFARI (1891–   ), Emperor of Ethiopia and Eritrea, son of Ras Makonnen and great-grandson of Haile Melekot, King of Shoa, educated at Harrar. In 1916, when his cousin Zauditu became empress of Ethiopia, Taffari was made regent, heir to the throne, and Ras, or Prince of Rases. In 1923 he obtained admission to the League of Nations for Ethiopia, and in the following year he made a tour of the European capitals. Because of his administrative ability and activity in effecting administrative reform he gradually gained more power and in 1928 had himself declared king (Negus), taking the name Haile Selassie. When Zauditu died in 1930, Taffari became emperor as Haile Selassie I. In the following year he granted a constitution to his subjects. Despite the efforts of the League of Nations and of the major European powers to forestall war between Italy and Ethiopia, hostilities broke out in 1935. When the capital, Addis Ababa, was taken in May, 1936, Haile Selassie was forced to flee, going to England via Palestine. Although dethroned, he continued to solicit aid from the League of Nations, making a dramatic personal appeal before the assembly on June 29, 1936. During the Italian occupation of Ethiopia between 1936 and 1941, he lived in exile in England. In 1941, during World War II, Haile Selassie was restored to the throne with the aid of the British, who drove the Italians from Ethiopia. The former Italian colony of Eritrea was added to his dominions in 1952 by the terms of a United Nations decision providing for an Ethiopian-Eritrean Federation. Haile Selassie made an official visit to the United States in 1954.

HAIL MARY. See AVE MARIA.

HAILTZUK, a group of Indian tribes native to the coast islands of British Columbia from Gardner Channel to Rivers Inlet, of the Wakashan linguistic stock. Their culture is almost identical with that of the related neighboring Kwakiutl (q.v.) tribes.

Ewing Galloway

Haile Selassie

HAINAN, an island of Kwangtung Province, China, situated in the South China Sea due s. of the Liuchow peninsula. Hainan Strait, about 15 m. in width, separates the peninsula from the island, which adjoins the Gulf of Tonkin on the E. Between its N. and s. extremities, Hainan has a length of about 160 m. Its extreme width is about 90 m. The s. half of the island is traversed by a series of mountain chains. Wu-Chi-Shan, the highest of these chains, has a maximum elevation of about 6000 ft. above sea level. Extinct volcanoes are numerous throughout the mountainous region. Many of the slopes and valleys of s. Hainan are covered with dense tropical vegetation. Except for occasional mountainous outcroppings, the N. portion of the island consists of level plains. Hainan contains rich mineral deposits, including gold, tin, iron, lead, and silver, but the economy is predominantly agrarian. Among the leading crops are rice, rubber, coconuts, sugar, betel nuts, and pineapples. Large numbers of hogs, cattle, and ducks are raised. People of Chinese origin comprise the bulk of the population of Hainan. Several unfriendly aboriginal tribes, locally designated the Maiu and Lois, inhabit the more remote areas of the mountainous region. The Maiu tribes originated on the Chinese mainland; the other grouping has marked physical similarities to the Igorots of the Philippines, and speak the same language. A Chinese possession since 111 B.C., Hainan was occupied by the Japanese in February, 1939, during the Sino-Japanese War. The island was returned to the control of the Chinese government following the unconditional surrender (August, 1945) of Japan in World War II. In May, 1950, during the Chinese Civil War, Communist troops captured Hainan from the Nationalists. Kiungshan (q.v.) is the administrative center and Hoihow (pop., about 22,000) is the chief seaport. Area, about 13,000 sq.m.; pop., about 3,000,000, about two thirds of whom are Chinese.

HAINAUT, province of s.w. Belgium, formerly a part of the medieval county of Hainaut. During the 14th century and part of the 15th, Hainut was united to the county of Holland and in the 15th century it came under Spanish domination along with the rest of the Netherlands. The Sambre and the Schelde are the chief rivers of the province. Mons, the capital, and Charleroi (q.v.) are the principal cities. Farming, stock raising, coal and iron mining, and the manufacture of iron and steel products are among the important industries of the province. Area, 1436 sq.m.; pop. (1948 est.) 247,299.

HAIPHONG, the chief seaport of Tonkin, North Viet-Nam, situated on the Songka R., about 16 m. inland from the Gulf of Tonkin and about 63 miles S.E. of Hanoi. It has modern facilities for the handling of water-borne freight and is the site of a French naval base. French, British, and American cargo carriers visit Haiphong regularly. Among the principal exports are iron, coal, rice, grain, cattle, tea, and castor oil, and the leading imports are machinery and tools. A railway line extends from Hanoi to Haiphong. Haiphong is also linked to Hanoi and other interior points by road and inland waterways. Various industrial enterprises, including zinc and coal mines, textile plants, and chemical works, are located near or in the city. Pop., about 73,000.

HAIR, collective term for slender, threadlike outgrowths of the epidermis of mammals (see SKIN), forming the characteristic covering of those animals. No animals other than mammals have true hair, and all mammals have hair. Even such apparently hairless mammals as rhinoceroses, elephants, and armadillos have hairs around the snout, at the tip of the tail, and behind each scale, respectively. Whales and manatees have hair only in the embryonic state. When the individual hairs are fine and closely spaced, the coat of hair is called fur; when soft and kinked and matted together the coat is called wool. Coarse, stiff hairs are called bristles; when they are also pointed, as in the hedgehog and the porcupine, they are called spines (or, popularly, quills). The term hair is sometimes extended to include any similar structure, especially the "hairs" forming the pubescence of certain plants.

Individual hairs are composed chiefly of the horny scleroprotein known as keratin, and contain neither blood vessels nor nerves. They usually contain pigment (except in the case of albinos), but sometimes also contain interstitial air bubbles which give the hair a silvery color. The shaft of the hair consists of modified epithelial cells arranged in columns surrounding a central medulla, and covered with thin, flat scales. The root of each hair is contained in a tubular pit in the epidermis, called the hair follicle. The hair grows from the bottom of the follicle and is nourished by the blood vessels in a papilla which extends into the follicle and, for a short distance, into the root of the hair. A minute muscle, the *arrector pili*, is attached to each hair follicle;

under the control of the autonomic nervous system the muscle contracts to make the hair "stand on end". Most mammals other than man possess *tactile hairs,* usually growing from the upper lip and eyebrows, with their roots set in erectile tissue richly supplied with sensory nerves.

In man the development of the hair begins in the embryo, and, by the sixth month, the fetus is covered by a growth of fine hair, the *lanugo.* In the first few months of infancy the lanugo is shed, and is replaced by hair, characteristically coarse over the cranium and the eyebrows and fine and downy over the rest of the body. At puberty coarse hair develops in the armpits and over the pubic region in both sexes; in males the hair over the upper lip and the lower jaw begins to grow coarse to form the beard. The rate of growth of the hair varies with the age of the person and with the length of the hair. When a hair is short, its rate of growth averages about 3/4 inch per month; by the time the hair is a foot long, the rate of growth is reduced by one half. The fastest growth is found in women from 16 to 24 years of age. See also HAIR DISEASES.

In anthropology the form of the hair is one of the most important and reliable characteristics of race. The nearly black hair of Negroes, Papuans, and Melanesians is characterized as *wooly;* it grows from a curved follicle, which imparts a spiral twist, and is flat or tapelike in cross section. The hair of the Chinese, Japanese, Eskimos, and American Indians is straight, coarse, long, and almost always black. It grows from a straight follicle; it is round in cross section, and has an easily distinguished medulla. The hair of Ainus, Europeans, Hindus, and Semites, called *wavy* hair, is intermediate between the straight and the wooly types. It grows from a straight follicle, but has a slight tendency to curl; it is oval in cross section and among individuals exhibits a wide range of color, from light blond to black. See RACES OF MANKIND.

HAIRBIRD. See CHIPPY.

HAIR DISEASES, disorders of the hair shaft or hair follicle, causing abnormal growth or abnormal or premature falling of the hair. Certain abnormal conditions such as dull or dry hair are caused by physical or chemical agents; too frequent use of permanent-waving chemicals or of shampoos or lotions, especially those containing alcohol or free alkalies, often cause such conditions. Diffuse falling of the hair, ordinarily a normal phe-nomenon, may reach abnormal proportions after a fever higher than 103°F. (39.4°C.), during a debilitating disease, or as a result of surgical shock. The cause of excessive hairiness is obscure, but in several cases it has been traced to tumor of the adrenal cortex, or to disorders of the pituitary body, the thyroid gland, and the ovary (qq.v.; see also HORMONES). Premature graying of the hair is associated with anxiety, shock, and deficiency diseases (see VITAMIN), and in certain cases with hereditary factors. *Alopecia,* or baldness, is also due principally to hereditary factors. Certain forms of baldness may, however, be due to other causes: *alopecia prematura,* in which the hair of a young person falls out without preliminary graying, may also be caused by seborrhea (q.v.); *alopecia areata,* in which the hair falls out in irregular patches, is believed by doctors to be caused by inflammation, nerve disorders, or local infections.

Infections of the hair follicle also cause a variety of hair diseases. *Tinea favosa,* or favus (Lat., "honeycomb"), is caused by the fungus *Achorion schoenleinii;* it is characterized by the formation around the mouths of the follicles of small crusts which frequently resemble a honeycomb. *Tinea trichophytina,* or ringworm (q.v.), is caused by fungi of the genus *Trichophyton.* These diseases have been treated successfully by epilation (i.e., removal of the hair from the affected follicles), cleansing with soaps or oils to remove encrustation, and application of parasiticides. Treatment by X rays has also been successful in some cases.

Hairy parts, particularly of the head and pubis, are subject to troublesome infestations by minute insects and mites. See, for example, CHIGGER; LOUSE.

HAIRDRESSING, the process employed in lending greater beauty to the hair of the head. The process includes a specific arrangement of the hair, and may also include cutting, curling, perfuming, bleaching, dyeing, powdering, or waxing of the hair, and the addition of false hair or a headdress or other adornment.

Hairdressing has been practiced from prehistoric times and among all types of peoples from the most primitive to the most highly civilized. Statuary and bas-reliefs of the ancient Assyrians, Persians, and Egyptians show that these people subjected the hair of head and beard to a number of decorative processes, including curling, anointing, and dyeing, and adorned the hair with ribbons and

Joseph Fleisher

EARLY HAIRDRESSING STYLES FOR WOMEN. *Top, left to right: Ancient Egyptian; ancient Greek; medieval European; "coiffure à la frégate," Louis XVI period. Bottom, left to right: Empress Eugénie waterfall; Madame Récamier, early 19th-century French; Queen Victoria; headdress with a chignon, a popular style in the 1890's.*

with ornaments of gold and silver. In the above-mentioned nations the use of the wig was common for the purpose of concealing baldness. In ancient Egypt feminine hairdressing, as revealed by sculptures and mural paintings, was extremely elaborate. Three styles of feminine hairdressing prevailed: the hair was divided into numerous locks or tresses, each thickly plaited; into numerous long parallel braids grouped into two masses, the smaller falling in front of the shoulder, the larger, behind; or into two broad and flat braids, one on each side of the head, the back hair being cut short.

Among the early Hebrews a head of thick hair was held in esteem; baldness rendered a man subject to suspicion of leprosy. In later times the Jews regarded long hair on a male as evidence of effeminacy. During the time of the ancient Jewish kingdoms, Jewish women wore their hair long, sometimes curling or plaiting it. After the Exile in the first century A.D., Jewish women cropped their hair at marriage, a custom which survived among the orthodox until recent times.

Among the Greeks, male children in general wore the hair long, but cut it short on attaining the age of eighteen; the men wore it short and curled in small ringlets. In Sparta, however, the reverse of the general practice was true: the boys wore their hair short and the men wore it long. Greek women dressed their hair elaborately. They parted it in the center of the crown, then brought it down over the temples and carried the two divisions toward the back, and finally fastened the two sections over the point where the part began, or tied them into a tuft or knot on the back of the head; the tied mass of hair was usually enclosed by a hood or net. Curling of hair was so general in Athens that it gave rise in that city to a new industry; the first hairdressers in history flourished in Athens. After the 4th century B.C., styles in male hairdressing showed a growing tendency toward simplicity, but the coiffures of women became more and more elaborate. The early Romans wore their hair long; after about 300 B.C. the custom of wearing it short prevailed. Roman women of the period of the

Republic wore their hair in a simple and natural style; those of the period of the Roman Empire adopted forms of headdress that varied from the elaborate to the fantastic. When a woman did not have sufficient hair of her own for the number of curls and plaits desired, she added false hair, usually blonde, taken from captive members of the Germanic tribes with whom Rome was at constant war. In early Christian times a form of hairdressing known as the tonsure was adopted by the Roman Catholic Church for its priests, to indicate their dedication to the service of God.

The early Britons wore their hair and beards long, but after the Roman conquest of Britain in the 1st century A.D., the Britons adopted the Roman custom of shaving and also the style of cutting the hair short. The Saxons, who ruled England in the 9th, 10th, and part of the 11th centuries, wore their hair long and parted at the front of the head. The Danes, who were masters of England from 1016 to 1042, generally wore their hair long. After the Norman invasion (1066) of England the style of wearing the hair very long prevailed among both women and men, including members of the clergy and soldiers; both these classes had generally previously worn their hair short. During the Plantagenet period (1154–1399) the hair was worn somewhat shorter. From the 13th to the 16th century it was worn cut short, but was kept bushy at the sides, cut close over the forehead, and curled just below the ears. From the 13th to the 15th century, women's hair was usually worn in a covering of gold network known as a caul; the hair was sometimes curled and ornamented with jewelry. During the first decade of the 15th century, women's hair was either permitted to hang down the back in curls, or was confined within a jeweled caul or tightly covered by a headdress such as a turban. In the time of Henry VII (1485–1509) a profusion of hair, with heavy side locks, was considered fashionable. During the reign of Henry VIII (1509–47) it became the fashion for men to part their hair in the center and comb it straight down the sides of the head. With the accession (1558) of Queen Elizabeth came the introduction of large and elaborate coiffures for feminine wear that were the forerunners of the gigantic coiffures worn in England and on the Continent during the 18th century (see below). From about the 17th century, hairdressing in England closely followed fashions on the Eu-

ropean continent, and is referred to in the account of European hairdressing below.

From the earliest period to the 14th century, hairdressing customs differed at different times among the various peoples of central and western Europe. Among the early Celts and Germans, with the exception of the Germanic tribe of Saxons, short hair was worn only by slaves or as a sign of disgrace by those convicted of violating some tribal law. Both Celts and Germans wore the hair long and tied up behind the head. By the end of the 8th century the long-haired style generally prevailing among Germanic tribes had changed in the particular tribe known as the Franks. Their famous king Charlemagne and his immediate successors wore their hair short. The Saxons, on the contrary, who had been wearing their hair short, beginning with the 9th century began to wear it long; it was permitted to hang down over the shoulders or was tied up and fastened with a pin. In France and elsewhere in Europe in the 11th century and later, the custom prevailed of forming the hair into one or two cues; these were bound up by ribbons and made to lie over the shoulders from the back.

Elaborate coiffures for both men and women came into vogue in Europe at the end of the 14th century. The method of hairdressing shown in portraits of King Henry IV of France, and of his minister of finance the Duc de Sully, is typical of the style in which men of quality dressed their hair during the late 16th and the early 17th century. The beard was combed out and elaborately curled, and by the use of a gum was made to extend out from both sides of the lower lip into a stiff, fanlike shape; the moustache was curled and, also by means of some glutinous medium, was held rigidly up and away from the mouth; the hair of the head was combed back straight up from the forehead. In the early portion of the reign of Louis XIV (1643–1715) in France, and during the reign of Charles I (1625–49) in England, the hair of men, worn long, was perfumed and, to prevent it from being blown about by the wind, was tied with ribbons into long and heavy locks. The wearing of wigs came into fashion in France in the 17th century. The vogue was introduced by Louis XIII, who wore an elaborately curled wig to conceal his baldness, and was continued by Louis XIV, who wore a towering wig in order to make himself appear tall. From royalty the fashion spread to courtiers and other members of the French nobility, and

Mexican hairless dog

from France to other parts of Europe and also to America. Charles II of England adopted the fashion during his period of exile in France, and brought it to England with him when he was restored to the English throne in 1660.

In the last two thirds of the 17th century and in the first part of the 18th, hairdressing styles for women were simple; toward the middle of the 18th century, however, feminine coiffures in France, which were the models followed in the rest of Europe and in England, grew more and more elaborate. In the reign of Louis XV they became lofty constructions of curls stiffened with wire, cloth, or other materials; on top of the huge edifice of hair was placed a cap or hat decorated with flowers or plumes. In the reign of Louis XVI the style became even more extravagant. The extreme was perhaps reached by a hairdresser of the late 18th century who devised the *coiffure à la frégate,* a high vertical structure of hair held in place by gigantic combs and adorned with jewels, the whole crowned by the model of a ship of war of the period.

The French Revolution brought about simplicity in the hairdressing styles for both men and women. After the beginning of the 19th century, men in Europe and America generally wore their hair short. In the first part of the 19th century, women arranged their hair in a series of ringlets which they permitted to fall to the sides of the head, and which they gathered around the back of the head with a ribbon. Later in the century, elaborate hairdressing styles for women came into vogue again; their chief feature was the use of the chignon. During World War I it became fashionable for women to wear their hair cut short. In recent years women's coiffures have been styled with simplicity and greater regard for individual taste, and considerably less regard for rigidly followed extremes of fashion.

HAIRLESS DOG, the general name for several species of dogs whose bodies are completely or almost completely devoid of hair. The principal breed of this type is the Mexican hairless, indigenous to Mexico and believed to have been brought there by the Aztecs (q.v.), who settled in the valley of Mexico early in the 14th century. The Aztecs reputedly came from Asia, supposed also to have been the place of origin of the dog. The dog is sometimes known as the "biche", the Aztec word for "naked". The Mexican hairless dog is an active dog no larger than a small fox terrier. It has a slender head and narrow skull; eyes that are yellow, hazel, or dark in color; a slender, well-arched neck; a smooth, soft, unwrinkled skin of any color and from which the hair is almost entirely absent; and a long, smooth tail. Some Mexican hairless dogs have a tuft of hair on the top of the head and a little hair on the lower half of the tail. The dog is bred principally on the west coast of Mexico. It is exhibited in the toy class in dog shows in the United States.

Other types of the hairless dog exist in various other parts of the world. The Chinese crested dog greatly resembles the Mexican hairless, and so does the hairless dog of South America, which is found as far south from Mexico as Peru; and the Rampur dog of southern India has many of the characteristics of the Mexican hairless. Types of the hairless dog are also found in Turkey, Japan, and Africa.

HAIRSTREAK, common name for any butterfly in the genus *Thecla* of the family Lycaenidae, which contains the copper butterflies (q.v.) and the blues. The hairstreaks, which have wing spans of from 1 to 2 in., have characteristic hairlike markings on the undersides of their wings. Their caterpillars feed on the leaves, flowers, buds, and stems of plants.

More than fifty species of hair-streaks are found in North America. The common hairstreak, *T. melinus,* found throughout the U.S., is ¾ in. long with a wing span of 1½ in. Above it is dark gray, bordered with black, white, and orange; below it is lighter gray, streaked with orange and marked with black oblongs, with an orange patch at the rear angle of each back wing. The front wings are smooth bordered; the rear wings are wavy bordered with a thin tail at the rear of each. The caterpillars, which are greenish-gray, feed on hop seeds, hopvines, and bush clover, as well as on many weeds.

HAIRTAIL, a name for the cutlass fish (q.v.).

HAIRWORM, Hair Eel, Horsehair Worm, or Horsehair Snake, common names for any brown, elongated, thread-thin worm in either of two families (Mermithidae and Gordiidae) of the Threadworm phylum. These common names were originated by superstitious people who believed that horsehairs turned into these living worms when dropped into water. Hairworms when young live as parasites within the bodies of insects; later they leave their host near water and become nonparasitic, aquatic adults, several inches in length. Fully mature hairworms sometimes reach a yard in length.

Hairworms of Mermithidae are Nematodes (q.v.), often found 2 or 3 ft. below the ground in wet soil as well as in fresh water, and commonly appearing above the ground in large numbers after a rain. Unlike other Nematodes the middle portions of their body cavities are solid, fat-containing organs from which the gonads, and the female eggs, draw nourishment. The best-known species is *Mermis nigrescens.*

The family Gordiidae contains a large number of hairworms which resemble Nematodes but differ in so many points that they are often considered a separate class, Nematomorpha. They do not have the typical lateral line and the dorsal nerve cord; their nervous system consists of an anterior mass of nerve tissue and one ventral cord. The body cavity is lined with epithelium and swells, at the posterior end, into an excretory *cloaca* into which, in both sexes, the paired genital ducts open. The female gordiid lays masses of eggs on plants or on rocks underwater. The larvae hatched from the eggs have special boring organs with which they puncture the skin of an insect living near the water. Larvae of *Gordius robustus,* the best-known species, are parasitic on crickets and grasshoppers and mature within their host; larvae of the genus *Parachordodes* bore into midges; if the midges are eaten by beetles, the threadworms mature in the bodies of the beetles. When adult, the hairworms bore out of their host and enter fresh water, or, in the single genus *Nectonema,* salt water. Hairworms in Gordiidae are also called "Gordian worms" because they are often found in knotted clusters reminiscent of the "Gordian knot".

HAITI, an independent Negro republic of the West Indies, occupying the w. third of the island of Hispaniola (q.v.). A boundary extending 193 m. from N. to S. separates Haiti from the Dominican Republic (q.v.). The capital and chief harbor of Haiti is Port-au-Prince (q.v.). Other important towns are Gonaïves, Port de Paix (qq.v.), and Cap-Haïtien Aux Cayes. Area, 10,714 sq.m.; pop. (1955 est.) 3,305,000, of whom about 90 percent are Negroes and about 10 percent are mulattoes. The population includes about 2000 white residents of foreign nationalities.

Haiti is characterized physiographically by thickly forested mountain chains and isolated mountain passes, interspersed with fertile valleys. Loma Tina, the loftiest peak in the republic and the highest point of the West Indies, rises to an altitude of about 10,300 ft. above sea level. The coasts are elevated, for the most part, and greatly indented, forming many natural harbors. The numerous rivers, most of them short, swift and unnavigable, have their sources in the mountains. Several large lakes are also found.

Palace-citadel of Henri Christophe, 19th-century ruler of northern Haiti

Haiti has no active volcanoes, but destructive earthquakes are frequent.

The climate is hot and humid in the low-lying portions of Haiti, the temperature during June, July, and August rising to about 95°F. In the mountains the weather is considerably cooler, the average temperature for the summer months being about 77°F. The greatest concentration of rain occurs between May and October, when hurricanes are not infrequent.

Haiti has a luxuriant tropical flora. Trees, growing in abundance on the mountain slopes and river banks, include the West Indian cedar, Haitian oak, shortleaf yellow pine, logwood, silk-cotton tree, mahogany, lignum vitae, royal palm, rosewood, satinwood, and calabash. Among the numerous fruits are guava, orange, grapefruit, mulberry, lime, breadfruit, and mango, which grow wild. The cacao and coffee plants also grow wild, as does the coconut palm. Several varieties of cactus are found in arid coastal regions. The larger fauna is notably deficient in Haiti. Insect life is richly represented by the sand fly, mosquito, blowfly, chigger, tick, ant, scorpion, cockroach, spider, and centipede. Butterflies abound in late summer. Waterfowl, such as geese, flamingos, pelicans, wild ducks, egrets, and snipe, have their habitat along the shores. Other birds are the hawk, white owl, kingfisher, woodpecker, pigeon, and dove.

The forests of Haiti are rich in timber of commercial importance. Mineral resources, almost entirely unexploited, include gold, silver, copper, iron, nickel, tin, antimony, coal, sulfur, gypsum, and porphyry. A large bauxite deposit, discovered in 1943, was leased to American interests for development. The country is almost exclusively agricultural, its rich soil being well adapted for cultivation. Most of the agricultural production is carried on by small farmers, and is largely for domestic consumption, although the country has a greater variety of export crops than any other region in the West Indies. Coffee is the principal crop; other important crops are sugar cane, cacao, bananas, cotton, tobacco, and sisal. Rice is produced in sufficient quantity to meet domestic requirements. Livestock in a recent year included about 1,000,000 goats, 200,000 cattle, and 14,000 sheep. Industries are small-scale and devoted to the processing of molasses and sisal, the refining of sugar, and the distilling of rum and other alcoholic beverages. Handicraft articles are made from sisal and mahogany.

The balance of trade in Haiti shows a slight preponderance of exports over imports Exports, valued in a recent year at $31,500,000, are chiefly coffee, cacao, raw sugar, bananas, cotton, sisal, and timber. Handicraft articles and essential oils are also exported. The principal imports, valued in the same year at approximately $27,240,000, are machinery, foodstuffs, cotton manufactured goods, cotton textiles, soap, and mineral oils. The bulk of Haiti's trade is carried on with the United States, which furnishes approximately 90% of Haitian imports and absorbs about 60% of the exports.

Steamship lines connect Haiti with the United States and Europe. Nearly 650 vessels totaling more than 500,000 tons enter and clear Haitian ports annually. The republic has almost 1000 m. of highways and secondary roads suitable for motoring. Two American-owned railroads cover a combined distance of 180 m. Air services are maintained with the Dominican Republic, Cuba, Puerto Rico, Jamaica, and the United States.

Roman Catholicism is the official religion of Haiti; most of the clergy are French. The practice of voodoo (q.v.), however, is widespread. About 95% of the people have an average cash income of about four dollars a year, and the illiteracy of the population is estimated at over 90%. Although elementary education is free and compulsory, actual school attendance is far below enrollment. The official language is French, but the majority of the people speak a patois called Creole French. In 1942 instruction in the English language became mandatory in all Haitian schools. About 100 elementary schools staffed by some 1200 teachers have a combined enrollment of approximately 90,000 pupils. Secondary education is furnished by 6 national lycées and 15 private schools. Other institutions of learning include 60 farm schools for boys, 8 urban schools for boys and girls, and 2 normal schools. The University of Haiti, the National School of Law, the National School of Medicine, and the Central School of Agriculture provide academic, professional, and advanced vocational training without tuition. The educated elements of the population are culturally oriented toward France.

Haiti is governed according to the provisions of the constitution of 1950. Executive power is vested in a president, who is elected by direct popular vote for a six-year term. The president is not eligible for two successive terms. A bicameral national assembly, con-

Pan American World Airways

IN PORT-AU-PRINCE, HAITI

Above: Notre Dame cathedral, seen from the park facing it. Right: Hotel La Gaieté, an example of early Haitian architecture.

sisting of a 21-member senate and a 37-member chamber of deputies, exercises legislative power. Senators and deputies serve six-year and four-year terms respectively. For administrative purposes the country is divided into five departments.

History. The independence of Haiti was proclaimed in 1804 by the Negro general Jean Jacques Dessalines (q.v.), who assumed the title of emperor. (See HISPANIOLA.) In 1806 Dessalines was assassinated, and for some years thereafter the N. part of Haiti was held by Henri Christophe (q.v.). In the S. part of the island a republic was established by the mulatto Alexandre Sabès Pétion. Upon the death of Christophe in 1820, Jean Pierre Boyer (q.v.), Pétion's successor, consolidated his power throughout the whole island. In 1844 the E. part of the island declared its independence, forming the Republic of Santo Domingo, now the Dominican Republic (q.v.).

The subsequent history of Haiti was characterized by a series of bitter internecine

struggles for political ascendancy between the Negroes, descendants of African slaves, and the mulattoes, descendants of Africans and the early French settlers. In 1849 the Negro president Faustin Élie Soulouque (q.v.) proclaimed himself emperor as Faustin I, and for ten years ruled in a despotic manner, attempting on several occasions to annex the Republic of Santo Domingo. At the beginning of 1859 the mulatto Nicholas Fabre Geffrard restored republican government; he remained in office until 1867.

Disorder persisted, however, leading finally (1915) to intervention by the United States. Under American occupation, order was restored to Haiti, and on August 12, 1915, Philippe Sudre Dartiguenave was elected to the presidency by the Haitian congress. Six months later the U.S. Senate ratified a treaty with Haiti by which the United States, for a period of ten years, agreed to render economic and political assistance designed to develop the natural resources of the island republic and put its government on a firm foundation. An insurrection against United States authority was put down in 1920. The assistance treaty, upon its expiration, was extended for another decade. Despite widespread improvements achieved under the American occupation, Haitian hostility to outside interference manifested itself in periodic uprisings. In 1931 a resolution was adopted by the lower house of the Haitian congress denouncing the original assistance treaty with the United States and retroactively invalidating all acts performed under the treaty extension of 1926–36. The United States then made provision for a transfer to native Haitian authority of all controls except those of finance and police.

In 1932 the Haitian congress unanimously rejected as unsatisfactory a proposed American treaty outlining the transfer of police functions to Haitian control and the withdrawal of U.S. marines in 1934, two years in advance of the previously specified date. In response to Haitian charges of American financial domination, the U.S. Department of State issued a report showing the favorable condition of Haiti's finances after seventeen years of American control in contrast with the economic situation prevailing prior to the establishment of U.S. authority. In 1933 a new agreement was negotiated between the foreign ministers of the United States and Haiti. The new instrument, taking the form of an executive agreement, and not requiring ratification by the Haitian congress, provided for the complete transfer of the police establishment to Haitian control by October 1, 1934, and for the evacuation of U.S. marines within the following month. Financial clauses of the agreement provoked fresh resentment in certain quarters of Haiti, and on November 16, 1933, Haitian president Sténio Joseph

Vincent communicated with President Franklin Delano Roosevelt of the United States requesting the immediate cessation of the American financial administration in Haiti. The U.S. reply indicated the impossibility of this action until such time as Haiti could devise a refunding arrangement satisfactory to American holders of some $12,000,000 in Haitian bonds.

In 1934, at a conference in Washington, D.C. between President Roosevelt and President Vincent, an agreement was worked out for the elimination of American control in Haiti. Opposition developed in the Haitian congress, however, and the plan was not ratified. The nineteen-year American military occupation of Haiti was terminated on August 15, when U.S. marines were finally withdrawn. Throughout the next three years, Haiti experienced the economic repercussions of the world-wide depression. In 1937 President Vincent charged that several thousand migrant Haitian workers who had crossed the border of the Dominican Republic in search of employment had been massacred by Dominican troops. The accusation was denied by Rafael Leonidas Trujillo (q.v.) Molina, the Dominican dictator, who maintained that the incident had been merely a border clash. The Haitian president then appealed to the United States to mediate the dispute. A commission composed of representatives from the United States, Mexico, and Cuba undertook to investigate the situation, and on the basis of their findings the Dominican Republic agreed to indemnify Haiti.

In 1939 President Vincent took steps to maintain himself in office beyond the expiration of his second term and to augment his semidictatorial powers. Confronted by strong popular opposition in Haiti, however, and by pronounced disapproval from the United States, Vincent reversed his stand and announced that he would not seek re-election. The Haitian congress thereupon elected Elie Lescot to the presidency.

Meanwhile, Haiti's relations with the Axis powers (Germany, Italy, and Japan) were steadily deteriorating. In August, 1941, Haiti ousted all Nazi consular officials, and shortly afterward the assets of German and Italian firms blacklisted by the U.S. government were frozen by a Haitian decree. Following the December 7th surprise attack by Japanese air units on Pearl Harbor, Hawaii, President Lescot, with unanimous approval of the Haitian congress, declared war on Japan (December 8) and on Germany and Italy (December 12). Early in 1942 Haiti permitted U.S. antisubmarine aircraft to make use of the Port-au-Prince landing field, and took effective steps to curb domestic pro-Axis espionage. Throughout 1942 plans were developed for American supplementation of the Haitian economy, hard hit by the war.

In 1943 the Haitian-American Agricultural Development Corporation, called SHADA, made promising strides in the cultivation of sisal, lemon grass, the cacao plant, and the rubber-bearing Cryptostegia vine. The development program, employing some 75,000 Haitians, was one of the most comprehensive agricultural enterprises in the Western Hemisphere.

On April 20, 1944, President Lescot's term of office was extended by the Haitian national assembly for a period of seven years. The following year, in consequence of tension arising from rumors of a secret agreement between President Lescot and Dominican President Trujillo respecting the cession of Haitian territory to the Dominican Republic, a stringent censorship was imposed on letters, cablegrams, and publications. Haiti signed the charter of the United Nations on June 26, 1945, becoming one of the original fifty-one members of that association of states. Growing political disturbances in the country culminated, on January 11, 1946, in a military *coup d'état* which ousted President Lescot from office. Three days later Lescot fled to Miami, Florida. On August 16, Dumarsais Estimé was elected president of Haiti.

Haiti signed the Inter-American Treaty of Reciprocal Assistance in September, 1947, and the charter of the Organization of American States in April, 1948. A $4 million loan to finance irrigation, drainage, and flood-control projects was granted to Haiti by the U.S. Export-Import Bank in 1948.

Aided by the Dominican government, the Haitian revolutionary movement became restive during the first half of 1949. Dominican interference in Haitian affairs continued despite repeated protests by the Estimé government. The domestic crisis grew increasingly acute, and on Nov. 15 the president declared a state of siege. In May, 1950, a new emergency, resulting in part from opposition to the state of siege, forced Estimé to resign. A military junta ruled the country pending national elections, which were held on Oct. 8. The Haitian soldier Paul E. Magloire, a former member of the junta, won the presidency by a large majority. Though Haitian labor supported his candidacy, Magloire suppressed the

trade-union movement after his inauguration. In December a new constitution was promulgated.

During 1951 the Magloire government sought to strengthen the national economy by encouraging the importation of foreign capital. The administration's chief accomplishment during the year was the settlement of a wide range of differences with the Dominican Republic.

In July, 1952, Haitian trade unionists united, with government approval, in the National Labor Union of Haiti. This organization, again with official support, subsequently succeeded in raising the minimum daily wage from $.70 to $1.00. Living costs increased during the year, but economic conditions, responding to public-works programs, U.S. Point Four Aid, and expanding foreign trade, were generally stable.

Haiti was damaged heavily by hurricanes during 1954 and 1955. Loans totaling $17 million were negotiated in 1955 with the U.S. Export-Import Bank and the International Bank for Reconstruction and Development. The loans only partially remedied the effects of the hurricanes and of chronic mismanagement of public works.

During 1956 Haiti suffered from economic difficulties and from public disorders occasioned by varying interpretations of the constitution. According to one interpretation, President Magloire's term of office extended only to May 15, 1956; according to another, it ended on Dec. 6; according to a third, it was to last until May 15, 1957. Magloire's refusal to vacate the presidency on May 15, 1956, provoked rioting in Port-au-Prince and other cities. The rioting was suppressed following the declaration (May 22) of a state of siege in the cities affected. Popular resistance to Magloire's rule mounted during the succeeding months despite efforts by the government to stifle dissent. On Dec. 6 he relinquished the presidency but immediately proclaimed himself commander in chief of the armed forces and chief of state. The labor movement retaliated by declaring a general strike. Though hundreds were arrested, the strike continued, paralyzing business activity and aggravating the economic situation. On Dec. 12 Magloire resigned as chief of state; he was succeeded by Joseph Nemours Pierre-Louis, chief justice of the Haitian Supreme Court.

HAJJ or **HADJ** (Ar. *hajja,* "to make a pilgrimage"), term designating the pilgrimage to the Kaaba (see MECCA), or sanctuary of Mecca. Every Mohammedan whose means and health permit is bound to perform this pilgrimage at least once in his life. The visit to the Kaaba may be made at any time, but the full rites of the Hajj can be carried out only in the twelfth month of the Mohammedan calendar, known as Dhu'l Hajjeh, or month of pilgrimage.

The pilgrims first assemble at several appointed places near Mecca in the beginning of the holy month. They start the rites by bathing. Each pilgrim then assumes the ihram, or sacred habit, which consists of two white cotton wrappers, completely devoid of needlework, one of which is thrown across the back, leaving the right shoulder and arm uncovered, and the other of which is draped about the loins from waist to knees. The head remains bare, and the slippers must cover neither the heel nor the instep. After he has assumed the ceremonial garb, the pilgrim must not shave any part of his body, anoint his head, pare his nails, or bathe until the end of the pilgrimage.

Arriving at Mecca, the pilgrim proceeds at once to the temple and begins the holy rites there by walking seven times around the Kaaba, starting from the corner in which the black stone is fixed. This ceremony, called the Tawaf, is followed by the Sai, in which the pilgrim runs between the two hillocks of Safa and Marwa. These ceremonies, accompanied by prayers, are repeated daily. The next rite occurs on the ninth of the month; the pilgrim stands in prayer and listens to a sermon on the hill of Arafat. All of the succeeding night is spent in holy devotions. Next morning, at daybreak, the pilgrim proceeds to the valley of Mina, where he throws seven stones at each of three pillars for the purpose of putting the devil to flight. The pilgrimage is completed with the slaughtering of a sacrificial animal. Most Mohammedans combine with the Hajj a visit to Mohammed's tomb at Medina.

HAKE, common name for any of several soft-rayed, marine, acanthopterygian fishes in the Cod family (Gadidae) and in the family Merlucciidae which was formerly included in the Cod family. Fish of both families are carnivorous.

The hake in Gadidae, which are also called codlings, are found on both sides of the North Atlantic Ocean, and are characterized by stringy, narrow pelvic fins attached to the throat and trailing in the water. This feature has led to the English name "forkbeard" for the common European species, Urophycis

blennoides, also known as "hake's dame". The squirrel hake, Phycis chuss, is the common American species and is about 2 ft. long. This fish, and the white hake, P. tenuis, are sought by fishermen for their oil and for their air bladders, used in the manufacture if isinglass.

The Merlucciidae, or true hake, are found on both sides of the Atlantic Ocean, in the Mediterranean Sea, and in the Pacific Ocean, off the U.S., Chile, and New Zealand. The common European hake, Merluccius merluccius, is a slender fish, reaching 4 ft. in length, and has a long, pointed snout. Unlike the silver hake, or whiting, M. bilinearis, found off N. New England, it is not valued as food.

The name hake is also applied to the kingfish (q.v.), or northern whiting, Menticirrhus saxatilis.

HAKEA, genus of Australian evergreen shrubs and small trees, belonging to the family Proteaceae. A few species are grown as garden shrubs and trees in California. They are drought resistant and can withstand light frost. Cultivated hakeas are usually grown from seeds or cuttings. The cushionflower, H. laurina, is a short tree or tall shrub which bears large, globular flowers having crimson petals and yellow styles. H. elliptica is a compact, white-flowered shrub. H. suaveolens is a tall shrub with small, fragrant, white flowers, and needlelike leaves.

HAKIM, AL-, or (Ar.) ABU-'ALI MANSŪR AL-HĀKĪM (985–1021), sixth Fatimid (q.v.) caliph and third caliph of Egypt (996–1021). His acts against the Christians and Christian holy places in Jerusalem aroused the general resentment in western Europe which culminated in the First Crusade (see CRUSADES). In 1016 he proclaimed himself the incarnation of the Deity, and was accepted as such by the Druses (q.v.). Al-Hakim met his death by assassination.

HAKKAS (Chinese, "guests" or "strangers"), term applied to a migratory people of southern China. Their origin has not been proved; they may be descended from the Burmese or Siamese, or from the aboriginal inhabitants of northern China. The Hakkas have always been persecuted by the natives of the regions in which they have settled. They differ from the Chinese in dress and customs, and speak a distinct dialect, related to those of southern China. Their women are not secluded, as many Chinese women are, nor do they bind their feet. The Hakkas are a thrifty, industrious people, engaging chiefly in agriculture, and working as quarrymen, stonemasons, porters, and barbers. When for a period they have been free from persecution, as under the Han dynasty (206 B.C.–220 A.D.), several Hakkas have attained high public office. During the Tang dynasty (7th to 9th centuries) they settled in the mountains of Fukien and during the 13th century they fought in the Chinese imperial army against the invading Mongol armies of Kublai Khan. They were again persecuted, after the 14th century, under the Ming dynasty, and moved to Kwangtung. The Hakkas have produced many noted scholars, such as Hung Hsiu-ch'üan (1812–64), leader of the Taiping Rebellion (q.v.).

HAKLUYT, RICHARD (1552?–1616), English geographer and writer, born near or in London, and educated for the ministry at Westminster School and Christ Church College, Oxford. While a student he became interested in geography and exploration, particularly in relation to the New World. His knowledge of these subjects made him so well known that in 1577, after receiving his M.A. degree, he was appointed public lecturer on geography by Oxford University. A book, *Divers Voyages Touching the Discoverie of America,* which he wrote in 1582, attracted considerable attention and influenced the government to appoint him chaplain to Sir Edward Stafford, English ambassador to France. On instructions from Sir Francis Walsingham, Queen Elizabeth's secretary of state, Hakluyt devoted himself in Paris to collecting information on Spanish and French voyages to America. In 1584, as a result of the material he compiled, he wrote *A Particular Discourse Concerning Westerne Discoveries* and three years later translated the journal of the French colonist René Goulaine de Laudonniere as *A Notable Historie Containing Foure Voyages Made by Certayne French Captaynes into Florida.*

Hakluyt returned to England in 1588 and a year later finished his greatest work, *Principall Navigations, Voiages, and Discoveries of the English Nation,* a compilation of the accounts of sea captains and explorers, including fact admixed with such fantasy as a description of the anatomy of sea monsters and the topography of regions still unexplored. The book was received with great acclaim and Hakluyt collected material for a new, enlarged edition which was published in three volumes (1598–1600). His work was regarded favorably by Queen Elizabeth, who gave him many preferments, including an

appointment as archdeacon of Westminster in 1603. After the accession of James I in 1602, Hakluyt was influential in procuring a royal patent for a Virginia colony and was one of the adventurers in the London or South Virginia Company. His last book was a translation of Hernando de Soto's explorations in Florida, *Virginia Richly Valued by the Description of Florida Her Next Neighbour* (1609). Many of Hakluyt's manuscripts, unpublished at the time of his death, were used by Samuel Purchas in his book *Pilgrimes.*

HAKODATE, seaport and city of southwestern Hokkaido Island, Japan, situated on a rocky promontory forming the eastern end of the bay of Hakodate, an inlet of Tsugaru Strait. The harbor is one of the finest in the world, spacious and easily accessible. Hakodate was opened in 1859 to foreign trade. For many years it was used by Russia as a winter port. Although it has lost its former rank in international shipping and trade, Hakodate is still important in interisland communication. Fishing is one of the chief industries. Exports from the city include fish products, sulfur, rice, and timber. Pop. (1940) 203,862.

HALAKAH, or HALACHA (Heb., "practice" or "rule"), in Judaism, the body of traditional law which is based on rabbinical decision and is supplementary to the Scriptural law contained in the Pentateuch, the Law of Moses. Handed down orally by the highest rabbinical authorities, these supplementary laws were first written in the Talmud (q.v.) during the first five centuries of the Christian era, and in the Midrash (q.v.), or Scriptural exegesis, begun about 200 A.D. The Halakah is the purely legal content of these works, the illustrations and amplifications of the ethical, political, and religious principles involved being set down in the Haggada (q.v.). After the completion of the Talmud, the Halakic and Haggadic elements of the great compilation were extracted and, with amplifications, used by themselves.

HALBERD or **HALBERT,** a weapon consisting of an ax blade and a spear mounted on the end of a long handle. It was an important weapon in the wars of middle Europe during the 15th and early 16th centuries. The handle, which was usually 5 to 6 feet in length, enabled a soldier on foot to reach an armored man on horseback, using the ax to cleave through the armor, and the spear as a weapon of defense to keep the man on horseback at a distance. The ax blades were often formed in a variety of artistic shapes. In the late 16th and early 17th centuries, as complete armor was gradually discarded and firearms were developed, the ax, or cleaving element, in the halberd was gradually displaced by the spear as an offensive weapon.

HALBERSTADT, city of the former State of Saxony-Anhalt, Germany, on the Holzemme R., 56 miles N.W. of Halle and 29 m. S.W. of Magdeburg. The earliest record of Halberstadt dates from 820. In the 10th century the city was made a bishopric of the Holy Roman Empire, and in 1813 it was annexed by Prussia. The Gothic cathedral, built in the 13th and 14th centuries, contains many valuable medieval objects of art. In the Liebfrauenkirche, or Church of Our Lady, which dates from the 12th and 13th centuries, are fine reliefs and mural frescoes. Many of the old private residences in Halberstadt are decorated with wood carvings. The chief industries in the city are the processing of foods, tanning, and the manufacture of paper, rubber, machinery, gloves, and cigars. Following World War II the city was included within the Soviet zone of occupation. Pop. (1946) 47,652.

HALCYON DAYS, days of serene peace. The term is derived from the ancient Greek legend that the "halcyon bird", or kingfisher, nests at sea during a fourteen-day period, encompassing a week prior to and a week after the winter solstice, when the weather in the northern Mediterranean Sea is customarily calm. See HALCYONE.

HALCYONE, in Greek mythology, daughter of Æolus, and wife of Ceyx. Their conjugal life was so happy that, according to one version of the legend, Halcyone dared to compare it to the marriage of Zeus and Hera, thereby incurring their divine wrath; in another version of the story, Halcyone cast herself into the sea after her husband had been drowned. In both versions the gods transformed Halcyone and Ceyx into kingfishers, and granted a period of calm to the seas at the winter solstice, when these birds were then believed to mate. See HALCYON DAYS.

HALDANE, J(OHN) B(URDON) S(ANDERSON) (1892–   ), English biologist, son of John Scott Haldane, born at Oxford, and educated at Eton and at Oxford University. After teaching at New College, Oxford, and at Cambridge University, he was appointed professor of biometry at University College, London, in 1936. He did research work for

the British admiralty between 1940 and 1944. Haldane was elected a Fellow of the Royal Academy in 1932, and was elected an honorary member of the Academy of Sciences of the U.S.S.R. in 1940. He is the author of a large number of books, many of which were intended for the general public as well as for biologists. His writings include *The Inequality of Man* (1932), *My Friend Mr. Leakey* (1937), *The Marxist Philosophy and the Sciences* (1938), *New Paths in Genetics* (1941), *What Is Life?* (1948), *Everything Has a History* (1951), and numerous scientific papers.

HALDANE, JOHN SCOTT (1860–1936), British physiologist, born in Edinburgh, and educated at the universities of Edinburgh and Jena. After 1912 he served as director of a mining research laboratory which was affiliated with Birmingham University after 1921; in connection with mining and industrial diseases caused by poor ventilation, he conducted extensive researches in respiration. Among his most important contributions were his discovery that breathing is regulated by the concentration of carbon dioxide in the respiratory center of the brain, and his methods of determining the amount of oxygen and carbon dioxide in blood. Haldane founded and became joint editor of the *Journal of Hygiene.* Among his writings are *Mechanism, Life and Personality* (1913), *New Physiology* (1919), *Respiration* (1922), *Materialism* (1932), and *The Philosophy of a Biologist* (1935).

HALDANE, RICHARD BURDON, VISCOUNT HALDANE OF CLOAN (1856–1928), British philosopher and statesman, born in Cloanden, Perthshire, and educated at the universities of Edinburgh and Göttingen. He was called to the Scottish bar in 1879, was elected a Liberal member of Parliament in 1885, and in 1905 became a cabinet minister, serving as secretary of state for war. As war secretary Haldane completely reorganized the British army, and established the Territorial Army, the Officers' Training Corps, and the scientific research department. As chairman of the royal commission on university education in 1910, he made recommendations which resulted in higher education in Britain becoming available to a larger portion of the population. He was created viscount in 1911 and became lord chancellor in the next year. In consequence of his known admiration for German philosophy and his attempts to reach a peaceful understanding with Germany, he was not included in the coalition cabinets of World War I; during this period, however, the value of his army reforms was fully proved. In 1924 he became lord chancellor to the first British Labour government. In the field of philosophy Haldane examined the doctrine of Georg Wilhelm Friedrich Hegel (q.v.) in relation to subsequent scientific discoveries. His books include *The Reign of Relativity* (1921) and *The Philosophy of Humanism* (1922). Haldane's influence on the spread of education was widely recognized. His *Autobiography* was posthumously published in 1929.

HALE, EDWARD EVERETT (1822–1909), American writer and Unitarian clergyman, born in Boston, and educated at Harvard College. He was pastor of the Church of the Unity, Worcester, Mass., from 1846 to 1856, and of the South Congregation Church, Boston, from 1856 to 1901. From 1903 until his death he served as chaplain of the U.S. Senate. Hale, who was a son of the journalist Nathan Hale, is known for his fictional writings, and for his abolitionist sympathies during the period immediately before the Civil War; his best-known work, the short story *The Man Without a Country* (1863, published in *The Atlantic Monthly*), is believed to have added to the strength of the Union cause. Hale wrote almost seventy published works, and for a time was editor of the magazines *Old and New* and *Lend a Hand*. He was also a member of the National Academy of Arts and Letters. His writings include the story *Ten Times One Is Ten* (1870), which led to the formation of many charitable organizations; the story *In His Name* (1873); *A New England Boyhood* (1893), reminiscences of New England life; *If Jesus Came to Boston* (1894), an attempt, in fiction, to reconcile religion with rapidly changing social conditions; and *Memories of a Hundred Years* (1902).

HALE, GEORGE ELLERY (1868–1938), American astronomer, born in Chicago, and educated at Massachusetts Institute of Technology. Hale engaged in research at the Harvard observatory and the University of Berlin, returning to the U.S. in 1888 to organize the Kenwood observatory in Chicago, where in 1889 he invented the spectroheliograph (q.v.). In 1892 he was appointed associate professor of astrophysics at the University of Chicago and, in 1895, organized the Yerkes observatory there, of which he served as director until 1904. In 1904 he organized the Mt. Wilson observatory, and served as its director until 1923. Hale was active in many scientific bodies, among them the National Research Council. He was a foreign member of the

Sir Matthew Hale

Institute of France and the Royal Society of London. While in retirement he was engaged in the development of the spectrohelioscope. Hale also conceived and helped to design the world's largest telescope. The instrument, a reflector with a 200-inch mirror, was installed at Mt. Palomar Observatory in 1948 and posthumously named the "Hale Telescope" in his honor. His writings include *The Study of Stellar Evolution* (1908), *The Depths of the Universe* (1924), and *Beyond the Milky Way* (1926).

HALE, JOHN PARKER (1806–73), American statesman, born in Rochester, N.H. His political career began in 1832 when, as a Jacksonian Democrat, he was elected to the New Hampshire legislature. From 1843 to 1845 he was a member of the House of Representatives; during this period his independence and vigor in the antislavery cause eventually brought about his expulsion from the regular Democratic Party, and in 1845 he led a powerful and successful personal campaign to influence the elections in his native state. As as independent Democrat, he was a senator from 1847 to 1853, the first antislavery man to be elected to that body; later, as a member of the Republican Party, he served in the Senate from 1855 to 1865, and consistently supported Lincoln's policy. From 1865 to 1869 he served as U.S. minister to Spain.

HALE, SIR MATTHEW (1609–76), British jurist and statesman, born in Alderney, Gloucestershire. He was called to the bar in 1637, and had a long public career, including service as a Justice of Common Pleas (1654)

Jacques Halévy

and in Parliament from 1654 to 1660. In 1660 Charles II knighted him, and appointed him chief baron of the Exchequer, and from 1671 to 1676 he was chief justice of the King's Bench, then the highest judicial office. As a member of Parliament, Hale shared in the triumph of the Parliamentary party under Cromwell, and he supported the Commonwealth after the execution of Charles I. However, he had labored to bring about a settlement between the king and Parliament, and eventually took an active part in the restoration of Charles II.

Hale's private studies included investigations in classical law, history, the sciences, and theology. He exercised considerable influence on the legal thought of his time, and his *Analysis of the Civil Part of the Law* furnished Blackstone with an outline of his Commentaries. Other works of his include *De Portibus Maris* and *A History of the Common Law.*

HALE, NATHAN (1755–76), hero of the American Revolution, born in Coventry, Conn., and educated at Yale College (now University). He taught school from 1773 until shortly after the outbreak of the American Revolution in 1775, when he became a lieutenant in the Continental Army. The following year he was promoted to a captaincy. While stationed near New York City with Knowlton's Rangers in early September, 1776, Hale volunteered to perform spy duty behind the British lines on Long Island. Disguised as a schoolmaster, he secured vital military information, but on September 21, before he could return to safe territory, he was captured. The next morning he was hanged by the British as a spy. His last words are supposed to have been: "I only regret that I have but one life to lose for my country". A statue of Nathan Hale stands in City Hall Park, New York City.

HALEAKALA (Hawaiian, "house of the sun"), a mountain on the island of Maui in the Territory of Hawaii. It is 10,032 ft. above sea level, and contains on its summit the largest extinct volcanic crater in the world. This crater is 20 m. in circumference and 2720 ft. deep; its floor contains 16 reddish cinder cones from 400 to 900 ft. high. The view from the summit is considered the finest in the Territory, and the windward slopes, which contain a series of gorges through which run rapid streams and waterfalls, are a source of water for the irrigation of the arid isthmus connecting the two halves of the island. See HAWAII NATIONAL PARK.

HALES, STEPHEN (1677–1761), British physiologist, born in Bekesbourne, Kent. Although a clergyman of the Church of England, Hales is best known as a physiologist, chemist, and inventor. Hales' interests were wide. His investigations are reported in his famous work, *Statickal Essays,* which was published in two volumes. The first, *Vegetable Staticks* (1727), deals with the physiology of plants; this work has caused Hales to be recognized as the founder of the science of plant physiology. The second volume, *Haemostaticks,* (1733) embodies his researches on the mechanics of blood flow. By means of animal experimentation, Hales was able to show that the circulating blood exerts pressure; see BIOPHYSICS. Hales also investigated reflex actions and demonstrated that they depended on the existence of the spinal cord. His other researches dealt with the behavior of gases, methods of ventilating ships and large buildings, the technique of determining ocean depths, and the processes of food preservation. In addition to his other works, Hales wrote anonymously *Admonition to the Drinkers of Gin, Brandy, etc.* (1734).

HA-LEVI, JUDAH. See JUDAH HA-LEVI.

HALEVY, JACQUES FRANÇOIS FROMENTAL ELIAS, originally surnamed LÉVY (1799–1862), French composer, born in Paris. He received his musical education at the Paris Conservatoire, where he studied counterpoint, fugue, and composition with Cherubini. In 1819 he won the Prix de Rome with his cantata *Herminie.* He later was professor of harmony and of composition at the Conservatoire. He first received recognition with the production of his satirical opera *Le Dilettante d'Avignon* (1829) and his ballet *Manon Lescaut* (1830), but not until his grand opera *La Juive* was produced in 1835, at the Paris Opéra, did he achieve importance as a composer of operas. This success was followed by another, in the same year, the musical comedy *L'Éclair*. Although Halévy wrote more than thirty operas, his fame as a composer rests mainly with *La Juive,* an opera made famous by the Italian tenor Enrico Caruso, who first appeared as Eleazar at the Metropolitan Opera House, New York City, in 1919.

HALFBEAK, common name for the small tropical fish in the family Hemiramphidae, closely related to the flying fish and in general form resembling the garfish (q.v.) but having the lower jaw prolonged far beyond the upper jaw, which is short and weak. Halfbeaks are found swimming near the surface in both salt and fresh water. They subsist on algae. The common species, *Hyporhamphus unifasciatus,* found off the s. Atlantic coasts of America, is about 13 in. in length, of which almost 3 in. is lower jaw. It often leaps out of the water, obtaining the necessary leverage by placing the tip of its lower jaw under a floating object. Other species, especially those in the genus *Euleptorhamphus,* found off Bikini Atoll, fly by spreading their fins after a leap. Many flying fish have a jaw structure similar to the halfbeak when young and they are sometimes considered descended from primitive halfbeaks. In Siam halfbeaks of the genus *Dermogenys* are cultivated for fish fights and are second only to the fighting fish (q.v.) in endurance. Fish of this genus utilize their beaks while fighting and engage in active "swordplay" but rarely draw blood. The fight continues until one or both of the participants are too exhausted to continue.

Halfbeaks are called gars (q.v.) in the U.S., garfishes in Australia and New Zealand, and escribanos (writers) or balaos (dancers) in the West Indies.

HALF DOME, or SOUTH DOME, a granite mountain in the Yosemite valley in central California, 8852 ft. above sea level and about 5000 ft. above the floor of the valley. It is one of the most imposing peaks in the Yosemite National Park (q.v.).

HALF LIFE, in a simple chemical or physical decay process, the time necessary for half of the material originally present to decompose. The half life of a reaction can be calculated only for those processes in which the rate of decomposition is directly proportional to the amount of the substance decaying. Radioactive decay is an important instance of decomposition of this type. For example, the half life of plutonium (q.v.) is 24,100 years. An ounce of plutonium will be reduced to one half ounce after 24,100 years, and after another 24,100 years one half of the half ounce, or one quarter of an ounce, will be left. The decay proceeds indefinitely, and it is therefore meaningless to consider the time necessary for the total disintegration of a radioactive substance. The half life of the radioactive isotope of carbon with atomic mass 14 is 5100 years; that of phosphorus-32 is 14.3 days; of nitrogen-13, ten minutes; and of polonium-212, three ten-millionths of a second. See RADIOACTIVITY.

HALFTONE. See PHOTOMECHANICAL PROCESSES: *Photoengraving.*

HALIBUT, common name for either of two species of flatfish (q.v.) in the genus *Hippoglossus,* related to the flounder. Halibut are longer, thicker, and heavier than any of the other flatfish, and differ somewhat in development. The upper, dark-brown side of the halibut corresponds to the right side of its embryo to which the left eye has migrated during development. The white underside corresponds to the left side. The dorsal and ventral fins also migrate so that they are situated at the new top and bottom of the adult fish. Unlike other flatfish, the result of the young halibut's development is a completely symmetrical fish.

The maximum size of the female is 7 to 8 ft. in length and 400 lbs. in weight; the male reaches a maximum weight of about 40 lbs. The flesh of the halibut is excellent food and the oil of its liver is even richer in vitamins A and D than cod-liver oil. Halibut are active and voracious, feeding principally on shellfish, but devouring other fishes whenever they have the opportunity. They are sexually mature at twelve years of age and live for more than thirty years. Their age may be determined by

The Atlantic halibut

Canadian National Railways

Old clock tower overlooking Halifax harbor, in the city of Halifax, Nova Scotia

the organic deposits in their ear bones (otoliths) which are laid down in seasonal rings. A female twelve years of age deposits 200,000 to 500,000 eggs at a time; one twenty years of age deposits 2,750,000 eggs; and older females produce even more. The eggs are laid in water at a depth of 900 ft. and drift with the currents at the same level until the birth of the young. The fish live in shallow water until sexual maturity, when they go down to depths of several thousand feet in search of food. Halibut are found in cold portions of the N. Atlantic and Pacific Oceans, and halibut fishing is a major industry in Canada and N. United States. In 1924 these two countries established the International Fisheries Commission for the Study of the Pacific Halibut, *Hippoglossus stenolepis,* the more important of the two species, found along w. North America from N. Alaska to Oregon, and off Hokkaido, Japan. The Atlantic halibut, *H. hippoglossus,* is found off Newfoundland s. to Massachusetts, and off Greenland, Iceland, the British Isles, and Scandinavia.

HALIFAX, chief Atlantic seaport of Canada and capital of the province of Nova Scotia, situated on a peninsula which juts out from the s.e. coast of Nova Scotia. The city is built on a hill overlooking Halifax Harbor, formerly Chebucto Bay, which is composed of two large basins, the harbor proper and Bedford Basin. The landlocked harbor has an area of 13 sq.m. and a minimum depth of 30 ft. Founded in 1749 as a British naval base intended to rival the French port of Louisburg, Halifax has retained its naval importance and is now commercially important as well. A naval dockyard covering an area of 14 acres extends along 2700 ft. of the waterfront. The city is a port-of-call for some thirty-six steamship lines, connecting the city with American and European ports. Harbor and dockage equipment include storage plants and facilities for the transshipment of goods. Halifax is the Atlantic terminus for several important railways, and is served by an airport. Goods manufactured or processed in the city, principally for export, include sugar, oil, wood products, skates, confections, spices, paint, varnish, cordage, paper boxes, clothing, nuts and bolts, fish, and fish products. Other exports include lumber, flour, and agricultural products. Manufactured goods are imported from the United States and Great Britain, and rum and fruit from the West Indies. Machine shops, shipyards, and insulating and steam-packing works are also located in the city. Dalhousie University, founded in 1818, the government house, the provincial parliament, and the Citadel, one of the older forts in the city, are among the interesting public buildings. On December 6, 1917, during World War I, a great part of the city was destroyed and hundreds of lives were lost when a munitions ship collided with another ship in the harbor and exploded. Halifax is an archiepiscopal see for the Roman Catholic Church and an episcopal see for the Anglican Church. Pop. (1951) 85,589.

HALIFAX, municipal, parliamentary, and county borough of West Riding of Yorkshire, England, located 7 m. by rail s.w. of Bradford. The borough was part of the royal manor of Wakefield in the 11th century. In the 15th century Halifax became a center for the cloth trade and in the 17th century was granted two markets and two fairs. It was incorporated in 1848 and became a county borough in 1888. Among notable buildings of the borough are the Heath Grammar School, founded in 1585; the Piece Hall, which was built in 1799 for the display and sale of piece goods; and the Rose and Crown Inn, on Black Lane, where Daniel Defoe is reputed to have written parts of *Robinson Crusoe*. The manufacture of cotton, woolen, and worsted goods and of carpets, iron, steel, and machinery are the most important industries in Halifax. Pop. (1951 prelim.) 98,376.

HALIFAX, CHARLES MONTAGU, EARL OF (1661–1715), English statesman and poet, born in Northamptonshire. He entered Parliament in 1689; in 1692 he became a lord of the Treasury, and in 1697 first lord of the Treasury and prime minister, a post which he held until 1699. Montagu was appointed auditor of the Exchequer in 1700, and, though twice impeached (1701 and 1703), retained this office until the accession of George I in 1714, when he again became first lord of the Treasury and prime minister.

In 1692, Montagu induced Parliament to float a loan of a million pounds, which became the basis of the permanent national debt of England. He was also active in the formation of the Bank of England in 1694, and in 1695 carried through a reformation of the currency, appointing Isaac Newton as warden of the Mint in charge of this work.

His reputation as a poet rests largely on his collaboration with Matthew Prior in writing *The Town and Country Mouse*, a parody of Dryden's *Hind and the Panther*. He was also active as a wit and patron of literature in London, and was an intimate of such men as Addison, Steele, and Congreve.

HALIFAX, EDWARD FREDERICK LINDLEY WOOD, 1st EARL and 3rd VISCOUNT (1881–), British statesman, born in Devon and educated at Eton and at Oxford University. He was a Conservative member of the House of Commons from 1910 to 1925. After holding a number of minor posts in the government, he became viceroy of India in 1926. He inaugurated a policy of co-operation with Mohandas Gandhi (q.v.) and did much to assuage the anti-British prejudice of the other Indian nationalist leaders. In 1931 he returned to England; in 1934 he succeeded to the viscountcy of Halifax, and in the following year became Conservative leader in the House of Lords. He was appointed secretary of state for foreign affairs early in 1938, and played an important role in the negotiation of the Munich Pact (q.v.). From 1941 to 1946 he was ambassador to the United States. He was created Earl of Halifax in 1944, and in the following year he served as a member of the British delegation to the United Nations Conference on International Organization, held at San Francisco, Calif. He is the author of *Indian Problems* (1932); a number of his important addresses were collected and published under the titles *Speeches on Foreign Policy* (1940) and *American Speeches* (1947).

HALIFAX, MARQUIS OF. See SAVILE, GEORGE.

HALITE or **ROCK SALT,** the mineral form of common salt, with the chemical composition sodium chloride, $NaCl$. Halite is a common mineral, formed by the drying of enclosed bodies of salt water; subsequently the beds so formed have often been buried by the rock strata formed from other sedimentary deposits. Beds of halite range in thickness from a few feet up to one hundred feet, and have been found at great depths beneath the surface of the earth. This mineral is often found associated with gypsum, sylvite, anhydrite, calcite, clay, and sand. Halite is widely disseminated over the world; in the United States notable deposits are found in New York, Michigan, Ohio, Kansas, New Mexico, and Utah.

Halite crystallizes in the isometric system, usually in the form of cubes, and shows perfect cubic cleavage. It is colorless and transparent when pure, but is often tinted yellow, red, blue, or purple by impurities. It has a hardness of 2½ and a specific gravity of 2.16.

Since World War II approximately three million tons of rock salt have been mined in the U.S. each year. For uses of the mineral, see SALT.

HALL, ASAPH (1829–1907), American astronomer, born at Goshen, Conn., and educated at Central College and the University of Michigan. In 1862 he was appointed aid in mathematics at the U.S. Naval Observatory. He was later promoted to a full professorship there, holding this position until he retired in 1891. From 1895 until 1901 he was professor of astronomy at Harvard. Hall is chiefly known for his discovery, in 1877, of the two moons of the planet Mars, *Phobos* (Fear) and *Deimos* (Terror).

HALL, CHARLES MARTIN (1863–1914), American chemist and inventor, born in Thompson, Ohio, and educated at Oberlin College. In 1886, while still a student at Oberlin, Hall became interested in the production of aluminum, which was then very expensive as the result of inefficient methods of extraction from its ores. Eight months after his graduation, Hall developed the first practical process for extraction of aluminum by means of electrolysis. In 1889 the Pittsburgh Reduction Company (later the Aluminum Company of America) was founded for the purpose of producing aluminum by the Hall process. Hall became vice-president of the company in 1890.

The process of aluminum manufacture in use today is essentially identical with the process developed by Hall; a similar process was developed independently by the French chemist Paul Héroult, probably a few months later. As a result of this process, aluminum has become an inexpensive metal, one of the basic materials in the American industrial economy. See ALUMINUM.

HALL, GRANVILLE STANLEY (1844–1924), American educator and psychologist, born in Ashfield, Mass., and educated at Williams College, Union Theological Seminary, and Harvard University, and in Berlin, Bonn, Heidelberg, Leipzig, and London. After teaching psychology at Harvard, Williams, Antioch College, and Johns Hopkins University, he became in 1889 president of the newly founded Clark University in Worcester, Mass. Under his guidance considerable work was done in educational research at the university during its first twenty years. Hall contributed to numerous educational journals, and was instrumental in the development of the new science of psychology. His work in this field shows the influence of William James (q.v.), under whom he studied while at Harvard. In 1887 he was the founder of the *American Journal of Psychology;* he resigned the presidency of Clark in 1920, but continued writing until his death. Hall's books include *Adolescence* (2 vols., 1904) ; *Jesus, the Christ, in the Light of Psychology* (2 vols., 1917) ; *Senescence, the Last Half of Life* (1922) ; and *Life and Confessions of a Psychologist* (1923). See EDUCATION.

HALL, JAMES (1793–1868), American writer and jurist, born in Philadelphia. After serving in the War of 1812, he settled in Shawneetown, Illinois, where he established a law practice and in 1825 became a judge of the Circuit Court of Illinois. He also became editor of the *Illinois Gazette* and later of the *Illinois Intelligencer,* and in 1830 founded the *Illinois Monthly Magazine,* the first literary magazine to be published west of Ohio. Hall is known chiefly for his books dealing with life in the West. His works include *Tales of the Border* (1835), *Legends of the West* (1832), and a *History of the Indian Tribes* (1836–44).

HALLAM, ARTHUR HENRY (1811–33), English poet and essayist, born in London, and educated at Cambridge University. At Cambridge he became friendly with Alfred Tennyson, who wrote the poem *In Memoriam* following Hallam's early death at Vienna. The literary works of Hallam were collected in *Remains in Prose and Verse* (1834).

HALLAM, HENRY (1777–1859), English historian, born in Windsor, and educated at Eton, at Christ Church, Oxford University, and at the Inner Temple. He practiced law until 1812, and then retired on the income from an inheritance and a government sinecure as commissioner of stamps. He devoted the rest of his life to historical research and writing. Hallam's historical judgments were often somewhat narrow, for he wrote as a devoted follower of Whig principles, and as a man accustomed to accepting 19th-century points of view as valid for all periods; however, his work opened new branches of historical study, and was marked by accuracy, conscientiousness, and thorough research in source material. His major works were *The View of the State of Europe during the Middle Ages* (1818), *Constitutional History of England* (1827), and *Introduction to the Literature of Europe in the Fifteenth, Sixteenth, and Seventeenth Centuries* (1838–39).

HALLE, or HALLE AN DER SAALE, city of Halle District, East Germany, on the Saale R., 21 m. by rail N.W. of Leipzig. In the 9th century Halle was a fortress. It early became known for its valuable saltworks, and received a charter as a town in 981. During the 13th and 14th centuries Halle was a free city of the Hanseatic League (q.v). After the Treaty of Westphalia in 1648, Halle became a part of the electorate of Brandenburg. The University of Halle was founded in 1694 by Elector Frederick of Brandenburg (later King Frederick I of Prussia) and has long been noted as a center of Protestant theology. Among the noteworthy buildings in Halle are the medieval town hall, the 12th-century St. Moritzkirche, and the 16th-century Marienkirche. The principal product of Halle is salt, which is obtained from salt springs on an island in the Saale R. Other important industries include brewing, sugar refining, printing, the making of machinery, and processing of foodstuffs. Halle was the birthplace of the composer George Frederick Handel, a statue of whom stands in the city square. Following World War II the city was incorporated into the Soviet Zone of Occupation. Pop. (1946) 222,505.

HALLE, ADAM DE LA. See ADAM DE LA HALLE.

HALLECK, FITZ-GREENE (1790–1867), American lyric poet and satirist, born at Guilford, Conn. In collaboration with his friend Joseph Rodman Drake, he wrote the satirical sketches *The Croaker Papers*, which were published in the New York *Evening Post* in 1819. Halleck commemorated the death of Drake in his best-known poem, "Green Be the Turf above Thee". His books of verse include *Fanny* (1819), *Alnwick Castle, with Other Poems* (1827), and *Poetical Works* (1847).

HALLECK, HENRY WAGER (1815–72), American army officer, born in Westernville, N.Y., and educated at the U.S. Military Academy at West Point. He was an expert in military fortifications and in 1846 wrote *Elements of Military Art and Science,* which was later used during the Civil War as a training manual for volunteer officers.

Halleck served on the west coast during the Mexican War. He resigned from the army in 1854, and had a successful career as a lawyer and industrialist until the outbreak of the Civil War, when he re-entered the army with the rank of major general. He commanded the Department of Missouri and planned the Western campaign of 1862. In July, 1862, he was appointed general in chief of the armies of the United States, and held this post until 1864 when he was superseded by General Ulysses S. Grant. He served as chief of staff of the army until 1865. This administrative post he filled with great success, although he has been generally ranked as a poor field commander. His writings in-

clude *Bitumen: Its Varieties, Properties, and Uses* (1841), *A Collection of Mining Laws of Spain and Mexico* (1859), and *International Law, or Rules Regulating the Intercourse of States in Peace and War* (1861).

HALLEL (Heb., "praise"), in the Jewish ritual, a selection from the Psalms, chanted as part of the liturgy during certain festivals. The more frequently used selection includes Psalms 113–118, and is known as the Egyptian Hallel, presumably because of Psalm 114, beginning "When Israel went out of Egypt . . ."; it is sung in synagogues on the first two days of Passover, on Pentecost (*Shabuoth*), on Tabernacles (*Sukkoth*), and on each morning of the eight days of Hanukkah. The Egyptian Hallel is also sung at the close of the domestic Passover service and is, presumably, the hymn sung by Jesus and his disciples at the end of the Last Supper (Mark 14:26). A second Hallel, the Great Hallel, includes Psalms 120–136, or may be Psalm 136 alone; it is sung at Passover and during Tabernacles. Originally, the Hallel consisted either of Psalms 113 or 114; the Psalms now included in the ritual are later additions, made about 160 A.D.

HALLELUJAH or ALLELUIA, a Hebrew expression meaning "Praise ye the Lord", which has been retained in hymns and liturgies of the Greek Orthodox, Roman Catholic, and Anglican churches. The Roman Catholic Church omits it from the liturgy in seasons of penance, as during Lent or on vigils of festivals. Musical composers of religious and semireligious music have made much use of it; a notable example is the "Hallelujah Chorus" in George Frederick Handel's oratorio *The Messiah.*

HALLER, ALBRECHT VON (1708–77), Swiss poet, philosopher, scientist, and theologian, born at Bern. A precocious youth, he had mastered several languages and written copiously in English and Latin by the time he was ten. He studied medicine at Tübingen and Leyden. He visited London, Oxford, and Paris and then went to Basle, where he studied first mathematics and then botany. He practiced medicine in Bern for a short time, but his botanical and anatomical researches led to his being offered a professorship in medicine, anatomy, surgery, and botany at the University of Göttingen in 1736. While at Göttingen, he conducted a monthly journal, the *Göttingische Gelehrte Anzeiger,* to which he contributed more than 12,000 articles in many fields of knowledge. He also

Albrecht von Haller (from an old print)

interested himself in religion, and succeeded in having a Reformed church erected in that city. Haller resigned his chair in 1753 and returned to Bern where he held various municipal and state positions, and where he wrote three sections of a projected *Bibliotheca Medica,* which was uncompleted at the time of his death. During the last few years of his life he was addicted to the use of opium.

Haller made many discoveries in botany, anatomy, physiology, and surgery; his best-known discovery was the distinction between sensible and irritable tissues, and his demonstration of the fact that irritability is a property of all living tissue, whereas sensibility is limited to tissues supplied with nerves.

Haller wrote a descriptive poem *Die Alpen* ("The Alps", 1729), and three philosophical romances *Usong* (1771), *Alfred* (1773), and *Fabius and Cato* (1774). His greatest work is the medical treatise *Elementa Physiologiæ Corporis* ("Elements of the Physiology of the Human Body", 1757–66).

HALLEY, EDMUND (1656–1742), English astronomer, born in London, and educated at Oxford University. At the age of nineteen he devised a new method for determining planetary orbits; and at the age of twenty he went to St. Helena, where he observed the southern skies and catalogued 341 stars of the Southern Hemisphere. The *Catalogus Stellarum Australium* (1679) won for him the name of the "Southern Tycho" (after the Polish astronomer Tycho Brahe), and election to the Royal Society. He visited Isaac Newton in 1684 to discuss the problem of gravity, and encouraged Newton to write the *Principia,* which Halley published in 1687 at his own expense. On a voyage on the Atlantic Ocean, which lasted from 1698 to 1700, Halley studied the magnetic variation of the compass, recording his results in *A General Chart of the Compass* (1701). He was made astronomer royal in 1720, and began an eighteen-year study of the complete revolution of the moon through its ascending and descending nodes.

Halley's name is best known in connection with the comet called Halley's comet. He applied Newton's law of gravitation to all available data on comets that had been observed and calculated parabolic orbits for twenty-four of them. Struck with the similarity of the comets of 1531, 1607, and 1682, he calculated that they were all the same comet, moving in an elliptical orbit, and reappearing at intervals of about 75½ years. He predicted that the comet would reappear late in 1758 or early in 1759 and the comet was seen on Christmas day in 1758. Since then the comet has returned in 1835 and 1910. Halley's comet was the first for which an elliptic orbit was calculated, and thus the first comet which was proven to belong to the solar system. Later astronomers were able to trace the comet's history, and it is believed to have been seen in 240, 467, and 625 B.C. Halley's *Tabulæ Astronomiæ* was published posthumously in 1749.

HALLGRÍMSON, JÓNAS (1807–44), Icelandic lyric poet, born at Steinsstadir and educated at the University of Copenhagen. Through comparison of the works of the principal German poets and of contemporary Icelandic writers, Hellgrímson became convinced that the form of the Icelandic language currently employed in the writing of poetry was stilted and almost unintelligible, both because it made use of outworn and complex figures of speech, and because it had been corrupted by the addition of many Danish and German words. In his poems Hallgrímson employed the pure form of Icelandic used in the days of the classical period of Icelandic literature (see ICELANDIC LITERATURE: *Classical Period*). Although all the lyric poetry Hallgrímson wrote fills only one small volume, his work was instrumental in setting up the new standards for the Icelandic language thenceforth followed by all Icelandic authors. Many of his poems and essays were first published in the periodical *Fjöenir*, which he helped to establish at Copenhagen in 1835.

HALL OF FAME FOR GREAT AMERICANS, a structure on the campus of New York University, in the Bronx, N.Y., erected in 1900 for the purpose of honoring Americans who have made signal contributions to the welfare or culture of the United States. A semicircular, open-air colonnade 630 feet in length, with a massive substructure, the Hall is designed to house 150 bronze tablets and busts. Its erection was made possible through the donation of $100,000, later increased to $250,000, by the American philanthropist Helen Miller Shepard.

Quinquennial elections to the Hall of Fame are conducted by a committee of 100 prominent Americans representative of the 48 States. Candidates, who may be nominated by any U.S. citizen, must have been dead at least 25 years and must have been citizens of the U.S., either through birth or naturalization. Agreement of three-fifths of the committee is necessary for election. The original plan provided for the selection of fifty persons at the first election, held in 1900, and for the election of five persons every five years thereafter until the full capacity of 150 had been reached. At the election of 1900, however, only twenty-nine names were chosen.

The following is an alphabetical list of the names of the individuals who have been elected since the erection of the Hall: John Adams, John Quincy Adams, Louis Agassiz, Susan Brownell Anthony, John James Audubon, George Bancroft, Henry Ward Beecher, Alexander Graham Bell, Daniel Boone, Edwin Booth, Phillips Brooks, William Cullen Bryant, William Ellery Channing, Rufus Choate, Henry Clay, Samuel Langhorne Clemens (Mark Twain), Grover Cleveland, James Fenimore Cooper, Peter Cooper, Charlotte Saunders Cushman, James Buchanan Eads, Jonathan Edwards, Ralph Waldo Emerson, David Glasgow Farragut, Stephen Collins Foster, Benjamin Franklin, Robert Fulton, J(osiah) Willard Gibbs, William Crawford Gorgas, Ulysses Simpson Grant, Asa Gray, Alexander Hamilton, Nathaniel Hawthorne, Joseph Henry, Patrick Henry, Oliver Wendell Holmes, Mark Hopkins, Elias Howe, Washington Irving, Andrew Jackson, Thomas Jonathan ("Stonewall") Jackson, Thomas Jefferson, John Paul Jones, James Kent, Sidney Lanier, Robert Edward Lee, Abraham Lincoln, Henry Wadsworth Longfellow, James Russell Lowell, Mary Lyon, James Madison, Horace Mann, John Marshall, Matthew Fontaine Maury, Maria Mitchell, James Monroe, Samuel Finley Breese Morse, William Thomas Green Morton, John Lothrop Motley, Simon Newcomb, Thomas Paine, Alice Freeman Palmer, Francis Parkman, George Peabody, William Penn, Edgar Allan Poe, Walter Reed, Theodore Roosevelt, Augustus Saint-Gaudens, William Tecumseh Sherman, Joseph Story, Harriet Beecher Stowe, Gilbert Charles Stuart, Booker Taliaferro Washington, George Washington, Daniel Webster, George Westinghouse, James Abbott McNeill Whis-

The Hall of Fame on the campus of New York University. The library is behind colonnade.

tler, Walt Whitman, Eli Whitney, John Greenleaf Whittier, Emma Willard, Frances Elizabeth Willard, Roger Williams, (Thomas) Woodrow Wilson, Wilbur Wright.

HALLOWEEN or **ALLHALLOWS EVE,** name applied to the evening of October 31, preceding the Christian feast of Hallowmas, Allhallows, or All Saints' Day. The observances connected with Halloween are believed to have originated among the ancient Druids (see DRUIDISM), who believed that on that evening Saman, the lord of the dead, called forth hosts of evil spirits. The Druids customarily lit great fires on Halloween, apparently for the purpose of warding off these spirits. Among the ancient Celts (see CELTIC PEOPLES AND LANGUAGES), Halloween was the last evening of the year, and it was regarded as a propitious time for examining the portents of the future. The Celts also believed that the spirits of the dead revisited their earthly homes on that evening. After their conquest of Britain the Romans added to the Halloween traditions features of the Roman festival held on November 1 in honor of Pomona, goddess of the fruits of trees.

The Celtic tradition of lighting fires on Halloween survived until modern times in Scotland and Wales, and in the concept of ghosts and witches still common to all Halloween observances. Traces of the Roman harvest festival survive in the custom, prevalent in both the United States and England, of playing games involving fruit, such as ducking for apples in a tub of water, and in the decorative use of pumpkins which are hollowed out, carved to resemble grotesque faces, and illuminated by candles placed inside.

HALLSTATT CULTURE, the culture characteristic of the first stage of the Iron Age (q.v.) in Central and Western Europe and the Balkans. It received its name from the village of Hallstatt, in Upper Austria, where a necropolis containing over 2000 graves and a great number of artifacts was excavated between 1846 and 1899. The period covered by the *Halstatt epoch* extends from about 1000 to 400 B.C.

Halstatt culture was characterized by elaborate funeral rites, involving, at different stages of the epoch, both cremation and inhumation. In general the age was marked by an increasing use of iron and an increasing skill in iron work, though occasionally older, Bronze-Age materials and techniques reappeared Hallstatt art has endured mostly in the form of iron and bronze work and pot-

tery, used as grave furniture, and decorated in symmetrical, repetitive, geometric patterns. In the few instances when artists took forms from nature, they distorted them into standardized geometrical shapes. See ARCHEOLOGY.

HALLUCINATION, the perception by an individual of an object which does not exist in his physical environment, or the experiencing of a sensation for which there is no external stimulus. Hallucinations occur in people particularly when they are under mental or physical strain. Common examples are hearing a doorbell ring when no one has rung the bell and becoming aware of a person in a room when there is actually no such person in the room. However, the frequent and persistent occurrence of hallucination of such vividness and seeming reality that the individual is convinced of their validity is a symptom of a mental disorder; see PSYCHOLOGY, ABNORMAL.

Hallucinations may be induced by suggestion in hypnosis (see HYPNOTISM) or by the administration of certain drugs, notably mescaline (see MESCAL) and lysergic acid diethylamide, known also as LSD. These drugs are currently important in neuropsychiatric research. It was discovered in 1955 that a new chemical, called Frenquel, counteracts the hallucination-producing effects of LSD and mescaline. Frenquel was found to be effective also in suppressing hallucinations associated with delirium tremens (q.v.) and mental disorders. Compare ILLUSION.

HALLWACHS, WILHELM (1859–1922), German physicist, born in Darmstadt, and educated at Strasbourg and Berlin. While he was a teacher of physics at the universities of Leipzig, Strasbourg, Giessen, and Dresden (he was made professor at Dresden in 1893), Hallwachs conducted researches on ultraviolet light. He is best known for his discovery in 1888 that a negatively charged body is discharged when ultraviolet light falls on it in a vacuum. This phenomenon, known as the Hallwachs effect, formed the basis for important discoveries, made about fifteen years later, in the field of photoelectricity.

HALMSTAD, seaport and capital of Halland County, Sweden, located at the mouth of the Nissa R. on the Kattegat, 76 m. by rail S.S.E. of Gothenburg. Halmstad is known to have existed as a fortified town during the 13th century. Until 1658, when it became part of Sweden, Halmstad was under Danish control. Among the most important industries of the town are fishing, the quarrying of granite, shipbuilding, brewing, and the manufacture of clothing, jute products, wood pulp, and paper. Pop. (1947) 32,474.

HALO, a term applied to certain phenomena of light diffraction caused by ice crystals in the atmosphere between the observer and the sun or moon. The commonest form of halo is a circle of colored light surrounding the sun's or moon's disk at an angular distance of 22° from the disk. A secondary halo caused by the diffraction from ice crystals sometimes is seen outside the primary halo at a distance of 46° from the sun or moon. Colored images resembling the disk of the sun and called *parhelia* or *sundogs* are also sometimes seen spaced 22° from the sun in a vertical or horizontal direction.

Halos are larger in diameter than the *coronas* seen around the sun or moon in hazy weather. Coronas are caused by the diffraction of light in water particles. Coronas are similar to rainbows (q.v.) and *fogbows*. The latter occur when sunlight strikes a fog bank, producing a colored arc about 40° in radius.

HALO, in religious art. See NIMBUS.

HALS, FRANS (1580?–1666), Dutch portrait and genre painter. He is generally regarded as one of the greatest masters of the art of portrait painting. There are no existing records of his life or work prior to 1616, in which year Hals painted the large "Banquet of the Officers of St. George's Shooting Company" (Haarlem Museum). This work, although more detailed than his later paintings, displays the overflowing vigor of Hals' style. His paintings executed between 1620 and 1640 are, for the most part, renderings of popular street types, itinerant musicians, and fisherboys, whom he portrayed with great vivacity and humor. Such well-known examples as the "Laughing Cavalier" (1624) in the Wallace Collection, London, and "La Bohémienne" (1630) in the Louvre, Paris, are characteristic of this period, and typify his most exuberant as well as his most popular manner.

Among his sitters were members of the most distinguished families of Holland, and such well-known contemporaries as the French philosopher René Descartes and the Flemish painter Sir Anthony Vandyck. Hals also received eight commissions to paint large portrait groups of the burgher guards and other corporations. They were executed at various periods of his life and the last two, done in 1664 and picturing the "Regenten of the Old Men's Almhouse" and the "Regentessen of the Old Women's Almhouse", are

"Singing Boy with Flute," by Frans Hals

considered his greatest, both as contemporary documents and as works of art.

His late work is characterized by a limited color range of black, flesh tints, and silvery whites and an amazing virtuosity of brushwork; because of the rapidity and directness of his manner every stroke is clearly visible in his work. The famous "Hille Bobbe" painted in 1650 (Berlin Gallery) is a typical example, as are a number of sharp, searching portraits done at this time.

Despite his early fame and successes Hals was in great poverty during the last years of his life, and was often dependent on a municipal dole. He left a painted record of life in Haarlem unapproached by any other Dutch painter. His paintings influenced the entire Haarlem school of the 17th century. His work is represented in virtually every important museum of the world.

HALSEY, WILLIAM FREDERICK (1882–   ), American naval officer, born in Elizabeth, N.J., and educated at the U.S. Naval Academy at Annapolis. He was given the nickname "Bull". He was commissioned an ensign in the U.S. Navy in 1906 and advanced through the ranks to rear admiral in 1938, vice-admiral in 1940, admiral in 1942, and fleet admiral in 1945. During World War II Halsey led the attacks against the Japanese on Marshall and Gilbert islands in January, 1942, and became commander of the Allied naval forces in the South Pacific in October,

1942. He led the naval action in the Philippines in 1944–45, and in July, 1945, commanded the bombardment of Japan from the sea. He was released from active duty in December, 1946, and retired in April, 1947.

HÄLSINGBORG, or HELSINGBORG, seaport city of Malmöhus Province, s. Sweden, located on the Öresund, or the Sound, opposite Helsingör, Denmark, with which it is connected by railway ferry. The modern city was established in the early 15th century near the site of the old town, which was known as a trade center as early as the 9th century. A ruined fortress is all that remains of the old town. The city belonged to Denmark until 1658, and after a period of conflict between Denmark and Sweden, it finally passed into the control of the latter country in 1710. Hälsingborg is an important port and one of the leading manufacturing centers in the country. It is located near the only coal field in Sweden and near large clay deposits. Among the principal industrial establishments are sugar and copper refineries, breweries, superphosphate works, potteries, and rubber factories. Pop. (1947) 69,051.

HALSTED, GEORGE BRUCE (1853–1922), American mathematician and educator, born in Newark, N.J., and educated at Johns Hopkins University and in Berlin. He was professor of mathematics at several institutions, including the University of Texas, St. John's College, Kenyon College, and Colorado State Teachers College. Halstead furthered the knowledge of non-Euclidean geometry (see GEOMETRY), translating the papers of such workers in this field as János Bolyai and Nikolai I. Lobachevski. He wrote on mathematics, philosophy, and formal logic for scientific magazines, and was a collaborator in the preparation of *The Century Dictionary and Cyclopedia*. His books include *Elementary Synthetic Geometry* (1892), *Non-Euclidean Geometry* (1900) and *Rational Geometry* (1904).

HALYS. See KIZIL IRMAK.

HAM. See MEAT.

HAM, in the Book of Genesis of the Old Testament, the second of Noah's three sons who repopulated the earth after the deluge. According to the genealogy presented in Gen. 10, Ham fathered four sons, the progenitors of the southern peoples of the earth. Cush became the ancestor of the Ethiopians; Mizraim of the Egyptians; Canaan of the Canaanites, the pre-Israelite inhabitants of Palestine; and Phut of an African people inhabiting Libya. In the Psalms, Egypt is re-

ferred to several times as the "land of Ham", evidently because of this Biblical genealogy, and the name of the Egyptian deity, Ammon, may well have been derived from the same source. Philologists and ethnologists recognize a distinct North African family of peoples and tongues which they term the Hamitic, classifying it as co-ordinate with the Aryan and Semitic families. See HAMITES.

HAMA, a city of Syria, situated on both banks of the Orontes R., about 120 m. by rail N. of Damascus. Its principal products are wool, silk, and cotton textiles. Pop. (1944) 71,391.

HAMADAN, capital of Hamadan Province, N.W. Iran, situated in a fertile region, about 180 miles s.w. of Teheran. The city of Hamadan contains a number of bazaars, several mosques, and two tombs of special interest, one claimed to be that of the Biblical Mordecai and Esther, and the other, that of the Arabian philosopher-physician Avicenna. The city is known for the manufacture of rugs, leather trunks, and copperware. It is the center of the Iranian shellac and leather trade, and is commercially important because of its position on the principal route between Bagdad and Teheran. The city is believed to occupy the site of the ancient *Ecbatana*. During World War I Hamadan was the scene of fighting between Russian and Turko-German forces. The Russians captured the city in 1915, were expelled by the Turks in 1916, but regained control in the following year. The Iranian government later resumed possession of Hamadan and other Iranian towns held by Russia. British troops en route to the Caspian Sea occupied Hamadan for a time in the spring of 1918. Pop. (1942) 104,000.

HAMADRYAD (Gr. *hama,* "together with"; *drys,* "tree"), common name applied to the sacred baboon and to the king cobra (qq.v.).

HAMAL, a star of the second magnitude in the constellation Aries (q.v.). It is the brightest star in this constellation, and is also called *a* Arietis. Hamal is about eighty light years from the earth.

HAMAMELIDACEAE. See WITCH HAZEL.

HAMAN, or AMAN, in the Book of Esther of the Old Testament, an Amalekite who was the chief minister of the Persian king Ahasuerus. When Mordecai, a prominent Jew, refused to pay homage to Haman, the minister attempted to have all the Jews in the kingdom massacred. His plans were foiled by Esther, the Jewish consort of Ahasuerus, and

Staats-Herold Corp.

The city of Hamburg on the Elbe River, Germany

Haman was hanged on the gibbet he had prepared for Mordecai. See ESTHER, BOOK OF.

HAMAR (formerly STORHAMMER), county seat of Hedmark County, Norway, located on Lake Mjösen, N. of Oslo. The town was founded in 1848. It occupies the site of a town established in 1152 by Nicholas Breakspear, who was papal legate to Norway and Denmark before his election in 1154 as Pope Adrian IV. All that remains of the old town is a ruined cathedral. Modern Hamar is a railroad junction and the center of the richest agricultural area in Norway. The condensing of milk, and the manufacture of boilers and locomotives are the most important industries in the city. Pop. (1950) 11,507.

HAMATH. See HAMA.

HAMBORN. See DUISBURG.

HAMBURG, successively a constituent state of the German empire and the Weimar Republic, an incorporated territory of the Third Reich, and, after May 23, 1949, a State of the Federal Republic of (West) Germany. The state consists mainly of narrow strips of territory contiguous to the lower reaches of the Elbe R. and of several islands of the Elbe and the North Sea; it is bounded by Schleswig-Holstein on the N. and by the new state of Lower Saxony on the S. The capital, largest city, and chief seaport of the state is Hamburg (q.v.). Other noteworthy communities are Cuxhaven, also a seaport, situated at the mouth of the Elbe, and Bergedorf. The state includes also a number of rural districts, in which large crops of fruit and vegetables are raised and dairy products are produced. Shipping and related industries are the principal source of wealth. The state contains numerous manufacturing enterprises, confined mainly to Hamburg. As part of the German empire, the state, officially known as the Free and Hansa City of Hamburg, comprised the capital, Cuxhaven, Bergedorf, the islands, and several outlying enclaves. Portions of Prussia, including Altona and twenty-seven rural districts, were incorporated into the state in 1938, giving it continuous boundaries. In May, 1945, following the collapse of the Third Reich in World War II, the state was occupied by British troops; it subsequently formed part of the British occupation zone.

Hamburg is governed according to the provisions of the constitution of 1952. By the terms of that document supreme authority is vested in a House of Burgesses consisting of 120 elected members; executive authority is exercised by the Senate, a twelve-member body elected by and from the House of Burgesses.

Area, 288 sq.m.; pop. (1950) 1,605,606.

HAMBURG, capital of the state of Hamburg (q.v.) Federal Republic of (West) Germany, the principal seaport, chief commercial center, and second-largest city of the country, and formerly the largest seaport on the European mainland. The city is situated on the N. branch of the Elbe R. at its confluence with the Alster R., about 75 miles inland from the North Sea and about 178 m. by rail N.W. of Berlin. In addition to vast accommodations for the receipt and discharge of transocean freight, the distribution facilities of the port include rail and inland-waterway connections with all major points in the interior of Germany. More than 16,200 vessels, with a net tonnage of nearly 18,925,-000, entered Hamburg in a normal year prior to the outbreak of World War II. Imports and exports totaled about 17,690,000 tons and about 14,975,000 tons, respectively, in normal years. Hamburg is also an important manufacturing center. Shipbuilding and related industries flourished prior to and during World War II, but many of these enterprises were extensively damaged by Allied air raids. Other leading industries of Hamburg include food processing, jute spinning, brewing, and the manufacture of distilled spirits, soap, furniture, wall paper, tobacco products, fertilizer and other chemicals, motor vehicles, bicycles, sewing machines, precision instruments, machinery, and textile products.

Hamburg consists of an old section, situated on the E. side of the Alster, a new section (*Neustadt*) on the w. side, and several suburbs. The old section, which contains the heart of the commercial district, is traversed by numerous canals. The main thoroughfare of Hamburg is the *Neuer Jungfernstieg,* around which center the better shopping, hotel, and residential districts. Among the outstanding features of the city are the many bridges spanning the canals; the Inner Alster and Outer Alster, artificial lakes created by a dam at the mouth of the Alster; the ancient ramparts, converted into a system of gardens and promenades around the old section of the city; and the *Hopfenmarkt,* the principal public square. Noteworthy ecclesiastical edifices are the church of St. Peter, parts of which date from the 12th century; the churches of St. Catharine and St. Jacob, both medieval structures; the church of St. Michael, a building in the Renaissance style with a lofty spire (431 ft.), completed in 1762; and the church of St. Nicholas, a Gothic structure with a spire 482 feet in height. The spire of St. Nicholas is one of the highest in the world. Other imposing buildings are the Rathaus, an elaborate edifice in the German Renaissance style, the Exchange, and the *Deutsches Schauspielhaus.* The city has a number of exceptional educational and cultural institutions, including the University of Hamburg (founded in 1919), a nautical school, a school of marine architecture, a museum of natural history, a public art gallery, an industrial art museum, a botanical museum, botanical and zoological gardens, and a municipal library.

Hamburg originated as *Hammaburg,* a fortress established by the Frankish emperor Charlemagne about 808 as a defense outpost against neighboring pagan tribes. Extending his campaign to convert the pagans to Christianity, Charlemagne founded a church in the vicinity of the fortress in 811. The church quickly became the center of Christian civilization in N. Europe and, as such, was subject to frequent attacks by hostile natives. Hamburg was designated an' archbishopric in 834. In 847, two years after the town was sacked by Norsemen, the seat of the archbishopric was transferred to Bremen. Despite destructive raids by the Danes and Slavs, Hamburg endured and, in 1189, received a charter from the German king and Holy Roman Emperor Frederick I Barbarossa. Among other things, the charter, an award for services rendered during the Third Crusade, granted the town important commercial privileges. Defensive alliances concluded with Lübeck in 1241 and with Bremen in 1249 led to the formation of the Hanseatic League (q.v.). By decree of Maximilian I, Hamburg became a free city of the Holy Roman Empire in 1510. The struggle between the Hamburg followers of Martin Luther and the Roman Catholic Church resulted in victory for the former in 1529. During the Thirty Years' War, the commercial prosperity of the city declined disastrously. A brief revival, initiated by the establishment of trade ties with the United States in 1783, was terminated by the Napoleonic Wars. Napoleon's forces occupied the city in 1806. Re-established as a free city after his downfall, it became a member of the Germanic Confederation in 1815. Hamburg recovered swiftly from the effects of the French occupation and continued to expand, despite a destructive fire in 1842. The city was a member of the North German Confederation from 1866 to 1871, when it became a constituent state of the German

Empire. A popular uprising in Hamburg in November, 1918, on the eve of the German surrender in World War I, heralded the overthrow of the German empire and the formation of the Weimar Republic. An important submarine base and center of the Nazi war effort during World War II, Hamburg was the target of frequent Allied air raids. These raids devastated extensive industrial and residential areas. British troops occupied the city in May, 1945. Pop. (1946) 1,384,106.

HAMDEN, a town of New Haven Co., Conn., situated 5 miles N. of the city of New Haven. The principal industries in the town are the manufacture of wire and wire rope, organs, concrete and concrete products, machine-shop products, textiles, automobile accessories, steel, garment fasteners, building materials, flour, and dairy products. Hamden was settled about 1638 and incorporated in 1786. Pop. (1950) 29,715.

HAMELN, a town in Lower Saxony, Germany, situated at the confluence of the Hamel and Weser rivers, 33 miles S.W. of the city of Hanover. The town contains many specimens of medieval and Renaissance architecture. The principal public buildings include the Hochzeitshaus (marriage house), adorned with fine gables; the town hall; the church of St. Boniface; and the Rattenfängerhaus (ratcatcher's house), containing murals depicting the legend of the pied piper. The chief industries are shipbuilding and the processing of chemicals, sugar, tobacco, and leather. The town developed around the 9th-century abbey of St. Boniface. In 1259 Hameln was sold to the Bishop of Minden, but the transaction did not meet with the approval of the townspeople, who, after a violent battle, placed themselves under the protection of the duchy of Brunswick. Hameln was a member of the Hanseatic League (q.v.). It was taken by the Swedes in 1633, and by the French in 1757; in 1806 it became a part of the kingdom of Westphalia, and finally passed to Prussia in 1866. After the defeat of Germany in World War II, Hameln was incorporated in the British zone of occupation. Pop., about 32,000.

HAMILCAR (270?–28 B.C.), surnamed BARCA ("lightning"), a Carthaginian general, the father of Hannibal (q.v.). In 247 B.C., the sixteenth year of the First Punic War (see PUNIC WARS) between Carthage and Rome, Hamilcar was appointed commander of the Carthaginian forces in Sicily. Establishing himself on Mount Hercte (Ercte), he made plundering attacks in all directions, sending his privateers along the coast of Italy as far N. as Cumæ. For three years he withstood Roman efforts to dislodge him from this position. In 244 B.C. he occupied Mount Eryx (Monte San Giuliano), whence he harassed the Romans until 241, when the defeat of the Carthaginian admiral Hanno compelled Hamilcar to abandon Sicily. While in Sicily, Hamilcar had made various commitments to his mercenary troops, which, after his return to Africa, he was unable, through lack of support from the government, to fulfill. The troops thereupon revolted, and were joined by some African tribes. The Carthaginian politician, Hanno the Great, attempted vainly to suppress the uprising. Hamilcar was then summoned, and succeeded in defeating the rebels, capturing their towns, and bringing their leaders to punishment. Appointed commander in chief of the army, Hamilcar formed the plan of establishing a new empire in Spain, from which he could launch a major attack upon Rome. He began his Spanish campaign in 237. After spending nine years in Spain, he was killed in battle against the Vettones, an Iberian tribe.

HAMILTON, county seat of Butler Co., Ohio, situated on the Great Miami R., 25 miles N. of Cincinnati. It is served by two railroads, and maintains a municipal airport. The city is an important manufacturing center and the trading center of a rich farming and stock-raising area. Industrial establishments in Hamilton include paper mills, woolen mills, foundries, machine shops, and factories manufacturing bank vaults and safes, heavy machine tools, motors, auto parts, paper-mill machinery, lamps, chemicals, prefabricated houses, stoves, sugar-refining machinery, tin cans, felt, and ladies' apparel. The city is the site of several business colleges, and contains two hospitals. Hamilton is commemorated in *A Boy's Town* by the American author William Dean Howells, who lived there as a boy. The city developed around Fort Hamilton, a stockade built on the site in 1791 by Gen. Arthur St. Clair, first governor of the Northwest Territory. The town was laid out in 1794 and named Fairfield. In 1796 the fort was abandoned, and the town was later renamed Hamilton, becoming the county seat in 1803. It was incorporated as a village in 1810 and as a city in 1857. Pop. (1950) 57,951.

HAMILTON, seaport town and capital of the Bermuda Islands, situated on Great Sound,

Main or Bermuda Island. The town possesses an excellent landlocked harbor. Hamilton was founded in 1790. Pop., about 3000.

HAMILTON, county seat of Wentworth Co., Ontario, Canada, situated at the w. extremity of Lake Ontario, 40 miles s.w. of Toronto. It is served by five railroads, and by Great Lakes and ocean-going steamers, and maintains a municipal airport. The Hamilton harbor is landlocked, and is one of the largest and best equipped on the Great Lakes. With its abundant water power, derived from nearby falls, and natural gas obtained from fields in the vicinity, Hamilton has become one of the most important manufacturing centers in Canada. It is also the center of a noted fruit-growing area, and has the largest open-air market in Canada. The manufacture of steel, iron, textiles, and electrical equipment are the basic industries in the city, and the more than 500 industrial establishments, including the largest agricultural-implement factory in the British Empire, produce a greater variety of products than any other city in Canada. Many of the industrial plants in Hamilton are operated by U.S. capital. The city is the site of a Provincial Government Normal School, and McMaster University, founded in 1887. It is an episcopal see of the Anglican Church and of the Roman Catholic Church. Among the hospitals in the city are the Ontario Hospital, for the mentally ill, and the Hamilton Mountain Sanitorium, for persons with pulmonary diseases. Dundurn Castle, in Hamilton, contains a museum of local history. The city maintains a park system covering approximately 2000 acres, which includes bathing beaches, golf courses, and botanical and rock gardens. Hamilton was first permanently settled in 1778, and incorporated as a city in 1833. Pop. (1951) 208,321.

HAMILTON, a burgh of Lanarkshire, Scotland, situated about a mile from the confluence of the Clyde and Avon rivers, and 11 miles s.e. of Glasgow. The inhabitants are chiefly employed in neighboring coal and iron mines and limestone quarries; market gardening and the embroidering of muslin are minor industries. Among the prominent structures of the town are the burgh buildings, with a clock tower 130 ft. high; and the county buildings, executed in the Grecian style. Hamilton furnishes the title to the premier peer of Scotland, the Duke of Hamilton and Brandon. Two miles north of the town is the famous Bothwell Bridge, where the Covenanters were defeated in 1679 (see

Covenanters). Pop. (1951 prelim.) 40,173.

HAMILTON, Alexander (1757–1804), American statesman, born on the West Indian island of Nevis, the son of James Hamilton, a Scottish trader, and of Rachel Fawcett (Faucette) Levine. In 1769, after the death of his mother and the bankruptcy of his father, he entered the countinghouse of Nicholas Cruger at St. Croix, where he exhibited such ability that in two years he was entrusted with the entire charge of the business. With the aid of funds advanced by friends to further his education, from 1772 to 1774 he studied at a grammar school at Elizabethtown, N.J., and then entered King's College (the present-day Columbia University).

Hamilton's advocacy of the cause of the American colonies against England began at a public meeting in the "fields" (now City Hall Park) in New York City, with a brilliant, well-reasoned speech urging the calling of a general congress of the colonies. He also wrote, anonymously, two pamphlets, *A Full Vindication of the Measures of Congress from the Calumnies of Their Enemies* (1774) and *The Farmer Refuted* (1775), in answer to Loyalist pamphlets signed "Westchester Farmer". His pamphlets were at first attributed to such leaders as John Jay and Robert Livingston; when his authorship became known, they brought Hamilton wide recognition.

On the outbreak of hostilities in the Revolutionary War, Hamilton became a captain of artillery, and served with distinction in the battles of Long Island, White Plains, Trenton, and Princeton. His courage and ability won him the notice of General Nathanael Greene, who introduced Hamilton to George Washington with a recommendation for advancement. In March, 1777, Washington made Hamilton his aide-de-camp and confidential secretary. He acquired great influence with Washington, both as friend and as adviser, but he was ambitious for military glory, and took advantage of a rebuke from the general to resign his post in 1781. He remained in the army, however, and, taking command of a regiment of infantry, distinguished himself at Yorktown.

In 1780 he married Elizabeth, daughter of General Philip Schuyler, allying himself with one of the most influential families in New York. At the close of the Revolution he left the army and studied law at Albany. He served a term in Congress in 1782–83, and then returned to the practice of law, becoming one of the most eminent lawyers in New York City.

In 1786 he took a leading part in the Annapolis Convention, called to deal with the problems of interstate commerce and other matters not covered by the Articles of Confederation, and drafted the resolution which led to the assembling of the Constitutional Convention at Philadelphia in the following year. At the Constitutional Convention his two fellow delegates from New York were antifederalists who outvoted him on every measure; nevertheless, Hamilton presented his plan of a strongly centralized federal government to the convention. His plan involved representation based on wealth and property, and absolute veto power vested in the executive; its aristocratic principles were rejected by the convention, but its forms were largely adopted. Although he was unable to obtain the form of government he desired, Hamilton turned his energy and ability to securing ratification of the constitution adopted by the convention. He conceived and started the series of essays which were published in the New York *Independent Journal,* and which were subsequently collected and published under the title of *The Federalist* (q.v.). Fifty-one of the eighty-five essays were written by Hamilton, and constitute the works by which he is best known.

Shortly after the establishment of the new government in 1789 with Washington as president, Hamilton was appointed secretary of the treasury. Finding public credit in disrepute, official accounts of the state treasury deficient, and the national economy in a generally unhealthy condition, Hamilton instituted a series of reforms and wrote reports that have strongly influenced the administration of the national government since that time. His reports on public credit raised materially the low concept of national honor of the time, and were instrumental in securing the passage of measures for the funding of the public debt. In a report favoring the establishment of a national bank, he advanced the principle of the "implied powers" of the Federal government under the Constitution, which later greatly influenced the decisions of the Supreme Court. His report on manufactures was notable as one of the first departures from the economic theories of Adam Smith, and as the genesis of the American protective policy; it advocated the establishment of a protective tariff and bounties to be paid in the encouragement of manufactures from the surplus funds derived from the tar-

Alexander Hamilton

iff. Hamilton was also largely responsible for the organization of the entire administrative structure of the government, and his reports on subjects outside the immediate scope of his department illustrate his versatility and ability as a statesman.

In 1795 Hamilton resigned from the cabinet, and, after declining appointment as chief justice of the U.S. Supreme Court, returned to his law practice in New York City. He continued his activities in political matters, however, and, with a series of essays signed "Camillus", defended Jay's Treaty (q.v.) as the best that could be obtained. Washington respected his ability and judgment and consulted him often. In 1798, at Washington's insistence, Hamilton was appointed major general, second in command of the army organized when war with France seemed imminent. Hamilton was the leader of the Federalist Party (q.v.); he supported John Adams for the presidency, but after the latter's election they became political opponents and Adams expelled Hamilton's friends from the Cabinet and other offices.

In the election of 1800, which was thrown into the House of Representatives because Thomas Jefferson and Aaron Burr had received equal numbers of electoral votes, Hamilton exerted his great influence in favor of Jefferson, who had always been his chief political opponent (see DEMOCRATIC PARTY), rather than favor Burr, whom he considered to be a man of dangerous ambitions. In 1804 Hamilton was instrumental in the defeat of Burr as candidate for governor of New York State. After his defeat Burr forced a quarrel on Hamilton and challenged him to a duel. Although he strongly disapproved of dueling, Hamilton felt obliged to accept the challenge, and they met at Weehawken, N.J., on the spot where Hamilton's eldest son had been killed in a duel three years before. Hamilton was mortally wounded and died the next day.

HAMILTON, ANDREW (1676?-1741), American lawyer, born in Scotland, famous for his defense of the publisher John Peter Zenger (q.v.). He was attorney general of Pennsylvania in 1717, a member of the provincial council from 1721 to 1724, and a member of the provincial assembly from 1727 to 1739. In 1734, when Zenger was charged with having published seditious and libelous material in his newspaper, Hamilton was summoned to his defense. In an eloquent address to the jury, he argued that the material was true, and had been published in the interests of public welfare, and therefore could not be regarded as libelous. He won an acquittal, and thereby succeeded in establishing the precedent for freedom of the press in the American colonies.

HAMILTON, EMMA (1761?-1815), English beauty, celebrated as the mistress of Lord Nelson. She was born Emma Lyon, in Great Neston, Cheshire. At the age of about twenty she became the mistress of Charles Greville (1749-1809), and under his tutelage she studied dancing, singing, and acting. In 1784 Greville, who had fallen into debt, agreed to send Emma to his uncle, Sir William Hamilton, the British ambassador to the court of Naples, who desired her as his mistress; in return, Hamilton paid off Greville's debts. Within a short time Emma became the favorite of the court, confidante of Queen Maria Carolina, and the chief liaison agent between the queen and the ambassador. In 1791 she visited England with Hamilton, and during their stay they were married.

Her first meeting with Lord Nelson (see NELSON, HORATIO) took place two years later; in 1798 she rendered invaluable assistance to him by obtaining supplies needed for his campaign on the Nile. In 1800 the ambassador, Lady Hamilton, and Nelson returned to England together, and in the following year she bore Nelson a daughter, Horatia Nelson Thompson. Upon her husband's death in 1803,

Lady Hamilton received a lifetime income of £800; soon afterward she went to live with Nelson. Two years later, when Nelson was killed at the battle of Trafalgar, she received his Merton estates and an annuity of £500. Despite these bequests, her extravagant habits and penchant for gambling soon left her penniless. She was imprisoned for debt in 1813; regaining her freedom after one year, she went to Calais, France, where she died in penury.

HAMILTON, SIR IAN STANDISH MONTEITH (1853-1947), English soldier, born in Corfu, and educated at Wellington College and in Germany. He entered the army in 1873, served in the Afghan War from 1878 to 1880 and in the South African revolt of 1881, and later participated in expeditions to the Nile and to Burma. He rose to the rank of major general in 1901, at the close of the Boer War, and then acted for one year as chief of staff to Lord Kitchener and for another as quartermaster general. During the Russo-Japanese War he accompanied the Japanese forces as a British observer. In 1914 Hamilton was promoted to the rank of general. He spent the first months of World War I as commander of the English Home Defense Army, and in 1915 was selected to lead the Mediterranean Expeditionary Force. After his failure to land troops successfully on the Gallipoli peninsula (see GALLIPOLI CAMPAIGN), he was relieved from command there and returned to England. Hamilton wrote a considerable amount of prose and verse; his books include *Gallipoli Diary* (1920) and *The Soul and Body of an Army* (1921).

HAMILTON, PATRICK (1504-28), Scottish theological reformer and martyr, born probably in Glasgow, and educated at the universities of Paris and Louvain. He adopted many of the views of the Protestant reformers (see REFORMATION), and after returning to Scotland began to preach at the University of St. Andrews. In 1527 his heretical views were brought to the attention of the archbishop of St. Andrews, and Hamilton fled to Germany He spent some time with Martin Luther (q.v.) at Wittenberg, and studied at the newly established University of Marburg, where the Protestant doctrines were taught. During this period he wrote the *Loci Communes,* a treatise known also as "Patrick's Places", setting forth the arguments for ecclesiastical reform. Later, he returned to Scotland, and was invited to present his views at an ecclesiastical conference at St. Andrews. After a disputation lasting almost a month, a council of bishops convicted him of heresy, and he was burned at the stake on the same day. Hamilton's martyrdom gave great impetus to the Reformation in Scotland.

HAMILTON, SIR WILLIAM ROWAN (1805–65), Irish mathematician and astronomer, born in Dublin, and educated at Trinity College, Dublin. He was appointed to a professorship at this college and spent the rest of his life in the study of mathematics at the observatory at Dunsink, near Dublin. Hamilton is known mainly for his work in vector analysis, in optics, and in dynamics. In the last-named field he introduced *Hamiltonian functions,* which express the sum of the kinetic and potential energies of a dynamic system; they are of great importance in the development of modern dynamics and quantum mechanics. Hamilton was Astronomer Royal for Ireland (1828) and was knighted in 1835.

HAMILTON COLLEGE, an institution of higher learning for men chartered in 1812, and situated at Clinton, N.Y. The curriculum includes preprofessional courses in medicine, dentistry, law, journalism, business, music, teaching, and theology, and general courses in the liberal arts and sciences, leading to bachelors' and masters' degrees. The facilities of the college include an astronomical observatory and notable collections of scientific specimens. In a recent year, the faculty comprised 57 professors and instructors, and the student body numbered about 600.

HAMILTON RIVER, principal river of Labrador, Canada, rising in the inland plateau region of Labrador, flowing generally N.E. for about 600 m., and emptying into the Atlantic Ocean through the salt-water body, Lake Melville, and its ocean extension, Hamilton Inlet. About 220 m. from its source the Hamilton descends from the plateau to a narrow and high-walled valley. At that point are located Grand Falls. Because of numerous rapids the Hamilton R. is mostly unnavigable. Formerly the river was known as the Grand River; an alternate name for it in its upper course is the Ashuanipi.

HAMITES, a group of Caucasian peoples, originally of northern and northeastern Africa and the Canary Islands. Anthropologists are in dispute about the precise ethnological definition of the Hamites; they generally define the group as comprising the Berbers of N. Africa, the Fulah, Tuareg, and Tibbu (qq.v.) peoples of the Sudan, the ancient Egyptians and the major Ethiopian tribes, and the Guanches, an extinct people of the Canary Islands.

The typical Hamite is over medium height and has dark-brown skin and curly, black hair. Some Hamites, such as the Berbers, occasionally have blond characteristics, arising probably from albinism or consequent upon invasion by Teutonic nations; others, south of the Sahara, show the effect of mixture with Negroid peoples. Some ethnologists have attempted to link the Hamites with the Mediterranean peoples, thus tracing their provenance to the heart of Europe.

Unlike the Semites (q.v.), with whom they are related in both biological character and language, the Hamites are in the main agricultural rather than pastoral peoples. They are responsible for the oldest extant writing in the world, the hieroglyphic inscriptions of the ancient Egyptians, and were the earliest engineers and architects in massive stones.

HAMITIC LANGUAGES, a family of languages which originated in N. Africa. It comprises ancient Egyptian (which, in the form of "Coptic" or "neo-Egyptian", survived until the 17th century A.D.), extinct and surviving dialects of the Berbers (q.v.), a group of languages called Cushite, which are spoken in regions bordering the Red Sea by such peoples as the Somalis and the Gallas (qq.v.) and a small group of isolated branches, such as the language of the Hausa (q.v.). In the north, Hamitic-speaking peoples are geographical neighbors to speakers of the Semitic languages (q.v.); the two families are closely related, and may have had a common parent in a primordial linguistic entity called Hamito-Semitic. In the south, largely conjectural relationships with the languages of the Hottentots have been described.

Hamitic speech is in the main inflectional, though the prefixes and suffixes used to form derivatives have a much smaller range than those of inflected Indo-European languages. Suffixes are affixed to nouns to express number, gender, and case, while both prefixes and suffixes are used in conjugating verbs. Arabic, a Semitic language, has influenced the formation of tenses, which normally express not time but the completion of or failure to complete an action. Hamitic nouns form distributive plurals, in which objects are distinguished as individuals; collective plurals, in which objects are regarded as a unity; and generic plurals applied to undifferentiated masses, such as grass and water. Hamitic languages have two genders. In some, especially that of the Masai (q.v.), the genders of nouns are based not on sex, but on size or strength. In the majority, however, the genders were origi-

J. Arthur Rank Organization

Hamlet, portrayed by Sir Laurence Olivier

nally personal and neuter; in time the personal became restricted to masculine, and the neuter came to include feminine.

Ancient Egyptian hieroglyphic writing, a transcription of the earliest known Hamitic speech, represents the oldest extant script in the world. Characters derived from a cursive form of these hieroglyphs survive in the ritual language of the Coptic church (see COPTS). Most of the written Hamitic languages, however, are today transcribed in borrowed Arabic scripts, such as that of the Hausa, or in recently introduced transliterations in Roman letters.

HAMLET, a tragedy in five acts by William Shakespeare, first acted before 1602 and first printed in 1603; an improved version was printed in 1604, and the play was included in the edition of Shakespeare's plays known as the First Folio (1623).

The setting of the play is Denmark. The king of Denmark has been murdered by his brother Claudius, who has married the king's widow, Gertrude, and himself become king. At the opening of the play, Hamlet, Prince of Denmark, son of the slain king, learns of the murder from the ghost of his father. Hamlet is a man whose intellectual habits keep him from acting quickly and boldly; although he realizes it is his duty to avenge his father's

death by slaying Claudius, he cannot decide upon a plan of action. The conflict within him between his need for action and inability to act drives him to the verge of suicide. He has been in love with Ophelia, daughter of Polonius, a court official, but after he discovers the cause of his father's death, his manner toward Ophelia becomes so strange and rude that she believes him mad, a belief shared by the king and the queen. Hamlet visits his mother's chamber to reproach her bitterly for marrying Claudius, and kills Polonius, who is spying upon them from behind a wall hanging.

The shock of her father's death at the hands of the man she loves drives Ophelia mad and she drowns herself. Her brother Laertes swears vengeance upon Hamlet. The king turns to his own ends the hatred of Laertes for Hamlet, and arranges a fencing match between them. The foil which Laertes is to use in the match is poisoned; and in case Hamlet should escape death by means of the poisoned blade, the king prepares a poisoned drink to offer Hamlet during the match. However, the king's plans go awry. During the contest, the queen drinks a toast to her son from the poisoned cup. Laertes wounds Hamlet, but Hamlet also wounds Laertes, with the same poisoned blade, which comes into his hand when the opponents inadvertently exchange swords. Both the queen and Laertes die. Hamlet, mortally wounded, is at last aroused to decisive action. He turns upon Claudius, stabs him, and then dies.

The source from which Shakespeare drew the material for this tragedy was an English play, no longer extant, reputedly by Thomas Kyd. This play in turn was based on material in *Historia Danica*, a history of Denmark to 1186 written by the Danish historian Saxo Grammaticus (q.v.). The story of Hamlet as related by Saxo Grammaticus was known in England in a French version, the fifth book of *Histoires Tragiques* (between 1559 and 1570) by François de Belleforest. According to the Danish historian, Hamlet, also called Amleth or Hamleth, was an actual person, the son of Horvendill, King of Jutland in the 2nd century B.C., and his Queen Gerutha. Horvendill was killed by his brother Fengo, who then married Gerutha; to save his own life, Amleth pretended to be insane. Also according to this chronicle, Amleth's mother, overcome by her son's reproaches, helped him kill Fengo. Modern Danish historians consider the narrative in the work of Saxo Grammaticus to be fictitious.

Hamlet is one of the most complex and life-like characters created by Shakespeare. Volumes have been written by scholars and critics in an attempt to interpret the character of the Danish prince, and particular attention has been directed to the problem of whether Hamlet is really mad, his mind unhinged by the responsibilities he could not meet, or whether he only pretends to be so. The question has never been definitely settled; the consensus of critical opinion in recent times is that the melancholy Dane is not actually mad, although under emotional stress he sometimes so appears. In recent years, also, a psychoanalytical explanation of his conduct has been given considerable credit. According to this theory, Hamlet's desire to slay his uncle arises not from his need and duty to avenge his father, but because Hamlet suffers from an abnormal love for his mother and an abnormally jealous hatred of any man whom his mother loves.

Hamlet is generally considered the greatest of Shakespeare's plays and one of the greatest in all dramatic literature. The most eminent of English and American actors have played the part of Hamlet; they include Richard Burbage, David Garrick, Edwin Thomas Booth, Sir Johnston Forbes-Robertson, John Barrymore, Maurice Evans, John Gielgud, and Sir Laurence Olivier. The play has often been used as the basis for an opera; the most eminent composers who have written operas on the story are Domenico Scarlatti, with *Amlete* (1715), and Ambroise Thomas, with *Hamlet* (1868). The story was also the subject of the overture-fantasia *Hamlet* (1888) by Peter Illich Tchaikovsky. In 1948 a notable motion-picture version of the play was produced by Sir Laurence Olivier, who also played the leading role.

HAMLIN, HANNIBAL (1809–91), American political leader and 15th Vice-President of the United States, born in Paris Hill, Me. He studied law and was admitted to the bar in 1833. Hamlin was active in politics in Maine and served for several terms as a Democratic member of the Maine legislature. From 1843 to 1847 he was a member of the U.S. House of Representatives, and from 1848 to 1856 was U.S. senator from Maine. His antislavery convictions made him instrumental in securing passage in the House (1846) of the Wilmot Proviso (q.v.) providing that slavery should never exist in certain territories Congress was then proposing to purchase from Mexico. Hamlin joined the newly formed and antislavery Republican Party in 1856 and, as a Republican, was the same year elected governor of Maine; in 1857 he resigned to run as candidate for the U.S. Senate, in which he again served until 1861. From the latter year until 1865 Hamlin was Vice-President of the United States in the administration of Abraham Lincoln, and was one of Lincoln's important advisers during the Civil War. From 1869 to 1881 Hamlin was again a member of the U.S. Senate, and from 1881 to 1882 he served as U.S. minister to Spain.

HAMLINE UNIVERSITY, privately controlled, coeducational school of higher learning, located in St. Paul, Minn., and affiliated with the Methodist Church. It was founded and opened for instruction in 1854. The university offers programs of study leading to the A.B., B.S., and M.A. degrees in the liberal arts and to the B.S. degree in nursing and in medical technology. The School of Nursing was organized in 1940. Through a co-operative arrangement with American University, students may spend a semester in Washington, D.C. The library contains 70,000 bound volumes. In the spring term of 1956 enrollment totaled 1206 full-time and 24 part-time students, and the faculty numbered 105. The endowment was $4,815,822.

HAMM, city of North Rhine-Westphalia, Germany, located at the confluence of the Ahse and the Lippe rivers, 19 m. by rail N.E. of Dortmund and 25 miles S.E. of Münster. The city was a member of the Hanseatic League (q.v.). Hamm is principally an industrial center, and contains machine works, wire factories, leather works, chemical works, and breweries. In the vicinity are coal mines and thermal baths. Hamm was one of the most heavily bombed German cities during World War II. Following the war it was included in the British Zone of Occupation. Pop., about 60,000.

HAMMARSKJÖLD, DAG HJALMAR AGNE CARL (1905–), Swedish statesman and United Nations official, born in Jönköping, and educated at the universities of Uppsala and Stockholm. He served as undersecretary of the Department of Finance of the Swedish government and as a member of the economic advisory board from 1936 to 1946, when he entered the diplomatic service as finance specialist in the Foreign Office. In 1947 he participated in the organizing conference of the European Recovery Program and in 1948–49 was vice-chairman of the executive committee of the Organization for European Economic Cooperation. Named Swedish deputy foreign minister and cabinet minister without portfolio in 1951, Hammarskjöld was (1952–53) a

The hammerhead shark (Sphyrna zygaena)

member and chief of his country's delegation to the United Nations. On April 7, 1953, he was elected secretary-general of the United Nations, succeeding the Norwegian statesman Trygve Lie.

HAMMERFEST, the northernmost town of Europe, situated on the island of Kvalö, in the county of Finnmark, Norway. The sun remains above the horizon there, day and night, from the 13th of May to the 29th of July. Hammerfest is the rendezvous of the fishing fleets which operate in the Kara Sea and in the waters along the coasts of Spitsbergen. Salted fish, cod-liver oil, fox skins, and reindeer skins are exported from the town. Pop., about 3500.

HAMMERHEAD or **HAMMERHEAD SHARK,** common name for any shark in the genus *Sphyrna,* characterized by a flattened projection on either side of the crown. The eyes are situated at each end of the rudderlike projections, which enable the shark to maneuver skillfully when chasing its prey. The hammerhead is a voracious, fish-eating shark which reaches a length of 16 feet; it has been known to attack man. It is found in all warm seas and comes as far north along the Atlantic coast of the U.S. as Massachusetts. The female hammerhead incubates its eggs within its body cavity. Five species are known.

HAMMERSMITH, a w. metropolitan borough of London, England, on the left bank of the Thames R., 6 miles w.s.w. of St. Paul's Cathedral. St. Paul's School, one of the leading public schools of England, founded in 1509, and Kelmscott House, the residence of the Victorian poet and artist William Morris, are within the borough. Industrial establishments in Hammersmith include boatbuilding yards, machine shops, oil mills, and distilleries. Area, 3.6 sq.m.; pop. (1951 prelim.) 119,317.

HAMMERSTEIN, OSCAR (1848–1919), German-American operatic impresario, born in Stettin. At the age of sixteen he came to the

U.S. and settled in New York City, where he procured employment as a cigar-maker. He invented a cigar-making machine and a number of other contrivances from which he derived a huge fortune. He wrote three plays, for which he also composed the music, and in 1870 he leased the old Stadt (afterward the Windsor) Theatre to present his work. Twenty years later, he built the Harlem Opera House, and followed that successively with the building of the Columbus Theatre, the Harlem Music Hall, the Murray Hill Theatre, the first Manhattan Opera House, the Olympia, the Victoria, the Republic, and the Harris Theater.

In 1906 he built the second Manhattan Opera House, which became such a serious rival of the Metropolitan Opera House that in 1910 the Hammerstein interests were purchased by the Metropolitan with the understanding that Hammerstein would not produce opera in the U.S. for ten years. He left immediately for England, and in 1911 he built the Kingsway Opera House in London. This enterprise was a failure and Hammerstein returned to New York to build the Lexington Opera House, in which he intended to produce operas. He was prevented from doing so by the intervention of the courts, which forced him to keep his agreement with the Metropolitan Opera House.

Hammerstein did much to overcome the inertia of the American public toward opera. His casts were always brilliant, including such famous names as Nellie Melba, Luisa Tetrazzini, Mary Garden, and John McCormack. He is credited with placing French opera in the American repertory. He also produced the American previews of *Salome* by Richard Strauss, *Louise* by Gustave Charpentier, and *Pélleas et Mélisande* by Claude Debussy.

HAMMERSTEIN, OSCAR, 2nd (1895–   ), American librettist, grandson of the operatic impresario Oscar Hammerstein, born in New

York City, and educated at Columbia University. He displayed considerable talent, both as a lyricist and actor, in amateur theatrical productions at Columbia. After working in a law office for a year, he made the theater his career, initially as a stagehand. He began to write books and lyrics for musical shows in 1919. In *Wildflower* (1923), his first success, he introduced the "musical play", i.e., drama set to music and, unlike musical comedy, employing realistic dialogue. All of his subsequent successes were of this genre. In 1927 he adapted Edna Ferber's novel *Show Boat* (1926) for the musical stage in association with the American composer Jerome Kern. The production earned high approbation. Hammerstein achieved his greatest triumphs in collaboration with the American composer Richard Rodgers. Their first work, *Oklahoma* (1943; Pulitzer Prize, 1944), an adaptation of the American dramatist Lynn Riggs' *Green Grow the Lilacs* (1931), won extraordinary critical and popular acclaim. Even more successful was their *South Pacific* (1949; Pulitzer Prize, 1950), generally regarded as one of the best musical plays ever written. Also in collaboration with Rodgers, he wrote *Carousel* (1945), *Allegro* (1947), *The King and I* (1951), *Me and Juliet* (1953), and *Pipe Dream* (1955). Among Hammerstein's other more popular productions are *Rose Marie* (1924), with music by the American composer Rudolf Friml, and *Desert Song* (1926) and *New Moon* (1928), with music by the Hungarian-American composer Sigmund Romberg. Highly popular songs for which he wrote the lyrics include "Oh ! What a Beautiful Mornin' ", "People Will Say We're in Love", "Some Enchanted Evening", "Indian Love Call", "Ol' Man River", and "The Last Time I Saw Paris".

HAMMETT, DASHIELL, in full SAMUEL DASHIELL (1894–   ), American detective-story writer, born in St. Mary's County, Md. He left school at the age of thirteen and traveled in many parts of the United States, holding a variety of positions. During World War I, he served as an ambulance driver in France. For eight years after the war he was a private detective; the experience gained during this period furnished much of the material which he later used in his novels. The first two of these, *Red Harvest* (1929) and *The Dain Curse* (1929) met with immediate popularity, but not until the publication of *The Maltese Falcon* (1930) did Hammett win recognition as the forerunner of a new school of detective fiction.

He is noted especially for realism and unconventional directness of character delineation and dialogue; for a shocking impact of plot narration, often involving detailed description of acts of sadistic brutality; and for a sophisticated cynicism of social attitudes. *The Glass Key* (1931) was written in a similar vein, but in *The Thin Man* (1932) Hammett introduced a note of gaiety and humor into his previously grim writing.

Many of his novels were later made into popular motion pictures, and he spent some years writing screen plays in Hollywood. Several radio serial programs were based on the characters Hammett had created in his novels. Among these were "The Thin Man"; "The Adventures of Sam Spade", based on the central character of *The Maltese Falcon;* and "The Fat Man", based on another important character in the same novel. During the late 1940's and early 1950's allegations of procommunist activity were leveled against him; in 1951 he served a six-month prison sentence for contempt of court.

HAMMOND, a city of Lake Co., Ind., situated on the Grand and Little Calumet rivers, about 20 miles S.E. of the center of Chicago, Ill. It is served by eleven railroads and is connected with Lake Michigan by a canal. The city is an important commercial and manufacturing center of the surrounding Calumet district, one of the richest industrial regions in the world. In addition to extensive railroad repair shops, industrial establishments in Hammond include printing and bookbinding plants, and large plants producing fabricated steel, railroad cars and equipment, soap and soap products, surgical equipment and supplies, chemicals, punch presses, industrial and tire chains, and agricultural machinery. The city also contains iron and brass foundries, feed mills, and factories manufacturing candy, metal toys, and clothing. It was first settled by George Henry Hammond, who established a meat-packing plant there in 1868. The town, originally called State Line in reference to its situation on the Indiana-Illinois boundary, received its present name in 1873. It became a city in 1883, developing rapidly from that time into the most important slaughtering and packing center in the State. Pop. (1950) 87,594.

HAMMOND, JAMES BARTLETT (1839–1913), American inventor, born in Boston, and educated at the University of Vermont. He served as a war correspondent for the Union Theological Seminary in the Civil War, and later studied in Germany. In 1880 he patented one of the first typewriters to be constructed on scientific principles and to have true alignment. He commenced manufacture of this machine in 1884, and amassed a large fortune from its sale.

HAMMOND, JOHN HAYS (1855–1936), American mining engineer and financier, born in San Francisco, and educated at the Sheffield Scientific School (Yale) and the Royal School of Mines at Freiburg. In 1880 he took part in a U.S. Geological Survey of the California gold fields, and later worked as an engineer for Cecil Rhodes in the gold mines of South Africa. In 1896 he was imprisoned and sentenced to death by the Boers, because of allegedly hostile acts, but was soon released. He then returned to the United States, where he engaged in mining and irrigation enterprises. He was designated special representative of the U.S. government to the coronation of King George V in 1911. He was a member of many scientific bodies and a fellow of the American Academy of Arts and Sciences. Hammond lectured at Columbia, Harvard, Yale, and Johns Hopkins universities.

HAMMURABI, HAMMURAPI, or KHAMMURABI, King of Babylon, and the greatest member of the first Babylonian dynasty. Historians differ as to the date of his reign: some give the dates about 1955 B.C. to 1913; others a century or two earlier; the most recent researches indicate that he ascended the throne in 1728 B.C. He conquered the Amorites and Elamites and extended the territory of Babylon to Susa and the Persian Gulf, and ordered the construction of numerous palaces and temples and two great canals. Hammurabi is most famous, however, for his codification of contemporary Babylonian laws and edicts.

His codification, the earliest complete legal code (q.v.) known to history, was engraved on a block of black diorite nearly eight feet high. The block, broken in three pieces, was found at Susa in 1901 and, in restored form, is today in the Louvre, Paris. Under a bas-relief depicting the king receiving the code from Shamash, the sun god, there are 16 columns of text on the obverse side and 28 on the reverse; the code contains in all 282 paragraphs. It begins with direction for legal procedure and the statement of penalties for unjust accusations, false testimony, and injustice done by judges; then follow laws concerning property rights, loans, deposits, and debts, domestic property, and family rights. Penalties were imposed for injuries sustained through unsuccessful operations by physicians, and for damages caused by neglect in various trades. Rates are fixed in the code for various forms of service in most branches of trade and commerce. Many of the laws were based on the principle of equal retaliation; thus, if a man knocked out the eye of another his own was to be knocked out, or if he knocked out the tooth of another, his own teeth were to be similarly treated. The Code of Hammurabi is strictly a civil code; it contains no laws concerning religion. In effect, the laws of the code seek to protect the weak and the poor against injustice at the hands of the rich and powerful; the code is a particularly just and humane set of laws for the time in which it was promulgated.

HAMMURABI, CODE OF. See HAMMURABI.

HAMPDEN, JOHN (1594–1643), English statesman and political leader, born in London, and educated at Magdalen College, Oxford University. In 1621 he was elected to the House of Commons, where he shortly became associated with the antiroyalist faction led by Sir John Eliot. Hampden opposed the general loan which Charles I authorized in 1626 without Parliamentary sanction. In retaliation, the government imprisoned him during part of the following year. His opposition to the king's usurpation of the prerogatives of Parliament reached a dramatic climax when, in 1637, he refused to pay the "ship money", a tax levied by Charles I for support of the royal navy. Brought to trial for this offense, he eloquently defended his position, but the case was decided against him. He was one of the five Parliamentary leaders whose attempted seizure, in January, 1642, by command of the king, precipitated the Great Rebellion (q.v.). After the outbreak of hostilities, Hampden served on the Committee of Public Safety and raised a regiment of infantry in Buckinghamshire, his home county. He was mortally wounded in a battle at Chalgrove Field, near Oxford.

HAMPDEN, WALTER, stage name of WALTER HAMPDEN DOUGHERTY (1879–1955), American actor, born in Brooklyn, N.Y., and educated at Brooklyn Polytechnic Institute and Harvard University. He made his theatrical debut at Brighton, England, in 1901, and from 1904 to 1907 was leading man at the Adelphi Theatre, London. In the latter year he returned to the United States, where he subsequently demonstrated remarkable versatility, performing in a wide variety of roles. Notable plays in which he appeared include *A Doll's House* (1907), *The Tempest* (1916),

Hamlet (1918), *Cyrano de Bergerac* (1923), *Richelieu* (1929), *The Admirable Crichton* (1931), *Ethan Frome* (1938), *Arsenic and Old Lace* (1942), and *Henry VIII* (1946). His interpretations of the roles of Hamlet and Cyrano are generally regarded as his greatest. He also appeared in motion pictures.

HAMPDEN-SYDNEY COLLEGE, school of liberal arts for men, located in Hampden-Sydney, Va., and owned and controlled by the Presbyterian Synod of Virginia. It was founded in 1775 as the Hampden-Sydney Academy by the presbytery of the Presbyterian Church of Hanover, Va., and the first classes were held in 1776. In 1783 the Virginia General Assembly incorporated the school under its present name. Among the petitioners for incorporation were the noted Virginia patriots Patrick Henry and James Madison. Amendment of the charter in 1919 permitted the Presbyterian Synod of Virginia to assume full control of the college. The A.B. and B.S. degrees are conferred. The library contains 41,000 bound volumes. In the spring of 1956 student enrollment totaled 351, the faculty numbered 27, and the endowment was $1,500,000.

HAMPSHIRE, or HANTS. See SOUTHAMPTON (England).

HAMPSTEAD, a metropolitan borough of London, England, 4 miles N.W. of St. Paul's Cathedral. It is situated on a range of hills, the greatest elevation (443 ft.) being on Hampstead Heath, a favorite holiday resort of Londoners. Hampstead has literary and artistic associations with the poets Alexander Pope, John Gay, Lord Byron, John Keats, and Leigh Hunt, the essayists Joseph Addison and Richard Steele, the lexicographer Samuel Johnson, the novelists John Galsworthy and George du Maurier, and the painters John Constable and George Romney. Area, 3.5 sq.m.; pop. (1951 prelim.) 95,073.

HAMPTON, WADE (1818-1902), American army officer and statesman, born in Charleston, S.C., grandson of the planter Wade Hampton. He studied law at the University of South Carolina, but did not enter practice, devoting his time to the management of his extensive estates. He was a member of the South Carolina legislature from 1852 to 1861. At the outbreak of the Civil War he raised and equipped at his own expense a force known as the Hampton Legion, which participated in the first battle of Bull Run and the Peninsular campaign. He was commissioned a brigadier general in 1862 and major general in 1863. He was of great assistance in the cavalry raids of James Ewell Brown ("Jeb") Stuart (q.v.) and after Stuart's death in 1864 assumed command of the entire cavalry corps. He was promoted to the rank of lieutenant general in 1865. Hampton was elected governor of South Carolina in 1876 and reelected in 1878. He served in the U.S. Senate from 1879 to 1890, when he was defeated for re-election. From 1893 to 1897 he was U.S. Commissioner of Railroads.

HAMPTON COURT, a palace built near the village of Hampton, Middlesex, 15 miles from the center of London, by order of Thomas Cardinal Wolsey in 1515. He presented it to Henry VIII in 1526, and the palace was used as a royal residence until the reign of George II. Since the time of George II the former palace has been occupied by needy persons of good family recommended by the king. Two of the five original quadrangles of the building remain. The edifice, which contains one thousand rooms, is built of red brick with stone facings and is one of the outstanding examples of Tudor architecture. In Hampton Court Edward VI was born, Queen Jane Seymour died, and Charles I was imprisoned before his execution. The picture gallery, royal apartments, the park, and the gardens covering forty-four acres are open to the public and constitute a popular holiday resort for Londoners.

HAMPTON INSTITUTE, in full HAMPTON NORMAL AND AGRICULTURAL INSTITUTE, a co-educational institution of higher learning, founded in 1868 at Hampton, Va., by the American Missionary Association, for the purpose of educating Negroes and Indians. In 1870 it received a charter from the State. It is a private corporation, administered by an interdenominational board of seventeen trustees. The instruction comprises courses in liberal arts, trade, agriculture, domestic science, and teaching. The expenses of tuition are met by voluntary contributions, but students who are unable to pay their board are required to make a return in labor. The most noted graduate is Booker T. Washington (q.v.), of the class of 1875. In 1954 enrollment totaled 1207, including 1152 full-time students; the faculty numbered 116. The institute had an endowment of $12,307,754.

HAMPTON ROADS, the channel through which the estuaries of the James, the Nansemond, and the Elizabeth rivers of Virginia flow into Chesapeake Bay. It extends between Old Point Comfort in the N. and Sewell's Point in the S., and is an important

European hamster

commercial waterway of the eastern United States, broad, deep, and ice-free throughout the year. The cities situated on its shores, Norfolk, Portsmouth, and Newport News, are leading ports and, together with the neighboring communities, comprise the Port of Hampton Roads, created in 1926. Forts Monroe and Wool guard the entrance from Chesapeake Bay. Hampton Roads is one of the principal rendezvous of the U.S. Navy, which maintains a vast naval base and supply stations at Norfolk. It is noted also as the site of two historic naval engagements of the Civil War. On March 8, 1862, the frigate *Congress,* the sloop of war *Cumberland,* the steam frigates *Minnesota* and *Roanoke,* and the ship *St. Lawrence* were in the roadstead, when the *Merrimac* (or *Virginia*), an iron-clad Confederate craft, attended by several small escorts, steamed into Hampton Roads from Norfolk and attacked the Federal fleet, destroying the *Congress* and the *Cumberland* before retiring. Federal losses during the engagement amounted to 286 persons, and the Confederates lost about a dozen men in the encounter. On the following day the famous contest between the Federal *Monitor* and the *Merrimac* took place. See MONITOR.

HAMPTON ROADS CONFERENCE, an informal conference held in Hampton Roads on Feb. 3, 1865, in an attempt to bring the Civil War to an end. The meeting took place on board a steamer, the *River Queen,* between President Abraham Lincoln and Sec-retary of State William H. Seward, representing the United States, and Alexander H. Stephens, John A. Campbell, and Robert M. T. Hunter, of the Confederate States. No agreement was arrived at after a four-hour talk, and the Confederate representatives returned to Richmond.

HAMSTER, common name of any of the small, Old World rodents in the family Cricetidae, characterized by large cheek pouches for the transport of food, by thick fur, and by a long tail. Hamsters are voracious animals which attain a body length of one foot. They do much damage to crops. The hamster lives in a many-chambered burrow, four to five feet below the surface of the ground, in a cultivated field. It uses one of the chambers of its burrow as a storage room which it fills with grain in the summer and fall. In winter the hamster hibernates; its sleep is not continuous and it often wakes to feed on its stores. The female bears several litters a year and produces as many as eighteen young in one litter. The young leave the parents and construct their own burrows two to three weeks after birth. The fur of the hamster is used by man to line coats, and the flesh is sometimes eaten. Three genera of hamsters are found in Europe, two in Asia, and one in Africa. Hamsters were imported into the U.S. for use as experimental animals in medical research; they are currently valuable in investigations of malignant growths, especially of mouth cancers. In 1956 it was discovered that hamsters can be infected with the common cold (see COLD, COMMON). This discovery is of great significance to cold-virus research, as the hamster is the first small laboratory animal found to be susceptible to colds. Hamsters have recently become popular as children's pets.

HAMSUN, KNUT, pseudonym of KNUT PEDERSEN (1859–1952), Norwegian writer, born in Lom. As a youth he worked for a living successively as a clerk, salesman, shoemaker's apprentice, coal trimmer, and country schoolteacher. At the age of twenty he enrolled at Christiania (now Oslo) University, with a view to becoming a journalist. Soon he gave up this attempt and emigrated to America, where he spent two years, chiefly in Minnesota and Wisconsin, working at various occupations and doing some writing. In 1884 Hamsun returned to Norway and in 1886 again went to the United States, where he worked as streetcar conductor in Chicago, farmhand in North Dakota, and lecturer on literature before Scandinavian residents of

Minneapolis. In 1888 he returned to Norway, and thereafter gave his full time to writing.

Hamsun rose to the front rank of Scandinavian writers with the novel *Hunger* (1890), a work dealing with the psychological effects of starvation. It was followed by a number of other novels, about ten in all, including *Mysteries* (1892), *Pan* (1894), and *Under the Autumn Star* (1907). Typical of this first creative period are Hamsun's main characters, negative types who pose as severe critics of civilization. Highly individualized and impulsive, and hating organized society, they generally escape to remote places to avoid their responsibility.

A group of later novels reveal Hamsun as a socially minded author. The novels *Children of the Time* (1913) and *Growth of the Soil* (1917) avoid concentration on the problems of maladjusted individuals and take up various problems of society as a whole. *Growth of the Soil,* considered Hamsun's greatest novel, treats of peasant life. In the year (1920) that it appeared in English, Hamsun received the Nobel Prize for literature. In his later novels, however, including *Vagabonds* (1930) and *The Ring is Closed* (1937), Hamsun returns to the depiction of the rootless, wandering individual of modern society.

Hamsun had strong antidemocratic views throughout his life. He was an admirer of Prussian militarism in World War I. In World War II, he openly expressed his sympathy with the Nazis, and was the only Norwegian writer of first rank who publicly welcomed their invasion of Norway in April, 1940. After the war (1946) he was tried for collaboration, but owing to his old age his sentence consisted only of an $85,000 fine.

Other novels by Hamsun include *A Wanderer Plays on Muted Strings* (1922), *The Women at the Pump* (1928), *The Road Leads On* (1937), and *Look Back on Happiness* (1940). He is also the author of several plays and of a volume of lyrics, *The Wild Chorus* (1903).

HAMTRAMCK, a city of Wayne Co., Mich., surrounded by Detroit with the exception of the N.E. portion, which adjoins the city of Highland Park. It is an industrial center, noted principally for the manufacture of automobiles and automobile accessories. Other important industries in the city are stonecutting and the manufacture of paints and varnishes, radiators, pottery, electrical supplies, alloy and metal products, and tools and dies. Hamtramck, incorporated as a village in 1901 and as a city in 1922, is named

in honor of Col. John Francis Hamtramck, who commanded the fort at Detroit after its surrender by the British in 1796. Pop. (1950) 43,355.

HAN, a river of China, one of the chief tributaries of the Yangtze R., and a main artery of trade of central China. From its source in the S.W. portion of Shensi Province, the Han flows generally S.E. across Hupeh Province, emptying into the Yangtze at Wuhan. The river, about 900 m. in length, is navigable by river steamers for about 300 m. above Wuhan and by smaller craft throughout most of its course. A number of important commercial cities, including Siangyang and Hanchung, are situated on the banks of the Han.

HAN, a Chinese dynasty, founded by Liu Pang (247–195 B.C.), a soldier of fortune who became Duke of P'ei, later Prince of Han, and subsequently the acknowledged emperor of the country, about 202 B.C. The capital was at Changan (now Sian in Shensi Province), but later, about 25 A.D., in the reign of the fifteenth Han emperor, it was moved to Lo-yang (Honan) in Honan Province; hence arose the division of the dynasty into Western (Former) and Eastern (Later) Han. The Han dynasty came to an end in 220 A.D., when the Empire broke up into the "Three Kingdoms", one of which is known as the Minor Han (221–64 A.D.). In all, fourteen emperors ruled during the Former Han, twelve during the Later Han, and two during the Minor Han. For the achievements of the Han dynasty, see CHINA: *History.*

HANAU, a town of Hessen, Germany, situated on the Main R., 14 m. by rail E. of Frankfurt am Main. Hanau is believed to have originated as a Roman settlement. It became a city early in the 14th century, and was fortified in 1528. The newer, or industrial, portion of the city was founded in 1597 by Walloons from the Netherlands. Notable buildings are the church of St. Mary, mentioned at the beginning of the 14th century; the 17th-century church of St. John; the 17th-century town hall; and the house occupied by the brothers Grimm, the German philologists and mythologists, who were natives of the city. Hanau is an important industrial center, containing factories producing machinery, chemicals, clothing, paper, soap, and metalware. Pop., about 43,000.

HANCOCK, JOHN (1737–93), American patriot and statesman, born in Braintree, Massachusetts, and educated at Harvard College. After his graduation, in 1754, he joined

John Hancock

the mercantile firm of his uncle and guardian Thomas Hancock. On the latter's death in 1764, he inherited the business and a substantial fortune. He was elected to the Massachusetts legislature two years later.

Hancock first became embroiled with the British government in 1768, when customs officials seized his sloop *Liberty* for unloading a cargo of Madeira wine without paying import duties. His vigorous defense in the ensuing law suits won him wide popularity among the anti-British elements in Massachusetts. After the Boston Massacre of 1770, he served on the committee that demanded the removal of the troops from Boston. He was prominently identified with the colonial cause thereafter, working closely with Samuel Adams in the leadership of the Whig, or Patriot, party in Massachusetts. The fateful British expedition to Lexington and Concord, on April 18–19, 1775, had as one of its major objectives the capture of Hancock. He was specifically excluded, along with Adams, in the general amnesty offered to the Revolutionary leaders by the British two months later.

From 1775 to 1780 Hancock was a member of the Continental Congress, serving as presiding officer during the first two years. By virtue of this office, he was the first to sign the Declaration of Independence. He was the first governor of the State of Massachusetts, holding that office from 1780 to 1785 and from 1787 until his death. Although he was initially opposed to the Federal constitution, he later supported it and served as president of the Massachusetts convention which approved the document in 1788.

HANCOCK, WINFIELD SCOTT (1829–86), American soldier and politician, born in Montgomery Square, Pa., and educated at the U.S. Military Academy at West Point. He entered the U.S. Army in 1844 as a second lieutenant serving in the Indian country. During the Mexican War he commanded a company and became a first lieutenant, and by the outbreak of the Civil War had risen to the rank of captain.

In 1861 Hancock was given the rank of brigadier general of United States Volunteers, and assigned to command a brigade in the Army of the Potomac. He first led his troops in action at Williamsburg, and was prominent in the battles of South Mountain and Antietam. In 1862 he was made a major general of United States Volunteers; during this year he fought at the battle of Fredericksburg, and in 1863 at the battle of Chancellorsville. At Gettysburg, Hancock was in sole command until the arrival of General George Meade and, commanding the left flank and later the center of the Union troops, was largely responsible for stemming the main Confederate attacks. In 1864 he was especially conspicuous in the battles of the Wilderness, Spottsylvania, and Cold Harbor. The achievements of this year under General Ulysses S. Grant, and his service at Gettysburg, led to his promotion in 1864 to the permanent rank of brigadier general.

In 1866 he became a major general of the regular army, commanding the Department of Missouri, and participating in campaigns against the Indians there. He was then transferred to the South to supervise the rehabilitation of the States of Louisiana and Texas, but the moderation of his measures was opposed in Washington, and in 1867 he was relieved at his own request and assigned to command the Military Division of the Atlantic, with headquarters at Governor's Island, N.Y. From 1869 to 1872 he was in charge of the Department of Dakota. In the latter year he was reassigned to the Division of the Atlantic, where he remained until his death.

Hancock was active in the Democratic party, and carried on his political and military careers simultaneously. In 1880 he was the Democratic nominee for President, campaigning for election while on military duty, but was defeated by the Republican candidate James Garfield.

HAND, (BILLINGS) LEARNED (1872–   ), American jurist, born in Albany, N.Y., and educated at Harvard University. Admitted to the New York State bar in 1897, he engaged in private legal practice until 1909, when President William Howard Taft appointed him to the bench of the U.S. Southern District Court of New York. He served in that capacity for fifteen years. From 1924 to 1951, when he retired, he was a member of the U.S. Court of Appeals of the Second Judicial Circuit. One of the outstanding American jurists of his time, Hand achieved particular distinction through his liberal and illuminating interpretations of constitutional law. His writings include *Spirit of Liberty* (1952), a collection of his addresses and papers.

HANDBALL, a game of ball in which the ball is hit with the hand against a wall alternately by opposing players. The game originated in Ireland in the tenth century and has since been a favorite sport in that country. It was introduced into the United States by Phil Casey, an Irish handball star who emigrated to Brooklyn, N.Y., around 1882. Casey was world champion until 1900, when he retired. Soon afterward handball was organized as an amateur sport by the Amateur Athletic Association, and has since become one of the most popular sports in this country.

Handball is played on either a four-wall or a one-wall court. The four-wall game, which is the original form, is played on a court 46 feet long and 23 feet wide, with front and side walls 23 feet high and a back wall 10 feet high. The one-wall game is a relatively recent innovation, introduced on bathing beaches around New York City soon after 1900 and subsequently adopted all over the country because of the ease and low cost of setting up a court. It is the form of the game most popular among nontournament players, and has afforded an introduction to handball for the great majority of players in most of the large American cities. In the public parks and playgrounds of Greater New York alone, for example, over 1200 one-wall courts were in use in a recent year. In tournament play one-wall handball is played on a court 34 feet long and 20 feet wide, with a wall 16 feet high and somewhat wider than the court. A "short line" is drawn

16 feet from the wall in the one-wall game (or 16 feet from the front wall in the four-wall game) and a "service line" is drawn five feet behind the short line.

The ball used in both games is made of black inflated rubber; it measures 1⅞ inches in diameter and weighs 2.3 ounces. This ball is called a "soft" ball, though in nontournament play, particularly on one-wall courts, softer and larger rubber balls are often used. An alternate, somewhat less popular form of the four-wall game is played with a "hard" ball made of hard solid rubber and tightly wound yarn and covered with leather; in tournament play such a ball is permitted to be from 1⅝ to 1⅞ inches in diameter and from 1½ to 1¾ ounces in weight. The hardball game is played on a special four-wall court 65 feet long and 25 feet wide, with front and side walls 30 feet high and a back wall 12 feet high. The playing and scoring rules are identical for both soft-ball and hardball handball, except that players of the hardball game are permitted to kick the ball during a rally as well as to hit it with the hand. Gloves may be used in playing with either ball and are almost always necessary when playing with the hard ball; according to tournament regulations they must be made of a soft material, and may not include webbing on the fingers.

Any handball game, whether played as "singles" (two opposing players) or "doubles" (two opposing teams of two players each), begins with a service. The serving player, standing on the service line, bounces the ball to the ground, and hits it on the re-

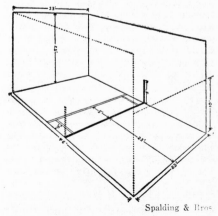

Spalding & Bros.

Diagram showing dimensions of the standard four-wall handball court

George Frederick Handel

bound against the front wall. The ball is in play if it is touched by the receiver before hitting the ground, or if it hits the ground behind the short line (and, in one-wall handball, before the back line at the rear of the court), and remains in play, being hit alternately by the opposing players or by either member of the opposing teams, until one team loses the rally by (1) failing to return a ball before it strikes the ground twice; (2) returning a ball so that it strikes the ground before hitting the wall (or front wall); (3) in the one-wall game, returning the ball so that it first strikes the ground outside the court; (4) in the four-wall game, striking the back wall above the 10-foot line. If the server makes a service fault (failure of the ball to bounce within the prescribed service area), he is permitted a second service; if he makes a second consecutive service fault, he (or his team) loses the rally. A number of other rules obtain which govern tournament play. In the four-wall game, for example, the ball may be hit and may rebound against any of the walls or the ceiling. In a one-wall doubles game a player is required to stand outside the playing area while his partner is serving. A served or hit ball which strikes the server or hitter or his partner costs that player or team the rally. Still other rules are sometimes adopted by agreement, particularly in nontournament play, but the main con-

ditions of both service and rally are the ones described above.

Handball is usually, and in tournament play invariably, played to a total of twenty-one points. A player or team holding service scores one point when he or it wins a rally; a receiving player or team scores no points upon winning a rally, but gains service (though in the doubles game both members of a serving team must be retired before the opposing team takes service). According to the rules of play, games must be won by at least two points; when two opposing players or teams tie the score at twenty points apiece, additional points are played until one player or team wins the game by gaining a two-point lead.

HANDEL, GEORGE FREDERICK (1685–1759), German composer, born in Halle, Lower Saxony. At the age of twelve he became assistant organist, and at seventeen head organist, of the Domkirche in Halle. In 1693, in deference to his father's wishes, he entered the university and completed a study of law. He then went to Hamburg to fill a position as second violinist, and later harpsichordist, in the opera-house orchestra. His first success as a composer came in 1705 with the production of his opera *Almira,* and he received a commission to write two more operas, *Nero* and *Florinda and Dafne,* produced respectively in 1705 and 1707.

In 1707 Handel visited Italy at the invitation of the Medici prince Cosimo III and stayed three years, acquiring a thorough knowledge and mastery of Italian styles and techniques of music. His reputation in Italy was made with the success of his operas *Rodrigo* and *Agrippina,* the solo cantatas *Lucrezia* and *Apollo e Dafne,* and the Italian oratorios *La Resurrezione* and *Il Trionfo del Tempo.*

He left for England in 1710 to produce his opera *Rinaldo,* which was so well received that Handel extended his visit to London; following a short stay in Hanover, he returned to England and remained there for the rest of his life. In 1719 he became a director of the Royal Academy but nine years later was forced to suspend activity when public taste turned from Italian opera toward more popular types of entertainment. This trend was due largely to the influence of the *Beggar's Opera* by John Gay (q.v.), a clever satire on the conventional Italian opera. Handel departed for Italy in search of new operas to produce, and to engage a new company of singers for the reopening of the Royal Academy, which took place in 1729. Competition in the field of entertainment was now overwhelming, however, and by 1737 Handel was financially bankrupt; in the same year he suffered a paralytic stroke and went to Aix-la-Chapelle, where he was brought back to health.

From 1738 to 1751 Handel entered into his final phase of creative activity, the composition of oratorios, practically all of which are considered masterpieces, the most famous being the *Messiah*. In 1751, while working on his last oratorio, *Jephtha*, Handel's eyesight began to fail, and by 1753 he became totally blind. He died seven years later and was buried at Westminster Abbey.

Handel was a prolific composer. His known works number 46 operas, 32 oratorios, 100 solo cantatas, 20 chamber duets, and concertos for various instruments, church music, songs, and sonatas.

HAND GRENADE. See GRENADE.

HANDS, IMPOSITION OF, in the Christian Church, the ritualistic touching with the hands in order to convey spiritual grace, employed in confirmation, ordination, and other ceremonies. The practice dates back to the beginning of the Church, and is a survival of the ancient belief that power possessed by a person could be transferred by the touch of the hand. Early instances of the belief are to be found in the Old Testament, as in Moses setting Joshua apart as a leader of the people by laying his hands upon him (Num. 27:23).

HANDY, WILLIAM CHRISTOPHER (1873–), American Negro composer, cornetist, and bandmaster, born in Florence, Ala. He was educated in the public schools, and by his father and grandfather, both of whom were clergymen. He began his musical career as a cornet soloist and bandmaster with minstrel shows; one of his earliest engagements was with the Chicago World's Fair in 1893. In 1900 he obtained a position as a music teacher at the Agricultural and Mechanical College in Huntsville, Alabama, where he stayed for two years. Handy turned to composition in 1907, and his first song published was *Memphis Blues*. He did a great deal toward bringing American Negro music to the attention of the public; among his many popular songs are *Loveless Love, St. Louis Blues,* and *Yellow Dog Blues*. He later founded a music-publishing firm.

HANGCHOW, the capital and chief commercial city of Chekiang Province, China, on Hangchow Bay, at the mouth of the Tsien-

tang R. and about 100 miles s.w. of Shanghai. The Grand Canal, for many centuries the principal artery of trade between N. China and the Yangtze delta region, terminates at the city. Because of the shallowness of Hangchow Bay, Hangchow is not accessible to ocean-going vessels. Most of the foreign trade of the city is routed through Shanghai. Flourishing commercial relations are maintained with inland points, however, chiefly by means of the Tsientang R., the Grand Canal, and a network of subsidiary canals. The city is also a thriving manufacturing center, producing tapestries, cotton textiles, silk fabrics, fans, objects of carved ivory, and processed rice. One of the most ancient cities of China, Hangchow is surrounded by massive walls with a circuit of about 12 m. The city was visited late in the 13th century by the Italian traveler Marco Polo, who characterized it as the most beautiful city in the world. Despite various vicissitudes, particularly the large-scale destruction caused by a revolution in 1861, Hangchow retains many noteworthy features, including ornate Buddhist temples, memorial halls, shrines, monasteries, and gardens. Pop., about 485,000.

HANGING, a method of inflicting capital punishment by suspending the condemned by the neck from a frame, consisting of two upright posts and a crosspiece, called a gallows. It is the accepted method of execution in many countries, including England, and in about one third of the States of the U.S. The cause of death in hanging is complex. Compression of the windpipe by the cord, obstruction of the flow of blood, and the stretching or tearing of the nervous structures of the neck all may play a part, especially when death is not instantaneous and is attended by violent struggling. Ideally, however, death is caused by the fracture or dislocation of the first three cervical vertebrae, which severs or fatally damages the spinal cord. To bring about this effect, which results in almost instantaneous death, the knot of the hanging noose is set behind the ear or under the chin, and the condemned is allowed to fall from six to eight feet before the slack in the rope is taken up.

Originally hanging was not a method of capital punishment, but of inflicting indignity upon the dead bodies of criminals; the practice of hanging an executed murderer in chains upon a gibbet (a simple gallows consisting of an upright post with a crosspiece at the top) near the place where his crime was committed continued in England until

well into the 19th century. The Germans of
the Roman era, however, used hanging as a
mode of execution, and passed it on to the
Anglo-Saxon peoples. It was first adopted
in England in 1214, when Maurice, a nobleman's son, was hanged for piracy. In time
hanging displaced other, more barbarous
modes of inflicting death. See EXECUTION;
CAPITAL PUNISHMENT.

HANGING GARDENS OF BABYLON, one
of the seven wonders of the world (see SEVEN
WONDERS OF THE WORLD), described by writers of antiquity either as a building or a series
of masonry arches, surmounted by a plantation of flowers, shrubs, and trees. The hanging gardens were built, probably in the 6th
century B.C., at the command of the Chaldean
king Nebuchadnezzar II, or of Cyrus the
Great, King of Persia. The plantation was
irrigated from a large reservoir located at the
top of the structure. Diodorus Siculas, a
Greek historian of the 1st century B.C., writes
that "this garden was four hundred foot
square, and the ascent up to it was as to the
top of a mountain . . . and the highest arch
upon which the platform of the garden was
laid was fifty cubits high, and the garden itself was surrounded with battlements and
bulwarks".

HANGNEST, the Baltimore bird (q.v.).

HANGUL or **CASHMERE STAG,** a deer,
Cervus cashmiriensis, closely related to and
resembling the red deer (q.v.) of Europe,
but larger. The male hangul stands 4½ ft.
high at the shoulder and has antlers which
reach 4 ft. in length. Hanguls dwell in the
forest regions of N. India, especially in Kashmir, at heights of 5000 to 12,000 ft. above sea
level.

HANKOW, a city of Hupeh Province,
China, situated on the N. bank of the Yangtze
R., about 500 m. from its mouth and at its
confluence with the Han R. The cities of
Hanyang and Wuchang, which, together with
Hankow, are known by the composite name
of Wuhan, lie on opposite banks of the Han
and the Yangtze. Hankow is at the head of
navigation of the Yangtze, and is accessible
to ocean-going vessels; this circumstance, the
navigability of the Yangtze by river steamers
as far inland as Ichang, and the navigability
of the Han for 300 m. above its junction with
the Yangtze, make Hankow the chief commercial city of central China. The commercial importance of the city also is enhanced by
its location on the railway from Peiping to
Canton. Among the principal cargoes handled
at Hankow are timber, hides, cotton, tea, and

silk. Hankow is one of the leading manufacturing cities of central China, producing steel,
textiles, flour, soap, cement, processed rice,
vegetable oils, and a wide variety of other
commodities. Pop., about 778,000.

HANNA, MARCUS ALONZO, known as MARK
HANNA (1837-1904), American politician and
businessman, born in New Lisbon, Ohio. After one year at Western Reserve College (now
University), he entered his father's wholesale grocery business. He was singularly successful in this and other enterprises, including
the coal and iron business, the operation of
railway and steamship lines, and banking.

Beginning in 1880, he became increasingly
active in the Republican Party. At the Republican National Convention of 1888 he
managed John Sherman's unsuccessful attempt to win the Presidential nomination. He
secured the Presidential nomination for William McKinley at the Republican National
Convention of 1896 and, as chairman of the
Republican National Committee, managed
the subsequent campaign. McKinley won by
the largest popular plurality accorded a
Presidential candidate up to that time.

In 1897 Hanna was appointed to the U.S.
Senate by Governor Asa S. Bushnell of Ohio.
He was elected to the post in the following
year and re-elected in 1904. One of the most influential advisers of President McKinley, Hanna advocated and secured, during the latter's
administration, a lasting alliance between the
Republican Party and corporate business interests. Hanna also favored friendly relations
between capital and labor, and was one of
the founders of the National Civic Federation. During Theodore Roosevelt's administration, Hanna headed the conservative faction of the Republican Party.

HANNAH, or ANNA, in the Old Testament,
the wife of Elkanah and mother of the
prophet Samuel (q.v.).

HANNIBAL, city of Marion and Ralls
counties, Mo., on the Mississippi R., 120 miles
N. of St. Louis, in a rich agricultural area. It is
served by three railroads and by river steamers and barges. The Mark Twain Memorial
Bridge spans the Mississippi at Hannibal to
Illinois. An airport is situated 4 miles N.W. of
the city. The principal industries in Hannibal
are the manufacture of shoes, rubber heels
and soles, precision tools, stamped-metal
products, coin-handling supplies, foundry
products, shipping crates, casket hardware,
beverages, stock feed, soap and soap products,
automobile accessories, optical supplies, cement, lime, and concrete blocks. In addition,

Hannibal and his army crossing the Rhone River during his famous march on Rome

Hannibal contains railroad repair shops, woodworking shops, and plants processing dairy products. In the vicinity of the city are deposits of shale and limestone. A dam on the Mississippi s. of Hannibal aids river navigation and assists in the control of floods. The city is the site of Hannibal LaGrange Junior College (Baptist), established in 1858, and the Hatch Dairy Experimental Farm, maintained by the State and Federal governments. Hannibal is noted as the boyhood home of the author Mark Twain (Samuel Langhorne Clemens), who lived there from 1839–53. A statue of him stands in Riverview Park, overlooking the river, and the house in which he lived is maintained by the city as a memorial. *The Adventures of Tom Sawyer* and *The Adventures of Huckleberry Finn,* two of Mark Twain's most celebrated works, have their setting in Hannibal. Hannibal was first settled in 1818, and was incorporated as a city in 1845. Pop. (1950) 20,444.

HANNIBAL (247–183 B.C.), Carthaginian general, the son of Hamilcar Barca (see HAMILCAR). At the age of nine Hannibal accompanied his father on the Carthaginian expedition to conquer Spain. Before starting, the boy vowed eternal hatred for Rome, the bitter rival of Carthage. From his eighteenth to his twenty-fifth year Hannibal was the chief agent in carrying out the plans by which his brother-in-law Hasdrubal (q.v.)

extended and consolidated the Carthaginian dominion on the Iberian peninsula. When Hasdrubal was assassinated in 221 B.C., the army chose Hannibal commander in chief. In two years he subjugated all Spain between the Tagus and Ebro (Iberus) rivers, with the exception of the Roman dependency of Saguntum (Sagunto). After a siege of eight months, however, Saguntum was taken. The Romans branded this attack a violation of the existing treaty between Rome and Carthage and demanded that Carthage surrender Hannibal to them. On the refusal of the Carthaginians to do so, the Romans declared war on Carthage in 218 B.C., thus precipitating the Second Punic War.

Hannibal then commenced his march on Rome. In the summer of 218 he left New Carthage, Spain, with an army of about 90,000 foot soldiers and 12,000 cavalry and a considerable number of elephants carrying baggage and later used in battle. He crossed the Pyrenees and the Rhone R., and traversed the Alps in fifteen days, beset by snow storms, landslides, and the attacks of hostile mountain tribes. After recruiting additional men among the friendly Insubres to compensate for the loss of troops sustained in transit, Hannibal subjugated the Taurini, a tribe hostile to the Insubres, and forced into alliance with himself all the Ligurian and Celtic tribes on the upper course of the Po

R. He next vanquished the Romans under Publius Cornelius Scipio Africanus (see SCIPIO AFRICANUS, PUBLIUS CORNELIUS) in two important engagements. In the following year he inflicted a crushing defeat upon the Roman consul Gaius Flaminius (see FLAMINIUS, GAIUS) at Lake Trasimenus (Lago di Trasimeno). After his victory he crossed the Apennines and invaded the Roman provinces of Picenum and Apulia, recrossing thence to the fertile Campania, which he ravaged.

The Roman general Quintus Fabius Maximus Verrucosus (see FABIUS), surnamed Cunctator ("Delayer"), sent from Rome to oppose Hannibal, adopted a highly cautious strategy. Avoiding any decisive encounter with the Carthaginian troops, he nevertheless succeeded in keeping Hannibal at bay, thus giving the Romans the opportunity to recover from their military reverses. Hannibal wintered at Gerontium, and in the spring of 216 took up a position at Cannæ (q.v.) on the Aufidus (Ofanto) R. There he almost completely annihilated a Roman army of 90,000 men under the consuls Lucius Æmilius Paulus and Gaius Terentius Varro.

After the battle of Cannæ the character of the war underwent a change. Hannibal needed reinforcements, which the Carthaginian government refused to furnish, and he also lacked siege weapons. He marched on Neapolis (Naples), but failed to take the city. The gates of Capua, one of the Italian cities which had fallen to Hannibal in consequence of his victory at Cannæ, were opened to him, however, and there he passed the winter of 216–15. In 211 Hannibal attempted to take Rome, but the Romans successfully maintained their fortified positions. The Romans then retook Capua, the loss of which cost Hannibal the allegiance of many of his Italian allies, and put an end to his hopes of further replenishing his army from their ranks. After four years of inconclusive fighting, Hannibal turned for aid to his brother Hasdrubal, who forthwith marched from Spain. Hasdrubal, however, was surprised, defeated, and slain by the Roman consul Gaius Claudius Nero in the battle of the Metaurus Metauro) R.

In 202, after an absence of fifteen years, and with the military fortunes of Carthage rapidly declining, Hannibal was recalled to Africa to direct the defense of his country against a Roman invasion under Scipio Africanus. He met Scipio at Zama; his raw troops fled, many deserting to the Romans; his

veterans were cut down; and Carthage capitulated to Rome. Thus ended the Second Punic War.

After a peace had been concluded with the Romans in 201, Hannibal immediately set about making preparations for a resumption of the struggle. He amended the Carthaginian constitution, reduced corruption in the government, and placed the city's finances on a sounder basis. The Romans, however, charged him with working to break the peace, and he was obliged to flee Carthage, taking refuge at the court of Antiochus the Great, King of Syria. With Antiochus he fought against the Romans, but when the Syrian monarch was defeated at Magnesia (Manisa) in 190, and signed a treaty with Rome pledging to surrender Hannibal, the latter escaped to Prusias, King of Bithynia. When his surrender was once more demanded by the Romans, however, Hannibal, all hope at last exhausted, took the poison which he carried on his person for such an emergency. See CARTHAGE; ROME: *History*; PUNIC WARS.

The life and times of Hannibal have been graphically portrayed in *Salammbô*, a historical romance by the 19th-century French novelist Gustave Flaubert.

HANOI, largest city and administrative center of North Viet-Nam, situated on the Coi (Red) R., about 75 m. inland from the Gulf of Tonkin. An important transportation junction, Hanoi is a railroad hub for lines extending from the port of Haiphong to Kunming, China, and from Nacham to Saigon. The trading center of a rich agricultural area, Hanoi has industrial establishments engaged in rice milling and in the production of textiles, bricks and tiles, china, leather goods, soap, and chemicals. Handicraft products include embroidery, jewelry, and articles inlaid with mother-of-pearl. Points of interest include *Petit Lac,* the lake which separates the European district from the native quarters; the pagoda of the Great Buddha, on an island in the lake; the citadel, former headquarters of the French colonial governors; and the University of Hanoi.

Long a strategically important Annamese town, Hanoi was made the capital of French Indochina in 1887. It was occupied by Japanese troops during World War II. Following the restoration of French control in Indochina, Hanoi figured prominently in the ensuing hostilities (1946–54) between the Communist-led Viet Minh and the French Union forces; see INDOCHINA: *History*. In accordance with the terms of the truce agreement (July,

1954), France evacuated Hanoi in October, 1954, and the city was occupied by Viet Minh forces.

Pop. (1951 est.) 217,000.

HANOTAUX, ALBERT AUGUSTE GABRIEL (1853–1944), French statesman and historian, born in Beaurevoir, Aisne, and educated at the École des Chartes. He was for a while a teacher, and in 1879 entered the foreign ministry. In 1885 he was a member of the staff of the French embassy at Constantinople; from 1886 until 1889 he served as a representative in the Chamber of Deputies. In 1894 he became minister of foreign affairs, and, with the exception of a ten-month period in 1895, held this office until June, 1898. A distinguished historian, he was elected to the Institute of France in 1897. During World War I Hanotaux was an active propagandist for the Allied cause; in 1921 he became a delegate to the League of Nations. His historical writings include *Histoire de la France Contemporaine, 1871–1900* (1903–08) and *Histoire Illustrée de la Guerre de 1914* (17 vols., 1915–26).

HANOVER (Ger. *Hannover*), successively a kingdom of Germany, a province of Prussia, and, after November 1, 1946, a part of the newly organized state of Lower Saxony in the British Occupation Zone of Germany. The province covered an area of 14,953 sq.m. and had a population of about 3,500,000. It extended from the Harz Mountains on the s. to the North Sea on the N., and from the Netherlands on the w. to Prussian Saxony, Brandenburg, and Brunswick on the E. The city of Hanover (q.v.), now the capital of Lower Saxony, was the administrative center of the former province. Other important cities of Hanover Province were Osnabrück, Hildesheim, Wesermünde, Wilhelmshaven, Harburg (now Harburg-Wilhelmsburg), Lüneburg (qq.v.), Göttingen, Emden, and Celle.

Rich mineral deposits, including coal, copper, lead, silver, and iron, occur in the region, which is noted also for its pastoral enterprises and manufactures. Among the leading industries of this portion of Lower Saxony are shipbuilding, ironmaking, brewing, and the manufacture of machinery, cutlery, cotton and linen textiles, and tobacco products. The principal agricultural products include rye, flax, potatoes, hops, tobacco, and sugar beets.

Hanover was established as a kingdom in 1814 by the provisions of the Congress of Vienna, the peace conference that terminated the Napoleonic Wars. It had been officially known prior to that time as the electorate of Brunswick-Lüneburg. The electorate, which was formed in 1692 from the territories of the house of Brunswick (q.v.), gradually acquired, in popular usage, the name of its capital city, Hanover. Ernest Augustus, the first elector of Hanover, or Brunswick-Lüneburg, married Sophia, granddaughter of James I of Great Britain. In 1714, George Louis, their son and the second elector of Hanover, ascended the British throne as George I (q.v.). For nearly 125 years thereafter, both Hanover and Great Britain were ruled by the same sovereign. The electorate was involved in the War of the Austrian Succession (see SUCCESSION WARS) as an ally of Austria, in the Seven Years' War (q.v.) on the side of Prussia, and in the French Revolutionary Wars as part of the anti-French coalition of European powers. In 1803, during the Napoleonic Wars, the electorate was occupied by the French. Napoleon I incorporated part of it into the new kingdom of Westphalia in 1807. In 1810 the remainder of the electorate was added to Westphalia, but later that year Napoleon withdrew a portion of the territory and united it with France. The electorate was restored to George III in November, 1813, shortly after the expulsion of the French armies.

For an extended period following its transformation into a kingdom by the Congress of Vienna, Hanover was the scene of bitter political strife between liberal political groupings and the monarchy. Several revolutionary uprisings in 1831 were quelled, but continuing liberal pressure forced the promulgation of a liberal constitution in 1833. The last joint ruler of Great Britain and Hanover was William IV (q.v.). Because Hanoverian law prohibited succession of a woman to the throne, Victoria, who succeeded William as sovereign of Great Britain in 1837, was denied the crown of Hanover. The title passed to Ernest Augustus, Duke of Cumberland and son of George III. The reign of this ruler, who immediately abrogated the constitution of 1833, was marked by a renewal of the revolutionary movement. In 1848 Ernest Augustus was compelled to liberalize the government. During the reign of Ernest's son George V, the kingdom was allied (1866) with Austria against Prussia in the Seven Weeks' War (q.v.). By the terms of the treaty of Prague, which ended the war, Hanover was annexed and made into a province by the Prussian kingdom. The province was occupied by British troops following the collapse of the Third

Staats-Herold Corp.

The new town hall in the city of Hanover, Germany

Reich in World War II. On November 1, 1946, after the formal liquidation of the state of Prussia, Hanover was merged with the former states of Brunswick, Oldenburg, and Schaumburg-Lippe to form the new state of Lower Saxony.

HANOVER, successively the capital of the electorate, the kingdom, and the Prussian province of the same name and, after November 1, 1946, the capital of the state of Lower Saxony in the British Occupation Zone of Germany. The city is situated at the confluence of the Leine and Ihme rivers, about 78 miles S.E. of Bremen and about 158 miles W. of Berlin. A junction point of two trunk-line railway systems, Hanover is one of the major commercial centers of N.W. Germany, with an extensive trade in coal, timber, grain, hides, wine, horses, and local manufactures. The leading industrial products of the city are machinery, hardware, asphalt, glass, furniture, pianos, processed foods, chemicals, oilcloth, and tobacco products. Printing establishments, railway repair shops, breweries, and distilleries are also located in Hanover. Altstadt, the old section of the city, has many medieval features, including nar-row streets, gabled houses with overhanging balconies, and the Markt Kirche, a brick structure dating from the 14th century. The oldest ecclesiastical edifice in Hanover is the Kreuzkirche, constructed about 1300. Among other structures are the former Rathaus, a Gothic-style edifice built between 1439 and 1455; the former royal palace, completed in 1640 and now utilized as a museum of art; and the Herrenhausen, formerly the summer residence of the royal family of Hanover. The city has a number of outstanding historical museums, libraries, lyceums, technological institutes, and other cultural and educational institutions.

An obscure village originally, Hanover first assumed importance in 1241, when Duke Otto, founder of the house of Lüneburg-Brunswick (later called Hanover) granted it a municipal charter. The town became a member of the Hanseatic League (q.v.) in 1481. In 1636 the Lüneburg-Brunswick family established residence in Hanover. Although serving as the seat of government of the electorate and, later, of the kingdom, Hanover grew slowly. The commercial and industrial development of the town began after the annexation of the kingdom by Prussia, in 1866. During World War II Hanover was a frequent target of Allied air raids. The city was captured by United States forces in April, 1945. Pop. (1946) 355,484.

HANOVER COLLEGE, an institution of learning, founded in 1827 in Hanover, Indiana, under the auspices of the Presbyterian Church, as Hanover Academy. It was chartered as a college six years later, and in 1880 was made coeducational. It offers courses leading to baccalaureate degrees, in the liberal arts, law, education, and home economics. In a recent year the student body numbered about 640 and the faculty 36; the endowment was about $4,000,000.

HANSA, THE. See HANSEATIC LEAGUE.

HANSEATIC LEAGUE or HANSE TOWNS (from Old High Ger. *hansa,* "league"), synonymous designations applied to a federation of N. German towns which was initiated during the 13th century for the protection and enhancement of mutual commercial interests. At the peak of its ascendancy, the League was a potent force in the politics of Europe. The federation developed as a result of conditions peculiar to medieval Europe, including the gradual emergence of free towns (see FREE CITY) and merchant Guilds (q.v.); the disintegration of centralized authority within Germany; the expansion of German colonization, influence, and trade in the region E. of the Elbe R.; the consequent stimulation of N. German trade with England and the continental ports on the English Channel; and the prevalence along the main arteries of trade of pirates and highwaymen.

As early as the beginning of the 13th century German merchants who had settled on the Baltic island of Gotland created a mercantile association, consisting of Cologne and twenty-nine other towns. The Gotland association secured important trading privileges abroad, notably in Russia, England, and Flanders. In 1241, while the Gotland *hansa* was in the ascendancy, the town of Lübeck, a rival commercial center, completed a treaty with Hamburg providing for joint control of the route between the Baltic and North seas. This alliance, which was strengthened by another agreement some years later, gave the signatories a powerful position in the commerce of N.W. Europe. In consequence of these developments, the sphere of influence of the Gotland association gradually diminished. The Lübeck-Hamburg union was immeasurably strengthened in 1252, when highly advantageous commercial treaties were arranged

with Flanders. Thereafter, Bruges, the chief city of Flanders and a leading mercantile center of Europe, figured significantly in the development of the League. Rostock and Wismar concluded an alliance with Lübeck in 1259 for common action against bandits and pirates. Less than a decade later, the merchants of Lübeck and Hamburg acquired the right to establish trading organizations in London, where Cologne merchants had previously enjoyed a monopoly. About the same time, the mercantile interests of Lübeck and Hamburg obtained full or partial control of trade between Germany and the coastal towns of E. England, particularly Boston and Lynn. Attracted by the mounting influence and prosperity of the Lübeck-Hamburg union, various other N. German towns, notably Bremen and Danzig, became affiliated with the organization. Other mercantile leagues of German towns, grouped on a regional basis, gradually accepted the hegemony of Lübeck and its allies. Among these regional leagues was one comprising certain towns of Westphalia, the Rhineland, and the Low Countries; another consisting of the trading center of Saxony and Brandenburg; and a third made up of Prussian and Livonian towns. The federation, officially designated as the Hansa in 1343, soon included more than eighty-five towns.

The Hanseatic League launched its first major political undertaking when, in 1362, it declared war on Denmark in retaliation against Danish seizure (1361) of Visby, on the island of Gotland. Eventual victory over the Danes, who were compelled in 1370 to grant indemnities, strategic territories, and other concessions, tremendously increased the power and prestige of the League. Shortly thereafter, Richard II of England confirmed his government's preferential commercial treaties with the Hanse Towns. The following century was a period of unexampled prosperity for the association. It created new centers of trade and civilization in N. Europe, contributed to the development of agriculture and the industrial arts, perfected a system of weights and measures, and constructed canals and highways. Intimidated by the naval establishment of the League, many sovereigns of Europe sought alliances with the organization. At no time, however, did the League, which was democratically ruled by a diet composed of delegates from the member towns, succeed in creating a centralized governmental structure. This circumstance, the source of frequent internal dissension, contributed eventually to the disintegration of the League. The process of disintegration, which began toward the close of the 15th century, was accelerated by a variety of other factors, primarily the rise and consolidation of sovereign states in other parts of Europe, the discovery of America and a new route to India, and the growth of Dutch and English sea power. Increasing friction between the League and England culminated, in 1589, in English seizure of sixty-one Hanseatic vessels. The outbreak of the Thirty Years' War in 1618 was another severe blow to the tottering organization. By 1630 the League comprised only Lübeck, Bremen, and Hamburg. This attenuated union endured for thirty-nine years, but the three cities retained nominal political independence and the traditional designation of Hanse towns until the revocation of these privileges, in 1934, by the government of the Third Reich.

HÄNSEL UND GRETEL, an opera in three acts, with music by Engelbert Humperdinck (q.v.) and text by Adelheid Wette. Considered one of the most important post-Wagnerian German operas, it shows a strong Wagnerian influence and, like many of Wagner's operas, is based on German folklore.

In the story, the two children Hänsel and Gretel are sent by their mother into the woods to pick strawberries. They lose their way and fall asleep near the hut of a witch, who captures them and takes them into the hut, where she plans to bake and eat them. The children suspect the witch's motives, however, and when the witch asks Gretel to open the oven door and look in, Gretel pretends to be clumsy and asks to be shown how it is done. As the witch is peering into the open oven, Hänsel and Gretel push her inside and bake her into a gingerbread.

Hänsel und Gretel was first performed at the Weimar Hoftheater, Dec. 23, 1893; in America, it was first performed in New York City at Daly's Theater in 1895, and many times after 1905 at the Metropolitan Opera House.

HANSEN, GERHARD HENRIK ARMAUER (1841–1912), Norwegian physician, born in Bergen, and known for his discovery of the bacillus of leprosy, technically called, after him, "Hansen's Disease". Hansen began his studies of leprosy at the Bergen Leper Hospital, of which he was assistant medical officer. Having proved that the disease was contagious (although medical opinion now states that it is slightly contagious and only in the tropics) Hansen was given financial backing by the Medical Society of Christiania to enable him to continue his investigations of the disease. The bacillus of the disease was discovered by him in 1871, and was named, after him, "Hansen's bacillus". He was instrumental in having the Norwegian government take measures to reduce the incidence of the disease in the country, and his policy of isolation of lepers is thought to have had the same general effect throughout Europe. See LEPROSY.

HANSEN, NIELS EBBESEN (1866–1950), American horticulturist, born near Ribe, in Denmark. He was brought to the United States by his parents in 1873, and was educated at Iowa Agricultural College and the University of South Dakota. From 1891 to 1895 he was professor of horticulture at Iowa Agricultural College and from 1895 to 1937 he was professor of horticulture at the South Dakota Agricultural College and Experimental Station. Hansen made horticultural studies in various parts of the world, including Russia, Turkestan, Lapland, and Japan, for the U.S. Department of Agriculture. In 1934, at the invitation of the Soviet government, he made a scientific tour of E. Siberia.

Hansen originated many new varieties of fruits, of which the best known is the Hansen hybrid plum (plum-cherry) now grown extensively in the prairie States of W. United States. He introduced Turkestan, Siberian, Cossack, and other alfalfas into the United States, and originated a method of field hybridization of hardy alfalfas. He imported Siberian sheep from which a tailless breed was developed. His works include *Handbook of Fruit-Culture and Tree-Planting* (1890).

HANSEN'S DISEASE. See LEPROSY.

HANSE TOWNS. See HANSEATIC LEAGUE.

HANSON, HOWARD (1896–   ), American composer and educator, born in Wahoo, Nebr., and educated at Luther College in Wahoo, at the Institute of Musical Art in New York City, and at Northwestern University. In 1916 he was appointed professor of theory and in 1919 dean of the Conservatory of Fine Arts at the College of the Pacific in Stockton, Calif. In 1924 he became the director of the Eastman School of Music in Rochester, New York. He did much to stimulate interest in American music by organizing composers' concerts and festivals. Of his compositions, the best known are the *Nordic* and *Romantic* symphonies, and the opera *Merrymount,* produced by the Metropolitan Opera House in 1933.   V